MALCOLM WILLIAMSON

A MISCHIEVOUS MUSE

Anthony Meredith
and Paul Harris

with a foreword by
Peter Williamson

OMNIBUS PRESS

LONDON / NEW YORK / PARIS / SYDNEY / COPENHAGEN / BERLIN / MADRID / TOKYO

ISBN: 978.1.84772.102.0
Order No: OP52129

Exclusive Distributors
Music Sales Limited,
14/15 Berners Street,
London, W1T 3LJ.

Music Sales Corporation,
257 Park Avenue South,
New York, NY 10010, USA.

Macmillan Distribution Services,
53 Park West Drive,
Derrimut, Vic 3030,
Australia.

Every effort has been made to trace the copyright holders of the photographs in this book but one or two were unreachable. We would be grateful if the photographers concerned would contact us.

Type management by John F Saunders

Printed by Gutenberg Press, Malta

A catalogue record for this book is available from the British Library.

Visit Omnibus Press on the web at www.omnibuspress.com

CONTENTS

I have written to apologise for my scandalous behaviour… The inner turmoil that I have had for some time exploded into the outer air. If I shocked the bourgeoisie, tant pis! I never knew any worthwhile artist to have a quiet, tidy, inward-looking mind. The artist's duty is to look out on the world, and, by whatever method, to change it. The tactics of appeasement are not for the artist… I should like people to care for, or at least react to, my music; but I have not written in blood and sweat so that people should say 'Isn't he nice!'

Malcolm Williamson to Jonathan Still, 1984

FOREWORD

by Peter Williamson

SIX MONTHS AGO, maybe more, I was invited to write a foreword to this biography of my father. Keeping to family traditions, I exceeded my deadlines. This was not, however, just procrastination, an inherited gene. The problem was this: how does one – anyone – introduce a book about Malcolm?

I grew up with and without him. Years on, what I remember is a father who flitted in and out of my life, a few moments that now bring tears to my eyes and many years when my only association with Malcolm was through the occasional clipping.

I once asked my father what his ambition was. His answer was that people who cared about music would listen to his works long after he was gone. This had nothing to do with preserving his name. What mattered was that the music that he spent his life writing continued to give people pleasure and joy.

Four years after his death, his music is heard occasionally and he is remembered only as a talented eccentric. Both the man and the music deserve better. Thanks to the remarkable research, affection and writing underpinning this biography, Malcolm's life has now been put into proper focus, and the pleasure and joy his music offers clearly revealed. Hopefully these pleasures and joys will begin to be more widely shared in the coming years…

INTRODUCTION
and Acknowledgements

THE MUSES IN ANCIENT GREECE were serious-minded young women, even though they served under that most light-hearted of deities, Apollo. If ancient art is anything to go by, there was not a mischievous one among them. Their faces reflect their wide responsibilities – not just music, but poetry, literature, dance, astronomy and philosophy.

Muses are still hard at work 2,500 years later, promoting the highest intellectual and artistic aspirations, encouraging the human spirit to 'ascend the brightest heaven of invention'. It is the muses who select that small group of people who are more artistically creative than the rest.

Malcolm Williamson was one of their chosen ones, his entire life surrendered to expressing in tangible form the intangible workings of his imagination, his muse constantly by his side. Unfortunately Malcolm's muse had certain idiosyncrasies unusual in her calling. She was more skittish than most, more fun-loving and mischievous, refusing to take human endeavour consistently seriously, delighting in her own perversity, and, as such, as much a trial as a blessing. Malcolm's professional career reflected this, and so too his private life. He achieved much, but the muse's gifts came to him at great personal cost.

Such a situation, of course, makes for a highly interesting pilgrimage through life, ideal for biography. The biographers, moreover, are also helped in having a protagonist who was not only sometimes misled by his muse as he pursued a passionate search for truth and self-fulfilment, but was himself a personality of great complexity. A story inspired by a mischievous muse may not possess an easily unravelled plot or a fairy-tale ending, but there is much compensation in its inherent capacity to be both entertaining and moving. The same is true of the music.

Malcolm Williamson once wrote of Lennox Berkeley's work:

> We are presented with three options: the saddest is not to know it at all; the middle way is to know it well enough to be charmed and dazzled by its glittering surface and easily observed skill; the last and best is to succumb to its timeless beauty and persist in exploring its depths and inconveniences. This last may seem to be an act of faith, like patient excavation in unlikely soil beneath a hot sun. Take your faith that you will

uncover treasures, take your delicate brush, and you will find that, even if the treasures are deep and concealed, they are there to be claimed...

These three options are equally applicable to the Williamson legacy, and our ambition in writing the first biography has been to play a part in encouraging a general movement from option one and two to option three. There are certainly great treasures to be uncovered, even if, at the moment, all such excavations are indeed an act of faith. In our endeavours to ease the way for the faithful, we have been very lucky in receiving generous help on all sides.

Our starting-point was Malcolm Williamson's long-time publisher, Josef Weinberger, where John Schofield and Gerald Kingsley could not have been more helpful, and Lewis Mitchell has nurtured the project throughout, furnishing score after score and recording after recording. Soon we were pointed in the direction of the family. We could not have written the book without the enthusiastic support and deep generosity lavished on us by Dolly, Peter, Brenda, Tammy and Clare (in England) and Marion and Diane (in Australia). We are most grateful also to the wider family in Australia; and to Peter for contributing a foreword.

Malcolm's many friends have also been extremely forthcoming with help, prominent amongst whom have been Michael Armstrong, Christopher Austin, Ken Bailey, Mario Bois, Michael Brimer, Brian Brown, Nigel Butterley, Janet Canetty-Clarke, April Cantelo, Phyllis Champion, Lord Dynevor, Dobbs Franks, Tony Gray, Marion Grimaldi, Elizabeth Lamb, Michael Hoffenberger, Jayne Kempster, Sybil Michelow, Brian Shaffer, Robert Solomon, Jonathan Still, Valerie Thurston, Graham Wade, Lady Wilson, Marguerite Wolff, Richard Womersley and Yuval Zaliouk. Simon Campion, Malcolm Williamson's other major publisher and his partner for nearly thirty years, was understandably reluctant to talk in detail so soon after his death, yet has also kindly provided us with help.

We cannot write too highly of the support we have received from Music Sales and Omnibus Press. We would particularly like to thank Chris Butler, Chris Charlesworth, Philip Conway, George Goble and Sarah Bacon.

We are also very grateful to Richard Adeney, John and Ursula Alldis, Peter Alexander, Kenneth Alwyn, the Revd. Patrick Appleford, Judy Arnold, Margaret Ashby, Peter Bahen, Lewis Baldacchino, Professor John Bailey, Isla Bannister, Richard Baker, John Barker, David Barr, Alison Bauld, Martin Beaumont, David Bellamy, Elinor Bennett, Sir Richard Rodney Bennett, Tanya Berry, Brian Blake, Eduardo Bennarroch, Morwenna Bowen, Nicholas Braithwaite, David Bray, Mike Brewer, Thomas Brezinka, Peter Broadbent, Richard Broome, Alan Burgess, Esther Burri, Guy and Valerie Butler-Henderson, Jean Burrow, Grayston Burgess, Rupert Burchett, Don Burns, Anthony Burton, Margaret Cable, Anthony Caesar, Teresa Cahill, Kerry Camden, Dr Alexandra Cameron, Simon Carrington, Sally Cavender, Lyle Chan, Geoffrey Chard, Margaret

Humphrey Clark, Nia Clark, Dr Nicholas Clark, Conrad Clarke, Phillip Clarke, Tamsin Clarke, Paula Clarkstone, Richard Cock, Jean Cockburn, Stephanie Cole, Francis Coleman, Clare Colvin, Sue Compton, Roger Covell, John Cox, Rita Crews, Martin Dales, John Davis, Peter and Meriel Dickinson, Dawn Dodd-Noble, George Dreyfus, Father Jim Duffy, Vanessa Duscio, Colin Dunn, John Michael East, Lauren Edwards, Ross Edwards, Frank Ehlers, Jackie Ehlers, Michelle Ehlers, Geoffrey Elborn, Brian Elias, Osian Ellis, Audrey Ellison, Barbara Elsy, Angela Embleton, Andrew Fardell, Peter Farquhar, Ronald Farren-Price, Ros Farren-Price, Tony Fell, Jim Ferguson, Duncan Ferns, Paul Fenson, Elaine and Martin Feinstein, Christopher Field, Christopher Finzi, Michael Finnissey, Mark Fleming, David Flood, John Freeman, John Fryatt, John Gardner, Sir James Galway, Ruth Gerald, Bligh Glass, Alexander Goehr, Dr Joan Gomez, Colin Graham, Cy Grant, Edward Greenfield, Peter Greenhill, John Grover, Denise Grocke, Omri Hadari, Robin Haig, Louis Halsey, Derek Hammond-Stroud, Richard Hand, Heather Harper, Donald Hazelwood, John Hawkins, Marie Hayward, Morgan Hayes, Ken Healey, Marcus Hearn, William Hennessy, Joy Hill, Reg Hill, David Hillman, Kenneth Hince, Alun Hoddinott, Kate Holloway, Catherine Hope-Jones, John Hopkins, Eva Hornstein, Rebecca Hossack, Cecily Huckfield, Alyson Hunter, George Hurst, Father Duncan Hyslop, Antony Hopkins, Donald Hunt, Georgina Ivor, David Jones, Iris Kells, Belinda Kendall-Smith, Brian Kay, Tom Kennedy, Christopher Keyte, Richard King, Justice Michael Kirby, Dame Leonie Kramer, Michael Johnson, Brenda Last, Crispin Lewis, Brian Ley, James Litton, Robert Lloyd, James Loughran, Ray Lovely, Hilary Lowinger, Rose Lutyens, Gerard McBurney, Sir Charles Mackerras, Michael MacNally, Jane Manning, Mary Marshall, Christopher Martin, Nita Maughan, Kevin Mayhew, Sir Peter Maxwell Davies, June Mendoza, Father Meredith, Dr John Meyer, Richard Mills, Donald Mitchell, Kathleen Mitchell, Geoffrey Mitchell, Christopher Morris, Stephen Moore, Lee-ann Nazzari, Antonietta Notariello, Hayward Osborne, Brother Reginald, Carol Oakes, Max Olding, Erin O'Neill, Sarah O'Neill, Patricia O'Neill, Wendy O'Reilly, Ross Nye, Ruth Nye, Ian Partridge, Pam Patch, Marisa Pepper, Nigel Perrin, Sue Phipps, Graham Pike, Margaret Piper, Edmund Pirouet, Vincent Plush, Kenneth Pont, Richard Popplewell, Kevin Power, Debbie Price, Janyce Pringle, Gwenneth Pryor, Dr Ralph Reader, Marisa Robles, Betty Roe, Clover Roope, Ned Rorem, Barry Rose, John Rose, Eric Roseberry, David Rudkin, Piers Russell-Cobb, John Rutter, Catherine Sandbach-Dahlström, Antony Sanders, Jimmy Sangster, Susan Sayers, Peter Sculthorpe, Andrew Sievewright, Peter Shaffer, Elinor Shaffer, Geoffrey Shaw, Ned Sherrin, Frank Shipway, Alan Simmons, Chris Smythe, Patricia Sharland, Maggie Shapley, Vincent Shaw, Pru Skene, Graeme Skinner, Larry Sitsky, Michael Smetanin, Larry Smith, Maurice Smith, Stephen D Smith, Fiona Southey, Chris de Souza, David Squibb, Barrie Steinberg, Pauline Stevens, Roger Stone, Derek Strahan, Margot Strickland,

Rosamund Strode, Eva Sutton, Sue Sutton, Roderick Swanston, Maurice Tapley, Sheila Tapley, Jeremy Taylor, Rick Terry, Gerald Towell, Basil Tschaikov, Jean Thiel, Patrick Thomas, John Todd, Andrew Toovey, Phillip Truckenbrod, Robert Tucker, Lynn Tungate, David Tunley, Judith Tydeman, Jeremy Walker, Professor Kim Walker, Robert Walker, John Warrack, Martin Wesley-Smith, Dr Allan Wicks, Fay Weldon, Felix Werder, David Whitehead, Bill Whitfield, Yvonne Widger, Bram Wiggins, Jenny Wildy, Margaret Wilkinson, Greta Williams, Elizabeth Wilson, Gerard Windsor, Sara Wood, John Woolfe, Guy Woolfenden, David Wright and Bryan Youl.

We are most grateful for help with photographs from Dolly, Peter, Diane and Tammy Williamson and Marion Foote; from Josef Weinberger Ltd; and from Christopher Austin, Michael Brimer, Lord Dynevor, Antony Gray, Morgan Hayes, Justice Michael Kirby, Elizabeth Lamb, June Mendoza, Sybil Michelow, Kenneth Pont, Prudence Skene, Robert Solomon, Richard Womersley and Yuval Zaliouk. We have endeavoured to find out and advertise all illustrative sources, but would be grateful to be told of any areas in which we have failed to acknowledge properly other people's labours or work, despite out best intentions and efforts. Any such omissions will be rectified in any subsequent editions.

Finally, our grateful thanks for constant support to Heather and Jo Meredith, who have borne with great fortitude the introduction of a second (and equally time-consuming) Malcolm into their lives. Meanwhile Michael Meredith, with great generosity and much Trojan zeal, has offered perceptive criticisms on the whole of the manuscript to its great advantage. *Nil desperandum Teucro duce et auspice Teucro!* For all, our thanks.

Anthony Meredith and Paul Harris
Akeley and Buckingham
July 2007

For
APRIL CANTELO
who sang the music
with such distinction

and in memory of
DOLLY WILLIAMSON
(1930-2007)

Quis desiderio sit pudor aut modus
Tam cari capitis?

I

1 BESSIE'S BOY

Sydney, 1931–46

MALCOLM WILLIAMSON WAS BORN IN SYDNEY at the time that the famous Harbour Bridge was nearing completion.[1] Indeed, he was so close to it that he was within howling distance. In retrospect this can be seen as a most appropriate omen. Yet his parents could have little imagined that their first child would one day grow up to become their country's most gifted composer and, like the bridge itself, enjoy the possibility of enduring fame.

The Williamsons were a well-established Sydney family. Malcolm's father, the Reverend George Williamson, was employed in the early 1930s as a curate at St Clement's Church in Mosman, just minutes away from the harbour. For him and his young wife Bessie, the progress of the bridge had been followed with the same source of wonder and pride as the approach and arrival of Malcolm. It was a momentous occasion when the bridge's two sections were joined together; and Malcolm himself was there on the North Shore headland, in his pram at four months old, to glimpse the opening ceremony along with three-quarters of a million other Sydneysiders.

Malcolm was a fourth-generation[2] Australian, yet the Williamsons took as much pride in being British as any other Sydney family of the period. In 1931 the Harbour Bridge was less a symbol of nationhood than a token of the power of the far-flung British Empire. King George V might be a distant figure, but he enjoyed automatic respect; his son, Edward, Prince of Wales, was as popular as a film star. Even the arrival around the time of Malcolm's first birthday of England's most aggressive cricket captain, Douglas Jardine, failed to do

---

1 21 November 1931

2 Malcolm's great-grandfather, David Williamson, was born in Inverness in 1834, came to Sydney on the *Gresham* in 1859 and married Charlotte Wagner in 1868. Charlotte had emigrated from Cork with her elder sister in 1863.

Bessie Wrigley on her wedding day, 1929

The Reverend George Williamson

The young Bessie

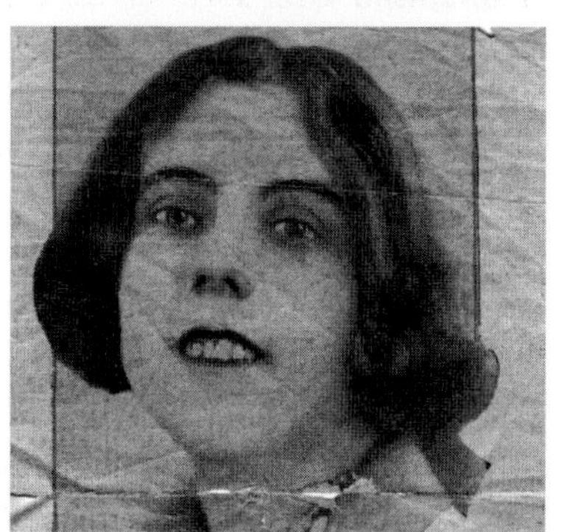

Malcolm and (right) with his father

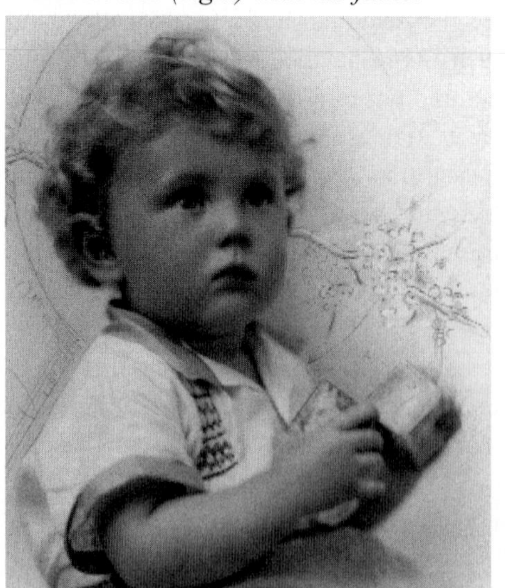

permanent damage to the two countries' special relationship. The Revd. George took the game seriously and was devoted to Don Bradman, but, for all his fierce outrage at the infamous 'bodyline' tactics, he and Bessie continued to look upon England as the mother country and would talk of a journey there as a visit 'home'.

For the little boy growing up in the harbour suburbs there were dramatic reminders of the all-embracing reach of the mother country in the ocean liners passing under the new bridge to and from their berth at Pyrmont. As the Williamsons' usual means of transport to the city centre was by ferry, there would be occasional sightings from water level of these giant ships. There was as yet little air travel to destabilise the romance of the six-week cruise to England, although Amy Johnson's solo flight to Australia in 1930 was a pointer to the future.

George and Bessie had settled in Raglan Street, Mosman, in 1929, the year of their marriage, close to St Clement's Church, where Malcolm Benjamin Graham Williamson was duly baptised.[3] Malcolm was an appealing child with curly golden hair and striking blue eyes. Even as a baby he possessed a strong personality, and Bessie doted on him. Bessie was a North Shore girl, born[4] at Neutral Bay and educated in the suburb of Gordon, the daughter of the owner of a flourishing store specialising in animal fodder. When she had first met George, at a tennis party at her parents' home, he was studying for the Church and his prospects looked promising, so Bessie quickly appropriated him.[5]

It soon emerged, however, that George's easy-going ways would inhibit his career advancement and frustrate Bessie's considerable social ambitions. Attractive and highly personable, Bessie had been a success at St Clement's and she was now looking forward to becoming a vicar's wife in an important Sydney Parish. Instead, in 1934, the Williamsons moved from the leafy hills of Mosman to St Mary's, twenty-five miles due west of Sydney on the dusty road to the Blue Mountains. St Mary's took its name from the Church of St Mary Magdalene, where George had accepted the post of Rector. It was hardly a coveted appointment. St Mary's had little to recommend it other than its simple little church, standing squat on a low hill. Though genteel inscriptions inside proudly commemorated an early Governor of New South Wales, its tombstones spoke of more humble folk, including transported convicts. To live at St Mary's, as Bessie would from time to time remind George, had always been a considerable penance.

---

[3] 26 January 1932. His godparents, the Revd. and Mrs Norman Fox, were friends of his father from his student days.

[4] Born in 9 February 1906, she lived with her parents many years in Macintosh Street, Gordon.

[5] Born in Petersham, NSW, in 1904, George Williamson trained at the Australian College of Theology, Moore Park, Sydney, qualifying in October 1927.

The thirty-year-old George bore such remonstration with gentle good humour.[6] He was well content at St Mary's, revelling in his scattered parish which included three other, equally remote, churches as well as the prison at Emu Plains in the foothills of the Blue Mountains. He especially enjoyed touring the countryside by pony and trap, and the chance to pause and chat with interesting passers-by, for George nursed an insatiable curiosity about his fellow men. Bessie was much less settled, but her frustrations were alleviated by the excitement of the birth of their second child, Marion.

In later life, as an expatriate struggling to assert his Australian roots, Malcolm was to exaggerate the harshness of St Mary's. It was a place, he said, 'between nowhere and hell', its climate as cruel as anything in central Africa, 'a great pocket of heat and humidity'.[7] He liked to remember that the lavatory was a shed at the end of the garden, with torn-up newspaper or paspalum[8] to hand; they used woodchips for the bath-heater and kept two sheep in the garden; badly treated prison gangs, which worked the roads, breaking stones, would sometimes leer at his father's accent – 'He talks flash, don't he!' Illness abounded, with occasional outbreaks of diphtheria; both he and his father caught scarlet fever. All in all, St Mary's was 'a place which had no right to exist at all'.[9]

He conceded that it was at St Mary's that music first mattered to him. In the church and the adjacent shack which served as a Sunday School there would be lusty choral singing, as his father led favourites like 'The Old Rugged Cross' and 'Fight the Good Fight'. Even so, said Malcolm, the music-making at St Mary's was motivated by 'a primeval desire to survive the hostile environment'. In such a forsaken place, 'where the summer is terrible and you can't have a bath and the loo had to be far from the house for sanitary reasons, people will turn in on themselves spiritually and artistically'. For that reason, he declared, even the very poorest possessed pianos.

But Malcolm's vivid imagination makes him an unreliable witness.[10] He could never resist painting a romantic picture, and the more florid the better:

---

[6] His family life was all the more precious to him after his own boyhood experiences. His father, who had been successful enough as a newspaper engineer to have a road named after him in his home town of Wagga Wagga, was tragically killed in an accident when George was only twelve. George's mother, too, had died young, leaving him to be brought up by her sister. He was grateful for the stability which his marriage and ministry had brought him.

[7] BBC TV feature film, *Malcolm Williamson Down Under*, 1975

[8] A coarse grass, which would have been growing all around St Mary's, but which, with its sticky seeds and long stringy stems, was ludicrously unsuitable for the task Malcolm here allots it. Malcolm always enjoyed being provocative.

[9] But there were consolations. The Victorian rectory, for example, was an attractive building, and Malcolm later mourned its passing.

[10] 'He had mother's characteristic,' writes his sister Marion, 'of making 4 plus 4 equal whatever they wanted it to equal! Malcolm never let the truth get in the way of a good story...' (March 2005)

Aged 4, at St Mary's

In the vicarage garden, St Mary's

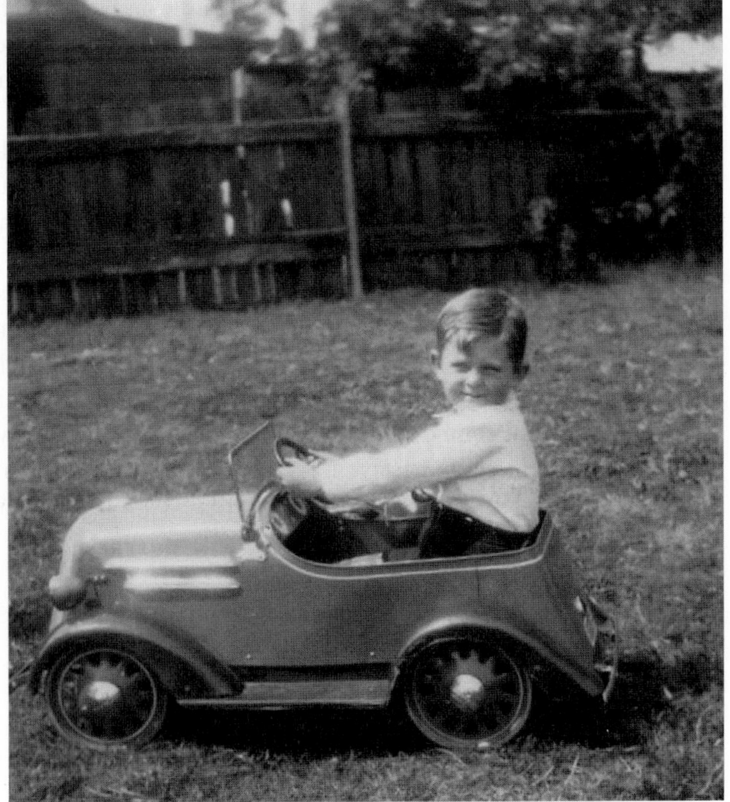

> Our family was poor, the piano our one treasure. Mum and Dad sang Schubert, Brahms and Mozart, playing the piano in turn.[11]

Alas for romance, there was no possibility that George gave moving renditions of *Der Erlkönig* to Bessie's artistic accompaniment, as Malcolm's sister Marion makes clear:

> I remember my parents later singing light musical comedy songs occasionally in the kitchen, but not together at the piano. I don't ever remember either my father or mother properly playing the piano… just a few basic chords, really.[12]

Nor were their financial circumstances quite so straitened as Malcolm suggested. He was simply attracted by the notion of parental poverty. It was, after all, the kind of thing expected in Lives of the Great Composers. There was a delightful piquancy in the idea of his mother going out to make ends meet: 'We bought liver at one shilling and sixpence from mother's speech and piano lessons,' he told one interviewer.[13]

But Malcolm was accurate in attributing his artistic temperament to his mother and his musical skills to his maternal grandmother, Mary Wrigley, who possessed a fine contralto voice. He had other musical forebears too. Manuscripts exist of songs written by his great-grandparents (the first generation of settlers) to words of their own. There is also, just possibly, a connection with Richard Wagner, German Wagners being a significant branch in his family tree. But Wagners have flourished in Germany with much the same regularity as Smiths in England, and the connection, though investigated assiduously by Bessie, remains unproven.

Malcolm's precocity soon became enshrined in family legend. As a baby he was said to have sat in his pram, grinning happily as he beat time to music on the radio. As a toddler he was inseparable from the piano, a Ronisch, and when he wasn't making music with it, he would sit beside it on the floor, gnawing away at its legs. The instrument survives, complete with Malcolm's teeth marks.[14] It was not long before Malcolm began to make up little pieces of music. 'The less said about the quality the better,' he was later to comment, 'but then I was only five'.[15] (This was one of his more conservative estimates. In other interviews he ascribed his earliest compositions to the ages of four, three and two.) Malcolm's gifts were all the more impressive for the haphazard nature of his early training. His first piano lessons, he used to relate, were given by the Sisters of St Joseph

---

[11] This recollection dates to 1995, when a friend of his schooldays, Robert Solomon, interviewed him for a possible biography.

[12] March 2005

[13] Robert Solomon

[14] As testified by its current owner, Wendy O'Reilly, one of his cousins

[15] *Daily Telegraph*, 29 April 1978

The vicarage, Concord

who ran a small school at St Mary's.[16] Bessie also gave her diminutive son some tuition, and it was not long before she realised that it was vital to find him proper professional help – useful ammunition in her battle to quit St Mary's. Told that he must find a new job to safeguard Malcolm's best interests, George speedily acquiesced, and in 1937, after just three years at St Mary's, the Williamsons returned to Sydney. Malcolm, who later maintained that much of his early life had been spent out in the bush, was not yet six.

George's new church – another St Mary's – was at Concord, just south of the Parramatta River a few miles from the city centre, a working-class suburb at the time. A cluster of gasometers[17] dominated the landscape and the air sometimes reeked of gas. George, who had always nursed a passion for cars, now acquired a small second-hand Wemys, with which he lent a little colour to the local landscape. Although the new Rector had been given a ramshackle bungalow, the Williamsons were delighted to be back in Sydney. Their home was comfortable enough with a useful verandah where the children could play. Moreover, a new rectory (another red brick bungalow) was soon being built on a plot near the church; Sydney's illustrious Archbishop Mowll unveiled and blessed the

---

[16] The Sisters of St Joseph were an order of nuns set up by Mary McKillop specifically to help the poor. Malcolm's sister Marion is sceptical about Malcolm's claims to have had lessons from the nuns, a claim made sixty years after the event and in the very year when the Pope visited Australia for the formal beatification of Mary McKillop. It could possibly be a romantic fiction.

[17] The Australian Gas Light Company's works were in Mortlake, Concord's twin suburb.

The bright boy of year 12, Mortlake School, 1940

foundation stone, a blue granite rectangle with the inscription picked out in gold.[18]

Encouraged by the episcopal stone, glittering away for all her friends to see and admire, Bessie soon tired of playing the humble vicar's wife. The social round, if pursued with determination, could be rewarding even in the lacklustre suburb of Concord. Before her marriage Bessie had played leading parts in amateur dramatics. Now in Concord church theatricals she could really indulge her passion for drama. As a devotee of Sybil Thorndike, Ruth Draper, Joyce Grenfell and Beatrice Lillie, she was a skilful comedienne and a beautiful speaker. George joined in too, under duress, and even played Henry VIII on one occasion. But Bessie was the star performer, her recitations as much admired as her ability to enliven the weakest of skits. She also began to give elocution lessons, exhorting the virtues of pure Thorndikian vowels. Bessie's burgeoning hobby offered Malcolm the bonus of regular family trips to the Sydney theatres, which he hugely enjoyed. Reading had become another passion, and he quickly made his way through his mother's drama library, steeping himself in

[18] The new rectory, like the old one, was in Brays Road.

Shakespeare, Chekhov, Ibsen and Barrie. He had also taken to writing his own poetry, celebrating the move to Concord with some simple hymns for his grandmother; at the age of eight he wrote her a passionate poem in blank verse about St Joan at the stake; in middle age he was still able to remember one of the stanzas of a childhood piece which had won Grandma Mary's warm approval:

> The silver sun sinks slowly in the west,
> The humble shepherd turns his flocks to rest,
> And day surrenders to oncoming night,
> As God commands.

Amid the excitement of her new life Bessie did not forget Malcolm's need for a competent teacher and he was soon having his first professional lessons on both piano and organ. Tom Leah, the organist at the Anglican church at Burwood, a short tram-ride away, proved exactly right for the task, kindly and yet demanding. Recognising unusual talent, Leah took a considerable interest in his young pupil and is remembered by the family as 'a great mentor to Malcolm'.[19] It was not long, however, before the pupil outshone the teacher, Tom Leah one day confessing to Bessie that Malcolm was now the better player.

Malcolm's talent on the piano brought him much attention at school (Mortlake Infants & Primary), his flamboyant performances of Percy Grainger's *Country Gardens* proving particularly popular with his fellow pupils and regularly arousing demands for more. Bessie was later to confirm that 'he was very popular at school naturally, because he could play so well'.[20] He was also showing considerable academic potential and after two years at Mortlake he was moved to an 'Opportunity School' two miles away at Summer Hill, where he was placed in a class which catered for children of high intelligence.[21]

Bessie, proud though she was of Malcolm's talents, was nonetheless anxious to control his increasingly obsessive nature, and there were big battles over his use of the piano, Bessie finally getting her way only by having a lock fitted so that she could put it out of use at certain times. Her mother, Grandma Mary, was rather more consistent in her encouragement, and Malcolm responded by writing her further religious verses and setting them to music. Grandma Mary still lived on the north shore, but had moved with Grandpa Benjamin to a large house[22] in Roseville, where on Sunday afternoons three generations of their large family

---

19 Malcolm's sister, Marion Foote. Malcolm himself was later to describe Leah as 'a very fine teacher, organist and pianist'.

20 Interviewed by Robert Solomon, 1992

21 Certain schools had 'opportunity' classes attached to them, which streamed specific academic abilities and inhibitions.

22 In Lord Street. The house, situated on a large corner plot, was owned by Grandma Mary's son, Sidney. Margaret Piper, Malcolm's cousin, writes: 'Grandmother had a lovely bedroom at the front of the house with a bay window. She always knelt beside her bed to say her prayers at night after combing out her long hair which she kept in a bun during the day...' Bessie was one of Grandma Mary's eight children, so Malcolm had many cousins in Sydney.

would congregate, providing a good audience for her powerful renditions of 'The Holy City' and 'Rock of Ages'. Malcolm's concentration would only last so long, and while his elders indulged indoors in religion and gossip, he preferred to lead the massed ranks of his many cousins in riotous games outside, jumping off the front verandah, roaring round the garden and generally doing it no good at all. Fortunately Grandpa Benjamin spent much of his time gardening (as a punishment, it is said, for an amatory indiscretion which tarnished the family's honour) so damage was never permanent.

The Williamsons had been in Concord only two years when the Second World War broke out. At first nothing much changed. There were occasional exercises simulating air-raids, when the family would wait together in the central hall for imaginary bombs. Gun emplacements sprang up in unexpected places, a fascination for an eight-year-old; rationing, however, was distinctly less thrilling, for Malcolm was keen on his sweets. Lack of petrol was also a nuisance in preventing the highly desirable weekend drives to rural Castle Hill, where he used to enjoy big lunches at Mrs Bailey's small café. The war in its first phase was curiously unreal, except for a few deprivations, and largely manifested itself in noisy farewells on the quaysides and patriotic music on the radio. Malcolm soon had his favourites. He could wring the heart out of 'The Maori's Farewell' – 'Now is the hour, when we must say goodbye' – and surely neither Hutch nor Layton and Johnstone could give quite such a flourish to 'Wish Me Luck As You Wave Me Goodbye'. He was too young to feel much of the communal anxiety as Sydney's young men went off to fight a distant war, but it was not to be long before he too experienced some of the anguish, at the announcements in his father's church of the latest parishioners to be killed and wounded. Malcolm was ten when the Battle of Britain resulted in particularly heavy losses of Australian airmen.

On the whole, however, youthful ebullience outweighed wartime anxiety. One of Malcolm's occasional playmates at this period was his young cousin Wendy Hill:

> My earliest impression of Malcolm was as a volatile, difficult child, given to flare-ups of bad behaviour. On one occasion, showing off his skills as a percussionist, he cracked a sugar bowl with a chicken bone! He would play the piano furiously, his sense of humour delighting us all. Often he used his own words for familiar songs. One line of his I still remember: 'My heart is like a stinking pig'.[23]

Wendy's elder sister, Margaret, has similar memories of his high spirits:

> Malcolm always entertained us with his outstanding pianistic skills and organising ability. A favourite game – no doubt to the annoyance of the adults – was 'Murder In

[23] July 2005. Wendy O'Reilly was the daughter of Bessie's sister Edith and one of a group of younger cousins which included Jack Hill, Winsome and Philip Wrigley. The older cousinhood featured Margaret and Reg Hill, and John, Ruth and Richard Wrigley.

With Marion and Diane, 1943

With Marion and a family friend, Anne Waddell, Sydney

Malcolm's first known composition

> The Dark'. There was also a form of noisy charades called 'Three Jolly Sailormen Looking for Work'. Malcolm was the invariable leader…[24]

Malcolm's leadership qualities led to an early domination over his young sister Marion. On one occasion, when George had organised a holiday exchange with another parson, allowing the family to spend time at Cooma in the Snowy Mountains, Malcolm decided that he would play scout leader and Marion his pack:

> First he insisted we dress for our parts. He pinched a whole lot of material so we could put tags on our socks. Then he christened me Miss Try-It – he was always very good on nicknames – and invented a series of scout-ish things to do – jumping, hiding and so forth. From my earliest days I can remember being led astray by him and told what to do…[25]

His lively manner and cherubic features made him a popular figure at his father's church, where, thanks to Tom Leah's tuition and despite his small size, he played the organ from the age of seven. He must have been a remarkable sight. But for the lack of wings, it could have been an overgrown and slightly plump angel sitting at the organ. His behaviour, however, was a little less than angelic. If, as sometimes happened, Marion was awarded the privilege of sitting beside him, he would feel obliged to entertain her:

---

[24] Margaret Piper, the eldest daughter of Bessie's sister, Edith Hill (July 2005)

[25] April 2005

Sometimes Dad would announce the next hymn and there would be an awful silence. Malcolm was in the middle of telling me a joke![26]

One token of Malcolm's precocious skills at this period survives, 'The Great Lady Waltz', which he composed at the age of ten as a birthday present for Grandma Mary. Not only is the main melody bright and original, but there is already an interesting key modulation, very much a characteristic of his later work. The Great Lady herself was to remain influential, and fifteen years later Malcolm wrote his First Symphony in her memory.

In 1942, around the time of 'The Great Lady Waltz', the war came more fully into everyone's lives. Sydney was shocked at the capture of 15,000 Australians on the fall of Singapore, and was thronged with American GIs, taking time off from training for the war in the Pacific. 8,000 arrived on the *Queen Mary* alone. Meanwhile the city had become the principal base of the British Pacific Fleet. By now most of the younger men in the family had enlisted; even Grandpa Benjamin gallantly signed up as a local warden and was busily checking the effectiveness of his neighbours' blackout. So George took the decision to join the Royal Australian Air Force, in which, at thirty-nine, he became a Flight Lieutenant and a padre.

Air Force life offered George a welcome change, for he was feeling more and more out of sympathy with the low-church hierarchies in Sydney. It was also a breathing-space in his sometimes difficult relationship with Bessie. George was content with simple pleasures: watching football and cricket, doing some carpentry and keeping a few hens; Bessie with her higher cultural ambitions tended to be dismissive of him as she set the family agenda. But George's posting to a Flying Training School at Deniquilin, three hundred miles south-west of Sydney, had one big drawback. It took him away from his young children. And there were now three of them with the arrival of Diane, eight years Malcolm's junior.

Soon afterwards Malcolm was entered for a boarding scholarship at Barker College, a Church of England school on the northern outskirts of Sydney which offered reduced fees for the sons of teachers and clergymen. Founded in 1890 and named after the second Bishop of Sydney, Barker College enjoyed a deservedly high reputation, and Malcolm's success in gaining a three-year award delighted his parents.[27] It was the kind of education which the family could not otherwise have afforded. For Bessie it must have been a considerable wrench to let her beloved son leave home. Theirs was an intense relationship of mutual adoration, but one in which feelings were volatile, quickly fluctuating between extremes and always stirred by a strong sense of competition. Bessie, for example, would recite poetry or a short story, while Malcolm accompanied her

---

26 April 2005

27 Bessie still recalled it with pride fifty years later.

on the piano, extemporising with whatever seemed most appropriate, each inspiring the other to ever greater histrionics. Through her precocious son Bessie was finding a new outlet for her own considerable artistic talents and she began to see Malcolm as a means to a more fulfilling and important life.

George's absence from Sydney reinforced his determination that Malcolm should go to Barker College, where he himself had taught briefly when a theology student. It might help stop the boy being over-mothered. With the uncertainties of war, too, it seemed a particularly safe environment, in a lush bushland setting close to the Ku-Ring-Gai National Park and the Berowra Valley. And Malcolm would not be far away, for Hornsby was in direct touch with central Sydney via the North Shore railway.

Barker College, for all its wartime merits, was far from the large and highly prosperous school it is today. In the economic slump of the early 1930s its roll had dwindled to only eighty pupils, and closure was imminent. However, a dynamic new headmaster, William Leslie, began to turn things around and by the time of Malcolm's arrival, in January 1943, there were three hundred and sixty pupils, a third of whom were boarders.

The choice of Barker had nothing to do with its music facilities, which, like those of most schools at this period, were negligible. There was one visiting teacher, the delightful Violet Turner, who soon after Malcolm's arrival (and the timing may be significant) decided to retire. Malcolm's memories of her were mixed:

> She was a charming old lady, but I cannot pretend she was of much quality. At eleven years old, my technique was considerably better than hers. The summit of our achievement was a Christmas concert where I played the piano for 'Tales From the Vienna Woods' for what was laughingly called The Waltz Choir. There was no harmony. It was all unison. And that was the end of The Waltz Choir…[28]

Her replacement, an elderly man called Henrie, enthusiastically provided the music for a school song. Malcolm was not impressed. There was no orchestra in the war years and Malcolm gave no thought to the brass band as it was linked to the compulsory cadet corps, which he hated.

But Bessie knew what she was about. She was not too besotted with her son to be unaware of his unattractive tantrums when his will was crossed.[29] If he was to become the Australian Beethoven and she to bask in glory as Beethoven's mother, he needed to acquire some self-discipline. The College might provide him with just the kind of steadying influence he now needed. Moreover, the headmaster was an avowed music lover, even though it was not the arts but muscular Christianity which dominated the school's life. Highly impressed by

---

28 MW to Robert Solomon, 1986

29 As a little boy, for example, he would kick the floor of a railway carriage in frustration that the train was not yet moving.

Malcolm's potential, Leslie had readily agreed with Bessie that he should be allowed out of school for extra tuition in Sydney every Saturday morning.

Even the shrewd Bessie, however, could not have planned what happened next. The greatest piano teacher at the Sydney Conservatorium was an elegant White Russian refugee with a formidable technique and fees to match, Alexander Sverjensky. As luck would have it, Sverjensky's son, Michael, was also at Barker, and one day, after not many months, there were cries of delight in the Concord rectory when Bessie received an exciting letter from Malcolm:

> Rosebud,[30] the most wonderful thing has happened! Alexander Sverjensky has been up here! And he played to me and I played to him![31]

Shortly afterwards Malcolm was given a scholarship to attend the Conservatorium every Saturday for free piano lessons with Sverjensky. At twelve-years-old and for the very first time, Malcolm would receive expert tuition.

Everything the Williamsons had heard about Sverjensky was impressive. He was rumoured to speak six languages and know everyone who was worth knowing. Born in St Petersburg, where his father was a railway worker, during the revolution he had left Russia with his family for a White Russian enclave in China, but returned later to his birthplace, studying for two years at the Conservatoire alongside his good friend Rachmaninoff. As a widely admired virtuoso pianist, he had toured Australia in the mid-1920s and eventually settled there.

A well-dressed and diminutive Jew, heavily bespectacled and with red hair surrounding a bald dome, Sverjensky both looked and acted the part of the imperious autocrat as he immersed his students in a heady mix of his Russian and French favourites: Rachmaninoff, Debussy, Scriabin, Medtner and Prokofiev. His lessons were of a pattern, always beginning with scales or a study, then some Bach, afterwards some Haydn, Mozart or Beethoven, and finally one of the Gallo-Russian post-romantics, or possibly Edward MacDowell whom he also loved.

For one of his former pupils, Alison Bauld, the whole Sverjensky mystique is still very vivid nearly forty years after his death:

> He was a phenomenal influence on pianists at that time. He was the teacher everyone at the Conservatorium wanted. Even pupils from other teachers wanted to change to him, which was very uncommon. He was in a different class! He really valued his students, enjoying dialogue with them on an even level – he wouldn't have been happy with a sycophant. He never raised his voice, but stimulated his pupils in a unique, mesmerising way. He was brimful with ideas! He would sometimes change direction and do something very unexpected – like one day asking me to read in

30 Rosebud was just one of Malcolm's many nicknames for his mother. Others included Mrs Wum and Primrose.

31 c.1943 (undated letter)

> French! He liked discussing ethics and emotions. It was all so exciting you remembered everything he said! And most of his female pupils were in love with him![32]

Malcolm adored Sverjensky. Here was a fellow obsessive, a kindred spirit and role model *par excellence.* He absorbed every delightful idiosyncrasy and worked at the piano with even greater fervour. His technique, which was to be outstanding by the time he was twenty, owed nearly everything to his six years with Sverjensky.

Alison Bauld fondly recalls several of Sverjensky's obsessions and rituals. He believed, for example, that a pianist should resist all outward display and be impervious to external distractions. To this end, while his pupils were playing, he would quietly come up from behind, pop chocolates into their mouths, and insist on no reaction. For Malcolm the *Clair de Lune* could never be the same without the surprise of a strawberry cream. Sverjensky's lessons lasted an hour, not a second more or less, with the first half-hour always a period of much greater intensity. ('One can only expect the brain to assimilate for half-an-hour at a time!') At two minutes to three every day he would walk down the hill to a milk-bar in Macquarie Street and restore his spirits with a chocolate milk-shake. A fine tennis player himself, he would strenuously urge his students to take up the game to improve their hand and eye coordination as well as their sense of rhythm. (Alas for Malcolm, tennis was something for which he had long since decided God did not intend him). The study of the piano, meanwhile, had to be given 200%, nothing more, nothing less. ('If you later lose 100% you can still operate at maximum capacity.') Above all, music needed passion! Sverjensky would talk with pleasure of a concert when his own passionate playing had encouraged a young man to propose to his girl friend. This kind of thing, he said, should happen more often!

Malcolm's first lesson with Sverjensky (later described as 'the most important thing in my life'[33]) was alarmingly inauspicious. His father, home for that particular weekend, had been sent to meet Malcolm at Wynyard Station and take him to the Conservatorium. Although they both arrived on time, there was confusion over the meeting-place and somehow they failed to locate each other. Eventually a friend happened to come across them, still anxiously searching, and brought them together, but Sverjensky greeted Malcolm's late arrival with icy displeasure.

It was not long, however, before Saturdays were very special occasions when, with a satchel full of music, Malcolm would catch the train at Hornsby, hardly noticing as it wended its way through interminable North Shore suburbs, his mind far away in the latest study score. Having crossed the old familiar harbour

[32] October 2005

[33] MW to Enith Clarke, Sverjensky's second wife, 7 September 1983

bridge and passed The Rocks, he would leap out at his destination into the arms of his mother. Off to meet the wizard, they would stride hand in hand along Martin Place and up the rise to Macquarie Street, all the while outdoing each other in the telling of funny stories, until, high above the city, on the edge of the tranquil Botanic Gardens, where cockatoos swooped from tree to tree and possums dozed before their night-time revels, they would make for the castellated nineteenth-century stable-block that was now the Conservatorium.

Sverjensky was quickly impressed with Malcolm. Here was not just enthusiasm but an exceptional talent worth nurturing. Malcolm quickly gained confidence and soon was not averse to testing the wizard's sense of humour, sometimes, for example, deliberately beginning pieces in bizarre keys.[34] There developed in time a strong friendship between Sverjensky's family and the Williamsons, Bessie remaining in contact for many years with Molly, his first wife, while Enith, Sverjensky's second wife, became one of a number of important mother figures in Malcolm's later life.

The pleasures of Saturdays went some way to ameliorating the discomforts of the rest of the week. Externally Barker College in January 1943 looked attractive, standing on a large, tranquil site stretching back from the Pacific Highway, with a new open-air swimming pool and two spacious sports ovals behind the school buildings. But, as the eleven-year-old Malcolm soon discovered, this was the age of bare walls, floors of linoleum and institutional paintwork. There were just two boarding houses, Plume House for the first year boys, and, on the other side of the central colonnade, Carter House. Dormitories seemed large and bare, home comforts entirely lacking. With the war on, boarding life was necessarily spartan. There were rosters for the pupils to clean the dorms; if the coke boiler failed and the water in the showers was cold, no-one made a fuss.

The tone of wartime Barker was set by its Headmaster, the hard-working William Leslie, who expected and achieved a high level of academic endeavour, and always led by example, happy to stoke a boiler or scythe an overgrown field. Malcolm was by no means typical of Leslie's intake which included tough boys brought up on cattle properties and sheep stations hundreds of miles inland from Sydney. Leslie's school catered for both brains and brawn. Intellectual and physical achievement, he believed, both depended on guts. A boy with guts would not only bring down the opposition with flying tackles but also solve his algebra. Guts led to good manners, honesty and an uncomplaining selflessness which meant that boys not only gave up their seats on trains but ate every morsel of their lumpy porridge. Leslie's stirring creed, as the school historian suggests, demanded obedience to a stern conformity:

> No slight breach of discipline would be tolerated, and boys coming into the school at once learned to adjust their ways to his expectations. The commanding voice was that of a man who, for all his bluff joviality, took himself seriously and expected others to

34 According to Nita Maugham, Sverjensky's assistant at the Con for several years

> do likewise… His values were direct and explicit. The national anthem was always sung; woe betide the boy whose hand strayed to brush away a fly. Standing to attention was no mere outward conformity; he regarded it as the bearing of those who were proud of their country and Commonwealth…[35]

Malcolm in later life tended to over-dramatise his four years at Barker in much the same way as his three years at St Mary's. He knew his Dickens, Thackeray and Bronte, so what could be more natural than to see himself, in childhood, in a haze of romantic oppression? In particular he would dwell on what he considered the excessive use of corporal punishment. His reminiscences are full of indignation:

> I was pathologically shy, and shyness is often taken for conceit. I do not believe I was conceited, but I recall a prefect caning me because he said that just because I played the organ in assembly I fancied myself as something out of the box, and he felt it his prefectorial duty to humiliate me…[36]

His memories of a senior boy being 'publicly thrashed (sixteen lashes) by Bill Leslie' blaze with outrage.[37] The boy, captain of the lst XV, had taken a toothbrush from the dispensary. Leslie explained to the school that the boy's parents had saved hard to pay the fees and, therefore, instead of expelling him, the usual punishment for theft, he was caning him. The punishment was carried out in awed silence. The boy came down the centre of the hall and climbed up onto the stage to meet the Headmaster, clad as usual in his gown. He bent down, unperturbed. On each stroke dust rose steadily upwards from the boy's trousers but he let out no cry. 'He took the thrashing without blenching,' wrote Malcolm, 'stood up like the mensch[38] he was and (final humiliation) had to shake hands with Leslie and walk down the aisle of the assembly to his seat.'[39] Malcolm's disgust accords with modern sensibilities but takes little account of the ethos of the 1940s when corporal punishment was as much a part of school life as caps, blazers, inkwells and copy-plate writing. It was he rather than Bill Leslie who was out of step with the times.

He was similarly extreme in his reaction to his Housemaster, the Deputy Headmaster, Leo 'Brose' Palmer, a well-meaning authoritarian who lived in Plume but was responsible for the running of both Houses.[40] Malcolm loathed his memory:

---

35 Stuart Braga, *Barker College*, p. 299

36 MW to Robert Solomon, 27 September 1987

37 They are also inaccurate. Sixteen was an exaggeration. The real number was eight.

38 As an adult Malcolm taught himself Yiddish, and enjoyed peppering his conversation with Jewish words.

39 MW to Robert Solomon, 27 November 1986

40 The nickname referred to a well-known boxer, Ambrose Palmer.

> I should like to have five minutes across the Styx to tell 'Brose' what I thought of him. I (or, rather, we) in Plume House, saw him swipe McAlister with such viciousness and power that that lovely dreamy lad fell to the floor and skidded, supine, the length of the dormitory. And for no good reason. Palmer then said to the 26 or so witnesses: 'Nobody is to say what he has just seen.' And, do you know, none of us did.
>
> The Plume House showers were like a military parade ground of backsides with horizontal purple stripes resulting from Palmer's caning of us in flimsy pyjamas.[41]

In another letter, similarly dated to the 1980s, 'Brose' still distressed Malcolm.

> Do you recall how we had to write home on Sunday afternoons, and 'Brose' Palmer looked at them to ensure that our script was worthy of the school? He was always assuring us that he did not absorb the contents, simply examined the style; so we always planned to write: 'Dear Mum and Dad, There is a self-righteous sadistic master here called Mr Palmer whom we all dread…' Alas, nobody, to my knowledge, ever dared write such a letter.[42]

By contrast, the recipient of these reminiscences, Robert Solomon, the school's outstanding athlete and a Rhodes Scholar, included 'Brose' in his list of the masters of whom he had fondest memories. He thought him stern but kind, genial and thoroughly professional. Malcolm's views, he believes, were those of someone who possessed only the two extremes of love and hate.

> I have no recollection of Malcolm or anyone else being treated unfairly by 'Brose'. And I spent a year in a dormitory with a bed next to his.[43]

Malcolm's highly coloured views of his schooldays reflect his lifelong pleasure in playing the role of the outsider, rejecting the values of the establishment and avoiding conformity with the feelings of the majority. He wished to be different. His hostility to his housemaster, like his own pianistic virtuosity, satisfactorily isolated him from the crowd.

So too did his emerging homosexuality. His daily life was dominated by the senior boys, who bestrode the school like young gods, and he found himself responding to them not only with awe but also, in some instances, with deep admiration. Forty years later he admitted having a serious crush on a tall senior boy who played good rugby and later went into the army.[44] He also claimed to have had an affair with the tough games-player who was publicly caned, and that this relationship included sex on Sunday nights at an assignation point somewhere between the two sports ovals. Fresh-faced and handsome, looking much younger than he really was, Malcolm would have had little trouble in attracting admirers.

---

41 MW to Robert Solomon, 27 November 1986

42 7 April 1987

43 August 2005

44 Interview with Robert Solomon, 29 July 1995

The games field was another area of school life in which he could indulge his passion for non-conformity. He was, in fact, a very enthusiastic swimmer, but to be a total failure on the games field was the only possible option for an outsider. In an interview in 1973 he was typically negative:

> In Australia I could never win. I was a total failure. I loathe competitive sports and the boarding school I was at, which was very fine in its own way, regarded competitive sports as an indication of manhood. It's so stupid I had, and still have, this fear of being put on a football field. I dislike physical violence enormously, and to this day I hate Saturday afternoon more than anything, for that is the time for sport… It has left me with a deep-rooted feeling of guilt that I'm opting out…

In athletics the only event he enjoyed was the bizarre one of cycling round a track as slowly as possible (feet not allowed to touch the ground).[45] Inclined to be a little plump and for ever joking that his sole exercise was at the keyboard, he soon acquired the nickname of 'Poddy'.[46] Yet it was only on the games field that 'Poddy' Williamson was a failure. Intellectually he showed outstanding potential. At subjects he loved, like Latin and French, he would regularly achieve 100%, though in those he disliked, notably science and geography, he would score as low as 8%. He so admired his scholarly Latin teacher John Duhigg that he sought him out in later life, planning to set to music the hymn Duhigg had once written for Barker.[47] He also admired a terse French teacher, Colin 'TAD' Taylor, the nickname referring to the frequency with which he would mutter 'Take a Detention'. But there were no detentions for Malcolm, a brilliant linguist, and he was to remain grateful to both men. Another important influence was a personable clergyman, Bruce McCarthy, one of the two resident masters in Carter House, with whom Malcolm eagerly explored spiritual matters. Barker College took its religion seriously if somewhat simply, its creed proclaiming 'a manly faith, seen in personal honesty and integrity, loyalty to crown and country, steadfastness of purpose'. With McCarthy Malcolm was able to probe deeper, becoming at one stage attracted to Catholicism and even nursing the idea of becoming a priest. He was likewise drawn to Judaism at Barker, enjoying discussions with another Carter resident, Asher Ginges, a cultivated Jew and English teacher who later lectured at Sydney University.

---

45 As he proudly told his son Peter

46 A young calf, or poddy, has a fat stomach.

47 Throughout his life he would proudly and accurately quote its opening stanza:

Aetatis primae tempora
Dum carpimus fugacia
Alumni usque carius
Canamus hoc collegium.

'May we pupils sing of our college with ever more affection, while we seize the fleeting moments of our youth.' It was written to be sung to the Old Hundredth psalm tune.

With Malcolm there was always a narrow dividing line between saints and sinners. He vilified 'Eek' Richardson, for example, although he was a lively English master who had inspired him to venture beyond Henry Newbolt and the other poets being taught in class. But when he proudly showed 'Eek' a book of modern verse and declared how much he was enjoying Brooke, Eliot, Sitwell and Dylan Thomas, 'Eek' cautiously suggested it would be better to keep to the examined syllabus. Malcolm never forgave him.

Malcolm's own poetry developed well during his Barker years. At thirteen he was writing with simple ingenuity:

Lamb
Gambol in a wood.
Damn
Man must have his food
Life
Young and pure and sweet
Knife
Man must cut and eat
Ah!
Slaughterhouse for thee
Baa!
Perverse misery.

Two years later he was aiming for greater profundity:

> ... embedded in a black-green lacquered earth chained to the sea
> The crescent waves are striving for the land...[48]

The Barker boys, for all the stern discipline, do not seem to have been cowed. Malcolm, for example, in telling a story criticising 'Brose' for wrongly accusing him and a fellow junior of sexual misconduct, gives an interesting glimpse of high spirits:

> Palmer caught us in the lavatory one night after lights out. We were making water-bombs with exercise-book paper, and giggling like mad. The next morning Palmer gave us a long and pious lecture on the bestiality of homosexuality... Palmer, like many charitable Christians, assumed culpability with no basis.[49]

The boys' practical jokes were sometimes quite daring. They played awful tricks on the Chaplain, Canon 'Mouse' Pain, on one occasion suspending a cicada, tied to a cotton thread, out of an open window, so that its screeching created havoc in his lesson. It was also not unknown for senior boys to have affairs with the maids. One maid, who was still serving meals although obviously pregnant, was called 'Ajax' after a famous racehorse, because she was right out in front.

---

48 Fragments of poems of his Barker College days, remembered by Malcolm in a letter sent to Emily Coleman, December 1956

49 MW to Robert Solomon, 27 September 1986

The atmosphere, then, was probably much more relaxed and enjoyable than Malcolm later cared to admit. Academically he was showing great promise and he passed his Intermediate Certificate in 1945, after which the College extended his scholarship for a further, fourth year. So much for his being a failure! As a pianist, too, he was more than making his mark. Indeed, as he himself put it later with a disarming lack of modesty, 'My scholarship was extended because I was something of a phenomenon'.

He had made his mark as a 'phenomenon' very early. It was a custom at Barker to stage a rowdy New Boys' Concert. The pupil preceding Malcolm tried to sing 'Lili Marlene' but after only a few tentative bars was heartily booed off the stage. Malcolm strode determinedly to the piano, ignored the ironic applause, and startled everyone with a rousing performance of 'Men of Harlech' which completely altered the atmosphere of the evening.

Keen to stay 'a phenomenon', Malcolm had enlisted the help of his friendly house matron to wake him up at 6.15 every morning, so he could practise for an hour on the piano in the Assembly Hall. Every afternoon Malcolm also managed forty-five minutes on the Dining Hall piano. His playing was not to everyone's delight, and he found it hard to forget one particular incident:

> A lovely guy came up one afternoon. It was near Leaving Certificate time and that poor guy was sweating in that artillery room under the Dining Hall and my music was driving him crazy. He asked me to stop and I seem to recall being beastly to him. I'd like that time over again so I could be more considerate…[50]

His practising in the Dining Hall was sometimes interrupted by a kitchen maid called Anne or 'Aniseed', who would often come up to gossip and flirt with him. But Aniseed's devotion was not fully reciprocated. When rudely told that he was tired of her hanging around him, she made her exit with impressive dignity. 'Williamson,' she declared, 'you are only a small part of my life at Barker College!' He treasured the remark.

It was not long before Malcolm was allowed to play the harmonium at morning assembly, his pleasure tempered only by the fact that it had seen better days. He also sometimes helped out on the organ at St Paul's Church, Wahroonga, where 'Mouse' Pain was Rector – part of Barker boarding ritual being the long march in Sunday best to 'Mouse''s morning service.

Bessie's best-laid plans worked well. The combination of Malcolm's weekly tuition from Sverjensky and hours of dedicated practice in his spare time at Barker saw a significant advance in his skills. By the age of twelve he could play competently half a dozen concertos from the classical repertoire.[51] He was also

---

50 MW to Robert Solomon, July 1995

51 Interview at Barker College, 1987

52 *ibid.*

busy composing. At Barker he usually sat by the swimming pool to write, often plunging in because he found the act of swimming helpful to creativity:

> Somehow the brain is liberated... something happens to the circulation of the blood from the neck to head... I've written some of my best music under water.[52]

There were the inevitable comments from passers-by as he sat lost in thought, but on the whole his privacy was respected and he also attracted his admirers. One of these was a friend called Drinkwater, unkindly nicknamed 'Fatty'.

> I'd play him my newest piece on one of the tacky pianos and he'd say 'Gee, Willy! Gee Willy! You should send that in!' There was an idea in people's minds that there was some big place in Sydney to which you sent pieces of music ...[53]

By the end of 1946 Bessie and George had to make a decision as to whether or not Malcolm, just turned fifteen, should remain at Barker for his Leaving Certificate or devote himself elsewhere to music. The decision proved an easy one. He had been making such good progress with Sverjensky that he was encouraged to take, and succeeded in securing, a scholarship for full-time study at the Conservatorium.

Malcolm's departure from Barker College was an emotional one, for there were many friendships he would really miss among both pupils and staff; besides, he had made his reputation there, was accepted as someone special, and had nothing more to prove. For all the harsh restraints of boarding life, he was strangely comfortable at Barker, gaining security from his membership of its enclosed order. At fifteen, too, he was less than certain that he would welcome every detail of his life coming under the careful scrutiny of his mother, now that he would again be living at home. Bessie's expectations were not necessarily all his. Nonetheless, the new challenge was undeniably exciting. He would be exchanging the jurisdiction of 'Brose' Palmer and Bill Leslie for that of the most famous musician in all Australia, Eugene Goossens, who had just arrived to take control of the Sydney Conservatorium. Instead of playing to 'Aniseed' or 'Fatty' he would have in his audience some of the best pianists in the land, even the great Goossens himself. And Goossens, so everyone was excitedly telling him, was something of a phenomenon...

---

53 Barker College, 1987

Malcolm's father during the war

The Wrigleys, 1952: Bessie with her parents, Benjamin and Mary; her brothers (l-r) Sid (a teacher), Eric (a travelling salesman) and Walter (a grocery store manager); and sister Edith (a comptometer operator). Walter was a fine tenor; all were musical.

2 THE STUDENT PRINCE

Sydney, 1947–52

THE END OF THE WAR, George's return and Malcolm's new scholarship all helped clarify Bessie's thinking. She had only just turned forty, but the possibility of a bright future was marred by a husband whose career offered little prospect of advancement. George was condemning the whole family to genteel poverty – hardly the best support for Malcolm's blossoming talents. Fortunately, as both Marion and Diane were now at school, Bessie felt able to take responsibility for the family's fortunes, and, as a result, in 1946 George gave up the ministry and, instead, agreed to support her in the running of a business.

She began by taking over a garage on the Parramatta Road, Annandale, a sop perhaps to George's love of cars, and, if so, a miscalculation. The failure of this enterprise within a year, however, only whetted Bessie's appetite for further challenges and by 1947, when Malcolm started at the Con, the Williamsons had acquired the Banister Overall Service, an industrial laundry offering a cleaning and mending service to a wide group of companies in and around Sydney.[1] Bessie, who had always been a fine seamstress, making clothes for herself and her daughters, quickly mastered the intricacies of industrial sewing machines and extended the business to include the manufacture of overalls, shirts and dust covers to her own design. George was assigned a lesser role, as she herself explained:

> My husband wasn't good at money matters or figures, so I ran things. He used to go round on a truck with a load of goods.[2]

George's affability proved helpful in attracting customers and keeping them happy, usefully complementing Bessie's creativity and shrewdness. The business prospered and grew.[3]

---

1 The Banister Overall Service was in Hill Street, Leichhardt.

2 Interviewed by Robert Solomon, Newcastle, 1992

3 It was too big an operation to be just a family business, but Bessie found jobs for her brother Eric and her brother-in-law Lloyd.

They were now living on the North Shore again, having moved from the Concord vicarage to Beauty Point, Mosman, not far from St Clement's Church where George had been curate. Their bungalow in Central Avenue[4] did not have views of the Middle Harbour, but it was close to a picturesque promontory whose tropical bush had not yet been totally tamed by developers. Across the nearby Spit Bridge lay the Pacific Ocean, just a mile away, and George would often take the three children to Manly Beach for an early morning swim.[5]

It was from Mosman, therefore, that Malcolm travelled every day to his full-time studies at the Con. There he continued to work with Sverjensky and began composition lessons with Alex Burnard, a former pupil of Vaughan Williams and friend of Percy Grainger.[6] The dominant figure in his life, however, soon became Eugene Goossens. The Con's new Director, who had also taken over the Sydney Symphony Orchestra, had been enticed to Australia by a salary higher than that of the Prime Minister. Now in his late fifties, Goossens was a cultured man who spoke several languages. As a conductor who had worked all over the northern hemisphere he brought a refreshing international vision to parochial Sydney. He was a friend of Stravinsky, Toscanini and Picasso and had been on close terms with Ravel. But for all his world-wide contacts and travels Goossens was as English as brown Windsor soup, exuding old-world *hauteur* from every pore and speaking in rich Churchillian tones. He was once one of England's most promising composers, often mentioned with Bax and Walton. He had trained under England's most charismatic conductor, Thomas Beecham. As he strode down the corridors of the Con, a camel-haired coat swinging from his shoulders, Goossens seemed the epitome of English elegance. Malcolm had a new role model.

On Goossens' arrival in 1947 the Con was still struggling to shake itself free from a reputation for dilettantism. There were about two thousand students, the majority part-time. Dilettantism and dedication existed side by side. Diane Collins, in her history of the Conservatorium, explains why:

> There were so many attractions: an enchanting building, the spectacular location, prestigious teachers. Just being there was a form of social credentialing. Isador

4 Central Avenue later became Pindari Avenue; the house has since been demolished.

5 Diane Williamson writes: 'Dad used to take us for a swim on Sunday morning before breakfast. Manly was about twenty minutes drive from home, and the pool was an inner harbour salt water pool formed by putting a shark net across the inlet. It was tidal; there was a pontoon we could swim to and there was a sandy beach.' (March 2005)

6 Burnard was as highly regarded as a composer and conductor - 'You seem to me to be exactly what the highest flight of Australian musical genius should be,' Grainger had once written to him - but his music fell from favour. 'One of the disgraces of Australia,' declared Malcolm in 1987, 'is that they didn't make the most of the late Alexander Burnard.' He much valued Burnard's book on Harmony and Composition. Malcolm was also taught by Livingstone Mote (Academic Studies), Edward Robinson (History of Music), Gladstone Bell (Chamber Music), Wilmer Johnson (Theory) and Joan Dawson Bell (Theory).

With Bronzy, 1947

In the Mosman garden, 1948

> Goodman[7] remembered one student – the wife of a grazier who was also the proprietor of a chain of butcher shops. The woman arrived each week in a chauffeur-driven limousine. At the first lesson Goodman ordered her to cut her very long fingernails and 'take off all that junk you're wearing'. He was referring to some large diamond rings that she frequently left behind, under the piano lid, when her lesson ended…[8]

Such eccentricities seemed quite natural in a building whose original function was to house the horses of a Governor-General yet whose exterior design was bizarrely modelled on two Scottish castles. Visitors to the Botanic Gardens, after a beer or two in the bright midday sun, might easily imagine El Cid galloping out to the fray from under those romantic battlements. The interior, however, was distinctly less the stuff of Hollywood epic. After thirty years' use as a music conservatory, the old building was forlornly inadequate: its concert hall in disrepair, its library equipped with only two tables and twelve chairs; there was a tiny common room for the students, and none at all for the staff.

When Malcolm had first studied at the Con, in his Barker College days, its Director had been another Englishman, Edgar Bainton, a devotee of Elgar and Vaughan Williams. Bainton's most significant initiative, as far as Malcolm was concerned, had been to create a permanent School of Opera,[9] a particularly important move at a time when there was no Australian Opera company, let alone an Opera House.[10] Malcolm's involvement in the Opera Group was wholehearted, its effect on his development considerable:

> At the Conservatorium I had to coach opera, play the piano for singing classes and opera production classes, and play the celeste in the opera orchestra. All this changed my outlook on music. Having, like most students, adored the piano works of Chopin and Beethoven, music which is closely written and has such marvellously composed inner parts, I came to see that I was wrong to despise the simple diatonic melodies of Italian opera. Only when I worked on these operas did I begin to learn what works in the opera house – to see, for example, what a genius like Verdi can achieve with simple arpeggiating accompaniments. And not only Verdi, but Donizetti, Bellini and the less significant masters, even Charpentier with his *Louise* – things like that I used to dread playing because the music was not pianistic and seemed to have only the most rudimentary interest under the vocal line – all this was instructive….[11]

Goossens' use of professional players and singers helped raise standards but inevitably they were variable. When the Sydney critics meanly accused a Con production of being second-rate, Goossens turned witheringly on their

7 A highly talented professor, rated by Neville Cardus as the best pianist in Australia.

8 *Sounds from the Stables*, p.114

9 The first opera Malcolm ever saw was Bainton's *The Pear Tree*, revived at the Con in 1944 with professional singers helping out the students.

10 It was Goossens who first pushed for an opera house and suggested the Bennelong Point site below the Botanic Gardens.

11 *Sadler's Wells Magazine*, Winter 1966

'gratuitous arrogance'. Would they prefer, he asked, annual productions of *The Student Prince*? Weren't they aware that three-quarters of a fresh loaf in Sydney's empty operatic larder was better than no bread at all?[12] With his critics suitably chastened, Goossens continued Bainton's practice of mounting two productions a year, still under the energetic direction of Hilda Mulligan, who not only had extensive professional operatic experience in Europe but had once been a pupil, it was believed, of Puccini. One absorbing production followed another. *Falstaff*, *Otello*, *The Force of Destiny*... Malcolm listened and learned as Hilda wove her usual magic. The last opera in which he participated (playing the celeste) was Goossens' *Judith*, still remembered today for the singing of the leading role by Joan Sutherland, a young Sydney secretary making her first stage appearance.

Meanwhile Malcolm's reputation as a pianist steadily grew. He had started from a position of strength, able at fifteen to play 'the Liszt E flat, the Grieg, three Mozarts, one Beethoven, Shostakovich, Prokofiev Third and things like that...'[13] He found it comparatively easy, therefore, to make a good impression at Goossens' exclusive Monday morning Diploma classes. Donald Hazelwood remembers one such occasion:

> Malcolm was asked to perform a section of a Rachmaninoff Concerto. He did so with great aplomb and Goossens was extremely impressed. 'How long have you been practising that?' he asked. We expected Malcolm to suggest something spectacularly short, but he was always the master of the unexpected. 'Oh, about three years,' he replied.[14]

By the time he was seventeen Malcolm was one of the Con's best-known students, his good looks and big personality making as much of an impact as his musical virtuosity. Eva Sutton, another of Sverjensky's pupils, recalls him as

> young and beautiful, gregarious, a good pianist and an outstanding student. All the girls were passionately in love with him.[15]

Malcolm's self-belief grew with the adulation.[16] He loved the brilliant opening to the Khachaturian Piano Concerto, for example, and would show it off at the slightest excuse.[17] Most of Sverjensky's pupils acquired an outstanding technique, but Malcolm excelled them all, helped by Sverjensky's insistence that

---

12 Rosen, *The Goossens*, p.311

13 Interview in *Musical America*, April 1971

14 December 2005

15 Eva Sutton (*née* Katz), August 2005

16 Malcolm did not find all the piano teachers at the Con so encouraging. He believed that Nancy Salas, the formidable devotee of Kodály, treated him and other students 'like dirt'. In strong contrast, he was devoted to Olga Krasnik, who exuded style both in her appearance and her playing.

17 Lewis Foreman, *Independent* obituary notice, March 2003

his future lay as a pianist rather than as a composer, and that he should therefore concentrate on becoming 'a second Edwin Fischer'.[18]

Sverjensky began to change his mind, however, when Malcolm was awarded the unique honour of a special scholarship to study composition on a one-to-one basis with Goossens. He was impressed, too, with Malcolm's cycle of Six Love Songs which he heard wonderfully sung by Joan Sutherland. This small triumph Malcolm was later to attribute modestly to the singer:

> The songs weren't important, except that she sang them so beautifully. Joan was delightful, extrovert and unspoiled, a very nice, quiet, gung-ho Australian girl. She had a glorious voice but at that time not many people recognized it. I don't think she was aware of how fantastic it was.[19]

Sverjensky also admired the range of Malcolm's writing. His violin lessons, for example,[20] had inspired a promising *String Quartet* and *Minuet*, while his battles with the French horn resulted in a study for that instrument, written for his friend and fellow student Barry Tuckwell:

> My teacher, Alan Mann, said I would never be any good [with the French horn] and why didn't I just forget it! But – perhaps to ease the blow – he suggested I write a piece for Barry to play. And so I wrote what I thought was a very difficult study. But Barry came into the studio, sat down and played it straight off, as if it were nothing![21]

Malcolm's compositional studies with Alex Burnard, therefore, had already proved fruitful when, in 1949, Eugene Goossens took over. Burnard might acidly comment that the Con would be better off without such flashy celebrities, but Malcolm received tremendous benefit from Goossens' sophistication and technical expertise, not least in studying with him his programmes with the Sydney Symphony Orchestra, which included first performances in Australia of works by Debussy, Delius, Clive Douglas, Grainger, Khachaturian, Mahler, Prokofiev, Ravel and Tchaikovsky.[22] He received, above all, some fascinating insights into Richard Strauss, whose intricate scoring and brilliant dramatic effects Goossens much admired.[23]

---

18 Sverjensky, who later gave the first performance in Sydney of Malcolm's First Piano Sonata, became a great enthusiast of Malcolm's work.

19 A talk given at Barker College, Hornsby, 1987

20 He was taught by the talented Phyllis McDonald, a short, plump lady with the thickest of spectacles, of whom Heifetz once declared, 'She looked like a devil but played like an angel'.

21 *Musical America* interview in the 1970s

22 There were also some interesting lesser-known pieces: Ghione's *Suol d'Aleramo*, Martinu's *Double Concerto for Two String Orchestras, Piano and Timpani*, Stravinsky's *Apollon Musagète*, the Britten-Berkeley *Mont-Juic* and Goossens' own first two symphonies and *Phantasy Concerto for Piano*.

23 Four works in particular: the *Rosenkavalier Suite*, *Symphonia Domestica*, *An Alpine Symphony* and *Metamorphosen*.

Equally inspiring, perhaps, were Goossens' tales of his younger days which would sometimes colour his tutorials. Assisted by his strong Russian Ballet connections, Goossens in the 1920s had entered the privileged, bohemian world of London's Bright Young Things. He knew everyone. There were stories of the Sitwells and William Walton; Aldous Huxley and Nancy Cunard; Augustus John and Virginia Woolf; Noel Coward and Serge Diaghilev. One story might be set at Stulik's Eiffel Tower Restaurant with Ivor Novello and Viola Tree; another at the Savage Club with Moiseiwitsch and Max Hambourg in the card room; or at home with his friends and neighbours Frank Bridge, Arthur Bliss and Edmond Dulac. He might be listening to A E Housman and G K Chesterton, discussing *The Ring* at George Moore's; to George Gershwin, embellishing his latest hits at Hoytie Wiburg's; to Stravinsky, waxing lyrical on Nijinsky at Sybil Colefax's or Karsavina at Jacob Epstein's; and to Olga Haley singing the songs of his life-long friend John Ireland at his Chelsea home. For Malcolm this insight into London's artistic past was an encouragement to dream big dreams. And then, beyond London, there were even more inspiring tales of Elgar, Sibelius, Debussy, Poulenc, Pavlova... Malcolm, who all his life had a great love of story-telling, avidly consigned the best tales to memory. He was very fond of one about Melba:

> Gene Goossens, standing in at the last minute for Beecham at one of Melba's farewell operas, rushed to the great lady's dressing-room only minutes before curtain-up to let her know that he had arrived. He knocked, hurried in, and found himself nose to nose with a sight to behold, Dame Nellie in her ample negligée. 'Oh! Gosh! I'm er... I thought er... Maybe I should... er see you later, Dame Nellie'!

Alexander and Molly Sverjensky

It is often wrongly stated that before Malcolm settled in England he had no knowledge of twentieth-century music beyond the period of Delius, Vaughan Williams, Bax and Bliss.[24] There can be no doubt that, at the very least, he and Goossens discussed Schoenberg and serialism. Goossens had been among the First Violins in that famous pre-war concert at the Queen's Hall when the promenaders violently hissed their disapproval of Schoenberg's Five Orchestral Pieces. Goossens later conducted the work himself and would often recall how he emptied the Hollywood Bowl with it. He did not immediately repeat the process at the Sydney Town Hall, but in 1950 Klemperer was there conducting Schoenberg's Theme and Variations. Malcolm therefore enjoyed much more adventurous music-making in Sydney than is sometimes suggested. In 1949, for example, he first came across Rawsthorne and Moeran:

> I found out that there was a very courageous chamber group in Sydney called the Collegium Musicum. Their evening meetings were held in a little attic room where they served coffee and biscuits. I can remember hearing – with Piers Coetmore – the Moeran String Trio, some Finzi and another piece which impressed me more than any – it absolutely knocked me out for six – the Rawsthorne Theme and Variations for 2 Violins. This little group of players, existing on a shoestring and goodwill, valued this work so much that they trotted it out one concert after another…[25]

Much of Malcolm's own music-making centred around the Young Musicians' Group of New South Wales, founded 'to foster friendly co-operation among students of music' and holding monthly meetings at the Lyceum Club in King Street. Malcolm as a committee member took responsibility for the organisation of concerts, in which he not only regularly performed but occasionally conducted his own choral works.[26] With a membership of around a hundred and fifty, the club had a lively, convivial atmosphere. One of Malcolm's best friends, violinist Brian Blake, was a fellow committee member:

> Richard Bonynge,[27] Joan Sutherland and Geoffrey Parsons were all guests. We used to hold extra meetings in each other's houses as well as in Paling's Music Store, the largest music store in Sydney with about fifty practice rooms attached. It was at Betty Allen's home that Malcolm met Joan Sutherland for the first time.[28]

---

24 It was an inaccuracy which Malcolm himself seemed to encourage. In 1973, for example, at a Sydney seminar he declared 'Stravinsky and Bartok were the avant-garde then [early 1950s] - and only like a distant echo over a distant hill one had heard about Schoenberg'.

25 Interviewed by Alan Poulton for his book on Alan Rawsthorne, p. 56

26 In February 1950, for example, he conducted a Christmas carol ('A Boy Was Born in Bethlehem') and a hymn of his own as well as Grainger's arrangement of 'Brigg Fair'.

27 'I remember Richard Bonynge played Haydn and Mozart quite wonderfully as a Con student,' wrote Malcolm to a friend in 1983, 'but it was a triumph against lack of technique; he was a pupil of Lindley Evans, and was as tight as a drum... Yet he was an extraordinarily good classical player. '

28 June 2005

Brian Blake's violin was the perfect foil for Malcolm's piano and the two of them spent much time together at Beauty Point working through the repertoire.

Eva Sutton was another regular visitor to Malcolm's home, often with her horn-playing brother Claude Katz:

> Malcolm and I would pound away at the two pianos! On one occasion he played second piano for me in a concerto competition sponsored by the ABC. I played a Beethoven Concerto and he played the 1st Shostakovich Concerto with that fine trumpet player John Robertson. I didn't get through but Malcolm made it to the finals at the Town Hall with the Sydney Symphony Orchestra under Joseph Post.[29]

Malcolm's role within the group was usually that of chief entertainer. Brian Blake remembers hilarious sessions around the Williamsons' piano at Beauty Point as Malcolm challenged his friends to keep singing 'Much Binding in the Marsh', the signature tune of Kenneth Horne and Richard Murdoch's popular radio show, while he moved swiftly from one key to another.

Family life at Beauty Point inevitably revolved around Malcolm, to the detriment of his sisters' considerable musical abilities. On some occasions there was no piano available for practice; at others there was a ban on making noise. It was hard for the teenage girls to be kept away from the radio and gramophone and it led to embarrassments at school where the current Hit Parade was, to everyone else, a topic of consuming interest. Marion also found discouragement elsewhere:

> I was good at sport, but Malcolm and mother tended to put sport down. Malcolm called me in quite a scathing way 'Miss Sports Girl'. I did well at it, it was my achievement, yet it wasn't recognised... Dad, however, would take an interest, and would sometimes take me along to cricket and football games...[30]

Malcolm was at his best when sharing his own interests with his younger sisters, and Marion and Diane remain grateful for his encouragement in literature and music:

> He was always taking us under his wing and introducing us to different authors. Robert Louis Stevenson, for example, and Thomas Hardy. Early presents from him often featured classical 78s: *The Nutcracker*, *The Miller's Dance*, *The Love for Three Oranges*... We learnt the Peter Warlock songs through listening to him, and several of his own – 'My Heart is Like a Singing Bird' and 'The Birthday Song'. His friend Betty Allen used to sing those beautifully. We learnt a great deal of music, by osmosis really. The Shostakovich and Prokofiev piano concertos, for example, outrageous works at the time, which we have loved ever since...[31]

A further impression of Malcolm in his college days comes from his cousin, Reg Hill.[32] The Hills, who also lived at Beauty Point and were involved in the

---

29 Eva Sutton, August 2005

30 Marion Foote, August 2005

31 Diane Williamson, July 2005

32 The son of Bessie's sister Edith

Banister Overalls business, saw much of the Williamsons:

> Malcolm's natural talent for composition when in his late teens was outstanding. He would compose music with appropriate lyrics, play them for us on the piano and sing – and have us in hysterics! On one memorable occasion at Beauty Point Malcolm emerged from his music room with a French horn, played some beautiful tunes and thereafter had us in fits of laughter with a succession of rude noises. He enjoyed having an audience. He would make us laugh, for example, with illustrated stories of 'The Dunny Man', the fellow with the horrible task of calling in the early hours to remove the 'nightsoil' bin from the outside toilet in the days before sewerage was available in Sydney. After entertaining us he would as often as not return to his room to work again. His dedication to his music was extreme. And we, as visitors, were always conscious of not disturbing him when he was in his music room.[33]

The peace and quiet his family afforded was helpful. In 1949, his last year at the Con, Malcolm, inspired by Goossens, completed three pieces for full orchestra: a Scherzo; a Lento; and a Theme and Variations.[34] And, even more impressive, there was a short score for an eleven-minute documentary film, *The Timber Getters*, a National Film Board production celebrating the harvesting of giant eucalypts from remote forest areas. The film survives, and what little music was allowed into the film is notable for some rich, though melodically unexceptional, writing for the strings.[35] Documentary film music, he had been firmly told by Goossens, should be as anonymous as faded wallpaper.

Malcolm was thriving on hard work, and at the same time enjoying and living college life to the full. Perhaps too much. His adolescence had been marked, on his own admission, by a series of hopeless love affairs with both sexes.[36] Now, as a confident seventeen-year-old, things were going much more his way, as Bessie could not but jealously notice. For some time she had been becoming anxious about Malcolm's growing bohemianism and a general carelessness towards the more routine side of life, though trying hard to convince herself that all was well. The closeness of some of Malcolm's friendships, both male and female, was both inherently worrying and threatening to their own special relationship. Whispered discussions with George began to take place. Something was wrong, but how best to put it right? Bisexuality was not a topic generally discussed in the 1940s, let alone understood.

George all this time had preferred to let matters take their course without interference. He had never, for example, sought to impose his religious beliefs on his children. Now, however, he was sufficiently aroused by Bessie's anxieties to encourage Malcolm to take spiritual matters much more seriously. Malcolm was to comment later:

---

33 July 2005

34 He also wrote that year a Nonet for Strings, Wind and Harp.

35 It reflects his current admiration for Bax, Vaughan Williams and Bliss.

36 Interview with Robert Solomon, 1993

The young pianist

> In my late teens my liberal father found me so lacking in any moral sense that for once he decided to take a firm hand and to have me confirmed into the Anglican church...[37]

Malcolm and his father would travel several miles every Sunday to the staunchly conservative Church of Christ, Turramurra. Malcolm took the High-Church ritual seriously, loved the use of Latin and again felt himself being drawn towards Catholicism. George's current hobby of reading Latin and Greek texts impressed him too, and from time to time he gave thought to George's suggestion that he should take an arts degree at university and not rule out the possibility of teaching. Malcolm had already completed his Leaving Certificate after private tuition[38] in Mosman, thereby opening up such an option.

Bessie agreed with George than an arts degree would be a useful safety net, though she continued to dream of Malcolm performing a musical high wire act with herself as Mistress of Ceremonies. But her pressures in this direction were

---

37 MW to Robert Solomon, 31 October 1986. On another occasion he commented 'My behaviour had been so wild they had me confirmed into the church.' (1967 interview with Hazel de Berg).

38 Bessie had found him an excellent private tutor in Roger Cornforth.

counterproductive. Some time in 1949, suffocated by too much advice, Malcolm ran away from home 'in a great but unsuccessful gesture of defiance',[39] turning up in Melbourne where he briefly found work in the sock department of the giant Myer department store. It is possible that it was a resultant family fracas which precipitated Malcolm's early departure from the Con, Bessie taking exception to his flight to Melbourne and believing that Malcolm was coming too much under the influence of the worldly Goossens, who, rumour had it, was not averse to enjoying himself down in King's Cross, the most raffish area of central Sydney.[40] Comments from one of Malcolm's cousins suggest that such an intervention from Bessie may well have proved decisive:

> Bessie always had a love-hate relationship with Malcolm. She would give generously to him, but at times withdraw financial support and make things hard for him. Their personalities were so similar in some ways – both wanted to be boss.[41]

His departure could alternatively have been provoked by a simple fit of pique, for it coincided with an end-of-year concert at which the Khachaturian Concerto, which he so fancied, was entrusted to Ron Grainer[42] and MacDowell's 2nd Piano Concerto (a great Sverjensky favourite) to Valda Whittingham.

Whatever the reason,[43] Malcolm left the Con in late 1949 soon after his eighteenth birthday. He had neither graduated nor taken the Performers' Diploma, though he achieved some excellent results in the exams of which records survive.[44] Now that he was free of College Malcolm could look more realistically towards Europe, the goal of every young musician of the period. It was with considerable excitement that he helped organise the party at violinist Pat Ryan's house as the Young Musicians' Group bade farewell to Geoffrey Parsons in January 1950, about to leave for England on the *Orcades*. Shortly

---

39 1975 BBC TV feature film *Malcolm Williamson Down Under*

40 It was also where the Sydney Symphony Orchestra had its rehearsal studios. Seven years later Goossens' infatuation with a King's Cross artist with a taste for witchcraft led to the tragic collapse of an otherwise glorious career. In his arrest at Sydney Airport for bringing in 'pornographic' materials (extremely mild by today's standards) he may well have been set up by jealous Australian-born rivals. Malcolm always complained angrily about the witch hunt against Goossens and later visited him several times in his London home.

41 Margaret Piper, May 2005

42 The composer of the 'Steptoe and Son' and 'Dr Who' theme tunes.

43 The Conservatorium's records of one of their most distinguished alumni would seem very brief, shedding no light on his departure. His current status there seems low, the web-site stating (in June 2007): 'Students accepted by the Conservatorium will be following in the footsteps of many past students who have become Australia's most respected and admired musicians, including Richard Bonynge, John Harding, Nathan Warks, Anthony Walker, Paul Ayres and Geoffrey Parsons.'

44 1947: Honours in Harmony (2nd year) and Piano Performers Grade 1 with a Distinction in Chamber Music (piano); 1948: Honours in History (2nd year) and in 1st Form results, with a Distinction in Aural training. 1949: Honours in History.

afterwards there was a similar send-off for Megan Braithwaite when she followed him on the *Himalaya*. And in February members of the Young Musicians' Group were informed that Malcolm was off to England that April in the *Mooltan*.

In February too, Bessie, ever anxious on her son's behalf, took Malcolm to an educational psychologist, Haigwood Masters. Such was the power of Bessie's personality that when the report came back she herself featured in it strongly:

> I hold a very high opinion of your mother's whole nature – she is herself sensitive, imaginative, artistic and I am perfectly satisfied, though I might find it difficult to convince her of this, that all your talents come from her. Her ear for pitch is excellent and it seems to me that you have inherited her abilities merely to a greater degree.

Having a mother of such quality, Malcolm was told, was especially useful in that it opened up a way out of his current 'problem':

> Your character is an essentially good and decent one, but it has just one weakness which is a very important one for the next seven or eight years. There is in you a very strong desire to be liked and a very strong desire to have people be kind to you, to have them want you and be nice to you. This quality is in every human being but in you it is developed to a dangerous degree…

Fortunately, continued the psychologist, there was help at hand:

> The one real safeguard against that characteristic causing you to be attracted into foolishness is your mother… Your mother has never let her feelings and emotions be let loose and that is the reason yours have grown and hers have been held back…

In what precise form that 'foolishness' had manifested itself, the report did not state, but it almost certainly related to his flight to Melbourne in the company of a boyfriend. The psychologist's recipe for Malcolm's salvation was via a draconian vetting system of those with whom he mixed:

> I feel that if you will really consult your mother on what you do and want to do, and on your friendships and bring home and let her see anybody you like or who interests you, man or woman, for the next seven or eight years you will have become so educated by your experiences of your mother's perception that you yourself will become a capable young man.

Malcolm was being treated like a little boy. Much as he loved and admired his mother, he was never going to submit to her guardianship. Nor was he impressed by the psychologist's lukewarm assessment of his potential as a musician:

> I cannot see him becoming a famous pianist, conductor or composer, but I can see him becoming locally famous in conducting, in composition, in teaching, in accompanying and very highly regarded as a pianist. I do feel that sometime you should study the voice so that you could teach this as well as the piano…[45]

---

45 The report constantly veers between second and third persons. It was generally addressed to Malcolm, in the second person, but sometimes, as here, deferred to Bessie, in the third.

Educational experts inevitably run the risk of their advice being discredited by subsequent events, but even if Haigwood Masters badly misjudged Malcolm's musical potential, he made two comments which would later be totally vindicated. Malcolm, he wrote, had a strong dramatic sense, could be good at acting, and therefore the musical field in which he could most expect success was possibly opera. There was also a shrewd reference to what would turn out to be a life-long inability to look after himself:

> No human being should need looking after all their life but many do, and until you learn to think practically and put common sense first, you will need looking after.

For Bessie this was the perfect cue. Three months later Malcolm was setting out for England with his mother beside him. It was to be a six-month trip, with George obligingly looking after Marion and the business in Sydney, and with Diane sent away to a boarding-school where she was extremely unhappy.

Disembarking in Italy, Malcolm and Bessie made their way through Europe, armed with letters of introduction from Goossens[46] and Sverjensky. A pause in Vienna allowed them to pay their respects to the spirit of Mozart; in Berlin to research (without success) the Williamson-Wagner connection; in Paris to breathe in the heady air of post-war serialism. From the moment he tasted his first croissant Malcolm was a committed, lifelong Francophile. He loved the whole Parisian atmosphere, the ubiquitous smell of stale Gaulloises, the sound of Piaf in nearly every bar, and cheap Simenon paperbacks which began his love affair with the French language. He also much enjoyed meeting the conductor and musicologist Frederick Goldbeck.

> He was very kind to me – we often sat for hours in a dimly-lit bar talking about music. It was very interesting to hear from a French-German Jew what contemporary British music looked like from the outside. He was very scornful of most things, but named four people who were figures of significance – Britten, Lutyens, Lambert and Rawsthorne…[47]

There was also another highly important name mentioned:

> Fred Goldbeck told me about an interesting young French composer, Pierre Boulez. I bought the lst and 2nd Piano Sonatas and I was initially very impressed. It was like a new world opening, which I found much more exciting than Schoenberg had ever been.[48]

Malcolm and Bessie joyfully celebrated their first night in London standing at the back of Covent Garden, watching opera. Shortly afterwards Malcolm tried

---

46 Goossens wrote: 'To whom it may concern. The bearer of this letter, Malcolm Williamson, has studied composition with me and, in my opinion, deserves every encouragement in his creative work. Both his originality and his industry make him very potentially a young man whose future will be well worth watching...' (28 October 1949)

47 *Alan Rawsthorne* ed. Poulton, p.56

48 'A Word With Malcolm Williamson', an interview with Belinda Webster (ABC Radio 24 Hours, November 1981).

Travelling abroad, 1950

With Bessie in Trafalgar Square, 1950

to make contact with Alan Rawsthorne, to see if he could arrange a few composition lessons.[49] Rawsthorne had developed his own individual neo-classical sound, and Malcolm was keen to learn more. Eventually he tracked him down at the entrance of the New Theatre[50] in Charing Cross Road:

> There at eleven o'clock one morning was this thick-set man with a canary-coloured waistcoat, a tweed suit, and a large tan homberg. Plucking up all my courage, I said, 'Mr Rawsthorne, sir!' He blushed and looked embarrassed because he felt himself to be such an obscure figure that he was astonished at being recognised! I continued, 'Can I come and study composition with you?' 'Well er, well er…' he mumbled and didn't know quite what to say. He wrote my name on the margin of *The Times* he was carrying and immediately hailed a taxi which disappeared in the direction of the French Club in St James…[51]

This setback led Malcolm to contact Elisabeth Lutyens, then in her early forties and not yet famous as 'Twelve-tone Lizzie' but still a considerable force in spreading the gospel of the radical European serialists. Malcolm's request for a few lessons filled her with sudden panic, for she had done no teaching before, but, needing the money, she agreed to see him and sat up all night drinking heavily, as she delved into her Hindemith primer on harmony. This, however, only muddled her, so she rang up Arnold Bax in the early hours of the morning, 'Arnie, what the hell is a major third?' His reply, perhaps affected by the time of the call, failed to calm her anxieties and so she put the question to Malcolm in her usual highly forthright manner as soon as she opened the front door to him. Not showing the slightest degree of surprise, he courteously gave her the answer.

Smoking and drinking with a speed Malcolm found hard to match, and dressed unusually smartly in a blue suit, Lizzie Lutyens devoted that first lesson to analysing her Chamber Concerto 1, a nine-minute serial work which demonstrated her interest in equal-part writing which she had picked up from Purcell.[52] It was the start of a most important friendship. 'If you were to undress my musical personality,' Malcolm was later to write to her, 'you would find the fingerprints of your own still there.'[53]

Malcolm's three months in London allowed him a good opportunity for making himself known in several important places, not least the BBC. 1950 was a golden age for television serials of popular novels, and Malcolm was invited to write music for Victor Canning's *The Golden Salamander*. The story of an art expert on the trail of priceless antiques in North Africa allowed him good scope for local colour, but unfortunately the serial and its score seem not to have survived.

---

49 By this time he had studied Rawsthorne's overture *A Street Corner* with Goossens, though it was not to have its Australian premiere till 1951.

50 Later the Albery, now the Coward

51 Poulton, p.55

52 M and S Harries, *A Pilgrim Soul*, p.89

53 *ibid.* p.165

On his final day in England Malcolm at last caught up with the hard-drinking and elusive Alan Rawsthorne, incarcerated in Shepperton by studio bosses desperate for a film score which had failed to materialize. Malcolm somehow managed to get himself taken down in a chauffeur-driven car to a secret hideaway where the composer was having lunch. Quite what Rawsthorne made of this unexpected intrusion is not recorded, but Malcolm stayed sober enough for some parts of their remarkable meeting to stay in his memory:

> I remember quoting to Alan – singing it over the table – the opening of Goossens' opera *Judith*, which uses nine tones of the chromatic scale, and something of Honegger, which uses ten and saying – over the potted shrimps – 'Here we are ... Goossens opens his opera with a big brave tutti using a series of nine...' and here he really cut me down to size. 'Oh,' said Alan, 'so what *you're* saying is – go the whole way!' Silence. And the silence was itself a devastating condemnation of the twelve-tone system! At the same luncheon I had the impudence to ask 'Do you think you write well for the strings?' He thought for an *eternity* and then very charmingly said 'Yes, I do, rather.' – an exact valuation![54]

The six-month reconnaissance had proved a great success. But back in Australia Bessie and Malcolm viewed it from different perspectives. For Bessie its purpose had been not merely to stimulate Malcolm's creativity but also to divert his attention from unsatisfactory relationships and wild living at home. It was now a question of his settling down in Sydney productively under her protective aegis. To this end a new house, in a higher-class area, seemed helpful, preferably one with a tennis court where Malcolm could indulge in manly exercise. Bessie's eyes fell on Killara, the best suburb in Sydney, a couple of miles to the west of Beauty Point. It was closer to her ageing parents, conveniently situated on the North Shore railway, and had an attractive church, St Martin's, at which George occasionally helped out. The family, therefore, speedily moved to a pleasant house on Pacific Highway, well set back from what was then a comparatively quiet road, and which met all Bessie's considerable requirements with the exception of the tennis court.

For Malcolm, however, who had tasted croissants in the Place Pigalle and munched hot chestnuts by a brazier on a foggy evening in Trafalgar Square, the delights of Killara and a house on the Pacific Highway soon palled. He had experienced something of the cultural riches of the old world, and now knew that it was there his future must lie. A battle of wills ensued, as Bessie, for all her resourcefulness, struggled to implement Haigwood Masters' strategies.

All was well for a short while, as Malcolm busied himself with several projects. He had, for example, acquired a commission for another short documentary film, *The Sturt Expedition*, the story of a famous exploration in the early nineteenth century by Charles Sturt up the Murray River across Lake

---

54 Poulton, p.56

Alexandrina.[55] He also ghosted an entry which Marion made to a competition run by an extremely popular children's radio programme, *The Argonauts*. In those innocent days children all over Australia were enrolled as Argonauts – each given a classical name and a place on board a particular ship – so they could have fun participating in Jason's artistic and musical adventures, hosted by 'Mr Melody Man', the popular Lindley Evans (who also taught the piano at the Con for forty years). Marion, who rowed at number 22 on the good ship Demodocus, was duly successful, received congratulations from 'Mr Melody Man' and was sent the much-coveted Purple Award.

Rather more important was a one-act opera, based on Virginia Woolf's modest little ghost story 'The Haunted House', a big challenge to his skills as a librettist, as time and place have a dream-like unreality and there is virtually no plot. Enough of the opera survives to show that Malcolm had heeded Goldmark's advice in Paris to familiarize himself with Benjamin Britten. It is a remarkably assured work for a nineteen-year-old, outstanding in its invention and sophistication, which is probably why it did not win first prize in the Young Composers competition for which it was written.[56]

This setback, coming at a time when Bessie was making frequent criticisms about his friends and homosexuality, may well have been the catalyst for Malcolm's abrupt departure from Killara to Melbourne, a break from the family which was to last on this occasion for over a year. It was, he declared much later, 'a very troubled time', and he deeply resented Bessie's well-intentioned attempts to bully him into social and sexual conformity:

> I had a great many crises, which I found difficult to surmount, and my parents were worse than no help at all in understanding what was becoming of me.[57]

His time in Victoria was by no means totally gloomy, however, and there were plenty of diversions. Peter Sculthorpe remembers Malcolm working as a pianist with the Borovansky Ballet (forerunners of Australian Ballet), meeting up with him in Hobart while on a month's tour of Tasmania.[58] There was also the pleasure

---

55 Also called *Inland With Sturt*, the sixteen-minute film was made as part of the 1951 Jubilee Celebrations commemorating the founding of the commonwealth in 1901. It still survives and is regarded today as a Film Australia classic. Its dating tends to be variable, 1952 (Film Australia Newsletter, 2003) and 1947 (Campion Press Catalogue of Williamson works, 1992) also being offered.

56 The score of *The Haunted House*, written in pencil in the first instance, shows signs of many erasures, as Malcolm worked towards the effects he wanted. He used just limited woodwind (flute, oboe and two clarinets), a harp and strings (with the cellos divided into three). The work is essentially tonal, but would have sounded very modern in Sydney in 1951.

57 Taped interview with Hazel de Berg, 1967 (Australian National Library)

58 Although there is no record of the Borovansky being in Tasmania in 1951-52, in Barry Kitcher's authoritative account of the company's travels, nonetheless the company was performing in Melbourne for a 20-week period while Malcolm was there, so Malcolm's temporary attachment to it seems most likely.

The first opera, A Haunted House, *1951*

of staying in Melbourne with Edward Brown and his sister Catherine, both enthusiastic musicians and to become lifelong friends. Malcolm would often talk about the day Edward burst into their house in great excitement, having just acquired some recently issued 78s of Rawsthorne's *Symphonic Studies*. On being told that Catherine was having a bath, he groaned in frustration, rushed upstairs with the portable gramophone and frantically wound up the machine while avoiding a volley of soapy sponges. 'Can't wait, love,' he explained as he stuck the needle in the groove, 'you've just <u>got</u> to hear this!' And thus the first

Australian performance of Rawsthorne's Symphonic Studies was given to a girl in a bath…

There was another even greater benefit in Melbourne than the opportunity of listening to the latest Rawsthorne. It was the home of Bernard Heinze, Ormond Professor of Music at the University Conservatorium, for thirty years the Director of the Melbourne Symphony Orchestra, and the pre-eminent figure in Australian music until the arrival of Goossens. Heinze, as Music Adviser to the Australian Broadcasting Corporation since its foundation in the 1930s, had enjoyed for a long time a controlling interest in all six state symphony orchestras as well as responsibility for the ABC concert seasons which dominated Australian classical music. Malcolm had first come across him as a young boy, for Heinze, taking it upon himself that post-war Australia would not be musically illiterate, had relentlessly toured all the big cities during the war, conducting series after series of children's and youth concerts. From the many Heinze performances Malcolm heard in Sydney, he retained most vivid memories of *The Dream of Gerontius*, *Belshazzar's Feast* and Delius's *Sea Drift*. He would also often talk about the impact of Heinze's first Beethoven Festival in Sydney in 1943, which was followed by an equally exciting Brahms Festival and a Festival of British Music.

So when the opportunity came to study with Heinze, Malcolm seized it eagerly. Heinze taught him a great deal by exploring the orchestration and structure of Malcolm's own compositions. They also pored over key works in the classical repertoire together, and Heinze kindly lent Malcolm many scores which were currently unavailable at the time in Australia. And at every single session

Taking leave of his grandmother, Mary Wrigley (the 'Great Lady'), 1952

Heinze went out of his way to heap praise on his pupil. At a dangerously unbalanced stage in his life Malcolm thereby recovered his self-respect and sense of purpose.

Whereas Goossens was a man of few words, Heinze was a wonderful, compelling story-teller, who liked to hold centre-stage in every situation. Both conductors were passionate about their hobbies outside music. With Goossens it was mainly steam trains (he was said to be capable of taking over the controls); with Heinze it was postage stamps (he was said to have six million), grandfather clocks and much, much more. Heinze's enthusiasms matched Malcolm's for intensity, and the forty-year age gap between them was never a barrier.

Above all, Heinze taught Malcolm to think big, both in composition and as regards his career. He had conducted several times in Europe and had good contacts in England, which, he told Malcolm, he should not delay in using. Impressed by Malcolm's virtuosity on the piano, Heinze invited him to make his professional debut in Sydney in one of his own concerts, the choice of piece decidedly adventurous: Schoenberg's *Ode to Napoleon*, the chamber work for piano, string quartet and speaker.[59]

By this time Malcolm was back at Killara, all forgiven. Bessie and George had learnt from the experience of the past year. Artistic talent was not something which could be regularized, like the cleaning of a pair of overalls. It needed to be nurtured with considerable sensitivity. What Heinze was now saying about England was only what they had already heard from Goossens and Sverjensky. So Bessie began making arrangements for another voyage to England. She had tried to keep Malcolm with her in Australia, but the call of London was too strong.

> To go abroad, that was the thing. That was the way to make your name. To stay at home was to condemn yourself to non-entity. Success depended on an imprimatur from London... to be really someone in Australian eyes you first had to make your mark or win your degree on the other side of the world.... [60]

Bessie, however, was not prepared to let Malcolm loose on the other side of the world without anyone around to keep an eye on him. He had, after all, only recently celebrated his twenty-first birthday and, as Haigwood Masters had made very clear, he was far from ready to look after himself. And this time it was not a question of a mere six months; Malcolm's stay in London might extend to several years. So Bessie took the bold decision to uproot the whole family. She and George would settle in England with Malcolm. Marion and Diane would come along too.

---

59 Schoenberg had died only the year before, bitter and generally despised, the father of a new and controversially dissonant kind of music which rejected the traditional key system, in which certain notes of the scale have automatic priority, for one in which all twelve notes of the octave are given equal importance.

60 Alan Moorhead, quoted by Stephen Alomes, *When London Calls*, p.93

The family prior to departure, December 1952

The final farewell party over, the Williamsons left Sydney on board the *Otranto* on 6 December 1952. By the time they reached England six weeks later it would be 1953, Coronation year. The ship, as they quickly discovered, contained many others embarking with similar starry-eyed ambition, all part of that final great wave of expatriation flowing to Europe after the Second World War. It was a process which, as Stephen Alomes has explained, stretched back to Victorian times:

> Although no longer a colony, Australia [in the early 1950s] still seemed provincial, unable to appreciate the arts or to sustain full-time careers in them. Writers, artists, musicians and actors set out on a journey in search of new opportunities, while also following in the tracks of their predecessors. Their distinguished number had included the writer Henry Lawson, the painter Arthur Streeton and the singer Nellie Melba...[61]

The experiences and successes of pioneer expatriates like Lawson, Streeton and Melba were currently uppermost in Malcolm's mind. Henry Lawson had gone out in different circumstances: over thirty, a family man, hampered by deafness and drink. His two years in England, however, were a great success, encouraging some of his finest poetry, even though his return was marred by divorce, penury and prison. Arthur Streeton was similarly over thirty when he embarked for Britain, where he would stay more than twenty years, painting England, Venice and war-torn France with such distinction he would be knighted, on his final return, as Australia's greatest artist. Nellie Melba, an adventuress just four years older than Malcolm when she left Australia, spent even more of her working life in the old world, yet her returns to her homeland were always wildly

61 Alomes, *When London Calls*, p.7

celebrated, and, after she had died at Sydney, just months before Malcolm was born there, an enormous motorcade followed *Dame* Nellie Melba as she was taken to her final Melbourne resting-place.

Malcolm, therefore, had much on his mind as the *Otranto* eased itself out to sea between the North and South Heads. History was on his side, the experiences of many expatriates highly rewarding. Nonetheless the home town he was leaving behind would not be lightly forgotten. Though London now was calling, it could never be that Sydney would be anything but brightly glittering in the memory. It would not be very long, indeed, before he was writing his own pianistic impressions of places which meant much to him: the 'Pyrmont Dockside', where the great adventure began; the 'Harbour Bridge', his exact contemporary; 'The Botanical Gardens', the 'Harbour Ferry', the 'Central Railway', all part of his very being; and, most personal of all, 'A Morning Swim', with its memories of his father and sisters at Manly…

There was no time, then, for second thoughts, now that Sydney was receding. The *Otranto*, towering and majestic as it bade farewell to Bondi, Coogee and Maroubra, gave dignity and reassurance to the whole enormous enterprise. Besides, the London which was calling was that of Goossens, Rawsthorne and Lutyens; Beecham, Boult and Britten; the London of the brand-new Festival Hall and Victoria's ancient memorial for Albert, where Melba had bid farewell to Britain twenty-six years before; the London of Fonteyn and Gielgud, Coward and Helpmann; the centre of the cultured world; the siren voice which had once called Lawson, Streeton and Melba. Like that early visitor to Britain, Julius Caesar, he had already made a first short reconnaissance. Now he was coming again, fully intending to conquer the natives.

3 BREAKING FREE

London, 1953–55

AT CHRISTMAS THE WILLIAMSONS were a quarter of the way round the world. By the time Marion and Diane were dancing Scottish reels in the 1953 New Year celebrations, both Colombo and Aden were in their wake. 'Shipboard life,' wrote one fellow passenger, 'for all those who made the pilgrimage 'overseas' in the 1950s was, at times, like one long cocktail party.'[1] Malcolm contributed to this atmosphere by playing the piano endlessly in the liner's lounges, where Marion would often be part of an admiring audience:

> I can't remember exactly what he played, but it included Ravel's *Jeux d'Eau* and the *Alborada del Gracioso* with its Spanish rhythms and folk-like melodies; some of the more showy Chopin pieces; Sinding's *Rustle of Spring,* of course, which was in the repertoire of every aspiring pianist at that time; and there would have been plenty of Prokofiev and Shostakovich. It would all have been classical. Malcolm's love of dance tunes and songs from shows developed later.[2]

In the course of the voyage Malcolm became friendly with Ruth Cracknell, a young Sydney actress looking to further her career in London. Together they devised a poetry and music recital which around two hundred people attended, Ruth Cracknell reciting works by Australian poets, Shakespeare and Yeats; Malcolm playing Beethoven, Chopin, Ravel as well as some Goossens. It was all a huge success and afterwards everyone adjourned happily to yet another Landfall Dinner.[3]

Excursions at ports-of-call were always exciting. At Naples there was the traditional visit to Pompeii and Vesuvius, the Italian guides inadvertently furnishing Bessie and Malcolm with material for endless impersonations. And, as usual, the family ventured beyond the regular tourist routes:

---

1 Ruth Cracknell, *A Biased Memoir*, p.83

2 Marion Foote, April 2005

3 *A Biased Memoir*, p.87. Ruth Cracknell and Malcolm kept in regular touch until her return the next year to Australia, where she was to enjoy great success in theatre, films and television.

> The whole city was very romantic and seemed full of music! On the way to the Opera House, which Malcolm was keen to see, we came across two funerals, one for an adult, one for a child. The child was borne along in a white carriage drawn by grey horses. The opera house, when we got there, was closed for renovation. But somehow we were allowed in, which was a great thrill…[4]

With Europe experiencing a hard winter, the Mediterranean proved choppy and at Marseilles Malcolm and his sisters saw their first snow. There was much relief when the *Otranto* finally reached Tilbury,[5] where in swirling mist and sleet the Williamsons organised their thirty-two pieces of luggage and somehow fitted themselves into a hired car.[6] Later, as they made their way into central London, Malcolm and Bessie vied with each other in drawing attention to all the landmarks. 'Look! There's your first Lyons Corner House!' 'This is Holborn! Covent Garden's nearby!' 'There's the grimy old British Museum!' 'The hotel can't be far away!' Dirty and down-at-heel though London looked, they were very lucky they had not arrived a month earlier, in its historic four-day smog.

After a short stay in a small hotel the Williamsons rented two floors of a house[7] in Kensington from the brother of Richard Addinsell, composer of the *Warsaw Concerto*. As usual Malcolm's needs were paramount, Bessie giving him the biggest room, where a piano was quickly installed. Meanwhile his sisters, now aged seventeen and twelve, had the challenge of adapting to the English education system at a grammar school in Chelsea, Marion moving on after just one term to the West London School of Physiotherapy.

Money was extremely tight – Australians at this period were allowed to take only £100 in sterling out of the country – so George did some supply teaching. Malcolm, too, found work – at Harrod's in the boys' clothing and antiques departments – but after only three weeks he was fired. 'I was humiliated by the rich women,' he later declared, 'and was deemed not suitable material!'[8] However, his inclination to spend his lunchtimes playing noisy avant-garde pieces on the pianos in the music department may also not have endeared him to the management.

Malcolm next applied for a job at Boosey & Hawkes, Eugene Goossens' publishers. His interview there was not a success, but, by a coincidence so extraordinary it must cast doubt on the story's complete veracity, as Malcolm disconsolately reached the bottom of the publishers' staircase he came face to face with Bernard Heinze. The conductor quickly pushed him up the stairs again and straight into Erwin Stein's office, declaring in a manner which brooked no denial, 'Employ this boy, Erwin, employ this boy!' Malcolm was duly employed, a key event in his career, for Stein was not only Benjamin Britten's friend and

4 Diane Williamson, April 2005

5 14 January 1953

6 There were six of them, Aunt Alice (George's cousin) having boarded at Melbourne.

7 Essex Villas

8 1978 interview in the *Daily Telegraph*

With Marion and Diane, Trafalgar Square, 1953

publisher but also an outstanding teacher, and it was not long before Malcolm was benefiting from regular lessons. These complemented those which Malcolm continued to take with Elizabeth Lutyens.

Since his previous visit to England Lizzie had taken a cure for her alcoholism and become a splendid teacher.[9] Richard Rodney Bennett was one of her devoted pupils, and she saw much of Harrison Birtwistle, Alexander Goehr and Peter Maxwell Davies. Goehr, whose friendship with Malcolm began at Lizzie's, shared his admiration of her:

> Malcolm used to say 'If you get praise from Lizzie, you knew you were doing well'. She was deeply generous, but never fulsome. Lizzie was extraordinarily exotic and had a very foul tongue. But her eyes showed the expletives bore no relationship to what she was *really* thinking...[10]

Despite the twenty-eight-year age difference Malcolm soon became a friend as well as pupil, and there were invitations to tea at Lizzie's Blackheath home for his whole family. Lizzie was as much an inspiration with her outrageous wit and defiant bohemianism as with her teaching. Malcolm fell totally under her spell.[11] Although she always claimed that she never forced serial technique on her pupils, in fact she did so with messianic zeal, and it is no surprise that Malcolm's four compositions[12] of 1953-54 are all in stiff Schoenbergian style. The most original, the Two Motets, was taken on by Chappell and became Malcolm's first published work, despite the criticism that 'the preoccupation with form represses content'.[13]

For someone never suited to work from nine to five Malcolm was happy enough in the Boosey & Hawkes Music Hire Library. He and Peter Shaffer, an assistant in the publicity department promoting symphonic music, soon became close friends.[14] Shaffer, who would shortly make his name as a playwright with *Five Finger Exercise*, was five years older than Malcolm and a strong influence. As a homosexual Jew he had a distinctive outsider's view of the world.[15] He was also delightfully inventive. If he had letters to write, for example, which he feared would have angry repercussions, he tended to sign above a completely fictitious name, fielding the subsequent calls with considerable glee: 'Who did

---

9 It would not, however, be until William Glock's appointment at the BBC in 1959 that her work began to be regularly played.

10 January 2005

11 Malcolm's admiration was fully reciprocated. Christopher Austin writes: 'Robert Saxton once commented to me that Malcolm was the only former student of Lizzie's whom she never slagged off! She had such enormous respect for him.' (May 2005)

12 Variations for Piano (1953); Lento for Seven Wind Instruments and Piano (1953); String Quartet No 2 (1954); Two Motets, 'Tantum Ergo' and 'Pange Lingua' (1954).

13 *Music Review*, February 1955. The Two Motets also reflect Malcolm's growing interest in medieval music.

14 Peter Shaffer worked at Boosey & Hawkes from 1954-56.

15 Peter Shaffer's televised play *The Salt Land* (1955) about the founding of modern Israel made a strong impression on Malcolm.

you say wrote to you? Oh, Mr Peters! I see...! No, I'm awfully sorry, but he's not in the office at the moment... No, he won't be. You see, he's just gone off on his holidays... Oh, for a long time, I think... I'm not sure, but – and this is strictly between ourselves – I gather he may not be returning at all!'[16] Peter Shaffer's twin brother Anthony, equally good fun and later to be famous as the author of *Sleuth*, soon became another close friend, as in due course did Brian, the youngest of the Shaffers:

> Malcolm was devoted to my mother and would often visit her. He went to her 90th birthday party. He would call her Auntie Reka. She was a very outspoken lady, which may be why he liked her so much...[17]

By late 1954 Malcolm had been promoted to work as an assistant proof reader for Erwin Stein, whose lessons he was still enjoying. Whereas Lizzie's teaching was concerned primarily with 'different instrumental sounds and the harmonic sensuousness one could achieve with them',[18] Stein gave Malcolm new theoretical insights by analysing the traditional repertoire in the Schoenbergian manner. For Malcolm it was extremely exciting to be taught by someone who in his youth used to visit the Vienna Opera House with his friends Berg and Webern, often meeting up afterwards in a coffee house where Schoenberg would hold forth.[19] (Stein became so close a pupil and helper to Schoenberg that he was entrusted with the first theoretical explanation of the twelve-note method.[20]) For all his impressive contacts Stein was not an intimidating presence. He was more like 'an absent-minded professor turned publisher, never with the right spectacles on his nose',[21] exuding the warmth of old Vienna, from where he had fled in 1938.[22] Malcolm delighted in taking off his thick Viennese accent.[23]

To have two such fine teachers in itself justified the move to London, where Malcolm quickly felt at ease. Depressing after-effects of the war – bomb damage, coupons needed for sweets, and ration books for butter and sugar – were

---

16 Malcolm often dined out on the story, no doubt elaborating further each time.

17 Brian Shaffer, July 2005

18 Harries: *A Pilgrim Soul*, p.165

19 Donald Mitchell, quoted in Carpenter: *Benjamin Britten*, p.216

20 Something of Stein's teaching style comes across from comments of another pupil, Jonathan Harvey: 'He was a strict teacher and taught in the classical Schoenbergian manner: sentences, periods, Lied form, scherzo or minuet form etc. He did not mind what style I wrote in – it didn't concern him. The essential was to achieve a strong, classical structure. He was friendly and cheerful and his wife was always very kind... I was sometimes taken aback by his directness and the sharpness of his criticisms...' (JH to Thomas Brezinska, January 2003)

21 John Amis, quoted in Carpenter, *Benjamin Britten*, p.217

22 But he knew his own mind. On one occasion Malcolm rushed into Stein's office enthusiastically brandishing 'a beautifully engraved full score of Rawsthorne's Concerto for String Orchestra'. Stein, however, took one look at it and waved him away. Naively Malcolm had thought everyone must approve of Rawsthorne. (Poulton: *Alan Rawsthorne*, p 56)

23 Diane Williamson: 'The family saying of "So dear!" came from Erwin Stein.'

countered by the vivacity of London's cultural life. Malcolm and Bessie were now able to visit theatres they had only glimpsed on their previous visit, and there was, above all, opera on a scale unthinkable back in Sydney.

There was much to inspire the penniless young composer, up in the slips at Covent Garden in 1953. Joan Sutherland was singing minor roles in *Gloriana, Die Walküre* and *Carmen*, part of the steady progress towards her triumph in *Lucia di Lammermoor* in 1959. Covent Garden was about to become a 'Callas house', Maria Callas making her debut there, as a stunning Norma, just days before the Williamsons set sail for England. Malcolm's operatic ambitions were also spurred by productions of contemporary British composers. After Britten's *Gloriana* came Walton's *Troilus and Cressida* (1954) and Tippett's *The Midsummer Marriage* (1955).

Malcolm's tastes speedily grew more catholic. 1953 was a very good year for musicals. Sandy Wilson's *The Boy Friend* opened the day the *Otranto* berthed, and first nights quickly followed for *Guys and Dolls* and *The King and I*. He became a devotee of Richard Rodgers. He was also in London just as the 'kitchen sink' drama of John Osborne, Arnold Wesker and Joan Littlewood's Theatre Workshop brought a new social realism to the stage. It was the age of 'the angry young man'. The anarchic anti-hero of Kingsley Amis's *Lucky Jim* arrived in England only one year after Malcolm. A year later came James Dean's *Rebel Without a Cause*. The new movement, anti-establishment, anti-pretension and shocking to middle class sensibilities, was something with which Malcolm quickly identified. With it came a glamorised propensity for self-destruction. Dylan Thomas's posthumous success with *Under Milk Wood* mirrored James Dean's in *Giant*. The press revelled in the doomed Brendan Behan's drunken interruptions of his own play *The Hostage*. As a young London bohemian, Malcolm kept abreast of, and absorbed, the spirit of the times.

He was also a vulnerable participant in the sexual revolution, which was only just starting. Nearly five hundred men were prosecuted in the early fifties for sexual offences with consenting male adults in private. 1953 witnessed a police 'purge' of homosexuals on orders from the Home Office. 'Male vice' was being targeted after the defection to Russia of Burgess and Maclean, 'known to have pervert associates'. It was also the year in which John Gielgud was both knighted and arrested for cottaging. In 1954 came the much publicised Lord Montagu trial, and, on release from prison, Peter Wildeblood published his spirited plea for (previously unheard of) gay rights, *Against the Law*, in which he starkly stated the current dangers:

> A man who feels attraction towards other men is a social misfit only; once he gives way to that attraction, however, he becomes a criminal.

In 1957 the Wolfenden Report, disregarding the conventional ideas of the day, suggested that sex between two adult consenting males in private should no longer be an offence, but it was to be another ten years before this became law.

Meanwhile discrimination against homosexuals continued. Benjamin Britten was among several well-known figures in the arts to be interviewed by Scotland Yard.

Bessie's worries over Malcolm's unwillingness to conform had been the decisive factor in the decision to uproot the family. But she would have known it was always going to be something of a gamble. As long as Malcolm was living with the family in Kensington there was a certain, helpful restraint in place, but Malcolm's inclination was to roam. Only a few months after the family's arrival, for example, he had moved to Watford to stay with the Australian violinist Brian Blake, a former committee member of the Young Musicians' Group in Sydney.

Religion and music were their shared passions. Brian, a Catholic heterosexual, introduced Malcolm to Father Timothy Croghan at The Church of Our Lady Help of Christians, Rickmansworth, where he worshipped, and soon Malcolm was taking instruction.[24] His conversion to Catholicism took place on 15 July 1953 when he was baptised by Father Timothy, Brian Blake acting as his sponsor. Four days later he was confirmed and given the additional name of Christopher by Bishop Craven in Westminster Cathedral. Malcolm's family seem not to have attended. George, despite his own High Church leanings, was extremely upset at Malcolm's move to Rome. Bessie seemed less concerned, saying cheerfully 'Well, at least he didn't join the Salvation Army!'[25]

Malcolm had always been attracted by the colourful trappings, the language and rituals, of Catholicism. Its demands helped alleviate his insecurities. It was helpful to have the *mater dolorosa* as a mother figure with whom he would never quarrel, someone who would offer total forgiveness at confession time. Although he always struggled to be a conventional Catholic, regularly castigating the church for intolerance and humbug, and later moving to an inclusive Christian-Jewish-Islamic stance, his Catholicism was to remain one of the priorities of his life. Under every new piece of music he was carefully to write i.o.g.D., 'Let God be glorified in all things'.[26]

Malcolm derived considerable benefit in this period from friendship with two other Catholics, George Malcolm and Anthony Milner, both of them gay. Just turned forty, George Malcolm was at the peak of his profession as a harpsichordist, registering a huge hit with an LP *Bach Goes to Town*. He was also an important member of Britten's circle and a superb choirmaster at Westminster Cathedral. According to one observer, 'George Malcolm was not just Malcolm's religious anchor for a while, but did a great deal to try to hold him together and limit his tendency towards self-destruction'.[27] Anthony Milner was equally influential. A composer and teacher, six years older than Malcolm, he had already

24 Father Timothy was an Augustinian. Malcolm was also instructed by Father Brendan Fox.

25 However, Malcolm was to claim 'it was gratifying' that his conversion to Catholicism had so infuriated his parents.

26 *In omnibus glorificetur Deus.*

27 Sue Phipps, January 2006

enjoyed some success with a cantata, *Salutatio Angelica*. Milner's deeply-held religious views permeated all his music. He had played an active part in Malcolm's conversion, and subsequently, when they went off on weekend camping expeditions in the countryside, they were sometimes to be seen on their knees together saying the Rosary.

In due course, irked by the daily journey to Boosey & Hawkes, Malcolm moved back from Watford to rejoin his family, now living at a flat in Lyndhurst Gardens, Hampstead, although he continued to see much of Brian Blake:

> We went for several trips in my little car on which Malcolm would amaze me by his knowledge of British history. We couldn't afford hotels, so we tended to sleep in the car, the discomfort of which I hated but it seemed not to worry Malcolm at all. On one trip to Wales towards the end of 1953 we stopped at a pub in the Wye Valley and were amazed to find the locals singing in four-part harmony. On another trip we picked up two girl hitch-hikers who turned out to be Australian![28]

Together, too, they were constantly meeting fellow musicians. They spent one very pleasant evening, for example, with the young Australian pianist Noel Mewton-Wood, who had made a name performing with Bliss, Britten and Tippett, most recently touring and recording with Peter Pears. They were very shocked when, only two weeks later, Mewton-Wood, consumed with grief at the death of the man with whom he was living, committed suicide.

They had happier memories of a visit made to Howard Ferguson's home in Cambridge, where Malcolm played endless duets with their host. Ferguson, a great friend of both Finzi and Vaughan Williams, had only recently completed his own Concerto for Two Pianos. On another occasion Malcolm and Brian Blake came across Vaughan Williams, then in his eighties, at a rehearsal of the Bach's *St John Passion* at Dorking Parish Church:

> I had been longing to meet him. And now he was standing there! I was both terrified and thrilled! I wanted to go up and say 'I think you're absolutely marvellous!' There he was, the enormously tall master, rather stooped, with a pair of glasses; one felt he really could have afforded a much more decorative pair than those he wore clumsily and lopsidedly halfway down his nose. Ursula Vaughan Williams suddenly led us up and introduced us. He responded with a question. 'Will you move that piano please!' And he, bless him, tried to help us move a grand piano. There were no affectations with Ralph Vaughan Williams. Afterwards, at the bun fight in the parish hall, he was sitting there more or less completely ignored. He lifted a finger at me and said simply 'Great work!' He was completely lost. He hadn't come out of the atmosphere of the Bach rehearsal he'd just conducted…[29]

Malcolm much missed Brian Blake after he was appointed Leader of the Tasmanian Symphony Orchestra, and so too did the Catholic church at Rickmansworth. 'It is with great regret,' noted the parish magazine, 'that we record the imminent dissolution of the partnership of Brian and Malcolm…' In

---

28 June 2005

29 BBC Radio, 'Meet the Composer', February 1970

London, 1954

addition to playing regularly for Sunday Services, they had been involved in an elaborate summer pageant put on by the local convent, Malcolm not only writing the music and directing the action, but being the life and soul of what turned out to be a big party:

> I remember the pageant as a highly enjoyable occasion; firstly, because it was very well done, even if one touch of realism when the saint's ashes were dropped into the stream was a trifle vivid for Anglo-Saxon tastes! Secondly because, even if it hadn't been as spectacular as it was, the Soeurs de Jesus had provided gallons of champagne for lunch with the Cardinal, so that everyone was in a splendid mood for the celebration.[30]

30 Magazine of the Church of Our Lady Help of Christians, Rickmansworth, Easter 1970

Brian's farewell concert in Watford Town Hall included Malcolm's tuneful Minuet for Violin and Piano, written seven years earlier, before Elizabeth Lutyens and Erwin Stein encouraged a severer style.

In September 1954 Erwin Stein was part of Britten's entourage which went to Venice for the broadcast premiere of *The Turn of the Screw* and on his return he encouraged Malcolm to contact Britten. In the flat in Bloomsbury to which his family had now moved,[31] Bessie and Malcolm carefully rehearsed what he should say on the phone. Later on, with Bessie looking over his shoulder to ensure his very best writing, Malcolm followed up the initial contact with a letter:

> Dear Mr Britten,
>
> You were kind enough to show an interest in my pieces when we spoke on the telephone last Wednesday evening.
>
> I realise how very busy you are, but would it be some time possible to visit you and show you some things?
>
> I must tell you that I was deeply impressed with *The Turn of the Screw*. I cannot judge it dramatically, although I was most moved by it; but it appears to me to be a masterpiece, both beautiful and significant from purely the musical point of view. I do look forward to preparing it for publication, or at least helping to do so...[32]

As yet he had little of worth to show Britten, but that would soon change. In the meantime he was invited over to Aldeburgh, played Britten's grand piano in Crag House sitting room with complete assurance and departed, enthused by all the courtesy and encouragement which Britten and Pears had shown. Two months later the Williamsons were able to hear Peter Pears at Morley College sing one of Malcolm's songs, the joint winner of a competition which Pears had organised for young composers. Malcolm's 'Aye, flattering fortune', which relied 'on wide leaps and the brooding effect of close chromatic intervals',[33] tied with songs by Richard Rodney Bennett and Arnold Cooke. Imogen Holst's Purcell Singers participated in the concert, and it was extremely encouraging for the family to hear her afterwards enthusing about Malcolm's talents as song-writer. This praise from Gustav Holst's daughter was soon followed by exciting news. Benjamin Britten wished Malcolm to write a piano sonata for the Aldeburgh Festival. A sonata was an ambition Malcolm had long nursed. He had begun and discarded several. Now he would begin again in the new year, and dedicate it to his parents as a token of all they had done to support him.

The upturn in his fortunes was very timely, for Bessie had recently been made aware that a return to Australia would soon be necessary. The overalls business, left for over two years in the control of relations, one of whom had just died, was much missing her management skills. Malcolm was now twenty-three, five years short of the age at which Haigwood Masters had guessed he might begin to be

---

31 68 Ridgmount Gardens

32 6 November 1954

33 *The Times*, 23 December 1954. The lyric was by Thomas More: 'Aye, flattering fortune, look you never so fair'. It was never published.

able to look after himself, but Bessie could hardly be faulted if she now relinquished her self-imposed role of moral guardian in favour of rescuing the family business. Departure was fixed for February 1955.

George was quite sorry to go. He had found work in the church again, helping first at St George's, Hanover Square, where Handel had been a worshipper for many years, and then at St Pancras Parish Church.[34] George had also started a university course, Malcolm at once dubbing him 'The Professor', a nickname which endured. For the two girls the return to Australia was another challenging interruption in their education, yet philosophically accepted, for they had been brought up to believe that their own interests were usually not of paramount importance.

There was an emotional leave-taking at Tilbury, as the family embarked on the *Strathcaird.* There were no plans for Malcolm to follow them. He was making his way in England and that is where his future now lay. For his young sisters it was a poignant moment, as Marion recalls:

> It was one of what were to be several occasions when I thought I might well be saying goodbye to him for the last time.[35]

The family's return to Australia marked the end of a period of relative stability for Malcolm. Had Bessie known how much his lifestyle was about to alter, she would have been tempted to cancel the voyage home. But it was not so much the loss of the restraining family influence which precipitated the new crisis in his life as a major disappointment.

Malcolm had become increasingly interested in the music of Olivier Messiaen and was mortified at his failure to win a scholarship offering a year's study in Paris with him. Then in his mid-forties, Messiaen was not yet the cult figure he became in the 1970s, but his importance had been steadily growing since the appearance in 1949 of his huge orchestral masterwork *Turangalîla*, which had caused Malcolm to declare him as 'the most disturbing musical influence since Stravinsky'.[36] *Turangalîla*, he later wrote, had struck 'with the force of an elephantine torpedo'. With its boldly juxtaposed blocks of sound, its excesses in dynamics and brilliant colours, and the almost unendurable lengths in which it kept performer and listener at climax-point, Messiaen's music was 'like a heady wine, except that the ecstasy does not wear off'.[37] Suddenly Malcolm realised that the avant-garde of the 1950s were, in fact, old-fashioned:

---

34 Across the road from Euston Station, it is remarkable as a nineteenth-century copy of the Erechtheum in Athens, complete with its porches of caryatids.

35 March 2005

36 Malcolm Williamson: '*Turangalîla* is a Mighty Stillness' (*The Listener*, 3 April 1969)

37 Malcolm delighted in the utter confusion caused by Messiaen's idiosyncrasies: 'No voice cried in the wilderness announcing that in the 1950s a genius would appear whose music denied that Bartok, Webern and Stravinsky had ever existed. How could the critic explain that here was a fully-grown giant figure, at one and the same time a polished classicist and a romantic whose overt tastelessness – by current ideas of taste – would have made Massenet or Gounod blush?' (BBC Radio, 'Meet The Composer', February 1970)

> While one army of composers was straining to push Schoenbergian formulae to further extremes, Messiaen showed that a key was not simply something to lock the door that Webern closed; and while another army was trying pathetically to outwit Stravinsky's rhythmic and metric ingenuities, Messiaen invented stillness in music...[38]

Inspired by Messiaen's organ works, Malcolm had devoted himself in 1955 to the raising of his organ technique to concert standard and, with this end in view, had become assistant organist at the fashionable Church of the Immaculate Conception, run by the Jesuits in Farm Street, Mayfair. Malcolm delighted in the church's superb organ, situated loftily in a gallery at the western end of the nave, and learnt much from the long-serving organist, Guy Wietz, who had studied with Widor and was himself a distinguished organ composer. The church's fashionable clientele also appealed to him. It was here, he would tell friends, that Evelyn Waugh had taken instruction and been converted. It was also at Farm Street, he alleged, that Queen Mary had been converted and where Princess Margaret took instruction. 'I was present at Queen Mary's conversion, so I know! But you mustn't, of course, breathe a word about this!'[39]

Excited by the possibility of studying with Messiaen, Malcolm carefully collected some impressive testimonials to support his scholarship application to the French Government. From Erwin Stein:

> He is a highly gifted young composer of great promise and unusual intelligence... As he has a very strong inclination towards French music, I feel sure to participate in French musical life would be a great inspiration to him...[40]

From Lennox Berkeley:

> I have known Mr Malcolm Williamson for some time, and he has shown me several of his compositions. I consider him a particularly suitable candidate for a grant which would enable him to have a period of study in France. He is not only a gifted and promising composer, but an excellent all-round musician, who has a wide range of musical interests and would know how to take advantage of the different angle of approach to the musical problems of today that he would find in Paris.

From William Glock:

> He is one of the most talented of our younger musicians. I have heard several compositions of his and have suggested one of them for performance by the English section of the ISCM this season. I am also going to publish in *The Score* a most interesting article he has written on the late works of Stravinsky... His music shows a distinct originality and a discipline of feeling and technique that is rare at his age...[41]

---

38 Williamson, *The Listener*, 3 April 1969

39 MW to Robert Solomon, 1986. It was a good story, but Queen Mary had in fact died in 1953, just two months after the Williamsons arrived in England.

40 20 April 1955

41 26 April 1955

And from Benjamin Britten:

> I have great hopes in Malcolm Williamson's future as a composer. He has already shown signs of the attributes necessary to such a career; he is hard-working & painstaking; serious & cultured; and although he is still very young, his compositions show the qualities of a true musical imagination. He deserves every encouragement.[42]

But it was not enough, and Malcolm was desperately disappointed when he finished runner-up to Alexander Goehr for the coveted prize. Even today Goehr regrets the decision:

> He should have got the scholarship! As an organist and a Catholic he was much more suited to Messiaen's teaching than I was. Malcolm, used to getting his own way, took the disappointment very badly indeed. He was so thin-skinned that he could get stuck in a time warp and bear grudges for life![43]

Although Malcolm subsequently did visit Paris and studied intermittently with Messiaen, he never came to terms with the loss of this scholarship. When Goehr eventually returned to London he was shocked to see how much Malcolm had altered:

> His first troubled year was when I was in Paris. It was the first time he went wild, sometimes right out of control. He was behaving incredibly disreputably, constantly drunk and flaunting the homosexuality. I would sometimes find him in the mornings propped up against the front door of my Clapham flat, sitting there with the milk. Thereafter, it seemed to me, Malcolm's life was a patchwork of constructive periods and periods when he was out of control.

He had been unsettled too by Bessie's departure. He had missed her and the family more than he cared to admit, having taken their presence in England for granted for over two years. Underneath the exuberance and brash bohemianism lay anxieties aroused by Bessie's withdrawal. He felt guilty not to be with her, lightening her days as she applied herself tirelessly to revitalising the family business; guilty too for staying away from Grandma Mary, still living at Roseville with Grandfather Benjamin, and regularly sending him family news:

> The clock keeps ticking on very quickly, and as your mother will be fifty next week she says she is not going to have any more birthdays, so I tell her to change her birthday to 29 February leap year.[44]

The amusing Grandma Mary was no longer the strong figure Malcolm had always known. He was alarmed by her unsteady writing and news of physical incapacity:

> I can't go shopping now. I can't climb the hill, so I sit in my chair and crochet and watch the people passing and criticise my neighbour, the Dowager Duchess…

It was over three years since Grandma Mary had last seen her 'scallywag'. She

---

42 24 April 1955

43 January 2005

44 Mary Wrigley to MW, 31 January 1956

was fully aware of the temperamental problems militating against his talents, and was still doing her best to be supportive:

> We are all human and we all have so many weaknesses, but, like the prodigal son, we have a loving Father, ready and waiting to love and forgive. Malcolm, I pray for you every day, and, if I am worthy to have my prayers answered, you should be a very good man indeed...[45]

She was also praying that his financial struggle would be successfully resolved. She had been about to send a note or two in the post, but 'your mother said our money would be no good in London'.

Malcolm's finances depended on his job at Boosey & Hawkes, which he looked increasingly unlikely to keep much longer. His lunch breaks at The George (the legendary 'Glue Pot', with its large clientele from the BBC) were growing ever lengthier, and in the summer of 1955 he frequently absented himself from work. He spent several weeks in Devon, for example, taking in the Dartington Summer School. He had attended this important gathering since 1953, when he first became obsessed with Henry Moore's Reclining Figure in the Dartington Hall gardens.[46] Moore's sculpture had provoked ideas for an organ work, *Fons Amoris*. He walked round the figure day after day 'trying to make its spatial existence appear temporal',[47] something he then endeavoured to recreate musically.

Malcolm found the youthful and provocative atmosphere of Dartington wholly to his liking. 'I get a fair amount of kudos here,' he reported to Bessie in 1955. Younger composers already looked up to him. Peter Maxwell Davies was typical:

> I'd written a little piece called *Alma Redemptoris Mater* for wind sextet and generally people thought it not modern enough, but Malcolm gave me lots of support and encouragement, for which I've always been grateful.[48]

Richard Rodney Bennett, another young composer at Dartington, much enjoyed the liveliness of Malcolm's company. But he seldom found him easy; he was too intent to shock. ('He once told me nursed incestuous feelings for his father.') Bennett felt that Malcolm 'had a transistor missing'. Hence his various excesses:

> I met him through Lizzie Lutyens. We became good friends, but he tried to seduce me, which I found very alarming! I remember knocking over a table lamp![49]

---

45 30 January 1956

46 The site of Moore's serene and elegiac sculpture, at the top of the tiltyard terraces, had been chosen in 1946 with great care so that its curves would reflect the distant rolling hills. 'I wanted to convey a sense of permanent tranquillity,' commented Moore, 'a sense of being from which the stir and fret of human ways had been withdrawn.'

47 As he later told organist Joan Lippincott

48 August 2006. The reference is to the Summer School of 1956.

49 April 2006

Although he much enjoyed his summers at Dartington, Malcolm was never completely at one with the expectation there of a passionate commitment to serialism. He was searching for a more personal expression, as Richard Rodney Bennett recalls:

> When we were growing up, serialism was the way to go. We were all touched by the 12-tone technique. But Malcolm needed to shock and so struck out in a different direction, and was sometimes treated with contempt for this. We were both taken by the glamour of Lizzie and I was fascinated by Malcolm's early music. It was really tough, but it also had medieval influences, which nobody else was pursuing. His interest in Machaut pre-dated Max [Peter Maxwell Davies].[50]

Malcolm also absented himself from work to spend time with a French friend, a young violinist, Paul Daude, who was blind. They had met in Aldeburgh and Malcolm afterwards went back to Paul's home at Les Chevreuses in the Île de France, about half an hour from Paris. Malcolm breathed in the atmosphere with delight, reporting happily to Marion:

> I have a marvellous holiday here in the warm sun and lovely French countryside, though at great risk to my job in B&H. Mme. Daude cooks marvellously and turns on wonderful wines etc. Paul plays the violin to my piano. The villages where I live are mainly 10th century without baths, but otherwise more modern than in England...[51]

Grandma Mary also received a postcard:

> I am not pleased at the prospect of returning to Londres, but it must be. The sun knows how to shine in France as rarely in the English spring. All the trees blossom and the people are good and kind.

Diane, at school in Sydney, was told:

> Nobody speaks English at all so that is good practice. I shall have to go back to B & H in a day or two which is a curse. I am meeting musical people and speaking better French.

The 'musical people' included Paul's teachers at the Paris Conservatoire, where one of the professors offered help towards finding Malcolm a scholarship. But Malcolm's thoughts had already turned away from Paris and London to the warmth of southern France, and shortly afterwards he was basking in the sun at Cassis, which, he told his parents, was the loveliest place on the Côte d'Azur... That November Malcolm was back with Paul in Suffolk, staying at a cottage just outside Southwold. Happy and content, he sent his parents a picture postcard of the beach:

---

50 April 2006. Guillaume de Machaut (c1300-1377) was the most significant of the Ars Nova movement. His Messe de Nostra Dame is the earliest surviving complete setting of the Ordinary of the Mass. He was most influential in the development of the motet and secular song. In 1954 Malcolm wrote two motets...

51 The cards from the Île de France are all undated.

> Do you still not want to be in England? This village has all the romance of the countryside. I had a 24th birthday here and worked hard on my long organ piece…[52]

Malcolm's biggest friendship at this period, however, was with Peter Pears' niece, Susan, whom he had met through George Malcolm, a mutual friend. At the time Susan Pears was housekeeping for her uncle at his London home near Regent's Park. Both were immediately attracted to the other, and Malcolm was soon a regular visitor at 5 Chester Gate. Susan for her part found herself a regular visitor at the Jesuits' church in Mayfair, which Malcolm seemed to have made his own:

> We'd be out and about doing something quite different and he'd suddenly say 'Let's go to Farm Street!' I'd sit at his feet as he played! It would mostly be Messiaen, but some of his own music too, and he would improvise with great skill, usually in a Messiaen kind of way. I was struck by the severity of some of Malcolm's own compositions. It was so unlike him. It just came out in his music, but he was never severe as a person. Just mad and wild![53]

Susan was an accomplished pianist, and they would sometimes play together, but more often than not they would be out with their friends:

> There were wild evenings with much dashing from pillar to post, getting soaking wet and roaring with laughter. Going nowhere in the end, just dashing around… Mostly on foot, sometimes on bus or tube; and I had a bicycle on which we would occasionally try to wobble along together…

As a time-keeper she found him quite hopeless. It was useless making advance arrangements. He exulted in freedom from responsibility, and swept everyone else along with his infectious enthusiasm for whatever currently mattered most.

> It was extremely easy to fall madly in love with him, for he was so beguiling. He was like a wild, lovely creature from the woodlands. There was a childishness in him, which brought out everyone's maternal instincts. He was like Peter Pan, but with a strongly self-destructive streak added. He had a different way of looking at things from everybody else, which made them both more dangerous and exciting… Even in those days he was not very good at finishing things... he was too easily distracted. He was a man who just went where the wind took him. Practically every minute of the day. If he suddenly felt like a bit of sex in the middle of something – it didn't matter what – he just had it, wherever he was…

Susan's friendship with Malcolm was interrupted by a period when her uncle went abroad and she was working for Rosalyn Tureck. On her return to London her life was soon centred again around Malcolm. There were visits to theatres and films ('He was pretty well up on foreign art films') and a considerable amount of poetry reading: 'He adored French poetry and we somehow got

---

[52] Grandma Mary also received a postcard, explaining how hard he was working: 'The weather is mild – very clean and very clear air. There's a fire and piano and every comfort including not having to bath and shave. I shall go for a walk to post this and get more ideas for the music I'm writing.' (24 November 1955)

[53] January 2006

through a great deal of it.' He was drinking just as much as ever: 'Any spirits he could get his hands on.'

In June 1955 Sue introduced Malcolm to her father, Peter Pears' elder brother, and not long afterwards she and Malcolm announced their engagement.[54]

> It was simply assumed by everyone that it was going to happen, though my father was a little dubious. But when we visited him, Malcolm behaved impeccably – he could always do this when needed – even though he was furious we were expected to have separate rooms.
>
> Of course Malcolm had a difficult side – the one people probably remember. But there was this extremely warm side, this extremely energetic, wild but imaginative and wonderful side! Always clouded by the demon drink, unfortunately. But we nonetheless had a relationship for a reasonable length of time, because he was an utterly fascinating person…

No wedding date was ever fixed, but they had decided on the little Catholic Church in Aldeburgh rather than Farm Street, and Imogen Holst had already written them a song as a wedding present when, one day, it was all called off.

> I think it dawned on us both gradually. And then one day there were terrible recriminations and we said 'Come on! That's it! We're finished! We can't go on like this!' I think both of us knew from the start that we would have killed each other. He would have driven me to an early grave. I didn't have the skills to persuade him to lead a more moderate life. I was just seen as a nag.

In addition to the excessive drinking, there was Malcolm's promiscuous lifestyle:

> He had this wild energy, particularly in matters of sex. He was absolutely crazy! He would have a relationship with almost anything or anybody! In the end I gave up, because he was just as happy in a homosexual relationship as he was in a heterosexual one. He had a number of boys and he had a number of men. It was difficult to cope with… He had this one strong relationship, too, probably the straw that broke the camel's back as far as I was concerned…

In all the complicated circumstances of Malcolm's private life it was appropriate that the one composition of the period to be completed should be called *Fons Amoris*. The dedicatee of 'The Source of Love' might be expected to hold a special place in his affections. And so it proved. Malcolm had met him in January 1956. Up to that moment love had been simply a game of musical chairs. With the exception of Susan, there had been little sense of commitment, just a scramble for survival as the music suddenly stopped, followed by an optimistic new start. But Malcolm was now to attempt to settle down for the first time in his life. His definition of 'settling down' was hardly the conventional one, but he was in love, and with love would come the first important outpouring of music.

---

54 On 23 June Grandma Mary Wrigley wrote delightedly to Malcolm about the engagement: 'Thank you for sending *The Times*. I saw the name of a grandson of mine in it. Congratulations! No need to say how pleased I am to hear of your progress.'

Fons Amoris (c. MARCH 1955)
Lento Lord have mercy on us
ORGAN
Christ have mercy on us
Lord have mercy on us
Christ hear us
Christ graciously hear us
God, the Father of Heaven have mercy upon us
God the Holy Ghost have mercy upon us

4 LORENZO
London and Buckland, 1956–58

LORENZO, DEDICATEE of *Fons Amoris*, came from Brazil. He was in his early twenties, tall, slim, exuding an old-world elegance, and hopeful of one day becoming an important artist. After a comfortable South American upbringing – his late father had been a successful businessman – he had led a nomadic life for several years in Europe, having fallen out with his mother who had married a retired English army officer. Although his step-father was hardly a Claudius, Lorenzo felt much like Hamlet, outraged and powerless at what he saw as his mother's betrayal. His tirades against the pair could be extremely violent. On an occasion when his mother had stopped his allowance he wrote:

> The bloody bitch! However much I try not to, I still hate that low-bred-nanny-goat-on-heat. I could kill them both. Killing one's step-father isn't patricide is it?[1]

His difficult relationship with his mother had not been improved by two affairs of his own: the first with a London businessman; the second with Emily Coleman, a rich expatriate American, now in her mid-fifties, a Catholic convert and the kind of character who might have interested Henry James.

When they first met, in 1954, Lorenzo was immediately fascinated by Emily and her circle of artistic friends which included fellow Americans Peggy Guggenheim and Djuna Barnes. Emily was a forceful personality, numbering among her many lovers Dylan Thomas. T S Eliot had nicknamed her 'Little Annie Oakley' after the Wild West heroine who could outshoot most men.[2] She had once worked on the *Chicago Tribune* in Paris and written a novel about her time in a mental hospital, *The Shutter of Snow*, published in New York in 1930. Currently in the grip of severe religious mania, she was daily writing pages of Catholic poetry, which, she hoped, would bring her the fame she craved. She was convinced she was a genius.[3]

---

1 Letter to Emily Coleman, 19 February 1958

2 It was also a pun. She was living in Oakley Gardens, London, at the time. (Robert Fraser, *George Barker*, p.84)

3 Her friend Antonia White was not so sure.

Always eager to adopt promising young men and much taken by Lorenzo's ardent Catholicism and dog-like devotion, Emily determinedly assumed responsibility for the nurturing of his artistic talent. Their subsequent year-long romance was played out in some appropriately Jamesian settings, most notably Venice, where Lorenzo, temporarily overcome by doubts, had loudly declared in St Mark's Square that he would never again be able to attend Mass, and Emily, in bringing him to his senses, had delivered such a slap across his face that passing tourists stopped and waited for more. Such hysteria characterised their unlikely love-affair, which ended only when Emily, growing anxious at Lorenzo's seeming indolence, selflessly dispatched him to London, to further his career. There, in early 1956, he met Malcolm. It was love at first sight.

Their only problem was their poverty, Lorenzo having little ready money and Malcolm even less. He had just been fired by Boosey & Hawkes for writing derogatory comments about the firm, though for the moment he was kept on as a part-time proof reader. He also had one or two piano pupils and a small retainer at the Farm Street church, while Bessie was still sending him a small monthly cheque, and Gerald Finzi, a Boosey & Hawkes composer, had organised some grants for him. But, all in all, it did not amount to very much, and Malcolm's expensive drinking habits ensured a hand-to-mouth existence with cheerful dependence on the goodwill of others. Fortunately he and Lorenzo shared a talent for eliciting hospitality and it was not long before they were living together in a smart house in Notting Hill.[4]

Each was convinced he would inspire the other to higher things, and Malcolm was soon writing long letters to Emily Coleman on this theme:

> It is early on Monday morning and my brain is fuddled. Lorenzo is here in the room reading to himself and making his drawings. He has been excellent for me. He makes me work and after that fracas in the dirty pub and another the following night he has put more self-discipline into me.[5]

Malcolm was also keen to acquaint Emily with his own strong Catholic conscience:

> I have seen Father Belton[6] for 2 hours on Friday night. He is worried about two people of such propensities as Lorenzo and me. We shall go and see him tonight…

It was important for Emily to realise that he and Lorenzo were just good friends:

> I believe your real fear is not that you may be excluded from his love (in any case you *never* shall be!) but that he and I may be paving each other's way to hell. With all my

[4] Arundel Gardens

[5] 10 March 1956

[6] A Jesuit priest attached to the Church of the Immaculate Conception, Farm Street. Malcolm sought counsel from him regularly during this period along with another friend, Father Wood of The Oratory. Throughout his life Malcolm cultivated Catholic father confessors. (Another attraction of The Oratory was its organ, on which in 1958 Malcolm recorded *Fons Amoris*.)

Peripatetic in London

> power I shall try to prevent this out of my love for you both, and he will try (as he already is) in order to better articulate his immense affection for you.[7]

Emily was unlikely to have been fooled.

Malcolm was also shrewd enough to realise that Lorenzo's mother's goodwill was as important as Emily Coleman's. Lorenzo had hopes of acquiring money of his own. There was a flat in Buenos Aires which he was trying to sell, but he was beset by continual complications, and in the meantime handouts from his mother came only irregularly. So Malcolm encouraged him to mend this relationship, and in April, as part of the process, he was taken to meet her. He behaved impeccably, modestly talking up his prospects: in three days' time he would be playing *Fons Amoris* on the Festival Hall organ;[8] there was also a piano sonata which he would be performing at Aldeburgh in a couple of months. Lorenzo's mother was also impressed by the easy way he talked about his friends Peter and Ben. Peter, she was told, had recently asked him for a song cycle.

Later, Malcolm gave Emily an account of the meeting:

> Lorenzo's mother talked about music to me and played for me… We talked about parents and children, and careers of the latter against opposition of the former. I ended up with a different picture of Lorenzo's life from the one he had given me. She loves him greatly and has few illusions about him. I told her that I was convinced of his

[7] 13 March 1956

[8] 13 April 1956

> great gifts and that she was tying his hands by her treatment of him… During luncheon they both screamed away in the kitchen at each other in Portugese leaving me to eat alone. Lorenzo told me later that there was no argument, only normal civilised conversation…[9]

There was encouraging talk for a while of their being found a flat for which Lorenzo's mother would buy 'all sorts of things' and loan them a piano. But Lorenzo fell out with her again and it failed to materialise.

The Festival Hall performance of *Fons Amoris* had been brought about by Guy Weitz, the Farm Street organist. Impressed by a short work, *Epithalamium*, which Malcolm had written for the wedding of a friend,[10] Weitz introduced Malcolm to Ralph Downes, a fellow Catholic and the outstanding organist of the day. Malcolm played Downes *Fons Amoris*, a 13-minute devotional piece, strongly medieval and much influenced by Messiaen, based on the *Stabat Mater*.[11] Downes was as impressed as Weitz and invited Malcolm to play it at a forthcoming organ recital at the Festival Hall. It was his first public performance in England, an important and challenging occasion. Malcolm was so very nervous that Lorenzo, turning over the pages for him, kept muttering Hail Mary's. All went well and the reviews were favourable, an encouragement for his forthcoming appearance at Aldeburgh.

Malcolm's standing with Britten and Pears was extremely high at this time. He had cultivated them assiduously, and more and more caught their interest. So when Richard Rodney Bennett, five years his junior, sent an oboe piece to Britten, Malcolm was very jealous. Aldeburgh, he declared firmly, was *his* territory. So hands off! It was certainly a patronage worth protecting, one which was already bringing him several benefits. In May 1956, for example, he had free use again of the cottage at Royden, Southwold, which, on the whole, met with Lorenzo's approval. He reported to Emily:

> This cottage makes me think of your ranch in Arizona. One has to piss in the fields and the lavatory has no flush. The view from it is beautiful and serene. Malcolm hasn't shaved for days and is looking like a Nordic sailor. This used to be a smuggler's den. It has cellars unlike the other cottages in the neighbourhood. It looks very much as if it were one just now. On the table two mugs of tea and an open tin of condensed milk. 'Unfit for babies'. Do you think we should drink it?[12]

Having at long last completed the piano sonata, Malcolm now had plans for a first piano concerto, but was currently being side-tracked by a bizarre

---

9 14 April 1956

10 Choirmaster Louis Halsey. The wedding was in August 1955.

11 A quotation by the thirteenth-century poet Jacopone da Todi remained on the title page: *Eia Mater, fons amoris, me sentire vim doloris fac, ut tecum lugeam*. 'Mother, source of love, make me feel the power of your pain, that I may grieve with you.' Malcolm subsequently began to orchestrate this work, but completed only thirty-eight bars. The dedication to Lorenzo was dropped by the time Novello published it.

12 6 May 1956

commission, an invitation from the Countess of Lichfield to orchestrate some songs for a version of *Robin Hood.* 'The songs are hideous,' reported Lorenzo to Emily Coleman. 'The poor chap moans and moans as he works.' This first brush with the English aristocracy, however, appealed to Malcolm very much indeed. Lorenzo, although disgruntled at not being included in the week at Shugborough Hall, was amused by Malcolm's mounting excitement:

> He's beside himself with glee. 'I'm very glad,' he says, 'that Lady Lichfield considers me socially acceptable.' This is more snobbery than I can stand! I don't understand it! It doesn't tie up with his apparent free attitude to life. I spoke to Lady L on the telephone yesterday. She sounds charming and easy. I don't think Malcolm realises yet that countesses are women. His social humility drives me nuts![13]

Driving each other 'nuts' was soon part of a relationship in which quarrels abounded. Lorenzo was constantly jealous, and no doubt with good reason. Malcolm's musical preoccupations he also found frustrating. On one occasion, with his despair reflected in his erratic spelling, he confided to Emily:

> Music, music, nothing but music: semi-cuevas, adagios, chorus, simphonies, sonatas, sonatinas, concertos, pianos, harpsichords, Palestrina, Bach, List, Shuman, Bartok, ballet etc etc…[14]

But there were compensations. He was delighted to be introduced to Britten and Pears, finding Britten 'sweet, unassuming and extremely alive'.[15] He loved meeting celebrities and being paraded as Malcolm's most prized possession. The affection Malcolm and Lorenzo showed each other in public visibly shocked the staid population of Southwold. ('We were stared at by these monsters today as if we were exotic animals escaped from a London zoo'.) But the good times only threw the bad into greater relief, and his holiday at Southwold, as related to Emily, was becoming a nightmare:

> I'm in Alborough [sic], alone again, in a pub drinking bitters, thinking of you, your poems and all that has happened… What have I done? How reckless and greedy! I only blame myself. Malcolm is with Miss Holst talking music. His feeling for me increases as mine lessens. I can't stand it any longer. I'm beginning to hate him and have told him so. I long for you, my sweet mad poet. I deserve what I'm getting. I threw bricks at Malcolm today. Felt murderous. I envy Malcolm in too many ways. I feel inferior! Why? Am I?[16]

It was lucky that Lorenzo had Emily Coleman to write to, someone with whom he could let out his pent-up feelings of inferiority. The murder of Joe Orton was shortly to demonstrate the violence which could erupt from the envy of a non-achiever for his highly successful partner. Lorenzo, depressed to be left alone in an Aldeburgh pub, could share his frustrations with Emily:

---

13 Letter to Emily Coleman, 9 May 1956

14 15 May 1956

15 The comment was made at a later meeting, in September, when Lorenzo was taken by Malcolm to *The Turn of the Screw* at the Scala Theatre.

16 5 May 1956

> I might tear up my drawings… Done lots. But not very good. They're about to throw me out. Almost drunk. Terribly tired. Haven't really slept since Malcolm… Is he the devil?

The very next night at Southwold, Lorenzo was again communicating his isolation:

> It is 12.00pm. Malcolm has disappeared since 7.00. I'm alone reading your poems. Rather terrified. I'm afraid of the night. The clock is ticking…

Back in London, he found nothing much had altered:

> I'm alone in the flat. Malcolm has gone to give a piano lesson to a debauched-east-end-opera-singer-to-be. Your poem The Suicide is superb, powerful and moving. But I can't write about it as Malcolm has taken it with him…[17]

Although in criticising his new love Lorenzo was probably pleasing his former love, his bouts of unhappiness were real enough:

> I put in an ad. in the Kensington News for a flat… I do hope we get something. I can no longer stand the instability of the life I'm leading. I feel so tired for I'm never allowed to sleep in the morning once Malcolm is out of bed. He says he can't work if I don't get up. Can you beat it? He is a tyrant…[18]

On good days, at least, the tyrant was a very loving one. In the middle of June 1956, for example, when the two of them were spending time with Phyllis Jones, Emily Coleman's closest friend, at Rye,[19] Malcolm wrote very proudly to Emily of Lorenzo's artistic talents:

> Lorenzo has begun to paint!!!! On a large scale, canvas 24" by 20" and very many oils subtly and beautifully mixed and matched. He dedicates his life to art more than he would care to admit. He took a very good drawing of a woman in a pub and transformed it for his canvas. Now it is quite a different woman. The face is full of dignity and acceptance of tragedies, vibrant of flesh and spirit. Despite rather daring distortion, the composition is more than satisfactory. The colour scheme for the figure (head and shoulders) is a rising progression of brown to a muted white.. The sense of colour, composition and of perspective (and, to me, very important, of gravity!), which I missed in the little oils he did before, are all here. The background presents the strange paradox of Lorenzo's imagination…[20]

Four days later, on 18 June, they were both at Aldeburgh, where, after taking Holy Communion in the little church of Our Lady and St Peter, Malcolm played his sonata in a recital of twentieth-century music. Afterwards he wrote to Bessie:

---

17 7 May 1956

18 *ibid.*

19 West Street. An attractive redhead who never married, Phyllis Jones was also friendly with Antonia White, typing out all her books in the 1950s. Emily Coleman spent several years that decade living with Phyllis at Rye before moving to the retreat guesthouse at the Benedictine convent near Worcester, Stanbrook Abbey.

20 14 June 1956

> I have this morning played my sonata here. I was recalled 4 times with cheers!! Lovely place, lots of people to butter one up, and about time too![21]

The sonata was Malcolm's first statement of where he stood in the highly confused contemporary scene. He regarded it, he said, as his homage to Stravinsky, but the earlier, neo-classical Stravinsky rather than the Stravinsky of 1956, now favouring a severer, serial style.[22]

After Aldeburgh came the Ludlow Festival, Malcolm and Lorenzo staying at the Portcullis Inn for nearly six weeks. Malcolm had written incidental organ music for a production of *Everyman* in the Parish Church of St Laurence where a strong cast was headed by Sebastian Shaw.[23] It was a successful production, but Malcolm soon wearied of his subservient role on the organ, particularly in an Anglican church. The Catholics, as Lorenzo told Emily, were their chief concern:

> We've spoken to the local priest (a rather sweet old man covered in bird shit) about the possibility of using the Festival as an excuse for Malcolm to give a recital in aid of St Peter's, the Catholic Church. He is thrilled and so is Malcolm…[24]

The Anglican clergy, running the festival, were understandably less keen:

> Malcolm is causing quite a stir for the Anglican Bishop is against anything being done in aid of the Roman Catholic church during his Festival, but it is not in his power to stop us hiring the Town Hall. All he can do is fume and that he is doing with great intensity! Cutting Malcolm etc. They've been treating Malcolm abominably trying to reduce his already meagre fees.[25]

Wherever he went, Malcolm usually managed to generate a crisis. Ludlow was no exception:

> Malcolm has had a slight fling with an obese over-painted fun-loving lass who managed a rather bogus continentalised (Italian) club that catered for the few fast-living inhabitants of Ludlow. I didn't particularly mind, although I pretended to. He was most repentant back in London and has since behaved in a saintly manner…[26]

---

21 Malcolm repeated his success in London (October 1956) at one of the lunchtime concerts organized by the English Opera Group at the Royal Court Theatre. The Aldeburgh performance was broadcast, Malcolm receiving a precious £7 from the BBC.

22 Although the sonata makes few concessions to popular taste and is a deeply intellectual work with a serial base, there is a sensuous Williamson feeling for line and colour and, in the last movement, a wit and light-heartedness which make it distinctively his. The slow movement is deeply-felt but very dark, and *The Times* declared the work 'poker-faced'. By contrast the *Daily Telegraph* liked it: 'It remains one of his best pieces and a promise of what a talent so tuneful, nimble-minded, sharp-eared and fundamentally serious might do.' (John Warrack, 6 July 1964)

23 The Festival lasted from 9-21 July 1956. *Everyman* was an adaptation by Dennis Arundell of the play written by Hugo von Hofmannsthal for Max Reinhardt. The score, most of which survives in rough manuscript, inspired Lorenzo with the fascinating idea that Malcolm should write an opera on *Everyman* to a libretto by George Barker.

24 Letter to Emily Coleman, 28 June 1956

25 3 July 1956. Malcolm earned a precious extra £50 by taking over as organist at St Peter's throughout his stay.

26 Letter to Emily Coleman, June 1956

Petty's Barn, Buckland

The 'fun-loving lass' fared less well. When the club's owner, her lover, heard of the 'slight fling', he flung her out into the street, never to darken his doors again. The police were eventually called to break up the ensuing brawl.

Their itinerant life continued with another stay at the Dartington Summer School, where Malcolm taught composition and, with several other young composers, participated in practical workshops on film music.[27] With interesting people to meet, Lorenzo was again as content as the love-hate relationship would ever allow:

> Malcolm irritates me terribly at times. He is incredibly domineering and overpowering. I feel squashed very often, although I love his company…

Malcolm and Lorenzo had been drifting from place to place for over six months when a rapprochement between Lorenzo and his mother led to a significant change in lifestyle. She and her new husband had been living in a cottage in the village of Buckland two miles from Reigate, and now that they were going back to Brazil she offered to keep paying the rent so that Lorenzo could live there. By August 1956 he had moved in with Malcolm. Petty's Barn Cottage, though comparatively small, had great character and was in beautiful condition. There was an upright piano in the L-shaped sitting-dining room, and Malcolm soon found friends in Dorking where a Bechstein grand was made available to him. With Lorenzo to look after his daily needs, he could begin to write in earnest. His situation would have been perfect if Lorenzo had only gone out to work to ease their financial worries, but this suggestion was not met with

[27] The workshops, taken by Roman Vlad and David Drew, were also attended by Alexander Goehr, Malcolm Lipkin and Susan Bradshaw. Scores they had devised for three-minute sections of Eisenstein's *Battleship Potemkin* and Clair's *Entr'acte* were recorded and given in a performance synchronized with the films. (Glock: *Notes In Advance*, p.61)

Malcolm at Petty's Barn, drawn by Lorenzo

enthusiasm. Malcolm could hardly be critical. His own efforts outside the musical world had been very indifferent. For a few hours, for example, he had sold encyclopaedias. 'But then it rained at midday, so I gave up and went home.'[28]

A gay couple, living together in a noisy and flamboyant manner wholly contrary to the ethos of the 1950s, was quite a shock to the quiet Surrey village. It wasn't long before the cleaning lady handed in her notice – her husband, she said, thought it wasn't a safe place to work – and village gossip centred on the risqué songs with which Malcolm would entertain all-comers. Fifty years on, local legend still tells of the infamous duo touring round Buckland by taxi on the lookout for attractive male companionship.

Comfortably installed in the cottage, Malcolm settled down to composition, Emily Coleman's religious zeal providing the initial inspiration for two of the three minor works first completed. As Malcolm and Lorenzo currently represented Emily's most appreciative readership, her latest poems would arrive most days at Petty's Barn, and the receipt of 'The Blessed Organ at Middlemass' occasioned a particularly excited response:

> I went very early to Communion, due to the clock being fast, and came back to find your very lovely verses. It is not a long poem but it is quite perfect as it stands for

28 1966 interview

> musical setting. I shall put 'The Innocent' with it. I know I'm greedy but what would be better than another smallish poem by you on the martyrdom of St Stephen? That would make a triptych for the Christmas season.[29]

Emily duly complied and when Louis Halsey, who directed the Elizabethan Singers, asked Malcolm for something new, he was given Emily's triptych under the title of *Meditations*.[30] Emily also inspired a Mass for unaccompanied chorus, which he dedicated to her.[31]

There was another unusual source of inspiration for the third work, which later became known as the Third Piano Sonata: an approach by C F Colt, a Kent collector of early pianos. Colt, who belonged to a family which built prefabricated wooden houses, had started his collection in the 1940s, storing it at the Colt-built village hall at Bethersden, where he lived. Malcolm's commission, for a piece suitable for a fortepiano, was expedited in just three days, an indication of how much his research into these early instruments had fascinated him. In deference to Lorenzo, Malcolm gave the work a Portuguese title, *Pinturasinhas* ('little pictures'), and its movements Portugese headings. Although it proved a delightful twentieth-century homage to Haydn and greatly pleased Colt, it did not receive a public performance until 1993.[32]

Malcolm was side-tracked for a while by the possibility of writing a musical. 'He has been writing such beautiful songs lately,' commented Lorenzo, shortly before Malcolm's audition with a producer at the Scala Theatre. 'It will mean a lot of money if it comes off.' Fortunately it didn't, and Malcolm was able to revisit an important idea, his first orchestral work since coming to England. It was something he had explored earlier that year:

> While I was writing Fons I planned my next work (as I always do). It was to be a work for orchestra – a triptych on the subject of a martyr entering heaven. To be three sections:
>
> The agony & beauty of the martyr's death
>
> The song of the angels' welcome
>
> The coronation of the martyr…
>
> Then I was moved by the beautiful word 'Elevamini' – from the psalm 'Lift up your heads, o ye gates of brass, and be ye lifted up ye everlasting doors that the King of Glory may come in…' But I had to distort the psalm, as I conceived in a rather

29 MW to Emily Coleman, 28 April 1956

30 The work was completed on 18 October 1956 and performed at the Royal Festival Hall Recital Room on 14 December 1956. It is written in Malcolm's severest style and strongly contrapuntal, the first 'carol' using a 10-note serial row, the other two not serial, but harsh harmonically.

31 The Mass was started in mid-August 1956 and completed seven weeks later. Lost for fifty years, it has recently come to light.

32 C F Colt died in 1985, but his impressive Clavier Collection survives. As Sonata No. 3 'for fortepiano or piano or clavecin', the work was turned down by Ernest Roth at Boosey & Hawkes ('sales of piano music, unless it is purely educational, are very poor'). Antony Gray finally gave the sonata its premiere at Melbourne University.

Grandparents, Benjamin and Mary Wrigley

primitive way the gates of heaven being lifted up, not for the entry of the King of Glory, but that a martyr might receive his sweet reward of seeing the King of All Glory. Then I had a germ of an idea for the music and worked [on it] spasmodically but fruitlessly…[33]

By that December he had decided on Thomas More as the martyr to be celebrated, when news reached him from Sydney of the death of his much admired grandmother.[34] Thomas More's ascension was quickly turned into that of Grandma Mary Wrigley. The work, which became his First Symphony

---

33 MW to Emily Coleman, April 1956

34 George, in writing to Malcolm of his grandmother's death, gently encouraged a return home: 'In Australia the govt. has increased the quota of Australian music to be played. Consequently we are getting tripe such as no self-respecting broadcasting station would play. I think you ought to explore the field out here through Australia House.' (15 December 1956)

(subtitled *Elevamini*), was accordingly dedicated[35] to 'The Great Lady' and such was his affection for his grandmother that by mid-February 1957 the structure was fully in place and he was working feverishly on the orchestration. *Elevamini* was completed in March, Lorenzo reporting to Emily:

> He is walking on air! He is taking it tomorrow to his publishers.[36] It ought to mean a retainer of 5-10 pounds a week.

Erwin Stein's support ensured that Boosey & Hawkes would indeed publish the work, but early attempts to woo concert managements for a first performance failed. Seizing upon this, Lorenzo, who was very bored with the country, urged a temporary return to London, which resulted in their imposing themselves on some friends in Belsize Park, in Thurloe Square, and, later at the Chelsea home of the ever-supportive Derek and Barbara Beck. For Lorenzo, life in London could never be boring. There were too many fascinating people. He was, for example, introduced to Edith Sitwell:

> She is one of the most beautiful of women with the most expressive non-existing eyes I've ever seen. She is warm, talks wittily about her majestic self and is eternally surrounded by young poets who in turn at various cocktail parties she introduces as the white hope of English poetry. She is covered in black satin, green brocade and aquamarine. I like her.[37]

Eventually, still without a first performance for the symphony, they returned to peaceful Buckland, from where Lorenzo reported gloomily to Emily Coleman's son, Johnny:

> Autumn is here, the roses are dead and the falling leaves do not make me think of the Phoenix. I am tired, very tired of it all. Schubert is being played, poached-egg-fed

---

35 It was an impressive dedication: *In memoriam M.E.W. Memento etiam, Domine, famulorum famularumque, qui nos processerunt signo fidei et dormiunt in somno pacis.* (Also remember, oh Lord, those of your servants, male and female, who went before us holding aloft the standard of faith and who now sleep in peace.)

36 Boosey & Hawkes. Malcolm was later to explain the work in programmatic terms: In the first movement (Lento) the opening of the gates could be heard, and the progress of the soul upwards until 'at the summit of the hill the gates of brass thunder out' and the soul is given 'quiet and tranquil release'. In the second movement (Allegretto) the dance-like cross-rhythms of the scherzo suggested the joy of the saints and angels at the approach of a new soul, and the trio signified 'the benediction of the blessed Virgin' over its approach. In the final movement (Lento assai – Allegro) 'the everlasting gates lift up and beyond them are heard the ever-varying rhythms of angelic dance' until a climax in which 'the soul is embraced in celestial clarity among the angels and saints'.

37 Letter to John Coleman, 16 August 1956. The Sitwell connection was assiduously cultivated. In 1957 Edith Sitwell was writing to Malcolm about a private recital he hoped to give her: 'I am so unhappy about this; but alas I shall not be able to have the great pleasure of hearing you next week. I fainted yesterday. The doctor says I have a tired and strained heart, and he has advised me to go to bed every night at 8 o'clock. What a bore! I had particularly looked forward to hearing you, and it was so very charming of you to offer to play for me. I look forward very much to seeing you and Lorenzo when I am a little better, even if the doctor is still sending me to bed like a baby. Best wishes to you both.' (15 August 1957)

> Malcolm is snoozing by the fire and Emily's poems are on a table. Snug? Country life, bucolic bliss, love. SHIT!!! The garden is going wild, the apples are rotting on the trees and 99 plates are waiting to be washed in the kitchen…

The more Malcolm began to achieve at Buckland, the more he wished Lorenzo were similarly productive. He had tried hard to get him an exhibition, promoted by a new friend, David Archer, whose Parton Press had helped poets like George Barker and Dylan Thomas and whose bookshop had exhibition space on the first floor:[38]

> The exhibition is in the balance. Archer partly enthusiastic, Deakin[39] extremely so and pushing like mad. Archer has no opinions or tastes really; he is asking other people to comment, apparently with good results. I've persuaded Antonia [White] to come and meet Archer on Friday so that I can gently introduce the subject…[40]

But Lorenzo's output was worryingly limited. The more Malcolm put pressure on him, the less he seemed able to achieve, and perhaps it was just as well that the exhibition did not materialise. Malcolm, however, continued to believe in him and would regularly give Emily progress reports:

> I am working frantically hard with Lorenzo's excellent stimulus. I wish I stimulated him. He has at least begun to draw again. Did a very good one of me today. He has collected several passionate and some discriminating admirers (Barker very much so)…[41]

George Barker, the anarchic and Rabelaisian poet, was another new friend. As a young man in the 1930s he had briefly allowed himself to be seduced by Emily Coleman, and his complicated love life was a constant topic of conversation at Petty's Barn. Barker, who is said to have fathered no less than seventeen children, had enjoyed a big critical success in 1954 with *A Vision of Beasts and Gods*. Malcolm had initially been looking for poems from Emily Coleman for a song cycle commissioned by Peter Pears, but the right words eluded him. For a while he considered some 'cowboy poems' of hers:

> The last batches are a rich harvest that any composer would be thrilled to have. But I do think that the word 'gay' which keeps occurring is not the thing to offer dear Peter Pears…[42]

In the end Malcolm decided to use poems from George Barker's *A Vision of Beasts and Gods*. Although they avoided the kind of language which had earlier involved Barker in charges of obscenity, they are (with the exception of a poem on the death of a famous bullfighter) hard for the non-specialist to understand. The first song, for example, is an invocation to a 'loving hydra' to lean out of the

---

38 The basement contained a coffee bar run by Henrietta Law (later Henrietta Moraes).

39 John Deakin, the Bohemian artist and photographer, who lived with David Archer

40 April 1956

41 10 February 1957

42 April 1956. At one stage in her life Emily Coleman had been married to a cowboy.

human breast and persuade an ant to instruct the human race. But Malcolm, steeped in modern verse, admired Barker's wittily allusive style:

> I have bought nearly all Barker's work and have taken a great liking to it. Much is enigmatic and even too deliberately so at times, but it has the stuff of greatness…[43]

It was, however, hardly ideal song cycle material.

In late February 1957 Malcolm was invited to dinner by Peter Pears. The intention was that he should play the new songs, but Malcolm arrived at Chester Gate with something of even greater interest, several of Lorenzo's line drawings, which, he suggested to Pears, might make good cover illustrations for his scores. 'Dismantled Doll' he felt was just right for *A Vision of Beasts and Gods*. ('Peter adored Dismantled Doll,' he later informed Emily proudly. 'He kept looking at it and chuckling.') For *Meditations* he suggested a drawing of Phyllis Jones 'with her arms crossed and head turned away'. After dinner he played Pears the song cycle. Pears masked his disappointment, not wishing to spoil the evening, but it was to be ten years before he gave *A Vision of Beasts and Gods* its single public hearing.[44] As for Lorenzo's drawings, *Meditations* was never published, and the cover of *A Vision of Beasts and Gods* contained someone else's design.

George Barker quickly became one of the more regular visitors to Petty's Barn, often accompanied by Betty Cash ('Cashenden'), with whom he was living intermittently. Malcolm greatly admired the beautiful Cashenden, and, anxious that Barker was not treating her well, secretly gave her a favourite St Christopher medal. Another visitor was the novelist Antonia ('Toni') White, a close friend of Emily Coleman's since the 1930s, when she, too, had fallen for George Barker's youthful charms. As emotionally unstable as her friend, Antonia White had emerged in the 1950s from a long period of writer's block and mental illness with three highly praised autobiographical novels, which Malcolm devotedly read and re-read. He also loudly extolled the virtues of her most recent book, on her two cats, Minka and Curdy. Lorenzo, who had quickly attracted Antonia White's maternal instincts, regularly furnished Emily with details of her visits:

> We had Toni, Barker and Cashenden to dinner two nights ago. It was a very successful evening. Toni looked very elegant in black and white and spotted grey. Toni having left, George was shown my drawings by Malcolm. He liked them so much he never stopped winking at me for the rest of the evening.[45]

For the last two hours of his visit Malcolm pounded the piano as George Barker bellowed Irish songs.

A happy summer of touring round the country followed. First to Aldeburgh; then to Cheltenham; later to Wilfrid Mellers's summer school at Attingham Park,

---

43 MW to Emily Coleman, June 1956

44 A radio broadcast, 3 October 1968, with Viola Tunnard (piano).

45 Letter to Emily Coleman, February 1957

Shropshire;[46] and finally the Dartington summer school of 1957, where the participation of Stravinsky caused Malcolm and Lorenzo great excitement.

Largely to please Peter Pears, Malcolm had agreed to take part in an Aldeburgh Festival competition for composers under twenty-five, the prize for the best setting of a poem by Blake being £25. Malcolm's 'The Fly' was one of four pieces chosen to be sung at a concert by Pears, at which the winner was to be announced. Cornelius Cardew and Alexander Goehr had written two serious philosophical songs; Michael Nuttall an appealing cradle song. Malcolm's piece, by contrast, was light and witty, the fly's erratic hopping and buzzing being brilliantly represented in the piano part. He was naturally disappointed when Britten and Pears evaded decision-making and awarded the four finalists £6 5s 0d each. The young, radical-thinking Alexander Goehr hated the whole event:

> It was abominable! Like a public school prize-giving! We were all called up, one after the other, to receive our miserable prize! I was fairly rebellious at that time and refused to get up and be patted on the head like a schoolboy! Eventually, however, Malcolm, who was sitting next to me, gave me such a shove I simply had to go![47]

In addition to his success with 'The Fly' Malcolm also had a Trio for Clarinet, Cello and Piano performed at the same concert.[48] The *Manchester Guardian*'s Colin Mason, finding it 'forthrightly tuneful, simple in form and texture, though making use, very loosely, of some sort of serial technique', came to the encouraging conclusion that Malcolm was 'the most originally and variously gifted of the rising generation of composers'.

In 1957 Malcolm's Second Piano Sonata (*Ianua Coeli*) was commissioned by the young pianist Robin Harrison for the Cheltenham Festival. Harrison had first approached Benjamin Britten, who suggested he try 'the very promising Malcolm Williamson', an experience Harrison found most interesting:

> He was something of a wild character at the time! He brought me the manuscript day by day as he wrote it, in almost illegible pencil on huge orchestral paper with small, narrow staves! One day I said to him, 'Malcolm, what is this note here? I can't read it. Is it an F or an F sharp?' 'It doesn't really matter,' he replied. 'It's the sweep of the thing that's important. Do whatever is more comfortable!'[49]

---

46 For which Malcolm wrote a bizarre Concerto for Soprano, Oboe, Cor Anglais, Cello and Organ. Anthony Milner, who was to conduct the work, reacted strongly to its late arrival: 'I have not yet received the score of your Attingham work. If it does not arrive by Wednesday next I will not be able to take the responsibility of directing it. There will be no time to learn new scores at Attingham. I have a heavy programme of rehearsals and lectures. So hurry up. After all, you're not nearly so busy as I am.' (22 September 1957)

47 January 2005

48 The performers were Harrison Birtwistle (clarinet) John Dow (cello) and Cornelius Cardew (piano). It is a work requiring considerable technical expertise – the clarinet writing is often very high and very quiet.

49 January 2006

The five-movement work[50] was well received, both at the Festival and later London concerts, where Harrison again played it. Colin Mason was strong in its praise:

> Genius is a dangerous word, and it is easy, as somebody once said, to be a genius at twenty-five (which is exactly Williamson's age); the difficulty is still to be one at forty. If I had to gamble on the chances of any young English composer's coming through those fifteen years as Britten has done, my stake would be on Williamson.[51]

Mason went on to make comparisons between the two:

> *Ianua Coeli* presents a fusion of serial technique and clear, simple tonality, slightly similar to, although certainly in no way suggested by, that extraordinary fusion of them in Britten's magnificent Canticle No 3, 'Still Falls The Rain' – a work to which Williamson's may also without absurdity be compared in stature…

For all such supportive comments, Malcolm would have continued in relative obscurity but for a new, important ally, Sir Adrian Boult. Introduced to Malcolm by Gerald Finzi in 1955, Boult was at once won over to his cause. Just as 'Ben and Peter were quite fascinated by Malcolm Williamson when he first came on the scene',[52] so too the less susceptible Adrian Boult was sufficiently moved at first meeting the impecunious young composer to present him with one of his overcoats, a gift so treasured that Malcolm would wear it in all weathers. Malcolm had revered Boult ever since attending one of his Beethoven series. No other conductor, he believed, could match him, with the possible exception of Bruno Walter. Now that he had achieved this unexpected friendship with his idol, Malcolm followed his every word. When warned by Boult about his bohemian lifestyle and told to do some exercises to keep fit, Malcolm responded so vigorously that he wrenched his shoulder and had to spend three days in bed.

Boult's support was helpful in winning over BBC Radio's music department, whose backing was all-important to a young composer. On Boult's advice, Malcolm sent a double request to the BBC in August 1956:

> It is now over a year since my *Two Motets* for chorus were accepted by the BBC for broadcasting. I have heard nothing since then from you about their promotion. Could you please let me know what is being done about them. I can provide you with any number of copies. The Purcell Singers (Imogen Holst) and the Elizabethan Singers (Louis Halsey) have expressed their willingness to broadcast them.

---

50 Malcolm wrote in July 1957: 'I conceived Ianua Coeli as a memorial piece to Gerald Finzi and at the same time as a devotion to the Blessed Virgin to whom belongs the title 'Gate of Heaven'. There are throughout the work two conflicting ideas, one of earthly sorrow, the other of heavenly peace. The musical material reflects this conflict which resolves in the last movement with a fusion of all that has gone before.' The sonata, initially called 'Pavanes and Sarabandes', its three movements based on the Rosary, was amplified for Harrison at Cheltenham into five movements, but later, in 1970-71, reduced back to three. 'The original was much better from every point of view,' declares Harrison. 'He spoilt it when he rewrote it! There was a wonderful, very beautiful slow movement!'

51 *The Spectator*, 26 July 1957

52 Colin Graham, January 2006

Could you tell me please how I proceed to having an audition as an organist? I played my own organ work, *Fons Amoris*, in an ICA programme at the Festival Hall earlier this year and I am keen to broadcast it, as well as other classical and contemporary music, particularly the Messiaen organ works.

A day later Boult enclosed a copy of this letter to the BBC's Head of Music Programmes (Radio), Maurice Johnstone:

I do not know whether you are interested in the organ; I am afraid I find it the least interesting of instruments, but this young man has, I think, got something to say. If you have time to glance over this letter and return it, I would be most grateful. If you would add a suggestion of whoever in your department is now looking after the organ, I think I will inflict on him an introduction for Malcolm Williamson...[53]

A broadcast of the Two Motets quickly followed and Malcolm was at once accepted as an accredited BBC organist.[54]

Boult was helpful again in 1957, several months after the completion of the First Symphony, generously offering the assistance of the London Philharmonic Orchestra to its cause. He had, he said, a spare afternoon rehearsal coming up in September. He could give the symphony a run-through then; and there would probably be time for another shorter piece, if Malcolm had one... Boult would not have had a 'spare' afternoon available at such long notice. He was altruistically subsidising the occasion.

Malcolm reacted as Boult intended. He had no other 'shorter piece', so he would write one! All he needed was a starting-point. A few days later Lorenzo happened to be discussing his family, several of whom came from Santiago. From the city the conversation moved to the saint who had given it his name. In the middle of a discussion on the good St James, who after his martyrdom helped the Spaniards in their battles with the Moors, Malcolm realised he had the subject he was needing for Sir Adrian's second piece. He would write an overture on *Santiago de Espada*, 'St James of the Sword'! As time was short, for a starting-point he borrowed the lyrical tune he had composed fours years earlier for a convent pageant at Rickmansworth. A histrionic and highly attractive seven-minute overture was quickly completed. Malcolm knew instinctively how to bring out the best from Boult's fine orchestra.

The Symphony also won much praise after the private performance at the St Pancras Town Hall.[55] There were several complimentary comments about its ethereal nature, the achievement in the outer movements of a strange sensation

---

53 15 August 1956

54 The First Piano Sonata, however, fared less well. 'We are not prepared to promote performances of this work,' wrote the BBC's Harry Croft-Johnson on 22 May 1956, though earlier, at the time of Boult's intervention, he had written to his colleagues quite encouragingly about it: 'I have just seen a remarkable piano sonata by Williamson, recently published...' Malcolm's disappointment was offset by performances given in Sydney in 1957 by his old teacher Alexander Sverjensky.

55 18 September 1957

that time and space were no longer real. Much was made of the work's programme, with the brass skilfully suggesting the brazen doors of heaven and angelic trumpeters. The influence of the neo-classical Stravinsky was suggested, and Malcolm himself declared his debt to Rawsthorne's *Symphonic Studies*.[56] In fact, *Elevamini* is pure Williamson, an early creation displaying what one critic was to call his 'bitter-sweet, highly chromatic and utterly unique palette'.[57] It also stands by itself quite satisfactorily without any programme, especially the central movement, the jazzy allegretto, which quite eclipses everything else, displaying great powers of invention.

Some listeners found the symphony's tonal base too facile for their taste, and as Malcolm could never cope with criticism he was extremely upset. Soon after the private performance Boult wrote to him:

> My thanks for your very kind letter – I'm so glad that the rehearsal was really useful to you. It must be a frightful ordeal to hear what you have only imagined and I'm so glad you were able to get some experience out of it… I'm sorry you've had a knock about the pieces. Did any composer in history not have advice from a candid friend to scrap something that turned out to be the most important?[58]

Malcolm's 'knock' came, most disappointingly, from Lizzie Lutyens, who wrote a long, critical letter, merely congratulating him for the occasion 'and the achievement it acknowledged'. She found the overture 'fairly ripe corn'. In his symphony she felt the orchestration did not do the ideas justice. Its 'inherent drama, power and contrasts' were 'blurred not clarified'. It was a harsh judgement, a reflection perhaps of her disappointment that the pupil had moved a long way stylistically from his tutor. But there was more to it than that. The criticism of the music served to introduce an attack on his current lifestyle. As a reformed alcoholic Lizzie was doing her best to shock Malcolm away from self-destruction:

> One cannot, I know, do creative work for more than a short period per day, and time must be allowed and budgeted for, to let ideas simmer and gestate. When to force out and when to wait… this is all part of the self-discipline of the artist. During the simmering hours then, without some routine activity, what can one do but booze? I've seen this dual activity – creating and boozing – kill so many. In the weakest (many who shall be nameless) the talent dies; in the strongest, like Dylan, the body dies. Surely the 'vie boheme' coupled with booze, religion, guilt and sex (rather than love) is awfully old-fashioned and démodé… I think waste a blasphemy, and still think the honour of being a composer demands the dedicated life…[59]

It was a brave statement, made in love, aimed at helping Malcolm out of a way of life into which she herself had encouraged him. Adrian Boult played a much gentler variation on the same important theme:

---

56 Poulton (ed.): *Alan Rawsthorne*

57 Richard Morrison, *The Times*, 4 March 2003

58 25 September 1957

59 22 September 1957

> Mrs Beckett[60] tells me you are easing up on the spirits – this is wonderful, and must have been terribly hard to begin with. But I hope that is behind you now, and will get easier and easier as time goes on…[61]

It is likely that Mrs Beckett had said something very different, and considerably less encouraging. But Boult knew that Malcolm responded better to encouragement. His letter was full of it: the orchestra had really enjoyed playing both works; the first violin would happily spend an hour with him talking over the fiddle parts; he himself would try to find him some film work to give him financial security and time for other composition.

Boult had helpfully invited to the rehearsal many of the most influential people in the BBC music department, and Malcolm wrote anxiously to one of them, Harry Croft-Jackson. While he felt 'his ambitions had been realised under Sir Adrian's excellent and sympathetic reading', he had been disappointed that reactions had been mixed and that someone had said the symphony was 'an organist's orchestration'. Croft-Jackson wrote back reassuringly that César Franck's symphony laboured under the same criticism but 'looks like being in the running for a long time to come'. He made no comment, however, about any future BBC performance.

So Boult approached the BBC. He wished, he said, to include either the symphony or the overture in his concert with the BBC Symphony Orchestra next February. The suggestion caused some anxiety. 'I don't think the poor man will have enough rehearsal,' declared one senior official. The Symphony was therefore deemed impractical, and *Santiago* was quickly vetted by the BBC's commissioning panel. Although the work is essentially easy on the ear, it does contain some dissonances which might have sounded dangerously avant-garde to the panellists of the 1950s, who were still trying to protect listeners from Boulez, Stockhausen, Nono, Henze and Messiaen. In only a few years a completely different set of standards would prevail and works written with traditional tonal centres, like Malcolm's, would rapidly change from being avant-garde to old-fashioned. But for the moment music with even a scent of the unusual could be suspect. *Santiago* was rejected and Boult was furious. Who were these so-called experts, he wrote back, who were contradicting the opinion of a conductor on a work he had recently performed? Did not the BBC frequently accept recommendations from seasoned professionals? What had suddenly changed? Maurice Johnstone quickly capitulated. 'Our criticisms do not amount to *total* rejection,' he declared anxiously. Although the overture was not suitable for a *Sunday afternoon* concert, it could now be included in the Third Programme on a *Saturday night*…. And, of course, he and all his colleagues 'looked forward to altering their opinions on the basis of this performance'. 'I certainly hope you will be able to alter your opinions,' replied Boult tersely. 'I can see nothing

60 Gwen Beckett, his loyal, long-serving secretary.

61 25 September 1957.

controversial in the overture at all!' Thanks entirely to Boult's patronage, on 8 February 1958 *Santiago de Espada* became Malcolm's first orchestral work to be broadcast. Boult thereafter conducted *Santiago* regularly with the London Philharmonic Orchestra. The work is dedicated to him.

Malcolm next turned to his piano concerto, which, he told Lorenzo, he was dedicating to him as a birthday present. The bored Lorenzo was only mildly appeased, for Malcolm's obsessive approach to his work was creating considerable domestic tensions:

> I'm having infernal rows with Malcolm. It's unbearable. I was in such a state of HATRED today that I couldn't go to communion. Malcolm drives me insane… The situation in this house is chaotic…[62]

In an attempt to alleviate his frustration Lorenzo took a job. He had earlier tried teaching at the Berlitz School, which hadn't worked out. He now found employment in a bookshop in Oxford Street, but was too anxious about being spotted there by his friends to last long.

Meanwhile Malcolm's final work on the piano concerto,[63] begun when he first met Lorenzo, was interrupted by the news of his grandfather Benjamin's tragic death, which, as he told Emily, aroused great feelings of guilt:

> You must say a lot of prayers for me and for Lorenzo! He misses you greatly. Say some prayers for my grandfather who either killed himself or was accidentally killed by a train last month. Nobody knows, except he was 84 and profoundly unhappy at being in a rest home… I have felt so upset about the implications of this incident… Father Belton assures me that Grandpa could only have taken his life under sufficient duress to qualify as insanity or senility. Anyhow the loss was terrible for my family… One feels a terrible guilt. My affection for Grandpa was not considerable…[64]

Grandpa Benjamin, who had run a local grocery store with great flair, was a lively character. Malcolm, indeed, may well have inherited some of his wilfulness, charm and native wit. But having lost the family's goodwill by his own waywardness, Benjamin failed to recover it, even in death. Bessie's account to Malcolm of her father's death was factual and cautionary:

> He was tucked into bed at 8.00pm by the matron of the hospital where he was staying. We think he waited till she was gone, and rose, put on his slippers and gown and with his two sticks went out of the back door across the lawn about ten yards to the hospital fence. The hospital side fence adjoins the railway line. He then pushed old palings out and got through the fence and on to a stretch of land 6 feet wide. From this land there

62 Letter to Emily Coleman, November 1957

63 As usual Malcolm had several projects going at the same time. Emily Coleman's poems were a constant challenge. He had recently set her carol 'My Jesus, Crying in the Wood' for tenor, chorus and piano: 'The piano part is just bell effects which increase in dissonance and frequency as the otherwise consonant music intensifies,' he wrote to Emily in December. 'The odd-numbered stanzas are a naïve modal melody which varies and elaborates each time it appears...' The carol would seem not to have survived.

64 19 December 1957

> is a ten foot almost perpendicular drop to the line. In the half dark he lost his footing and fell to the culvert by the rail track. We think he then tried to pull himself up by grabbing a railway sleeper and got too close to the line. The 8.19 train came along and he turned to see it and his right side was struck… He died at the North Shore hospital an hour later without regaining consciousness… We are all sure he was only wandering and had no intention of taking his own life… His mental state was 100% though he was depressed. He rebelled that grandma went first and left him to fend for himself. She was his slave… Think of the living and the future and learn from others' mistakes… Keep happy…[65]

Emily Coleman, having only just received Malcolm's anguish over his grandfather, now received Lorenzo's over Malcolm. It was prefaced quite inconsequentially:

> Darling sweet and longed for Emily,
>
> I am alone tonight. Malcolm is in London. I miss his company. You know how I hate being by myself. I'm just starting a book that I don't think will cheer me up. Kafka's Castle… I hate this cottage as much as I love yours, but I'm determined to stick it out up to when mummy comes back…[66]

And then the bombshell:

> Malcolm, I don't know how to begin, has apparently fallen in love with an American Jewish girl… So sweet! So American! So companionable! A regular kid!…

A colourful paragraph of high invective was followed by another of introspection:

> I had no moral reaction at all. I was too busy trying to find out why, why and how he had mustered enough courage to be so cruel to me whom he loved so dearly… I was so confused and just like a dog reacting to his master's changes of tone… I still love him though.

Lorenzo might have been even more worried if he had known the full background, for Dolly Daniel was not, in fact, a new girl-friend at all, but someone whose friendship with Malcolm went back much further than his.

Dolores Danielovich came from a closely-knit Jewish family. Her father, Jacob, had emigrated from Lithuania to America in the early years of the twentieth century, her mother, Leah, from near Minsk after the First World War. In the 1930s they had moved to Minnesota, where Jacob had started a clothing store; Dolly was born at Hibbing, soon to become famous as the birthplace of Bob Dylan. At the time when Malcolm was visiting Europe with Bessie, Dolly was studying at the University of Minnesota for a degree in journalism, but shortly afterwards, on graduation, she too felt the urge to explore Europe. Spending regular periods abroad, Dolly took several different secretarial jobs with the American forces, first in Germany and then in London. Intelligent,

---

65 13 November 1957

66 2 December 1957

articulate and cultured, she had met Malcolm in 1954 on her first stay in England, thanks to a mutual friend, Peter Shaffer.

The two were living in Earls Terrace on Kensington High Street, Dolly in a room in the basement, Peter Shaffer in a flat upstairs. Dolly found Peter Shaffer highly entertaining ('he was such a great actor!') and they shared a strong interest in music.[67] It was this which led to Dolly meeting Malcolm for the first time:

> There was a piece of music – it may have been by Britten – that Peter was insistent I should hear, but of which he could not find a recording. So he said he would invite a composer friend of his around, someone working with him at Boosey & Hawkes, a fine pianist who would be able to play the piece to me.[68]

Malcolm arrived in the early evening in a playfully difficult mood:

> I had made a light supper, just bacon and eggs, but he refused to eat anything, drank lots of coffee and made facetious comments about what a strange time of day it was to be eating breakfast. He played the piece, and that was that…

But Dolly had, in fact, made a big impression. ('She had the most beautiful eyes I had ever seen. Then there was the voice, the humour, the incredible warmth…'[69]) When they next met, he announced that she would marry him, though it was at a large, boisterous party and he was not exactly sober. The moment passed. Dolly for her part was at once attracted by his relish for life. His black and white outlook, with no greys in between, made him highly amusing company. She began to see more of him in her second stay in England, when she was working for the USA Air Force at South Ruislip in an office dealing with top-secret special investigations, the excitement of which soon met its match in Malcolm.

It was only in late 1957, two years after her work in Ruislip had begun, that Lorenzo first met her, 'rather liked her' but was quickly consumed with fierce jealousy. Her vitality and charm, he realised at once, had totally captivated Malcolm. And there was something unbelievably beguiling about that sexy American accent… Perhaps, he thought, the situation could be salvaged if Malcolm were given new proof of his own great value? And so he now posted off letters to Somerset Maugham and the Brazilian Ambassador to London, urging them to commission an opera. Malcolm, meanwhile, oblivious of all these anxieties, was in the highest of high spirits. When Lorenzo went down with 'flu a week before Christmas, Malcolm cheerfully brought him hot drinks and insisted on reading him the exploits of Minka and Curdy.[70] Encouraged by this

---

67 Peter's knowledge of works being played on the radio was often remarkably impressive, though his twin brother Anthony mischievously suggested to Dolly it was all a clever trick, Peter having swotted up the relevant details beforehand in the *Radio Times*.

68 Dolly Williamson, March 2005

69 MW interviewed by Ian Woodward in 1973

70 Malcolm wrote admiringly of Antonia White to Emily: 'Toni humbly says of all her work that she has a small talent and merely reproduces incident. She seems oblivious to the fact that from actual incidents she creates an artistic structure, planned and executed with

show of affection, Lorenzo still hoped for the best, his vague, delusional plans for a literary future inspired by Antonia White. After Christmas, he told Emily, he would start writing down ('every day from 10 to 1 and from 2 to 5') some of the most interesting incidents in his life. There were quite a few, as she knew.

Emotions were very mixed at Petty's Barn over Christmas: Malcolm in a state of euphoria over Dolly; Lorenzo nursing feelings of betrayal. Dolly was one of several visitors who also included Antonia White,[71] the moody young poet Dom Moraes and his future wife, the ebullient Henrietta, Francis Bacon's model who was steadily destroying her beauty with drink and drugs. Amid the hilarity and confused festivity Lorenzo was fairly sure that Malcolm had asked Dolly to marry him. 'It's all rather vague,' he told a friend, 'for I'm not being informed by trustworthy informers'.[72] Meanwhile, as soon as Christmas was over, he postponed writing his autobiography and used his Brazilian connections to acquire a job in a shipping office in the City. Further defensive manoeuvres included a programme of cultural self-improvement:

> Since I know so many poets but nothing about poetry I shall try to read more in order not to seem too ignorant in comparison with Malcolm whose knowledge is phenomenal.[73]

He made a start with Edith Sitwell's book on Alexander Pope. ('Malcolm shares her great admiration for him.') And having failed to extract opera sponsorship from Maugham and the Brazilian Ambassador, he applied to the *Daily Mirror* and asked Emily Coleman to approach a rich friend.

In the new year of 1958 Lorenzo revised his thoughts on Buckland. While Dolly was working in London, it was important to keep Malcolm in Surrey. He was relieved that Malcolm was busily engaged on several projects: a short orchestral piece for a French competition; a violin sonata which he promised to dedicate to Lorenzo's father-in-law; and a ballet score based on Antonia White's novel, *The Sugar House*, of which Lorenzo hugely approved:[74]

> Malcolm and Toni spent a whole day yesterday writing the synopsis of the ballet Sugar House. It is stupendous. He has already started to write the music. He has already asked Boosey & Hawkes to contact a choreographer with whom to collaborate. I'm thinking of designing the costumes. I wonder if I'm capable of it. I also thought of asking Francis Bacon to do the décor. Do you know his work? His last exhibition in London was magnificent...[75]

---

immense imagination and presented in beautiful subtly varied prose. Her gift is a great one...' (19 December 1957)

71 Antonia White stayed for a couple of 'wild weekends' at Petty's Barn this period, enjoying the lively company of 'the boys'. She found them in cheerful chaos, amused at the lack of basic domestic items like cutlery and linen. (Jane Dunn: *Antonia White*, p.360)

72 Letter to John Coleman, 19 December 1957

73 *ibid.*

74 None of these projects was completed.

75 Letter to Emily Coleman, 15 February 1958

Emily received a totally different viewpoint of the project from Antonia White, who nursed considerable reservations about the balletic potential in the story of her disastrous first marriage:

> Don't think I'm not immensely flattered by Malcolm's wanting to do the ballet. I'm enormously touched and pleased. No, it's the seeming impossibility of turning it into a ballet… the mediums are so different and I spent 2 days working hard at it before Malcolm and I got down to our five hour grind, which left both of us limp and worn out. I couldn't bear him to put all that work into it and then find it just wouldn't fit into ballet form.[76]

Antonia White's fatigue was compounded by the tensions evident between Malcolm and Lorenzo, for both of whom she felt concerned. Lorenzo was now putting all his hope on St Joseph, a new father figure. It gave him great temporary solace, despite Malcolm's cynicism, as he related to Emily:

> Malcolm tells me that St Joseph is the patron of virgins. This seems rather ironic, him practically being a sex maniac. I do so want to be pure! Maybe St Joseph will help me more than others have! I don't love Malcolm in the way one loves a lover, but he does me, and therefore his struggle is great, although his passion has subsided somewhat…[77]

Meanwhile Lorenzo busied himself more and more in Malcolm's affairs. He was indispensable, he thought, as Malcolm's business manager, so he played a leading part in the negotiations going on with Eileen Joyce to take on the now finished piano concerto. The Tasmanian-born pianist, who like Malcolm had trained in Australia before coming to England, was at the height of her career, an internationally acclaimed concert hall figure, famous for her Norman Hartnell gowns. With a repertoire of fifty perfectly memorised concertos, Eileen Joyce at once appreciated the maturity of Malcolm's writing and the boldness of the melodic lines. The concerto promised well. But she had been brought up to haggle over terms, so her offer of £50 for a year's exclusive rights was not particularly generous. In his delight at being given £20 on account,[78] Malcolm accepted the offer, but on later being told that he had short-sold his concerto, asked for triple the fee. Joyce, an implacable foe once crossed, imperiously withdrew. Lorenzo was as outraged as Malcolm:

> Having been turned down, she and her rich husband wrote an extremely rude letter to the publishers stating among other things that 'Mr Williamson was using a work of art as a mere means of making money'. What do they think he lives on? Pigs!!![79]

---

76 23 February 1958. She also struggled with the emerging ballet score. 'I don't understand Malcolm's music,' she told Emily, 'but like you I believe in him.' (Dunn: *Antonia White* p.361)

77 20 February 1958

78 'He appeared to need a little financial leg-up,' wrote her agent and husband, Christopher Mann of this handout, to John Andrewes at Boosey & Hawkes (20 January 1958).

79 Letter to Emily Coleman, 22 January 1978

The work was too good to languish unplayed for long, and two months later Arthur Wilkinson, the organiser of the Cheltenham Festival, was promising Malcolm an early performance with the Hallé:

> I am grateful too for the suggestion from Donald Mitchell that you play the work yourself, and I have noted that you will be quite happy if we were to ask Katin or Katchen to play it…[80]

For the time being Lorenzo seemed secure again. Donald Mitchell, later to found Faber Music when Benjamin Britten parted from Boosey & Hawkes, was on the Cheltenham Festival Committee and in this capacity he and his wife visited Malcolm one weekend, ensconced with Lorenzo in some style in an Islington flat. Malcolm cooked them an excellent meal, and it was altogether a very happy evening, Malcolm clearly on his best behaviour and Lorenzo absolutely charming. There would seem to have been no clouds on their horizon. Eventually Donald Mitchell suggested some music, but instead of the Piano Concerto Malcolm started up on Gershwin's 'Someone To Watch Over Me', embellishing the song with the richest of harmonies and singing the lyrics sweetly to Lorenzo with no outward sign of mischievousness:

> There's a somebody I'm longing to see,
> I hope that he turns out to be
> Someone who'll watch over me.
> I'm a little lamb who's lost in a wood,
> I know I would always be good
> If he would watch over me…

Malcolm's ability to 'always be good' was of course minimal, whoever was watching over him. The tense situation with Lorenzo needed only one big incident to cause an explosion and it happened one weekend in March 1958 when Dolly paid a visit to Buckland. Getting up in the middle of the night, the jealous Lorenzo dramatically seized a knife and slashed through her car's tyres. Next morning, as the AA man repaired the damage, Lorenzo indulged in a long tirade, before returning drunkenly to bed. Malcolm and Dolly very quietly left the cottage for good shortly afterwards. Later that day Lorenzo wrote dejectedly to Emily. If he had played Hamlet in 1956, he was now the self-pitying Richard II:

> I'm sitting on the floor alone amidst the scattered debris of my pastels and my line drawings. I destroyed them last night in an attempt to alleviate the pain Malcolm is causing me by creating a new one. All I've succeeded in doing is to populate the vacuum left by Malcolm with a thousand ghosts…
>
> Malcolm calls this cottage his 'Sugar House'. I've always loathed it, but he loved it. We both hate it now. At least on that we are still united. I shall go to London tomorrow… I wonder if he hates me…[81]

---

[80] 14 March 1958.

[81] March 1958

Fortunately he had just received a cheque from his father-in-law so there was not a problem with the outstanding bills for gas and electricity…

> I'm bursting with unshed tears, for I've given up crying for Lent. It's the first time I've given up anything for Lent. It is very difficult indeed, for I always was a cry-baby.

With considerable more resource than either Richard II or Hamlet, Lorenzo now adapted to changed circumstances, finding a middle-aged painter in need of inspiration and with accommodation to spare near Canterbury. Malcolm, he had heard, was on the continent, but he knew not where.

Malcolm was initially at Lourdes – with a companion – celebrating the centenary of St Bernadette's vision which had led to the establishment of the famous sanctuary. He would return regularly in future years, not merely as a pilgrim but as a helper. From Lourdes he crossed over to Franco's Spain, staying at first in Barcelona ('I have never seen a more beautiful city except Paris'),[82] from where he wrote lengthy letters to 'Senorita Dolores Daniel', who had agreed to drive over for a rendezvous at Tours in central France. His frank and amusing letters told her of wild evenings, often fuelled by cognac, in dockland bars, and of a furtive, madcap departure from Barcelona:

> I went out with a very pukka English boy late in the afternoon and took him to meet Jesús. We drank some champagne and I said goodbye to Jesús, raced back to the hotel in a taxi just in time to get the English boy to smuggle my bag out of the back door and race off to take a train to Tossa de Mar. In my haste to get the train I left 200 cigarettes & my Spanish dictionary in the taxi. The train unfortunately never appeared, so after a lot of palaver I asked for a ticket to anywhere, and got one to Sitges.[83]

From Sitges, the St Tropez of Spain, Malcolm continued expounding to the 'much-missed and much-loved Dolly' his latest adventures, which included a useful encounter with a local painter called José:

> Next morning I went out to look at Sitges, and nearly went out of my mind because of the beauty of the town and beach. I walked for ages along the Esplanade. Suddenly a bearded young man approached and, thinking I was someone else, talked to me in German. He blushed at his mistake. We then talked in French and he took me for drinks on the beach, showed me a marvellous place for lunch, then took me to a pension which was half the price of mine. We are sharing a room there.

That evening José introduced Malcolm to a club where he could play the piano. The next night, out by himself, Malcolm met two waiters from the hotel he had abandoned:

> 'Drinkee?' they called. I said Yes, if they paid. We went to a café called El Cable and had a hilarious evening. They are nice boys but goad all the time. I met there a negro entertainer called Billy King, who told me he was world-famous.

82 MW to Marion Foote, 5 April 1958

83 13 April 1958

Next day Malcolm avoided all the English tourists by visiting 'a low bar', owned by a friend of José's, where he was overcome by longing for Dolly on hearing the radio play their song, 'It's almost like being in love'. That night, with José, the two waiters and several other new friends, Malcolm revisited El Cable to see Billy's act:

> He played the harmonica abominably for about an hour and then danced superbly. Needless to say, he had competition from the drunken Spaniards who wanted rock'n roll and cha cha cha all night. We went on to a low bar about 3 a.m. where José succeeded in selling some watercolours…

There Malcolm discovered that the beautiful young wife of a Dutchman shared his love of American musicals and Ella Fitzgerald. But whenever they tried to sing their favourite numbers, Billy King, cross at being ignored, would interrupt with his harmonica:

> I got rather tight and was not terribly polite to Billy in the end, but he was much tighter and didn't mind. José took me home, forbidding me to sing. But I felt like singing, so I went down to the beach and sang all our favourite songs very loudly and, I thought at the time, very beautifully. I said lots of prayers for you and me, and I watched the sunrise... I reeled back to bed about 6.30 am and I was woken by José at 12 to go to Mass. Afterwards I had lunch. Now I'm sitting at El Cable with a cognac…

Quite remarkably in all the circumstances, Malcolm somehow managed to get himself from Sitges to Tours at more or less the time at which he and Dolly had agreed to meet. Tours' shrine of Saint-Martin had been venerated by pilgrims on their way to Santiago de Compostela for many centuries, so the town was a fitting setting for the start of what he hoped would be a new personal pilgrimage. For all his interest in the likes of Jesús and José, Malcolm had decided that his future lay with Dolly. And he told her so, again and again, as they admired together the magnificent Gothic Cathedral and the famous cedar tree, planted outside by the Emperor Napoleon. He kept on with his protestations as they moved to Bourges, on the Loire, where there was a further Cathedral to inspect in addition to some very ancient Roman walls. 'France in Spring is fabulous and agreeably hot,' he reported blandly to his father from the Art Deco gardens of the Près Fichaux. It was delightful to be in France with the added flexibility of Dolly's car. Having planned, for example, only a short stop at one venue, they had stayed several days because there was such good bouillabaisse. But the idyllic holiday came to an abrupt end one morning in the heart of the Beaune wine district. They were off at the start of a day's outing, their picnic already organised, when Malcolm decided he would like to sample a local Burgundy. Dolly pointed out that it was still early in the morning; the wine could surely wait till later. Malcolm thought this totally unreasonable and hotly demanded she stop the car. So Dolly pulled to a halt and Malcolm leapt out. She waited patiently for him to come back, but he didn't. So she began to drive around, looking for him, but he had vanished without trace. Left alone in a country whose language she did not speak, she was not best pleased, especially when a further two days of searching and waiting produced no result. When she eventually returned home, anxious and dejected, she at once telephoned the Derek and Barbara Beck in great distress. Malcolm had gone missing! Had they by any chance heard anything of him? They had indeed, and he was soon on her doorstep, as contrite as could be. He really was terribly sorry. Please would she still marry him?

But the holiday drama made Dolly all the more aware of what she already knew: with his heavy drinking and impulsive waywardness Malcolm could never be the ideal husband. She needed time away from him to think things through. For the moment they ceased to see each other, and six months later she went back to New York.

Malcolm, who was never pleased to be thwarted in his desires, was extremely upset at this setback. London, however, still offered a multiplicity of attractions, and, only two months after Malcolm's dramatic return from France, Emily Coleman received a letter from Lorenzo, written somewhat eccentrically on the back of a packet of Senior Service cigarettes, with some surprising news:

> Malcolm is back! Thinner, browner and sweeter. I was near to collapse, looking cadaverous and very drunk when I met Malcolm by chance in Piccadilly Circus five days ago. Incredible coincidence… He and Dolly have had a terrible quarrel 'to end all quarrels', says Malcolm.[84]

A second packet of Senior Service gave further news of the reunion:

> Am at present in a studio while Malcolm practises the Stravinsky for the Festival Hall next week. Malcolm has just interrupted me to say 'Wish it were one of those beautiful Australian nights when we had a house by the sea and I had a wonderful piano to practise on: which later my mother sold in order to pay for the psychiatrist's bill'[85]

A third packet, this time of just 10 Churchman's, announced enigmatically:

> It happened at about 8.30 p.m.

To what extent they were now together again in London is unclear. But a few weeks later, just before Clive Lythgoe was to play the First Piano Concerto with Barbirolli at the Cheltenham Festival, Lorenzo accompanied Malcolm to Edith Sitwell's Hampstead home to meet her secretary Elizabeth Salter. A writer of detective stories, Elizabeth Salter had just completed the book of a musical and was keen to collaborate with Malcolm. He had agreed to do so, and a further session took place, which Lorenzo also attended. He was also able to report to Emily on the return to England of Bessie, who had travelled across the world to hear the Piano Concerto. Lorenzo, who knew that Malcolm was dreading the visit, was an amused onlooker:

---

84 5 June 1958

85 This was clearly a total fiction on Malcolm's part. Bessie would have had neither the need nor the inclination to sell the piano.

Cheltenham Festival, 1957
Left to right, Ralph Vaughan Williams, John Barbirolli, MW, Clive Lythgoe

> Malcolm's mother is here, fat, witty, white-haired, good-looking, well-dressed, charming and hard. Her accent is not as perfect as Malcolm's, a few au's are to be heard. She hands out sixpences to Malcolm. He is bursting with rage![86]

Perhaps it was Bessie who saw to the second break with Lorenzo. Whatever its cause, he was not around by the time the Piano Concerto had its premiere. Even so, the event was full of drama. John Barbirolli, for example, took exception to Malcolm's manuscript score, carelessly scribbled down amidst the chaos of Petty's Barn, and complained to the publishers, Boosey & Hawkes:

> You say there is no time now to make a hand-written fair copy, but surely someone should have thought in time that it would be quite impossible for anybody to rehearse a modern new score from such a pencil manuscript as was submitted. Should your new photocopy be beyond my capacity to read, I can only suggest that Mr Williamson conduct the work himself.[87]

The rehearsals proved equally emotional. The first day the Hallé went through the work at Manchester, the orchestra four times broke into spontaneous applause. At the end of the final rehearsal, at Cheltenham, there was yet more applause from the orchestra, this time led by Barbirolli himself.

It is indeed a very striking concerto, written in Malcolm's most popular manner, his first work to be wholly tonal since he began studying with Lizzie Lutyens. Its first movement boldly begins and ends with an adagio; then comes a stylish nocturne, taking the concerto's initial theme into much darker regions; and finally a rondo, full of rhythmic subtlety and a glorious main tune. A review in the *Gloucestershire Echo* gives some indication of the surprise it caused in 1958 and why it was given a prolonged standing ovation:

---

86 27 June 1958

87 Letter to John Andrewes, 21 June 1958

> This concerto, though it uses an orchestral technique that has absorbed all of Walton and after, looks back emotionally and intellectually to Rachmaninoff, Grieg and Chopin, rather than Bartok, Stravinsky or Rawsthorne… Is it any the worse for that? That depends on your view – the world may be a very grim place nowadays and young composers may feel they must go into it armed with portentous adagios written on the twelve-tone system, but there is also time to look round and enjoy life, which is what Mr Williamson seems to be doing…'[88]

For Malcolm, however, there was only one person whose viewpoint mattered:

> Vaughan Williams was at the performance. I sat several rows behind him and was terribly worried because in the loud bits he'd pick up his ear trumpet and in the soft bits he'd put it down. But it was very clear afterwards that he had heard the work and he was very nice about it in his own down-to-earth way. It was like one carpenter talking to another…[89]

The highbrow critics were rather less enthusiastic than the carpenters, Desmond Shawe-Taylor inveighing against 'the shamelessly cheap tune in the finale' and struggling to come to terms with the popular idiom:

> Last year he gave us a piano sonata with a religious programme called Janua Coeli, which had some lush passages (he is an admirer of Messiaen) but was fairly severe in its general impact. This year, gaily shouting 'Flectere si nequeo superos, Acheronta movebo' he has stormed the depths, so to speak, of the popular post-Rachmaninoff concerto style… I doubt if he will care to be reminded of this garish concerto ten years hence…[90]

This, however, was a minority view. The concerto did much for Malcolm's reputation and – a real token of its acceptance – was chosen for next season's Proms.

The Cheltenham success was the culmination of everything achieved at the Buckland cottage. But Lorenzo had finally disappeared from Malcolm's life. There would be no more emotional reunions in the shadow of Eros. That December Malcolm told Emily:

> I have not seen or spoken to Lorenzo for months now. We parted friends but it was difficult for me to be tough while he was clinging and affectionate. The trouble, apart from things emotional, is that he tried to project his life into mine, would not work at either his own drawings or for money, and just roamed about promiscuously without the remotest desire to be a Catholic, as far as I could see. I hear it rumoured that he is going to Rio on Monday. He will stay there until the family return in late Spring.[91]

For Lorenzo, life with Malcolm had been damaging. Antonia White, writing to Emily Coleman, in the aftermath of the first parting, was fearful for him:

---

88 19 July 1958

89 BBC Radio, *Meet The Composer*, February 1970

90 *New Statesman*, 26 July 1958. It was a sign of the times that Shawe-Taylor felt his readers could cope with the Virgilian quotation, 'If I can't impress Heaven, I'll woo Hell instead.'

91 31 December 1958

> He cannot, as you say, live on his own. But he must some day. And he should have some kind of job... Otherwise he'll just drift, and I'm afraid he's got into the habit of drifting – it's this damned pub life which Malcolm can stand, but I feel is bad for Lorenzo. Malcolm used to try and stop him at Buckland but, once launched into a pub, he goes on and on. I couldn't afford to stand drinks at his rate. Lorenzo goes straight through a bottle of sherry without realising he's done it. I know it's because he's miserable. There is something so innocent about him, whatever he does. I think St Joseph is looking after him. And he is so honest about himself and such a loving person: I fear he will always get hurt…[92]

Two years later Lorenzo was briefly sighted running a small art gallery near Leicester Square, seemingly more in funds, but less secure in spirit. From there he posted 'Malcolm Williamson' a copy, in faltering hand, of a short and incoherent poem, his first. He was never to reveal himself as an artist or writer in the way which both Malcolm and Emily had hoped.

But Lorenzo could claim some vicarious successes. For all the wildness of the Buckland period, Malcolm in his two years with Lorenzo did manage to produce his first major works: a piano concerto, a symphony and an overture. The concerto, in particular, was not idly dedicated to Lorenzo. In its lyricism, high spirits and dramas, it could be seen as a celebration of their life together. With Lorenzo more often than not beside him, Malcolm had made a promising, if erratic, start as a composer of consequence. And the achievements of this period were to look all the more impressive when set against the wastage of the next eighteen months.

---

[92] 31 March 1958

Alyson Hunter's evocative photo-etching, 'Opening Time at the Colony Room Club'

'Miss Winnie's', Limehouse, just before its demolition, 2007

5 LIMEHOUSE BLUES

The East End, 1958–59

IN THE SUMMER OF 1958, as excitement after Cheltenham subsided, Malcolm began to address the problem of finding a new home after several nomadic months in which he had been taxing his friends' goodwill. He had little income, was living on credit and was no longer being subsidised by Bessie. 'There will be no more payments,' she had written to him in an unsuccessful manoeuvre to force him home to Australia. 'I want you to be self-supporting at the old age of 26 years…'[1] So when he was offered an organist's position at an East End church, with free accommodation in the nearby rectory,[2] he took it. At the very least it would be an interesting change from Surrey's stockbroker belt.

The Church at which he became organist, St Peter's, Limehouse, was high Anglican rather than Catholic, but the priest-in-charge was a fellow spirit. Father Christopher Christian, despite his love for incense and high church ritual, was one of London's trendier vicars and would rarely be seen without a pair of jeans underneath his cassock. He had worked as a printer, teacher and journalist before ordination in middle age and arrival two years ago at the parish. Like Malcolm, he had 'quartered around London pretty thoroughly'. Interviewed for a London magazine, he impressed with his detailed local knowledge:

> He knows not only the riverside but all the pubs and restaurants whose fancy past gave glamour and magic to the words East End. The settings are cheap and rough… He assures me that with or without table linen the food is tastier than its West End equivalent.[3]

Father Christopher was undoubtedly instrumental in drawing Malcolm to Limehouse, though precise details of the move are no longer known. Susan Pears sees it as a typical piece of impetuosity:

---

[1] 13 November 1957. Payments ceased after January 1958.

[2] Stainsby Road, E 14

[3] *What's On In London*, 1961

> Someone must have told him that Limehouse and the Isle of Dogs were interesting areas worth exploring; that something wonderful was going on there! So he dived in to see how he could bully people into doing what he wanted! But he was also an acerbic character, who didn't keep relationships going for any length of time. He had a way of upsetting people… hence the frequent changes of scene.[4]

The parish was in the heart of what had once been Chinatown, the fabled haunt of itinerant seamen, awash with sinister opium dens, gambling rooms and taverns, a romanticised version of which had been widely promulgated by Anna May Wong's *Limehouse Blues*.[5] Situated immediately to the north of the Isle of Dogs, the area had developed in response to the heavy commercial shipping on the Thames; Charles Dickens' godfather had been a rigger and chandler living in Garford Street alongside St Peter's Church. In the 1950s enough of the old Dickensian atmosphere had survived the ravages of war for Malcolm to take delighted interest in local literary associations: the robbery in a Chinatown churchyard in *Our Mutual Friend*, for example, and the opening of *Edwin Drood* in a Limehouse opium den.

But change was afoot. St Peter's, a forlornly neglected late Victorian building, the absolute antithesis of the Jesuits' impressive 900-seat church in Mayfair, would soon be knocked down to make way for the dockland redevelopment which culminated in Canary Wharf.[6] St Peter's had been built for the labourers of the West India Docks, and the Dockmaster's House was still adjacent, but many of its parishoners' modest dwelling places were now overgrown bomb sites in the slow process of being transformed into blocks of ugly flats. Limehouse, for all its current Dickensian 'dirt and squalor',[7] was fast losing its old identity, the Chinese restaurants in West India Dock Road the most tangible remains of its colourful past. One building, however, continued to remain aloof from the changes of time, St Anne's Church, a baroque masterpiece built by Nicholas Hawksmoor, which shared a parish with lowly St Peter's and whose organ (a Gray and Davison from the Great Exhibition of 1851) Malcolm regularly played.

Malcolm's new home, St Peter's Rectory in Stainsby Road, was half a mile from both churches. It backed onto the dreary towpath of the Limehouse Cut, once a busy eighteenth-century canal built to save the large sailing barges from having to round the Isle of Dogs. Malcolm's high spirits were not at all affected by his drab new surroundings and he at once settled happily at the rectory, which had become distinctly lively ever since Father Christopher opened it up as a refuge for a large number of teenage boys in the process of rehabilitation after trouble with the law. Malcolm was soon on excellent terms with them all despite their pursuit of unappealing practical jokes, like cooking cat food for supper.

---

4 Susan Phipps (*née* Pears), May 2005

5 The classic film had come out twenty-five years earlier.

6 St Peter's Church was closed in 1968 and demolished in the 1980s.

7 *What's On In London*, 1961

Shortly before moving into the rectory in 1958 Malcolm had begun his involvement in a promising musical theatre project with Ned Sherrin and Caryl Brahms, then at the start of their long and fruitful collaboration. Sherrin was a young television producer, soon to be famous for devising, producing and directing the ground-breaking satirical television programme *That Was The Week That Was*; the diminutive Brahms, then in her late fifties and an established writer and critic, was author of a novel about Shakespeare, *No Bed For Bacon*, which Sherrin had recently dramatised and supplied with lyrics.[8] In their search for a composer they happened to contact Boosey & Hawkes. Did the publishers by any chance have on their books a young, educated musician with a gift for melody and an interest in musicals? Indeed they did.

The first meeting with Malcolm occurred not long before the dramatic tyre-slashing incident at Petty's Barn. The venue, an empty BBC Television studio at Lime Grove set up for the 'Tonight' programme on which Ned Sherrin was currently working, had been chosen to save money on piano hire. Malcolm arrived, dishevelled and hung-over. 'I ought to warn you that I'm an alcoholic,' he declared cheerfully before urinating against the studio's cyclorama. Somewhat taken aback, Sherrin and Brahms outlined the plot (later the starting-point for Tom Stoppard's film-script *Shakespeare in Love*): Lady Viola, a young girl infatuated by Shakespeare, disguises herself as a boy player and in due course inspires *Twelfth Night*. There was a sub-plot about Francis Bacon.

Malcolm's initial response – £25 up front before a note was played – went down badly with Sherrin and Brahms, but they persevered. It was soon clear that Malcolm was very much at ease in the idiom, although he later stressed its problems to Emily Coleman:

> Some of my very best melodies have gone into two musicals written for a ghastly woman called Caryl Brahms. The 32 bar popular song is not easy to write and one has to imagine the staging all the time…[9]

Sherrin and Brahms, for their part, found Malcolm equally 'ghastly', his promising songs offset by his signal unreliability. 'Quite early on,' wrote Sherrin, 'Malcolm showed signs of trouble. His musical gifts were sabotaged by appalling behaviour.'[10] However, the score was completed, and, just before the premiere of the Piano Concerto, a demonstration tape of the first eight songs was made by soprano Marion Grimaldi, with Ned Sherrin himself singing Will Shakespeare and Malcolm at the piano.

Marion Grimaldi was already an established West End favourite. Noel Coward had created a part specially for her in *After The Ball* and subsequently took a strong interest in her career. She had been a very moving Polly Garter in the original production of Dylan Thomas's *Under Milk Wood*. Malcolm found

---

8 *No Bed For Bacon*, a collaboration with S J Simon, had been published in 1941.

9 31 December 1958

10 Sherrin, *Autobiography* p.242

her sympathetic and loved writing for her voice. She recalls that he was delightful to work with, 'very patient, understanding of any difficulties and very encouraging', though away from the music 'a gypsy, all over the place'.[11] The tape survives to show how close they all came to a big success. Malcolm had produced an extremely tuneful score, sensitively responding to the book's wit and gentleness. Although Shakespeare was given two songs which immediately suggested *My Fair Lady*, the score otherwise leant more towards Julian Slade than Lerner and Loewe.

Despite Malcolm's unprofessional behaviour he was soon collaborating on a second Sherrin-Brahms musical, *Make with the Mischief*, a reworking of *A Midsummer Night's Dream*, for which he wrote fifteen numbers. Taking its cue from 'we are spirits of another sort', *Make with the Mischief* offered a black fairy world, the demo tape's Oberon and Titania being Cy Grant (famous for singing the BBC News in calypso) and Lucille Mapp. Malcolm's score was broad stylistically, Oberon and Titania bringing proceedings to a hilarious climax with 1950s calypso and rock'n roll. The air of mystery and romance, however, was captured by an earlier era. Oberon's 'Love Juice' is every romantic ballad ever crooned by Al Bowlly; Hippolyta's 'Fly Time', beautifully sung by Marion Grimaldi, is as graceful as anything by Ivor Novello; Demetrius and Lysander's 'We are yellin' Helen' out-Porters Cole Porter. Rachel Roberts, fortifying herself and Malcolm with liberal quantities of port throughout the recording session, attacked Hermia's show-stopping songs with all the vitality of a Welsh Ethel Merman. It is hard to understand why *Make with the Mischief*, with all the ingredients for success, failed to find a theatre. But at least it can take pride in inadvertently making a contribution to the history of English opera. Only months after Malcolm privately played the highlights of *Make with the Mischief* to Britten and Pears at Aldeburgh, an alternative version of *A Midsummer Night's Dream* was being hatched…

While Sherrin and Brahms were seeking to place both shows with theatre managements, Malcolm looked round for a source of regular income. He had become an occasional participant in bohemian Fitzrovia and Soho, mixing comfortably with the artists, musicians and down-and-outs who haunted the districts' favourite pubs. Through various contacts – Isobel and Alan Rawsthorne, Elizabeth Smart and George Barker, and Dom and Henrietta Moraes – Malcolm had often visited one of Soho's most colourful establishments, the Colony Room Club; and there, from October 1958, he began to work in the evenings as a pianist.

The Colony Room Club had become a legend in just ten years. Its simple premises consisted of a single first-floor room up a steep, dark staircase in Soho's Dean Street. Its walls were bright green. There was a bar at one end and a piano at the other. Its owner, Muriel Belcher, a Jewish lesbian with a black girlfriend,

[11] June 2006

Carmel, would sit on the bar stool by the entrance, either welcoming members and guests or telling them to 'fuck off'. With the help of Francis Bacon, who acted as her 'hostess' for £10 a week, she soon established the club as a bohemian hideaway with a strong artistic bias, importantly offering continued drinking from 3.00 pm onwards for those coming in from a bibulous lunch.

Malcolm's lifelong habit of peppering his conversation with colourful language was nurtured in the Colony Club, where 'fuck' and 'cunt' were often almost as much in evidence as the definite and indefinite articles. Once asked by the manager of a smart French Riviera hotel why she sat by the swimming pool, but rarely went in, and then for barely a minute, Muriel Belcher replied famously, 'Don't be a cunt, dear. I only go in for a piss'. One of her many foibles was only ever to use feminine pronouns. Speaking of Peter O'Toole in his most famous film role she declared, 'If she was any prettier, dear, they'd have had to call it "Florence of Arabia"'. Presiding at the Colony Room bar was Ian Board, whose bright red nose, it was said, went pure white at his death. Board, who ran the club after Muriel Belcher, delivered ready witticisms in fine camp style. On one occasion an inoffensive little man, who had somehow erroneously wandered in from the outside world, eased through a crowd at the bar and asked for peanuts. 'Pea-nuts! Pea-nuts!' responded an outraged Board. 'You boring, dreary little cunt, this is The Colony Room Club not London Zoo! Fuck off!'[12]

Malcolm loved the camp and coarse atmosphere. The provision of non-stop background music may have been something of a chore, but he would have a long line of drinks lined up on the piano to alleviate his suffering. It was at the Colony Room Club that he perfected his upper-class English accent, and where, too, vodka became his preferred drink. 'When in doubt the serious drinker reaches for vodka,' wrote club member Richard Whittington, 'because it tastes of nothing at all, so it does not sicken the person the next day when taken as a restorative.'[13] Malcolm's ability to play the popular tunes of the day with a flourish made him popular with the Club's clientele. His favourite song, Doris Day's 'Secret Love', a gay anthem at the time, he could imbue with the spirit of Rachmaninoff. Alexander Goehr was full of praise for his talents:

> Some of the best performances of my own piano music were by Malcolm, a lovely classical pianist, musical through and through. But he was a wonderful bar pianist too, and right in his element at The Colony Room. He found it a good place to pick up men. Women too![14]

Malcolm was proud of the Colony Room Club and took every opportunity to show it off. Lizzie Lutyens' daughter Rose remembers Malcolm taking her there with her brother and sister:

---

12 Richard Whittington, *Colony Room Club 50th Anniversary Art Exhibition*

13 *ibid.*

14 January 2005

> We drank a lot and mother was furious when she found out we'd been there! Malcolm was quite a drinker. He used to go round our house after parties to finish up what people had left.[15]

Her brother, Conrad Clark, has stories of similar wildness:

> He was very young when we first met him and very naughty! He took us all to the Tria Tria – a gay club in Piccadilly. I think my mum and dad were away on holiday with William Glock at the time. We all got terribly drunk! Malcolm would regularly come over to the house at King Henry's Road. He knew all the Rodgers and Hart songs and we would sit round the piano, sing, chain-smoking and drinking! He was always the life and soul of the party![16]

But only until he was overcome by the alcohol. Richard Rodney Bennett, who had a flat in Soho at the time, would sometimes be visited by Malcolm, completely drunk, at two in the morning. Like many other good friends, he found the drunkenness something with which he couldn't cope. Peter Maxwell Davies likewise has painful memories of meeting an inebriated and abusive Malcolm in a tube train, a grotesque parody of his usual charming self.

One of the new drinking friends was the writer and television journalist Daniel Farson, a Colony Room member who also chose to live in Limehouse around this time. Farson, a prodigious drinker but in his mid-thirties still keeping his fair good looks, led an alarmingly risky sex life, regularly picking up rent boys and being robbed by them. The great-nephew of Dracula's creator, Bram Stoker, Farson could become a total monster when drunk and was often chased down the stairs of the Club by an outraged Ian Board, an umbrella vigorously in use. Farson lived on the Limehouse waterfront and bought a pub which, as The Waterman's Arms, he turned into a loss-making Music Hall. Even Judy Garland sang there.

A somewhat more productive friendship was that with Father Geoffrey Beaumont,[17] a great friend of Father Christopher. The hard-drinking Father Geoffrey had come to national prominence in 1956 when Weinberger's published his *Folk Mass*, written much in the style of a Hollywood musical. A long-playing record had quickly become a bestseller, and the score was to enjoy multiple reprints over the next twenty years. Father Geoffrey had composed the work a few years earlier when Chaplain at Trinity College, Cambridge, and its accompaniment there by the university's Traditional Jazz Band had led to it sometimes being known as a 'Jazz Mass'. Beaumont's ideas, revolutionary at the time, soon led to the formation of the influential Twentieth Century Church Light Music Group.

---

15 October 2005

16 October 2005

17 Geoffrey Beaumont had arrived in south-east London in his fifties, when appointed vicar of St George's, Camberwell in 1957. He later entered the monastic Community of the Resurrection at Mirfield, where he died in 1971.

Malcolm had not been long in Limehouse before he met Beaumont and immediately identified with the ideals of the Light Music Group. He found Father Geoffrey engagingly approachable.[18] Like Malcolm, Father Beaumont was at his happiest music-making in crowded public bars, a cigarette dangling from his mouth, a new pint waiting for him on the piano. 'Eer!' exclaimed an aggressive plumber, accosting him on one occasion. 'Fancy finding a flipping parson in a pub!' 'Eer!' responded Father Geoffrey amiably. 'Fancy finding a flipping plumber!' Malcolm was later to comment:

> I lectured with Geoffrey Beaumont and we became great friends. Ours became a mission through music. This music wasn't practised so much in church. In fact it was practised in sleazy bars, gay bars, in houses where the pianos fell all to bits, if there was a piano at all. The words were essentially Christocentric, but in the vernacular. Often Geoffrey used words with puns in them. This was basically, shall we say, 'whaling captain' language, but it helped to get the point home in the East End.[19]

St Peter's was soon showing two very different musical trends. On the one hand, in accordance with Father Christopher's high church ambitions, Malcolm continued to explore Messiaen's revolutionary organ music, his own two organ works of the Limehouse period[20] reflecting a solemn, intellectual approach, underpinned by great technical expertise. Barry Rose, a leading young cathedral organist at the time, recalls:

> I met Malcolm at Limehouse and thought him a genius at the organ. The instrument at St Peter's was tiny, but his skill on it was amazing. He was a real improviser, of course; he could make up pieces which matched any moment. He painted the most wonderful musical pictures…[21]

On the other hand, the influence of Father Beaumont and the need to attract and enthuse a new congregation led Malcolm to evolve his own popular 'folk' style, exhibited for the first time in *Adoremus*, a short Christmas cantata for alto, tenor and organ. Less simplistic than Father Beaumont's music, it is the forerunner of many light church works which Malcolm was to write in the 1960s, notable for a sophisticated simplicity in the manner of John Rutter (who was shortly to appear on the scene). The needs of the St Peter's congregation proved a helpful catalyst, as Malcolm was often to acknowledge:

> The Broadway style was the parishioners' musical vernacular; they couldn't cope with more difficult things. I took traditional texts and set them to different rhythms so that the singers would rethink the meaning of those texts. The tunes often had five or seven beats in a bar to teach rhythmic flexibility. I used some Latin and some theology, and all those things were mixed up into a hybrid type of music. It was a

18 Patrick Appleford, a leading member of the Light Music Group, described him as 'The humblest priest I've ever met'. (November 2005)

19 Interview with MW in *Music Ministry*, October 1974: 'Pioneers Of Pop, Ten Years Later'

20 *Résurgence du Feu*, dedicated to Father Christopher Christian and the congregation of St Peter's; and the unpublished *Variations on Veni Creator* (both 1959)

21 May 2006

> music that would speak to the parishioners and draw them forward beyond their known capacities.[22]

Most of Malcolm's popular music for St Peter's was written for the moment and subsequently lost. He was too busy with other things to write it down carefully for possible publication. In the evenings he was at the Colony Room Club; and many lunchtimes were spent in the Limehouse local, 'Miss Winnie's', where Malcolm and Father Christopher would entertain the Rectory's latest young charges and vice-versa.[23] There were also occasions when Malcolm would earn a few pounds helping friends. In May 1959, for example, he went to Oxford, having been asked by Lizzie Lutyens to coach the chorus songs she had composed for a production of Euripides' *The Bacchae* at the Playhouse. Inevitably there was a crisis. Malcolm spent two days on the Wadham College organ making an emergency re-recording of Lizzie's difficult score. Still, as he told Bessie, 'there was some dough, thank goodness'.

Malcolm's hopes of making large sums of money rose a little with the news that *No Bed For Bacon* was to be produced for three weeks[24] at the Bristol Old Vic, the theatre from which Julian Slade's highly popular *Salad Days* had started. Its excellent cast, led by Marion Grimaldi and Derek Godfrey, was directed by Frank Dunlop, then resident at the theatre. Marion Grimaldi remembers that the show's many strengths were offset by bickering:

> It was a good company; everyone worked very hard; the show went extremely well at Bristol, and there were offers for it to go to London. But we were all very stupid. Frank Dunlop was a very good director, but he enjoyed stirring people up, and perhaps we became too volatile. There were spirited exchanges about one song, 'Pick up Your Quill, Will' which several of us thought owed too much to *My Fair Lady*.[25]

Tempers steadily frayed as the first performance neared, and eventually, as Caryl Brahms has described, there was a serious incident at the Old Duke, fifty yards up the road from the theatre:

> The 'waywardness of Williamson' reached its climax after a Saturday morning rehearsal.[26] There had been some disagreement... We went to a pub to talk it over. A miracle: Malcolm bought his own drink at last, a pint of Bristol beer, which he proceeded to pour over my head. I was quick enough to stop Ned, a big man, from hitting him... The smell of beer did not leave me all that sweltering weekend.[27]

The disagreement, as Marion Grimaldi remembers it, centred on 'Pick up Your Quill, Will':

---

22 *Music Ministry*, October 1974. Malcolm was helped in his endeavours by the young Vernon Handley, another of Adrian Boult's protégés, whom he persuaded to work at St Peter's for a while as choirmaster.

23 The Conant Arms, Stainsby Road

24 9-27 June, 1959

25 June 2006

26 According to Ned Sherrin the incident in fact took place after the dress rehearsal.

27 *Too Dirty For The Windmill*, p.196-97

> There were several of us having a discussion at the theatre, Frank, Malcolm, Caryl and Ned, and the topic, as usual, was having such a derivative song so early in the show. Several of us felt that it needed changing and Malcolm was happy to do a rewrite. But Caryl wouldn't hear of it! 'Well, of course, Marion,' she said to me, 'If you're not happy with the show, there's a very good understudy'.

The suggestion did not upset Marion Grimaldi at all, for she knew that her understudy, good actress though she was, couldn't really cope with the songs. Malcolm, however, felt that Marion had been hugely insulted and took his revenge.

> He came rushing back to my dressing room afterwards, horror-struck. 'Marion, I've done something terrible! I've poured a pint of beer all over Caryl!'

Unsurprisingly Caryl Brahms was hugely indignant. '*Now* do you see why I can't work with Malcolm!' she complained to Marion Grimaldi. Both Brahms and Sherrin had had enough of him and, rather than pursue the strong possibility of a London run, they began negotiations for a new score from another composer.

Caryl Brahms, however, showed a greater generosity of spirit only weeks later, when she wrote to Ninette de Valois about Malcolm's lst Piano Concerto, to be played at the Proms that summer. Brahms, a former ballet critic who had written a book about Robert Helpmann, urged de Valois to listen to the Concerto: 'I think that rhythmically and melodically Malcolm Williamson would be the right composer for a ballet.'[28] It was prophetic advice.

Malcolm planned a big excursion from Limehouse to hear the concerto, to be played again Clive Lythgoe. It would be good for the boys of the Rectory to have their first experience of a classical concert, and they would enjoy it all the more if fortified with a few glasses beforehand at Miss Winnie's. Only hours before the concert, however, his plans for a riotous night went sadly awry when Clive Lythgoe injured an arm and was unable to play, Malcolm being forced to deputise. The prospect of playing the piece without practice to a packed Albert Hall, even after a lunch-time in Miss Winnie's, was daunting, but the alternative was the cancellation of his very first Prom. He was ashen-faced as he made his entrance. The conductor John Hollingsworth looked equally stressed and anxious, and the BBC Symphony Orchestra distinctly uneasy. Malcolm could so easily have made an utter fool of himself. This was a somewhat bigger challenge than 'Secret Love' in the manner of Rachmaninoff. But this was the moment for which Bessie had laboured long and hard. This was the future Sverjensky and Goossens had seen for him. Encouraged by initially hitting a high proportion of correct notes, he relaxed into the piece. The showman took over and he began to enjoy himself. The jazzy finale went particularly well and audience roared its approval, the orchestra rising too and joining in the long and loud applause. Malcolm took his bows with suitable modesty, smiling enigmatically. Only he knew that he had just played Lorenzo's birthday present.

---

28 30 June 1959

The critics next day were kind. It was perfectly understandable, they said, if the composer displayed signs of nerves when deputising at the last minute. But the work itself was too overtly attractive to please everyone, and only the more conservative elements exulted in its tunefulness. The *Daily Mail* felt it was 'a pity so few composers touch Williamson's form'.[29] The concerto, it said, was 'tough, genial, sentimental and deliberately common'. The *Daily Telegraph* found it 'stylish', declaring that 'there is an intelligent mind behind the playfulness and the craftsmanship is distinguished and, in the field of instrumentation, original'.[30] But others struggled to understand why he had chosen to pursue a direct and immediately comprehensible style, forsaking his 'chosen straight and narrow path of advanced modernity'.[31] Noel Goodwin was typical:

> Why is it that only the shallowest and dullest new music is thought fit for the Proms? Mr Williamson calls his work 'light-weight'; it is positively transparent as a pastiche or mock-imitation of Rachmaninov diluted with Richard Addinsell. Maybe the composer stuck his tongue in his cheek, hoping for another *Warsaw Concerto* hit? But his growing reputation as a serious composer takes a knock from it…[32]

Even Colin Mason had reservations about the great tune in the last movement and was a little less fulsome than usual:

> We shall need another chance to reconsider this controversial work by an erratic young composer who in natural musical talent and liveliness of invention is probably more gifted than anybody in this country since Britten…[33]

In the circumstances 'erratic' was a generous description of Malcolm's Limehouse years. The acclaimed performances of the Piano Concerto at Cheltenham and the Proms barely disguised the general lack of creativity: just two musicals in 1958; just two short organ works and *Adoremus* in 1959. The great promise of 1957 had fallen away. Anxious friends could do little to help. Marion Grimaldi, for example, could not begin to understand what motivated the self-destructive lifestyle. 'I didn't know what he was running away from, why he couldn't begin to sort himself out.'[34]

Few friends knew that the past two years of exceptional disarray coincided with the period in which Malcolm had been urging Dolly to marry him. Although she had gone back to America, his determination had not altered. Over Christmas 1958 he had sent her his love with a succinct telegram:

> LOVE AND MARRIAGE etc HORSE AWAITS CARRIAGE[35]

---

29 Charles Reid
30 Donald Mitchell
31 *The Times*
32 *Daily Express*
33 *Manchester Guardian*. Malcolm was paid £23 12s 6d for performing the work.
34 June 2006
35 26 December 1958

Dolly's family, however, still strongly opposed him, and Dolly herself, torn by conflicting loyalties, stayed away for the first half of 1959 as a test of their respective feelings. Time would modify them, she believed, if marriage wasn't right. But time failed to do so. Thoroughly miserable in America, Dolly returned to England at the end of June 1959, just after the last performance of *No Bed For Bacon* in Bristol and just before the triumph at the Albert Hall, which she was able to share with him. Much had happened to Malcolm in the six months since she had last seen him, but it was soon painfully clear to her that, for all his new arrangements in Limehouse and at the Colony Room, Malcolm was badly letting himself down and dissipating his talents. Marriage really seemed no nearer.

On the first Sunday in January 1960 Malcolm was as usual at the organ of St Peter's. At this particular Evensong his Christmas Cantata *Adoremus*[36] was finally being sung for the first time. Its inspiration, Father Geoffrey Beaumont, was not only present but preaching, an occupation which always gave him a good thirst. For some hours afterwards, therefore, Father Geoffrey and Malcolm entertained everyone at Miss Winnie's with extracts from *Adoremus*, the *Folk Mass* and whatever else happened to come into their heads. The new decade seemed to be being ushered in with the old irresponsibility.

Four days later, however, Dolly Daniel, who was working in a USA Navy office in west London, returned from lunch to be met excitedly by a friend and fellow secretary, given an armful of flowers and hurriedly led to her desk. There, propped up against her typewriter, was a note saying 'Mr Williamson rang through to say you're getting married on Saturday'. Dolly at once contacted Malcolm to thank him for the flowers and to beg him not to be so foolish again. Nothing, she said, had essentially changed. 'Indeed it has!' he replied. 'I've bought a licence, and been given a special dispensation to marry you from the Vatican itself!'

It was a defining moment. Dolly had done her best to do what her parents wanted. But she loved Malcolm, and in his own endearingly irresponsible way he had shown the constancy of his feelings. She was certain now that he desperately needed her love and her strength, if he was to make something of his huge talents. The excitement of this challenge, one of such epic proportions, finally overwhelmed any further misgivings and she found herself no longer protesting. Just two days later, on 9 January 1960, she and Malcolm were married at the Limehouse Registry Office.

---

36 'The mixing of the very elementary musical ideas,' wrote Colin Mason who was present, 'with more refined and sophisticated ones was generally successful – most notably in the first movement, an Ave Maria, which also contained a short prelude and postlude for organ with strange birdsong effects in the manner of Messiaen.' (*Guardian*, 5 January 1960)

Toccata on D (or Daniel hurrying to the lion's den before closing time)
Americana

A wedding gift

II

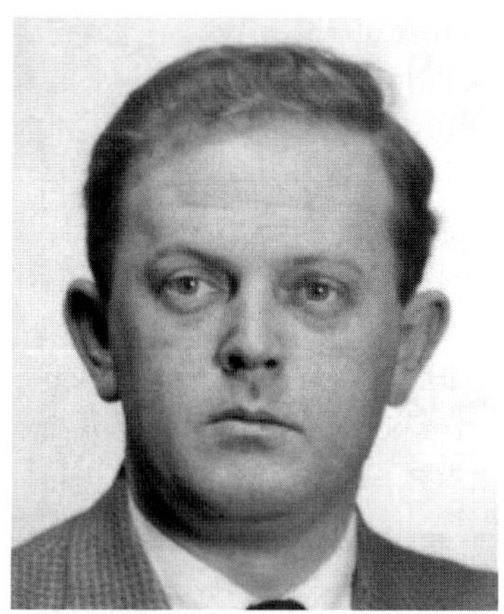

6
DOLLY
London, 1960–62

IN *NO BED FOR BACON* the heroine wanted life *her* way:

Things that other people do
Are not the things I want to do.
So much domesticity,
It's not for me! Not for me! Not for me!

Malcolm had agreed with her, preferring a bohemian life regardless of convention. Yet, paradoxically, as a bohemian, he had always retained a sneaking regard for the trappings of worldly success: wealth, celebrity and social position. Domesticity with Dolly was an expression of this alternative side of Malcolm's complex nature, just as it was of his sexuality.

The Limehouse wedding was a joyful occasion, the bride resplendent in a cream outfit belying the speed of its acquisition, the groom dapper in his best double-breasted suit, one of the identical made-to-measure outfits which Lorenzo had insisted on ordering for the two of them. There had been a flurry of telegrams between London and Sydney, but although Bessie sent her good wishes, she was not best pleased, unable to attend the wedding, let alone to vet the bride. The small group of wedding guests did, however, include Malcolm's sister Marion (now a qualified physiotherapist and currently in England). The Best Man was Derek Beck, though Anthony Shaffer in his autobiography later claimed the office.[1] His twin brother Peter was in New York, where *Five Finger Exercise* had just enjoyed a successful opening on Broadway, and, on hearing of the wedding, sent Malcolm and Dolly 'love and kisses':

> How wonderful! I'm so very glad for you both. I know you will be very happy. It's really marvellous news! You both deserve every possible happiness and blessing and I hope you will get them all.[2]

[1] He also erroneously suggested that Malcolm was the worse for drink at the ceremony. (*So What Did You Expect?* p.164)

[2] 20 January 1960

There was a reception at the Rectory, a continuation at Miss Winnie's and a meal in the best Chinese restaurant in West India Dock Road, after which (remembers Brian Shaffer) the 'distinctly convivial wedding party' returned to Miss Winnie's.

Dolly's only concern was her relationship with her parents. After a few days of marriage she sent them what she described as 'both the saddest and happiest letter' she had ever written: she was in despair over how the marriage might be hurting them; but the last two years, 'despite separation, meeting other people and leading very different lives', had convinced her and Malcolm of the rightness of it all:

> You know me well enough to realise that I don't do anything without putting a great deal of thought into it – and particularly when it is undoubtedly the biggest step in my life. Both of us have turned ourselves inside and out over this and we know the problems ahead, but more important is that we love one another very much and know we will make it work.
>
> If you ever give your son-in-law a chance, you will like him very much. He is good and gentle and kind, and I have all the faith and respect in the world for him. He has loved you both for a long time just through hearing about you, and I hope you will not turn your backs on him.[3]

Her mother responded with immediate, if secret, support, but it was to be some time before her father accepted the marriage.

Dolly had outlined Malcolm's prospects to her parents in glowing terms, and with some justification. Although his contract with Boosey & Hawkes had come to an end, he had now signed up with Chappell, gaining thereby a useful weekly subsistence allowance. He was already in negotiations over a series of piano studies of increasing levels of difficulty, taking as their theme some of the most famous cities in the world.[4] He had just received £200 from the doyen of theatrical impresarios, Bertie Meyer, to write a score for a musical based on George du Maurier's *Trilby*, for which there was every likelihood of production in London and New York. There was also a remunerative contract with Hammer Films. With Dolly herself in regular work and Malcolm moving into the first-floor, one-bedroom flat she was currently renting in West Brompton, the demands of domesticity could be met with a certain degree of optimism.[5]

Malcolm at once gave up his work at the Colony Room Club and before long ceased to be the organist at St Peter's. At twenty-nine he was able to devote himself to full-time writing in a way previously not possible, although he continued taking in a few composition pupils, and for a couple of years occasionally lectured at the Central School of Speech and Drama. He was at a

---

3 12 January 1960

4 These *Travel Diaries*, published in 1961, in addition to Sydney featured Naples, Paris, London and New York.

5 61 Redcliffe Gardens, SW10, close to Earls Court, not far from the Fulham Road.

Wedding day: January 9th, 1960

turning-point. If he failed now, he would struggle to find excuses. But failure was something he never even considered.

There was a good start, a successful completion of a score for *The Brides of Dracula* in which Malcolm made splendid use of the organ and included a tempestuous section for piano and orchestra. This opportunity had come through John Hollingsworth, who had conducted Malcolm's Piano Concerto at the Proms the previous year. Hollingsworth, the music supervisor of Hammer Films, had recently looked after *The Curse of Frankenstein*, *Dracula* and *The Revenge of Frankenstein*, and when James Bernard was unable to help him over *The Brides of Dracula*, Hollingsworth remembered Malcolm. The creation of music by the split second was something Malcolm always found irritatingly

Wedding day: with Brian and Anthony Shaffer

Wedding group: Father Christopher Christian between Malcolm and Dolly; Marion next to Dolly; Vernon Handley far right

restrictive, but Hollingsworth was delighted with what he considered a very professional job: grand guignol with a touch of class.

Indicative of the new Malcolm was the completion of his three-movement *Sinfonia Concertante* (essentially a Shostakovian concerto, with piano and three trumpets in constant dialogue with the string orchestra), which he had pondered on at Petty's Barn, played with at Limehouse but only now completed, dedicating it to Dolly and stripping it of the religious references inspired by Emily Coleman. He had called it initially *Laudes* ('Praises'), and each movement had been piously titled (*Gloria in excelsis Deo*; *Salve Regina*; and *Gloria Patri*). But the *Sinfonia*, as written, would seem to relate as easily to Dracula's Brides as the Queen of Heaven and God the Father.[6]

Money was tight, but Malcolm was no longer drinking to excess and he and Dolly celebrated the success of *The Brides of Dracula* by taking a short holiday in mid-June, a late honeymoon at the seaside resort of Noli on the Italian *Riviera delle Palme*, where their hotel had its own private beach. As Dolly was now pregnant, Noli had been chosen for its peace and quiet, and they were not disappointed; it was not much more than a little fishing-town, though its mediaeval castle hinted of a more glorious past and Malcolm was soon extolling the church of San Paragorio with its twelfth-century True Likeness of Christ on the Cross.

They spent time too in Florence, from where Malcolm sent George 'a picture of the most beautiful city I ever saw'. He heard Mass at 7.00 am in the Duomo, and with Dolly visited the Medici Palace, gazing in awe at Gozzoli's 'Journey of the Magi' before giving in to temptation and shopping on the Ponte Vecchio. Florence proved the highlight of a glorious honeymoon. Malcolm told George:

> The devastating depth of culture and tradition is visible at every corner. Michelangelo statues to the right and left. The people are beautiful, food exquisite, wine marvellous.[7]

Back in London, despite the lack of people, food and wine of quite such excellence, Malcolm's euphoria at impending fatherhood was undiminished. Preparations for the baby's arrival preoccupied him, including the need to put their precarious finances under yet more pressure by finding a larger flat, suitable for three. They settled, eventually, on Lyndhurst Gardens, Hampstead,

---

[6] The first movement is developed from the chant-like motif (with F sharp dominating), the only obviously religious part of the work. Serial in style, it is extremely rhythmic, full of irregular metre and lively interplay between soloists and orchestra. Exciting and absorbing, the movement ends on a complex chord based on F sharp: a sense of homecoming. The dark slow movement, in turns lyrical and declamatory, exudes the spirit of Shostakovich, as does the final *Presto*, which, in loose rondo form and with a short piano cadenza, caps its unpredictable progress in a serene coda in an undeniably tonal F sharp major. There is homage to Stravinsky as well as Shostakovich. An uncommissioned work, it would not be performed until 1964 (by Norman del Mar and the BBC Scottish SO).

[7] 24 May 1960

a road Malcolm knew well from his parents' stay in London.[8] The rent, at £45 a month, was a huge commitment and, as such, a statement of intent that Malcolm was at last going to calm down and do himself justice.

The baby arrived safely in September, his parents' friendship with Peter Shaffer resulting in that Christian name. Among the many expressions of congratulations was a note from the ever-supportive Adrian Boult:

> Delighted to hear of the family addition, and I hope the Hampstead home will be in every way a success. I told the agents that I know you had had a successful year, and in any case, you were not the kind of man to take on a liability you couldn't comfortably meet!
>
> Please remember that any musician who wants to talk to me about anything is a first priority! And naturally you are well in the front now! Come any day you like to fix with Mrs Beckett and we can always go out for a meal or something if you want to talk quietly…[9]

Life with the new baby could not have been more idyllic, the Hampstead flat (one of four in a dignified, late Victorian building, which has since been demolished) proving ideal. There was a good communal atmosphere, and Malcolm and Dolly quickly made friends with the family of David Storey, who had just achieved a big success with his novel *This Sporting Life* and lived in the garden flat. Their other neighbours included a genial retired English gentleman who played the horses and drank.

Malcolm, however, did not join him. He was so proud and so anxious at becoming a father that he decided to take a cure for his alcoholism. Dolly is unequivocal about the motivation:

> The family did it. He took a cure before Peter was born, because of his new situation. Malcolm may have been an oddball father at various times, but he went over the moon at the prospect of having children and gave up drinking entirely because of the family.[10]

Lizzie Lutyens put him in touch with Dr Yerbury Dent, an addiction expert whose cure had already given her eight alcohol-free years. Malcolm was lucky in the timing. A year later Dent was dead, and the cures which he had developed in the 1930s, based on the use of apomorphine, largely died with him. The drug, an offshoot of morphine, had been developed a hundred years earlier by the same laboratory which discovered aspirin and heroin, but its medical use had tended to be only as an emetic.[11] It helped take away the nightmare effects of

---

8 January 2006. The flat was just across the road from the one (No.3) rented by George and Bessie.

9 4 September 1960

10 March 2005

11 Dent's treatment, because it induced vomiting, was simply seen as an aversion cure and, as such, poorly regarded. It is currently used in Parkinson's Disease therapy, and also for sexual enhancement.

*With Dolly and Peter,
Lyndhurst Gardens*

alcohol withdrawal, stabilising the body's metabolism. Malcolm was also lucky that whereas Lutyens[12] had to stay in Dent's clinic for regular injections of apomorphine over several days before revulsion took effect, he himself, despite ten years of alcohol abuse, simply took tablets at home, and, as Dolly remembers, for a remarkably short period:

> We cancelled a three-day weekend away so he could take the tablets and the vodka. I don't remember him getting very sick and it didn't take long before he was saying 'I don't want any more. I just don't want it.' Nor did he take the pills for very long. It wasn't an on-going thing. I had been preparing for a dreadful period of withdrawal over many days, but mercifully this didn't happen.[13]

The remarkable Dent cure did not guarantee lifelong freedom from addiction, but its effects seemed miraculous:

> Malcolm was so good about not drinking. He would happily fix drinks for other people. We had a table in the living room that had bottles on it. Sometimes, when he'd open wine, he'd smell it and say 'Tell me if this is nice. It smells as if it's good.' If we were out at a dinner party, and they served something suspect like a salad with a bit of wine in the dressing or strawberries and cream with a bit of brandy, he would signal me across the table to taste it first, and if I nodded 'no', he wouldn't touch it. He really was amazing.

Aware, perhaps, that this quality of life might be transitory and that time was therefore precious, Malcolm devoted all his considerable energy into providing for Dolly and the family, frequently ignoring basic needs like sleep and recreation. Writing music became, in a way, a new form of addiction. William Burroughs, the Beat generation novelist (and also a member of the Colony Room Club), who was treated successfully by Yerbury Dent for drug addiction, when asked about possible psychological changes, replied:

> The experience of addiction and withdrawal does change people. It's like being in prison for a long time. Nobody who hasn't been there knows what the experience means. But it does make some changes to you.[14]

In Malcolm's case the change made him a workaholic. Conditions in the Hampstead flat were by no means perfect – Malcolm did not have his own study but worked instead at a dining table in a small annexe off the sitting-room – but in the next two years he was to write three full-scale concertos and much else. Difficulties over meeting deadlines no longer existed; and he was always writing more rather than less.

Late in 1960, for example, he was asked by the distinguished organist Dr Allan Wicks for a small work of a secular nature. Malcolm presented him

---

12 Her addiction was to gin. Malcolm used to tell the story (which sounds a somewhat tall one) that during the period when revulsion was being induced, if she turned on a tap, she would find gin coming out...

13 December 2005

14 An interview with Dr John C Kramer, *Journal of Psychoactive Drugs*, January 1981

with an immense, six-movement Organ Symphony.[15] It was a formidable piece, so full of elaborate instructions and challenging time changes that Wicks had to practise it long and hard. When Malcolm eventually came up to Manchester to hear it, he gave it everything:

> It's a piece of huge pyrotechnics, demanding much sweat of the brow! When I had finally finished playing it to him, pretty exhausted by it all – it's a thirty-five minute work – he said quietly 'Yes, Allan! That's marvellous! But, you know, you could always play it much more relaxed, like Brahms…[16]

The Organ Symphony was shortly followed by another extravagant work, an Organ Concerto,the first of his three Hampstead concertos, commissioned by William Glock.

Malcolm had already had some lively contact with Glock through his Summer Schools at Dartington. Recently appointed Controller of BBC Music, Glock was determined to introduce the country to the latest European developments, offering strong new support for serialism. He was already furthering the careers of several of Malcolm's more radical contemporaries but he viewed Malcolm himself a little warily, puzzled by Malcolm's return to tonality in his First Symphony and *Santiago da Espada*. However, on Boult's advice, Malcolm made a careful approach to Glock about the possibility of a BBC commission, and it was not long before the BBC's Controller, impressed by Malcolm's new seriousness of purpose, was inviting him to his home to hear his recordings of the American serialist, Wallingford Riegger. The warmth of the new relationship was expressed in an immediate commission of an organ concerto for the Proms, with Malcolm as soloist.

The work was not only dedicated to Boult but also used his initials ACB as the basic thematic material.[17] Scheduled to conduct the work with the LPO and anxious to do it justice, Boult arranged for Malcolm to play to him as much as he had completed six months in advance of the rehearsals.[18] The session took place at Dyneley's studios, a young Australian friend of Malcolm's, Michael Brimer, playing the orchestral reduction on a second piano:

> It was difficult stuff to be sight-reading, and my piano score had an extra stave on top containing a condensed version of the rhythm of the percussion section. Malcolm

[15] It was an extension of ideas formulated in *Fons Amoris*, the movements bound together serially, but, wrote Malcolm, 'not twelve-note serialism in the Viennese sense – the derivations come from medieval music and its modally-framed serial use of plain-chant shapes...' (programme note)

[16] May 2005

[17] He also allowed Boult's initials to dictate the key sequence of the three movements. The addition of the missing semitone to complete the minor third which contains Boult's initials also allowed him permutations on that most famous of all mottoes, BACH.

[18] In the light of Malcolm's known difficulty in meeting deadlines, it is possible that Boult, in asking for this session as early as 27 March, was helpfully nudging him in the right direction.

> expected me to knock the percussion part with my knuckles on the front of the upright piano! I remember Boult looking at me somewhat curiously over his glasses! Afterwards Boult whispered a little anxiously to me, 'I don't think I shall conduct any more premieres!' We had a second session with him later, going though the whole concerto.[19]

Boult's anxieties and painstaking approach reflect the considerable demands this highly experimental work makes on both players and audience, Malcolm confidently blending his introspective, strongly medieval serialism with extrovert and jazzy rhythms suggesting Constant Lambert. Each section of the three movements is highly distinctive, with the organ displayed against different orchestral combinations. In the first it is pitted against the brass, harps and percussion, and seldom can the Albert Hall organ have produced such a massive sound.[20] After this 'atonal battery' the second movement supplies 'a kind of tonal soothing syrup',[21] the strings alone supporting the organ in a remarkable *Largo sostenuto* which owes more to Mahler than Stravinsky or Schoenberg. The third movement begins with an organ cadenza of great power and breadth, after which the soloist finally meets the entire orchestra, the work coming to a gloriously rich conclusion in which Malcolm draws together the materials and colours of the earlier movements and crowns them with a long, sustained melody, optimistic and affirmative, 'a juicy tune' according to one critic,[22] yet founded on the all-important motto ACB.

Michael Brimer was present at the first performance[23] and subsequently sent his mother an account:

> All seats were sold so I had to queue from 2.45pm for standing room. I was fairly near the front of the queue so I managed to get right against the rail in front. The programme was the Beethoven 8th symphony, Myra Hess playing the 4th Beethoven piano concerto, the 3rd Brandenberg Concerto, Malcolm's Organ Concerto and Ravel's Daphnis and Chloe. Myra Hess played beautifully even though she's a very old lady now – a very little person. But her playing was so poetic. Malcolm's concerto did what I expected and shocked everyone, rather. He got a good reception, but the criticisms in the papers have been awful! Times, Telegraph and Daily Mail all damned it, Manchester Guardian praised it, and today the Sunday Times and Observer have given it faint praise and found lots of faults. The Telegraph even went so far as to say

---

19 February 2006. Brimer, later to be Ormond Professor and Dean of the Music Faculty, Melbourne University, first came to know Malcolm through Bessie, with whom he found himself travelling back to Australia in 1958. Bessie had been in England for the Cheltenham Festival.

20 The movement opens with a cadenza on the tympani on the notes ACB. After a dramatic and mysterious *Andante*, an exciting battle rages, or, as Malcolm later expressed it, 'jagged non-symmetrical utterances pile up contrapuntally'.

21 Felix Aprahamian, *Sunday Times*, 10 September 1961.

22 Edward Lockspeiser, *The Listener*

23 8 September 1961

Lyndhurst Gardens, 1962

> 'But is it right that he should be allowed to treat the queen of instruments like this?' And the Daily Mail had a big heading 'This won't do, Mr Williamson!'[24]

Malcolm was later to remark sardonically:

> The first performance was received with enthusiastic abuse by the more conservative elements of the British organ world for being too venturesome, by Baroque enthusiasts for its use of the romantic organ, and by some critics for not being sufficiently venturesome. It recovered.[25]

A typically encouraging letter from Adrian Boult was some compensation for all the criticism:

> I'm quite sure that no executant has ever before had such a handsome and charming compliment paid to him by a composer: there is so much more than the dedication that you have given me. I can't adequately thank you, and only hope that you felt the performance, though suffering as most first performances do, conveyed enough of your message to satisfy you for a first effort – there is so much more in a first performance than just reading new notes.

Boult had clearly found it hard to come to terms with the concerto's vivid stylistic contrasts:

> As I said to you, I can see the beauty of the slow movement, and I can share something of the excitement and vitality of the others, but I can't expect to take it all in, as music, at my age, I suppose; and I was ashamed that you spotted wrong notes which I hadn't heard at all. I suppose it is impossible to keep up with the times when

24 15 September 1961

25 1975 sleeve notes for the Lyrita recording

one is past 70, but I count it a great privilege to have taken part in this show – and to be in on a major work of yours…

The work obviously made a fine impression, and your playing was terrific in the best sense of that word![26]

The premiere of this controversial piece coincided with the completion of his second Hampstead concerto, a full-length work for piano and strings in three movements, written in a remarkable eight days as an entry for a competition sponsored by the University of Western Australia. If the Organ Concerto was a message from a young man determined to shock and impress the musical establishment, the new work, his Second Piano Concerto, was a much more personal piece, an expression of his current happiness and security, exuding Shostakovian high spirits.[27] Uninhibited yet completely cohesive, sophisticated yet strongly melodic, the concerto unsurprisingly won the £500 lst prize in the competition, was cheered at its Perth premiere, and has remained one of Malcolm's most popular works ever since.[28]

Such financial successes were a blessing and, in May 1961, combining business with pleasure, Malcolm was able to show Dolly round Paris in springtime. Bessie and George in Sydney received a picture postcard showing second-hand bookstalls beside the Seine:

This should make you nostalgic! We are having a wonderful week. We've been to Versailles to see the fountains; to Chartres, most impressive and beautiful; I have been visiting musicians and publishers. On Sunday talked to Messiaen… My French is improving hourly. I can even do my musical business in French…[29]

Later the same year, when Dolly took Peter to New York to see his grandparents, and Malcolm remained in London, his letters to Dolly were full of the excitement of the period:

Your two letters have been enchanting, and your news is excellent. I rush to every mail for others. I'm sure Momma is marvellous with Crumbum.[30] It was darling of

[26] 9 September 1961

[27] The first movement, though full of Gershwin syncopations and elan, is in classic sonata form, with a careful development of the first and second subjects (the first lively and humorous, the second a flowing cantabile of considerable tonal ambiguity, with hints of the middle-east.). The central slow movement is a wonderful contrast, a threnody which abounds with augmented intervals predominant in Jewish chants, a reminder that the work was dedicated to Dolly's first cousin, Elaine Goldberg (a talented pianist). Malcolm's response to being welcomed at last into Dolly's family had been to immerse himself in Jewish culture and history, and his new passion for Judaism is clearly reflected in this poignantly beautiful movement. There is also joyful Jewish folk music in a tumultuous finale, imbued again with the spirit of Gershwin.

[28] 3 May 1962, with Michael Brimer as soloist with the University of Western Australia String Orchestra, conducted by Frank Callaway. Malcolm later wrote a chamber version, for piano and string quintet.

[29] 25 May 1961

[30] Malcolm's name for Peter

> your father to buy the potty. Can't wait to see it. The house seems very empty, particularly at night and feeding times. I'm missing you both very much...[31]

He was working on several different projects, which included a ballet score (for the Royal Ballet's David Blair), two musical comedies and a number of film commercials.[32] Anthony Shaffer, currently in advertising, had put the film work Malcolm's way, but though this was financially helpful, it wasn't a medium with which Malcolm was comfortable. He tended to over-write:

> I finished the film on Tuesday, working at a hell of a pace and the recording was fixed for this afternoon. It took a lot of arranging, and copying the harp part took for ever. Anyway the session was a failure, and tonight I could die. The director looked like the end of the world as the players grappled with the music, saying it was too hard to play straight off, but at least they loved it...
>
> [And later] The second recording session for the film is tomorrow. Due to their miscalculation I have had to write two more minutes' of music, and due to my own complicated style rewrite several harp passages...[33]

Malcolm was too disorganised to cope easily with the mechanics of everyday life, and preferred, in Dolly's absence, to find refuge in other people's homes. For a short while he stayed with one of Dolly's friends, Marion Cronheim:

> Darling!
>
> In great haste. Just got out of bed at Marion C's where I came after the film on Tuesday. Film a great success. Got bad flu and got home to find central heating failed, so Marion kindly took me in and spoilt me endlessly...

He was still optimistic about the prospects of the musical *Trilby*, for which Teddy Holmes, a Director of Chappell, had asked for a demonstration disc. Malcolm had by now completed the whole score apart from the overture, but seems to have fallen out with his collaborator, Harold Purcell, who was responsible for the book and lyrics.[34] *Trilby*, the melodrama of a young artist's model being turned into an operatic star by the mesmeric genius of the evil Svengali, was much to Malcolm's taste, but he and Marion Grimaldi, who was hoping to play Trilby, were both fretting over Purcell's apparent loss of interest at this critical time:

> Teddy is screaming for Trilby. I said OK and fixed all tomorrow for a rehearsal, and all Friday for the recording. Three sessions with Harold and still no new lyrics. Marion and I took the words of an Italian song by Pergolesi and fitted it to the aria... Marion and I have assembled an emergency chorus...

---

31 4 November 1961

32 All were mentioned in an interview in the *New York Morning Herald. Ballet for One*, which survives complete in piano reduction form, was to be choreographed for Blair by Alfred Rodrigues. However, the project would seem to have ended in disarray, Malcolm not completing the orchestration.

33 8 November 1961

34 Purcell had contributed to many films and musicals over the years, working with stars like Hermione Gingold, Cicely Courtneidge and Anna Neagle.

> [And later] The Trilby session was a great success. I finally got together my bunch of singers and they were excellent. Teddy came to the session and was pleased. Harold managed to find time, between writing the lyrics he hadn't done, to be absolutely overbearing and dominating all day, and got everyone's back up, or at least mine and Marion's. Marion sang like an angel. Excellent dramatic work. I worked solidly, conducting, playing and even singing from ten to six thirty with ten minutes for lunch. But we got the whole score in the can. It is really much better than I thought. Afterwards, the recording engineer congratulated me – you know, the usual professional thing – saying that it was better than My Fair Lady…[35]

Though, disappointingly, nothing was to come of *Trilby,* Malcolm was too busy to be too disappointed.[36] When he was not writing, he was often teaching, and Dolly was given details of his current efforts at the Central School of Speech and Drama as well as with a new piano pupil:

> Yesterday's class was a sensational success. Marion gave a brilliant recital. She encored them with Polly Garter's song,[37] and they clapped for almost five minutes. Some of the students took me out afterwards and generally made a flattering fuss… My cheque came through from the Central School saying the lectures were a tremendous success and 'looking forward to having you again next year'…
>
> I have a new pupil, a boy from the Central School. He is not quite a beginner, and I am trying him out. I gave him the Crumbum book.[38] And he came back with the little pieces very thoroughly studied. It may I suspect just be a momentary enthusiasm for music, and I have given him due warning about waste of my time. He is very poor, but must pay as a guarantee of seriousness…

Malcolm's friendship with Lizzie Lutyens was now all the stronger for their shared experiences of Dr Yerbury Dent's cure for alcoholism, her criticisms of his First Symphony long since forgiven. Lutyens had written incidental music to another Greek tragedy, this time Aeschylus's *Oresteia* at the Old Vic, and Malcolm loyally attended:

> Had fabulous evening. Extra ticket at last minute. The Oresteia is just terrific. 3 and a half hours in the theatre but you don't notice. Lizzie's music is excellent, but very difficult.

---

35 13 November 1961.

36 'Bertie' Meyer had been a London theatrical manager and impresario for over sixty years, famous for the building and running of the Cambridge and St Martin's theatres. But though he paid Malcolm a further £200 to maintain his option over the score, at 84 he no longer fancied risk-taking and eventually let *Trilby* drop. Some pieces of Malcolm's score miraculously survive, including Trilby's aria, revealing a strongly operatic atmosphere. Highly melodic and written with a sensitive feeling for Victorian melodrama, *Trilby* clearly had much potential.

37 Marion Grimaldi had enjoyed a great success as Polly Garter in the original London production of Dylan Thomas's *Under Milk Wood.*

38 Malcolm had dedicated his *Travel Diaries* to various family members: Sydney to Diane; Naples to Marion; London to Peter; Paris to Peter's new sister, Tamara; and New York to Dolly. They are highly attractive miniatures, ideal for student pianists.

Shortly afterwards Malcolm took off for Paris, to discuss a possible radio performance of his new *Jazz Mass*, recently the centre of a great public outcry after being banned in England by the Catholic Church. The work had originated from a request for a Mass in a popular idiom by Kevin Mayhew, the young choirmaster of St Anselm and St Cecilia, Holborn. Malcolm had quickly produced *O Rex Israel*, a cantata for soprano, choir and organ, which he offered to Mayhew augmented with some of his other existing Church Light Music pieces. Mayhew began rehearsals, and a recording was arranged with the BBC. But just before the scheduled performance, Cardinal Godfrey, reflecting embattled conservative opinion at the dawn of the Swinging Sixties, decided that the Catholic Church should make a stand against such tasteless modernisation of its ritual.[39] As soon as Malcolm's Mass was banned, a mole (perhaps Malcolm himself) informed the press, and shortly afterwards the *Daily Mail* was expressing national outrage:

> ARCHBISHOP BANS MASS
>
> 'WE THINK HE IS A SQUARE,' SAYS CHOIR LEADER:
>
> An angry choirmaster called the Archbishop of Westminster a 'square' yesterday.[40] He said so after the Archbishop, Cardinal Godfrey, had approved a ban on his Mass with a modern beat. 30 disappointed choristers had been rehearsing the 'jazz' Mass for weeks. Priests heard it, even monks heard it, and they all like the music with a touch of Broadway in its lilt.

Malcolm, sensing some useful publicity, soon joined in, telling *The Times*:

> I'm most annoyed about this! I have been writing church music since I became a Catholic when I was 21. This Mass took me two years!

Two weeks might have been more accurate, but no doubt it felt like two years to him in the heat of the moment. A subsequent television debate, in which Malcolm argued his case against a Catholic Cathedral organist, was equally heated, made excellent viewing and led to the invitation to Paris.

But Malcolm nearly failed to get there on time, as he told Dolly:

> What a trip! I bought my ticket at 3.30 yesterday and only got it by the skin of my teeth due to a BEA strike. Raced home and had sweating fits of nausea and thought I was dying. I packed what I could and ordered a minicab to the terminal. It was over an hour and ten minutes late, and so I had to take it to the airport! 25 shillings! Got there to be told that my booking was cancelled, but after giving an emotional performance I was rushed onto a plane carrying my own luggage – no nonsense about Customs. Would you believe it, at 3.30 I'd had a fight to get a BEA booking and yet there were eight empty seats in my section of the plane…[41]

---

39 At the end of October 1961

40 In fact Kevin Mayhew had said nothing of the kind. A reporter, at the end of a telephone conversation with him, had said 'I suppose you think the Archbishop's a square?' to which Mayhew had merely chuckled.

41 17 November 1961

That crisis over, things suddenly seemed much better:

> I went mad with delight on being in France and it goes on this morning. I'm the smartest man in Paris in my gorgeous new corduroy trousers, gift from my lovely wife and son! Thanks a million. Marion gave them to me, and the Varese is really just what I wanted…

The trousers were a thirtieth birthday present:

> I had a quiet birthday, but enjoyed myself walking the length of Paris soaking up coffee. Phyllis[42] bought me truffle-chocs, but they are almost too rich and delicious to eat.

The *Jazz Mass* furore produced even more publicity than he'd hoped. Interviewed in Paris by the *New York Herald Tribune*, Malcolm gave colourful descriptions of the congregation at St Peter's beating out the rhythm to his cantatas on tin cans and saucepans, while he pulled out all the stops on the Limehouse organ. As a talker he had few rivals. He was made for television chat shows:

> 'I have deliberately tried to replace the conventionally pious by something with shock value,' said Mr Williamson today in Paris as he had a cup of coffee and a pastry in a café. 'I am trying, through a mixture of serious and popular, to restore the power that church music once had but has lost by becoming too pious. The life of Christ is full of shocking stuff, but people have heard it told so often in the usual church music that they come to church with a feeling of smug self-righteousness.'[43]

Having attacked (and presumably alienated) many churchgoers, he turned on the avant-garde. It was good, he said, for a composer to be above and ahead of the people; but not too far ahead; a composer's job was to lead people down a road they knew in order to bring them to something new. But those who deliberately wrote music for the future – he named no names – were fraudulent. He, by contrast, was a socialist in his music, because he wished to work for the people:

> Music needs a wide public, it mustn't be aimed at a small snobbish coterie. The barrier between light music and serious music is artificial. Some stylistic fusion is going to come. But it makes life very difficult if you think this, as I do, and try to do the fusing. I am sick of the critics acting so superior when they hear anything sounding like light music. Why, if it comes to the point, shouldn't music be vulgar as well as noble? Picasso isn't noted for good taste. Good taste is a curse![44]

In speaking further to reporters and on radio Malcolm was equally articulate and controversial, determined to capture everyone's attention and little worried that, in attacking good taste, he was in fact attacking much of his own music. His sole concern was to create the maximum publicity for the broadcast of his Mass on

---

42 Dolly's friends Tom and Phyllis Bodin were putting him up.

43 *New York Herald Tribune*, 25 November 1961

44 The *Melbourne Sun*, January 1962

French Radio and in this he was so successful that he felt he owed it to himself to prolong his stay:

> Darling,
>
> Have been having a marvellous time here, and due to circumstances within my control I am staying over until next Wednesday…

This meant three additional days of French cooking:

> We went out to lunch yesterday in a very good restaurant, said to be the oldest café in the world. On the fixed menu I had 12 snails and a sort of stew of goat's meat. Very good. I shall do what shopping I can for snails, paté and marron. Marion C wants all these things too, so I shall get what I can and you gels can divide the spoil when you return…

Meanwhile Dolly herself was given some simple shopping instructions:

> Bring me back some bran muffins. By that I don't mean a deep-freeze full of food. But some bran muffins would be gorgeous…

In addition to good food there was good music:

> We went to three concerts. Bach by the excellent Stuttgart players, Beethoven by the Concerts Colonne, mixed, and Monday night Phyllis and I heard a modern music evening with a superb Stravinsky performance…
>
> Our hours are very bohemian here. We went to three operas in three nights. Gounod's *Mireille*, which starred Andrée Esposito, a fabulous soprano and an excellent actress. I love the music! We saw her again last night in *La Boheme*, which I also loved… Phyllis and I saw then *The Trojans*. Mostly magnificent, all spectacular, making Covent Garden look like a village charade…

Other highlights were meeting Nadia Boulanger and a Mass at the Church of St Esprit, where Jeanne Demessieux 'played superbly'.[45] Malcolm later gave her a copy of his early organ work *Résurgence du Feu*.

Malcolm returned to Paris with Dolly on musical business in the summer of 1962, his chief purpose being to go over his new Third Piano Concerto with Philippe Entremont. The French pianist had persuaded the ABC to commission a concerto from Malcolm to be played on his next Australian tour. This was the first time the Australian Broadcasting Commission had supported a composer working overseas, a sign of Malcolm's increasing stature.[46] Charles Moses, the ABC's General Manager, writing to Malcolm from Sydney, had made clear what an important opportunity this was:

> The commissioned work is envisaged as a concerto giving plenty of scope for a soloist of Entremont's capacity. The orchestral part of the score should be practicable under normal conditions, offering no undue obstacles to performance by the average professional orchestra. It could be scored for medium or full orchestra. We would suggest a minimum performing time of 25 minutes… Our Music Department is convinced that the combination of your composing talent and Entremont's performing

45 The legendary Jeanne Demessieux was for thirty-one years the organist at St Esprit.

46 There was a useful completion fee of £200.

ability could achieve a success which would greatly enhance this country's musical prestige.[47]

Eight months later, Malcolm and Dolly returned to Paris a full two months before the August completion date with a two-piano score of the last of the Hampstead concertos, a magnificently tuneful four-movement work lasting well over the stipulated twenty-five minutes. Their week in Paris, as reported on a postcard to Bessie, could not have gone better:

> We saw Faust here on Monday. I thought of you and how you'd love it. All your (and my!) favourite tunes. The production was spectacular. We are exhausted after a pleasant week of shopping and seeing people. I played my concerto on 2 pianos with Philippe E. who said he was delighted. The weather has been perfect and the food beyond belief…[48]

But even if the weather had been foul and the food poor, they would probably still have been in high spirits for Dolly was again pregnant and Malcolm ecstatic at the thought of a second child. On their return they said a sad farewell to the flat in Hampstead, and in July moved into a three-bedroomed flat[49] in Bryanston Place, not far from Marylebone and Paddington, and close enough to Grosvenor Square for Dolly to be able to walk to work. In October 1962 their daughter Tamara was born and soon joined little Peter in the new flat, which, though ideal for babies, was less perfect for a busy composer. Sherwood Court was a modern block of flats with only modest sound-proofing, so the neighbours were soon making outraged complaints about the noise from the piano at all times of the day and night. Good relations were only restored when Malcolm obtained a special piano from Chappell which could, at the switch of a lever, muffle the sound.

The Hampstead years had been good ones in so many different ways. This was the period, for example, when Malcolm first established links with a new publishing house, Josef Weinberger, a company which would prove extremely important to him in the development of his career. His relationship with Boosey & Hawkes had never been easy after his dismissal as a full-time and a highly difficult employee. Since the death of Malcolm's greatest supporter at Boosey & Hawkes, Erwin Stein, the firm's distinguished Chairman Dr Roth (who had been publisher, counsellor and friend to Richard Strauss, Stravinsky, Kodály, Bartók and Britten) no longer concealed the disfavour with which he viewed much of Malcolm's work. Of the First Symphony he wrote patronisingly:

> I believe, rightly or wrongly, that you have overreached yourself and that the work is too ambitious. I think I told you at the time that nothing is more difficult to write than a slow movement or any piece of slow music. A young man, however ingenious, should be well satisfied if he succeeds in writing one slow movement in a symphony:

47 3 October 1961

48 28 June 1962

49 Sherwood Court

Tamara with her proud parents, 1962

> but you wrote practically three and (judging of course only for myself) the effect is certainly not what you intended...[50]

Roth was similarly dismissive of the lst Piano Concerto, which, like the Symphony, was eventually published by the firm despite Roth's lack of confidence in it:

> Concerning the Piano Concerto I have told you all I have to tell. I quite understand and appreciate your optimism that what has happened in every case would not happen in ours. However, I must be allowed to be more sceptical. Once you have a number of successes beyond London, Cheltenham and Australia I will look at the Piano Concerto with friendlier eyes. At present I regret I cannot publish it.

Although Roth had agreed to publish the *Sinfonia Concertante*, his brutally honest remarks about the Organ Concerto were instrumental in encouraging Malcolm to move, first to Chappell and then to Weinberger:

> It is a difficult piece to listen to. What worries me most is that I cannot find in it your individuality, although I notice with a certain satisfaction that you have freed yourself

[50] 4 April 1961

> from the influence of a certain period of Stravinsky. I cannot, however, quite see what has replaced this influence.[51]

Chappell, therefore, published both the Second Piano Concerto and the Organ Concerto, as well as the *Vision of Christ Phoenix*, an exciting and difficult organ work written for Coventry Cathedral and given its first performance there by Malcolm.[52] Several small choral works were also taken on by Chappell, but in this field there was strong competition from Weinberger's, whose Director, Otto Blau, had taken a great interest in Malcolm's *Jazz Mass*, championed by one of best 'pluggers' in the music industry, Dougie Foss. Weinberger's main business was in operetta and musicals, but they had branched out into Church Light Music, and Father Geoffrey Beaumont's *Folk Mass* was currently one of their biggest sellers. In 1961 Foss, who, legend records, liked a drink and would sometimes end the working day travelling home to Hove comatose in the Brighton Belle, negotiated a deal whereby Chappell ceded to Weinberger Malcolm's new and highly tuneful Cantata for Easter, *Procession of Palms*. It was an odd thing for Foss to do, as he was employed by Chappell, but he liked Malcolm and felt Weinberger was more likely to exploit the work. His judgement was quickly vindicated, *Procession of Palms* soon being widely sung in churches all over the world, and several other pieces[53] in similar style were also published very successfully by Weinberger, who began to take an active interest in Malcolm's more serious work.

Through Weinberger Malcolm met John Alldis, the leading singer on Father Beaumont's *Folk Mass* LP, who had just formed the John Alldis Choir,[54] a highly talented group of young singers, the perfect outlet for both his light and serious choral work. John's wife Ursula remembers being struck at once by Malcolm's strong personality:

> He was fascinating! A one-off! It was just as if electric sparks were coming out of him! He must have been very wearing to live with, and it needed someone very special to cope with him, because he was so over-the-top, and such a prima donna! He loved being in the limelight and was a real attention-seeker![55]

---

51 28 December 1961

52 *Vision of Christ Phoenix* was subsequently assigned to Boosey & Hawkes and the Organ Concerto to Weinberger.

53 These included *O Rex Israel*, the heart of the 'Jazz Mass', plus *Harvest Thanksgiving*, *Easter Carol* and settings of the *Agnus Dei* and 'Jesu, Lover of My Soul', which all did well after release on LP.

54 Singers included Ian Partridge, Robert Tear, John Shirley-Quirk, Grayston Burgess, Barbara Elsy, Joyce Millward and Pauline Stevens. Geoffrey Mitchell remembers the heady early days of the John Alldis Choir in 1962: 'We decided to do three introductory concerts at Holy Trinity, Kensington. Each was to have a new work to interest the critics. The first had Lizzie Lutyens' *Lichtenstein Motet*, a very hard piece. The press went wild! Then we had Sandy Goehr's *Two Choruses* and the third concert was Malcolm's *Symphony for Voices*. The choir was immediately asked to make a recording; we did Malcolm's lighter works and the Symphony, with Malcolm himself on the organ.'

55 February 2006

At one of their early concerts at Holy Trinity Church, Kensington, the Alldis choir gave the first performance of Malcolm's *Symphony for Voices*,[56] a serious work in which the attention-seeker comes out very clearly, not just in the hyperbole of the title (for a setting of five poems for unaccompanied choir) but in the choice of poems themselves. The Sydney-born poet James McAuley was one of the outstanding intellectual figures in Australia at the time.[57] In using five of his poems Malcolm had determined to court attention, ignoring the fact that, taken out of their original context, they made very little sense. The music is attention-seeking too in its demands for virtuoso singing and exceptionally detailed ensemble blend.[58] Far removed from the world of Church Light Music, it draws instead on the traditions of Britten and medieval chant, and so successfully that it has remained a popular work with choirs. David Drew wrote of the first performance:

> It is the best work of Williamson's since he made the hazardous channel crossing from so-called serious to so-called light music some years ago. Here he is back on the shore from which he set out, and seems to be much the wiser...[59]

Not really. He would never stay on one shore for very long, for consistency was not in his nature. He was too light a spirit, too much a creature of whimsy, too childlike in his openness to the latest enthusiasm. The stylistic inconsistencies of 1961-62 were to remain with him all his life, a token of his volatile personality. The serious *Symphony for Voices* was in marked contrast to the light *Jazz Mass*; the dramatic Organ Concerto to the skittish Second Piano Concerto; the difficult Organ Symphony to the easy *Travel Diaries*; and the intellectual *Vision of Christ Phoenix* to the crowd-pleasing *Trilby*. As his work gathered a furious momentum throughout the 1960s, it was characterised by a consistent determination to be inconsistent.

Perhaps the greatest stylistic synthesis was achieved in his early operas, the commission for the first of which arrived in 1962 as a deserved climax to all the hard work of the past two years. Great was the rejoicing in Sherwood Court when Sadler's Wells Opera invited Malcolm to collaborate on an operatic version of Graham Greene's recent novel, *Our Man In Havana.* Now, at last, thought Malcolm, he had something with which to impress Dr Roth, and even

---

56 2 May 1962

57 McAuley was in some ways a mirror image of Malcolm in the 1950s: a witty conversationalist; a jazz pianist; a former church organist and choirmaster; a promiscuous bohemian; and a heavy smoker and drinker. He had even converted to Catholicism at the same time as Malcolm. 'I adored Jim McAuley,' wrote Malcolm later. 'He and I had love-feasts as fellow Catholics and hate-feasts politically. Jim always squashed me by saying, 'Oh you *are* a naïve political animal'. He was a jazz pianist of sorts. Gough and Margaret Whitlam used to do a song-and-dance act at end-of-term cabarets and Jim accompanied them on the piano...' (Letter to Robert Solomon, 1986)

58 Joseph Stevenson, John Alldis biography (Allmusic)

59 *New Statesman*, 25 May 1962

though the project had only been agreed in outline, and there was not even yet a librettist in place, Malcolm wrote excitedly to the publisher. Alas, the portentous tones of the reply were hardly an encouragement:

> I have read most of 'Our Man in Havana' which is certainly quite an entertaining book although Graham Greene's manner of writing is not exactly to my taste. What I cannot see in it is a libretto for an opera. To start with I have not discovered any loveable character in it and I think a theatrical piece without a lovable character is doomed. Therefore, unless the librettist has sufficient freedom to transform at least some of the characters and is clever enough to write a libretto which gives the music sufficient elbow room, I could not persuade myself that this is really a desirable subject for music...[60]

It was good if cautious advice, and, in trying to persuade Peter Shaffer to write the libretto, Malcolm was probably taking heed of it:

> Talked to Petie last night. He thinks he is too busy to do Our Man at the moment, and anyway Greene walked out of Five Fingers, told Gielgud he hated it.[61] But he wants to do it. I rang Peggy Ramsay[62] who suggested William Plomer, who did Gloriana for Britten...[63]

For a while, however, Malcolm deferred on making a decision, and, as the Hampstead years ended, he was able to pause for breath and enjoy the celebrity which the commission from Sadler's Wells was bringing him. One interview in particular, in *The Guardian*, gives a good glimpse of Malcolm at thirty on the brink of fame. Asked how he set about writing a piece of music, a question which would have reduced many a young composer to anguished monosyllables, he offered an eloquent response:

> 'If one wrote like Wordsworth,' said Williamson, 'going out for long contemplative walks before producing each small phrase, life would be impossible. I don't compose at or with a piano – partly by design: I have a very bad piano. A musical idea comes usually as a contour, and one shapes it, chisels it, defines it more accurately. The best pieces – the pieces I think are my best – are usually worked out through doubts and depressions. When something comes easily one fears that it's written on technique alone.' He paused. 'Every piece is more difficult to write than the last.' He went to a bookcase, found a copy of T S Eliot's *Four Quartets* and quoted from it:
>
> And so each venture
> Is a new beginning, a raid on the inarticulate
> With shabby equipment always deteriorating
> In the general mess of imprecision of feeling,
> Undisciplined squads of emotion.

---

60 28 December 1961

61 Shaffer's highly successful play *Five Finger Exercise*, directed by John Gielgud, had been first produced in July 1958

62 Peggy Ramsay was the most influential theatrical agent in London after World War Two. She represented and nurtured many of the best-known stage writers and, for a time, represented Malcolm.

63 MW to Dolly Williamson, 13 November 1961

> Williamson paused reflectively. 'I don't know what emotion is. A fortnight ago I decided to try and write music intuitively, in the mood I was at the time, glum, sad or nostalgic, whatever it was: rather in the manner of a Hollywood film of Liszt or Chopin. It was nonsense. I threw it away.'[64]

Fame, then, was something which Malcolm was beginning to enjoy and exploit. Much had changed in the past three years. His old bohemian friends might quietly mock his new-found domesticity, mutter about 'uxoriousness' and bemoan the loss of his outrageous wit and behaviour, but the workaholic of 1961-62 had achieved a professional reputation unimaginable in the Limehouse days. A few years earlier there had been suggestions that, if he could only harness his talent, he could be the next Benjamin Britten. Now, with that talent at last productively harnessed, his future prospects were looked upon with renewed interest. Such was his apparent facility and such his originality and scope, he might, indeed, be the new Britten. It was a remarkable leap forward, and friends like Kevin Mayhew put it all down to Dolly:

> She really sorted him out – she was thoroughly good for him – she was the one person who could keep him under some sort of control.[65]

She was, in short, the single most important influence in the whole of his creative life. Domesticity, so feared in *No Bed For Bacon*, had really proved its value.

There was one song in that musical which had always amused him but which he now saw very differently: 'She Would Distract A Man', a duet in which Shakespeare, sounding very much like Henry Higgins, rebuts Lady Viola's every suggestion that a woman could be good for a man:

> She'd supercharge a man!
>
> She'd sabotage a man,
> If any man should treat a woman as a friend!
>
> How well she'd steer a man!
>
> She'd domineer a man,
> She'd hoity-toit him and exploit him to the end!
>
> She would be there! He would be fired!
>
> She would be everywhere except where's she's required!

If Malcolm had been ambivalent about the debate at the time he had set it to music, he was no longer so. In his current situation the Shakespearean arguments sounded distinctly flawed. Did he feel 'sabotaged'? Of course not! 'Supercharged'? Certainly! He had never felt so confident and or so equal to anything. Did he feel 'exploited'? Hardly! 'Steered'? Certainly! As he thought about *Our Man In Havana* and tried out a few ideas on his muffled piano in Sherwood Court, he felt supremely secure. Even this great undertaking, so worrying to Dr Roth, could be successfully completed. *She* would be there! *He* would be fired!

---

64 David Wainwright, *The Guardian*, 19 July 1962

65 January 2006

UR MAN
HAVANA
A New Opera by
With Librett
ased on the Nov
il Cantelo
nley Bevan
en Brannig
Millward
owman
d Herincx
ric Shilling

7 CENTRE STAGE

London, 1963–67

THE 1960s WERE A DIFFICULT TIME for writing opera. However confident Malcolm might feel, he was living in an era when the old certainties had been swept away, tradition being replaced by diverse experimentation. His early years in England had seen several important attempts at redefining what a modern opera might be: Berg's *Wozzeck*, largely to be declaimed rather than sung, its atonal score characterised by huge skips in pitch, the very antithesis of a conventional vocal line;[1] Stravinsky's *The Rake's Progress*, opposing atonality with a neo-classicism which offered its own advanced and often dissonant harmonies, meanwhile utilising the eighteenth-century format of set numbers and recitative; Walton's *Troilus and Cressida*, its neo-romanticism generally considered old-fashioned despite the somewhat cautious melodic invention; Michael Tippett's *The Midsummer Marriage*, an 'opera of operas', offering orchestration of Wagnerian proportions and allusive references to great works of the past; Weill's *The Threepenny Opera*, nostalgically reflecting the late Weimar cabarets, sardonic and stridently sentimental; Poulenc's *Dialogues des Carmelites*, substituting lyrical declamation for recognisable tunes. Ideas certainly abounded in the 1950s, but there was little synthesis. Whereas in lighter music a continuous stream of development had seen nineteenth-century operetta move into the art form of the modern musical, opera was struggling for identity and, in the process, in danger of becoming little more than an intellectual plaything, of no relevance to the general public. The confused situation facing Malcolm in 1963 was well expressed by *The Observer*'s Peter Heyworth:

> There can be no doubt that whatever else may have been achieved, the post-Webern avant-garde has yet to develop a language sufficiently rich and comprehensible to serve an opera house. As a result, for the first time in 250 years, there is today no generally accepted operatic style. Style is no longer something that an operatic

[1] All the works quoted had their first performances on a British stage in the 1950s.

> composer can take for granted. Today he must start by asking himself 'What manner do I want to write in?[2]

But this was to ignore the most successful post-war writer of opera, Benjamin Britten, perhaps on the grounds that his highly personal musical language was nothing but a remarkable one-off, unlikely to be developed by those coming after him. Malcolm as a young man had carefully assimilated Britten's new operas: *Billy Budd*, *Gloriana*, *The Turn of the Screw*, *Noye's Fludde* and *A Midsummer Night's Dream*; and much of Malcolm's recent vocal writing reflected this influence, his song cycle *Celebration of Divine Love*, for example, being closely related to the Canticles. So strong, indeed, was Malcolm's admiration that he made a conscious effort to keep well away from Britten's operas during the eight months he was working on *Our Man In Havana*.[3]

Malcolm's ambitions and abilities, however, were different from Britten's. Above all, he yearned for a greater communication with the general public. Britten's genius lay not so much in weaving strong melodic lines as in the sensuousness of his sounds, the richness and aptness of his orchestrations, which, backed up by strong structure and symbolism, offered immense pleasure to those prepared to explore this new world with suitable determination. Although Malcolm followed Britten in retaining the traditional operatic forms of sung recitative, arias, choruses and dances, he preferred to appeal more directly to his audiences, offsetting his austere, Brittenesque recitative with such strong melodic lines that comparisons with Puccini and Richard Strauss were frequently made. Peter Heyworth felt that Malcolm was going even further, attempting 'to enlarge opera in the direction of the musical'. This was an exaggeration. Malcolm's intentions were simply for a modern style which engaged rather than alienated the public, a work which contained enough reference points with the stage musical to attract a new audience into the strange and more rewarding world of serious opera. Critics like Edward Greenfield rejoiced at this boldness:

> The supersensitive may rebel as they have done so often with Verdi and Puccini, but anyone who has concern for the vitality of modern opera – in serious danger of being sucked down the serialist plughole – must applaud.[4]

Fortunately Malcolm was too preoccupied with the challenge before him to worry much about current confusions, as he settled down to work in September 1962 in the new flat in Bryanston Square[5] with Sidney Gilliat, his librettist.

---

2 7 July 1963

3 'Musical precedents for most situations occur in the Britten operas, and I was so afraid of imitating these masterly works that I avoided hearing them while composing. Undoubtedly Britten's name will be mentioned in any good notice my opera may get...' (MW, *The Spectator*, 12 July 1963)

4 *The Guardian*, 1 July 1963

5 As the flat was an unsatisfactory working-place, Malcolm would often seek out alternatives. For *Our Man In Havana* he sometimes used a cottage near Cranleigh owned by Ursula Alldis's family. They also had a bungalow on the south coast at Angmering, where he could work and swim.

Graham Greene's choice, Gilliat had been in films since before Malcolm was born, working nearly forty years as a screenwriter, producer and director, so he was well experienced in the adaptation of novels, if not for the opera house.[6] Although an unusual choice, he could not have been bettered, not least as someone far too experienced and successful to be overawed by a world famous author or headstrong young composer.

After completing 1,250 pages of manuscript, Malcolm finished the opera in May 1963, on schedule, a month and a half before the premiere. 'I was nearly blind when I finished it,' he told a reporter.[7] Shortly afterwards he took the score down to Bournemouth, to go over it with James Loughran, who was to conduct the performances at Sadler's Wells:

> It was very pleasant working with Malcolm when he came down to my house on the south coast. He was full of music and mischievous fun. After dinner the first evening he said, 'We won't get dressed tomorrow until we've been through the whole score'. We never did get dressed that day and spent it all in our pyjamas, working![8]

Malcolm had long since known who his singers would be and he had familiarised himself with their particular qualities, producing roles which were tailor-made for Raymond Nilsson, April Cantelo, Owen Brannigan and Eric Shilling. As regards the two great Sadler's Wells basses, for example, he knew that Brannigan would relish a low D and Shilling a high A, and so provided them. Nilsson, an Australian tenor, had preceded him at the Sydney Conservatorium, where Malcolm had first heard him sing in several of Edgar Bainton's operas before Nilsson departed for Europe.[9] Owen Brannigan and April Cantelo, two of Malcolm's most important friends and allies, both had helpful experience in the Britten operas; only three years earlier, as Bottom and Helena, they had sung in the first performances of *A Midsummer Night's Dream*, and Brannigan, the original Noye, had created several other roles at Aldeburgh.

As press interest intensified in the days before the premiere, Malcolm responded with his customary delight at being in the spotlight, presenting meanwhile the kind of clean-cut image which would have been unthinkable a few years earlier:

> Small, dapper, incisive of speech with a darting glance and a ready smile, thirty-one-year-old Malcolm Williamson looks more like a prosperous accountant than a talented musician.[10]

---

6 Gilliat was the business partner of Carol Reed, who had directed the recent film of *Our Man In Havana* from Green's script. Gilliat's film credits included the Hitchcock classic *The Lady Vanishes*; he collaborated with Frank Launder in over forty smart, witty British thrillers as well as the *St Trinian's* films. He adapted a Saki novel for a Malcolm Arnold television opera.

7 Interview quoted by the Sydney *Sun-Herald*, 30 June 1963

8 July 2005

9 Nilsson had settled in America, where he had married a high-powered space scientist.

10 *Sun-Herald*, Sydney, 30 June 1963

He explained how he and Gilliat had solved the problems of the novel by giving extra importance to the hero's friend, Hasselbacher, the loyal doctor becoming the loveable person Dr Roth had rightly insisted the story needed (and who, as played by the avuncular Owen Brannigan, became even more loveable); there had also been a heightening of the relationship between the hero (Raymond Nilsson), a seller of vacuum-cleaners and the fabricator of a network of imaginary spies, and Beatrice (April Cantelo), the spy sent out by MI5 to support him; and the hero's name had been changed to Bramble, 'because if you sing "Wormald" it'll sound like "Worm" half the time'.[11]

It was clear from his comments that Malcolm had enjoyed considerable input in the casting. Early on he had unsuccessfully promoted the claims of Marion Grimaldi and, in his determination to 'co-opt the cast from musical comedy as well as the opera', he had made one remarkable approach:

> I invited Noel Coward to repeat his film success as Hawthorne, the imperturbable MI5 agent. Mr Coward replied that he'd considered opera before but decided his voice was too good for it...[12]

He was more successful with the appointment of John Alldis as chorus-master, and from his friend's choir Joyce Millward was chosen as Milly, Bramble's daughter, whose spendthrift ways resulted in him reluctantly becoming a spy. It was a bold move[13] to choose an unknown singer for so important a role and the *Evening Standard* took up the story eagerly:

> A blonde Lolita wiggled her hips on the stage at Sadler's Wells today – and virtually walked away with the new opera, *Our Man in Havana*. Joyce Millward, an unknown young soprano, plays the star role of Milly... Today was one of the final rehearsals... Afterwards members of the cast clustered around Joyce offering their congratulations. Milly is the first opera role that honey-blonde blue-eyed Joyce has played...[14]

Malcolm was on hand to add his thoughts:

> It was hell to find a singer who could combine the looks of a 17-year-old with the vocal stamina and virtuosity of a soprano in her middle 30s. Joyce does it. She even looks beautiful when she is singing – and that's really difficult...

Malcolm's relationship with his singers was always strongly supportive. Caring for them so much, he could be very volatile in rehearsal, particular as regards the orchestral playing and James Loughran, his conductor, found the final days very tense:

---

11 *Queen*, 6 March 1962

12 *Town*, 3 June 1963

13 It was not as rash a choice as it sounded. Very early on in the project, in trying out ideas with John Alldis's choir, he had used Joyce Millward as a soloist on a preliminary tape. She subsequently auditioned at Sadler's Wells and hers was the voice he heard thereafter as he wrote the part.

14 1 July 1963

> Malcolm proved terribly fussy over orchestral detail. Although he was extremely gifted as an orchestrator, his string writing was often very demanding for the players, and he was always insistent that it was absolutely precise…

As the premiere on 2 July 1963 approached, amongst the good wishes was a telegram from Graham Greene, who had watched one rehearsal from a seat next to James Loughran in the pit but had otherwise kept well away. Adrian Boult sent ‘every kind greeting’, Peter Shaffer his love. Alexander Goehr, John Gardner and Lizzie Lutyens offered support along with Father Christopher from St Peter’s, Limehouse: ‘Petertide greetings and good wishes from all’. Sidney Gilliat wrote:

> Bear up tonight. All may not yet be lost. Think my music is fine but not so confident about your words.

His telegram ended with a quotation from the end of Act One, as Bramble prepares to send off to London by morse code the names of the three agents he has just invented:

> ‘May that which follows be happy!’

Raymond Nilsson, the distinguished Australian tenor

Set design for Our Man in Havana *by Carl Toms*

*Owen Brannigan, Raymond Nilsson and April Cantelo (*Our Man in Havana*)*

The five initial performances[15] could hardly have gone better, Gilliat's convincing narrative bringing out the very best from Malcolm, a score that abounds in melody, atmosphere and imagination. Several critics, J W Lambert among them, found the opera more satisfying than the recent film:

> The sad absurdity of the story of the little vacuum-cleaner man caught up – as he plods along with his job, his memories of a worthless wife, and his care for a silly daughter – in a network of spying and counterspying comes across very clearly, aided by a beautiful performance by the tenor Raymond Nilsson, long a Covent Garden *comprimario*, which in terms of characterisation made much better sense than that of Alec Guinness.[16]

Some of the sterner critics struggled to come to terms with Milly's lilting waltz, which would indeed have served Mitzi Gaynor well in *South Pacific*, though Edward Greenfield seemed not to mind:

> At last a new opera with tunes as memorable as anything in a Richard Rodgers musical! *Our Man in Havana* has characters clear-cut enough to let you see them develop musically and dramatically, yet requires no studying of learned essays. It has a good story; the atmosphere is beautifully judged; and its choruses have you annoying your neighbours to Cuban rhythm. It is an opera, in short, that takes you by the scruff of the neck and doesn't let go.[17]

Opera was equally supportive:

> How rare to find a modern opera that makes no excuses, that demands no indulgence for the composer's musical or philosophical hobby-horses, that fuses theatrical and musical appeal together with the directness of a Verdi! But here it is, and my first praise to Malcolm Williamson is for the sheer boldness of his conception – an opera on a present-day plot, in straight dramatic form and in a readily comprehensible musical language…

It was felt that the novel's biggest challenge – the emergence of tragedy from comedy – had been well met:

> Later come the serious scenes, centring on Hasselbacher – his superb lament after his laboratory has been ruined, his death by shooting and the ensemble-elegy for him. What helps to unify the score and the drama, making it clear that comedy and death belong to one tale, is the sequence of exotic (and beautiful) Latin-American numbers interspersed in the opera…

---

15 There were just three more performances the following year. Contemporary opera was a big box office risk, particularly at Sadler's Wells which catered specifically for a non-specialist audience with a liking for operettas and traditional operas sung in English. But the paucity of performances was compensated by a live BBC broadcast (30 June 1964). Although Malcolm's operas hardly accorded with William Glock's advanced tastes, the BBC's Director of Music was extremely supportive, broadcasting all five of his full-length operas.

16 *Christian Herald*, 4 July 1963

17 *The Spectator*, 6 July 1963

Colin Mason, editor of *Tempo*, persisted in comparisons with Britten, declaring *Our Man In Havana* 'the most promising first opera by an English composer since *Peter Grimes*'.[18] Malcolm, he wrote, had shown a similar abundance of musical invention and sense of the theatre as Britten in *Peter Grimes* at exactly the same age. The deft handling of comedy and tragedy reminded him of *Albert Herring*; in its establishment of several musical planes, which rarely overlapped, it mirrored *A Midsummer Night's Dream*. Mason was always supportive, but Peter Heyworth, a champion of serialism and the avant-garde and not a natural ally of Malcolm's at all, nonetheless conceded that the score had 'undeniable variety and engaging gusto', Malcolm showing 'the sort of genuine feeling for the theatre that some senior British composers so notably lack…'[19] Even more encouraging were the comments of the young composer Alan Ridout:

> Just a line to say how magnificent I thought 'Our Man in Havana' was. It seemed to me to have everything one could hope for in an opera: drama, vitality, colour and beauty. I found the generosity of the music quite overwhelming. Congratulations on a unique and memorable work.[20]

There were inevitably a few dissenting voices, and it was often Malcolm's sense of humour which was questioned. The opera is alive with musical witticisms. Milly, for example, asks for help in her homework. 'What's the capital of Iceland?' she asks. 'Reykjavik rings a bell,' responds Beatrice, and at once a bell is heard in the orchestra. (It was later removed.) At every mention of Lamb (*Lamb's Tales From Shakespeare* being a crucial part of the plot) there is a decidedly audible orchestral bleat. A snatch of a sailor's hornpipe is heard just before a mention of Nelson, and on several occasions the cellos become wonderful vacuum cleaners.

The use of a contemporary novel by so distinguished a writer also caused some misgivings. *The Times*, while acknowledging Malcolm's 'real operatic talent' and 'highly coloured and ebullient score', saw the libretto as 'a travesty as a representation of a great novel'. Graham Greene at once sent the newspaper a letter in Gilliat's defence:

> To me the opera was in no way a travesty of the novel, and I admired the great skill with which the libretto had compressed the action and yet brought out every political point… As the author of the film-script may I say I infinitely preferred Mr Gilliat's libretto?…[21]

He had been similarly positive immediately after the first performance:

---

[18] The comment suggests how much Malcolm had assimilated English ways over the past ten years. But he would never be fully acceptable as 'English', just as the Australians would no longer consider him fully 'Australian'.

[19] *New York Times*, 4 July 1963

[20] Letter to MW, 5 July 1963

[21] *The Times*, 3 July 1963

With Edith Sitwell at a London performance of English Eccentrics

'I liked it,' said Graham Greene as he sipped a glass of red wine backstage after the premiere. 'I was very pleased. The libretto was excellent, the music brilliant. I liked it better than the film… I think they conveyed exactly what I intended the book to say...'[22]

Havana's successor was being planned even before the first performance. Benjamin Britten had asked Malcolm for an 'operatic entertainment' for six singers and a small orchestra to be performed under the aegis of the English Opera Group at the Aldeburgh Festival of 1964, and later at the City Temple Hall as part of the City of London Festival.[23] 'What we really want,' Peter Pears had explained to Malcolm, 'is an anti-opera.'[24]

Malcolm did not find it easy to find a theme fulfilling the requirements of the commission. Eventually, however, realising that Pears was after something Brechtian, he proposed an adaptation of a book of essays by Edith Sitwell, *English Eccentrics*, a survey of people in past centuries with the strangest of habits, both comic and tragic. Sitwell, herself, of course, was a present-day eccentric, and Malcolm was devoted to her:

She was like a little girl that you wanted to cuddle because you adored her and just couldn't help it. She was extremely tall and with a strange queenly face. She framed

22 *Opera*, August 1963

23 In June and July, 1964

24 MW, programme note to the Trinity College of Music production, 1990

> herself with extraordinary clothes which suited her very well. There was not a shred of affectation about her, only an amount of irreverent humour, that spirit of irreverence which goes with a true sense of proportion.[25]

Britten and Pears were at once pleased with the idea, for they too admired Edith Sitwell and had worked with her before at the Aldeburgh Festival. Britten had warmed again to Malcolm now that he was no longer drinking, and had been impressed by his contribution to a surprise 50th birthday present, when Malcolm, Richard Rodney Bennett and Nicholas Maw had each written a variation on a Britten theme.[26] The 50th birthday telegram Malcolm and Dolly had sent him was also well received. ('I'm feeling 150 at least now!' he replied.) Early on in the writing of *English Eccentrics* Malcolm sought Britten's active help:

> Dear Ben,
>
> It was charming of you to write a letter about the little birthday pieces. And thank you for your offer of help. May I take you up on it, please? I have pressing libretto (not librettist) problems and your advice would be invaluable. I know that you are even busier than usual, and I don't expect that I shall see you for more than a moment, if that, at RFH 'Gloriana', but if I could see you soon at almost any time and place for a short while, it would help immensely. If you are weighed down, ignore this for goodness' sake, and I shall try to get Jeremy[27] on the phone.
>
> Love,
> Malcolm[28]

Britten responded with a long, helpful telephone call.

While Malcolm was engaged on his preliminary work on *English Eccentrics*, he was also in the throes of writing a ballet score for Robert Helpmann. Now in his fifties and at the height of his powers as an actor, director and choreographer, Helpmann had just returned to his native Australia to create an original work for the newly formed Australian Ballet, which he would be running with Peggy van Praagh. *The Display* was a dance drama centred upon an Australian lyrebird, a somewhat bizarre idea which had originated (as Helpmann loved to tell) through his friendship with Katharine Hepburn:

---

25 BBC Radio: 'Meet The Composer', 19 February 1970

26 *Reflections on a Theme by Britten*. It was played at a MacNaughten concert in the Mahatma Gandhi Hall, London, 25 October 1963. The work was based on a theme written in 1959, the *Tema Seriale* in Pars II of Britten's *Cantata Academica*. Two days later Britten responded: 'My dear Malcolm, I was very touched and pleased by the Tarantella you wrote for the other night. Thank you more than I can say for having done it. In spite of your doubts, I liked it a great deal, and anyhow the gesture was something that meant a great deal to me. You know, I think, how much I admire your work – and this was a real compliment. And I look forward now to the Eccentrics more than I can say. Do keep in touch, won't you, and anything I can possibly do to help I will certainly happily do. With love and thanks to you and to your wife whom I was so happy to meet.'

27 Jeremy Cullum, Britten's secretary.

28 12 November 1963

Kathleen Gorham and Barry Kitcher in The Display *(1964)*

> I was touring Australia with my very dear friend Katharine Hepburn.[29] One of her fans gave her a book about lyrebirds in Sherbrooke Forest. Every Sunday morning she would knock on my door, drag me out of bed and drive us up to Sherbrooke Forest, just outside Melbourne, where we would go looking for lyrebirds.[30]

For a long time they met with no success. Then one day Hepburn was shown where the lyrebirds lived:

> After that all our spare time was spent in the forest, watching the birds performing their display. We were totally hooked. We even rehearsed our lines there. When the company moved to Sydney I got a phone call from a friend who'd just spotted a lyrebird running around Sherbrooke Forest with a gravelly Katharine Hepburn voice, reciting Shakespeare…

Helpmann's stage lyrebird was almost as elaborate as the real creatures running around Sherbrooke Forest, practising their imitations of Katharine Hepburn. It was constructed out of bamboo, nylon and horsehair, with a leather strap harness, two wings, a garment for the chest, a collar to go with it and a beautifully made head-dress with a beak, feathers and two large eyes, as well as a sixteen-feet-long tail, built on a hinge, so that the dancer could pull a small handle and open it out spectacularly into a huge fan.[31] It sounds an unlikely ballet costume, but most of the dancing in the forty-minute piece came not from the lyrebird but a group of

29 In three Shakespearean plays with the Old Vic Company in 1955

30 Kitcher: *From Gaolbird to Lyrebird*, p.244

31 *ibid.* p.245

young people picnicking in a forest. Helpmann's story had strong sexual undertones and ended in rape. It was wildly melodramatic, and when the ballet appeared in New York a few years later, Clive Barnes had fun with it:

> *The Display* is a kind of bird-gets-girl ballet. A young lady, oddly attracted by lyrebirds, goes on an unfortunate picnic. Australian youths drink beer and test their muscles. The girls watch admiringly. One boy is an outsider to this sporting life. The heroine flirts with him. He kisses her and their embraces are roughly interrupted by the intrusion of the gang who, with untypical lack of Australian sportsmanship, beat him within a centimetre of his discouraged life. He quickly recovers, races after the girl, and – apparently – rapes her. This experience has an odd effect upon her, and she then gives herself to the lyrebird, who presumably has been standing in wait. She appears to be something of an ornithologist…[32]

Helpmann, however, knew what he was about, and Malcolm responded to the scenario with an appropriately theatrical score, full of the atmosphere of the bush, which Helpmann took back to Australia in great excitement. Meeting his company for the first time in Adelaide, 'a slim, elegant figure in a cool safari suit… with a shock of dyed blonde hair and a lei of gold chains around his neck,'[33] Helpmann carefully outlined the story before handing Malcolm's score to the company's pianist, Jessie Clarke:

> 'Take it home and study it', he told Jessie. 'It is a most difficult score. The pianist in London struggled with its strange irregular rhythms and countings'. Jessie took the score, opened the page, put it on the lectern and played it perfectly from the first note. 'It goes like this,' she said as she worked through the complex rhythms, 'And this is how you count it'. When Jessie had finished, there was a long silence as Helpmann stood before the piano. We could see he was flabbergasted.[34]

The Display, premiered at the Adelaide Festival in March 1964, proved a huge success, becoming Australian Ballet's signature work for many years. The applause at its first performance lasted fifteen minutes and Helpmann took twenty curtain calls. Barry Kitcher, who danced the lyrebird, remembers 'an abrupt and utterly deafening outburst of acclamation' washing over the cast as the audience went wild. 'The applause, the whistles, the cries and stamping of feet was overwhelming…'[35]

Malcolm's score was much praised for capturing the woodland scene with its 'realistic bird calls and strange dissonance'.[36] Roger Covell, the influential critic of the *Sydney Morning Herald*, wrote of it:

> It has the distinction of intrinsic qualities of technical resource combined with theatrical fluency and sense of gesture to a degree probably unprecedented in any music specially commissioned for ballet use in this country. It is a highly melodic, rhythmically supple score, eclectic in its derivation, difficult to play well but always in deft allegiance with the mood of the stage action… The opening and closing

---

32 *New York Times*, 1971.

33 Barry Kitcher *op. cit.* p.243

> sections pay an occasional undisguised tribute to the Stravinsky of *The Fairy's Kiss* and, most of all, to Britten's *The Prince of the Pagodas*. But to point out these allegiances is not to depreciate the quality of the music, merely to indicate its approximate area of texture and style…[37]

But Malcolm missed all the excitement, unable to travel to Australia because of his involvement in the Sitwell opera, *English Eccentrics*. His librettist this time was Geoffrey Dunn, another unusual but excellent choice, suggested by Britten and Pears. Dunn had spent nearly forty years in the theatre, as a singer, director and actor (with a special line in eccentrics). Tall, elegant and just as theatrical as Robert Helpmann, he had recently been successfully translating and adapting operas and operettas at Sadler's Wells.[38] An excellent tenor, he had first met Britten and Pears when singing with the London Intimate Opera Company just before the war; his seasons of music hall at the Players' Theatre were further useful experience for *English Eccentrics*.

Helpmann, back in England, had expressed an interest in directing the opera, so one day he and Malcolm set off in their usual high spirits to see Edith Sitwell at her Hampstead flat. She was confined to her bed, not at all well, but she rallied strongly in their presence:

> Williamson asked her why titled ladies were sometimes Lady Mary Smith and sometimes Mary, Lady Smith. In the latter case, Edith explained, she is a dowager. 'But Tennyson was always known as Alfred, Lord Tennyson.' 'Ah, but then he *was* a dowager!' And her delighted laughter rang out, disturbing Shadow the Siamese cat, who lay on her bed.[39]

Edith Sitwell's support was not enough, however, to convince Britten and Pears that they wanted Helpmann at Aldeburgh. Malcolm would often tell the story of his efforts to counter Helpmann's low standing there:

> When I first suggested to Peter Pears that Bobby might direct *Eccentrics* he sighed deeply. 'Must you really use him, Malcolm? He's so terribly *vulgar*!' Next time I saw Bobby, therefore, I put it to him straight: 'Look, Bobby, if you want to work at Aldeburgh, I think you're going to have to tone down your act!' Bobby smiled and shook his head. 'Forget it, Malcolm, forget it. At Aldeburgh I'd be about as welcome as lockjaw in a cock-suckers' picnic!'[40]

---

34 *ibid.*

35 *ibid.* p. 248. The work was to be performed by Australian Ballet a further 321 times. Although it has not been performed since 1983, only *Don Quixote* and *The Merry Widow* have received more performances.

36 *Sydney Morning Herald*, 16 March 1964

37 *ibid.*

38 Dunn had been responsible for successes like *La Belle Hélène*, *La Vie Parisienne* and *The Gypsy Baron*. In his day he had been an excellent tenor, a star in the music hall for thirty years.

39 Glendinning: *Edith Sitwell*, p.353

40 A story retold by several of Malcolm's friends.

The director eventually chosen was another former dancer, the amusing Billy Chappell, whose fund of stories of the Vic-Wells Ballet with Constant Lambert, Ashton and de Valois fascinated Malcolm. Chappell (who was also an accomplished artist and stage designer) brought to *English Eccentrics* the same choreographic finesse and sense of style he had given many West End revues and comedies.[41] He also coped well with Malcolm's outbursts, refusing to take him too seriously. (On the first night he sent 'Loving wishes to the greatest eccentric of them all.')

With its small cast the opera requires versatile performers, and Malcolm was very lucky that April Cantelo, Owen Brannigan and Raymond Nilsson were again available, joined by John Fryatt, Anna Pollak and Michael Maurel. John Fryatt remembers the fun they had:

> There were six of us doing 36 roles! It was more like a revue. The changing was desperate, and we got to know each other well! It was a nightmare behind the scenes! Peter Rice's design was wonderful – it was really a rubbish heap and he would continually go out to real rubbish dumps and bring back more rubbish to add to the set…[42]

April Cantelo has similarly happy memories:

> It was an absolute joy to do, because there were so many parts. We were much busier offstage than on, changing! I had a ball as Princess Cariboo. I enjoyed that immensely.[43]

The opera begins with Malcolm's Brechtian chorus of four singers, who from time to time, from a raised platform in the pit, comment on the action, the device proving particularly helpful in conveying something of the flavour of Sitwellian language with its strikingly bold metaphors and similes.[44] Each of the two acts begins with an ensemble of eccentrics, historical accuracy giving way to the need for characters to interact. The tone is set by a discussion between Lord Petersham, who has a different snuff-box for each day of the year, and Miss Tylney Long, who delights in tall hats and is distressed to find herself outdone by rivals who end up twenty, and even thirty, feet high. 'I could weep for vexation and mortification!' They are joined by old Thomas Parr, married first at ninety-three, 'and then marriage became a habit', who in turn is complemented by the Countess of Desmond who fell to her death from an apple tree ('a curious prank for a gel of my rank') at the age of 140. Further eccentrics in the opening scene include Lord Rokeby, who washes incessantly, and Lady Lewson who cannot bear the sight of water. There follow two extended scenes, one comic, the

---

41 Chappell, for example, directed the first performance of Anouilh's *Ring Round the Moon*, which epitomised stylish romance in the 1950s.

42 January 2006

43 August 2005

44 There is a similar device in Weill's *The Seven Deadly Sins*. The quartet all came with top-class Alldis pedigree: Barbara Elsy, Pauline Stevens, Ian Partridge and Christopher Keyte

other tragic. The comic scene introduces the hopeless but flamboyant Romeo Coates:

> The story of Romeo Coates, the bogus mulatoo actor, gives Williamson an opportunity to turn Latin-American. Romeo's rumba rhythms are infectiously delightful, while his blues – in which he appeals to the audience that has mocked him – is a touching moment of illumination, sensitively sung and acted by John Fryatt...[45]

The First Act ends with the tragic tale of Sarah Whitehead, unaware that her brother has been hanged for forgery and believing the Bank where he worked, which she visits every day, to be defrauding her.

The Second Act is likewise in three sections. After a hilarious miscellany of eccentric quacks ('Visit my Temple of Health and Hymen,' sings Dr Graham, 'Sleep on my Celestial Bed! Fertility guaranteed!') comes an extended comic scene featuring a serving girl who passes herself off as the Javanese Princess Cariboo:

> Williamson tells us the truth about Mary Barker on her first appearance, for the tune she sings to herself is a folk-song that reveals her English heart. The pseudo-orientalisms of her disguise are quaint; only gradually do we realise that they're also sad. Her dream of exotic glamour is part of the 'truth' about her: which is why she can inspire the stodgy representatives of the Establishment to emulate her dreamy lyricism in the lovely trio-lullaby that hovers precariously between laughter and tears. Her final cadenza, after she's been unmasked, asserts the truth, even as it pricks the bubble, of her dream...[46]

The final scene is the tragic tale of Beau Brummel's senile decline, which, said *The Times*, 'Williamson fills out to a heart-rending Verdi-like climax'. Raymond Nilsson's study of a once great royal favourite reduced to distracted, penurious exile was full of moving pathos.

The opera was received extremely well, but Malcolm's elation lasted only to a moment in the second half of the first performance when he spotted that Britten had not returned to the box he always shared with Pears. His absence may well have had nothing to do with the opera, but it seemed a very public rebuff, and Malcolm was mortified. Dolly recalls:

> No explanation was ever forthcoming. Malcolm was unbelievably distressed and hurt. It was something he never really was able to forget. [47]

Worried that Britten might have felt the opera was too flippant, Malcolm took every opportunity to stress its underlying seriousness:

> Superficially at least the material is comic, but, as with eccentricity, the comedy spills over into tragedy. Those who consider themselves less eccentric than the rest of the world find the eccentric entertaining, but shun him or her if there is any suggestion of intimacy. The characters in this opera are all ultimately unacceptable to others.[48]

---

45 Wilfrid Mellers, *New Statesman*, 26 June 1964

46 Wilfrid Mellers, *ibid.*

47 May 2006

48 *Radio Times*, 4 June 1964

English Eccentrics, *Aldeburgh, 1964*

He later wrote:

> The opera is set in winter and I was centrally preoccupied with death – the death of the leaf which is going to be re-born.[49]

Some of the more perceptive critics brought out this side of the opera. Andrew Porter wrote:

> Williamson has a way – a warm and likeable way – of putting himself into a work. He is high-spirited and brims with fun and invention; but he is also a poet, with a serious melancholy side. There is a vision of eternity behind the passing show... under the gay eccentric parade lies the sorrow of things.[50]

Porter's praise was part of a large chorus of critical approval:

> – Mr Williamson has provided a scintillating score, fluent, easy on the ear. It projects the text clearly – in ensembles as well as solos – and is always apt to the situation...[51]
>
> – It is a diverting, highly ingenious entertainment for the sophisticated, with outstandingly skilful and resourceful music...[52]
>
> – Using a wide variety of rhythms and speeds, Williamson's style is easy on the ear, and kind to the voices. There is no straining for outré effects, no fractured atonal

---

[49] *Sadler's Wells Theatre Magazine*, Autumn 1966

[50] *Financial Times*, 15 July 1964

[51] Felix Aprahamian, *Sunday Times*, 14 June 1964

[52] *Musical Events*, July 1964

> grimaces; but there is most certainly a composer of real value at work. The scoring, small in scale, still manages to create a wealth of atmosphere, from seedy decay to potty ebullience…[53]
>
> – It is evident that Malcolm Williamson is the most naturally gifted of our young operatic composers; gifted with fluency and fertility in the best way, the way that opera composers need: with a sense of timing and pace, climax and progression, for the theatre; with the ability to set words that they sing naturally and never seem awkward. Also that he has mastered all the techniques available to opera composers today, from Stravinsky and Britten to Richard Rodgers… The whole performance with a first-rate cast is a *tour de force* and it should not be missed…[54]

Edith Sitwell herself, now a frail seventy-six, followed the project with enthusiasm, cabling her good wishes and being taken in a wheelchair by ambulance to one of the London performances.[55] She had hoped very much to entertain the cast afterwards, as John Fryatt remembers:

> We were all invited back to her home, and given sherry and very stale biscuits. After a while it was announced that she was unfortunately indisposed and would only be able to see one of our number. Anna Pollak was chosen to go up and see her. When she came down, quite soon afterwards, she whispered dramatically to us, 'She's drunk!'[56]

April Cantelo, however, remembers a slightly more successful visit, during the rehearsal period:

> Three or four of us went with Malcolm to meet Edith Sitwell at her Hampstead home. It was a very moving experience, although she was immobile and did not look well.[57]

Ian Partridge recalls four of them sitting at the end of the bed, desperately trying to institute some conversation.

Only a few months later she was dead. Malcolm went to her funeral at the Church of the Immaculate Conception, Farm Street, familiar to him from his time as assistant organist. He wrote to Benjamin Britten afterwards:

> I felt very sad, as I'm sure you and Peter do. She went peacefully, I'm told, but the last week of her life some idiot let her read a violent personal attack on her, and she was extremely distressed. One wishes that the critic concerned might know that she read him, if only accidentally…[58]

The problem between Britten and Malcolm, if problem there was, had passed. That Christmas, only six months after *English Eccentrics*, Malcolm was thanking Britten for his Christmas card and kind comments he had made in an article in *The Times*:

---

53 Norman Kay, *The Guardian*, 14 June 1964

54 Andrew Porter, *Financial Times*, 15 July 1964

55 Her brothers Osbert and Sacheverell were also there, so too Graham Greene.

56 January 2006

57 August 2005

58 29 December 1964

Your words about my generation of composers were very generous. Thank you so much. Must work harder!

The performances of *English Eccentrics* had taken place at the same time as the premiere of the Third Piano Concerto in Australia, precluding the possibility of Malcolm making a first return to Sydney since his departure twelve years earlier. The concerto, written for Philippe Entremont in 1962 on the ABC's commission, had a difficult beginning. Entremont had been scheduled to play the work under Bernard Heinze on his Australian tour of 1963. The pianist, however, had written to Malcolm in some embarrassment that illness had prevented him learning the work properly and so he would not be playing it:

Il est hors de question pour moi de ne pas rendre complète justice au concerto. Ou je le fais de mon mieux, ou pas du tout.[59]

Shortly afterwards the ABC contacted Malcolm, suggesting that the concerto was, in fact, unplayable. While Malcolm in great dismay consulted Adrian Boult, controversy over the concerto's cancellation raged in Sydney with letters appearing in the *Morning Herald*:

The proposed abandonment of the performance at the Sydney Youth Concerts of Malcolm Williamson's new concerto is indeed a catastrophe, and the public will surely look to the ABC to make other arrangements for its performance at an early date. All too little is known here of the work of this very brilliant Sydney composer, and it is time that his Organ Concerto was also heard in Sydney…[60]

Bernard Heinze, far from pleased at what he believed to be very shoddy treatment, pointedly substituted in his programmes the First Symphony (*Elevamini*), thus giving it its first public performance.[61] Boult, meanwhile, busied himself behind the scenes to prove that the concerto was certainly was not beyond a virtuoso's technique, and in June 1964, John Ogdon flew out from Britain to play the work with the Sydney Symphony Orchestra. The young Ogdon, who only two years before had been joint winner with Ashkenazy of the Tchaikovsky Prize in Moscow, had a formidable technique and scored a considerable triumph in Sydney, with Bessie, George, Marion and Diane proudly present.[62]

Roger Covell was suitably impressed:

It is a gusty, uninhibited virtuoso work… The piano part hurtles and glitters, clatters and sings, and is in fact fearsomely difficult. The orchestral writing has some

---

59 Philippe Entremont to MW, 23 July 1963. He expressed heart-felt unhappiness at the situation, but did not discuss any future date for the concerto.

60 Donald Peart, a member of the Sydney University Music Department, 14 September 1963

61 Melbourne Symphony Orchestra, 13 November 1963. Boult had broadcast it on 8 February 1958.

62 2 June 1964. Ogdon was later to record Malcolm's Sonata for Two Pianos with Brenda Lucas.

John Ogdon with Malcolm's sisters and parents after the premiere of the 3rd Piano Concerto, 1964

> brilliantly effective strokes and is complicated enough in metre to be a test of the ability of conductor, orchestra and soloist to keep themselves together. Yet another of the attractive qualities of the concerto is its rhythmic liveliness and resource. The busy, nimble opening figure of the first movement and the vigorous syncopations of the finale are the work of a man who genuinely feels and enjoys the sudden gulps and hiccups of displaced metre and their insistent invitation to movement and dance…[63]

Soon afterwards Ruth Nye and Malcolm gave the first two British performances, when the critics, on the whole, were similarly positive.[64] 'What an attractive and likeable piece it is,' declared Michael Kennedy,[65] and Gerald Larner similarly found it

> a most enjoyable work and unmistakeably Malcolm Williamson in its colourfulness, its tunefulness, its never-a-dull-momentness and its close (but not obsessive) thematic unity.[66]

---

63 Covell: *Australia's Music*, 1967, pp.176-77

64 Ruth Nye recalls: 'Malcolm was going to give the first British performance himself, but by some curious chance I had the opportunity to play it three weeks beforehand. I didn't want to steal his thunder so I rang him up. He at once said 'Go ahead! You play it! You'll do it much better than I anyway!' It was a typical example of his warmth and generosity.' (August 2005)

65 *Daily Telegraph*

66 *The Guardian*, 17 February 1966. Larner was writing of a Williamson/Boult performance at Manchester with the Hallé.

The Times, however, saw the concerto in terms of 'symphonic jazz' and issued cautionary advice:

> Symphonic jazz has had a chequered history. Composers on both sides of the Atlantic have attempted various ways of combining elements of the two traditions or of achieving some measure of cross-fertilisation, yet even when the two mix they rarely fuse. Many of these attempts made a great impact when first heard, but comparatively few have established themselves. Now one of Australia's most prolific and gifted composers Mr Malcolm Williamson is challenging history by giving jazz idioms a vital share in his technique…[67]

The critic had to concede that the work was attractive:

> No-one can doubt its originality and integrity; it is vivid, exciting and compelling. His ideas are good in themselves, brilliantly developed and forcefully projected. In defiance of contemporary fashion he does not scorn the gift of expansive melodic writing and every movement has 'a big tune' worthy of Rachmaninoff himself.

In 1964, the year of the Third Piano Concerto's first performance, Malcolm accepted a commission from Yehudi Menuhin for a Violin Concerto to be played at the Bath Festival the next June. When Malcolm had been working on it for three months, Menuhin, having heard nothing, wrote cautiously:

> I do not want to intrude, be a busybody and look in at a secret and mysterious process before my time is due; on the other hand if you would like to show me anything, I would be more than curious and interested.[68]

His curiosity was satisfied, and the full score arrived on time in May. There was a mild moment of panic when Menuhin rang up to say that one section was unplayable and would have to be rewritten. Malcolm, who had little time for rewrites, was plunged into deep gloom until there came a further call. 'Malcolm, I was wrong! I can see now how it can be played! Don't change a note!'

The Concerto was dedicated to Edith Sitwell's memory, as Malcolm explained at the time of the first performance:

> It was to have been dedicated to Edith Sitwell, but tragically it must now be in affectionate memory of that great woman. The middle movement is at once a Rondo and the Scherzo, as buffoon-like and light-hearted as the outer movements are solemn and threnodic... But this, I feel, is one occasion where a memorial piece can contain light-hearted music without any lack of reverence. The work, which grows out of one germinal motif announced at the opening, centres on the note D.[69]

The rondo-scherzo, thought Desmond Shawe-Taylor, was suggestive of Edith Sitwell 'in her character of a famous tease', and he praised the outer movements for 'unconstrained lyricism and communicative power'.[70] Another of the

67 17 February 1966

68 24 December 1964

69 *Radio Times*, 10 June 1965

70 *Sunday Times*, 20 June 1965

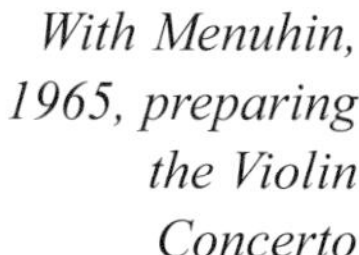

With Menuhin, 1965, preparing the Violin Concerto

concerto's supporters was Neville Cardus, who had followed Malcolm's career with interest ever since 1946, when he had been sent a song by Malcolm, then aged fourteen.[71] Cardus pointed out the work's rhythmic and harmonic originality, praised the slow movements in particular for their imagination and concluded

> Here, maybe, is at last the composer destined to give a centre and a focal point to Australia's creative musical activities.[72]

The Concerto received mixed reviews, not everyone realising that in associating the solo instrument with his beloved Edith Sitwell, Malcolm had deliberately given it a distinctive character reflecting the old-world values for which she stood. Cardus, reviewing a later performance, understood this and explained the resulting stylistic contradictions:

> The concerto engages interest throughout despite – perhaps because of – a curious contradiction in styles. For the better part, the solo violin is written in a manner which is traditional; the virtuoso cadenza figuration is as familiar in method as anything

---

71 Cardus wrote: 'Your manuscript of Hannacker Mill reached me only yesterday. At a first glance I am very much pleased with it, especially because of your avoidance of any commonplace or tasteless features. And I congratulate you on your choice of Belloc's poem... I'd like to show it to one or two Sydney vocalists and perhaps shall be able to persuade one of them to sing it at a recital... Please tell me something of your music studies. Who is your teacher?' (October 31 1946)

72 *The Guardian*, 17 September 1965

> conceived or executed by the nineteenth-century Paganini-haunted fiddlers. So with relaxations into suave phrases, sometimes quite beautifully lyrical. But the orchestration operates in another and later-time dimension, not atonal but not in entirely harmonious agreement with the general tone and diction of the soloist. The orchestra, in fact, provides a background of contention on the whole, except for a warm eloquent preliminary unison and a surrender to a peaceful and conventional close.[73]

There was another work, this time for organ, also written in memory of Edith Sitwell, which Simon Preston played at the Aldeburgh Festival in 1965. Peter Pears had contacted Malcolm about it the previous year:

> We are going to do your 'Young Girl'[74] at Edith's memorial here in the Festival – also a new Searle setting of 'Canticle of the Rose' and Michael T's 'Weeping Babe' & Ben's Canticle 3. Wm. Plomer is reading some poems, and I have asked Lennox to write possibly a piece for Organ or a Horn Fanfare! If you felt like writing an Organ Prologue and Epilogue to start and end the occasion that could be lovely – but not long – 3 minutes each at the most. What do you say? Love, Peter[75]

Malcolm subdued his natural desire to write something more fulsome and, in the event, his *Epitaphs for Edith Sitwell*, developed from a phrase in the Violin Concerto, lasted only a minute over Pears' instructions.

He was given more scope in the commission of two short operas for amateur groups, *The Happy Prince* and *Julius Caesar Jones*. *The Happy Prince*, written for the Farnham Festival of 1965, was Malcolm's own re-working of Oscar Wilde's fairy tale about the self-sacrifice of a 'happy' prince and a little swallow.[76] Its strong moral – that taking thought for others may be scorned in this life but will be rewarded in the next – was beautifully pointed by a carefully delineated score in which certain recurring melodic intervals were used to delineate particular characters, the mayor's music being a formal sequence of fourths, for example, and the swallow's a tiny melody of four notes always trying to rise and for a long time never managing to do so. Nearing the opera's completion, Malcolm felt confident enough to run it past Benjamin Britten:

---

73 *The Guardian*, 11 February 1967

74 Malcolm had set Edith Sitwell's poem 'A Young Girl' for unaccompanied choir in 1964, the commission from the Thames Concerts Society coming via Louis Halsey.

75 Undated letter from The Red House, Aldeburgh

76 According to a local booklet about the Farnham Festival, Malcolm wrote *The Happy Prince* in just three weeks, telephoning the Festival's director, Alan Fluck, each day to discuss progress. Fluck later recalled Malcolm's first visit to inspect the church: 'I can well remember the Rector, Hedley Wilds, standing in the middle of the church and Malcolm Williamson saying 'there we will have the flames of hell' and he pointed to the pulpit. 'Then the little bird can flutter down here' and there was the composer fluttering down the nave. Hedley was saying 'Why not? Why not?' and dear Mary Joynes [the choir mistress] was wondering what I had landed her with.'

When it's ready I'd like to send you a copy of my children's opera on Oscar Wilde's *The Happy Prince* – a one-acter for schools. I concocted my own libretto – a bit of a cheat really as most of the dialogue is there for the taking. Do you approve of O.W.'s fairy tales? I used to play Liza Lehmann's Monologues with Piano for my mother to recite them and I still adore them.[77]

Britten was too busy to accept an invitation to the first performance on 22 May 1965, but Malcolm was nonetheless pleased by its strong sense of occasion. The various episodes in the story were acted out in different areas of the church, all suitably lit at the appropriate moment. Most spectacular of all was the sight from the nave of distant angels, adroitly illuminated on high behind the reredos. The costumed crowd, denied easy movement by the limitations of the Parish Church, were effectively positioned on a raked stage and treated like a Greek chorus. The Festival's director, Alan Fluck, was delighted by every aspect of the production:

All the critics turned out in force and from them the following morning we knew we had helped launch one of the finest of all children's operas – as if we hadn't realised long before anyway![78]

Malcolm had always admired Britten's *Let's Make An Opera*, and ever since attending the premiere of *Noye's Fludde* in 1958 had wished to write a work involving both children and adults. The opportunity arose when a good friend, John Andrewes of Boosey & Hawkes, asked him for an hour-long opera for the Finchley Childrens' Music Group and Malcolm responded with *Julius Caesar Jones*, for which he created with Geoffrey Dunn an original libretto set in London's suburbia. The setting reflects his own changed circumstances, for in late 1964 the Williamsons had moved to a large, detached house in East Sheen. *Julius Caesar Jones*'s Mortimer Rise would seem to have much in common with Malcolm's new home in Hertford Avenue, built in the 1930s as part of an attractive development for the well-to-do middle classes. The story, however, is completely fictitious with points of contact with both *The Turn of the Screw* and *Lord of the Flies*, as a group of children, in an exciting change from their daily routine, create among themselves a separate life of the imagination, played out at the bottom of the Mortimer Rise garden. The attractive score (resourcefully employing just ten instruments) offers the characteristic Williamson mix of melody and astringency, and even manages to surmount one of the least promising openings in operatic history, as Mrs Everett questions her sister, Mrs Whyley:

Nora! Nora! Why don't we give the children a party? A summer party to start off the holidays? Nora? Summer parties are just the thing: easier and safer than winter-term parties; fewer epidemics….'

---

77 29 December 1964

78 Booklet accompanying the Argo recording of 1966.

Recording The Happy Prince *with Richard Rodney Bennett*

The first performances, at the Jeanetta Cochrane Theatre, went very well, helped by direction from Billy Chappell,[79] sets by Peter Rice, and singing from April Cantelo, Norma Procter and Michael Maurel. LPs were later issued of both operas (Malcolm and Richard Rodney Bennett supplying the accompaniment for *The Happy Prince,*) and they subsequently enjoyed considerable success in many parts of the world.

Malcolm's prolific output was all the more impressive in that he was also maintaining a parallel career as a performer. When working on *Our Man In Havana*, for example, he still managed to give organ recitals at the BBC, the Festival Hall, Coventry Cathedral and the Belfast Festival. Similarly he took time off *English Eccentrics* to give several performances of the Gershwin Piano Concerto with Charles Groves and the Royal Liverpool Philharmonic Orchestra and his own Third Piano Concerto with Adrian Boult and the Hallé,[80] and often gave concerts with singers like Owen Brannigan, Nancy Evans, April Cantelo

79 Chappell's involvement in the shaping of the opera was considerable, just as it had been in *English Eccentrics*. Four months before the first production he had written to Malcolm: 'I am very anxious to see the rest of the epic with the new libretto by G Dunn and look forward to a smashing dust-up between you and me around October 6th. I trust there will be no separate printing of the libretto till I have had a chance to have a look at it.' (September 1965)

80 Boult wrote to him after a tour of northern cities in 1966: 'It was very nice indeed having you with us all last week and we are most grateful for all your help in the way of taxis and porters and all the rest of it; it really was outrageous some of the things that happened, and I am very sorry you should have suffered in some of the hotels...' (22 February)

Suburban solidity: 32 Hertford Avenue

and Barbara Elsy.[81] For a time he and Richard Rodney Bennett performed at two pianos, their repertoire including much Messiaen, Stravinsky, Berkeley and Poulenc. 'He was great to work with,' comments Bennett. 'He had an extraordinary brilliance and it was always Malcolm who played the difficult bits!'[82] After one recital he wrote to Malcolm:

> Thank you for your nice letter. The whole concert was a delight to do and you were sensible to cajole me into doing No. V of the Messiaen; I was told my birdsong was ever so *libre et gai* if not especially *clair*. Your piece was divine and I loved playing it.[83]

Malcolm's flourishing career as a performer helped establish him financially; so too the move to the publishers Josef Weinberger, with whom he had been under contract since 1963, a firm small enough to be able to take a very personal interest in him. This close relationship with Weinberger's brought much-needed organisation to the chaos which had formerly surrounded his business affairs.

With money suddenly less of a problem, he and Dolly had been able to make the move to East Sheen on learning that the family was shortly to be augmented by the arrival of twins. The house in Hertford Avenue, to be the focal point of Malcolm's most productive period, was very much a symbol of all that had been achieved in the first five years of marriage, its parquet floors and oak doors and panelling exuding an appropriate air of solidity and style. Malcolm took over the front reception room as his study; the back garden, though not as long as that in

---

81 With Barbara Elsy, for example, he gave the first performance of *Celebration of Divine Love* (St James' Square, 8 April 1963). For this attractive song cycle he again turned to the poems of James McCauley.

82 April 2006

83 Undated letter. It contained a PS: 'Am planning to use a quote from your letter in a forth-coming brochure on me: "... so marvellous to play with..." M. WILLIAMSON.'

Julius Caesar Jones, was also a useful sanctuary for Malcolm when he had problems, as Dolly recalls:

> He was a quick writer on the whole, but he would often destroy what he'd written and start all over again. He would also sometimes go through anguish, and on such occasions he would spend a long time in the garden.[84]

On occasion he would even resort to the small front garden. His neighbours across the road still have memories of him pushing a mower along the lawn absent-mindedly, a pile of manuscript papers under one arm.

Never one to throw anything away, Malcolm now had the space to hoard. Soon his study was a reflection of his unrelenting work ethic; the glass-fronted corner cabinet full of scores; books and papers all over the room. Yet there was a certain amount of order in the disorder, and Dolly remembers it as a comfortable environment for creativity:

> The freedom of having a big room was helpful to him. It was pretty shabby but he liked everything in it, not least the favourite big chair which sagged almost to the ground. He had a small piano – we had a grand in the sitting-room for a time – but he worked on the small one. He heard all the music in his head, but he liked to try things out on the piano. If he got excited at some lovely tune, he would seek me out – usually I wasn't in bed if it was very late, for I'm a night owl – and cry 'Come and listen!' He was absolutely joyous when things were going well and might suddenly call me in. The children too, as they grew older. They would love to listen to him late in the evening, sometimes even quietly falling asleep as he played and played…

Malcolm's domestic happiness in these early years of marriage delighted Bessie, far away in Sydney, yet frustrated her too. The birth of her first grandchildren, Peter and Tammy, on the far side of the world was a reminder of her failure to keep her only son close to her. For such a good organiser of other people, used to getting her own way, she had somehow badly mismanaged things when they most mattered! Her emotions were accordingly all the stronger when she wrote to Malcolm with the news of the birth of Marion' first child:

> You may be father and husband and composer etc etc but now for the first time in your life you are an uncle! Diane is ecstatic as is your father. The first grandchild born in Australia. Wish you were having yours here in Jan. How is Dolly?[85]

Bessie was continuing to run the family business ('we have a very full programme now until Christmas with staff shortages and business rush, but we'll get through') but looking forward to life beyond it ('I'm going to be sixty in a year and a half. Then I'll live it up…'). Becoming a grandmother a third time had put her in good spirits, and she was her old artistic self – she had just written 'a beautiful pome' which she would send him 'for your next hopera'. Bessie was delighted with the names of Clare and Rebecca which had been chosen for the twins if they were girls.

---

84 March 2005

85 1 December 1964

> They are lovely. But what if you have two boys and they are thugs like West Side Story type and are champion wrestlers or boxers… whatever would you do? Maybe you'll have a string quartet to conduct and Dolly can do a song and dance…

The twins were expected in January. Before Christmas, however, Dolly was rushed from East Sheen to the premature baby unit of the General Hospital on the Harrow Road. A nightmare ensued. The twins had not been expected for another seven weeks and the hospital staff were unconvinced that Dolly's contractions had started; their attention, moreover, seemed focussed on a former staff nurse who was having a baby the same night. Eventually, at the very last minute, an elderly matron appeared and a doctor came rushing in, still buttoning up his coat… Dolly was at once aware, at the babies' birth, that all was not well.

> I think they showed me Clare for a second and then dashed away with her. With Rebecca I heard them say 'She looks terribly anaemic' after which they just disappeared, leaving me as I was for several hours. [86]

Rebecca died three hours later. Clare survived after spending five weeks in an incubator. At Rebecca's burial Malcolm stood in anguish beside the grave, holding the tiny coffin in his arms, unwilling to part with it. It was his first experience of death. 'Malcolm was beside himself with grief,' says Dolly. 'In the end, I guess the music may have saved him. It gave him an outlet...'

There were several big orchestral commissions to work on, the most pressing one, ironically, a celebration. The BBC were to inaugurate Radio 3 with a concert given by Adrian Boult and the New Philharmonia, for which Malcolm had agreed to write a three-movement *Sinfonietta*. Quite remarkably, in the fullness of his grief and anxiety, he wrote a bustling introductory Toccata and, for the finale, a delightfully cheeky Tarantella, archetypal Williamson. Tuneful and rhythmically highly inventive, this Tarantella always catches the attention. But the heart of the work is the central movement, an Elegy, in which hushed sounds of sorrow are interrupted by dissonance and despair. The work was dedicated to the three-month-old Clare, who inspired the joyful Tarantella as surely as Rebecca the heartfelt Elegy.

The stress under which the *Sinfonietta* was written showed as soon as Boult played it through with the New Philharmonia. Dolly was at this rehearsal, her anxiety mounting:

> The play-through was terrible – such a mess! The piece sounded so difficult – in places it seemed to make no sense and everyone was very unhappy. Then Sir Adrian took control, and started sorting it out. Calmly. He only had two and a half hours before he made the recording, but he was never flustered. And miraculously, the music gradually became cohesive – you could see where it was going. Sir Adrian seemed to know intuitively what Malcolm had been intending.[87]

---

86 June 2005

87 June 2005

Two days after it went out on air Boult wrote apologetically to Malcolm:

> Alas, I missed the broadcast[88] though I heard your charming reference in the interval talk – many thanks. We were settling down to enjoy the Sinfonietta and, at about page 6, I was just thinking how much better your clean and spare scoring was transmitting than Elgar's lush and over-ripe stuff, when we were invaded by 3 kids and 2 grown-ups![89]

The volume of work successfully accomplished at this period was immense. The *Sinfonietta*, premiered in March 1965, was just one of a remarkable sequence of first performances that year: in February, a series of *North Country Songs*, written for Owen Brannigan; in April, the Concerto for Wind Quintet and Two Pianos (8 hands), commissioned by Macnaghten Concerts for Alan Rawsthorne's 60th birthday;[90] in May, *The Happy Prince*; in June the Violin Concerto; in August the *Concerto Grosso*, a three-movement work for the BBC Proms;[91] and in September his forty-minute *Symphonic Variations*, commissioned by the BBC for the Edinburgh Festival.[92]

The proliferation of work inevitably heightened the usual complaints about lack of consistency, critics often choosing to give with one hand and take away with the other:

> In many ways his music is alive with brilliance and talent. He is never dull, has a flair for elegant melody, and orchestrates with assurance and sophistication. But stylistically he is a chameleon. What is Mr Williamson's purpose in ducking from style to style? Is he after some sort of symbolic 'universality'?[93]

Malcolm's ambition for music to be inclusive in an age when it was becoming more and more exclusive caused considerable surprise. So too his incorrigible desire to shock. His works in 1965 were nothing if not challenging. Critics naturally struggled to come to terms with shocks like the three fortissimo

---

88 *Musical Opinion* wrote of Malcolm's interval talk: 'This discourse was in every respect a delight, not only in respect of content – which included some choice comments and observations laced with sweetly acidic humour – but also as regards delivery: Mr Williamson is almost as gifted a speaker as he is a composer. According to the *Radio Times* he was down to talk about his new work; which he did, but about much else besides, including some words of explanation why, essays in serialism notwithstanding, he prefers to write tonally. And I loved his aside about those composers "busy re-writing Webern from memory".' (May 1965)

89 23 March 1965. Boult's letter suggests that the performance had flaws: 'I do hope the slow movement wasn't ruined in effect when you finally heard it? I have dropped a very fat hint to the NPO authorities about that...'

90 Malcolm was joined by Richard Rodney Bennett, Peter Maxwell Davies and Thea Musgrave at the Wigmore Hall first performance, Marcus Dods conducting the New London Wind Ensemble. Rawsthorne wrote to him afterwards: 'Unlike your contemporaries, after listening to a piece of yours, Malcolm, when one gets to the end one feels something has happened.' (Poulton, *Alan Rawsthorne*, p.58)

91 Given its first performance by Colin Davis and the London Symphony Orchestra.

92 Given its first performance by Vilem Tausky and the BBC Concert Orchestra, Usher Hall.

93 JC, *The Scotsman*, 10 September 1965, in a review on the *Symphonic Variations*.

orchestral chords of great dissonance which preface the serene conclusion of the Violin Concerto (a work in which Delius seems to be fraternising with Stravinsky). Similarly, having opened his *Symphonic Variations* with a long, sternly argued and serial first movement, allowing no melodic frivolity to diminish its intellectual rigour, he follows up with a Serenade and Aubade of such easy mellifluousness that Weinberger's also published them as a separate entity. And could the same composer really have written at much the same time the nostalgically romantic Aubade and the grittily intense Rawsthorne Concerto?

Malcolm had become what he always wanted to be, a big talking-point. A feature on his music in *The Times* at the height of this prolific period shows him offering typically trenchant comments on what he stood for in 1965:

> Real novelty, he believes, lies along the road which absorbs new things into tonality; there are, he declares, structural innovations in the works of Mahler, Reger and Schoenberg more far-reaching than the 12-note method, and he speaks with reverence of Messiaen as the inheritor of diverse French and German traditions united in his compositions.... It is the composer's responsibility, Mr Williamson declares, 'to be as clear as crystal'. 'I think of myself privately,' he says, 'as a 12-note composer who uses six or eight notes and keeps the others in reserve. If I use common chords and dominant seventh, I don't use them in a traditional way. But it would be dishonest to suppress my simple, melodic side; I adore writing tunes, and I adore inventing accompanying figures. I can't lose my love of a great apotheosis at the end, when the shining trumpets blow. But I've had an obsession with counterpoint, even if it's chopped up in pizzicato strings till it doesn't sound like counterpoint at all. I do like,

The 'Rawsthorne' Concerto soloists, 1965: Malcolm with Richard Rodney Bennett, Peter Maxwell Davies and Thea Musgrave

when I'm writing a piece, to have it in simplest form, to have two tunes coming together, sometimes with very sharp dissonance.'[94]

In early 1966 Malcolm was involved in an exciting new project, a new ballet, *Sun Into Darkness*, commissioned by Peter Darrell's Western Theatre Ballet[95] and premiered at Sadler's Wells that April.[96] Like *The Display* it caused much comment with the boldness of its story-line. It also attracted attention as the first full-length British ballet on a contemporary theme, and for having a scenario by David Rudkin:

> Peter Darrell engaged me as a scenarist on the strength of a somewhat scandalous reputation I had earned with my first stage play *Afore Night Come*. That play, premiered by the RSC in 1962, opened up a new visceral vein in what had till then been mainly a socialist-realist genre, the 'work' play…
>
> The idea for *Sun Into Darkness* had startling enough origins – in a bizarre carnival I witnessed while stranded (by motor-cycle breakdown) in a Dartmoor village in summer 1964…
>
> It was said in some quarters that *Sun Into Darkness* 'broke new ground'. That basically means that it was what Peter called a 'queer' ballet, overtly so at a time when gay sex was still illegal. I was around for some of the rehearsal process, and it was all leather-clad and cheesy…[97]

The critics were divided. Darrell, whose career was cut short twenty years later by AIDS, played an important part in liberating the dance world from its reluctance to discuss important social and sexual themes. *The Times* thought *Sun Into Darkness* loaded with significance:

> A young visitor, stranded by a broken motor-cycle, is dressed up as a joke as Lord of Misrule: but joke becomes reality and is followed by atonement, ending with a death not consciously intended. Mr Rudkin knows his Freud and his Frazer, and his Aeschylus too, and what is on the surface straightforward has depths of moral and social significance about justice, fear and order which work in the imagination like a time bomb…[98]

The influential Richard Buckle was equally supportive:

> Critics complained that after the hero asked for his motor-bike to be mended he did a *grand jeté*. They pointed out the ballet's improbabilities, and thought it absurd that in addition to a family more peculiar than the royal house of Thebes, they were given

---

94 'Malcolm Williamson on Writing Music', 19 August 1965

95 Peter Darrell founded Western Theatre Ballet (with Elizabeth West) in 1956. By the mid-sixties he had settled the company in London, where they supplied dance for Sadler's Wells Opera. In 1969 he took the company to Glasgow, where it became the Scottish Theatre Ballet (which he led for nearly twenty years), at the same time another WTB dancer, Laverne Meyer, founding Northern Ballet Theatre in Manchester.

96 It was given further performances at Sadler's Wells that autumn and returned briefly in 1967, after which is disappeared from the company's repertoire.

97 December 2005

98 14 April 1966

Simon Mottram and Donna-Day Washington in Peter Darrell's Sun Into Darkness

> rape, murder, fetishism, an orgy and a spot of the love which is now daring to speak its name in the House of Commons.
>
> I thought Darrell had brought off this very difficult feat: by which I mean that the lurid improbabilities were acceptable, that I was never embarrassed by the combination of crash-helmets and *arabesques*, and that I always wanted to know what would happen next...[99]

Others were offended by issues which they thought inappropriate for the stage:

> The Theatre of Cruelty invaded the ballet at Sadler's Wells last night! A story about a leather-jacketed stranger who is made drunk by a sinister priest, forced to have sexual intercourse with virtually all the village of both sexes, and finally lynched and unwittingly murdered by an effeminate boy who is in love with him...! Frankly all this struck me as nonsense...! Bestiality, flagellation and striptease...![100]

The *Evening Standard*'s Nicholas Dromgoole thought it 'the ultimate example of the sordid sex ballet' and hated the whole evening:

> At the end of the second act, after an earthy pas de deux with every sultry cliché in the dancing repertoire, the stranger drags the Wife behind a symbolic throne, while the orchestra in a series of staccato throbs provides the exact musical equivalent for the significant row of asterisks in a cheap novelette...[101]

99 *Sunday Times*, 9 July 1966

100 Oleg Kerensky, *Daily Mail*, 14 April 1966

101 5 July 66

Forty years on, memories of the ballet are still quite vivid. Dancer Robin Haig recalls Malcolm attending rehearsals.

> He seemed very interested in the production process, and was always very amenable. It seemed more like a danced play than a ballet. I did a 'strip' at one point and someone stopped my mother on the street at Perth, West Australia, to say that if I was reduced to 'doing that sort of thing' why didn't I leave London and return home![102]

Conductor Kenneth Alwyn remembers that the score, as first presented, showed signs of haste and contained some inaccuracies:

> It was a very black score – lots of notes – a difficult work! Malcolm attended the rehearsals, mostly on good behaviour but he did get irate when things went wrong. [103]

Alwyn's most vivid memory is not of the ballet at all, but of an organ recital which Malcolm gave in Belfast at around that time.

> It was being broadcast live, perhaps from a cathedral, and after he had finished playing Malcolm launched into a passionate political homily: 'My lovely Irish people – how can you fight one another?' and so forth. It was at the height of the troubles, and it didn't go down at all well!

David Rudkin has little affection for the project:

> To be honest, in devising the scenario's narrative process I did not dig deep enough into unturned soil within myself. To some extent I was retreading *Afore Night Come*, also my first TV play, *The Stone Dance*, which had since intervened. I thus don't look back on my work with Darrell with any sense of pride. It was a very mid-60s thing, and I fear it would play embarrassingly today. If I had been more bravely and honestly original at the start, we might have evolved a ballet that people would still be doing now.[104]

Perhaps the ballet was too rushed, fitted into an overbusy schedule, for there was a notable lack of contact between scenarist and composer:

> There was no specific working method: a couple of meetings with Peter, a postal to-and-fro of ideas, then drafts, until we had a workable scheme. I met Williamson only once, as I remember, and my impression was that he didn't consider me a collaborator of any significance. He may well have been right, given how little I now regard the work I did. I'm sorry to say that all I brought away from the meeting were his anecdotes and gossip. There wasn't any creative interaction between us at all. I fear I did not awaken in him music of any emotional depth.[105]

It is fair comment. It is a highly inventive score, full of lurid pyrotechnics as demanded by the scenario. There is a considerable feeling of Prokofiev in its quieter moments, but ultimately it lacks melodic strength; there are times when the emotional content deepens only for Malcolm to shy away, as if unwilling to face a greater involvement.

---

[102] February 2005

[103] April 2006

[104] September 2005

[105] David Rudkin, December 2005

Involvement requires time, and the sheer pace of Malcolm's life militated against him. In the month of *Sun Into Darkness*, for example, he participated in four radio programmes, gave the premiere of his *Six English Lyrics*[106] with Nancy Evans in Manchester and visited Berlin for performances of *Our Man In Havana* and Aldeburgh for his *Two Epitaphs for Organ*. He was also developing as a writer, his book reviews always pithy and entertaining.[107]

Busy as he was, Malcolm still found it hard to turn down interviews. When the Women's Institute heard of his forthcoming choral work *The Brilliant and the Dark* to be sung by its members, a reporter[108] from *Home and Country* was soon visiting Hertford Avenue even though Malcolm was hard pressed to complete his Five Preludes for piano for Antonietta Notariello to play at that summer's Cheltenham Festival. The magazine's emphasis was naturally on domestic matters:

> 9am – small Wellington boots on the front step, a friendly smile at the door, the fragrance of real coffee – and the taste of it in a room with beautiful comfortable furniture, a copper coal-scuttle full of magazines and a boy's tool-set on the mantelpiece. All this charm overlooked a tree-shaded garden splendidly equipped with swings of all sizes.
>
> 'How nice it looks out there,' I remarked.
>
> 'I suppose,' said Mr Williamson hopefully, 'you won't have to tell your readers about the old canvas swimming pool hanging on the line?' I wouldn't dream of it.
>
> Mr Williamson sat on a sofa against the window, by his work-table. I faced him from an easy chair through a cloud of cigarette smoke, charmed to find we shared the same vice – our only one, we assured each other…

A long, rambling interview was enlivened by the appearance of Clare and Dolly:

> I can't remember at what point in the interview we were joined, at floor level, by delightful creature with fair hair and bright eyes called Clare. She seemed to indicate that the one thing she had longed for all her life (fifteen months so far) was a green ball-point pen, so it was a good thing I had two. Mr Williamson remarked that he had found parenthood a terrific stimulus. 'Ever since Peter was born I've worked from 18 to 20 hours a day.' He met his wife in London. Mrs Williamson is American, dark-haired, very good-looking, and I fell completely for the cheerful way she seemed to suggest, as she replenished our coffee cups, that having a complete stranger around while she was up to her eyes in housework, was the most normal thing in the world…

---

106 One of the most immediately attractive of all his song cycles, the *Six English Lyrics* (a setting for low voice and string orchestra of poems by Waller, Tennyson, Christina Rossetti and Leigh Hunt) deservedly maintained a long popularity.

107 Of Frank Howes' *The English Music Renaissance* he wrote: 'When twelve-tone music is mentioned, there is a strong impression that Mr Howes doesn't quite get the point. But he is generous to Lutyens and Searle on musical grounds and, in a world where far too many people know far too much about twelve-tone technique, his lapse is not too grievous...' (*Sunday Times*, 11 June 1966)

108 Honor Wyatt, mother of actor Julian Glover

Another interview, aptly titled by the *Sunday Times* 'Excess Success', began with some random thoughts on drink ('he loves drinking so much he's given it up – he now drinks six coca-colas one after the other'), television ('he loves it so much he won't have one in the house') and P G Wodehouse ('he continually buys new copies as the old ones fall to pieces') before offering some useful insights into Malcolm's compositional life:

> Most of all Mr Williamson is excessive about work. He's 35 but already has an international reputation for his five operas and countless other pieces. 'I'm a compulsive composer and have been since I was five. I just can't fill up blank pages fast enough. I got through 825 pages for the orchestral score of my new opera, *The Violins of Saint-Jacques*, and fought like a cat with everyone. You've got to have good eyes and good health to be a composer. I compose from my heart, from my lungs, from my crotch. It comes out of what food I've eaten, what films I've seen. I sing and I dance as I write and my heart beats faster all the time.'
>
> He gets up at 6.30 each morning, drinks several glasses of lemon juice and honey, and composes till lunch. He's back at it after lunch till he falls asleep about eleven. When there's a panic he often works all night. 'I get a terrific feeling of pride and arrogance when I've worked through the night. Not that anybody knows, of course, except my wife. She's pretty bored really, but she always pats me on the back.'

The Violins of Saint-Jacques, Malcolm's finest opera, was his second commission from Sadler's Wells. Two years earlier, during *English Eccentrics*, Malcolm and Billy Chappell had chatted about possible further projects, Chappell suggesting Patrick Leigh Fermor's short novel from which the opera takes it name. As soon as Malcolm read the story, about a volcanic eruption on a Caribbean island at the turn of the century, he at once sensed its possibilities and asked Chappell not only to direct it but also to provide him with a libretto. Chappell later wrote about the creative process in his usual good humour:

> My apprehension increased when, during our preliminary discussions, Malcolm made me firmly aware of the librettist's role. 'You,' he told me, 'have to realise that the librettist is the slave of the composer. He must accept that he is to be trampled underfoot. He must be meek, submissive and totally obedient'.[109]

Interviewed on the same subject, Malcolm gave more details:

> Librettists always give me the first draft, at my request, in a very rough state indeed. Then I go through it with a blue pencil and I write new words of my own and reshape the whole thing. In every instance I have done this. I spend months doing this, constantly changing, and then I do a typescript myself. Then I start to compose. A lot of what comes in the first draft of the vocal score is with my own indifferent words which I then throw back at the librettist asking him to provide something better. To write a libretto requires the patience of a saint…[110]

109 *Musical Events*, November 1966

110 *Sadler's Wells Magazine*, Autumn 1966

Chappell's commitment as director meant he could ill afford to be meek and submissive:

> My two-headed role made me automatically challenging, defensive and eager to salvage every moment in the book with exciting directorial possibilities... The battle was prolonged, bloody, sometimes hysterical, never dull!

Two months before the first performance, in the heat of a particularly big argument, Malcolm declared he would ask the Sadler's Wells director and librettist, Edmund Tracey, to take over as his collaborator, Chappell taking refuge in a visit to Dublin, from where he wrote to Malcolm:

> My dear Carabosse,
>
> I received your letter of ill tidings and feel there is little to say about it except that I'm shocked and hurt at your unkind and unfriendly tone – and can only say if the little confidence you see in the words is carried through into your attitude to the production – then God help us all.
>
> There will be those who will much enjoy Tracey being brought in to salvage the ruin I have apparently made of the libretto, but as I see I am not supposed to have any feelings of any kind, I'll say no more.
>
> Really, Malcolm.
>
> PS I am sure I shall be more than thrilled with your music. As to words I prefer to reserve my opinion. Now I know why opera librettos are so ghastly and banal.[111]

Fortunately the quarrel was immediately patched up, for Malcolm needed the experienced Chappell, whose summary of the staging requirements show the vivid theatricality of the piece:

> The Prologue is set in the open sea in modern times. A fishing boat is discovered. The six fishermen, going about their business, are interrupted by the sound of violins. One old fishermen knows what that means. The island of Saint-Jacques, destroyed by a volcano many years ago, is rising from the waters, just as legend says it does every year in the month of the Carnival. Terrified, they row for their lives. The island slowly rises from the darkened sea. The scene gradually changes into the tangled jungle that covers the lower slopes of the volcano of Salpetriere, the setting for Act One.
>
> Act Two takes place first in the ballroom of Beausejour, the house of the Count de Serindan, the leading aristocrat on the island, and secondly in a picturesque street by the harbour. Act Three begins back in the ballroom. It is just before dawn, and a great languor has settled over the party. Not long afterwards comes the eruption: There is a sudden tremendous roar from the volcano. The walls of the ballroom crack open. Smoke and flames erupt through the windows. Darkness; flares of light; screams; confusion.
>
> An interlude leads to the last scene, where the solitary survivor, the young governess Berthe, is alone in a boat...

Scenically, therefore, the opera offered great scope and challenge. But, as Chappell was aware, there was a need to compromise spatially between the requirements of spectacle and the intimate nature of the love story:

---

111 26 September 1966

> Visually the opera needs a vast stage to cope with Peter Rice's tropical settings of the open sea, the jungles, streets and great houses of a volcanic island in the Caribbean in 1902, an island ruled by a French Creole aristocracy, kind yet autocratic, effete yet vigorous; these settings call for space. In opposition to this the intricate relationships of the characters demand an intimacy of treatment and performance, which the small size of the stage and auditorium at Sadler's Wells can only enhance.[112]

The love story was distinctly controversial. Sosthene, son of the Count de Serindan, loves Berthe, the family's governess, who loves Josephine (Sosthene's younger sister), who loves Marcel (who, unknown to most, already has a wife but is trying to persuade Josephine to elope with him)… In 1966 the love of woman for woman, expressed unequivocally in the opera, was a very startling topic for the stage, and in a pre-performance interview for the *Sadler's Wells Magazine* Edmund Tracey did his best to play it down. Malcolm, however, preferred to be explicit:

> Berthe is a sexual deviant and, like Lot's wife, is outside life. When the holocaust comes she gets left behind. This characteristic of sexual deviation makes her something of an observer, with additional awareness. She cannot procreate and is therefore outside the life stream and outside the death of the Saint-Jacques community.[113]

Tracey tried to modify this view:

> But surely, though Berthe begins as a sort of crypto-Lesbian with a crush on Josephine by the end of the second act she has managed to respond to Sosthene's declaration of love?'

Malcolm would have none if it:

> I wouldn't have thought she had matured at all! I think she is constant. It is Sosthene who has matured, and the romantic duet that he and Berthe have at the end of Act Two shows him no longer the supplicant that he was at the beginning, but a man who is determined to dominate Berthe. Berthe is unchanged. She never in fact says that she loves Sosthene. She wants warmth and comfort from him, but this doesn't change her at all. Not that I regard Berthe's deviant character in any way immature. She is simply a static character outside the growing lives of the others. She hasn't changed and she won't change, but she has had a terrible shock to discover that the little girl she loves is in love with a man. She is further shocked to discover that that man is married. She has to stop. She tries to persuade herself that she wants to stop, and she allows herself to be dominated by Sosthene, she warms to him very much, wondering at the change in him. But I feel that her heart is still with Josephine.

The situation is fully explored in the first act. Challenged by Sosthene that she does not really love him, Berthe sings softly:

> How can I explain to you
> Something I do not understand myself?
> A love that is not love, yet fills my entire being.

---

112 *Sadler's Wells Magazine*, Autumn 1966

113 *ibid.*

> Josephine is my sacred charge.
> Our friendship is an idyll, and like an idyll possesses
> Everything primitive and innocent.

Then comes an aria, one of the opera's great highlights, in which the luxuriance of Billy Chappell's language, matched by the richness of Malcolm's music, perfectly captures Berthe's passionate but threatened feelings.

> Each afternoon,
> When the cooling breezes swoon and die
> In the golden heat of the siesta hour,
> There we meet
> In our room beneath the roof of Beausejour
> And there we live in a magic world –
> a bubble of bright air.
>
> One side the sea,
> Where the white bright sun
> Burns like a phoenix on the vast horizon.
> The other side the woods,
> The tangled green of the jungle,
> And the cone of the volcano
> Trailing his plumes of smoke on the blue air.
>
> We are quite alone
> When the cooling breezes swoon and die
> In the golden indolence of the siesta hour.
> Each precious moment
> Like the falling petals of a summer flower
> Bestows sweet benediction on the hours we share –
> A bubble of bright air.

Divided strings hover above her voice, hinting at (but never quoting) the lovers' music in Verdi's *Falstaff*, while the aria is characterised by Malcolm's subtle modulations, his skilful ambiguity of keys reflecting the sexual ambiguities which lie at the heart of the opera.

As usual Malcolm wrote the score with those who would sing it in mind. Sosthene was specifically written for tenor David Hillman, who remembers rehearsing Acts One and Two with Malcolm and Billy Chappell still wrestling over the third act. Sometimes emotions in rehearsal could be volcanic:

> Malcolm turned up at one rehearsal to be shocked to discover that Billy Chappell had changed some of the words! It caused one of his famous outbursts! He became angrier and angrier, seized hold of my copy and started screwing it up, promising, as he did so, to withdraw the opera! He was extremely temperamental and would get very angry with almost everyone, except the singers.[114]

April Cantelo has only happy memories. Berthe was the favourite of her many Williamson roles, despite an anxiety about having to begin her

114 January 2006

performance with top notes sung offstage (as Berthe searched for the missing Josephine):

> There wasn't much which could be done about that, though I think Malcolm modified one note by a third. He wrote so beautifully for the voice, that I can't remember any other anxieties or problems, though everyone, when first seeing a role, would say 'Oh my God!' before realising that it wasn't quite as difficult as it at first had seemed! Malcolm was very stable at the time, very family-orientated. I had happy visits to their home. He cared a great deal about things going right for people in their lives. I found him extremely sympathetic and caring…[115]

John Fryatt, whose portrayal of the foppish Captain Joubert brought welcome comedy, agrees. He also remembers Malcolm's constant admiration for the singers.

> The music was wonderful to sing, really wonderful. And the staging so effective! The eruption of the volcano was done marvellously in the original production. It began with an armchair catching fire. There was huge smoke and excitement! In the revivals it was less effective. A blackout, and a few puffs of smoke at either end of the stage! That was all you got![116]

The premiere took place on 29 November 1966, Malcolm arriving at the theatre hobbling on a stick having embarrassingly just torn his Achilles tendon by trying to cheer Dolly up by doing silly jumps in the air. It did not prevent him taking some loud and enthusiastic curtain calls afterwards. *The Violins of Saint-Jacques* was very well received on its initial six performances and was equally happily revived over the next four years, at Sadler's Wells as well as on tour in Leeds, Stratford, Manchester and Glasgow, and finally, in 1970, at London's Coliseum (into which English National Opera had just moved).

The critics on the whole disliked its tunefulness. Desmond Shawe-Taylor, for example, bridled at arias as simple and appealing as Marcel's 'I have another world to show you':

> At such moments we feel *The Violins of Saint-Jacques* to be the grand opera that Ivor Novello would have written if he had enjoyed the benefits of full conservatoire training.[117]

The Times struggled to cope with Malcolm's ability to carry forward the traditions of the past:

> It was the refusal of Williamson's new opera to align itself with any of the recognisable stylistic concepts of music-drama in the 1960s that called the originality of the music into question… It is clear that this is the music he prefers to write, doubtless because it makes contact with audiences who stop at *Turandot*, but it is ostrich music! Peter Pan music! And we cannot help wishing that this extraordinarily talented composer will, as soon as possible, be his age and write adult creative music…[118]

115 August 2005

116 January 2006

117 *Sunday Times*, 4 December 1966

118 30 November 1966

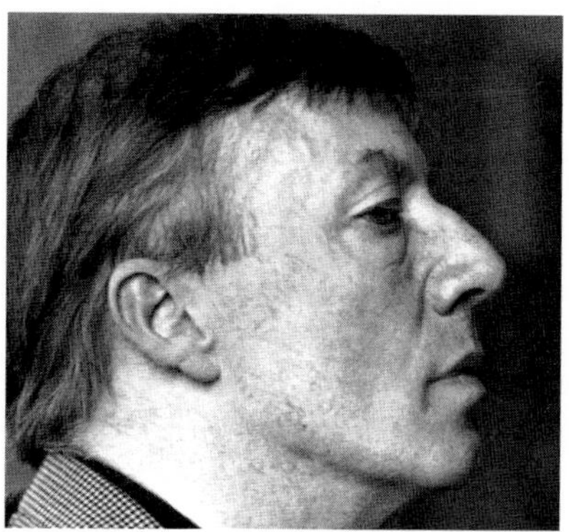

The multi-talented William Chappell

Glorious sets and costume designs by Peter Rice embellished the opera

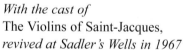

With the cast of The Violins of Saint-Jacques, *revived at Sadler's Wells in 1967*

Peter Heyworth summed up with grim irony:

> To hell with modernism and all its works, his score seems to proclaim. Why should a composer be afraid of a good square tune or a juicy harmonic sequence? Were Rossini and Donizetti, or for that matter Verdi and Mozart, too proud or too squeamish to give the public and the singers what they wanted? What opera suffers from today is too much art and too little success. Such seems to be the point of view underlying Mr Williamson's score![119]

Billy Chappell, writing to Malcolm after the first performance to send his love and thank him for the gift of a book, was unmoved by the mixed reviews:

> The notices for Violins were much as I expected. Smug, arrogant, narrow-minded and condescending – but I don't think we need bother. Public opinion is what matters and I haven't heard a single voice from the audiences who are not delighted with the piece – and seem particularly pleased with all the aspects that the half-baked critics carped about…[120]

The BBC's John Manduell was equally positive:

> I am writing to say how much I enjoyed last night. I hope you were pleased. Don't take any notice of the snobs.[121]

Not all the critics were hostile. *The Spectator*'s Charles Reid was particularly eloquent:

> Malcolm Williamson is being impeached up hill and down dale (a) for writing tunes in Richard Strauss-Puccini idioms, (b) for writing tunes that aren't good enough, and (c) for being so archaic as to write tunes at all.
>
> I heard the work twice with a lot of enjoyment (I wasn't alone in this) and spent some time with the vocal score to get those debated tunes more firmly in my head. They are of two kinds: heartstring tunes and frivolous ones. Of the heart-stringers the best is 'Let me one day return' sung by Josephine. The elegiac mezzo line (supremely singable, like most of Williamson's vocal lines) is supported by harmonies that have shade and warmth and cool and sadness in them. It so hooked me that I went back repeatedly to my piano for the pleasure of it. Strauss-Puccini idiom? Emphatically yes. And who cares? Why the guilty sackcloth and the weeping? What Mr Williamson proves is that the Strauss-Puccini seam isn't worked out; that a composer may exploit it still without copycatting, with an accent and palmprint of his own.[122]

Reid painted a vivid picture of the fevered festivities of the Second Act:

> For buoyancy (brilliance too) the Mardi Gras scenes are the thing. In a 1902 ballroom (French West Indies) Creole servants (bare feet and perruques) do an opening chorus as titillating as the sourbets and soursoups they're carrying by the trayful. An offstage band sets everybody gyrating with waltz suites whose provenance goes back as far as Weber and the young Chopin… Whether written in 1820 or 1966 a tune is a tune is a tune… Into the dance-cum-chorus complexities of the Mardi Gras Mr Williamson

119 *Observer*, 4 December 1966

120 8 December 1966

121 30 November 1966. Manduell was Chief Assistant, Music Programmes at the time.

122 9 December 1966

Hertford Avenue at the time of The Violins of Saint-Jacques

adroitly weaves up to a dozen alternating or combining strands of 'character' music (Jennifer Vyvyan's comic Mathilde, John Fryatt's pansy Joubert and Owen Brannigan's bumbling host are collectors' pieces) as well as haunting creole quartet music…

Edward Greenfield was another enthusiast:

> With the daring that takes the breath away Williamson has thrown aside all idea of writing an advanced opera in the interests of communicating with the widest possible public. The apparently guileless melodies and opulent orchestration hide a great deal of art and a great deal of structural cunning. With the help of his librettist he has turned an unlikely source into a richly emotional drama in which the relationships between characters come to life in big bold arias, duets and ensembles introduced Puccini-style. What is more Williamson has again shown that, like Puccini, he has a natural flair for creating atmosphere…[123]

In March 1967, not long after *The Violins of Saint-Jacques* had finished its first run, Malcolm enjoyed the sixth and last of his stage successes in this short five-year period, a ballet created by Frederick Ashton on the work written for the opening of the Third Programme, *Sinfonietta*.[124] Two years earlier Ashton had been impressed by *The Display* when it was brought to Covent Garden by Australian Ballet, and at a post-performance dinner he toasted Malcolm in

123 *The Guardian*, 30 November 1966

124 Billy Chappell sowed the seeds of this project. Once a fellow student with Ashton at Marie Rambert's dance school and a lifelong friend, Chappell had several times urged Ashton to consider using Malcolm's music, plying him with LPs.

Les Noces, *Covent Garden, 1966: with John Gardner, Bronislava Nijinska, Edmund Rubbra, Richard Rodney Bennett and John Lanchbery*

champagne and invited him home to discuss possible collaborations.[125] A few months later Malcolm was one of four celebrity pianists for the first night of the revival at Covent Garden of Nijinska's *Les Noces*, Ashton writing to him afterwards:

> Thank you so much for coming to thump out 'Les Noces'. You four greatly added to the success of the evening with your distinguished names and Mme Nijinska was most appreciative as indeed am I that you were able to find the time to collaborate with us.
>
> You must do a creation for us. What? Please think.
>
> Yours ever,
>
> Freddie [126]

The collaboration over *Sinfonietta* followed, Malcolm adding a short Prelude at Ashton's request. The ballet ('An attempt by the master to swing with the times'[127]) was unhelpfully influenced by Ashton's current infatuation for Martyn Thomas, who suggested a psychedelic lighting design, the 'set' simply being strange shapes and colours projected onto a blank screen upstage. Thomas, who himself had a liking for pink trousers and Mr Fish shirts, also encouraged costumes garish enough to cause a stir even on the King's Road.

Malcolm later gave Ashton's biographer an account of the collaboration:

> Freddie said 'I'm not musical like Mrs Chappell.[128] I have to sit up night after night with a wet towel on my head to absorb the music.' He was meticulous about minutage

125 Julie Kavanagh, *Secret Muses*, pp. 491-2

126 29 March 1966

127 Kavanagh, *Secret Muses*, p.491

128 William Chappell. Chappell was later to edit the letters of his lifelong partner, the painter Edward Burra, under the title *Well, Dearie*.

> down to a quarter of a minute and the ballet followed the [musical] structure so brilliantly that you couldn't tell which had come first.[129]

There were the inevitable pre-performance tensions. When Malcolm interfered one late rehearsal, suggesting the orchestra was playing the Tarantella too slowly, Ashton turned on him fiercely. 'All right! We'll do it at *your* tempo and *ruin* the ballet!'

Sinfonietta, which was given over sixty performances in 1967-68 by the touring company (today's Birmingham Royal Ballet) including several at Covent Garden, was far from the total failure ballet history has since declared it.[130] Critics were complimentary about the 'vigorous' score.[131] The Toccata was 'lively and capricious', the Elegy 'slow and lyrical', the Tarantella 'bracing and sharp'. John Percival loved the Elegy (which Malcolm had originally written for Rebecca):

> A long adagio for Doreen Wells and five cavaliers; strange, slow and remote, one of those solemn passages which Ashton always handles so well. Here given a crystalline, almost icy freshness.[132]

The Toccata, according to James Kennedy, inspired Ashton to provide 'a talented dancer (the small strong athletic Brenda Last) with more suitable choreography than any ballet has ever given her', while the Tarantella made for 'an effective, gay and highly musical finale'.

Malcolm himself was thrilled with Ashton's choreography, saw little wrong with the psychedelic lighting and quickly rushed onwards to new endeavours. As soon as *Sinfonietta* had been given its first performance, at Stratford-upon-Avon, he was on the South Bank for the opening of the Queen Elizabeth Hall.[133] Arthur Bliss, as Master of the Queen's Music, had asked Benjamin Britten to give an hour's concert of British music with the English Chamber Orchestra. Dances from *Gloriana* were to be the main feature, but also four new folk song arrangements. Three months earlier, just days before the opening of *The Violins of Saint-Jacques*, Malcolm had written to Britten:

> My dear Ben,
>
> Thank you for asking me to do the folk song. I'd love to. When should the score and parts be ready?
>
> As I am one of the few old-fashioned composers left who write in keys or modes, I should like to know what the other songs are tonic-wise, so that I don't overbalance the key sequence.

---

129 Kavanagh, p. 492

130 David Vaughan in *Frederick Ashton and his Ballets* suggested it was 'the banality of the music' which prevented its survival. The bizarre lighting and costumes were the likelier culprits. Brenda Last recalls that the music was anything but banal.

131 Alexander Bland, *The Observer*, 12 February 1967.

132 *The Times*, 11 February 1967

133 1 March 1967

> Rehearsals at Sadler's Wells are going bumpily but some daylight emerges.
> Gloriana [at Sadler's Wells] certainly triumphed all round! The Wells begins to look like a home for British opera. May it be a home of entertainment at the same time!
> Love to you both,
> Malcolm [134]

Britten replied with suggestions about keys ('and how wise you are to use 'em still!') wishing him 'a rousing success'. Two weeks before the opening of the Hall Malcolm sent Britten the full score of the three-minute arrangement of 'Mowing The Barley':

> I hope my manuscript makes sense to you, but you'll know what to do tempo-wise. There is a possible solo for Peter, except that a mezzo voice of comparable dramatic gifts would be required to balance it. Whatever you think.

Britten responded with warmth:

> My dear Malcolm,
> I've just been sent the score of 'Mowing The Barley'. It looks excellent and amusing and will, I know, be a very good end to our rather mad programme! Thank you so very much for doing it. Do you want to come to a rehearsal – Sue can tell you when they are.
> Yours ever,
> Ben [135]

If Malcolm had been angling for mezzo-soprano Nancy Evans to sing before the Queen, he was unsuccessful. Pears sang all four folk songs. But Malcolm was more than happy, for after the concert he was formally presented to the Queen by Arthur Bliss.

There was still no time for a break. As each commission was completed, another began.[136] The final two works of this period, *The Moonrakers* and *Dunstan and the Devil* exemplify Malcolm's ability to write at completely different stylistic levels. *The Moonrakers* is particularly important in being the first of his 'cassations', short and undemanding choral works for young people, designed to be a very gentle introduction to opera.[137] Commissioned for performance at the Dome in the Brighton Festival, *The Moonrakers* is written for three groups of singers – smugglers, villagers and Revenue Men – and is set in a

---

134 15 November 1966

135 Undated card from The Red House

136 The first work premiered after the opening of the Queen Elizabeth Hall was in fact Malcolm's *Serenade* for flute, piano, violin, viola and cello, which Australian friends Douglas Whittaker and Geoffrey Parsons had commissioned for a concert in the new Purcell Room. (8 March 1967)

137 *The Moonrakers* was first produced on 22 April 1967. In the 18th century the title 'cassation' was given to a divertimento-like work made up of several movements. Mozart wrote two seven-movement cassations.

village on the south coast in the 1780s. The synopsis, devised by Malcolm, is delightfully simple:

> On a dark night the villagers creep from their houses to wait at the dockside. As the church strikes two, the song of the smugglers is heard as their ship sails into the cove and ties up at the dock. Smugglers and villagers take barrels and kegs of brandy from the hold of the ship, and heave them through the village streets into the open country.
>
> The King's Revenue Men, patrolling the coast on horseback, are heard approaching. Hastily, the villagers and smugglers push their barrels and kegs into a large pond, just before the Revenue Men appear on the scene. 'What are you doing here?' ask the Revenue Men. Villagers and smugglers take on the expressions of country simpletons; they pretend to think that the moon's reflection in the pond is real gold, and that they can rake it to the banks.
>
> Convinced that all is innocent, the Revenue Men shrug their shoulders and ride away. When all is clear the smugglers return to their ship, and as the church clock strikes three sail out to sea, while the villagers return to their houses.

The enthusiastic family man:

(above) with Dolly, Dolly's parents, Peter, Tammy and Clare

(right) with Peter, Tammy and his father-in-law, Jacob Danielovich, 1966

Several hundred children turned up at Brighton's Dome for the first ever cassation. As pianist, director and general centre-of-attention, Malcolm was in his element, his enthusiasm and electric personality ensuring that the one-hour rehearsal was not just enormous fun but practically effective. First he taught the music, then put in the movements and gestures – the acting in cassations being as important as the singing – and finally merged the two. An eight-minute 'performance' followed, an exciting culmination to the workshop, with every available prop and costume being seized upon. No-one was allowed to sit and watch, not even the children's parents. Everyone had to participate. Total non-singers were put into an 'orchestra' to make simple sound effects.

Dunstan and the Devil, by contrast, was an hour-long opera for adults written for church performance, and, as such, clearly influenced by Britten's *Curlew River* and *The Burning Fiery Furnace* which just preceded it. The enthusiastic Festival Committee of the Berkshire village of Cookham (known mainly for Stanley Spencer and Kenneth Grahame) had raised £300 for a work featuring their church's patron saint, Dunstan. Malcolm, still working at a frenetic pace, decided to fit the attractive commission into his overcrowded schedule, not in the least concerned that his fiercest critics might make much of the fact that Cookham was something of a musical backwater. *The Observer*'s Peter Heyworth did not disappoint:

> You will not find Cookham listed among the European Association of Music Festivals and for that matter Malcolm Williamson's little opera *Dunstan and the Devil*, written for the church, is unlikely to feature prominently in the annals of twentieth-century music. But that anyone should find it odd that a village bent on festivity should enlist the services of a living composer precisely underlines what is troubling so much present-day music.
>
> No doubt the result is not great art. But Mr Williamson is exactly the sort of composer who thrives on commissions of this sort. Skilful, fluent and abundantly fecund, he would have felt perfectly at home in some minor eighteenth-century court, turning out a multitude of works for all manner of occasions from a funeral to a dance, and very well he would have done it. As it is, he is fated to live in a century that offers few functions to a composer of his sort and cruelly spurns everything that is not a masterpiece. But to my judgement Mr Williamson is often more at ease when he is fulfilling a modest commission such as Cookham offered…[138]

A modest commission indeed it might have been, but Malcolm took the same pleasure in writing for Cookham as for Aldeburgh or Sadler's Wells. Chris Smythe, a member of the commissioning committee, remembers him spending much time in discussion with the local director, exploring the scope of the work and optimum number of parts. Malcolm attended the auditions and also several rehearsals, always a flamboyant figure, sometimes mysterious in dark spectacles and with a camel coat slung over his shoulders, in the manner of Goossens:

138 21 May 1967

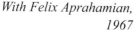

With Felix Aprahamian, 1967

> He was very agreeable, never interfering, nothing but supportive. He sometimes stayed on after rehearsals, in sessions when we put the world to rights, and I sensed on these occasions that he wasn't really as confident in himself as the outward show suggested.[139]

As usual he did his best to exploit the media. The opera, he announced to the *Maidenhead Advertiser*, would be 'camp and funny', the devil providing most of the laughter as, in various disguises, he attempts to tempt the saint.[140] But, as the final rehearsals took place, only he knew the *dénouement*. Malcolm was heavily over-committed – ten days before the Cookham premiere he was in Debrecen for Hungarian performances of *Our Man In Havana* – and tempers understandably became frayed as the singers faced the prospect of an opera with no conclusion. John Grover, vicar of St Dunstan's at the time, was one of the concerned onlookers:

> Malcolm was virtually writing out the last of the four scenes during the dress rehearsal. That's a lot of music! He and his wife and children stayed with us at the vicarage for two or three days during the time of the performances. They liked to go to bed very late and rise at midday, which didn't always fit in with a vicarage routine! We had a party at the vicarage after the first performance – a very lively affair indeed! My word![141]

---

139 September 2005

140 In one scene, for example, Dunstan is working in his cell on a pair of candlesticks as the devil come tempting. Dunstan takes his tongs from the furnace, chases the devil as he becomes a viper, a bear and a fox, and finally tweaks his nose.

141 September 2005

Such was Malcolm's reputation that the performances attracted most of the musical press. In view of the haste with which the opera had been assembled it was unsurprising that some critics, like Andrew Porter, were a little ambivalent:

> *Dunstan and the Devil* was too grandly described as an opera; it is a village-church-pageant, a miracle-play-cum-musical, closer in genre to *Noye's Fludde* than to *Curlew River*... The music? Deft, unelaborated, eclectic, a touch of gregorianism, chant reminiscent of the 'Noe from the Waters' section of *Gerontius* alternating with a lively catchy worksong for Dunstan that could drop straight into a musical...[142]

William Mann, by contrast, was extremely impressed:

> *Dunstan and the Devil* is a direct, scrupulously judged score; the composition is quite elaborate, with particularly enjoyable ensembles and choruses in varied moods. The music had radiance, even the keenly characterised devil's music, and even the passages where external influence seems incompletely digested (Dunstan's praising God in the accents of Nick Shadow, for example).[143] Williamson's expertise allows him to circulate fluently in musical climates of all sorts... Sophisticated persons might be dismayed by this newest opera, but it seems to me as much a *tour-de-force* as *The Violins of Saint-Jacques*...[144]

The Moonrakers and *Dunstan and the Devil* were an apt conclusion to a five-year period of richly diverse achievement. Malcolm's muse had rarely failed him, and now, at thirty-six, he was a composer and performer of real consequence. At last, therefore, after nearly fifteen years away from Australia, he could consider a return, for, like several other contemporary expatriates – Joan Sutherland, Charles Mackerras, Keith Michell and Leo McKern – he had an undeniable success story to tell. Accordingly, when a timely invitation for a short return was offered, he accepted it. He had left Sydney in 1952 on the slow-moving *Otranto*; he would return more speedily by aeroplane. In the new age of easy travel, expatriate Australians who stayed away long periods were viewed back home, at best, with wariness, though Malcolm, fully occupied with his non-stop labours, was naively unaware of this. Despite his long residence in Britain Malcolm still saw himself as Australian through and through. Others would see him very differently. Malcolm's long crisis of identity was about to begin.

---

142 *Financial Times*, 22 May 1967

143 In Stravinsky's *The Rake's Progress* the devil comes along in the form of Nick Shadow to tempt a country lad with promises of more excitements than he can even imagine. Mann has touched on one of Malcolm's greatest influences. At the time of *Violins* Malcolm declared *The Rake's Progress* 'a monumental masterpiece', the greatest opera of the century. (In the same context, Britten's music was 'superbly clear' and 'superbly theatrical'; Tippett had 'enormous flair for the theatre'; and he loved 'the lamentably neglected late works of Strauss – superbly theatrical pieces like *Arabella* and *Capriccio*'.)

144 *The Times*, 19 May 1967

8
A MONTH IN AUSTRALIA
The Canberra Festival, 1967

MALCOLM FLEW FROM HEATHROW full of optimism. He would enjoy being the leading guest at the three-day Canberra Spring Festival organised by Musica Viva, and a busy month away would also include making several guest celebrity appearances in other parts of Australia as well as recordings for the Australian Broadcasting Commission.[1] Although he was disappointed at leaving Dolly[2] and the children in England, he was keen to further his career in his home country and was justifiably proud of his achievements – his stage successes, the breadth of his published catalogue and his expertise as performer, lecturer and broadcaster – which no other Australian composer could begin to match.

He had, it was true, heard some disconcerting things about the 'tall poppy syndrome'[3] and Australian wariness towards expatriates, but the country was not yet subject to the fierce nationalism shortly to engulf it. Sir Robert Menzies, who had once famously declared himself 'British to the bootstraps', had only just retired as Prime Minister; two years previously Joan Sutherland, who had spent as long a time away in Europe as Malcolm, had been rapturously received on her return; and so many top-class Australian musicians were overseas in 1967 that a complete orchestra could have been made from them.[4] Yet there were already some signs of changing times. The Qantas Airways Boeing 707, on which Malcolm travelled out, had only recently changed its name and livery from The

[1] Musica Viva, one of the country's most prestigious musical organisations, was originally founded to bring the best of chamber groups to Australia.

[2] They had, however, spent that August together in America, Malcolm participating with the small ensemble which gave the first performance of his *Pas de Quatre* at the Metropolitan Opera Festival at Newport, Rhode Island.

[3] An Australian term for the national characteristic of being dismissive towards the successful out of envy. Expatriates were particular targets.

[4] The comment came from a frustrated member of the Sydney Symphony Orchestra. (Alomes: *When London Calls*, p.147)

Qantas *Empire* Airways. More ominously, the phrase 'cultural cringe' was being bandied about in Australia to describe an exaggerated deference to the old world in the arts.

One of the strongest opponents of the 'cultural cringe' was Roger Covell, music critic of the *Sydney Morning Herald* and a Senior Lecturer at the University of New South Wales, who was determined Australia should cease to be 'one of the final refuges of the arrière-garde in music'. Covell had just written an important book, *Australia's Music, Themes of a New Society*, which not only summarised the past but laid out a radical agenda for the future. If the 'cultural cringe' were ever to be eliminated, thought Covell, it would be necessary for Australian composers to ignore the avant-garde elsewhere in the world and develop music which was even more futuristic – serialism acting as a springboard for a radical post-serialism, rejecting all such traditional devices as 'conformist' melody, relative tonality and recurrent rhythm patterns. Covell's view was not an isolated one, but shared by growing numbers of Australians in higher education and the media. Malcolm was returning to a country which, far from being cosily conservative, was highly radical. As Derek Strahan has commented:

> Concertgoers might have been forgiven for concluding that there existed a national conspiracy to confuse, bemuse, abuse and only occasionally, and then inadvertently, amuse audiences with an unrelenting flow of works of unrelenting modernity, whose purpose, as stated in programme notes, was to educate, but never to do anything so vulgar as to entertain.[5]

Malcolm was looking forward to challenging Australia's new radicalism at the Canberra Festival, in which a series of chamber concerts would be a background to seminars organised by Covell himself. Malcolm had been taken to task in *Australia's Music* for scorning the determination of many young Australian composers to be up-to-date, Covell quoting some flamboyant and ill-considered remarks which Malcolm had made two years earlier:

> I abhor more than I can say the occasional signs from Australia that it is desirable to attain a European chic… I have seen a number of my fellow composers treating the musical profession as a rat-race, feeling a rivalry with the most progressive continental musical centres… In this race they see Pierre Boulez firing a Schoenbergian starter's pistol, and each feels he must win or perish. It is pathetic to see symptoms of this attitude in Australian music of today.[6]

Covell pointed out very reasonably that Malcolm himself was not averse to a pursuit of the chic; and that to hope Australia would ignore international musical trends was like wishing the scene of one's childhood always to remain as charmingly old-fashioned as it existed in the memory.

---

5 Strahan: *Australian Music Past, Present and Future* (Part 1) (Internet: Revolve: Australian Classical Music)

6 Malcolm was speaking at a conference on Music and Education in the Commonwealth, held at the University of Liverpool in 1965.

Covell then wrote at length on Malcolm's music, introducing him as 'a somewhat defiant conservative'. The problem for all conservative composers, he explained, was that 'writing in an idiom on its way to becoming fossilized… takes nothing less than genius to stand up to the comparisons of established masters of this idiom'.[7] He proceeded to analyse Malcolm's music, not wholly to its advantage, in this context: the Violin Concerto was 'sub-Prokofiev grotesquerie'; the *Sinfonietta* indebted to Prokofiev and neo-classic Stravinsky; the *Travel Diaries* had an 'obvious and honourable debt' to Bartok's piano music for children, the *Symphony For Voices* 'an obvious debt' to Britten. *The Display* paid tribute to Stravinsky and Britten. Ravel, Britten, Copland and Liszt were all there in the Third Piano Concerto, parts of which Covell liked – 'at least it's worth arguing about' – which was more than could be said for the First Piano Concerto, where the influence of Ravel was overwhelmed by that of 'composers of successful pop songs' resulting in a work 'which pleads for public favour with disarming frankness'. Covell had not seen scores of the three full-length operas, but he had heard *The Happy Prince* on LP and felt it 'soft-centred' despite its 'obvious debt' to Britten. Of the 'uninhibitedly eclectic' *Elevamini* Covell declared 'it would be hard to find a piece of music more generously derivative in idiom' and by way of proof cited Vaughan Williams, Nielsen, Britten, Stravinsky, Messiaen, Copland and 'Shostakovich-cum-Mahler'. Finally, in the book's appendix, Covell left the reader in no doubt as to where the true future lay. Whereas the five other speakers at the Canberra seminars (Nigel Butterley, George Dreyfus, Peter Sculthorpe, Larry Sitsky, and Felix Werder) were given an average of five musical examples each, the 'defiantly conservative' expatriate received just one. Fully aware, therefore, of the background to the Canberra Festival, Malcolm looked forward to some lively confrontations. There were important battles to be won.

He began badly. After flying in to Sydney on 11 September, Malcolm was rushed into a press conference, where jet-lag and an over-eagerness to make a big impression resulted in him being less than diplomatic. His attack on the Australian government's limited cultural objectives was a fair one, but the manner of its delivery made him sound insufferably opinionated:

> Cultural development should not hinge on the Sydney Opera House! We should be going to the grass roots – the children – and giving them opera in schools! The Government should pay huge, meaty commissions for children's operas. Then the next generation would grow up screaming for an opera house! The whole thing shouldn't centre on this building! If it crumbled tomorrow, we should still be able to have operatic life here. It's a pity to be building a great, flash opera house when the cultural situation is as bad as it is in Australia. These tiara'd ladies in their 20 dollar seats will want Sutherland and *Traviata*! I can't see them wanting horrible modern music![8]

[7] Roger Covell, *Australia's Music*, pp.171-178

[8] Sue Jordan, *Sydney Morning Herald*, 12 September 1967

George and Bessie

He stopped short of quoting Dame Nellie Melba's famous comment to Clara Butt on her fellow countrymen – 'Give em muck! It's all they can understand!' – but he made it quite clear that Australia, for all its hopes of a brave new opera house, was a cultural wilderness. Even when he had calmed down a little, he was still careless of giving offence:

> The composer, plump and pleasant, with slightly thinning blonde hair, tempered his criticism with good advice: 'Opera WILL find its feet here but only with lots and lots of financial support from the Government. Let's not have small inconsequential opera companies doing Gilbert and Sullivan and that muck.'

The next day, when the interview was fully reported in the national newspapers, Malcolm and Bessie had a chuckle over Gilbert and Sullivan's 'muck', for down the road from Blues Point Tower, where Bessie and George now lived, the Mosman Musical Society was currently putting the final touches to its production of *The Mikado*.

The Williamsons had moved into Blues Point Tower four years earlier. The tallest apartment block in Sydney, Harry Seidler's controversial building at McMahon's Point on the northern foreshore had initially so upset local opinion that the developers struggled to sell its 144 apartments, despite the attractiveness of the setting, two acres of parkland on the Paramatta waterfront.[9] The artistic Bessie, however, had at once seen the advantages of Blues Point – as had Rupert Murdoch, another of its early residents – and she and George bought a three-bedroom apartment on the twentieth of the twenty-five floors, facing across the harbour towards the heart of the city. Its far-reaching views included the nearby Harbour Bridge and, beyond, the unfinished Opera House.

Sydney's ambitious Opera House project was currently in absolute chaos, six years behind schedule, its estimated costs having risen from eight million dollars to fifty, its architect forced to resign, and the opening, once scheduled for 1963,

---

9 They had also acquired a cottage at Blackheath in the Blue Mountains just west of Sydney.

indefinitely postponed. Nonetheless Malcolm, as the most successful writer of opera in Australian history, nursed a proprietary interest in it as he gazed at it each day from Blues Point. The outer shell was at last complete, and though arguments were still raging about internal facilities, Malcolm looked forward eagerly to the day when he would participate in the Opera House's future.

So too did Bessie, her pride in Malcolm intensified by his long-awaited return. Diane remembers them both in a state of some exhilaration:

> Mother was extremely excited and proud of Malcolm's successes and they spent much time together in cheerful reminiscence, which would go on into the early hours, bedtime put off as mother would start on a new anecdote or Malcolm relate another funny story. We would move from room to room, with Malcolm and mother laughing and talking without pause…[10]

Though George had retired, Bessie was still very active, looking after the family and its business. Diane, now a full-time secretary, was living with her parents at Blues Point; Marion and her husband Brian were a couple of miles away at Killara. Brian was a cartographic surveyor but was currently working for the Banister Overalls Service, in which Bessie had given him a management job. The understanding was that Brian and Marion, who prepared the firm's monthly accounts, should eventually take the business over, but Bessie was reluctant to relinquish it.

For Marion and Diane it was frustrating that Malcolm was so busy catching up with old friends and furthering helpful contacts that they saw comparatively little of him; even when attending a large family dinner at Marion's, he spent most of the evening holding long conversations on the telephone. Diane, who at least saw something of him as she ferried him around Sydney in the evenings, eventually triumphed with Marion by taking him out to dinner at a restaurant without a telephone. Marion was disappointed by how self-absorbed her brother had become:

> He was very good with my young daughter when I visited Blues Point, but he was essentially preoccupied with his own affairs and probably, in comparison to his exciting life in the public eye, found us rather dull. He always made a great thing about his love for his family, but it didn't seem that he had a great interest in us in practice! He was not often to be found at Blues Point, and, when he was, he tended to be on the phone![11]

Malcolm's efforts to get to know Marion's husband Brian were only sporadic:

> Before our marriage Brian had spent two years in the Antarctic as a radio operator, surveyor and Base Leader, for which he received the Polar Medal. He wrote a book about his time there. I don't think Malcolm read it, but he keenly offered his help to get it published, though it came to nothing…

---

[10] June 2005

[11] July 2005

For Malcolm, each day was an important opportunity to further his career. While at Sydney, for example, he was heavily engaged with recordings for ABC. Nigel Butterley, who played the Sonata for Two Pianos with him, remembers the influence Malcolm wielded there:

> To the ABC in 1967, Malcolm was a big name, demanding immediate respect. The two-piano sonata, which we recorded for a broadcast, was, I'm sure, just one of several other works he recorded at the time. For he was Malcolm Williamson, and the ABC would agree to whatever he wanted to do![12]

Malcolm also rushed off to Melbourne for three days with Bernard Heinze, recording there his Second Piano Concerto, the piano part in *Sinfonia Concertante* and, at St Patrick's Cathedral, his Organ Symphony. Then came a hastily chartered flight to Newcastle, where the Conservatorium had organised a four-day 'Salute to Malcolm Williamson' and a Civic Reception hosted by the Mayor. Malcolm gave several talks but the highlight was a Newcastle Opera Workshop production of *The Happy Prince* at the Hunter Theatre, the first Williamson opera to be produced in Australia, for which Malcolm ran three workshops. Bessie, George, Marion and Diane took the Newcastle flyer down for the final performance. 'It was a memorable occasion for us,' remembers Diane, 'and very moving to see Malcolm come on stage at the end. Dad was very proud.'[13]

The object of wide admiration, leading a hectic bachelor life half a world away from suburban Surrey, Malcolm responded warmly to the relaxed, friendly atmosphere. As 'Guest of Honour' on ABC radio, he spoke approvingly of Sydney's youth and beauty:

> I've longed to be back in Australia... and now I'm here I'm stunned with admiration for so many things. The people – young people particularly – are terribly, quite exceptionally, good-looking, cordial and they're very forthright… It's extremely refreshing…[14]

No doubt he himself was equally cordial and forthright, but, as the interview shows, he was determinedly mixing business with pleasure, his priority to associate his name with the Opera House:

> When all the tumult and the shouting about the Opera House has died, and the Opera House has opened its doors, is the stable going to be full of live horses, or is it going to be a bejewelled museum for stuffed horses? Money should be poured into the commissioning of Australian operas, as well, of course, as Australian music… If a country is old enough to put up State Opera Houses, then it jolly well is old enough to engage its own composers to write for that Opera House; and it would be simply

---

12 Butterley found the two-piano sonata 'rather thickly written' but much admired the lyricism of his vocal writing: 'Malcolm had this wonderful ability to write something that was almost banal, almost ordinary, and then do something to it very unexpected in the harmony or the shape of the tune. To me that was his greatest skill.' (May 2006)

13 June 2005

14 24 September 1967

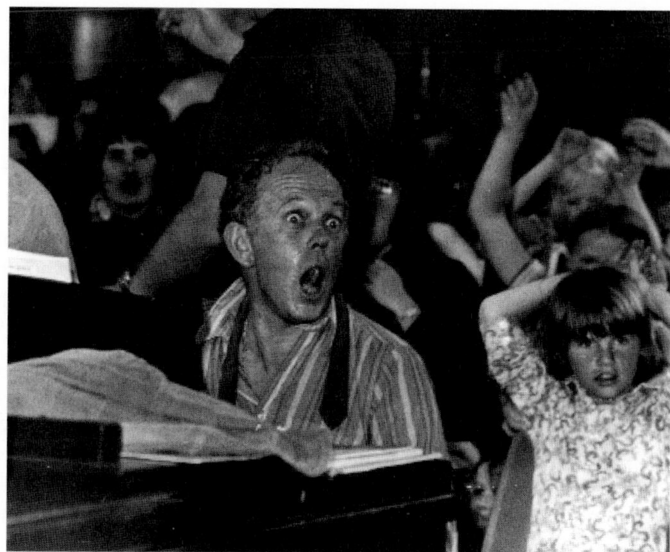

Business with pleasure: Malcolm was soon directing The Moonrakers *and other cassations all over the world*

> pathetic and laughable if Sydney Opera House, or any other Australian Opera House, were to open and survive entirely on the strength of the classics or imports of a contemporary nature…

Malcolm had made some good contacts in Sydney and there were strong possibilities of a commission for the opening. But reservations had been expressed about his long absence abroad, so Malcolm used every opportunity to stress his Australian credentials:

> Our Australian-ness comes through in our music as clearly as in the works of our painters. Of course, I don't mean that pieces of music with words like 'gumtree' in the title are necessarily more Australian than those with names like *Homage a Garcia Lorca.*[15] I mean rather that the brash, candid, no-nonsense character of Australia directs an Australian composer's thinking. He is fond of athletic exhilaration in music, and on the other hand is very self-conscious about the poetry of music.[16]

And so to Canberra. He was met off the plane by the Festival Committee's Chairman, Hazel Reader, who with her husband Ralph (a leading heart specialist) put Malcolm up at their home, Melrose Valley Farm, to the south of the city.

---

15 *Homage to Garcia Lorca*, a radical work for two string orchestras by Richard Meale, was described by Roger Covell as 'not merely a piece of music' but also 'a cataclysm'. Covell waxed lyrical about its strangeness: 'Whole passages of the music are, in essence, strikingly varied ways of articulating a twelve-note chord....' For Covell this was exactly the kind of work needed for Australia to rid itself of the 'cultural cringe'. The most radical of all his contemporaries, Meale had been invited to the Canberra Conference, but was unable to attend.

16 ABC broadcast, 24 September 1967

Hazel, who soon fell under Malcolm's spell, worked extremely hard on his behalf, forgetting about the toyshop she ran as she chauffeured him to, from and around the city and effecting in the process many useful introductions.

Well briefed by Hazel Reader and raring for the fray, Malcolm included in almost every interview a warning about the evils of music which failed to communicate:

> I worry about those who worship 'the newest'. The 'newest' can fade the fastest. It is very heartening to see a composer like Richard Strauss, who turned his back on 'the newest' after he formed his own personal style, attaining in the public mind much greater popularity today than his (rough) contemporary Arnold Schoenberg, who was passionately keen on being more 'modern' than tomorrow, being superficially original, and being newer and more shocking than what had gone before… It is a recurrent obsession with musicians that music should be something understandable only by them and only by a few of them. This is a particularly vicious contemporary musical disease, which is rampant in the 1960s in Australia….something the mature composer has to get over. He has to learn to communicate and practise communicating as clearly as possible rather than practising pulling the wool over people's eyes and making everything as obscure as he possibly can.[17]

The Spring Festival, enthusiastically supported by Prime Minister Harold Holt, was held at the newly-built Canberra Theatre complex, the severe concrete of the theatre's forecourt hinting at some of the music to come. The first-day audience, which included senior politicians and civil servants, seemed strangely formal and subdued on arrival, as if in readiness for possible ordeal by sound. Outside strong sunshine did its best to alleviate this heavy atmosphere, the magpies chattering noisily from the trees, and the rugged beauty of the Black Mountains, just a few hundred yards away, reminding Festival visitors of another, softer world.

Malcolm was encouraged by the presence of Bessie and Marion, who had travelled to Canberra to support him. They were particularly looking forward to seeing him participate in two of his recent chamber works: the Concerto for Wind Quintet and two Pianos; and the *Serenade* for Flute, Piano and String Trio. He was also to conduct a concert version of his cassation *The Moonrakers*, the whole audience acting as his singers.

Neither of the two chamber works suggests that Malcolm was as conservative as Covell intimated. The *Serenade* in particular shows him at his most enigmatic, by turns tonal and serial, providing his own unique answer to the confusions of the age. It has three titled movements, each describing (as Malcolm himself pointed out in a programme note) 'inanimate things which a child's imagination could imbue with life': a puppet theatre; a doll left out in the rain; and a toy circus with a carousel. In the first movement, written in elaborate sonata form,

---

17 This argument, articulated in more detail at the Conference, comes from an interview with Hazel de Berg, recorded on 8 October 1967 for the Oral Collection of the National Library of Australia.

dissonance lurks in every corner of the puppet theatre; there are strange harmonies, even in the central, more lyrical section, as the puppets perform their bitter-sweet dances; eventually, however, finally exhausted, they sink to rest in a very tonal conclusion. The drenched doll, by contrast, is given a lyrical and seemingly tonal melody of great beauty, but, as it develops, unexpected and dissonant notes punctuate its course. Malcolm provocatively stated in the Festival programme that this movement had 'the lyrical, circular and overlapping nine-eight feel of a Donizetti aria'; but, unlike Donizetti, it continually teases the ear as it floats in and out of consonance, with occasional highly tonal cadences marking the end of phrases. The toy circus and carousel of the finale display much of the razzamatazz of Malcolm's 2nd Piano Concerto, the opening based on strongly identifiable recurring rhythmic patterns (a feature much derided by the radicals) while occasional changes of metre help convey the playful character of the circus. It is an arresting, if acerbic, conclusion to a highly original exploration of a child's imagination.

But for the most of the critics present, Malcolm's two challenging chamber works were not nearly challenging enough.[18] Felix Werder's impenetrable sixth string quartet, by contrast, was roundly praised. Werder, a committed serialist who made few concessions to entertainment, was the senior of the six featured composers and much esteemed for having known the Schoenbergs personally as a boy, before fleeing from Hitler's Germany.[19] The other four composers, though also more 'advanced' than Malcolm and therefore more attractive to the critics, offered their own distinctive brand of modernity. Peter Sculthorpe, for example, like Malcolm, had experimented with serialism as a young man, only to develop in his own unique way outside it. By 1967 he had already created a specifically 'Australian' style with his *Sun Music* series, *Sun Music 1* (1965) depicting the power of the sun and the harsh desolation of the Australian landscape, *Sun Music III* (1967) incorporating for the first time traditional Asian music, from Bali. Although he had rejected serialism in the desire to uplift audiences, much of his work at the time was (wrote Covell) 'marked by a withdrawn, intensely personal

---

[18] Covell, for example, wrote that 'they required a good deal of agility and even virtuosity, but their musical value seemed to me much less'. (*Sydney Morning Herald*, 4 October 1967) Kenneth Hince found them 'fluent and professional, like his talk had been, but perhaps with less substance'. (*The Australian*, 3 October 1967)

[19] Werder was said by Covell to be someone 'who feels obliged to hide his more sensitive qualities behind a pugnacious assertive manner of speech and writing'. The same 'protective aggression' was evident in his music. (*Australia's Music*, p.183) Another critic described him as 'a storm centre in Australian music in the sixties': 'He creates tension so quickly in his works and remains on a high plateau for so long that emotionally one becomes detached through exhaustion. For these reasons Werder's work has often puzzled his audiences; they lack the stamina to follow his ideas through. Werder seems to expect from them the quick-wittedness and musical erudition he possesses himself.' (Radic, *Australian Composition in the Twentieth Century*, pp. 90-91). Covell thought Werder's Sixth String Quartet 'a brilliant and masterly work'.

quality' and he rarely exhibited 'the glitter of virtuosity so evident in much of Malcolm Williamson's work'. Of the other three featured composers, Nigel Butterley wrote music which was often deeply mystical and also reflected his interest in the ways recording technology could enlarge a work's scope; Larry Sitsky embraced experiments with music calculated by computer; and George Dreyfus, though deeply influenced in the 1960s by Boulez and Stockhausen, had such a sense of humour[20] that Covell sometimes despaired of him. ('His music is quite likely to slip on a banana skin of vulgarity.')[21]

In the seminars Sculthorpe and Werder discussed 'The Composer and New Sounds', and Butterley and Sitsky 'Composing For New Media', Malcolm sharing a platform with George Dreyfus on the more conservative subject of 'Composers for the Theatre'. Dreyfus, bassoonist with the Melbourne Symphony Orchestra at the premiere of *Elevamini* ('Sir Bernard introduced it to us, quite rightly, as a twentieth-century masterpiece') always found Malcolm highly entertaining:

> You could not but enjoy his comments about other composers! He was irreverent; entertainingly spiteful! His sharp tongue could always produce a good turn of phrase. He once said on television 'George Dreyfus wears his Australian-ness like a mackintosh'![22]

At ease with Dreyfus, Malcolm spoke well on modern opera at the seminar, though inevitably struggling to sound modest when his own achievements were in such stark contrast to the desultory situation in Australia. Larry Sitsky's one-act *The Fall of the House of Usher*, produced in 1965, was in fact the first successful presentation in Australia of an opera by a native composer. Dreyfus's 2-act opera, *Garni Sands* – despite its first act ending with one group of rebel convicts preparing to eat another – might have encouraged Covell to declare that Dreyfus was 'an operatic composer in the making', but it was yet to be produced. Critic Kenneth Hince, covering the seminars for *The Australian*, made a rueful comparison:

> Malcolm Williamson spoke fluently about his work in opera; he showed us a world of experience which contrasted cruelly with that of George Dreyfus who spoke after

---

20 He looks back on the 1960s with a certain amount of irony: 'I discovered European contemporary music in the 1960s. My compositions became very serious indeed and tunes were hard to find. I became Mr New Music of Melbourne...' (Australian Music Centre website, 2006)

21 Covell *op. cit.* p.193. The group was anything but parochial in outlook. Butterley had already spent a year in London studying with Priaulx Rainier; Sculthorpe, who was well-known outside Australia, had spent a year at Oxford and had recently returned from America after a period at Yale. Dreyfus had studied with Stockhausen at Cologne. It would be wrong, too, to suggest that personal animosities accompanied professional differences. Malcolm enjoyed long friendships with Peter Sculthorpe and Nigel Butterley and always appreciated the liveliness of George Dreyfus and Larry Sitsky. Nearly forty years after the conference all four remember Malcolm with much affection.

22 May 2006

Imitating Helpmann's sartorial elegance

him and who, like any operatic composer still working in Australia, has no theatre waiting for him.[23]

Attending Felix Werder's talk on 'The Composer and New Sounds', Malcolm grew steadily more irritated and restless. Eventually he could endure Werder's trenchant comments no longer and with angry cries of 'Bullshit' made a noisy departure from the hall.[24] His exit was all the more noticeable in that, inspired by Robert Helpmann, he was wearing the brightest of leopard-skin jackets. Unfortunately Werder, as the music critic of Melbourne's highly influential newspaper, *The Age*, was able to wreak full revenge, reviewing Malcolm's works thereafter quite mercilessly. He was to describe the First Piano Sonata, for example, as 'an amateurish, listener-insulting concoction by that anti-talent Malcolm Williamson'.

Even Werder and his supporters, however, were unable to deny Malcolm one moment of triumph at the Festival, when he conducted *The Moonrakers* with such passion that the audience demanded an immediate encore of themselves. Roger Covell, under a heading A TINY WORK OF JOY, wrote with real pleasure about it. The songs were 'simple and serviceable (which is not to say every composer would find it easy to hit on them)' and there were some delightful orchestral touches.[25] He emphasised Malcolm's own contribution as conductor:

23 3 October 1967

24 Nigel Butterley remembers the occasion vividly.

25 George Dreyfus, who played the bassoon in *The Moonrakers*, was so impressed that he wrote his own children's opera the next year.

> The finest performance undoubtedly was given by Malcolm Williamson, whose acting, miming, singing and 'encouraging' were wonderful to see. We can only be thankful that we have creative musicians like Malcolm Williamson who are willing to make music with children and adults and show them that it can be fun as well as exciting and beautiful.[26]

There was, however, a Parthian shot. *The Moonrakers*, wrote Covell, had much more musical value than Malcolm's two chamber works…

All in all, Malcolm suffered a big defeat at Canberra. With jealousy and parochialism rampant, the battle was always going to be difficult, but he did not help himself by his own naivety. Having been away from Australia so long, he would have been wiser to adopt a more cautious approach, but instead, everywhere he went, Malcolm insisted on haranguing whoever would listen with his articulate but highly dogmatic views on every topic under the sun, however sensitive or contentious. On the vexed issue of immigration, for example, he declared:

> There are teeming millions of starving, underprivileged underfed people in Asia and they would be less than human if they didn't look with longing eyes at this incredibly beautiful and tough country, which is waiting to be settled. And the attitude of white superiority, of hand-me-down Anglo-Saxon smugness, is going to do Australia nothing but ill…[27]

Unsurprisingly, he aroused much antagonism and came to be seen by many as a patronising and opinionated outsider. He was also believed, quite unfairly, to have betrayed the cause of serious music for commercial gain – behind his back he was known at the Festival as 'Welcome Millions'. Larry Sitsky explains:

> We all saw ourselves in our different ways as leading-edge avant-gardists. Our prevailing notion was that Malcolm had become an Establishment figure and had 'sold out'. Most of us welcomed him, but he always seemed to have a very large chip on his shoulder – he wasn't exactly unfriendly, but people reacted to him in a mixed sort of way. Some aspects of what he said irritated them. He once said to me 'Why are they so unfriendly?' I couldn't tell him it was because of his own attitude to them! He was kind of snooty. He kept on about being a pupil of Eugene Goossens. We all knew that, so it didn't help when he went on about it. He felt he wasn't treated with sufficient respect…[28]

Nigel Butterley has similar memories:

> We were all probably looking down our noses at Malcolm at the Festival! We were so avant-garde! Malcolm, by contrast, seemed old-fashioned! At this distance now we can look back and see how silly that was! But we were all really committed to the new music and new ideals…[29]

As Malcolm flew back to Britain in early October, he had much on which to reflect. He had made some valuable contacts, particularly in Sydney, even though

[26] *Sydney Morning Herald*, 3 October 1967

[27] Hazel de Berg interview, 1967

[28] June 2006

[29] May 2006

Conducting The Moonrakers, *Canberra, 1967*

the cranes still stood like guards over the empty shell of the opera house. Overall, however, with the notable exception of the ABC, he had been disappointed by the tepid response to his return. He had been billed at Canberra (without hyperbole) as 'pre-eminent in the British music world',[30] but the way he had been treated during the Festival hardly reflected this importance. Surprised and wounded, he now viewed his own country with considerable misgivings. He was unimpressed, too, by the low standing accorded to composers in Australia, which forced them to seek other employment. The visit, in short, had dispelled any thoughts he ever entertained of one day moving back with his family.

Instead, his head was full of new operas. The seminars had helpfully highlighted the scope and originality of his own achievements. Bessie too had stressed how central opera had become to his compositional life, and he himself had admitted as much at Canberra:

> My mother has a passion for the theatre; and while I had always enjoyed the theatre, never had I realised that I had any instinct for it until I had to write opera. And I discovered that this came to me more naturally and more congenially than any other form of music. And I've been writing operas since, more than anything else. When I've had commissions to write concert pieces, I've tried whenever possible to have the commission turned round so that I would be able to write an opera.[31]

He and Bessie had enjoyed several evenings together at the theatre, including *Il Trovatore* at the Tivoli, but most significant of all had been a visit to the little Independent Theatre in North Sydney, not far from their old Mosman home, where they had seen Strindberg's *A Dance of Death*. Strindberg, they both agreed, might provide exactly the right kind of material for his next opera.

So Malcolm was now planning an operatic future at two very different levels. On the one hand, encouraged by *The Moonrakers*, he would write more works for children, simple and direct cassations, to bring opera into schools; on the other hand he would turn to Strindberg for a hard-centred opera, as visionary and as modern as the Blues Point Tower. His first home-coming may not have turned out exactly as anticipated, but it had helped shape his immediate future.

---

30 The Canberra Conference programme had written of him: 'As a composer, pianist, organist and lecturer, he has established himself in a pre-eminent position in the British music world...'

31 Interview with Hazel de Berg, October 1967. *The Happy Prince*, for example, grew out of a commission for a short choral work.

9 STRINDBERG DRAMAS

Dynevor and Sadler's Wells, 1968–69

MALCOLM'S INTEREST in the Swedish playwright August Strindberg began with a chance discussion in 1964 between two critics, Philip Hope-Wallace and Edward Greenfield, hugely impressed by Malcolm's handling of Sitwell's *English Eccentrics* and debating what other literary sources might appeal to him. Hope-Wallace suggested Strindberg, and when, not long afterwards, Greenfield happened to be lunching with Malcolm and Dolly at their Sherwood Court flat, he put the idea forward. That afternoon they walked across to a bookshop in Baker Street, where Malcolm bought all the Scandinavian plays he could find.

The interest grew. In a Canberra interview three years later Malcolm described Strindberg as 'one of the greatest artistic influences in my life' and gave some insight into the reason for the attraction:

> Sweden to me is a very remote culture. I am drawn to its remoteness. My attraction to Strindberg is in the essential remoteness. A remoteness where human nature is laid bare. The whole of life, the whole of humanity is to be found in Strindberg.[1]

Remoteness is one of the themes of *The Dance of Death*, which Malcolm and Bessie had seen in Sydney, Strindberg's view of marital hell, played out on a rocky, wave-tossed island off a distant Swedish shore; and human nature is certainly laid bare in the misogyny and sexual frustration of *The Father* and *Miss Julie*, the works for which Strindberg today is best known. But, for operatic purposes, Malcolm was more interested in the plays of his later years, when he had turned away from realism to expressionism, often heavy with symbolism. Indeed, as Malcolm confided in an Australian interview, he had a play in mind:

> I've been cherishing for several years (and I hope in 1968 to write) an opera based on Strindberg's serene play *Easter*, one of his least tortured and most beautiful plays, but it's a very static piece with only one stage set (a Swedish bourgeois interior) and only six characters. The action is very interior, the conflict of people's hearts, and this is

[1] Hazel de Berg interview, National Library of Australia, October 1967

> the biggest challenge I've ever had: to write an opera without the appurtenances of the theatre, without the glamour of ballets and exotic settings and violent conflict. Very little happens on the exterior, it's all interior.[2]

What story there was – about a family struggling to cope with the father's imprisonment for embezzlement and the daughter's confinement in an asylum – certainly presented difficulties, and when Malcolm mentioned *Easter* at Sadler's Wells, it failed to generate any enthusiasm despite its ending of symbolic forgiveness and redemption. Strindberg, Malcolm was firmly told, usually spelt trouble at the box-office.

But once engaged in a new interest, Malcolm found disengagement impossible. On the train journeys to and from Cookham for the rehearsals of *Dunstan and the Devil* in 1967 Malcolm had begun teaching himself Swedish. A year later, after a few evening classes, he was fluent enough to enjoy the subtleties of Ingmar Bergman's production of *Ghosts* for the Swedish Royal Dramatic Theatre.[3] A Swedish-speaking friend, Patricia Sharland, remembers his gift for language:

> We would often speak and exchange letters in Swedish, which he had picked up very easily, for he had an extremely quick brain. He empathised with Swedish thinking. He would often quote Ingmar Bergman's comment that the Swedish were consumed by eroticism, loneliness and death.[4]

Undeterred by cautionary box-office stories, Malcolm began to look further afield for the right home for his first Strindberg opera. It emerged through the Welsh composer Alun Hoddinott, who in 1967 had commissioned Malcolm's song cycle *From A Child's Garden* for the Cardiff Festival of Twentieth Century Music. At that time Hoddinott had just taken responsibility for a new festival at Dynevor Castle, some twenty miles from Swansea. Dynevor, he told Malcolm, was an inspirational setting for music, its owner the young and enlightened Richard Rhys, 9th Baron Dynevor, who had inherited the family's 2,000 acre estate six years earlier along with a million pounds of death duties.[5] The 'castle' was, in fact, a seventeenth-century country house, rebuilt in the 1850s in glorious Victorian Gothic, each corner of the rectangular, three-storey building being given a tower in Disney style. It was set in romantic grounds partly landscaped by 'Capability' Brown and beautiful enough to have attracted artists like Turner, the park including the ruins of a medieval castle, a deer park and inspiring views of the Towy Valley. A first Dynevor Festival of films and music had been ambitious and successful[6] and Hoddinott urged Malcolm to consider writing

---

2 De Berg, ANL, October 1967

3 RSC World Theatre Season, Aldwych Theatre, June 1968

4 July 2005

5 The death duties duly achieved their purpose. Dynevor Castle had later to be sold by the family, the house and immediate grounds now being owned by the National Trust.

6 Musicians at the festival included John Ogdon, Michael Tippett and Johnny Dankworth, and Alexander Goehr wrote a string quartet for it.

something for 1968. Malcolm, though busy with other work,[7] agreed to a meeting with Lord Dynevor in London, where it was quickly decided that a Strindberg masterpiece, not *Easter* but *A Dream Play,* was exactly what Dynevor needed.

Malcolm's *The Growing Castle* (*A Dream Play* converted into a two-act chamber opera with piano accompaniment) was completed in just two months. His starting-points were Strindberg's Swedish text and Elizabeth Sprigge's English translation, but, as he wrote to Lord Dynevor, he soon discovered he needed to follow his own instincts:

> With the exigencies of the Dynevor stage and of operatic treatment I found myself obliged to create what was virtually my own version. As you know I read some Swedish, and for musical reasons I have had to use Strindberg's original to suit my musical requirements. This has meant doing my own translation in places, and more often capsulating whole passages into sentences of my own invention or into music…[8]

By spending two weeks in May at Dynevor, he was able to assess the requirements of the music room, where the opera would be presented to about a hundred people. During this time he wrote assiduously during the day in a cottage in the grounds, a former dairy, meeting up in the evenings with Lord Dynevor to discuss progress. His host was quickly impressed:

> Malcolm was such a huge enthusiast that I became fascinated by the whole project! Each evening we had long intense conversations. He was able to focus so strongly on the work in hand, but we also spoke about everything! His ability to quote – especially Shakespeare, but by no means exclusively – was phenomenal![9]

Malcolm later took himself off to a hotel on the seafront at Rhyl, where he continued to make good progress. In early June he wrote to Richard Dynevor promising a draft of the whole opera:

> I have just finished the closing scene. I'm glad that it's done, as I can scarcely work at it without tears. The first act is sketched throughout and I shall return to it tonight.
>
> Rhyl may not be uplifting, but I am able to turn inwards as there is no external attraction. I have a sort of studio in this hotel and by chance a filthy novel (bought on Euston Station) which is very long and not too interesting, so I am utterly happy.[10]

From Rhyl Malcolm went to stay for a few days at Nancy Evans' house near Aldeburgh, where the three other members of the cast (Jennifer Vyvyan,

7 In 1968 he also wrote two cassations, a Piano Quintet (played several times by Malcolm and the Gabrieli Quartet, together with the Elgar Quintet), and a song cycle, *From A Child's Garden*, using poems by Robert Louis Stevenson. Robert Tear and John Ogdon gave *From A Child's Garden* its first performance at the Cardiff Festival, and April Cantelo and Malcolm were soon giving further ones. Malcolm was still busy as a performer, on one occasion rushing to the Festival Hall to play Handel's Concerto in D Minor with the LSO as a last-minute stand-in.

8 6 June 1968

9 July 2006

10 Undated letter from the Westminster Hotel, East Parade, Rhyl

Geoffrey Chard and Benjamin Luxon) joined them for an initial look at the opera. *A Dream Play*, first produced in 1900, is a notoriously dark and difficult work, highly experimental and arguably the first stage work to dispense with the conventions of time and place. It is not often performed.[11] The characters are unhelpfully one-dimensional, insubstantial symbols which 'split, double, multiply, evaporate, condense, disperse and assemble'.[12] The original play had eighty parts distributed between eight actors, whereas Malcolm's four singers in *The Growing Castle* were to tackle eighteen roles, as well as act as choristers, lovers in Fairhaven and damned souls in Foulstrand. 'I suppose it could be said I've destroyed the play in order to rebuild it,' he later joked. 'I've had to drive a Roman road through the play. It's rather like writing the Lord's Prayer on a pin's head.' Malcolm himself was to provide the accompaniment, on 'a piano with a harpsichord stop'[13] together with a whole range of percussive effects. It was a sensible response to the limited space of the Dynevor music room, but even his virtuosity would struggle to disguise the thinness of the musical texture over two long acts.[14]

There was a necessarily short rehearsal period. After individual sessions with the singers Malcolm and the cast spent a week together in London before moving down to Wales. Geoffrey Chard, a fellow Australian who had just been singing Don Giovanni at Sadler's Wells and who became a strong friend of the family, remembers Malcolm being uncharacteristically difficult:

> Although usually very helpful at rehearsal, Malcolm was also quite temperamental. On one occasion, when we had met at Nancy Evans's, we were having a joke and he didn't like it at all. He would also phone us up, and go on for ages and ages about the complexities of the story. When we finally got to Dynevor it all became very fraught. He cancelled Peter Rice's interesting set designs – which were based around a spiral which turned around with blocks on it with different designs – and in the event we had virtually a bare stage – the audience had to use their imaginations! He also bawled me out for something, I can't remember what, which was most uncharacteristic of his usual attitude to his singers...[15]

The first of the six Dynevor Festival[16] performances took place on 13 August 1968. Despite a highly talented cast and all the care lavished on the music and text, Malcolm had failed to broaden the appeal of Strindberg's esoteric drama. The opening scenes (as outlined in Malcolm's own synopsis) set the tone:

---

11 It was, however, seen at the National Theatre in 2005, the same year that the RSC produced a new version of *Easter*.

12 Strindberg's own words (in his foreword to the play).

13 Desmond Shawe-Taylor, *Sunday Times*, 18 August 1968

14 Malcolm later orchestrated one section, Agnes' Farewell at the end of Act Two. It is a fine lyrical aria in its own right, but the contrast between the two accompaniments is most marked, the orchestration bringing so much extra colour and vitality.

15 March 2006

16 Other musical events at the 1968 Festival featured Josef Suk and Jan Panenka, Peter Katin, the Aeolian String Quartet, Osian Ellis and Margaret Price.

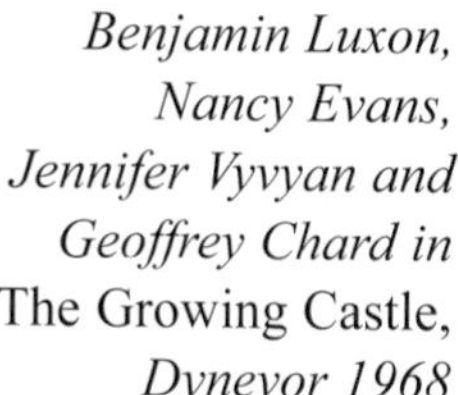

Benjamin Luxon, Nancy Evans, Jennifer Vyvyan and Geoffrey Chard in The Growing Castle, *Dynevor 1968*

Agnes, daughter of the Gods, has come to earth to see what the life on mankind is like. The setting of her visit is a castle, the roots of which are in the earth and which stretches upwards like a flower towards the sun where it will blossom in fire and die. Agnes first meets an Officer, imprisoned in the castle, and seeking freedom, love and life. In the castle is a cupboard with a trefoil pattern on the door. The (hidden) secret behind this door causes him to quarrel with an old woman, possibly his mother. The old woman is preparing for death and Agnes feels compassionate towards her. The scene dissolves to an alley behind a theatre. There is, although we do not see it, a stage door with a trefoil air-hole on the other side of which the officer's true love, Emilia, is to be found. The officer comes daily in youth and age to the trefoil door calling for Emilia who never comes. A light-hearted bill-sticker who has achieved his life's aim – to own a fishnet and a fish box of a particular shade of green – tells Agnes of the sorrows of the Janitress, who sits by the stage door. The Janitress herself, her wrist bound to the chair, sings of the sorrows of others and her own mission, to wear a shawl into which is woven the world's pain, and forever to listen to the plaint of others. Agnes feels perfectly able to assume the Janitress's duties…

It is difficult to see how any music could redeem such unpromising material. But Malcolm made no concessions to the dour tale, writing mostly in a severe style, his dissonant and angular melodic lines well matching Strindberg's pessimistic assessment of the human condition, but hardly offering a good evening's entertainment.

'Williamson has allowed a certain Scandinavian draught to blow through his naturally warm imprint,' wrote one critic accurately, yet – a sign of the perverse musical times – the majority of critics, ignoring the strong dissonances, found *The Growing Castle* quite lyrical, but then 1968 was the year when Stockhausen's *Kontakte* was given at the Proms and Berio's *Sinfonia*, Searle's *Hamlet* and Nono's *Until the Forests Burn* were premiered, none of them easy on the ear. Desmond Shawe-Taylor, perhaps over-influenced by the opera's genuinely lyrical ending, wrote (on the whole, misleadingly) of 'some rapturously soaring cantilena':

> The composer has a lyrical vein that fearlessly skirts the abyss of banality and sometimes rises to a tuneful eloquence that is RARE in modern music. Though I felt that there was an underlying contradiction between his easy-going style and Strindberg's fierce obsessions.[17]

The opera is certainly not written in 'easy-going style', but William Mann supported Shawe-Taylor with comments of such remarkable inaccuracy that one can only wonder whether he was writing from memory of *The Violins of Saint-Jacques*, having broken down on the way to *The Growing Castle*:

> There is a quantity of ravishingly beautiful vocal melody in it, old-fashioned, tonic-and-dominant, dodo-music which, incredibly, lives and breathes and has reality. A sedan-chair overtaking a GT in the Monte Carlo rally could not rouse greater surprise. Other composers use this language more novelly, but with no less verve (Paul McCartney with outstanding originality, Malcolm Arnold often to spirited effect); Williamson re-evokes it, gaslight, antimacassars and all, not trying to update it or, Tiny-Tim-fashion, make us smile wistfully at our days before yesterday. The best music in *The Growing Castle* includes, among many examples, a chorus that would not disgrace Mozart and a vocal monologue, at the end, as beautiful as anything in Strauss' *Ariadne auf Naxos* – or so you are compelled to believe at the time, in my own case totally unwillingly, since to write new music in this old-curiosity-shop manner seems as valueless as to write a tract on the servant problem or female suffrage. You may disapprove of the music he sometimes writes but you cannot doubt that he is the most talented composer of his generation…[18]

Overall, therefore, the dissonant *Growing Castle*, though not dissonant enough for many critics, achieved considerable approval, and Malcolm felt that

17 *Sunday Times*, 18 August 1968. Malcolm also commented on the singing in the Dynevor music room: 'The impact of four huge operatic voices in a small auditorium makes the walls feel like rubber.'

18 *The Times*, 19 November 1968. Mann was writing of the London premiere, a Macnaghten concert performance at the St Pancras Town Hall, with Jane Manning, Meriel Dickenson, Geoffrey Chard and Michael Rippon.

With Geoffrey Chard and Lord Dynevor at Dynevor Castle

he had proved the Jeremiahs wrong. Strindberg *could be* both good box-office and ideal material for opera.

The cast loved it. Nancy Evans, whose several roles included The Janitress, Ugly Edith and The Poet, wrote afterwards:

> Darling Malcolm,
>
> I can't ever thank you enough for all you have given me, in allowing me to be a part of the incredibly beautiful creation of *The Growing Castle*. Your encouragement has given me renewed vocal and spiritual joy.[19]

Meriel Dickinson, who replaced the unwell Nancy Evans in one of the Dynevor performances and took over the role in London and the Richmond Festival, similarly declared:

> *The Growing Castle* was wonderful to perform…hugely challenging… beautifully written for the voice.[20]

Jennifer Vyvyan, meanwhile, found the whole experience so moving that she struggled to come to terms with its immediate aftermath, as Malcolm reported to Richard Dynevor:

> Jennifer rang this morning. She left Dynevor and straight away went to Pitlochry where she had a nervous collapse – wept all day, fucked up her recital and crashed her car – all due, she claims, to *The Growing Castle*. She can't wait to do it again.[21]

---

[19] Dynevor, August 1968

[20] April 2006

[21] 27 August 1968

She did not have to wait long, for a number of performances in London had already been arranged, at St Pancras Town Hall and Australia House, where the basement was converted to a 450-seat theatre. There, at considerable expense,[22] in an appealing setting of Australian gothic, the opera was well received, Malcolm winning much praise for his efforts as a one-man orchestra. He was particularly delighted with the enthusiasm of the Swedish Ambassador and soprano Elizabeth Söderstrom, 'who hoped to perform it in Stockholm in the near future'.[23]

For the family there were very happy memories of Dynevor. Dolly, the children and Ranghilde, the Norwegian au pair, not only stayed with Malcolm at the Castle for the fortnight of rehearsals and performances but for a week's holiday afterwards. They had their own house in the grounds, full of such old-world character that Dolly was surprised, on her first visit to the scullery, by a sinkful of baby bats. She also remembers the day Tammy met Dynevor's female ghost:

> One afternoon Tammy tacked on to a party being shown round the house. The tour took them to the castle roof – I remember Tammy up there with them, a little figure waving at me. When she came down, she asked, 'What happened to the strange lady, the one in olden-day dress who was up on the roof with us, but didn't stay with our party?' 'A lady in an olden-day dress?' I asked. 'What on earth was she doing up there?' 'Oh, nothing,' said Tammy. 'She just smiled at me, and then disappeared.'[24]

Malcolm's sister Diane, who was in England at this time, temporarily working in Fleet Street, also spent a happy weekend at Dynevor:

> The castle was in a lovely setting and I remember wandering around watching deer grazing; also Jennifer Vyvyan, drifting around the garden in the daytime, lost in another world. I loved the opera. There was a small stage at the end of the room, with an extension made through a large window to allow the singers to go off and on. The staging was highly effective, particularly at the end when the character played by Jennifer Vyvyan returned to the gods by fire. It was so realistic I was quite shocked, and relieved when she returned to take a curtain call![25]

Diane stayed with the family in East Sheen for a short while, finding the atmosphere on the return from Dynevor settled and cheerful, but Malcolm's health was a concern to her:

> Malcolm at times suffered from severe headaches, such that the doctors even suspected he had a brain tumour. While he had the headaches, he didn't write. Nonetheless, he was still marvellous company, listening to records, reading, telling the children stories he'd made up. During one of these episodes when I was there, the

22 Geoffrey Chard repeated his Dynevor roles. Neil Easton replaced Benjamin Luxon. As a member of the Australian Music Association, Chard had helped in the organisation of the event.

23 *Sadler's Wells Opera Magazine*, Spring 1969

24 July 2005

25 September 2005

apple tree in the garden was in fruit and in an effort to save some money, he decided we should collect the apples and make apple sauce. We would all gather in the garden while he climbed the tree and threw apples for us to catch. Then we adults would peel and slice saucepans of apples and freeze the sauce while Malcolm related funny stories to us. He was a hard taskmaster and rarely allowed us time off. Then suddenly, the house was silent, and Malcolm was back at his desk, composing. His headache had gone.

The three children, now aged four to eight, grew up in a home where their father's work was always pre-eminent. There now was a television, but the volume was always kept low. Likewise with the radio. Pop records were to be played only when Malcolm was out of the house. Although the three children saw a reasonable amount of their father, he was often preoccupied, even at moments of supposed leisure. Tammy can recall few meals which were not interrupted one way or another:

> If Dad didn't have something preoccupying him, he would hold forth and be very amusing. Meals were also a useful time for Mum and Dad to discuss day-to-day necessities. But often the phone would ring and he'd disappear into his study and that would be the last we'd see of him! We developed a kind of system whereby Mum would either send one of us to ask a question or she'd scribble a note, like 'Shall I serve the roast or shall we have it cold tomorrow?' He was so involved with his work that sometimes, when the phone hadn't even rung, he would still get up, go next door and start playing the piano. And one by one, as we finished, we would leave the table and go to join him and stand around. If it was a simple piece, something we knew, something he'd been working on for a time, we'd all start joining in. When it was something new, we'd simply listen. 'That's nice!' we'd say at the end, and he would be delighted. We rarely had any meals which started and finished with everyone at the table! It wasn't an unhappy situation at all, for to us it all seemed quite normal…[26]

The children took it as a matter of course that he would always be composing, always have something going on in his head, and, as Tammy recalls, there were physical manifestations of this:

> Dad would be sitting in an armchair, seemingly very relaxed, yet his fingers would be drumming on the corners of its arms. He was for ever feeling the corners of a chair or a table, as if he was working out the mathematics of some music. He wasn't aware of doing it. And sometimes his fingers weren't actually moving yet you could sense the vibrations, like electricity, at the end of his fingers.

Smoking was an integral part of Malcolm's hyperactive life and Peter seldom saw his father without a cigarette:

> He was a compulsive smoker. Unable to concentrate without. I remember meals where he couldn't get through a course without a cigarette. He made quite a lot of efforts to give it up. He tried acupuncture, for example, and a hypnotist.[27]

Malcolm was keen that his children had the opportunity to learn an instrument, and, like Malcolm Arnold before him, sent them for lessons to the redoubtable

---

[26] March 2005

[27] March 2005

Adele Franklin, a great family friend.[28] Tammy recalls anxious visits to her home:

> We weren't particularly keen but from the age of about five we had to go once a week to Adele Franklin, a terrifying personality to us kids! She was about six feet tall, wore high-heeled lavender suede boots, had a deep voice and a tiny little Yorkie called Polly-Sue who had ribbons in her hair and used to sit on her lap, and she'd pick at the After Eight mints… And if you played a wrong note she'd say 'Poor Beethoven! Poor Beethoven!'

Tammy was to persevere with the piano for another ten years, and, at one period, as part of her musical education, Malcolm encouraged her to be his page-turner.

> It made me aware how strong his hands were. He had quite small hands – he could just stretch an octave – You looked at his hands and wondered 'How did he do that?' Especially when he was playing the organ. He was doing a concert once, and I was meant to be learning to turn the pages, so I was sitting next to him, and it was incredible – his feet and hands were going all over the place – and sometimes, to reach, he had to lift himself off the seat. It was all so beautifully co-ordinated. This incredible sound would be coming out…

Having a famous father tended to provoke unusual situations. When the film of *Chitty Chitty Bang Bang* came out in 1968, Clare and Tammy had been very frightened by Robert Helpmann's sinister Child Catcher. 'You really don't want to be frightened of *him*,' protested Malcolm afterwards. 'It was only Bobby Helpmann. He's a charmer.' So he rang him up. 'Bobby, it's Malcolm. Would you please tell Tammy and Clare, who've just seen *Chitty*, that you're really very charming! Here they are!' 'But I'm *not* charming at all!' hissed Helpmann down the phone to the girls. 'And what's more – I'm coming to *get you*!' There were also moments of wild hilarity. While writing the score for *The Horror of Frankenstein* Malcolm would delight the children by rushing like a ghoul around the house, plastic fangs sticking out from his mouth.

But there were long periods when he was locked in his own thoughts. Dolly had very soon become used to the difficulty of getting through to Malcolm on mundane matters. There was once, for example, a problem with the central heating.

> As I went out of the house one day, leaving Malcolm working on his music, I reminded him about the plumber. 'If he rings, please tell him he's done a lousy job which needs doing all over again.' On my return I asked if the plumber had rung. 'Oh yes,' he said. 'What did you say to him?' I asked. 'Oh, I told him that everything was just fine.' He had seemed to be listening to me and taking in what I was saying, whereas in fact he hadn't heard a word! It was something I slowly had to adjust to…[29]

Malcolm's musical world absorbed him day and night:

---

28 The dedicatee of the first cassation, *The Moonrakers*

29 October 2005

> We'd sit up in bed reading at night. I would have my book, and Malcolm would have a score. I can remember him on one occasion absorbed in a Stravinsky score. I said something to him and he didn't hear me, he was so engrossed. I tapped him on the arm and said 'Can you really hear that the way I'd hear it in a concert hall?' 'Of course,' he said. 'Every note.'

Malcolm's pride in Dolly and the family was as intense as ever, and still very much his primary professional motivation. But the onset of the Strindberg operas coincided with a period of change. The weeks at Dynevor had been less than totally happy for him as he struggled to come to terms with a resurgence of homosexual feelings. The bisexuality of the 1950s had given him very little pause for thought. But now with his family responsibilities came guilt.

The admiration for Strindberg only added to his confusions. Strindberg extolled the ideal of the poet-artist, a free spirit unrestrained by convention on his pilgrimage through life. Poet-artists were hardly at ease in the bourgeois comfort of suburban south London. In *Julius Caesar Jones* Malcolm had taken a first step, introducing into the placid and unquestioning suburban environment the possibility of a wilder life, partly lived in the imagination and partly for real. In *The Growing Castle* he had gone much further, suburban certainties giving way totally to the wild disorder of the imaginative life. There are several points in *The Growing Castle* which suggest that Malcolm had discovered in Strindberg situations and debate which reflected his own inner state. Often these are where the writing is at its most accomplished. At the opera's highly lyrical conclusion, for example, when Agnes parts from the androgynous poet, with whom she has fallen in love, she expresses the essential loneliness of the artist pilgrim, resorting to acts of renunciation because of the compulsion of the journey of discovery:

> Now I am going;
> Now the hour has come to leave both friend and place.
> How harsh the loss of all I loved!
> How deep regret at all destroyed!
> The human soul is cleft in two,
> Emotion by wild horses torn.

Another fine section occurs halfway through the First Act, where the opera at last comes to life, the music adopting the quasi-lyrical tone which so moved Shawe-Taylor and William Mann. Agnes at this point is persuading a disillusioned lawyer (one of Strindberg's many self-portraits) to take a chance on marriage. Malcolm, it seems likely, may also have identified with the lawyer, the text smacking as much of 1960 as 1900:

First comes the Lawyer's distinctly ambivalent definition of love and marriage:

> One joy there is in life, a sweet joy, the fairest joy and the most bitter, it is called love. Love is called marriage; marriage is called home; the highest joy, the lowest, the sweetest and the most bitter.

Agnes puts some pressure on him:

> Let us taste this sweetest joy; you know love's dangers, you know the stumbling stones; let us make trial of love.

The Lawyer's uncertainties are met, and eventually overwhelmed, by Agnes's determination:

> – I am poor.
>
> – If there is love, can poverty hurt us?
>
> – You may hate all I love; I may desire what you despise. We may grow tired of one another.
>
> – Children will come, renewing our love.
>
> – Will you take me? Poor, ugly, despised, discredited?
>
> – Let us entwine our lives with love.
>
> – So be it!
>
> – So be it![30]

But Strindberg does not allow married love to flourish. Soon afterwards the husband and wife are having arguments. By the end of Act One the lyrical 'One joy there is' has been totally discredited. Dissonance reigns.

If *The Growing Castle* was an opportunity for Malcolm to explore and appease the new uncertainties welling within him, two new cassations, commissioned for the Brighton Festival of 1968, reflected the continued pleasures of fatherhood. *Knights in Shining Armour* and *The Snow Wolf*[31] were a natural extension of the imaginative fun he would have from time to time with his children in Hertford Avenue. Clare remembers an occasion when Dolly was out with Peter, and Malcolm left in charge of her and Tammy.

> He really didn't know how to deal with us! He went round the house looking for things to do, ending up in a rusty old shed in the garden from which he extracted an grotty orange bath mat! This at once became an Orange River, and he wrote us an operetta of that name, with a story involving a grandmother and her grand-daughter. We went off to his study while he wrote it out. He then rehearsed it with us and we performed it, twice, once for Michael Rich and his wife, great friends who lived nearby, and then for Mum and Peter when they returned.[32]

As his cassations became more and more well-known – he eventually wrote one for the last night of the Proms – so Malcolm tended to declare that he wrote them in the first instance for his children. This was not really so. Singing in private was one thing, acting in public quite another. None of them, Dolly included, felt comfortable with Malcolm's exhibitionist demands in rehearsal.

30 Text by permission of Josef Weinberger Ltd

31 Sponsored by Watney Mann, one of the pioneers of industrial patronage of the arts in the 1960s. Trevor Russell-Cobb was the inspiration behind Watney's sponsorship which had earlier embraced *The Happy Prince* and the *Concerto for Wind Quintet and Two Pianos*. Russell-Cobb's sons, Piers and Fabian, took part in the Brighton Festival cassations, Malcolm later dedicating the two new works to them.

32 January 2006

Dolly remembers on one occasion discreetly tip-toeing towards the exit as a rehearsal was beginning only to be halted by a familiar voice crying out across a crowded room, 'And where exactly do you think *you're* going?'

The contrast of these simple and immediately appealing cassations with the intricacies and anguish of *The Growing Castle* is startling, even though his scenarios include some quiet Strindbergian symbolism. In *Knights in Shining Armour*, for example, set in medieval times, there is a symbolic treasure chest, hidden deep in a forest. It motivates the first entrance of the knights, who come galloping in with a song which, being made up of melodic sequences and repetitive rhythms, is easy for untrained singers:

Shining helmets, shining mail!
Shining armour must prevail!
Guarding treasure locked away!
Saving all against a rainy day!
Silver hidden in a chest!
Golden virtue manifest!
Shining helmets, shining mail!
Shining armour must prevail!
Guarding treasure locked away!
Saving all against a rainy day!

Meanwhile, hiding in the bushes, are some dastardly robbers who, using the same harmony, now sing, ostinato-like:

I wonder, I wonder if we can get at it!
It must be worth having, it must be, it must be!
I wonder, I wonder if we can get at it!
It must be worth having. It must be gold!

The two ideas are then dramatically combined, with the knights and robbers in effective counterpoint. The fun continues with the robbers prising open the chest as the music goes into a minor key, and out pop the seven deadly sins together with many deadly dragons and hydras. Then more drama – the robbers, about to be killed by the monsters, are saved by the sudden arrival of the knights. The opening music returns, and the knights repeat their song; the robbers at the same time sing in bogus penitence while the cowed deadly sins add a third strand to the texture with a delightful series of falling octave 'oo-ooh!'s. The cassation ends with the robbers plotting another attempt on the symbolic chest. The moral of this simple story? Money is the root of all evil, and some people never learn!

In May 1968 Malcolm spent two weeks at the Brighton Festival working on three cassations at the Palace Pier Theatre.[33] Hugo Cole was present at one session:

> Every day a fresh batch of up to 250 primary school children arrives to find an empty theatre with stage and auditorium available for their use; and 10 professional actors

[33] It was a big commitment. He also conducted evening performances of a youth production of *Julius Caesar Jones*.

> (specially assembled for the season) ready to lead, organise and encourage them. There are three works specially written by Malcolm Williamson; and a professional director and specialist in children's drama, Marjorie Sigley, to teach them to rehearse and perform.
>
> Yesterday it was *Moonrakers*, which was rehearsed for two hours and then performed. The story calls for two separate choruses, two sound effect sections and a percussion group. The whole theatre was in use, with human waves plashing up between the front rows of stalls, with smugglers' boats laboriously negotiating the gangways, and with the Revenue men up in the balcony with their horses (the whole of Brighton pier seemed to vibrate to the sound of their hooves). The first hour or so was spent rehearsing the music; which consists mainly of three tunes, one of which goes into canon and one bar of recitative. Just one child out of this operatically innocent audience knew what the word meant.
>
> Malcolm Williamson's music is marvellously apt to the occasion and the children learnt it quickly. Though, as happens so often in opera, the rhythms began to stagger when action was added, and never fully recovered. But the point of this two hours is to achieve a lively, rather than tidy, end result. The performance was certainly fully alive…[34]

Malcolm's reputation was such that most of the music critics called in at the Pier to sample these workshops. Sean Day-Lewis summed them up for the *Daily Telegraph*:

> The stalls were filled with Primary School children who gave a predictably blank response when Mr Williamson asked them if they had ever sung in opera before. 'Gosh!' reacted the composer, 'but you have been in plays and this is just like a play with the music telling you what is going to happen.' This was accepted and soon the stalls were ringing to the sound of crying seagulls, clopping horses, sea swishing and splashing – all part of his short opera in praise of smugglers, *The Moonrakers*. It was discovered that even the tunes were not difficult to sing, though they were difficult to play with the composer hammering on what he good-naturedly called 'the most broken down piano in Brighton'.[35]

William Mann clearly enjoyed his participation in *Knights in Shining Armour*:

> Knights, robbers and ferocious monsters are rehearsed separately in their moves (though everyone has learnt to sing all the music) before they converge riotously in performances that occupy the auditorium as well as the stage. Everybody takes part, parents and teachers as well as children (and music critics – I thoroughly enjoyed playing the piano while the composer conducted and co-ordinated the production). Part of Williamson's idea is that there should be no audience, only participants – Wagner would have been delighted at this fulfilment of his theories.
>
> The third mini-opera is *The Snow Wolf* about a trans-Siberian train which chuffs round the auditorium gangways and then breaks down, whereupon a group of children secretly get out and are left behind, playing happily with a pack of lonely and unexpectedly friendly wolves.

---

34 *The Guardian*, 3 May 1968

35 30 April 1968

> Williamson himself regards his mini-operas as instant disposable music, designed to be forgotten half an hour after the show is over, and only intended to help the children enjoy Mozart or Wagner more intensely when eventually they begin their opera-going… It is a wholesomely modest attitude… Human memory has made sure that only uninventive music is as disposable as your paper handkerchief or beer-can…[36]

For Malcolm it was an important fortnight. Working alongside several experts in school drama, he was able to garner ideas, taking in what did and didn't work, preparing himself for developing this special genre in the future. It was an exhausting time, but he liked working with the young and found it therapeutic. As a child who had never fully grown up, he had a natural understanding of youthful imaginations.

Inevitably the cassations brought him further comparisons with Britten, which, however flattering, upset him. At Brighton he struggled to mask his exasperation:

> He admits he may have been influenced by Benjamin Britten but is not sure. 'Anyway,' he says, 'There were others before Britten! It is a fallacy to think that Britten invented children!'[37]

Britten, whom he had once so admired, would now have nothing to do with him. No-one is quite sure why. Malcolm, it seems, disgraced himself in some hot-headed way. He may well have rashly taken sides at the time when the Earl of Harewood was excluded from Aldeburgh after leaving his wife Marion (Erwin Stein's daughter and a friend of Britten's) for Barry Tuckwell's sister. Malcolm's friendship with the Tuckwells dated back many years, and Harewood, it is said, was a significant factor in Malcolm's productive relationship with Sadler's Wells Opera. In October 1968 Peter Pears gave a first performance of *A Vision of Beasts and Gods*, the cycle based on George Barker's poems written in Buckland ten years before. It would seem a placatory offering. Pears was for ever trying to pick up the pieces of broken relationships, and always had much warmer feelings towards Malcolm than Britten.

For the moment Malcolm was enjoying such success that the goodwill of his biggest rival hardly mattered. In the summer of 1969 came a further triumph, *The Brilliant and the Dark*, a choral work which was given three sell-out performances at the Albert Hall. An hour-long 'operatic sequence', it was set to words by Ursula Vaughan Williams for an event involving all 9,000 of the Women's Institutes scattered throughout England, Wales, the Channel Islands and the Isle of Man. The Marchioness of Anglesey, as chairman of the National Federation of Women's Institutes at the time, explained the background:

> Every three years the Institutes work towards a National Event. In 1964 it was decided that the next National Event should be a musical one, the first since Ralph Vaughan

36 3 May 1968

37 Interview with Sean Day-Lewis during the Brighton Festival (*Daily Telegraph*)

> Williams had been commissioned in 1950. We wished to present a work by a leading British composer and, with generous financial help from the Carnegie United Kingdom Trust and the Arts Council, this was made possible. We were exceptionally fortunate that Malcolm Williamson accepted the commission…[38]

The Brilliant and the Dark celebrates the lives of British women during the past thousand years, showing their *brilliant* achievements and *dark* moments of tragedy. Originally a chronological sequence of scenes, it evolved into a succession of musical groupings showing participants in relationship to each other rather than time. A group of embroiderers, whose work illustrates the story, acts as the linking chorus.

To allow the participation of as many choirs as possible, Malcolm wrote the music at varying levels of difficulty, sometimes in unison and sometimes using two and three parts. The first auditions were in the form of fifty County Festivals which took place over four months in 1968 and selected for further consideration some two hundred choirs, eighty soloists and fifty pianists. All of these auditioned later at twelve Regional Festivals, attended by Marcus Dods who had the unenviable job of selecting eight soloists, eight pianists and forty-eight choirs to perform at the Albert Hall. He then held courses for the choir conductors and distributed notes on the work. In addition to all this, arrangements had to be made for actors, dancers and costumes:

> From Westmorland to Kent, from Breconshire to Cambridgeshre members have been making 700 costumes, accessories and scenery to the brilliant designs of Peter Rice… The 120 actors and 30 dancers, all volunteers from East Sussex and Hertfordshire, have been rehearsing under the dynamic direction of John Cox.[39]

Janet Canetty-Clarke, who was one of the pianists chosen to accompany the eight embroiderers and who worked on many other projects with Malcolm, retains happy memories of every aspect of *The Brilliant and the Dark*:

> It was a fantastic piece of music, Malcolm at his very best, with Richard Strauss his inspiration. It was one of the most exciting things that amateurs have ever done. And in the end it was all due to Malcolm! We loved it. We absolutely loved it! At first, of course, some of the choirs said, 'We don't like this – it's horrible!' But gradually the music took hold of them, became part of them and they thought it amazing.[40]

After learning and rehearsing the music locally, the thirteen hundred participants came together at 2.00pm the day before the concert for the first orchestral run-through:

> It took place at the Henry Wood Hall and was both exciting and hilarious! It was an amazing experience to hear Marcus Dods and the English Chamber Orchestra bring it all to life in vivid colours. Malcolm, of course, was beside himself with anxiety, sometimes erupting in great anger as he charged around the orchestra – 'Take the

38 Concert programme, 3 June 1969

39 *ibid.*

40 April 2005

trombones out!' 'Alter this dynamic!' – brandishing his red pencil like a dagger and rushing from player to player. It was mostly balance he was concerned about – changing the dynamics. He was so supercharged we expected any moment to see steam coming from his ears ! Marcus coped very well with Malcolm in moods like this. He knew how to handle him.

The first performance took place on 3 June 1969. Just before it began there was, as Janet Canetty-Clarke recalls, a big last-minute panic:

> Peter Rice went rushing round all the embroiderers, who were sitting around the Albert Hall with their needles at the ready, shouting 'Take your watches off, you stupid women!' We all admired Peter Rice, but the handsome director John Cox was the one that all the WI fell in love with – they were two wonderful characters. Marvellous!

The audience was naturally a friendly one, and the critics proved equally warm, completely disarmed by the whole event. Stanley Sadie wrote in *The Times:*

> Williamson was the right composer for this project. The style has to be within the scope of small local choirs; he pours out long, fluent diatonic melodies, with a pastoral air or a whiff of the sea, with imaginatively dancing rhythms, once with an

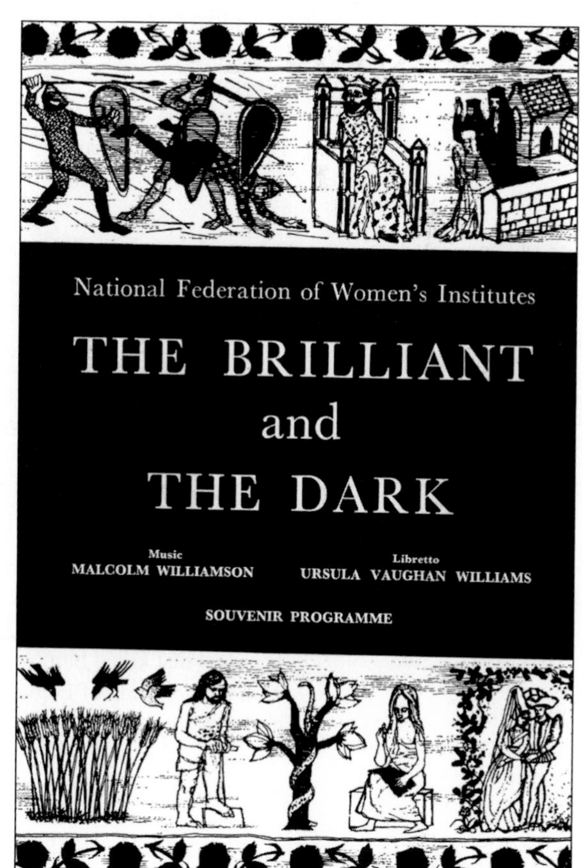

National Federation of Women's Institutes
THE BRILLIANT
and
THE DARK
Music
MALCOLM WILLIAMSON
Libretto
URSULA VAUGHAN WILLIAMS
SOUVENIR PROGRAMME

> apt touch of the cloister; and with darker hints here and there. There are memories of other composers (the Novice's Song is gorgeously Straussian) but it could hardly have been otherwise; and Williamson handles the women's voices, solo and choral, with the greatest skill and variety…[41]

Malcolm was thrilled with the performances, the culmination of his many great successes in the 1960s. But despite its fine qualities *The Brilliant and the Dark* subsequently suffered for being written only for women's voices and it has not found a place in the choral repertoire. Nor have its most outstanding sections so far found a life of their own. The splendid feminist aria 'We are one half the nation, still in bondage' certainly deserves attention. So too the eighth and final section, Lachrymae, a magnificent statement on the futility of war, a woman's view of man's folly, which links the World Wars with the Crimean War, the Crusades, the Civil War and, its *pièce de resistance*, the lament for Harold after the Battle of Hastings.

The ending of Lachrymae, in simple two-part writing, is particularly striking. The Saxon women have been surveying the battlefield:

> The flight of arrows
> Came like birds
> Flock on flock
> In autumn migration.
> Birds of prey
> That fell on their quarry.
> The tall men are carrion
> The king is dead.

Edith, the King's mistress, queries bleakly:

> Where is the King?

The Saxon women cannot help her:

> We must search the fields
> Where we gleaned the harvest
> For the marred bodies,
> For our sons,
> For our husbands.

Edith responds:

> He sleeps
> With the arrow that blinded him
> The steel that killed him,
> With the gold ring of England
> And the cloak of my love.
> No sunrise for England
> No waking from death.

---

41 4 June 1969

Then, in moving counterpoint, as the Saxon women repeat 'We must search the fields', Edith sings

> The winged arrow
> has given him night
> and night is his kingdom
> where he must sleep

at which Malcolm brings proceedings to a conclusion with some gentle chords of reverie in a serene A major, achingly sad, expressing the cumulative anguish of centuries of senseless bereavement. At all three performances the Albert Hall stayed hushed for many seconds afterwards, no-one wishing to break the spell.

The Brilliant and the Dark was a considerable achievement, but Malcolm was soon given pause for thought by an anxious Adrian Boult:

> Mrs Beckett tells me of another brilliant success last night and today's Telegraph confirms it – and so I send congratulations, but perhaps you will forgive me if I send a warning too. Mrs B says that both of you looked dreadfully tired. Why? Surely you are in a position to do just the kind of work and the amount of work that you can comfortably take on, and no more? Do listen to an old fogey who has been through all this, and try and decide how and when and how very often you must say no to people. No one else can do it and the whole world is quite ruthless in its pressure until you decide how and when to draw the line....[42]

Malcolm, however, continued to draw no lines. In the early months of 1969, in addition to writing two scores for Hammer Films (*Crescendo* and *The Horror of Frankenstein*) he also took on several smaller commissions which he might have done better to have declined: a setting of Oscar Wilde's 'On Hearing the Dies Irae Sung in the Sistine Chapel' for the John Alldis choir; carol arrangements for CBS Records; ' A Word From Our Founder', a humorous item for the 1969 Hoffnung Festival; and music for a large number of simple ditties like 'Going to the Zoo' and 'Silly Billy' for children learning English in schools around Stockholm.

He was also engaged on a symphony and an opera. Malcolm's Second Symphony was commissioned by the Bournemouth Symphony Orchestra for its 75th anniversary and given its first performance in October 1969, just four months after Boult's worried letter. But no amount of cautionary advice would have stopped him writing it, for it was a project which meant too much to him, exploring (like *The Growing Castle* and *The Brilliant and the Dark*) a growing obsession, the concept of pilgrimage – 'the intrinsic goodness which lies in being a pilgrim'[43] – and at the same time saluting a precious friendship with the Nobel Prize-winner, Pär Lagerkvist, one of Sweden's most important literary figures, highly respected as a poet, novelist and playwright. Malcolm subtitled the symphony *Pilgrim på havet* ('Pilgrim at Sea'), the title of a recent Lagerkvist book, the second in a trilogy of stories inspired by the legend of the Wandering Jew, condemned for his sins to roam the world until the Second Coming.

42 4 June 1969

43 Programme note, 3 June 1969

Lagerkvist's pilgrim is Tobias, a mercenary, who boards a ship for the Holy Land and meets up with a defrocked priest, an old man of the sea, who persuades him that love is greater than faith; and the goal of the pilgrim less important than the voyage itself.[44] The sea on which they travel is Lagerkvist's symbol for life and death. 'You'll win no rest for your soul except from the sea, which itself never rests – it's cruel and hard and restless, and yet gives peace…'[45]

Malcolm was fascinated by the metaphysical nature of Lagerkvist's narrative, and his twenty-two-minute, one-movement[46] Second Symphony is, in effect, a tone poem of Tobias's travels and discoveries on the sea of life and death, 'boundless and sufficient in itself'. Lagerkvist's unorthodox view of a god who was good and evil, light and dark, incoherent yet full of meaning, upset the established church but intrigued Malcolm, whose visits to Lagerkvist's Stockholm home were in themselves in the nature of a pilgrimage, the disciple visiting the master. Inspired by Lagerkvist, Malcolm wrote of 'the compulsion which is in us to sever the rope that holds the anchor, and to go where there is nowhere to go',[47] which was to have important repercussions on his future life and work. So too Lagerkvist's emphasis on the connection between pilgrimage and society's outsiders, with whom Malcolm identified closely. In an explanatory programme note on the Second Symphony Malcolm wrote:

> Our century has written the word *refugee* in immense letters across the world, and the word shows no indication of being eradicated. The refugee is a compelled pilgrim, and through his rejection he shines with dignity.[48]

The ideas of pilgrimage and refuge were further strengthened by the symphony's dedication to Constantin Silvestri, Bournemouth's Romanian conductor, who died just as Malcolm was beginning the work, and from whose initials he took his germinal idea. Prevented from travelling widely by his communist rulers, Silvestri had been forced to leave Bucharest for a career in the west. Silvestri's life had strong resonances, in Malcolm's mind, with Lagerkvist's compelled pilgrim.

Slow and ruminative throughout and founded on serial procedures, the Second Symphony invites the listener into a strangely remote sound world. Here

---

44 Lagerkvist's ambiguous religious position influenced Malcolm's. Strong Catholic though he was, Malcolm more and more subscribed to the belief that the divine was greater than a single faith. He already considered himself as Jewish as his family, and had taken very seriously the Jewish education of his children, teaching himself some Yiddish in the process, and he was to embrace more faiths as he grew older. His emphasis on a multi-faith deity might sit awkwardly with his continued devotion to the Virgin Mary, yet it was to underpin much of his subsequent writing.

45 Lagerkvist, *Pilgrim at Sea* (tr. Naomi Walford), Random House, 1964

46 Unlike Sibelius' Seventh Symphony, one of his possible starting-points, Malcolm's Second contains no scherzos nor does it advance to a distinct conclusion.

47 3 June 1969

48 3 June 1969

is the remoteness which initially attracted Malcolm to Swedish culture in general and Strindberg in particular. Indeed, there is a severity stretching beyond Lagerkvist to Ingmar Bergman, whose views of the artist-poet's pilgrimage also much interested Malcolm.[49] The Symphony may also be a subconscious response to the pain inflicted by suggestions in Australia that his music was 'soft-centred'. No critics would be able to say that of this deeply meditative work. Nor did they. Amid the many declarations of critical approval, Andrew Porter dubbed the symphony 'a heroic spiritual statement', commending it for being 'full of quiet ostinato backgrounds against which varied and highly memorable incidents come and go in massive timelessness, ever reforming in new patterns and relationships'[50] The symphony was subsequently championed by several conductors and, enthusiastically promoted by Weinberger's, enjoyed international recognition for several years.

Sweden was also the inspiration for a less happy work, Malcolm's new opera, *Lucky-Peter's Journey*, based on one of Strindberg's easier plays.[51] Ever since the critical success of *The Growing Castle* Malcolm had wanted to prove the experts wrong by producing a commercially successful Strindberg opera. By the time he visited Stockholm in the autumn of 1969 for a production of *The Growing Castle*,[52] he was delightedly preparing for just such a challenge, but it was one in which he was to overreach himself with dreadful consequences, realising all Boult's worst fears. In December 1969, his judgement warped by weariness, his self-belief strengthened to the point of pig-headedness by a decade of almost continuous success, Malcolm perpetrated one of the worst disasters in English operatic history, as *Lucky-Peter's Journey*, presented with much pomp by English National Opera at its new home at the London Coliseum, proved once and for all that Strindberg (even at his least portentous) had great potential for box office catastrophe.

---

49 Bergman's films had helped foster Malcolm's interest in Sweden ever since *The Seventh Seal* and *Wild Strawberries* in the 1950s. Bergman's more recent films, though less full of the symbolism Malcolm so much admired, were concentrating on aspects of the artist-poet's pilgrimage, 'the harrowing separateness of people, the intractable privacy of men and women even in love'. (David Thomson, *The New Biographical Dictionary of Film*, p.75)

50 *Daily Telegraph*, 1 November 1969

51 *Lycko-Pers Resa*, first performed in Stockholm in 1883, has been popular in Sweden, but its first English performance only took place over seventy years later, in Scarborough...

52 At the Stora Theatre, 26 September. Jennifer Vyvyan repeated the role of Agnes, this time with Ailene Fischer, Robert Bateman and John Barrow. It was part of a 'London Week', brought to Sweden with help from the Swedish Institute. Malcolm had also visited Copenhagen and Göteborg in 1969. His diary was full of the names and telephone numbers of Swedish musical contacts. He had become by this time a great expert in Strindberg's other artistic interests, as a composer ('simply appalling') and a painter ('He did quite extraordinarily anticipate a lot of what Kandinsky was later to do, a lot that Paul Klee was later to do...') He was also 'drenching' himself in Swedish folk music. (BBC Radio, 17 December 1969).

Malcolm had been approached three years earlier by ENO, who were looking for an operetta, a follow-up to *The Merry Widow* and *Orpheus in the Underworld* but with specific Christmas appeal. The company's artistic adviser, Edmund Tracey,[53] was to be Malcolm's librettist and he made it very clear that their commission was for an unpretentious 'light-weight work' with wide audience appeal:

> Malcolm was immediately fired by our ideas. The first thought was that the structure of the piece should follow the lines of the operetta or musical and be in dialogue-and-numbers form. In the course of our first discussions Malcolm said he would like to aim at a piece with the density of *La Bohème*, i.e. lyrical and in the best sense popular.[54]

For a while both favoured the story of Dick Whittington, and they met several times at Hertford Avenue to work at it. Malcolm's sketches of their rough synopsis survive. Act One would be set in six varied scenes, including Holloway and the London quayside. Act Two would open with a chorus and ballet at the Barbary coast, where there would be fun with the Pasha and Fatima, and would end at the Mansion House with another ballet and chorus. It clearly had potential to be exactly the kind of light-hearted Christmas show the management envisaged, and Tracey worked hard on a full libretto:

> I waited with some apprehension to see what Malcolm would think. He was busy with *The Brilliant and the Dark* and *The Growing Castle*, so his decision hung fire, but when we got down to working at the details it became clear that he was as unhappy about it as I…

Malcolm had an alternative suggestion. There was a fascinating early work by Strindberg, he said, called *Lucky-Peter's Journey*, a fairy tale, part-fantasy, part-pantomine. It had all the qualities which they had most liked in *Dick Whittington*. Tracey read it and was suitably impressed. Then the first big mistake: they agreed to dispense with spoken dialogue and settle for a 'through-composed form' instead. Malcolm made a new translation, and between them they created a three-act structure out of the original five-act play, discarding certain scenes that seemed superfluous, conflating others, inventing much new material, and building a comic female double act for April Cantelo and Jennifer Vyvyan.

As usual the relationship between composer and librettist was a tempestuous one, Malcolm insisting that his word counted in all things – his second mistake, for his instincts were fallible. Edmund Tracey did not give way easily, but he did give way:

> Of my original libretto Malcolm set some scenes (e.g. the Robin's song) just as they stood. Others he contracted, retaining the overall shape, but taking only the lines he

53 In addition to his managerial role, Tracey was a fluent librettist who had made many English translations for the company.

54 *Opera*, December 1969

needed (as in the opening carol). Sometimes he fastened upon an image or phrase which pleased him and asked me to proceed from that point along different lines; once – as in the case of Peter's apostrophe to the ocean – he was seized with an irresistible musical idea – so I had the laborious task of fitting English words to existing music: the Spring Bird's song, with accompanying chorus, I wrote at the side of the piano in a state of high good humour one day last spring… The thing that always impressed me was his acute sense of what he wanted…

What Malcolm wanted was an opera, not a children's Christmas entertainment, and at the last moment he mischievously made sure he wrote what he wanted. He confessed in *The Listener*:

I began to feel like a dancer doing *jetés en tournant* with a noose about his neck. So there was nothing for it but to write precisely my own sort of opera, but weighted to the requirements of the management of the theatre...[55]

The two ideals were incompatible. Malcolm's comments to the press shortly before the first performance reveal how far he had strayed from the agreed commission:

The music itself contains set numbers, arias, trios and large contrapuntal ensembles, all of which are laid into a continuous symphonic stream. As the plot catapults forward, less a smooth narrative than a succession of highly charged scenes juxtaposed, the thematic material interweaves and the themes distort themselves, growing into new themes, superimpose themselves on each other to make ironies which may not be consciously perceived as such but which generate musical tensions. Only in the final ensemble of the opera does an extended release come with the septet and chorus which unite the human and the sub-human protagonists in illusory pleasure. The happy ending of *Lucky-Peter's Journey* cloaks an almost imperceptible Strindbergian question-mark.[56]

Edmund Tracey, realising things were going wrong, tried to bring in a director who might insist on late changes. Colin Graham not only directed regularly for English National Opera, but was also the much valued Director of Productions for Britten's English Opera Group.[57] He admired Malcolm's music, liked Strindberg's play and had found Malcolm's initial ideas, as laid out in his Production Notes, fascinating. He could never fully understand Malcolm's refusal to accept him as director:

---

55 5 February 1970. It would seem from this interview that, although Malcolm had thoughts on the opera stretching back to 1967, he actually wrote the score against the clock in 1969: 'The last essential dynamics were put into the orchestral score in November 1969 during the preliminary rehearsals, and, as the Sadler's Wells Opera gave me their official permission to base the opera on the Strindberg play in November 1968, I should say that I spent a year writing it. But this would be far from fact. In November 1968 I was working with intensity on a commissioned symphony, so my mind was not on opera...'

56 *ibid.*

57 Colin Graham had just directed a new production of *A Midsummer Night's Dream* and, not long before, had not only undertaken the premiere of Britten's *The Golden Vanity* but written the libretto. But instead of Graham Malcolm opted for the less experienced John Cox, who had worked with him on *The Brilliant and the Dark*.

> Malcolm told me to my face that he didn't want me to do *Lucky-Peter* because 'you would do all you could to make it a success'! By this strange and baffling statement I think he must have meant that my record as a director of so many other composers' world premieres would probably mean I would be leaning too hard on him to make alterations! Who knows? He never explained it beyond that to me…[58]

Graham's letter to Malcolm after their abortive meeting had been friendly but honest:

> …What you really need is a production assistant with not too many ideas of his own to act as your mouthpiece, in fact a stooge. I'm afraid I can't visualise myself in that capacity, even though I am, as I told you, always of the habit of working very closely with composers before the event.[59]

Graham's strong working relationship with Britten was clearly not a recommendation to Malcolm:

> You seem to have <u>such</u> deep-rooted mistrust of my 'position' with other composers and of my 'taste' that, even if you had not made me all too aware of your feelings, our relationship would be impossible. I quite understand your point that you resist me because of the management having forced me on you, but it obviously doesn't stop there…

In the event, *Lucky-Peter's Journey* was overseen by John Cox, a young director of much promise who was subsequently to do much distinguished work around the world. He was, however, brought in too late to be able to save Malcolm from himself.[60]

Had Malcolm been writing again for the Dynevor Castle music room, all might have been well. But instead of Dynevor he was in London's largest theatre, the 2,300-seat Coliseum,[61] where a jolly Christmas romp for children was being advertised, not 'a serious opera for grown-ups taking it easy'.[62] The critics were scornful and the public warily kept away. Thirteen performances had been scheduled and they all took place, but in a virtually empty theatre. Robert Lloyd remembers that 'one night we played to eight people in the house! There were 150 of us on stage and in the pit, and eight in the audience!'[63] April Cantelo suggests the figure might have been nearer fifty. Whatever the precise number,[64]

58 December 2005

59 Undated letter, written from Orford, Suffolk around May 1969.

60 John Cox became Director of Productions at Glyndebourne, Artistic Director at Scottish Opera and Production Director at the Royal Opera, Covent Garden.

61 The Sadler's Wells Opera Company had moved from Rosebery Avenue to St Martin's Lane in 1968, later changing the name to 'English National Opera'. But at the time of all Malcolm's operas they were already effectively the national company.

62 Edward Greenfield, *The Guardian*, 19 December 1969

63 January 2006

64 Richard Womersely, who watched three of the performances, thought that 'about a third full' was the lowest attendance.

Lucky-Peter's Journey proved a terrible failure and Malcolm's score, one of his best, has yet to be brought back to the stage.

Of all the critics who analysed the opera's shortcomings, none did so with more disappointment than Edward Greenfield, who five years previously had suggested Strindberg to Malcolm. For Greenfield, not only was *Lucky-Peter's Journey* not fulfilling its advertised purpose, but it possessed two major flaws. Malcolm's mistrust of temperamental tenors had made him give the part of the fifteen-year-old Peter to a baritone ('Chard made a dashing figure, but his Disney lederhosen outfit made one expect a voice much lighter'); and the book went too far from the original and lost coherence:

> Lucky Peter, immured in his tower from birth thanks to the protectiveness of his father, is given gifts by two magic characters, a Gnome who gives him a ring with which every wish will be granted; a Good Fairy, who gives him a vision of Lisa, the ideal love for whom he must search. Williamson and his librettist have omitted all mention of the first gift and that is a basic mistake. Only the vaguest hints are given of why and how Peter suddenly becomes the richest man in the world and later Caliph, of how he transforms winter into spring… The absence of a magic symbol disconnects the whole entertainment. One is left with a series of random happenings... The element of childish fantasy, so strong in the Strindberg, is almost eliminated, and the work of creating a childish fantasy from the rest made much more difficult...[65]

There was so much that was genuinely good, however, that Greenfield felt that with some judicious rewriting *Lucky-Peter's Journey* could still be successful as an adult opera. He cited the charming opening:

> Snow is falling on the cyclorama against an indigo sky as the curtain goes up… Shadowy cloaked figures bearing candles and an enormous shining star at once begin to sing Christmassy music. There is no robin (that seasonal essential has to wait till the next scene) but the Christmas-card picture is completed almost at once by the arrival of surpliced choirboys in procession. A final chink of sleigh-bells – musical tinsel. It says much of Williamson's skill in following Puccinian cliff-edge technique that for all those Hollywood trimmings (in fact because of them) he makes it a *magic opening.*

He also picked out the comic effectiveness of April Cantelo and Jennifer Vyvyan:

> The joke that certainly does come off, because it is so firmly based musically, is the equivalent that Williamson has devised to the pantomime pair of ugly sisters. The libretto neatly modifies the play so that there is a pair of rats in the first scene, a robin joined by a spring bird in the second, a pair of houris when the rich man is being milked for favours, a pair of saints in the final scene… The element of rivalry is genuine enough for everyone to have a whale of a time. The houri sequence with its haunting waltz theme is the most developed ('I speak as a friend,' each sings to Peter, behind the other's back) but all 4 sequences taken together give the opera a more distinctive element than anything in the whole piece.

---

65 *The Guardian*, 19 December 1969

But, for Greenfield, the opera's chief strength was where it mattered most, in its score:

> Musically at least the opera marks a consolidation of what Williamson has achieved in several of his previous operas, both in idiom and in operatic treatment. There is the easy transition into Richard Rodgers-style 'numbers' as in *Our Man in Havana*; the lightness of opera-cum-revue which marked *English Eccentrics*; the rich Straussian texture supporting sweet seamless melody as in *The Violins of Saint-Jacques*; the matching of apparently lightweight manner with a deeper undertow as in the previous Strindberg opera *The Growing Castle*…
>
> Musically there is a comparable thread holding the score together – the 'Land of Pleasure' theme which gets transformed in the most unlikely but highly effective and immediately recognisable ways. It first appears when the Gnome and the Good Fairy are talking to Peter in the first scene. Peter looks out to the world he has never visited and with elation sings 'Have you ever stood alone by the window in the tower?' The tune then keeps re-emerging, whether in Cuban rhythm at the rich man's party or sour and compressed for a chorus of beggars… It got hooked on me so completely that I was humming it for days. With at least a couple of other 'grand tunes', Puccini-style, the houris' waltz theme and an 'uplift' theme like a Williamised hymn tune, you have an opera which, whatever else it is not, is exceptionally sweet on the ear.

Understandably pleased with his score, unused to failure and wounded by the smallest criticism, Malcolm was quite unable to see the flaws of the opera, and behaved with an utter lack of restraint in the face of the critical onslaught: the disaster was not his fault nor that of his singers; he had been unsupported by the management all along; in their crass ignorance they had impeded him at every turn, failing time and again to listen to what he was saying… He raged on and on, before turning abruptly on his heel and slamming the door behind him, little realising that he would never again be welcome at the ENO or, indeed, be offered a commission anywhere in the country. The word soon spread that Malcolm Williamson was to be avoided. At thirty-eight, he had written his last opera.[66] Malcolm had so much more to offer the professional stage, but from 1970 he would simply write cassations for children. These were very worthwhile endeavours, and he would bravely declare that the Ditchling village hall was every bit as exciting as the London Coliseum. But it wasn't, and Malcolm's highly vulnerable personality would never fully recover from the traumas of *Lucky-Peter's Journey*.

66 *The Red Sea* (1972), written for children on a summer course, was essentially an enlarged cassation.

10 PILGRIM TRAVELS

From America to Africa, 1970–73

THE FAILED OPERA not only marked the end of a decade but a turning-point in Malcolm's creative life. Whereas in the 1960s he produced a continual flow of high-quality works, in the 1970s a growing lack of self-belief meant that he struggled with every new piece. He remained externally ebullient, rarely revealing any inner turmoil, but his compositions over the next four years were, by his previous standards, quite modest: a fine song cycle, an ineffective symphony, an enigmatic concerto, four sparkling cassations and several interesting but essentially minor works.

In the 1970s he began to travel much more widely, at home and abroad, seeking to promote performances of his large body of work; it was a significant change of lifestyle, allowing him less time for writing. In its stead he found enjoyable employment staging his cassations with young people, and also, for a while, running his own touring company, Castle Opera, to further his more serious shorter works. Constantly on the move, living off his wits and selling his wares wherever and however he could, he was a curious mixture of circus showman, travelling salesman and compelled pilgrim.

His continuing activities as a performer complemented this increased emphasis on travel. The early months of 1970 were typical. In February he was at the Queen Elizabeth Hall, broadcasting a recital, 'Meet The Composer', in which he introduced music of his choice and accompanied April Cantelo, Shirley Chapman and Jennifer Vyvyan.[1] In April he played his Organ Concerto at the Festival Hall with Adrian Boult and the LPO. In May he gave an organ recital at the Camden Festival (Howells' Sonata, Tournemire's *Symphonie Sacrée*, and six Bach choral preludes) and a piano lecture recital at University College, Cardiff,

[1] The choice included songs by Purcell, Handel and Vaughan Williams, three Bach choral preludes and Messiaen's *O Sacrum Convivium*.

with much Messiaen, Rawsthorne's *Ballade* and the Second Piano Sonata of the contemporary Finnish composer he was currently championing, Usko Merilainen.

As he approached forty, he also began to explore more seriously his talents as a writer. His book reviews showed an incisive use of language, and one of them led to an important friendship with the Master of the Queen's Music, Sir Arthur Bliss. It began with an unexpected letter from Bliss in the summer of 1970:

> Your generous appreciation of my 'Memoirs' in this morning's *Sunday Times* pleased my wife and myself so much that I must break my rule of never replying to newspaper notices, and tell you what satisfaction it is to have the kind comments of a fellow composer and of a so much younger one.
>
> I can perfectly understand how each generation of composers *must* start off on quite a different track from their predecessors, and indeed feel a somewhat contemptuous dislike of their methods – hence all the more is my appreciation.
>
> With all best wishes to the future of your own music…[2]

At 79 Bliss was still very active, producing a Cello Concerto that year and, for the Queen, several short pieces celebrating Prince Charles and Princess Anne. Bliss had the leisure and the private means to write as he pleased, unworried by the need for sponsorship. Malcolm, by contrast, continued to live a hand-to-mouth existence, spending many weeks in 1970 relentlessly touring round Sweden for the Swedish government, directing cassations in schools and teaching English (with his 'Hallo Everybody!' songbook). He might tell Nancy Evans grimly that tackling two or three hundred children at a time in Swedish was 'a fortifying experience!'[3] but he very much enjoyed the linguistic challenge, and, despite an exacting schedule, made sure he could pursue his interest in Strindberg. Richard Dynevor received a postcard from Stockholm:

> I visited Strindberg's last home where one can study his MSS and much else of great interest. His experimental materials as a chemist, for example. This photo [Strindberg with two of his daughters] was probably taken by himself with processes of his own invention. I've met some Str. scholars. The G.C. in Dynevor Castle is written about in their society's archives…[4]

Malcolm returned to Sweden later that year, having organised a holiday exchange with a Stockholm family. Dolly, who drove there and back, remembers the journeys chiefly as examples of Malcolm's remarkable ability in packing the car:

> A sense of spatial awareness is connected, apparently, with musical composition – both involve the right side of the brain. At any rate, what Malcolm managed to fit into our estate car – a not particularly large Datsun – was amazing! It was tight enough going there, what with Malcolm, the *au pair*, the three children and myself! But at a wonderful store in Stockholm we bought a huge rug, a chair, a bedside table, and

---

2 14 June 1970

3 April 1970

4 23 April 1970

several other bulky items. And somehow Malcolm, by dint of his remarkable packing skills, got all of it in, as well as all of us and the rest of our luggage![5]

A trip to Holland for performances of *The Happy Prince* at The Hague[6] was followed by the American premiere of *The Growing Castle* with an American cast in New York. Dolly, prevented by illness from travelling, wrote in determined support to Malcolm, who was staying with her parents in Brooklyn:

> Darling,
>
> It's even worse not being there than I thought it might be. All evening I've been calculating what the time would be in New York and wondering what you are doing at that minute and how the weather is and who will be there, and trying to imagine it outdoors and wishing so very much I were with you, both to be with you and see the production. It's less than an hour before you are due to start and I'm sitting 3,000 miles away with the first night jitters… I'm hearing it all in my head and aching to be there. Do get through from Princeton late tonight![7]

Malcolm was visiting Princeton to finalise a year's appointment as composer-in-residence at the Westminster Choir College, later to become part of Rider University. The appointment was a bold new step for the comparatively small college, training around four hundred music students, postgraduates[8] as well as undergraduates. Malcolm was an excellent acquisition with his passionate interest in all kinds of church music, his skills on the organ and his breadth of knowledge of past and present American music.[9] His lighter works were currently in use in many American churches.

For Malcolm the appointment was financially helpful, temporarily taking pressure off his compositional life, and it fulfilled his ambition for further academic involvement after his short stay in Canberra three years earlier. Dolly, however, was anxious. For Malcolm to be away from London for most of a year was to risk losing touch with the professional musical world. The disruption to family life was also considerable. The two girls were to have a year's schooling in America, but Peter's London Prep School preferred him to convert to boarding.[10]

---

[5] December 2005

[6] The Holland Festival, 16-19 June 1970

[7] 4 July 1970

[8] It offers postgraduate study in voice, organ, piano, conducting and teaching.

[9] He impressed on interview with his detailed knowledge of American composers like Virgil Fox and Richard Felciano. 'I have great admiration for the originality of Richard Felciano,' he wrote in 1974, 'but I can't help feeling that he stands out as a sort of highbrow reaction to Father This and Sister That strumming their guitars... The pieces of Felciano that have interested me most are the pieces that don't have tapes but use living human bodies. When we stop using living human performers in worship and when we start using tape recorded this, that, and the other, I'm fed up.' (*Music Ministry*, October 1974)

[10] Peter was at Colet Court. The next year Malcolm dedicated *6 Wesley Songs for the Young* to 'the boys of Colet Court, St Paul's School, London'. It was one of several popular books of his hymn settings published in the 1960s and early 1970s by Weinberger's.

They arrived in Princeton in September 1970, settling in to a house on the College's attractive twenty-acre campus,[11] where they were delighted to find themselves looking after Poppy, a border collie, whose owner was away on a sabbatical. Malcolm's brief as composer-in-residence was threefold:

> To bring to the campus the excitement of a composer who is internationally recognised; to acquaint the student body with as many of the composer's works as possible; to allow selected students to work with the composer on a one-to-one basis.[12]

It was also agreed he should give a series of talks on contemporary music.

From the very first Malcolm was a great success, as James Litton[13] remembers:

> He was warmly welcomed by the students. He had a particular ability to recognize immediately the strong and weak points of each student, to reinforce naturally strong abilities and increase confidence in areas where students were insecure. He always found the proper place for students who may have lacked the highest vocal or instrumental ability. In workshops or performances of his cassations these less talented students were given just the proper role to make the most of their individual abilities. These experiences have been remembered by many of Malcolm's students decades later, and several have gone on to become musical leaders or outstanding teachers in their communities.[14]

Dr Joan Lippincott, Head of Westminster's Organ Department, also has happy memories:

> When I think of Malcolm, I remember his enormous creative energy, not just in and about his own compositions but in his enthusiasm for the work of others. I remember especially Malcolm's convincing us at Westminster to play the complete works of Messiaen in one year, in organ performance classes, in recitals and in chapel. He wrote programme notes for many of these events and drummed up support everywhere on the campus, as well as making the reception of the works exciting.[15]

Michael Cordovana, choral director of Washington's Catholic University of America, was another friend from this period:

> What a genius! Not just as a composer, but also as an organist and pianist! And so too, what a very kind and considerate gentleman he was! The students adored him.

---

11 540 Ewing Street

12 *The Princeton Packet*, October 1970, quoting the new College President, Dr Ray Robinson.

13 Chairman of the Church Music Department and a member of the organ faculty at Westminster, Litton co-ordinated Malcolm's programme and worked closely on all aspects of it with him. He had first come to know of Malcolm's music when studying with Allan Wicks at Canterbury. Litton and Alec Wyton were largely instrumental in Malcolm's appointment. Wyton was a visiting Professor at WCC, Organist and Choirmaster at the Cathedral of St John the Divine in New York City, and Headmaster of the Cathedral Choir School.

14 August 2006

15 June 2006

> Nothing was too petty for his consideration and understanding. He was a magnificent teacher.[16]

Malcolm revelled in being a celebrity on the Westminster campus, his ego flattered and his inner self reassured. Socially he loved to be surrounded by young people; intellectually he was in his element in academic surroundings; musically he was able to give dazzling recitals and enjoy performances of his own creations. In a special Williamson Festival in Washington, for example, eight compositions were to be heard in four different venues.[17]

The most important one of these, *In Place of Belief*, a new forty-minute song cycle for six-part chorus and piano duet, proved too difficult for the choir preparing it, so Michael Cordovana was hastily called in to organise another first performance, which took place at the Catholic University of America.

> The cancellation was embarrassing as the work had been commissioned by the Kindler Foundation. Fortunately it was holiday time and I was able to get sufficiently long rehearsals for six very talented students. A man at the Embassy helped us with the Swedish pronunciation! It was a terrific undertaking and we had a magnificent time doing it. It was, in the end, a great success and received wonderful notices…[18]

In Place of Belief was, like the Second Symphony, inspired by Pär Lagerkvist, ten of whose early poems provide the cycle's text. Malcolm wrote of them:

> The poems which appeared in 1919 are to do with a countryman's and a bereaved father's attitudes to the transience of nature and of human life, a refusal to believe in the permanence of death. The title indicates Lagerkvist's defiance of the conventional comforts and answers of religion.[19]

Only six years on from the tragedy of Rebecca, Malcolm fully empathises with Lagerkvist's reflections on the death of a young child and the thoughts it provokes on the uncertainties of the human condition. This is his most personal utterance, the poems inspiring a bitter-sweet musical setting which takes them to

---

16 February 2006. Malcolm had always enjoyed teaching, and throughout his time at East Sheen, despite all his other commitments, had managed to help along some students of particular promise. John Hawkins was one such pupil: 'He was a wonderful teacher, very giving, very generous. He put much stress on motivic development, encouraging me to be extremely disciplined so that each idea was developed to its maximum. He had great admiration for Poulenc ('a great genius, don't you think?'), Webern and Messiaen, talking about them very often, particularly as regards economy. 'Be very economical with your building blocks,' he would say. Haydn too! He made me analyse Haydn to see just how economical he was with his material.' (July 2005)

17 10-11 January 1971. Following a Sunday evening service at Washington National Cathedral, Joan Lippincott played his Organ Symphony and the Introit from his Mass of Christ the King. The service also contained his *Te Deum* and several of his hymn settings. Elsewhere the Sonata for Two Pianos was played by Alice and Arthur Nagle, while the National Gallery hosted his Quintet for Piano and Strings.

18 This success (on 15 January 1971) led to Cordovana (later a distinguished Professor of Music at the CUA) producing *The Happy Prince* ('a gem of an opera') and *The Growing Castle* ('terrific too').

19 Programme note, 1971

new emotional heights, strangely beautiful harmonies floating in and out of the world of tonality, as the six-part chorus mourns, reflects, pleads, questions, cries, rages and, in the poignant final moments, grudgingly accepts. The cycle shows Malcolm at his most typical, employing the richest musical textures at times of greatest distress, when emotion is rawest. Nowhere is this more evident than in the unaccompanied 'Come with a dream to your father's side',[20] an imaginary monologue in which the father asks his little child about the world beyond the grave.

> Was it spring when you went, was it winter, was it fall?
> And is all there unmoving and peaceful?
> You must tell me it all, heavy grief weighs my breast,
> You must tell me all that you know, my sweet one.
>
> Did the birds sing in the dawning hour, when sunlight touches all,
> Did returning twilight dim the daytime's ending?
> Did a wind pervade the trees, like the winds that murmur here
> When it darkens, this impalpable small sighing.
>
> Or is all suffused with light, without darkness, unlike here,
> Without anguish for the great, the unimagined?
> Was your heart not ever heavy, like my heart which bears alone
> A single grief desiring no forgetting.
>
> Were the pathways dim and narrow, far from the glittering squares,
> Was there darkness for the desolate and quiet?
> I ask you not for gladness, I ask you but for grief.
> You must tell me all that you know, my darling.
>
> I shall go soon, soon the pathway, the very path you took,
> But I find it all a lengthy, lengthy journey.
> Let me bless you, little child, who reached down here to earth.
> I go far from this world like one unseeing.

Malcolm gives this poem a setting of great calm and beauty, yet the peacefulness is subject throughout to much harmonic side-stepping; peace can never be taken for granted; it is always wafer-thin.[21]

For Malcolm the premiere of *In Place of Belief* was the highlight of his year at Princeton and ensured that he would always retain fond memories of his days at Westminster Choir College. Dolly, however, never really settled, and looks back on the period with mixed feelings:

> I didn't want to be there at all. I had a bad feeling about going and I didn't like it, despite the fact that my parents and my sister were in New York only sixty miles

---

20 The tenth poem in the published score, but the ninth in the fine ABC recording of 1974, which gives Malcolm's definitive version. Initially Malcolm set the Swedish words, but, happily, he later translated the poems himself. (Text by courtesy of Josef Weinberger Ltd.)

21 *In Place of Belief* is, by any reckoning, a superb work of art, the finest of Malcolm's many fine song cycles. But it demands choral singing of the very highest level. Anything less could result in chaos. Perhaps that is why it currently languishes in obscurity...

> away. I guess I wasn't very involved in the organisation Malcolm had gone to. They seemed mainly born-again Christians. I was the first Jew one of them had ever met![22]

There was also the distress of Malcolm sliding back into the emotional mayhem of the 1950s. James Litton remembers Malcolm bringing up the subject of his confused sexuality:

> Following several weeks of our work together at WCC, Malcolm began to discuss his sexuality conflicts with me. I made it clear that if his year at WCC were to be a success, he must be completely professional, regard his colleagues as professionals, and treat the highly impressionable students as students, and not as close friends, always being aware where the dividing line should be. He was not always happy with this advice, and since he was a few years older than I, would tell me that I should listen to him! Still, as far as I know, there was never an infraction of any sort during his time at WCC. I always realized that Dolly was concerned and may have thought otherwise. I, of course, cannot speak of his lifestyle away from Princeton...[23]

For Dolly there was the added concern that, for the first time since they were married, other commitments and interests were cutting across the writing of music:

> Malcolm was teaching a great deal, so it wasn't a particularly creative time. I don't have strong recollections of him writing at Princeton. I can usually picture him writing – at a desk or table, or that sloping device he had at Hertford Avenue – but not at Princeton. I can see the sprawling one-storey house we had, but I can't put Malcolm into any of the rooms.

It was certainly a less productive time than usual, for the major work, *In Place of Belief*, had been largely completed before he left England.[24] At Princeton Malcolm wrote only *Peace Pieces* (for organ) and *Genesis*, a splendid seven-minute cassation in which three groups of singers represent God, half the world and the other half of the world.[25] Dolly, aware of the correlation between Malcolm's vigorous work ethic and his commitment to the family, was understandably anxious, though as supportive as ever. Richard Rodney Bennett, who was also in America at the time, is full of admiration for all she achieved:

---

22 July 2005. James Litton writes: 'It is true there were at the time several students whom Malcolm called 'the God Squad', who came from very limited fundamental backgrounds, but he won many of them over, and made a major change in their lives. But most of the students have been very dedicated and hard working, talented budding musicians, and Malcolm delighted in his work with them.' (August 2006)

23 August 2006

24 On 11 May 1970, four months before moving to Princeton, Malcolm wrote to Arthur Nagle, Vice-President of the Kindler Foundation, 'I'm assuming that you and your wife will play the piano parts of the new work, *In Place of Belief.* I'm well advanced with the piece and may be able to show you something of it in June...'

25 Each participant was urged to bring either a musical instrument or a saucepan lid. *Genesis* was commissioned by Dr Marilyn Keiser, when she was associate organist at the Cathedral of St John the Divine in New York. The premiere was given in North Carolina (where Dr Keiser was by that time working) by young choristers (conducted by James Litton) attending a summer camp in the Carolina mountains.

During this period I was at the Peabody Conservatoire, Baltimore, and so began to see more of the two of them again. I liked Dolly enormously. She was a strong lady with the strength to save Malcolm from himself, but not in the sense of being bossy. She wasn't head prefect! Just a strong lady, who was marvellous for him.[26]

Dolly was much relieved as Malcolm's year drew to its conclusion. In his last term, by way of thanks, the College's finest singers presented *The Happy Prince* and *Dunstan and the Devil*. James Litton, who directed *Dunstan* and also played *The Vision of Christ Phoenix* in his final Faculty Concert, emphasises the far-reaching nature of Malcolm's achievements at Westminster:

Largely as a result of Malcolm's residency the entire curriculum for Church Music was revised, and this curriculum proved the basis for the education of many young musicians whose experience at WCC has greatly influenced the direction of the church music profession in America during the past several decades.[27]

Malcolm had little time, however, on the return to England in June 1971, for nostalgic reminiscences of America, having to turn very quickly to a long-neglected commission for a short cassation for the last night of the Proms. He had been thinking of a possible biblical theme while he was in Princeton – about Moses and the crossing of the Red Sea – but had abandoned it as impractical. He needed a new idea very quickly, but none came, and, meanwhile, there were other commitments. He had, for example, promised his friend Elizabeth Lamb (one of the soloists in *The Brilliant and the Dark*) that he would participate for four days in her local festival at Holme Cultram in Cumbria.[28] It proved a blessing, for there, not far from Hadrian's Wall, he suddenly found a perfect topic for his Proms cassation: the Scots on one side of Hadrian's Wall, the English on the other, with a third group of singers, the Vikings, intervening. Time was now perilously short, but Elizabeth Lamb again came to the rescue. As she and her husband were off on a three-week singing tour, she invited Malcolm and the family to take over the house. While Dolly occupied the children with some determined sight-seeing, Malcolm worked away at his new idea. *The Stone Wall* was completed in Cumbria on 7 August, and, with hours rather than days to spare, the score was delivered to an anxious Colin Davis.

Five weeks later,[29] on the last night of the Proms, the audience found in their programme a map designating various areas of the Albert Hall to the Scots, English and Vikings. Their evening began with a rehearsal. First Colin Davis, with Malcolm at a piano, took the promenaders through the cassation. Then the whole audience, all six thousand of them, were asked to stand up and sing their

26 April 2006

27 August 2006.

28 Elizabeth Lamb recalls: 'On 29 June at the Church of St Mary's I sang several of Malcolm's pieces to his accompaniment: The *6 English Lyrics*, some Wesley hymns, *From A Child's Garden*, the Epiphany Carol and an aria from *Violins of Saint-Jacques*. He also played one of his sonatas and the Five Preludes.' (September 2005)

29 18 September 1971

way through it, this time accompanied by the BBC Symphony Orchestra. Richard Baker (in lavender shirt, fawn suit and grey top-hat) led the English; Malcolm (wearing a bright tam-o-shanter) the Scots.[30] Participation was total and predictably boisterous.

The piece begins fiercely. 'Northern savages!' sing the English to the Scots. 'Southern savages!' reply the Scots to the English. And the word 'savages' is bandied back and forth. The English are given the first tune:

Divided we should always stand.
United we should fall.
Our only hope of self-defence
Is if we build a wall.

– while the Scots are jeering with an ostinato set to the word 'savages'. As the English start building the wall, it is the turn of the Scots to sing out the same melody:

United we should always fall
Divided we should stand.
Let's build a great dividing wall
To keep them off our land,

– the English meanwhile providing an accompanimental ostinato of 'stone on stone on stone on…' As the Scots[31] join in the building of the wall, the arriving Vikings are given their own melody:

Fire and sword and battleaxe
Kill the Scots and Sassenachs!
Fire and sword and arrow shots
Kill the Sassenachs and Scots!

– while the English and Scots, busily building, take on the 'stone on stone on' ostinato. The Vikings sing a second verse as the building continues. Then comes Malcolm's big coup. The wall has been completed and, by way of celebration, he gives the English and Scots a noble tune in the bright key of E major, magnificently moving:

Not a stone is left.
Let our labour cease.
Praise the god of stone.
May we now have peace!

Peace, of course, is not possible while there are dastardly Vikings around. And with a reprise of the 'Fire and sword and battleaxe' they come swooping

---

30 'I found Malcolm Williamson a delightful man,' recalls Richard Baker. 'During the interval I was talking to prommers and interviewed Malcolm in that area we called no man's land – between the orchestra and the prommers. I must have introduced him as Malcolm Arnold because the next day I received a funny postcard from him on the subject!' (March 2006)

31 Perhaps the haste in which *The Stone Wall* was written was responsible for the exclusion of the actual builders of the wall, the Romans.

down on the wall-builders, who, in horror, sing 'Savages' and 'Vikings!' in counterpoint. A glorious battle follows, the Vikings being pelted with stones from the wall, before, in another musical coup, Malcolm gives the fleeing Vikings an arresting song of lamentation, the orchestra answering them at the end of each line with a mocking glissando:

> We should have kept aw–ay.
> It would have been far cannier.
> Let's sail the other wa–ay
> Who'd want to rule Britannia?

The Vikings sail off into the distance and the Scots and English, left alone at the site of the dismantled wall, join together in a noble reprise:

> Not a stone is left.
> Let our warfare cease.
> Praise the god of stone.
> May we now have peace!

Malcolm has one surprise left. Far, far out at sea, the chastened Vikings contribute, ever so *pianissimo*, one last 'May we now have peace!' before peace itself is signified with a sweet E major chord, dying away very slowly and softly.

The Stone Wall, simple and sophisticated, proved one of the highlights of the evening, five minutes of sheer joy, after which the massed singers gave the orchestra, Colin Davis, Malcolm and themselves a long, standing ovation. But unfortunately, for all its success, *The Stone Wall* failed to find favour where it most mattered, in the higher reaches of the BBC. There was a move afoot to 'improve' the Proms, to get away from the vulgarity which was felt to have come in with Malcolm Sargent. *The Stone Wall* had been a sop thrown by the radicals to appease the conservatives, and its huge success was looked upon with disdain rather than pride. The highbrow critics were so scornful that Malcolm, in much distress, even queried his future. 'Shall I give it all up?' he asked Janet Canetty-Clarke miserably. Even though the television coverage throughout Europe and the speedy issue of a Last Night of the Proms LP had ensured *The Stone Wall* the immediate popularity it deserved, it has yet to be heard again at the Proms.

The pace did not slacken. The first of a series of visits to America took Malcolm to Washington where the Catholic University performed *The Growing Castle* and he gave an organ recital. This included *Peace Pieces*,[32] written at Princeton and dedicated to James Litton. Its third section, 'Peace in Solitude', was, as Malcolm explained, inspired by the Swedish landscape:

> I was thinking of old age and loneliness. But also, having come from the hot inclement summers of Australia, I had become very obsessed with northern Sweden. There I saw the Baltic go into deep winter into what seemed a sleep of eternity, the moment preserved in ice, capped with snow. The inspiration was from Francis Thompson's poem 'The Hound of Heaven'.

---

32 22 October 1971, National Shrine of the Immaculate Conception

In the USA, 1971

> The pulp so bitter, how shall taste the rind?
> I dimly know what time in mists confirms
> Yet ever and anon a trumpet sounds
> From the hid battlements of eternity.[33]

Peace Pieces was part of his increasing need to find some time and space for himself:

> By coincidence, every ten years of my life I seem to return to the organ, where I can write at my most interior and personal. I've retreated into this wonderful, magic and isolated world and written the most complex music I've ever written at all, because I knew that very few people would play it. I don't really care if very few people play it…[34]

Such personal music apart, Malcolm cared passionately about the promulgation of his work, and he was accordingly delighted to sign on with an agent in New Jersey, Phillip Truckenbrod of Arts Image, through whom he hoped to establish himself in America. Soon he was travelling all over the country: to a

33 *Malcolm Williamson Down Under*, BBC Television, 1975

34 *ibid.*

Genesis *in the USA*

conference in Atlanta to demonstrate his cassations; to New York for discussions on *The Happy Prince* and *Dunstan and the Devil*, which were being performed the following Easter;[35] to the Carolinas for more cassations; to Louisville, Kentucky for a recital, more cassations, and an *ad hoc* ballet based on his *Twelve New Hymns*, culminating in 'a ticker-tape procession to Crown Him with Many Thorns.'[36] In Chicago he met Byron Belt, an influential radio programme host; in Washington a Strindberg expert (Donald Burnham), Olivier Messiaen and his wife and Ursula Vaughan Williams, he and Ursula enjoying a 'not bad' performance of the *Sea Symphony* under Susskind at the Kennedy Centre.[37]

Phillip Truckenbrod exploited the cassations most effectively, particularly in his own state of New Jersey. Malcolm even coped in the black ghettoes of Newark, telling Weinberger's Richard Toeman on one such occasion:

> Tonight I feel somewhat chewed up since I've had four days of *Knights in Shining Armour* with the Newark and Trenton schools... The schools are rowdy in the depressed areas and it is not easy to handle them, but we get some sort of performance.[38]

He experienced a somewhat easier time at the Benedictine Theological Seminary in Ramsey, New Jersey, where a group of young priests and their mentors acted out *Genesis*. Malcolm was on top form:

---

35 At the Cathedral of St John the Divine with the same student casts which had performed at WCC a year earlier.

36 MW to Richard Toeman, 9 October 1972

37 MW to Richard Toeman, 14 March 1972

38 MW to Richard Toeman, 9 October 1972

> It's not really a workshop, it's a fun-shop!... please, just a soft chaos noise!... here now, group one, you cannot be doing fish music when everyone else is doing their bird thing!... One half of the world, come here! Now start to be the Light and Darkness!... Careful there! Keep your extremities in, or you will be trodden on by God![39]

Phillip Truckenbrod, one of his strongest allies at this period, remembers Malcolm as a lively figure, popular with everyone:

> He often stayed with us, sometimes by himself, sometimes with his family. We used to take Dolly to the airport to visit her family in Brooklyn. She was always very tolerant, proud and supportive. He liked to give the impression that there was something slightly scandalous going on, that he was philandering rather more than he actually was! One night when he was staying with us, he'd gone to bed, but heard one of my friends arrive, and so joined us in his drawers! He wanted to be involved in all the gossip.[40]

These promotional travels were extremely costly, but his publishers usually paid for them. Richard Toeman, who had taken over as Weinberger's Managing Director, found Malcolm very touchy on the subject, often grumbling that in undertaking such visits he was compensating for Weinberger's inadequacies, when the real reasons for his constant travels had to do with his need for space. In October 1972 Toeman received a typical harangue:

> Over this much-discussed travel allowance, you must know that I have to work myself very hard and use money that I do not possess in order to promote. I also must find time that I do not have. The expending of energy is colossal; and I do not like in these circumstances having to bargain with you over the travel allowance, as I have had to do. For your private information the cost of the Arts Image publicity and getting performances etc has taken every dollar I earned here in October/November. I left the fees in Truck's hands and he has used the money prudently, but it all went except a handful of cents and I cannot complain or reveal to Dolly what has happened. Truck is vastly cheaper than any of the other USA agents, and I believe does more. He is getting my music known, which is important...[41]

When Richard Toeman suggested caution, Malcolm threw a tantrum:

> I'm tired of being treated like an idiot, who must be guided by experts to be saved from himself!

In addition to the USA there were flying visits to Finland, Holland, Belgium and long stays in France, particularly Paris, where he had found a promising contact in a cultured young publisher, Mario Bois, married to a leading ballerina at the Paris Opera Ballet, Claire Motte; both became important friends. There were also the regular travels around Britain, wherever engagements might take him.

---

39 MW, as reported by Carolyn Raney, *Music*, February 1973

40 August 2006

41 14 March 1972

One of his most important English assignments in 1972 was at Dartington Hall, where he supervised a new forty-five-minute 'opera', *The Red Sea*. Sponsored by the Devon Education Authority, it was written to a specific brief: a simple opera around which a week's workshops could be organised for singers and instrumentalists aged 14-16, leading to two performances. *The Red Sea* was really an extended cassation, abandoning most of the traditional operatic conventions; it was performed in the round, without sets, designed costumes and stage lighting; the large orchestra[42] was positioned at either end of the hall, the young singers in between; there was no conductor, the strongly-knit rhythmic score being held together by three people beating time at different vantage points.[43] The audience was expected to join in, not only with refrains and chorus verses, but with simple actions at key moments.

Hugo Cole was one of the many critics who made the long trip down to Devon to keep an eye on Malcolm's latest venture:

> The story is simply that of the flight of the Israelites from Egypt. All is made to centre round the crossing of the Red Sea, and this vital episode came off brilliantly. Human waves covered the middle of the sports hall, parting for the Israelites (white tee-shirts), rising to engulf the Egyptians (red and yellow). The threatening advance of the Egyptians was musically and dramatically thrilling; the whole of this sequence was most imaginatively produced and, as so often, Williamson rises to the big dramatic moments with his ability to invent striking and memorable motifs that instantly establish a mood, and to build up large structures from simple musical ingredients. The chorus of rejoicing that follows is one of Williamson's happiest inventions...[44]

Purists could grumble that the two performances, at the Dartington College of Arts and King Edward VI School, Totnes, exuded a rough and ready atmosphere, but, as Hugo Cole concluded, 'for the children taking part, it's the sense of involvement in a new sort of magic that will remain'.

Malcolm also loved the magic which smaller festivals could bring, especially those which centred on historic rural churches.[45] In 1972 he began to participate annually at Mayfield in Sussex, which conveniently boasted a Church of St Dunstan's, and he continued to visit the Holme Cultram Festival, for which he wrote an extended cassation on a Christmas theme, *The Winter Star*. Its conductor, Andrew Sievewright,[46] recalls:

---

42 Allowing for the unpredictability of school orchestras, Malcolm stipulated only 'high, middle and low instruments' without further specification. They were supported by pianos and percussion

43 Geoffrey Baggs, *Western Morning News*, 17 April 1972

44 *The Guardian*, 18 April 1972

45 In 1972, for example, Malcolm also played his *Epitaphs for Edith Sitwell* at Beecles Church, and the Haydn and Handel organ concertos with the English Sinfonia at Wangford, Suffolk.

46 His first contact with Malcolm's music had been as conductor of the Carlisle and District choir in *The Brilliant and the Dark*.

Genesis *at Holme Cultram*

> The Holme Cultram Festival was started by an enthusiastic Catholic clergyman – it was a one-man show, and very much out of the way. As well as *Winter Star*, we did *Dunstan and the Devil* and *The Happy Prince*. I was very fond of Malcolm, but his company was very exhausting! He would sit up to two or three in the morning, smoking and talking! He could be very difficult, but also had a lovely sense of humour. He was full of stories. He would tell of the occasion he had given his all at a recital in Carlisle Cathedral, ending with the hugely difficult *Vision of Christ Phoenix*. Afterwards a lady came up to him. He was expecting a modicum of praise. But not a bit of it! 'I wonder if you ever knew a Canon Snodgrass?' she enquired. [47]

One year, not long before a performance, Malcolm approached Andrew Sievewright urgently. 'You can't conduct in a shirt like that,' he told him and insisted on their rushing out to one of Carlisle's less salubrious areas:

> There, at a hippy shop which he seemed to know quite well, he bought me a dreadfully gaudy patterned yellow shirt! He was so delighted with it that, despite my embarrassment, I just had to wear it!

The formation of Castle Opera in 1972 was a further potential link to local festival music-making. It came about through a meeting with a dynamic young music administrator, Prue Skene, who had most recently been organising a tour for Richard Rodney Bennett as well as a visit to Australia by Britten's English Opera Group:

> Malcolm had this idea of touring his operas under the banner of Castle Opera and asked me to help. He was the Director, I was the Manager, and Lord Dynevor the

47 September 2005

> Patron! The thing was run very informally – we didn't set it up as a company or anything. It was basically just run by Malcolm and me![48]

After his cantankerous break with English National Opera, Malcolm saw the development of his own company as a possible alternative way forward, particularly as so many friends in the operatic world were prepared to participate in it, giving it immediate credibility. In the long term he might write new works; in the short term he had at his disposal ten short operas and cassations. The first venture was a single performance one Sunday evening in early June 1972 of *Dunstan and the Devil* at St James's Church, Piccadilly, featuring soprano Madge Stephens and tenor Kevin Miller, both Australians pursuing successful careers in England.[49] A press release explained the general background:

> Castle Opera takes its name from Dynevor Castle in Wales; it was in that castle that Williamson's *The Growing Castle* was first performed in 1968. The company fulfils the composer's aim to form a company for the mobile presentation of opera in unusual settings as well as in theatres and opera houses. Future appearances of Castle Opera include an appearance at the Cheltenham Festival on June 9 where it will present the world premiere of Williamson's latest work, a symphony for voices.[50]

This was his Third Symphony ('*The Icy Mirror*'),[51] commissioned by Sir Arthur Bliss, and its appearance at Cheltenham might have been good publicity for the fledgling Castle Opera, if only the work been even vaguely attractive. Unfortunately much of it is very sombre indeed, and the text for the four soloists and chorus incomprehensible without previous study, the theme of man's misuse of the environment getting lost in the chorus's confusing interaction with a harvest goddess, a prisoner and a pair of lovers. Associating the Third Symphony with Castle Opera was an extremely ill-judged piece of opportunism, for it had absolutely nothing in common with the exciting operatic product linking amateurs and professionals, adults and children, for which, like *The Music Man's* Professor Harold Hill, Malcolm was currently trying to drum up support:

> Anything with a roof over it can be an opera house. It's a great thing to mix skills, virtuoso singers with children, for instance. The kids bring to an opera zest and enthusiasm which impress the professionals, and *they* have the skills which impress the children.[52]

---

48 July 2006

49 Other friends included baritones John Barrow and Robert Bateman; pianists Janet Canetty-Clarke and Michael Rich; conductor Kenneth Pont (who brought along his Mayfield Festival Chorus); Sister Daphne Walker (Director of Music at the Catholic School at Mayfield) who provided percussionists; and the designer Ronald Searle's daughter, Kate.

50 Press release, late May 1972

51 It was performed at Cheltenham Town Hall on 9 July 1972, with the Cheltenham Bach Choir and Festival Chorus and BBC Northern Symphony Orchestra, conducted by John Hopkins. Jennifer Vyvyan, Margreta Elkins, and the two baritones Robert Bateman and John Barrow were the soloists.

52 MW, *Sunday Telegraph*, 4 June 1972

Directing Dunstan and the Devil *at Mayfield*

Working on a cassation

Castle Opera at Le Touquet, 1972:

(left) pianists Janet Canetty-Clarke and Michael Rich, with Prue Skene

(below) with Prue Skene

The family at Le Touquet, 1972

Much more in sympathy with these ideals was Castle Opera's biggest undertaking in 1972, a week's participation in Le Touquet's first summer music festival. This involved two performances of *Dunstan et Le Diable*, preceded by cassations performed by local children; and two concerts in which Malcolm's singers[53] combined with the French National Television Orchestra,[54] conducted by Castle Opera's Yuval Zaliouk, in performances of *The Red Sea* and *Six English Lyrics*. In addition to directing all the cassations and operas, Malcolm also played his Second Piano Concerto.

53 April Cantelo, Madge Stephens, Margreta Elkins, John Barrow, Robert Bateman and Kevin Miller. Michael Rich and Janet Canetty-Clarke were the pianists.

54 *Orchestre National De L'ORTF*. The *Office de Radiodiffusion Télévision Française* ran French radio and television at that period.

Despite Prue Skene's best efforts and Dolly's presence as a backstage helper, the week did not go smoothly. The company of twelve inauspiciously spent their first night in a down-at-heel hotel annexe lacking both telephone and bathroom. Malcolm and Dolly, having on a preliminary visit been shown a large gym where *Dunstan and the Devil* would be performed in the round, were now told it would be performed in a horse stadium, covered in sawdust, as the gym was booked for a ping-pong match. Eventually, after day-long discussions, it was conceded that they could use the *Palais de l'Europe*. 'But what about the poor people who have already booked tickets?' asked Castle Opera. 'Don't worry!' came the reply. 'Tickets have not yet gone on sale.' Tension mounted with another day-long negotiation, this time over payment to the singers after a last-minute discovery that one of the concerts was to be broadcast, while Malcolm and Yuval Zaliouk, expecting to rehearse with the orchestra in Le Touquet, were not best pleased to have to travel to Lille 200 kilometres away. This, however, had some advantages, for Malcolm's warm feelings towards a handsome but disorganised Festival official were also not contributing to the smooth running of the event.

Malcolm, as Janet Canetty-Clarke remembers, nearly broke his twelve-year abstinence from alcohol in Le Touquet:

> We had a party at the end of the week in a restaurant, Chez Isadore, all of us sitting around an extra-long table. Malcolm was very eager to have a drink that evening, but Dolly discouraged him. She was an amazing woman – she didn't make a fuss, but she won her point. Malcolm kept on soft drinks.[55]

Janet also remembers an amusing incident which arose because Prue Skene, mistrusting the organisers, had insisted on the company being paid in cash:

> The glamorous Prudence, in charge of receipts and payments, had a little box stuffed full of francs, which one evening she was dispensing in a room at the back of the restaurant. Various female singers and helpers went in, one by one, to be paid. Later that evening a local tart came up and asked us how we managed to get so much work – she thought we were women of the night! Malcolm loved that!

Castle Opera made a few other appearances, notably with *The Red Sea* at the Fairfield Halls,[56] but the project lacked financial backing. Malcolm made a presentation to the Arts Council in October 1972, but it came to nothing. He expected support from Weinberger's, but they, quite understandably, felt unable to meet this commitment. Malcolm eventually admitted to being £1,000 out of pocket on the venture, and that was probably a conservative figure. The problems were not just financial. Malcolm's materials were inappropriate for his vision, the shorter operas being far too musically sophisticated for easy collaboration

---

55 April 2005

56 In April 1973 with April Cantelo (Pillar of Cloud), Margreta Elkins (Pillar of Fire), David Bowman (Moses) and John Cameron (Pharoah). Tom Hawkes directed. On a separate day at the Croydon Festival there was a 'Malcolm Williamson Evening' at which Malcolm directed *Genesis* and *The Red Sea*.

between amateurs and professionals, and, as such, uncomfortable partners on the same bill as the simple cassations.

Castle Opera's attempts to reconcile the irreconcilable were a reflection of his own struggles. Sexually, he was again at the crossroads, uncertain of future directions. Professionally, too, the wide scope of his creative endeavours continued to cause confusion. It could range from 'Sing a Song! Ding a Song!', in a schoolroom in a remote Swedish village outside Ystad, to the *Ode to Music* (words by Ursula Vaughan Williams) sung by London school choirs in the Festival Hall to the accompaniment of the LSO;[57] from the comforting warmth of a Christmas cantata, *The World At The Manger*,[58] to the icy brilliance of a *Partita for Viola on Themes of Walton* for Yehudi Menuhin.[59] He himself, meanwhile, might one moment be cajoling two hundred children and their parents in an opera-workshop in Totnes, and the next playing with Richard Rodney Bennett the accompaniment to *In Place of Belief* on its first broadcast or with Gwenneth Pryor[60] his Concerto for Two Pianos and String Orchestra at the Queen Elizabeth Hall.

The double piano concerto, written in 1972 for an Australian commission, exemplifies the convergence of opposites in Malcolm's work at this period, an ethereal central *Lento* being contrasted with two wildly percussive outer movements.[61] The *Lento*, strongly influenced in technique by Messiaen, is full of luscious string writing and crunching parallel chords on the pianos, and contrives to be both ravishingly beautiful and strangely static, the journey of a pilgrim travelling nowhere. By contrast the first movement is 'nerve-wracking in its

---

57 The five-minute *Ode to Music*, which celebrated the 50th anniversary of the Robert Mayer concerts for children, is still popular with choral groups in north America, but less so in Britain and Australia. Tuneful and richly scored, it deserves full rediscovery.

58 Commissioned by the Leicester Philharmonic Society and given its first performance at the De Montfort Hall, 6 December 1973. A highly attractive twenty-five-minute cantata for soprano, baritone, SATB chorus and organ (or piano duet) in six sections, *The World at the Manger*, currently languishes in inexplicable obscurity.

59 'We were totally in awe of Dad's talent,' says Clare. 'We'd come home from school and he'd be in the living room with Yehudi Menuhin. "Put on a smile!" Mum would whisper – I was a moody little girl! – and I'd go in!' (January 2007)

60 Gwenneth Pryor had come from Australia two years earlier. Her mother was a good friend of Bessie's, so Gwenneth contacted Malcolm just before she was about to play his 5 Preludes in a South Bank concert, suggesting a meeting. 'Bit busy at the moment,' said Malcolm. 'Would this afternoon be all right?' It was the beginning of a long friendship.

61 But in this apparent clash of opposites there is a hidden cohesion, as Sue Regan has pointed out: 'The concerto was commissioned by the Australian Arts Council and the Astra Chamber Orchestra for performance [Melbourne, 9 June 1973] by two American pianists, Charles Webb and Wallace Hornibrook. Using the musical letters contained in the names of the two pianists, Williamson constructed a twenty-note theme which forms the basis of the whole work. The theme appears in each movement in a fascinating variety of forms together with a modal ascending and descending scale as an additional unifying factor.' (Sleeve note, EMI LP, 1975)

moto perpetuo, jangling with insistent tension',[62] and the finale even tenser, a very grim-faced attempt at jollity. Malcolm declared that the work was inspired by the winter:

> Poetically the Concerto was suggested by various aspects of the winter – not the Australian winter with its geniality, but the northern winter, where the elements cannot be ignored when one is outside, and, when one is inside, it is the time of reflection, intimacy and expectation. For me the winter has a feeling of permanence, while the summer seems evanescent.[63]

It was unlike Malcolm to be so gloomy but the harshness of the outer movements of the double piano concerto were a reflection of his current mental state. He was close to a breakdown, as he himself acknowledged:

> I hadn't had a holiday for eight or nine years and I simply didn't know what was happening to me. It was such a curious sensation.[64]

Dolly, as usual, came to the rescue, organising a family holiday, ten days of rest at Dynevor Castle. In the calm beauty of Dynevor Malcolm made a temporary recovery, his two medicines his music and his children:

> I took a lot of Vaughan Williams recordings and a phonograph, and a lot of pop records for the children. We enriched ourselves with Vaughan Williams and my children taught me to dance after their manner – things like T-Rex, Blood Sweat & Tears and Gilbert O'Sullivan…

He needed longer, but soon he was off on his compulsive travels, this time to Africa, which he had long wanted to visit. Funded by the British Council, he stayed for three weeks at Lusaka, Zambia, with a friend of Dolly's, who remembers him as 'a whirlwind of huge energy, involving everyone with his plans and enthusiasms'.[65] His first commitment was a recital in the newly opened British Council Recital Hall:

> There was only an upright piano there and they couldn't tune it properly for some reason. Malcolm wasn't exactly thrilled about this, but he could see the funny side. He began with his First Sonata, then some Vaughan Williams, Rawsthorne, Brahms and Rodney Bennett, before concluding with his *5 Preludes* and some of the *Travel Diaries*.

Then came *The Red Sea* in the Anglican Cathedral, with novices from a local Jesuit Monastery playing the Egyptians, and members of the Lusaka Music Society the Israelites:

> Malcolm conducted proceedings with great gusto. It was very well attended, and he bewitched everyone as he spoke about the work, creating a wonderful atmosphere. Malcolm also played one of his piano concertos, this time on a grand!

---

62 Edward Greenfield, *The Guardian*, 1973

63 *Sydney Morning Herald*, 9 June 1973

64 1973 interview.

65 Jackie Ehlers, December 2005

But the highlight was a trip out into the bush, twenty miles from Lusaka. There were no theatrical facilities in the village of Chipapa, and so *Genesis* was rehearsed and performed in an open field. There was also a stop at Dar-es-Salaam in Tanzania, from where Dolly posted a card to Weinberger's Richard Toeman:

> It's hot, sticky and endlessly fascinating. It all seemed a great success and the British Council very happy. You should hear *The Stone Wall* in Swahili![66]

Malcolm had no financial problems in his sponsored visit to Africa, but a return to America, for the first performance of a work for chorus and organ, *Canticle of Fire*,[67] caused further antagonism with his publishers, Malcolm writing furious letters when Weinberger's declined to pay for travel about which they had heard nothing in advance. Richard Toeman, in regretting Malcolm's 'petulant' letters, kept doggedly to the facts:

> As regards your fare to the USA the terms of our contract say that the travel allowance is to be given after discussion about the various occasions. You at no time mentioned this journey in this context, and I imagined that the American Guild of Organists were paying your fare, since they have engaged and commissioned you. The very first we knew of the case was receiving a bill from the travel agent…[68]

Despite the escalating tensions in the relationship, Weinberger's had renewed Malcolm's contract in 1972 for another three years, with its useful retainer of £2,100 a year. Malcolm's regular criticisms of his publisher's shortcomings were an early expression of what was later to emerge as a serious persecution complex. Weinberger's could not have been more supportive at this period. They had always done their very best by Malcolm.

His altered state of mind comes over clearly in two press interviews given at this period. In the first, *The Guardian*'s Christopher Ford shares with his readers the problems he encountered in trying to get a rational response from Malcolm on some fairly basic questions:

> Sometimes it's hard to tell whether Williamson is being profound or simply provocative. He says he prefers a bad notice to none at all, but he has learned also to be a little wary of the press. Occasionally the bright phrases come out as readily as the smile that frames them; more often a question is received with a piercing stare, as he assembles the words, like notes, to express his thoughts; or it is answered with such long, vague pauses between sentences that you chip in with the next line of enquiry and the conversation gets out of phase. Then again he's apt to answer one question with another, or say something so improbable that you have to grope for context and example. He does not make for easy chat, not about music anyway. For instance: 'Strindberg has influenced me more than any composer. From his whole treatment of time one learns new things about rhythmic balance…'[69]

66 3 April 1973

67 20 May 1973, Manhattanville College, New York, organist Jean Thiel, conductor Ruth Branch

68 29 May 1973

69 'The People Who Are Malcolm Williamson', 8 July 1972

The confident young composer of the mid-1960s is now riddled with self-doubt:

> I'm one of the slowest composers I know… I just work long hours. I want to steady up and write very little. Writing's painful, because, if I want to write music, I cannot for example give up smoking and diet at the same time, and because there's a shortfall between the conception and the execution of any work one writes… I'd like to be somebody else – it would be nice to have the leisure to throw ink at politicians rather than at music paper… There's this awful feeling one has that it's really wrong to write music in this day and age.

The second interview, for *Woman and Home*, begins conventionally enough with a glimpse of life at Hertford Avenue:

> We open the great oak door of the Williamsons' home, and Malcolm disappears promptly into his study to answer a ringing telephone. As I take my coat off in the large parquet-floored hall I catch a glimpse of the au pair cleaning her room at the top of the stairs, and the children's nanny cooking in the kitchen. The children – twelve-year-old Peter, Tamara aged ten and Clare who is eight – seem to be everywhere…[70]

It continues unremarkably with references to Chimar ('the noisy but endearing beagle hound') and Malcolm's extra-musical interests – 'taxis, aeroplanes, Americans, Swedes, the French, fattening food, cigarettes, television soap operas, P G Wodehouse, cola, *The Guardian*, Noel Coward, off-beat people and after-shave lotion' – and a description of his working habits:

> Malcolm's day is long and hard. He jumps out of bed at 5.30 in the spring, drinks several glasses of lemon juice and honey and goes for a walk in Richmond Park. In the winter, because of the lulling effect of the central heating, he sleeps on until 6.30. When he returns from his walk he drinks heaps of coffee, looks at the newspaper, and then goes into his study to compose – all this before anybody else upstairs has stirred! Later, when the children come down, he will more than likely have coffee with them.

But then his depressed state of mind asserts itself as he soliloquises:

> Composing is a tremendous strain… it never ends… It's such a precarious life… 'Serious' music doesn't seem in tune with the way the world is now going… You must be prepared to have no money on Tuesday and be rich on Wednesday, spend it all on Thursday and the bills come in on Friday…

Towards the end of the interview Malcolm lets his guard down completely. He admits first to acrophobia, agoraphobia and dreams about crocodiles, sharks and snakes, and then to a fear of professional failure:

> He lives all the time, he says, with a feeling of inadequacy, whereas so many people he knows (a good many of them composers) live with a sense of triumph and fulfilment…

It was unsurprising that Malcolm, oppressed by such uncertainties, should be struggling to meet agreed deadlines and beginning to acquire a reputation for unreliability. His setting of Yeats's *The Death of Cuchulain* for The Scholars

70 Ian Woodward, *Woman and Home*, May 1973

(forerunners of the King's Singers) was one such saga of delay, as Stephen Varcoe recalls:

> We intended to have a run-through at a music club, but the score was so late we had to offer an 'open rehearsal' instead. It was a difficult score, requiring us to play a variety of different percussion instruments when we were not singing, and the audience was not at all happy with our stop-start efforts. We were still horribly under-prepared at the official premiere at the Queen Elizabeth Hall. It was meant to be memorised and staged. It couldn't be, and wasn't! Once again we had to tell the audience they would be watching what was really a rehearsal. There were some scathing reviews![71]

The King's Singers were a little luckier. Their commission, a nine-minute cantata for six unaccompanied voices based on a Grimms' fairy tale, *The Musicians of Bremen*, turned out very well eventually. Its first performance, in Sydney, was highly praised:

> This charming bit of lighter-than-air nonsense about four superannuated farm animals on trek to Bremen to get jobs as musicians, scaring the daylights out of two robbers on the way, has the quartet of singers meowing, bow-wowing, hee-hawing and cockledoodledooing while the other two play the heavies. One of Williamson's best pieces, it has sparkle, pace and a deadpan wit.[72]

Nevertheless there had still been problems. It had been agreed that the piece would be ready in February, before the King's Singers' departure for a three-month world tour. Instead it reached them in New Zealand just a week or so before the scheduled Sydney premiere in mid-May.[73] Two months earlier Malcolm had been in America, working for Phillip Truckenbrod. In a letter to Richard Toeman he alluded to his problems with the commission:

> I'm rising early here and labouring in hotel rooms on *The Musicians of Bremen*. It is progressing well, but of course I wish that I had finished it. I shall get to a piano nearer the end of the week… I shall get it done, and I hope satisfactorily, but the lateness alarms me. I cannot, however, expect to be other than late with deliveries when there is too much to do and when tension makes my very healthy body painful and unwell. I arrived here in knots, and am only slowly getting them undone…[74]

---

71 February 2006. The premiere was on 6 November 1971.

72 Maria Prerauer, *The Sunday Australian*, 21 May 1972

73 The project had started auspiciously with a visit by Simon Carrington to East Sheen: 'I remember spending a convivial morning at Malcolm's house discussing text possibilities, the voices, range and characters of my colleagues in the King's Singers and a reasonable time-table for the commission. The music was charming and the voicing skilful. The first performance in the old Sydney Town Hall was a success. We incorporated Malcolm's piece into our regular repertoire and performed it often over the next several years. It struck a chord with music lovers of every level and even now I meet people here and there who remember it with great affection – some of them highly sophisticated musicians whose tastes one might assume would favour more esoteric fare.'

74 14 March 1972

Under stress, rehearsing The Red Sea, *Croydon, 1973*

It was a period of constant tension. Less than a week before the start of the workshops in Devon on *The Red Sea*, there was no sign of *any* music. Michael McNally was one of the anxious organisers:

> Eventually we received a few scribbled notes, and Michael Lane, who was to supervise the production, attempted to play through and make sense of what Malcolm had provided. The whole event, at this stage, was nearly cancelled. Then two days before the course was starting the score finally arrived, albeit in a very scrappy state...[75]

The summer of 1973 was dominated by problems with a chamber work, *Pietà*, commissioned for a concert in the Purcell Room by the Athenaeum Ensemble (oboe, bassoon and piano) augmented by soprano Margaret Cable. Knowing that the Ensemble wanted something light with which to end the first half of the concert, Margaret Cable had suggested they contact Malcolm. At first all went well. Sue Sutton, the group's leader, recalls Malcolm being in splendid form when they visited Hertford Avenue for some pre-concert publicity:

> I made him a passion fruit sponge – one of his favourite dishes, and very Australian! He loved it and was extremely amusing and entertaining, telling us stories about his various exploits around the world. One was a performance in Africa where the piano kept slipping down the stage as he was playing.[76]

But the music wasn't forthcoming...

---

75 June 2005

76 January 2006

Malcolm was in the midst of an emotional breakdown which led, on his return from America, to a short period in hospital.

It was difficult for Dolly to know what was for the best. To ignore the fact of his gay relationships and the virtual leading of two lives, and to make excuses for the times he would stay away from home? Or to argue things out confrontationally with the attendant risks of escalation? It was important, at all events, that the problems should not reach the media. It was hard for her to cope with innocent questions about the marriage in interviews; hard, too, not to be nervous as Malcolm talked volubly to *Woman and Home* about their relationship:

> Dolly's a marvellous, normal, well-balanced girl – aren't you, darling! As a mother to the three children she's not obsessive in the J M Barrie sense. She says that I tend to have my head in the clouds, but have you ever known a marriage where one of the partners didn't have his or her head in the clouds? She is pathologically generous. In fact the entire family are generous to the point of idiocy… It's lovely! She copes with me beautifully, especially with my difficult ways when I'm composing. We both play a truth game, and Dolly knows by now, after thirteen years of marriage, when to tell the truth and when not. Nothing needs to be said. She's become good enough at drawing a veil over her true feelings if she thinks a particular moment is bad, and she's very good at knowing exactly when the moment is bad. But she'll always tell me and it comes at exactly the right time…

Malcolm acted the role of the ideal husband well, but Dolly in reality was far from coping 'beautifully' with his 'difficult ways' and was no longer capable of 'drawing a veil over her true feelings'. Only a month after their appearance in *Woman and Home*, the situation in Hertford Avenue was dire. They had no money, the children could not but be aware of all the arguments and tensions in the house, and Malcolm's ability to keep earning a living from his music depended on his overcoming his present emotional turmoil. His immediate future was a topic of endless debate. He was anxious to return quickly to America, preferably that summer but certainly in the autumn, the exact time when he had been offered a three-month contract as Creative Arts Fellow at the Australian National University. Inconclusive arguments about the best way forward raged on, and Dolly, who had initially seen three months at Canberra as an opportunity for retrenchment and reconciliation, felt more and more in limbo as nothing was decided. Under great stress herself, she confided in her occasional journal:

> Today has been frightful. We've had an all-day row over Malcolm's US trip in the fall. He will say nothing about it, so the dates and fees must be pretty bad, but he still seems committed to it – going all the way from Australia at a fare of $1000. I have lost heart about Australia, after the long excitement – it now seems it will revolve around Malcolm's US trip.[77]

She was particularly frustrated in her exclusion from his daily life. She no longer seemed to count. Since he had taken to his worldwide travels, Malcolm had tended to keep the decisions and details of his professional life to himself, and this, as Dolly could see and would tell him, was by no means always to his

[77] 13 June 1973

best advantage. But her valuable help was inevitably tied in to the domesticity he was no longer sure he wanted. He was moving, with diffidence and no little distress, towards the dissolution of a relationship which, as entries in Dolly's journal in the summer of 1973 suggest, was now close at hand. Even the resourceful and resilient Dolly had to face up to it:

> How does one start to get a divorce? Millions of people do it and it seems our incompatibility is complete. It will be hard to be alone. I will lose a lot of people. But I may gain some self-respect, instead of being an attachment…

Although she mused about it, divorce was certainly not something she wanted, however poor the current relationship:

> We can't even have a short phone conversation without rows and tension. I wonder if it can ever get better? It's so sad that he manages to turn away from him people who love him and want to help him! He cannot see that he does this – and goes on doing it. And after a time, people stop caring…[78]

A week later she was writing of two 'terrible days' in which she had been 'heated and emotional' and 'said terrible things and heard some'. They discussed a separation and the possibility that his time at the ANU might offer a natural break, but Malcolm seemed not to know his own mind:

> When I said how much I wanted to see Australia, Malcolm said it would be much better if I stayed here. When I agreed, he said it would be a pity for me not to see it and he wanted to show it to me. He would talk of how he hated Australia, and I'd say 'I know', only for him next minute to suggest he might go there for a year after all. He also talked of wanting to live in America, and when I said it might make him happy, he said he wouldn't think of living there permanently… One minute it was one thing, the next another. I could say nothing right…

Malcolm's indecision over the ANU's Fellowship was caused not so much by a desire to be difficult as very real anxieties about his reception there. It was now six years since his only previous visit home, in 1967. Even on the death of his father, a year later, he had been unable to return.[79] The earlier visit had been made

---

78 18 June 1983

79 George Williamson had died aged 64 in October 1968, just after the Dynevor performances of *The Growing Castle*. Bessie had written to Malcolm and Diane at the time: 'Marion phones me and we talk like Joyce Grenfell. "Are you all right?" And I say, "Yes, are you all right?" and we both howl our eyes out. But why? I have talked to hordes of very kind people who call on me and phone, and eulogise the saints for letting me off so lightly, with Dad's easy and smooth release, but it is still sad. No one can deny that he did everything in comfort, even dying, and had he lived to become a human onion, hating his existence and me mine, well... In the hospital bill it mentions a fee for oxygen so I assume they did put up a fight towards the end. Obviously it was so quick that they couldn't send for me but the Doctor assures me it was most peaceful. I am requesting that the ashes be scattered to the four winds. Hope you agree. Even that costs a dollar, but urns and niches run from $25 upwards to hundreds, and who knows whose ashes they are? Quite heathenish, I feel. I will, however, give something to Killara Church as a memorial, a book or vase or something, with name inscribed...' (30 October 1968)

at a time of massive achievement, in the immediate aftermath of many stage successes. Now he felt much less secure, unsettled by the failures of *Lucky-Peter's Journey* and Castle Opera, and unsure of himself at forty-one in the midst of a mid-life crisis. Even though there had already been considerable activity in Australia to arrange concerts, workshops and other events to mark his expected return, he prevaricated.

Meanwhile sessions with a psychiatrist proved unsatisfactory, not least, perhaps, because of his insistence that the children be involved. Malcolm, a polished performer on the psychiatrist's couch, was his own articulate self, inhibiting Dolly, who felt strangely tongue-tied and awkward:

> I felt myself a target. Everyone talked about my yelling, explosions, and anger, and I left drowned in inadequacy, feeling they felt I didn't give them love or comfort or care. I think I do – but why doesn't it come across to them?[80]

Glorious summer weather at the beginning of July at least allowed the children to let out pent-up emotions outdoors, but the tensions didn't lessen. Dolly reported Malcolm sitting in his chair all day, 'staring into space, headachy, gloomy, joining us for meals, but silent and irritable, speaking to me very little'. She wondered how many more days they could spend 'under the same strained roof'. The American organist and choirmaster James Litton was currently in England and staying with them, but it hardly lessened Dolly's feelings of exclusion:

> Malcolm had a taxman all morning and went to bed at 2.30 this afternoon, waking up at 6.30, after being up with Jim Litton until 3.30am. He's been like a bear all evening, a well-behaved bear, of course, not saying anything. Oh, for a good clean fight![81]

Eventually the tensions at Hertford Avenue helped persuade Malcolm to accept the Canberra post. Dolly and the children would go too, though, as she confided in her journal, the omens were not particularly auspicious:

> Australia is on again, and I am planning for the kids and myself, and Malcolm zooms into activity far into the future for his own American plans. Not a bit of help for us, but he pulls himself out of depressions amazingly quickly to finalize anything for the States.

She had reason to be critical. Malcolm's desire for a summer visit to America, which she thought 'unnecessary, unimportant and uneconomical', meant that the three children would fly out with her to Australia in early August and he would follow a week or so later, after spending time in the USA. It was not a good start for retrenchment and reconciliation.

---

[80] 29 June 1973

[81] 3 July 1973

11 BREAKING FREE

World Travels, 1973–75

DOLLY'S FIRST IMPRESSIONS of Australia were somewhat less glorious than she had anticipated. On arrival at Sydney she and the children were initially refused entry:

> I kept declaring, 'My husband is an Australian called Malcolm Williamson!' and the airport officials kept replying, 'We have no evidence of an Australian Malcolm Williamson!' It went on for a considerable time. There seemed no way forward. And then, eventually, I remembered that he had changed citizenship when there'd been some immigration problems in Britain. 'Oh hang on,' I cried. 'Maybe he's British now!' '*Ah*!' they said. 'He's a *Pom*, then! He *isn't* Australian at all!'[1]

The zealously obstructive officials who turned the family's first hour in Australia into such a nightmare were a reflection, perhaps, of the new sense of Australian nationhood which had come into being with Gough Whitlam's Labour Government.[2] The country's relationship with Britain was being redefined. Australians would no longer be 'British subjects'. The Queen was shortly to visit Canberra to put her assent to a document modifying her title to 'Queen of Australia and other realms'. There would no longer be any mention of her role as 'Defender of the Faith', thought inappropriate in Australia's emerging multicultural society.

With Marion and her family currently living in England, it had been left to Bessie and Diane to form the welcoming party, but the long wait at the airport had cooled the warmth of Bessie's welcome. 'She wasn't exactly a barrel of fun,' remembers Dolly. Peter recalls that as soon as they reached the flat his grandmother declared 'Well, *I'm* not hungry! I don't know what *you lot* are going to eat!' A tin of Campbell's cream of celery soup was eventually produced. 'Well, that's it!' said Bessie. 'And when it's gone, there isn't anything else!' Bessie had made arrangements to stay with friends elsewhere in Blues Point Tower, and it

1 June 2005

2 Although as an expatriate Malcolm would be damaged professionally by this, he always remained an enthusiastic Whitlam supporter.

was not long before Dolly and the children found themselves alone on the twentieth floor, jet-lagged, disorientated and with no more celery soup in immediate prospect.

Things quickly improved, however. Peter discovered that the way to his grandmother's heart lay through hours of mah-jong and showing an interest in her new passion for bridge. There was also the excitement of Diane taking him and Dolly on a two-day reconnaissance of Canberra. Bessie's initial lack of welcome probably reflected the pressures of her latest business enterprise, the transfer of books onto tape. This had started when she read a book onto a cassette for one of her bridge partners who was having eyesight problems. Soon Bessie was working briefly for the Royal Blind Society, reading textbooks onto cassettes, before creating her own organisation, the Australian Listening Library, for which she rented two rooms on the top of Blues Point Tower as office space. Her enthusiasm for raising funds, seeking permission from authors for the use of their books, auditioning readers and marketing the end-result showed characteristic Williamson flair.[3]

Malcolm flew in from New York a week later, far from relaxed. He was again unguarded in his responses to the reporters who met him at Sydney Airport, encouraging *The Australian* to run a front page headline 'HUMILIATED' COMPOSER GLAD TO ACCEPT FIRST JOB BACK HOME. There were similar tales of 'humiliation' in the *Sydney Morning Herald*:

> You want very much to come back and nourish yourself in your own country, but the humiliation of asking Australia to take you back, and being refused, is very terrible. I have done it quite often.[4]

This was not true. For many years Malcolm had forgotten all about Australia, but he had now cast himself in the role of martyr, and when he was in role play the truth could be distorted.

Two days later, having arrived at the Australian National University with the family, he surprised the *Canberra Times* with an attack on the forthcoming National Conference of Australian Composers[5] of which he was to be the chief guest:

> He says he will feel like an Aunt Sally, not a big brother, that such affairs are usually a load of hot air and that most of the business will be done, as always, in the bar and bedrooms. 'One of the rich and growing things in Australia is the sharp individuality of the talents developing,' he says, 'but most of the guys – and the girls – I want to meet, I shall meet in my own time.' He had declined to talk on a panel on the future of opera in Australia, one reason being that he does not want to talk about opera in a country where his own major works are not presented.[6]

---

3 The company is still functioning, though it has moved to different premises.

4 14 August 1973

5 'The Status and Role of the Australian Composer', a conference organised by the Canberra School of Music and supported by the Australian Council for the Arts.

6 *Canberra Times*, 16 August 1973

Arrival in Sydney, 1973

He unhelpfully aired his grievances over the Sydney Opera House quite regularly in public:

> Williamson is especially, and perhaps justly, bitter about Australia's neglect of his operas, which he regards as a substantial and important part of his life and work. It is not that Williamson needs Australia – he has had ample success in opera elsewhere – but the lack of response is a thorn in the rose of his success and a bitter gall in the midst of his sincere gratitude and pleasure at being here.[7]

Having joined the family in a pleasant house[8] on the ANU campus, Malcolm tried hard to forget the battles of Hertford Avenue and give the children a good time, knowing that both Peter and Tammy did not have long before they had to return to schools in England. The charms of Canberra helped lift his spirits. Founded as the only full-time research university in the country, the ANU, although now offering undergraduate courses, still exuded an appealing scholastic atmosphere, and Malcolm was soon making plans to involve himself in the Department of Scandinavian Studies. The university, moreover, lay in a most attractive setting, adjoining bushland, yet close to the city centre and Lake Burley Griffin.

In contrast to the bustle of Sydney the young city exerted a civilised calm, and Malcolm was quick to sing its praises to the *Canberra Times*. It was beautiful in 1967, he said, but it was stunning now. He was incautiously uncomplimentary, however, about Canberra's Carillon, a much admired gigantic musical instrument with 53 bells, dramatically situated on an island in the lake. A gift to celebrate the 50th anniversary of Australia's capital city and inaugurated by the Queen only three years earlier, it chimed pleasantly every quarter of an hour and gave

[7] Kay Lucas, *The Bulletin*, 8 September 1973

[8] In Liversidge Street

recitals twice a week. 'It impinges on the sounds of the countryside!' complained Malcolm. 'It's put music in the open air – our only form of escape left!'[9]

Malcolm was clearly on edge. One contributory factor was his uneasiness in following Don Banks as the Australian National University's Creative Fellow. Banks, a few years his senior and a successful avant-garde composer, had also lived in England for many years before returning to Australia for good. As the ANU's Creative Fellow in 1972 he had established an electronic music department at Canberra's School of Music and was now in charge of the composition teaching there. Malcolm's lack of interest in electronic music made him seem a dull conservative compared to Banks, whose lack of worldly success was said to be a mark of his musical integrity.[10]

Uncomfortable and on the defensive within the School of Music, Malcolm was all the keener to seize upon a fortuitous diversion. In his application for the Fellowship Malcolm had mentioned that his cassations had been used with physically handicapped children.[11] But Ken Healey, the ANU's Academic Registrar, misreading Malcolm's file, inadvertently contacted the Koomarri School at Tuggeranong in south Canberra, a non-religious state school with between fifty and sixty children with Down's Syndrome and other conditions of mental, rather than physical, handicap. Never can a clerical error have had a happier outcome.

By a strange coincidence Malcolm had stayed near the Koomarri School six years earlier as the guest of Ralph and Hazel Reader and had met some of the children at Tuggeranong's small Catholic church where he helped out on the harmonium. He was nonetheless full of misgivings, very much aware of his inexperience in the field of mental health, as he was introduced to a silent group of children, all extremely withdrawn and many exhibiting obvious signs of social maladjustment. It was a moment of truth. Instead of introducing himself and explaining why he was there, Malcolm simply smiled at them all, tip-toed over to the piano like a conspiratorial gnome and began pounding through an inspirational warm-up, putting on any number of funny faces as he encouraged the children to relax or move with the music. Most of them simply sat, earnestly watching the fascinating little man before them, the atmosphere perceptibly softening. 'You liked that? It was good fun wasn't it! Let's do some more!' And off he went into his first ever workshop with the mentally handicapped, using a simplified version of his cassation *Genesis*. Ken Healey looked on in admiration:

---

9 16 August 1973

10 Roger Covell commented in 1967: 'Banks is sometimes used to provide admonishing comparisons with Williamson's showiness and facility... the chances are that Banks gets more than tired of being told he has more integrity than, say, Williamson. The comparison, in any case, serves to bring into needless opposition two composers who between them illustrate some of the diverse possibilities of creative temperament...' (*Australia's Music*, pp.178-9)

11 Particularly by his friend John Andrewes of Boosey & Hawkes.

Meeting Hazel Reader, Canberra, 1973

Newly arrived at the Australian National University, Canberra

> He showed amazing courage. It must have been really daunting, but he was just naturally wonderful with them. He was truly miraculous, a magician. There was absolute genius in the way he led this and all the subsequent sessions… The Koomarri staff said they had never seen their charges relate socially with such enthusiasm. Somehow he knew instinctively how to unlock these children's great disabilities with the rhythms of his music.[12]

Thereafter musical therapy for the mentally handicapped became a passionate commitment,[13] the Koomarri School taking precedence over Canberra's music, as he immersed himself in the new challenge and began the long business of acquiring a scientific understanding of the children's problems. Ross Edwards, invited to attend a cassation workshop at the Canberra Conference, vividly remembers the experience:

> I was very touched not only by Malcolm's vitality but also by his great tenderness. He obviously had a genuine care for such children; *their* handicaps were *his* challenge.14

Alison Bauld was another composer invited to participate at the Koomarri School:

> The children were very difficult to handle, but we worked at a cassation – I think it was about a castle – for a long time, possibly as much as three hours. Malcolm was like a supercharged three-year-old! He was so highly enthused it was amazing. And wonderful. So much energy and so much generosity! Later he was filmed at the Koomarri, but there were no media people around when I was there. He was simply giving of himself to the children. They mattered. They mattered a very great deal.[15]

Dolly's fragile hopes that the time in Canberra might be one of refreshment and reconciliation were thwarted by Malcolm's desire for independence and the large number of professional commitments he accepted outside the ANU. Within a week of arrival at Canberra, for example, he was back in Sydney, as guest of honour at a weekend festival, held by the Conservatorium and featuring several of his works. 'Welcome, Malcolm!' wrote the Director Rex Hobcraft. 'This musical offering is the Con's way of welcoming you home.' Malcolm, in return, gave good value:

> Here he was, talking with candour and brisk humour about his rise as a composer in the 60s, a compactly built man, charged with an energy that flowed with the force of an electric current through his audience – high forehead, fair hair, twinkling eyes and expressive hands – he gave his account, coining highly individual phrases as he went along…[16]

---

12 May 2006

13 Malcolm's enthusiasm comes out in a letter to Richard Toeman: 'I'm doing a lot of therapeutic cassation work with mentally handicapped kids with wonderful results. The study is in its infancy. The cassations have to be simplified. I am also teaching therapists the use of opera as therapy. The Red Cross has given me terrific support.' (8 September 1973)

14 January 2006

15 October 2005

16 Vera Goldman, *Show Business*, 27 September 1973

Deep down Malcolm felt very vulnerable. 'There are many people waiting in this country to bring me low,' he confided to John Schofield at Weinberger's.[17] Ross Edwards, who was present at the concerts, deplored the lukewarm response:

> It was evident that some people who were jealous of his success overseas had poisoned wider opinion. This charming and typically Australian reaction, known as the 'tall poppy syndrome', understandably upset him and he became quite prickly for a while...[18]

The *Sydney Morning Herald* reported in the same vein:

> A self-righteous and fairly influential circle of local creative musicians find it strange at best and unfortunate at worst that Williamson who has been living in England for two decades should want to write melody-based music. One detects a whiff of sour grapes... Musical progressives, often cold, academic or rebellious at heart, who find their own 'masterpieces' turning into public disaster pieces, like to spread the deplorable view that composers such as Williamson, who win public acclaim and even affection, are really prostituting not just their talent but the integrity of contemporary music.[19]

Only two weeks into his residency Malcolm was telling Richard Toeman that he had not stopped night or day since his arrival and that, although he was meeting malice where he expected it, 'things have developed amazingly'. The Romanian-born conductor Sergiu Commissiona was touring the country with Malcolm's Second Symphony; several of his shorter operas were to be produced in different cities; and cassations had firm dates for Canberra, Sydney, Adelaide, Melbourne, Newcastle, Alice Springs, Darwin and Brisbane. A couple of days later there was more news:

> I'm writing this on the plane from Adelaide to Sydney. This week has been hectic, but it's getting to be so all the time. On Monday I did a Sydney TV appearance; on Tuesday an organ seminar, another TV and the best organ recital I ever played; on Wednesday in Melbourne I did a seminar at the University and rehearsals for 2nd Symphony with Commissiona. Thursday there was Genesis twice at a mental hospital, and the 2nd Symphony broadcast (greeted with unprecedented applause), Friday, *Genesis* with retarded children and a meeting in Adelaide to set up three-day festival...[20]

It was helpful that the ABC in the early 1970s still suffered from 'the cultural cringe', preferring Australian concert soloists who had made a mark overseas. The British-born conductor John Hopkins ('loving and helpful'[21]) was a particularly influential ally. Now in the last of his six years as ABC's Director of Music,[22] Hopkins devotedly helped initiate event after event for Malcolm and

---

17 17 September 1973

18 January 2006

19 Fred Blanks, 28 August 1973

20 8 September 1973

21 MW to Richard Toeman, 11 September 1973

22 1967-73. He subsequently became a distinguished Dean of the School of Music, Melbourne.

also commissioned a cassation, *The Glitter Gang*, Malcolm's first musical statement on behalf of the aboriginals. Set in the Australian bush, *The Glitter Gang* contrasts the innocence and generosity of the indigenous Australians with the deceit of two groups of European settlers. In a thought-provoking ending the aboriginals watch with awe and horror as the European Outlaws pollute their once clear stream and, having committed mass murder, ride off triumphantly with stolen gold. Hopkins himself conducted the first performance at an ABC concert, which also featured Malcolm's Third Symphony.[23] *The Glitter Gang* is one of Malcolm's best cassations, its strong anti-racist message as relevant today as it was at the time Gough Whitlam was trying to stir the national conscience on the issue of aboriginal rights.

But the more cassations he wrote, however good their quality, the more the critics of the 1970s derided his standing as a 'serious' composer. Feeling himself overworked and undervalued, pulled in different directions, professionally and socially, Malcolm grew more and more depressed. As usual, he took out his frustrations on Richard Toeman at Weinberger's. If his publishers had supported him better, wrote Malcolm, his music would have earned him a living without the need for wearing himself out in promotional efforts around the world. He resented the implied criticism that the failure to earn considerable money was the fault of the music itself; if it were promoted more vigorously abroad, things might be very different.

Richard Toeman answered the intemperately expressed letter with patience and concern:

> I am glad things are going well and your worst fears regarding your standing in your home country are not being borne out... I am sorry to see from your latest letter how depressed you have become. You cannot really doubt that we have always had – and shown – faith in you and in your music; apart from any direct financial considerations, the way in which we have published so many pieces that, by their very nature (no reflection on your music) are very slow and limited sellers should be ample proof of this; if not, then above all the personal commitment and special attention which you have enjoyed in our firm over the past 12 years are. If all this does not show adequate faith in you, then you must please tell me specifically what you envisage as doing so in the future.[24]

Typical of the 'slow and limited sellers' was *Pietà*, his dissonant setting of four Lagerkvist poems, which, five weeks after his arrival in Australia, he had at last managed to send off by express airmail. He told John Schofield:

> It is a vast, but not difficult piece. I feel terrible about the delay and it nearly killed me to write it. I am almost afraid to ask about the performance. It is difficult to have private moments to write. I get up at dawn and write and practise the piano. In Australia one can do with comparatively little sleep...[25]

23 Sydney Symphony Orchestra, February 1974

24 24 September 1973

25 24 September 1973. The last section arrived two days before the performance.

The two works completed by Malcolm on this visit to Australia could not have been more different. The tuneful *Glitter Gang* was a world away from *Pietà*, a progressive passacaglia, its sections based on the Stations of the Cross, a chromatic exploration of his worst uncertainties, a work whose esoteric beauty only reveals itself in stages. As entertainer and intellectual, Malcolm displayed a range given to few composers; but the split personality also suggested inner disquiet.

His problems only weighed on him intermittently. When he met up again with Nigel Butterley in Sydney, to play the two-piano concerto and the double sonata, he was in good spirits:

> We went down to the quay one day and got a ferry across the harbour to Cremorne Point. There we sat on some rocks and chatted – over some sandwiches – Malcolm at his most relaxed and amusing. He told me that the reason he had wanted to do the sonata with me back in 1967 was that he was keen on me. He was without his family that trip, lonely and frustrated. He had made some approaches – though it didn't go any further, for I was unsure of my own sexuality at that time. He told me that because I hadn't been interested, he had gone to bed with someone else instead. It was clear now, as we talked, that his life had reached some kind of crossroads.[26]

One of his first requests to Ken Healey in Canberra had been for an introduction to a sympathetic priest. Healey found him Father Augustine Watson, a Franciscan friar, attached to St Christopher's Cathedral. An urbane and highly educated man, with a brief to counsel and support homosexual Catholics, Father Augustine became an important friend over the next few years.

Malcolm's inner doubts were well concealed by an outer vivacity. He was ubiquitous and unsparing of himself, his days filled with a swift succession of interviews, piano and organ recitals, seminars, cassations and operas. A local Canberra reporter, watching him working energetically on a professional version of *The Growing Castle*, led by the admirable Ailene Fischer, dubbed him 'Supermuso':

> There stood Supermuso, resplendent in the sort of denim jacket and jeans you could find on the football terraces or at a rock concert. I call him Supermuso, because he is stretching into areas where the angels of contemporary music fear to tread. With a fervour which sometimes frightens observers, he has charged into his three months as Creative Fellow…[27]

An accompanying photograph showed Supermuso looking very tired, despite a florid shirt, with heavy bags under his eyes.

Whatever the event, there was always the same commitment. An interesting account survives of a 'jazz mass' Malcolm led at St Paul's Church, Manuka, an exciting occasion, but perhaps not the most appropriate expenditure of time for an international composer. It began with a rehearsal. Malcolm had brought along a choir of teachers and student teachers attending a music course at Canberra,

26 May 2006

27 Garry Raffaele, 25 September 1973

but, as he explained from the pulpit to the regular congregation, it was *their* voices he most wanted:

> This is the last night of the pre-Christian era! You are all slaves of the Romans! You are shackled together! Join arms with the person next to you and sway with the music! Now the sun of the world is rising. Bend down, DOWN, under the pews if you can. Raise your arm horizontal! That is the horizon. Lift your other arm slowly above it! That is the sun, the light of the world, coming now into the world. But keep singing! Stamp your feet too, if you can! Make your whole body take part in the Mass…![28]

The congregation relaxed. They were making fools of themselves, perhaps, but no more than their neighbours. They divided into two parts, singing Malcolm's antiphonal version of 'Jesus lover of my soul':

> Make it SOUND like a love-song! Wave your arms towards the altar! Show your desperate longing for truth and salvation and holy things! Christ is coming! Wave your hands and your handkerchiefs! You're in a ticker-tape procession for the Christ, down Broadway or somewhere…!

At this Malcolm wrenched off his tie and waved it high, encouraging a flurry of hands and multi-coloured handkerchiefs. The rehearsal over, it was time for the actual service.

> Three teenagers speared out their arms and bent their heads to form a triptych. 'Christ whose glory fills the skies,' the congregation sang, trying to match the unfamiliar rhythm and straining for one or two uncomfortable high notes. They moved up to take communion, while behind them the voices of the choir rose to the panelled ceiling in a jazz setting of the 23rd psalm, 'The Lord is My Shepherd'. The congregation responded, five beats to the bar, 'Alleluia, Alleluia'…

When it was all over, the elation was palpable. Only a few hurried out into the chill, overcast morning. Most went to the small church hall for coffee, the *Canberra Times* reporter among them:

> The face of an earnest, dark-haired woman lit up as she recalled the service. 'Some of us have been praying for a long time that something like this would happen at St Paul's,' she said, almost breathlessly.

Her response gives a clue to Malcolm's participation in such events. He needed the human contact and, with it, the encouragement which came from faces glowing with approval.

His successes, however, were often marred by the machinations of his opponents, which he took very much to heart. He reported to Richard Toeman that Maria Prerauer, was 'an implacable enemy' of his music.[29] She was on the

---

28 *Canberra Times*, 24 September 1973

29 5 October 1973. Maria Prerauer, a Sydney contemporary of Malcolm's, had been a highly talented soprano who furthered her career in Europe in the 1950s. In Malcolm's first year in London she was singing at Covent Garden in a season which included Kleiber's acclaimed *Wozzeck*. Having returned to Australia in 1960, after a pierced eardrum prematurely ended her singing career, she became a much respected music critic, her strong views leading to the nickname 'Maria Piranha'.

Arts Council Opera Panel, 'who have refused a penny for any production of any of my operas in Australia'. The Panel had prevented the Canberra production of *The Growing Castle* from being taken to the Independent Theatre, Sydney, for several performances at the time of the opening of the Sydney Opera House. There had also been the possibility of *Dunstan and the Devil* being toured to the Northern Territory, but the funding application for both projects was turned down by the Australian Council for the Arts. Had the excellent cast of *The Growing Castle* been able to perform at Sydney at the same time that Prokofiev's *War and Peace* was opening the Opera House in the presence of the Queen, the exclusion of Australia's foremost operatic composer from the new facility might have been noticed. His enemies had good reason to kill off the project.

The Queen opened the long-delayed Opera House in October 1973, little suspecting the farrago of jealousies, bitchiness and enlightened self-interest which had been going on behind the scenes. Nearly four years earlier, Malcolm, long promised a commission, had received sudden bad news from the Opera House's General Manager:

> May I ask if you would be willing to allow our tentative arrangements for commissioning an opera to be not proceeded with?'[30]

Although outraged by the use of 'tentative', Malcolm kept his peace, for a time hoping that Edward Downes, the first Musical Director, might consider *The Violins of Saint-Jacques* or *Our Man in Havana*, for in 1972 Downes had spoken encouragingly of 'a future in which each season would include one Australian opera at least'. It was not to be, even though three Australian composers did have works produced by Opera Australia in 1974.[31] 'It is not much use trying to persuade Downes to look at something of mine,' Malcolm wrote miserably to Richard Toeman.[32] He had reason to be feel mortified. Not only were his operas excluded, but the Sydney Symphony Orchestra, now resident in the adjacent concert hall, also ignored him in its opening season. His name was not even on the guest list for the grand opening.

Malcolm, however, had made expensive arrangements to be in America by the time the Queen arrived. His well-planned three-week diversion involved some hard work, as his report to Richard Toeman made clear:

> My USA tour included *Winter Star* in New Orleans and Dallas, *Peace Pieces* in ditto, a week of *Stone Walls* in New Jersey, *Canticle of Fire* in Princeton etc. It was enjoyable but fatiguing. *Red Sea* in North Carolina was excellent! I flew twice

---

30 22 July 1969. The turning-point had come with the formation of a new board to administer the Australian Opera Company. Up to that moment the Australian Elizabethan Trust, under the patronage of the Sydney Opera House Trust, had been supporting the long-standing verbal agreement to mount a new Williamson opera.

31 *The Affair* by Felix Werder, *Lenz* by Larry Sitsky and *Rites of Passage* by Peter Sculthorpe.

32 11 September 1973.

> through bad storms, making 26 flights in all in 3 weeks. One storm right up the eastern USA with lightning and thunder and driving rain was very alarming…[33]

But Malcolm usually managed to extract pleasure from his solo travels, however strenuous, seeing them more and more as welcome opportunities for the whole-hearted pursuit of a gay lifestyle. One of his dearest friends in America was Michael Hoffenberger ('Woo Woo'), a young organist whom he had first come to know during his time at Princeton, and who was living in Washington in a basement flat in the home of his uncle, Michael Cordovana (the conductor at the premiere of *In Place of Belief*). Malcolm was given his customary room on the house's top floor, but his first day back in Washington had been a hectic one and he hadn't heard that Hoffenberger had agreed to vacate the basement flat for one night to solve a crisis of accommodation for a visiting celebrity. Michael Hoffenberger still remembers the embarrassment this caused:

> It was one of those impossible nightmare situations when, try as I might, I just couldn't get a message through to Malcolm that I would not be in the flat that night. And so, in the early hours, as was his custom when staying with us, Malcolm quietly made his way down the stairs stark naked, from top floor to basement, before cheerfully letting himself into the flat and slipping into my bed. To his great surprise, however, he was greeted by an ear-piercing scream – it probably could have been heard in the White House – as the visiting celebrity, who happened to be very straight, was woken up by the unexpected presence of Malcolm in the all-together.[34]

This moment of embarrassment can be precisely dated, to 20 October 1973, as it happened to coincide with Washington's infamous 'Saturday Night Massacre', when President Nixon fired the Watergate Prosecutor, accepted his Attorney-General's resignation and paved the way for his own impeachment. It was the same day, too, on which the Queen formally opened the Sydney Opera House.

By the time Malcolm returned to Australia, in mid-November, Dolly had unexpectedly returned to England with Clare. She had intended to stay a little longer, to the official end of Malcolm's three-month residency, but flew back on receiving an SOS from Peter. Left in London without adequate care, he had in consequence suffered some problems at the school which he had just joined and was badly in need of support. Cross with herself for having allowed both Peter and Tammy to return independently to England while she stayed on in Australia, Dolly vowed that in the future, whatever the demands of her unstable marriage, the childrens' best interests must always come first.

Malcolm, staying on in Australia, busied himself with a relentless programme of workshops and recitals, his energy and crusading zeal undiminished as he found new excuses for not facing up to the mounting problems at Hertford Avenue. A reporter at Newcastle captured something of his mesmeric manner:

---

33 14 November 1973

34 March 2007

The Snow Wolf
on Australian television

> For two hours yesterday afternoon 100 students from Newcastle Conservatorium fell under the spell of a short, balding man with the wizardry of Cinderella's godmother… Within half an hour Williamson had a smuggler's boat, loaded with contraband, slipping into a village port… A girl student, standing on a chair to represent the village clock, signalled 2.00 am with her fingers as the ship slid past the lighthouse, portrayed by a second student with outstretched arms wrapped in a yellow mackintosh. A 'dog' ran down the village street. The sleepy villagers awoke and a posse of customs officers approached on horseback… 'Whip up your horses!' cried Williamson, slapping his thigh…[35]

A photograph shows him on a chair in histrionic pose, one leg high in the air, with a group of students mesmerised below. 'Quick! Get that contraband ashore!' runs the caption.

His three-month residency at Canberra, by contrast, came to a fairly tame conclusion, with little impact made at the School of Music.[36] One of the students of the period, Jim Cotter, writes:

> We heard he was in residence, but we didn't really see him. I think, from memory, we saw Malcolm only once in a lecture-recital context and perhaps a couple of times at concerts. He was reportedly going down spending time with the 'special needs' kids at Koomarri, which seemed very laudable, but it was quite different from his predecessor Don Banks, who had set up an electronic studio, created performances and taught the essentials of electronic music to the likes of me.
>
> It wasn't long before a whispering campaign began. Provincial egos seemed to be bruised because he was not engaging with the music scene in a way deemed 'appropriate'. I remember Don Banks speaking very highly of him and defending his

[35] Joan Cairnes, *Newcastle Morning Herald*, 11 October 1973. *The Moonrakers* was part of a successful concert involving six hundred young musicians, conducted by John Hopkins and including the *Ode to Music* and *The Stone Wall*. Less successful, on a separate evening, was a production of *The Red Sea*, the students becoming mutinous after a rehearsal which lasted six and a half hours.

[36] Other parts of the University, however, saw him differently. Hans Kuhn of the Germanic Studies Department wrote that December: 'My hope is that you have now recovered your old vigour – without using it quite so recklessly! But reckless or not, it is safe to say that no previous Visiting Fellow in the creative arts category has made such an impact on the Canberra scene and the ANU. And the Anglican church, I daresay!'

right to pursue his own project, especially to the students. But the same courtesy wasn't extended to him by others.[37]

Malcolm's first major commitment after his return was at Adelaide, where he directed a jazz mass for the Royal School of Church Music, conducted and directed *The Red Sea* at the Adelaide Festival Theatre, gave an organ recital, oversaw a performance of *In Place of Belief* and had fun with the cassation *Genesis*. From Adelaide he moved on to a two-day event, 'Music In The Round', at a country house twenty miles west of Melbourne, Chirnside House, Werribee Park. For the travel-weary Malcolm, Chirnside was a wonderful, if unreal, haven. Built in the 1870s in Italianate style for two brothers whose pastoral empire had made them a fortune, the sixty-room stately home was resplendent in its local bluestone, mosaic floors, gold leaf ornamentation and fine furniture. Its thousand-acre park included a lake and grotto as well as shepherds' huts, dairy and wool-sheds. For a time it had been a Catholic Seminary, when a chapel, theatre and dormitory were added, and it was now owned by the Victorian Government.

The event was organised by The Australian Musicians' Guild, a body recently founded by two hundred enthusiasts whose happy inspiration was to encourage others to enjoy good music in surroundings which would enhance the whole experience. Informality and discussion between musicians and public were the keynote. In the mornings the Royal Australian Navy Band played in the garden. There were also craftsmen giving practical demonstrations of the making of instruments. In the afternoons and evenings concerts were given simultaneously in five different venues: the theatre, chapel, billiard room, library and gallery. Every half-hour a new concert began and audiences could move around the house, experiencing music in different settings. There were sixty performers, with Malcolm the celebrity guest.

Malcolm's commitments included playing his Second Piano Concerto with the Melbourne Philharmonia and his Flute Serenade with a chamber group. He also had a session in the Chapel, taking some local schoolchildren through *Genesis*. His helper there was Simon Campion, five years his junior and the secretary of the weekend's organising body and assistant organist at St Patrick's Cathedral, Melbourne.[38] Each felt an immediate rapport with the other. Indeed, the shared rehearsal of *Genesis* in the Chirnside Chapel was to change both their lives, and they would ultimately spend nearly thirty years together.

From 'Music in the Round' at Chirnside House Malcolm moved on to Melbourne for a three-day festival in which his concert at the National Gallery with the Astra Chamber Orchestra included the Concerto for Two Pianos played with William Kimber.[39] The constant overwork and a flurry of gay one-night

[37] June 2006

[38] Simon Campion's other commitments that weekend included playing some Beethoven, Mozart and Bach as well as Messiaen's *L'Apparition de l'Eglise Eternelle*.

[39] The Astra Chamber Orchestra had given the work its premiere five months earlier, the pianists being Charles Webb and Wallace Hornibrook.

stands led to increasing tensions, pep pills, alcohol and, inevitably, a breakdown. It occurred at Melbourne Airport, where, rushing to catch a flight to Canberra, he found himself overcome by a fear of flying and unable to climb aboard. He was taken to Canberra by car, where he at once collapsed. At first he was thought to have heart problems, but it soon became clear that he was in the midst of an emotional breakdown, resulting in a total loss of confidence. He was about to be committed to a hospital psychiatric ward, when Dr Ralph Reader, with whom he had earlier been staying, offered to look after him at his farm. Heavily sedated, Malcolm slept for fourteen hours and was subsequently quietly cared for by Reader's wife Hazel. In retrospect, thirty years on, Reader believes the illness was perhaps less serious than he thought at the time:

> He was on the edge of a nervous breakdown, certainly. There was a lot of strife in his marriage. He resented, he told me, Dolly setting up engagements for him in England. But there was nothing seriously wrong with him, nothing clinical or psychological. He was not psychotic at all. It was purely behavioural, and it was transient. It didn't affect him in later life.[40]

Malcolm's obvious fears of everyone around him, however, were serious enough for recourse to psychiatric help, so he was driven to Sydney to see Dr Bruce Herriott, the Medical Superintendent at Sydney Hospital, whom he knew. Herriott referred him at once to Dr Bill Metcalf, an Honorary Physician specialising in Psychiatry, and Dr Ravich, another Sydney Hospital Honorary. Metcalf decided that a period of total rest was necessary, at least two weeks. Arrangements were therefore made for Malcolm to stay in the Koala Motor Inn, near Hyde Park in central Sydney, close to the ABC studios, where further work was scheduled. For the moment, said Dr Metcalf, there should be no contact with his family. Diane was to be told where he was, but she was not to tell anyone else, not even Dolly or Bessie. When the two weeks of solitude were extended to four, Diane had to cope with anxious phone-calls from Dolly in England and Bessie at nearby Blues Point, both in a state of some distress.

Malcolm, ensconced in a large apartment complete with a kitchen, received regular medical visits. He had been told to swim three times in the hotel pool, sit in the sun and cut down as much as possible on coffee and cigarettes. He swam and sunbathed, but he needed his cigarettes and the only concession he made to interminable cups of coffee was to water them down with ice cubes. Friends from ABC, led by John Hopkins, kept him informed of the recording of *The Violins of St Jacques* being made by ABC for a television production, something he had hoped to supervise.[41] Somehow, over three days, suitably sedated, he managed to make several recordings for ABC on the fine organ of the Sydney University

40 May 2006

41 The recording would use Australian singers except for April Cantelo, who was flown specially in from a concert tour of New Zealand.

Great Hall, the avoidance of traffic noise dictating that he worked through the middle of the night.[42]

Just before Christmas, Diane was at last allowed to explain to the family what had happened. Writing to Dolly in England, she tried not to be alarmist:

> Malcolm is very fit physically and has lost a little weight… My own theory is that he has had a serious emotional breakdown, signs of which were coming to the surface earlier this year. You mentioned this happening around Easter, I think. He appears to have lost all confidence in himself on one part, and yet is bursting with ideas for music, but can't settle to write. He seems to find it very difficult to meet new people and to overcome the extreme loss of confidence…[43]

Diane explained that she had visited Malcolm a couple of times in his Sydney retreat. The first occasion was in answer to an SOS:

> Malcolm rang me in a very distressed state, so I told him to contact Metcalf who was out. He had no valium left and as Mrs Metcalf had told him to take 2, I went in with some and stayed until he was a bit calmer. Took his washing home and returned it the next day. He seemed much brighter and business-like but in the same instant was tearful. His emotions seem to go up and down faster than a yo-yo.

Professional anxieties vied with personal ones. While resting at the Koala Motor Inn, Malcolm wrote to Weinberger's gloomily about 'the work load ahead from now until late May'. He had three important commissions to finish, one of which, *Perisynthion*, was a score commissioned by Robert Helpmann for the Australian Ballet, for which John Lanchbery, the company's Music Director, was asking for the parts by late January. Malcolm had made a start on it in Canberra, telling John Schofield:

> Today the first section went to be photographed and a copy will be airmailed to Richard [Toeman]. It is for a large orchestra. I'm on fire writing the ballet but wonder how I'll ever get it done on time.[44]

He didn't. He finished the long central section by the deadline, but the first part went mysteriously missing (Malcolm always blamed Weinberger's for this) and the third part was not completed. Helpmann, who had been choreographing bits and pieces as and when they arrived, eventually took fright, abandoned the Williamson score and re-set his steps to Sibelius' First Symphony, still retaining the title *Perisynthion*.[45] It was not a success. Malcolm did eventually finish the

42 'Works for Organ', subsequently issued as an LP by EMI Records, Australia, included *Peace Pieces* and *Little Carols of the Saints*.

43 22 December 1973

44 24 September 1973

45 The first performance took place on 21 March 1974. Malcolm wrote to a friend (25 February 1974) that there had been 'dirty work at the crossroads', ludicrously suggesting that his music had been rejected because it was 'beyond the capacity of John Lanchbery to conduct the score'. With equal inconsequence he mocked Helpmann's choreographic skills and his recent appointment as 'King' of Melbourne's big Moomba Festival: 'The truth seems to be that the crown lies uneasy on the head of His Majesty of Moomba. When *The Display* hit Covent Garden, Nolan, the company and I all got raves, while Bobby was slated for his choreography, and he does not wish a repetition of that...'

score, several months later, and its outstanding quality makes the disappointment of its late completion all the more bitter. It has never been danced, but it works well as a concert suite, as Dobbs Franks has demonstrated, and, more recently, Christopher Austin:

> Two tubular bells and two vibraphones create a signature sound. *Perisynthion* is a combination of fantasy, imagination and extraordinarily complex compositional rigour. It is masterly. The melodic invention is all based on interlocking chords you hear initially on the vibraphones. By using the vibraphones and bells there is something less concrete about the pitch – the whole piece structurally becomes a means of gradually solidifying that grammar. But from that chromatic grammar he is also capable of writing diatonic and pan-diatonic tunes. That degree of authority is very rare.[46]

Furious about the use of Sibelius and unable to see where the chief blame lay, Malcolm ill-advisedly sued the Australian Ballet, who, in turn, sued him for the return of half his considerable commissioning fee. Soon lawsuits were flying in all directions until, over a year after the Sibelius *Perisynthion*, Richard Toeman eventually persuaded all parties to withdraw legal action.[47]

Another of the commissions preying on Malcolm's mind was a cantata for soprano and string orchestra to be sung at the Proms in July by Elisabeth Söderström and based on the poetry of the Swedish Secretary-General of the United Nations, Dag Hammarskjöld, killed in an air-crash twelve years earlier.[48] Malcolm much admired Hammarskjöld's posthumously published writings on his solitary spiritual pilgrimage, but it was a token of his problems that he was unable to translate his enthusiasm into action.

The final commission, for a multi-part television series *Churchill's People*, came with an attractively lucrative contract from the BBC, but its twenty-six fifty-minute dramas, based on episodes loosely taken from *The History of the English Speaking Peoples*, would require huge quantities of music. There were rumours too that the budget was dangerously small, the scripts being farmed out to any number of different writers, and that Malcolm's agreement to write the score marked the end of a series of refusals.

Malcolm re-emerged briefly in England at the end of January 1974, to fulfil various commitments: a performance at the Queen Elizabeth Hall of his Concerto for Two Pianos;[49] a radio interview with Joseph Cooper; and an

46 Christopher Austin, January 2006

47 Malcolm felt this was a terrible betrayal by Weinberger's. ('I am not pleased that the House of Weinberger, instead of protecting its composer, runs for cover in the pious expectation that the composer will set the matter right.') But it was the right course and allowed Dobbs Franks to record it with the Sydney Symphony Orchestra. He tactfully chose a new title, *Astarte*.

48 Malcolm identified very closely with the highly cultured Dag Hammarskjöld, a theologian and multi-linguist, keen on music, art and poetry. Hammarskjöld had served as Secretary-General from 1953 until his death in 1961.

49 10 February 1974. With Gwenneth Pryor and the BBC Scottish SO under Yuval Zaliouk. They had previously spent two days rehearsing and recording the work for Radio 3 Scotland.

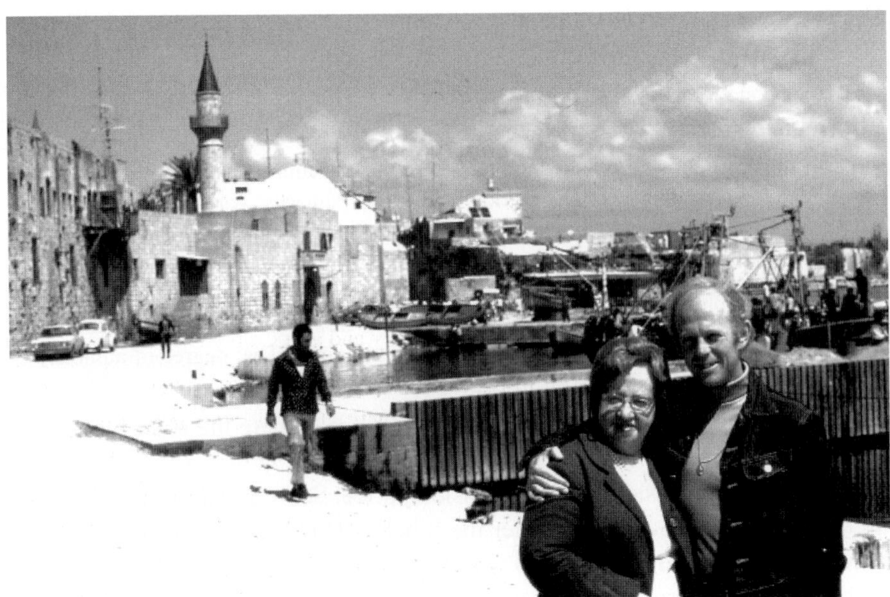

With Ahuda Zaliouk, Yuval's mother, in Akko's Muslim quarter near the harbour

Jerusalem, 1974

appearance at the first live British performance of his First Symphony (*Elevamini*).[50] But by the beginning of March he was in Paris, making arrangements through Mario Bois to do a series of cassations with *Jeunesses Musicales de France*.[51] He was soon writing to Richard Toeman from the Grand

50 Charles Groves conducting the Royal Liverpool Philharmonic Orchestra, Liverpool, 19 February 1974

51 Bois, who ran his own publishing business, also acted as Weinberger's French associate. There were now several editions of the cassations translated into French by Bois.

Hotel de Champagne ('Beat this for grandeur!') with an excitement which belied his problems over the unwritten Hammarskjöld cantata.[52]

Later that month Malcolm spent an equally happy time in Israel, where he played three performances of his Second Piano Concerto at the invitation of Yuval Zaliouk, Music Director of the Haifa Symphony Orchestra.[53] Zaliouk remembers no sign of emotional problems:

> He was in terrific form, real high spirits. My wife Sue spent a lot of time with him, talking into the small hours of the night. Neither she nor I remember any difficulties. Quite the contrary, he was for ever joking, and at the same time the visit to the Holy Land meant a great deal to him, both personally and as a Catholic.[54]

He stayed at the Hotel Shulamit in Haifa, close to Yuval Zaliouk's parents' home. Malcolm throughout his life had a homing instinct for a mother figure. Ahuda Zaliouk was perfect. Not only did she return the warmth of his affection, but she also happened to be one of Haifa's foremost piano teachers. Inspired by feelings of acceptance, Malcolm quickly composed on her Steinway ten graded teaching pieces, *Haifa Watercolours*, which he dedicated to her. These highly chromatic and vivid miniatures, with romantic titles like 'Bedouin Shepherd and his Black Mountain Goats' and 'Spring Flowers on Mount Carmel', successfully capture the sound of the eastern Mediterranean. Malcolm had fallen in immediate love with the sparkling colours of the busy town and would gaze in awe from the quayside of the grand harbour as Haifa rose before him in great shell-like curves towards the top of Mount Carmel. His *Watercolours* begin and end with the harbour at sunrise and sunset.

Malcolm saw much in a short time. Zaliouk drove him to the top of Mount Carmel to visit the Carmelite monastery on the site where Elijah threw the Baal pagans into the Kishon River. He also took him to Akko, Lake Galilee and the Druze villages Usphia and Dhalia, as well as the Arab-Christian village of Fasuta in Upper Galilee. At Fasuta a family friend prepared for Malcolm and the Zaliouks a huge Arab feast, which lasted a whole afternoon. Jerusalem's Western Wall (where he left a request note) and the Holy Sepulchre Church both made a strong emotional impact on him.

---

52 'I had a superb week with JMF. Delighted by the totally unexpected review in *Le Monde*... Mario was a great help all the way and JMF are *très enthousiastes*. They want more of the same. Two people (one from Lausanne the other from Nice) came to see my work and asked me to do cassation series, and JMF have asked me back... This is the direct outcome of my European trip Weinberger promoted. With this beginning in France (and thank you!) we go on....!'

53 Late March 1974. Yuval Zaliouk conducted, the rest of the programme consisting of Handel, Kodály and Mendelssohn. Back in September 1973 Zaliouk had been hoping Malcolm might complete his work on the Unknown Jewish Martyr for this visit, offering enticingly a recording by the Israel National Radio Orchestra, but it was not to be finished for another two years.

54 May 2006

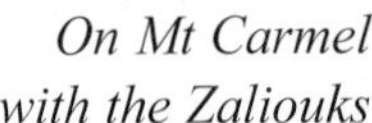

On Mt Carmel with the Zaliouks

In his happiness Malcolm sent several postcards to the family, strongly stressing Israel's free and liberating atmosphere but showing little concern for what was going on in England. He wrote to Dolly from Haifa:

> Darling,
>
> You'd love this place as I do. The air is fresh and relaxing. So far the Jerusalem weather has been very cold with rain and thunder but Haifa is very mild spring. The hills at the back of the picture border on Syria and out to the left the beginning of Lebanon. The feeling of freedom and youth here is incredible. Jerusalem is very touristic but absolutely astonishing and lovely. Love M

And again:

> Darling,
>
> Your cable arrived and was much appreciated! The audience enthusiastic about the concerto…. Haifa is small but I think magical. Jerusalem is like a whole world. Disappointed Americans abound, but it's a happy country. Love M[55]

Peter, about to start at a new school as a boarder and not particularly happy at the prospect, might have benefited from a word of encouragement from the father he had not seen for seven months but instead only received tributes to the freedom and beauty of Israel:

> I look forward to next visit here and we must all come. I love it all. There is an amazing free atmosphere and in spite of all troubles people are happy and excitable. You'd love the tiny Arab shops in Jerusalem and mixture of peoples and languages…
>
> You know this [the Golan Heights] is where the defensive fighting takes place, not far from where I am writing this. Mount Hermon comes in the Psalms. The colours do not exaggerate. It is like Spain but even more highly coloured and beautiful. A highly spiced mixture of Jewish and Arab, old and new cultures…
>
> This is very much your world, I think. I wish I could read Hebrew as you do, but each day I learn a few more words. It is a land of freedom and great beauty. You'd want to stay here for ever…[56]

55 23 & 25 March, 1974

56 23 & 25 March 1974

Fortified by the freedom, youth and beauty he encountered in the Holy Land, and seemingly unconcerned that not a note had been written of his Proms commission, now only five months away, Malcolm made another brief stop at East Sheen, where, perversely, he completed *Perisynthion* and spent time thinking about a Harp Concerto.[57] Like *Hammarskjöld Portrait* it was a work he very much wanted to write, inspired by an earlier chance visit to the Tomb of the Unknown Jewish Martyr in Paris. But, like the cantata, it remained unwritten. For the moment he could only create cassations with any ease, his newest one being written in French for use in workshops organised by the *Jeunesses Musicales*.[58]

Meanwhile the situation with Dolly remained volatile. In the Spring of 1974 they again tried counselling, but no effect, and, as Malcolm disappeared on his latest travels, Dolly was left in East Sheen to explore her feelings in depth on paper:

> Malcolm has said during a number of sessions that he finds the situation intolerable and that he must somehow do something about it. He also says at home that he doesn't want a divorce, or at least not enough to take action. 'But why don't you?' He also says he doesn't speak out because he doesn't want to hurt me. My God! He doesn't speak out that much in private, but when he has an audience the restrictions appear to be less. I find the situation intolerable as well. Why don't I say so at the sessions?[59]

Instead she tended to sit quietly and defensively as Malcolm levelled various complaints against her: that she couldn't distinguish between his social and business evenings; that she told him over and over what a bad husband he was; that she was 50% to blame for his breakdown in Australia and 100% for his impotence. Were all his problems, she asked herself, really (as he suggested) related to her 'screaming like a fishwife'? Didn't he accept some responsibility for what was going wrong?

Financial and professional pressures mounted with emotional ones, and the presence of Bessie[60] in England proved the catalyst in June for another major breakdown, this time Malcolm's loss of confidence being accompanied by an inability to walk. His doctor was reassuring. The walking problem was just the brain telling the body to stop working. Nothing, he assured Malcolm, was functionally wrong.

---

57 For which funds had been found by Geoffrey Chard and other friends who ran the Australian Music Association in London.

58 *La Terre Des Rois* (which later became *The Terrain of the Kings*) was first performed in France in the spring of 1975 under the auspices of the JMF, the dedicatees. It was for four-hand accompaniment with optional orchestra; it was set in the Camargue, its cast consisting of bulls, horses, birds and man (the enemy).

59 15 March 1974

60 'I assume that my mother has returned to Australia,' wrote Malcolm later, from the safety of France. 'I wish that I didn't feel resentment in me on account of what little my father left me.' (He could not understand why his father had left half of the business to Bessie and a quarter each to his sisters.)

A further period of separation was advised by his psychologist if the Proms commission was to be written, and, with the bank manager's help, it was arranged that Malcolm should stay at a quiet hotel at Pont-du-Crau, a small, nondescript Provencal town on the outskirts of Arles. For the family it would mean respite from constant dramas at Hertford Avenue, which only Peter, away at boarding school, managed to miss. As Malcolm set off for France, he wrote him a brief explanation:

> I didn't really have a chance to explain to you that I have to go away for a month on Tuesday because the years of overwork have caught up with me. I am physically well, but mentally and psychologically so exhausted that the doctors have commanded me immediate rest in solitude. I shall be back in time for your Bar Mitzvah. The Churchill music has kept me very busy but has gone so far successfully. This is a series of 26 TV spectaculars covering British history from pre-Saxon days up to the Industrial revolution.[61]

Malcolm used his period of solitude in Provence to try to take stock of his troubled state. Dolly was much in his thoughts and he sent her a long progress report:

> Darling!
>
> I guess love's love! I'm missing everyone so much. Your voice on the phone was wonderful to hear.
>
> Although I've been away only two days I can see how necessary it has been… I was terribly depressed after leaving & consumed with guilt about everything. I still feel (i) guilt and (ii) personal and artistic inadequacy. They are terrible feelings and until I can get over them I cannot go on. Money troubles are frightening, but I accepted them as God's punishment because I'm such a dreadful person. How can I explain to you that I do not feel you are to be condemned, judged badly or disliked, but that the condemnation, negative judgement and dislike is of myself for myself? This feeling of total failure goes very deep and has a completeness… You feel that I have rejected you. I have not. It is my own feeling of worthlessness that prevents me operating to an outside world… Until I can feel any justification for living I cannot be a proper father or husband, or fulfil myself as a composer… Feeling like that, how can I let you and the children love me when I don't deserve it?[62]

He was full of fear, he wrote, despite taking valium for the past eight months. ('It eases the pain of existing and puts the tensions of human relationships at a distance.') His outbreaks of aggression were simply manifestations of this fear. His travels, he explained, were an expression of his sense of failure. He could cope better in new places where acceptance was easier. Hence the arrangements made to spend the first months of next year as composer-in-residence at the University of Florida, a topic of much contention between him and Dolly. Another contentious issue was Malcolm's wish for the whole family to go to

---

61 16 June 1974. Yuval Zaliouk, who conducted the Churchill recordings, believed the music was excellent, just the right material for a Suite. But he found Malcolm's temper extremely unpredictable during the many recording sessions: 'We had quite a brush on one occasion.'

62 18 June 1974

Spain in August, for which there was no money. Dolly could see little justification for getting further into financial trouble. Malcolm, however, still pleaded for the holiday:

> If we do not go to Spain together, money or no money, I shall lose the last vestige of self-respect. I shall come back early to London with some money and in spite of all let's go. For the sake of the children, for our sakes, I know that the tax menace and other menaces make it impractical, but starting with our own honeymoon we have never been able to afford anything, and this is heart-breaking capitulation to fate. The holiday in Spain is my only hope – I mean it! This present sojourn is hard work, musically and psychologically.

An unsatisfactory telephone conversation followed. The more Dolly talked sense, the more depressed Malcolm became.

> Your saying that you were being pulled between Mr Moore [the bank manager] and Mr Muller [the tax adviser], that Spain is to be cancelled, that we shall be paying tax debts for months to come, that you do not like being the middle man, drives me into worse and more unproductive panics. I realize that you are worried sick too. But I am so far down I cannot see outside my own fear. You think that this is selfish?

He realized, he told her, his emotional breakdown was tied in with his overworking, but such were their financial problems there was no obvious alternative way forward:

> I cannot work at the rate I do and pursue publishers, agents and so on at the same time, and keep accounts as Mr Muller would wish, send out VAT invoices, answer letters and be a reasonable human being in the family or other social context. I cannot say I shall crack, because I have cracked! Even if the *Churchill* continues as well as it began, even if the *Hammarskjöld* is not the disaster I anticipate, I know that I am not coping with all the other important things that make life go on as it should… While I am only half-alive & cannot study the music I wish to study, read the books I need to

A return to Hertford Avenue for Peter's Bar Mitzvah, 1974

> stimulate me; while we cannot relax or take holidays, there is really no time for psychiatrists, for anything else, while the chase for cash becomes increasingly desperate, things can only get more desperate.

Malcolm could see no future. He clearly despaired of making progress through further sessions of psychiatry. He had been brought up to be self-centred, and, as such, he loathed the continual arguments to justify himself. The arguments were all the more painful in the hollowness of the self-justifications. 'I need to be alone and at leisure, to try to live by my own discipline.' It was not something he had achieved with any success in the past, as no doubt Dolly pointed out. Constantly letting her down and arguing from the weakest of positions, he found his guilt intolerable. He again broached the possibility of divorce:

> Along with every psychiatrist and doctor that I have seen in Australia and in England, Dr Franks thinks that one of two solutions is possible: (i) periods of separation or (ii) permanent separation. What do you think? For your sake and the children's sake the two cannot be reconciled. I should be the first to admit that you deserve a better husband and a happier married life, from which point of view permanent separation or divorce is practical as soon as possible. For the children's sake it is better that we stay together and have periods apart. Finance and the need to overwork to earn cut through all this. People make new beginnings, but not when one of them is a wreck as I am. Why should I wreck you further? You are fragile as well as strong. Why should I break you and waste more of your life?... I love you, but love and a life together are not the same thing.

Hammarskjöld Portrait, once he began writing it, proved a form of therapy with its gay subtext, for Hammarksjöld's inner struggles were Malcolm's own: the anguish of the pilgrimage through life, both sexual and spiritual; the fear of masochism; the guilt; the uncertainty; the temporary respite in the delights of nature; and, finally, the submission to the hope that there would be eventual answers, acceptance and forgiveness in following through to the end the compulsions of martyrdom:

> He will shed his jacket
> And with shirt-tail flapping
> Stands against the wall-face
> To be shot at.
>
> Do I fear an urge in me
> Thus to be murdered?
> Or within me,
> Is there darkly hidden
> One who only waits
> To pull the trigger?[63]

For all his worry and self-questioning at the little hotel at Pont-du-Crau, or perhaps because of it, Malcolm found that the cantata which had eluded him so

---

63 Malcolm's translation from the Swedish. His original Swedish version was the one sung by Söderström at the Proms, the singer pausing between each section to give the audience the sense of the passage.

long was now coming to him almost faster than he could write. On the third day he was reporting to Dolly that 'the *Hammarskjöld Portrait* is progressing at great speed' and he even anticipated finishing in time to turn back to the Churchill series on which he was currently well behind schedule:

> The quiet and solitude here is fine for working – the hotel is without character & swimming takes up about three quarter-hour periods of the day. I am taking a tiny walk after the evening meal, before breakfast and after what is laughingly lunch (I steal breakfast bread and dinner fruit to avoid lunch as I pay for only two meals & the French being French don't mind.) Walking is a real problem and I try to walk a little farther each time.

By the fourth day he was reporting that the cantata was 'coming along beautifully', although the psychosomatic illness persisted:

> I increase the walking distance each time, but it's a battle, particularly with my left leg. I've taken no valium since leaving London and all the time I'm sick with fear. Fear of swimming even if nobody's about, fear of going to an empty dining-room, or making the decision to go for a walk…

It was not long before he was back on valium and anticipating that *Hammarskjöld Portrait* would be a disaster. By now he had all five sections in short score and was addressing the orchestration:

> Today was all lightning and thunder. I went to Mass in the tiny village church and got drenched. But at least with no swimming and walking it was all Hammarskjöld. It's a huge work. Why do I write these things?

The orchestral rehearsal called by the BBC was only three weeks away, the Prom itself just five. He was already well past his deadlines:

> The failure to meet deadlines must not become a habit. There are always reasons. The ballet, the Churchill scores; it mustn't happen again, but until I am better it looks like becoming a habit.

Four days later he was able to send off the first completed section to Dolly, the central third movement, probably the most important of all with its reflections on Self, 'both the persecuted and the persecutor, the crucified and the crucifier.'[64]

> With some triumph the large third movement went off express. The people in the hotel have a photocopy machine so I put it all together, packed it and the old boy drove me into the post office. I hope that it's quick. I got up at 3.00 am today and worked on the second movement. I don't see how it will ever be ready. I cannot go on quicker than my brain will go and my legs are giving me quite a lot of pain.

The fourth movement was the last to be completed, a short, ghostly nocturne representing 'the troubled cloudy night that presages the Arctic winter', and

---

64 Dolly had the task of keeping the publishers confident that the score would arrive in time for the concert. An internal memo was circulated at Boosey & Hawkes on 21 June, when nothing yet had been received: 'Mrs Williamson will bring in by hand to the Hire Library sections of the full score as soon as she receives them... The first rehearsal is scheduled to take place on 14 July at Maida Vale studios.'

reflecting the anxieties of a desperate race against the clock, both in its brevity and tortured atmosphere.

With *Hammarskjöld Portrait* miraculously completed, Malcolm returned to England, not knowing his own mind, caught halfway between wanting his freedom and wanting the family he loved, consumed with guilt and 'numb with fear'.[65] He and Dolly were soon embroiled in disagreement over his wish to spend a year as composer-in-residence at the University of Florida. Malcolm wanted the family to come with him. Dolly, on the other hand, feared more damaging disruption to the children's schooling. She also pointed out that although they had all gone to Australia at Malcolm's explicit request, once there, they had seemed largely surplus to his requirements. In the event Malcolm would go out by himself to Florida after Christmas for just one academic term.

There were also differences of opinion over a possible television opera, on which Dolly had worked hard, preparing the ground in Malcolm's absence. Brian Culshaw, a good friend and Head of Music at BBC Television, had already opened up preliminary negotiations, but, as at Sadler's Wells a few years earlier, Malcolm insisted on going his own way. Whereas the BBC were looking for an accessible and tuneful work, Malcolm preferred something less popular, *The Document of Adam*, a gruelling exposé of mankind's failings, including the Holocaust. Such an unacceptable scenario, Dolly was convinced, was a foolishly wilful surrender of an opportunity which might never come again.

At the end of July the first performance of *Hammarskjöld Portrait* ensured a temporary diversion from the intensities of East Sheen, Malcolm writing for it an informative programme note, though taking care that it was not too self-revelatory:

> I chose a soprano voice with string orchestra to impose upon myself a challenge in blandness to the voluptuous coloration of the poems. The use of the strings is at times severe, at times more lush, and a solo violin hovers spirit-like over the textures.
>
> Musically and poetically cross-references abound. It seems futile to reproduce in a programme-note for a British audience the Swedish text which is being sung, or the official English version by W H Auden. It may, however, be worth quoting the opening verse, as a key to the nature of Hammarskjöld's attitude:
>
> *Herre – in är dagen,*
> *Jag är dagens.*
> Lord – the day is yours.
> I am of the day.

65 'I well remember when I completed the *Hammarskjöld Portrait* in Southern France,' Malcolm later wrote to Dr Michael Armstrong, 'that I returned to London full of self-contempt for the work, and only by stern persuasion did I attend the rehearsals...' (25 May 1983)

> Verbally, musically and ideologically this passage recurs during the work. Through the implorings, the bitter acceptances of suffering, the exuberance, and the quiet contemplation of nature, the thread of submission to a higher power is always present.

Malcolm's worst fears over *Hammarskjöld Portrait*[66] were not realized. Lennox Berkeley told Malcolm it was better than anything he himself had ever written;[67] the delighted Söderström subsequently sang it all over Scandinavia; even most of the critics were favourable. Joan Chissell in *The Times* loved everything about it. Desmond Shawe-Taylor in the *Sunday Times* found it the happiest example he yet had heard 'of the strongly lyrical talent of this composer, who goes his own way, indifferent to accusations of being behind the times'.[68]

To a modern ear *Hammarskjöld Portrait* sounds anything but 'behind the times'. In its day, however, bolder experimentation was widely preferred. Davidovsky's electronic synchronisations, Steve Reich's tape loops, and Ligeti's complex mechanical rhythms and electronic-sounding textures were typical of the period. Malcolm's premiere actually coincided with that of Stockhausen's *Across the Boundary* at The Roundhouse, in which a bassoon's strange snorts and grunts were amplified by tape-refraction. Shawe-Taylor had some wry fun at Malcolm's staunch refusal to be deflected from his own language by that of the more revolutionary composers:

> The merest *tricoteuse* of the musical revolution will know what insults to fling at the insolent fellow *en route* to his tumbril. There are key signatures in his score at one point rising to a voluptuous total of six sharps: disgraceful! No percussion whatsoever, not even the tapping of bows against wood; nothing left to chance or the whim of the performer; no fragmented syllables or mutterings or sudden screams in the highest register for the soloist. What are things coming to?[69]

He was full of praise for *Hammarskjöld Portrait*:

> Williamson's attitude to fashion is not so much defiant as serene. He has written for his soprano as gratefully and as beautifully as possible, and for his much-divided accompanying strings with a skill and variety that never do violence to their musical nature.
>
> The tone of the music is often passionately rich and romantic, at times even Straussian in its soaring lines and fondness for enharmonic modulation; at other moments joyous and sparkling (as in the dance-like second piece about the Swedish summer)… Any danger of cloying is offset by the freshness and grace of the vocal line, and even more by the skill and resourcefulness of the string writing. There is a continual abundance of harmonic, contrapuntal and textural interest, but the web of sound is never allowed to become fussy. The writing is often in six or more parts constantly and purposefully on the move. Such music is a gift that few sopranos of

---

66 The first performance on 30 July 1974, with the BBC Symphony Orchestra conducted by John Pritchard, was broadcast on Radio 3.

67 Dickinson: *The Music of Lennox Berkeley*, p.50

68 4 August 1974

69 4 August 1974

> our time have had the luck to receive; and Miss Söderström repaid her composer with singing that was both radiant and intimate.

The finest section of all, and Malcolm's most uninhibited rebuttal of those who endorsed strange snorts and grunts, comes in the third movement, the exposition of Self, when an emotional prayer for mercy is expressed in a rich Straussian *cantabile*.

> Be merciful
> Unto us.
> Be merciful
> Unto our conflict,
> That we
> Sensing thee, in fondness and faith,
> Pure-heartedness and faith-keeping,
> May follow thee,
> In honour and truth and hope,
> And see thy face,
> In stillness.

The deep tranquility of this prayer was an ideal to which, in his current agitated state, he could not himself begin to aspire. The concert over, Malcolm spent little time at home, quickly rushing up to Warwickshire where he was expected at Moreton Morell. Once a private country house, Moreton Morell had become an Agricultural College, which, in the summer holidays, was home to an annual summer school for music teachers. Malcolm had attended with Dolly for the first time the previous year. Visiting Moreton Morell was to become an important part of Malcolm's life and he made many strong friendships there. Ray Lovely, who had volunteered to collect him from Warwick Station, still remembers what a troubled spirit he was in the summer of 1974:

> The first thing we had to do was stop off at a tobacconist's where he bought vast quantities of cigarettes. He was obviously greatly on edge. When he got back and took the wrapper off the first packet, he discovered that it did not have the usual cigarette coupons, so he stormed back into the shop and demanded his money back. We then had to find another tobacconist. This time, thank goodness, they came with the necessary coupons and he was happy. But we still couldn't go to Moreton Morell. We had to make another diversion to a grocer's, where he bought the most enormous amount of coffee. Armed with huge quantities of cigarettes and coffee, he relaxed a little, but he didn't appear very much during the week's course. He kept himself to himself, until right at the end he did a cassation.[70]

Shortly afterwards he was told by his doctor he was suffering from nervous exhaustion and must take a rest. This was such alarming news for the BBC, anxiously waiting on music for various episodes of *Churchill's People*, that they offered to organize every aspect of a holiday in France, if he were to make a

[70] June 2005

further, significant contribution to the series. Malcolm duly wrote them twenty minutes of music, which took him to Paris, where he stayed with Mario Bois and Claire Motte, met a young American friend, Larry Smith (currently studying with Nadia Boulanger), and caught up with Elisabeth Söderström, as he reported to Boosey & Hawkes's John Andrewes:

> I lunched with the Belfrages and Elisabeth Söderström. She appears very keen to sing *Hammarskjöld Portrait* in France, although of course she'd sing 'Three Blind Mice' in a bathing suit if the fee was right. I took 'Tempo' with its review of Hammarskjöld for her, and she sat in front of everyone reading her notices quietly as luncheon proceeded…[71]

After sending the BBC a further eighty minutes of music, he travelled down to the *Alpes Maritimes*, to stay at the Hotel Le Logis Sant' Estello, a former farmhouse, just ten kilometres from Cannes in the village of Mandelieu la Napoule. At the attractive Mandelieu, set in a glorious forest of mimosas, with high mountains all around, Malcolm did his best to ignore the fierce Mistral and the pressing Churchill commitments by reading Proust in the original French. He told Richard Toeman:

> Maddingly the swimming pool is like an ice block; the hotel had claimed that it was 'climatisée', but she isn't, dat ole piscine! Dat ole Mistral, however, is active, and the weather constantly changing…[72]

Dolly was at the forefront of his thoughts, but he started several letters before eventually completing one:

> Darling,
>
> It was wonderful to be talking last night. Tammy sounded great and you sounded happy… It seems that our conversation about the Churchill, about your grasping the facts and then the nettle, helped me to slow down. Even on two cups of coffee a day I have not been able to slow down until last night. With the mogadon also, I got my first proper sleep since I left. I woke at 6.00am. Today there has been no mistral, a lot of sun and I lunched in the open air in jeans only. This evening I walked to the top of the mountain, and of course the views are incredible – at each turn you see new mountains appear and at each new height a different aspect of the Mediterranean. It is certainly peaceful and the fact that the air is so vinous makes it difficult to smoke, easy to observe the 'no smoking' signs which is a rule in Alpine forests.[73]

Solitude in the *Alpes Maritimes* allowed Malcolm a chance for genuine self-evaluation:

> A curious aspect of staying here is that one is forced to rest, or at least divorce oneself from the mountainous problems that grew from molehills; one cannot do anything about them, thank God; and I am my own worst enemy, being carried away by my

[71] 2 October 1974

[72] 11 October 1974

[73] 8 October 1974

enthusiasms and my grievances, so that I cannot sleep or really function as a person. We've been over this so many times already.

On one glorious morning, having risen at five and realized that breakfast would not be available for another two hours, he ventured outside and forgot his troubles:

> I climbed to the top of a mountain and saw the dawn. It was a stunning sight, but would have been more agreeable on a fuller stomach. Kierkegaard's father cursed God from the top of a mountain and Ibsen's Brand delivered some of his most moving protest speeches from another (presumably). I wonder how they had the breath to do it. I can understand Moses coming down with the tablets; it's easy to roll down even without them. I guess I lack the Everest spirit.

At night-time, however, the demons returned:

> Rest? Again I hardly slept. The second night in succession I dreamed of a death – last night my father in a coffin with a glass disc for me to look at him which by law I was forced to do. He kept laughing. I woke well before dawn. The hotel had given me coffee and a tiny stove, so I was working before sunrise. The wooden shutters are banging in a terrible gale… Ignore the crazy bits in this disconnected letter. I long to talk to you tonight.

Unable to swim or sunbathe because of the Mistral, Malcolm found it hard to relax. He had forgotten how to have a holiday, he told John Andrewes, because of all the years of compulsive work, and, as if to prove his point, had brought three projects with him: the Harp Concerto in honour of the Unknown Jewish Martyr; some piano pieces with a Provençal theme, *The Bridge That Van Gogh Painted and the French Camargue*; and a new cantata, *Les Olympiques*. Of his ongoing crisis, *Churchill's People*, there was no mention.

After a week without swimming he moved down to Cannes,[74] where he was able to sunbathe and catch up with his correspondence. A letter to Peter hints at the mayhem he had been causing at East Sheen:

> My dear Pete,
>
> It was super to talk to you by phone & I'm sorry to have missed your weekend at home. I hope that you enjoyed it…
>
> I had not foreseen this enforced rest that I am taking. I have had far too much work and problems associated with the work, including tax and so on, mount up and one has forgotten how to sleep and become literally sick in the mind. The girls have been very understanding about this, although I actually have no knowledge of it. The brain needs to be cleared and rested & I do not have the time and freedom to do it, at least until Sir Winston C's TV series is finished. This is hard on everyone in the house and thank God you are at school.[75]

But Malcolm seemed psychologically unable to complete *Churchill's People* with its associations with the old life, suburbia, domesticity and repression of his

---

74 Hotel Moden, Rue de Serbes

75 14 October 1974

gay self. Instead, he spent time on forging a French text, based on the writings of Henri de Montherlant[76] for his new cantata, even though he was not to complete the musical setting, for mezzo-soprano and string orchestra, for another two years. From Cannes he wrote to Dolly:

> I wish I had some mental relief. My energy is enormous. I worked on the Montherlant from before dawn and all day except for reading about 100 pp. of Proust which is rough going…

De Montherlant's suicide two years earlier had revived interest in his novels, not least a controversial one (*Les Garçons*) which told of two schoolboys having an affair in a Catholic boarding school. However, the work which most interested Malcolm, *Les Olympiques* (*The Olympics*), was an unusual medley of essays, stories and poetry, drawing on de Montherlant's experiences as a soldier in the First World War and as an athlete. *Les Olympiques*, the book, expounds the virtues of athletic prowess and deplores warfare for the necessary destruction of male beauty. *Les Olympiques*, the cantata, as chosen and arranged by Malcolm in retreat at Cannes, is a carefully contrived journey through life, from youthful athlete to serene old poet, its final section endorsing an explicitly gay philosophy: A slender young boy (*svelte garçon*) is sitting in the darkness, tired and awaiting death, his face like a carving by Michelangelo. He reminds the old poet of Hypnos, the classical god of sleep, who in legend fell in love with the handsome young Hyperion. The young boy, however, turns out not to be mortal, but the brother of the Spirit of Death. 'If the Spirit of Death is your brother,' concludes the poet, 'I am not afraid of the agony of dying.' Malcolm's *Les Olympiques* was to be a strong personal statement, a meditation on the trials and tribulations of being gay, the title itself unequivocally endorsing ancient Greek ideals of male physical perfection.

Malcolm was preparing himself for a new life in which he would, he convinced himself, re-find emotional stability. In one of his last letters to Dolly from the *Alpes Maritimes* he touched again on the subject of his illness. Mental instability 'or mind-sickness', he wrote, was ugly. He did not want the children to see more than they had already seen. It was important, meanwhile, that everyone began to accept the seriousness of his condition:

> I don't know what the expression is – 'cracked', 'crackers', 'crazy' – but that's what I went months ago. I am sick and tired of saying this while nobody listens or understands… People still treat me as a rational person – one is not. You do, Erskine does, Mr Moore, Mr Whatever-the-accountant's name is, even the Churchillian

[76] Malcolm later was to give a potted account of the writer in the score of *Les Olympiques*: 'Henri de Montherlant (1896-1972) returned from the war of 1914-18, in which he was wounded, to disillusionment with civilian life. He sought in association football and in athletics, to recover the comradeship he had experienced in war and to pursue the moral, intellectual and physical virtues which for him accompanied the struggle for excellence. His experiences and emotions were expressed in the two parts of Les Olympiques... The song cycle makes use of a prose litany and four poems from the first part.'

> people accept eccentricity. I have nowhere to go, no time to go anywhere to be put right. Why will nobody listen? I know how I should behave and I don't. I'm clinging to the edge of actual sanity while sinking into the quick-sands of insanity – and fast. The top-dressing of reasonableness that gets Churchill scores written with more or less the right arithmetic is thinning. You think that I imagine this? That I want to exhibit myself before the world as something crazy and so jeopardize our livelihood and our children's welfare? I want to be cool and rational, for God's sake, and get our emotional and economic life smooth, whether we are together or apart. My earning power will be zero if I'm put away, or get too much of a reputation for self-centred neurosis.

There was no obvious way forward for the moment, but he believed he would only find emotional stability and only be able to continue his creative life when removed from the pressures of traditional domestic life. He was Hypnos in need of Hyperion. He was the crucified and the crucifier. To be true to himself he had to be false to others, and, in particular, those dearest to him. But there were no quick solutions in such a confused and hurtful situation, for however fiercely Dolly might fight with him to try to re-establish the values on which their life together had been based, she still accepted him lovingly for what he was, imperfections, disloyalties and all.

It was both a relief and an anxiety for Dolly as Malcolm departed in early January 1975 for his term at Tallahassee, Florida. He was all the keener to be away as the first episodes of *Churchill's People* were just being screened and, to his chagrin, it was clear that the low-budget series was going to be a terrible flop, talked about only for all the wrong reasons. The fifty-minute playlets were attempting too much with too few resources and there was much unintentional comedy. The second episode, for example, featuring the Romans in Britain (one of whom was a toga-clad Arthur Lowe), prompted *The Guardian*'s critic to declare:

> The decline of the Roman Empire in Britain was amply explained by their fondness for studio discussions… The decision of the Saxon captive to seize a sword and run amok among the debaters is one that will strike a chord in every viewer's heart!… There are twenty-four episodes to come. As Macbeth remarked on a similar occasion, 'What! Does the line stretch out to the crack of doom? I'll see no more.'[77]

Alan Coren in *The Times* did see some more, but he struggled to take the saga of King Alfred seriously despite the best efforts of Alan Howard and Anna Massey as King and Queen and Brian Blessed as the Viking Chief:

> Last night we saw in the continuing saga of our island race how King Alfred, having been beaten by Danish invaders, sought refuge in an extremely small television studio. It was there, among the cardboard rocks and rubber grass of his beloved Shepherd's Bush, that Alfred came face to face for the first time with the coarse folk of Wessex. A terse, retarded folk, they eke out a poor living as character actors, pursuing their primitive belief that by slapping a bit of greasepaint on their cheeks and matting their wigs they could pass for west Saxons of the ninth century and that by

[77] Nancy Banks-Smith, 7 January 1975

Newly arrived in Florida, with (l-r) Edward Kilenyi, Elena Nikolaidi and Carlisle Floyd

> speaking in the accents of Hardy's peasants and rolling their eyes, could bring authenticity to a script in which the Danes screamed 'I'll mash yer face in!' at one another and English soldiers asked prisoners what their bleeding names were.[78]

The episode ended with Alfred gumming on a white beard, going deaf and holding 'a delightful sub-Beckett exchange with his decayed consort'.

Despite taking with him some of the later scripts of this ill-judged epic, Malcolm was in good spirits. He was relieved to be leaving behind many other worries, which 'gnawed' at him in London, not least his tax problems and the battle to achieve 'economic ease'.

> I don't mean the worries that have been thrown at you, like VAT and tax, but the worries about which we can do nothing, like Ponsonby & Weinberger's and lack of performances and so on, which bug me and hold up our prospects of economic ease out of my music.

Without such burdens he could luxuriate in his apartment[79] on the university campus, with sophisticated air-conditioning, a sun lamp and, most important, a swimming pool by the door. The University's School of Music was forward-looking, run by a popular Dean, whom he immediately liked.[80] There were some interesting faculty members too: pianist Edward Kilenyi, who had been taught by Dohnányi and to whose records he used to listen on the radio back in his boyhood in Sydney; the Greek mezzo-soprano Elena Nikolaidi, to whose concert in

[78] 21 January 1975

[79] 432 West Jefferson St., Apt 120

[80] Malcolm dedicated two of his Toronto psalms to the Dean, Wiley Housewright, and his wife Lucilla.

Sydney Bessie had once taken him, and one of America's most successful composers of operas, Carlisle Floyd.

Malcolm liked everything about the university but was less impressed by its immediate surroundings:

> Tallahassee is a really terrible town. It's a sort of southern (Georgia-Arkansas) type shanty town, rather than Floridian splendour. It's just got the enormous Uni and a couple of government buildings, then really tacky ghost-town crumbville. It has no centre, just about 6 shopping malls of limited glamour spread through the countryside and great stretches of sad, black residential districts of no character. It's like Randall Jarrell's 'Pictures from an Institution'... The height of culinary ecstasy in Tallahassee is 'The Garden Tearoom' in a shopping plaza about three miles away... North of here is the Swanee River (alias Swannee) where each year they have a Stephen Foster Festival with a beauty queen competition with the crowning of a Miss Jeannie with the Light Brown Hair...[81]

The School of Music made good use of his presence. In addition to a student production of *Our Man in Havana* a wide cross-section of his music was performed[82] during the course of the term, Malcolm telling Dolly proudly that he was on a big ego trip, with his music coming out of every nook and cranny of the Music Building:

> I have the impression that I am a different person here... The atmosphere of being a visitor and a Britisher [sic] gives one a flattering novelty value, added to which the students are singing Havana in the corridors and the cassations are a hit.[83]

There was a relaxed atmosphere on the campus – 'the student-Faculty relationship here is very good and uncomplicated, very adult'[84] – but even so he 'raised a few eyebrows' by sunbathing bare-chested in the Music School's courtyard between lectures and rehearsals.[85] His teaching won more universal approval, his Analysis lectures on Contemporary British Music (including six hours on *Our Man in Havana*) attracting an impressive number of Faculty members as he 'took off into far-away realms' with the brightest students he had ever taught.[86] It was not long before he was also involving himself in the English and Drama departments, offering stimulating help to groups studying Yeats and Strindberg.

In addition to all this, the University's Therapy Department showed great interest in the use of the cassations with the handicapped, asking him to lead seminars and give practical demonstrations. At the end of January he wrote happily to Dolly:

---

81 8 January 1975

82 It included *From A Child's Garden*, the Rawsthorne Concerto, *Pas de Quatre*, *The Brilliant and the Dark*, *Symphony For Voices*, the 2-Piano Sonata, *Elegy JFK*, *Six English Lyrics*, *A Vision of Beasts and Gods*, *Death of Cuchulain* and various cassations.

83 28 January 1975

84 MW to Dolly Williamson, 17 January 1975

85 *Tallahassee Democrat*, 14 February 1975

86 MW to Janet Canetty-Clarke, 1 March 1975

One of the many attractive cassation scores

> It's been two exhausting but exciting days. Last night for 2 hours I gave a teach-in about my cassations… This was followed by a 3-way *Snow Wolf* with about 200 students from music, education, therapy and psychology. It was all video-taped. Today about forty therapists came with me to Sunland – there are Sunland homes all over Florida – at Tallahassee and we did a very simplified *Snow Wolf* with a whole lot of patients, all non-ambulatory. This was tough. Many do not speak, some are blind, all are severely mentally handicapped, many spastic. One man slavers from his nose and mouth and tries to rip off his clothes, one has acute hydrocephalus and one tiny child has it – an enormously distorted head larger than her body. The train was wheelchairs being wheeled around the room. We got a good chuffle chuff chorus memorized and sung; and wolf howls. I guess that this was a big achievement. The room was suffocating with the central heating and terribly overcrowded… I also did some improvised arm, leg and body moves with clapping, noise-making and singing. It was great to see the patients (many old people) surprising themselves with what they could do… I am hoarse from shouting…[87]

Malcolm's successes at Florida boosted his fragile self-esteem, giving him much-needed reassurance. He was delighted when one of the Sunland nurses shyly revealed that she'd wanted to meet him ever since hearing *Vision of Christ Phoenix* in New York.

---

87 28 January 1975

> I guess I'm terribly insecure to be pleased from that coincidence. I so badly wanted approval for my work at the hospital today and nobody said anything afterwards. Then this evening Dr Madsen, the head of music therapy, casually told me that he was so pleased the students were so very excited about this new facet of music therapy. I asked him if he'd seen this sort of thing before. He said, 'Of course not; this is quite a new concept.' They now have three hours of my talks on video-tape. Why do we long to be loved?[88]

He was too busy to make much progress on big projects like *Les Olympiques*. He was also too comfortable. He loved the luxury of a good-quality stereo-player in his flat and was soon borrowing piles of LPs, especially of American music – Aaron Copland' s Clarinet Concerto was his constant companion, and he revelled in Roger Sessions and Roy Harris ('a terrific composer'). Stravinsky's Violin Concerto was another favourite and Benny Goodman's recording of the *Ebony Concerto*. He also took the opportunity to read widely, having found 'a wild Maoist bookstore at the edge of the campus where you buy for next-to-nothing second-hand books which include a great range of classics'. So he delved further into Proust ('like Shakespeare, Jane Austen, Ibsen and a few more, he gets into the blood and changes one's ideas for ever'), Ionesco and Gide ('rather remarkable although not a little diseased and over-ripe').

Dolly, meanwhile, was holding things together in London as best she could, appeasing the taxman, maintaining appearances while living on a shoestring and doing her best to keep the momentum going on a BBC project of a television film exploring Malcolm's roots. *Malcolm Williamson Down Under*, which would involve his returning to Australia for a few weeks later in the year, promised a big boost to his career.

Malcolm's letters were full of his own problems. He was anguishing whether to butt in on the production of *Our Man in Havana*:

> The production and the student singers are extremely good but the conductor is a let-down and the orchestra which could be good is under-rehearsed. So I'm in the apartment washing clothes and composing and getting it to be a little less untidy…[89]

The composing occasionally included *Churchill's People*:

> Like the skull on the mantelpiece to remind one of death, the Churchill schedule lies under my eyes and I view it with dread and loathing. [90]

The task seemed as unending as it was unsatisfactory, yet somehow he forced himself to complete his score for Oliver Cromwell, his seventeenth, but there were still another nine to go:

> A few melting tunes have flowed into the score but the show was unintelligible and crammed with dialogue, so I can't think it makes much difference. I'm so dispirited about this. It's got in the way of writing my own music for so long…

88 *ibid.*

89 27 February 1975

90 28 January 1975

He continued writing 'bits every morning at the breakfast counter' but that was about all, so progress was inevitably slow. The Churchill series provoked such great 'mental pressure' that he told Dolly he would willingly give up writing music for teaching. The pleasures of Tallahassee only served to emphasise his dislike for his chosen career. In 'heavenly' Florida he struggled to face 'the ghastliness of being a composer'.

The 'ghastliness' was tied in with his continued feelings of inadequacy, not just as a composer but as a husband. He was being pulled in two ways. Although he wrote to Dolly in utter sincerity 'I wish you and the children were here to share Florida with me' and said he was exploring the possibility of them all living in America in the future, he was at the same time settling comfortably into a gay lifestyle. His travels around America, for example, were constantly involving sexual adventures. Michael Hoffenberger has many stories of Malcolm's escapades – wild nights, for example, in Philadelphia ('nothing but sex, sex and sex'), a misjudged tryst with a tenor ('he found him especially delicious, but the tenor would not respond, for Malcolm was sexually out with some people') and a more successful pick-up of a well-endowed lorry driver at a wayside eatery on the road to Norfolk, Virginia. ('I, the holy innocent, had missed the eye contact going on across the tables, and had no idea what was happening, so when Malcolm was away an extremely long time in the toilet I eventually went to see if he was all right – bad idea.'[91])

But, for the moment, the gay life in America ran in parallel with his continued role in England as a heterosexual with problems to solve. He was still writing to Dolly with analyses of what was wrong with him as a husband, thereby letting her believe that finding a way forward together was something he was still taking seriously. He had never subscribed, he wrote, to the Australian he-man complex, in which the male was the aggressor in love who conquered the 'little lady like a caveman':

> I was never like that and early on believed that I had a terrible lack, and in almost no sexual relationship in my life have I ever been an aggressor except with you in early days.[92]

His confusion was all the worse, for their recent happiness together:

> How shall I ever discover what has been wrong? Suddenly in the time just before I came here a way seemed to have been found between us, but I do not know what caused this. It was so very agreeable and suddenly loving and easy. Do you have any idea why? I am certain at least that if I am fearful of you and/or uncertain within myself <u>of</u> myself (which is all the time) it is difficult to have the sort of aggression required to be a lover.

He perceived that at the root of his problems there was Bessie:

---

91 March 2007

92 3 March 1975

> An aggressive woman is to me something fearful and disagreeable. My mother would say that she in her life with my father was the aggressor and the decision-maker because he was so weak. I can see now that in any marriage she would have been the decision-maker and the aggressor. Maybe in the past I have (as the psychiatrist says) attributed these characteristics to you, not because they were yours, but because I should identify any wife of mine with Bessie's character. I suppose that I still fear her. I've not written to her for ages and I fear her sharp rebuke when I do write. I shall be more of a man and a better husband when I don't care what Bessie or anyone else says or thinks of me.

One particular reason why he currently feared her was his decision to start drinking again, a direct result of the three months in Florida away from Dolly. He was at a Tallahassee poolside party, as usual enjoying his status as visiting celebrity, when someone offered him a Saki. 'But I don't drink,' said Malcolm. 'Ah, come on! Saki's not a proper drink, not proper alcohol – Saki can do you no harm!' Dolly was not on hand to dissuade him by her very presence. He drank it, liked it, and quickly downed another.[93]

Peter had once, as a boy, asked his father why he didn't drink. 'I liked it too much,' he replied candidly. And now he liked it again. He convinced himself that this time he would keep it under control. But he couldn't. He began missing appointments.[94] Dolly remembers him ringing up from Florida clearly the worse for drink. At Weinberger's too the change was soon noted on his return, as John Schofield recalls:

> When I first met him, in 1972, he was completely off the drink. And then he went to America three years later and he suddenly started drinking vodka again. 'Oh,' he said to me, 'I'm just having a drink, but I can stop whenever I want to…' But that was that. He never stopped drinking to the end…[95]

It was a decision connected with his intention to break free. He had stopped drinking in 1960 when Dolly first became pregnant. Pride in his family miraculously changed his damaging lifestyle. But now, however much he still loved his children dearly, however much he still loved Dolly, in going back to a dependence on alcohol he was subconsciously making a statement of intent that suburban domesticity was no longer for him.

Fuelled by drink, on one occasion he steeled himself to tell Dolly this in a letter, though it was one written over several days, veering inconsistently, according to the mood of the moment, from the conciliatory to the belligerent.

---

93 An alternative story exists that Malcolm first started drinking again in Australia in 1973, after nearly being involved in a collision mid-air. The plane's captain, on landing, insisted on all the passengers being given a brandy...

94 'On Tuesday I was due to lecture on Strindberg and had it in my diary for Wednesday and failed to appear. This was terrible and everyone was pretty mad; I was pretty ashamed – you know the dreadful feeling of having missed an appointment. Next week I talk on The Dream Play to the Theatre Department and so hope to repair the damage a little.' (MW to Dolly, 17 February 1975)

95 March 2005

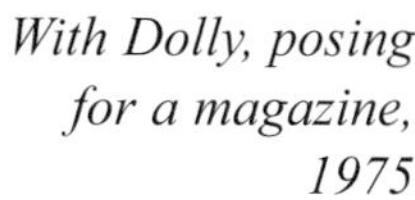

With Dolly, posing for a magazine, 1975

After a number of non-inflammatory topics, like the death of P G Wodehouse ('Poor PGW, who never thought about the afterlife, now he's entered it...'), he wrote at length on 'the distress of our unsuccessful marriage' with the need for him always to be apologizing and placating her as she criticized him for this and that:

> You will always resent my having any friends of my own and I shall always be hiding such friendships because they upset you. Shall we ever be any different? I do not care whether the fault is yours or mine or just the chemistry of the combination. A situation will arise in which you and I are both unhappy on account of each other. I do love you and I do miss you, but I am happy alone also, working and doing a job, seeing people and knowing nobody very well…[96]

On his brief return to England, with a separation of some form or other agreed by both of them, he was in a highly emotional state, and when he heard on the radio that Arthur Bliss had died, he completely broke down:

96 19 February 1975

> I burst into tears. I was still crying when the BBC rang up, and I went and did an off-the-cuff broadcast about him.[97]

Days later, at the Moreton Morell Easter School, he gave a highly emotional account of what he always considered Aaron Copland's masterpiece, *Vitebsk: Study on a Jewish Theme*. Graham Wade still remembers the concert:

> With Brian Brown (violin) and Sue McHugh (cello) Malcolm gave a deeply moving performance of Copland's *Vitebsk*. He prefaced it with a few comments on how the piece expressed the anguish of the Jewish people through the ages. Malcolm came over to us as a man totally possessed by music and life, in a conjunction both painful and deeply inspiring. It was a searing performance, unforgettable, a profoundly thoughtful experience to absorb.[98]

The course over, Malcolm gave a BBC talk on Messiaen and then rushed across to perform at Aldeburgh,[99] returning to East Sheen at four in the morning. Four hours later he caught a plane for Paris, prior to three months of cassations with his new-found allies, the *Jeunesses Musicales de France*. The departure, in April, was inauspicious. Dolly was away in New York, where she had flown on the death of her father. By the time of the funeral, Malcolm was back at the Provencal hotel in Pont-du-Crau where he had written much of *Hammarskjöld Portrait*, just about to begin his cassations with three hundred children in nearby Arles. He had thirty-eight different sessions of *The Snow Wolf* to direct along the Côte d'Azur, but, basking in the sun, he seemed oblivious of the hard work. By the time he reached Nice at the end of the month, he was 'hoarse and tired' but still loving the French way of life. He was even, most unusually, taking setbacks in his stride, as he told Janet Canetty-Clarke:

> There have been a couple of tiny catastrophes but not of the order that we connoisseurs have come to expect! Before the Côte d'Azur I was in Dijon for four days and just before we began the first show somebody had lost a nine-foot grand piano in a van somewhere in the middle of the town. By good luck two pianos of Czech origin unexpectedly arrived...[100]

When commitments in England interrupted his French idyll and caused a quick dash to East Sheen, Peter (still at school in Seaford) was sent some details:

> My visit was quite a rush. I got into London before midnight on Tuesday, spent half of Wednesday at BBC TV, went to a banquet at the Royal Academy of Arts where Princess Margaret was the guest of honour, spent all of Thursday doing *Churchill's People* recordings, and was two hours at home with the girls. Then off to Nice, for more *Snow Wolf*. Tomorrow is my last *Snow Wolf* on the Côte d'Azur and after church I fly to Corsica for a week, then Paris. I'm doing the last of the Churchills at the moment. Whoopee![101]

---

97 *Radio Times*, October 1976

98 May 2006

99 He played both his Second Piano Concerto and the first piano in Percy Grainger's *The Warriors*.

100 From the Villa Arson, 20 Avenue Stephen Liegeard, 27 April 1975

101 From the Villa Arson, 2 May 1975

In Corsica it rained but he didn't seem to mind. Peter received several postcards, the first from Bastra:

> This island is fascinating, even to the most callous tourist. I am in a hotel on the sea front a few yards from the Place de Gaulle. Today we animate *Le Loup de Neige* in Bastra's biggest working theatre...
>
> Tomorrow is Ascension Day and I shall take Mass in this church in Ghisonaccia. Corsica takes one's breath away at every turn. It is very rural and the cities are like sea-ports... I live in Abbazia, which is a hotel and bar and three houses. I got lost yesterday, luggage and all, in Vix, which is two bars and one house. Also a broken phone booth...[102]

Back in Paris, at the familiar *Hotel de Champagne*, Malcolm was working on an orchestral version of the *Terrain of the Kings*, having completed a new cassation, *La Colline and La Vallée*.[103] He was also writing with some indignation to Dolly suggesting that she could have held the Memorial Shabbath Service for her father in London at a time convenient to himself. At the same time, as if all was still well, he was telling her with delight that Mario Bois wanted them all to spend some weeks in the summer in his country house or Paris home.

From France Malcolm flew to Toronto, writing to 'darling Dolly' from the Muir Park Hotel, Toronto, telling of 'a week of horror' in a country 'knee-deep in crazy people'. He had met his commitment of delivering twenty psalms,[104] had given 'the best organ recital of my life' and overseen a production of *The Happy Prince*, but it all came at a price:

> I am fighting old battles and the newest and oldest, alcohol, is back in the ring. I drank brandy on the plane last Sunday, had some great slugs of it on Wednesday and Thursday nights this week & got tight on Friday night. Nothing since, but it's the old pre-Dent world. I've been to A A which I think is a dumb thing, but all that I have. And maybe I'm winding up my life, I don't know.[105]

He sensed a further onset of the furies, and, in his despair, warned Dolly to keep well clear:

> What I said at the airport about loving you was true, but I've bad news... I'm heading for a nervous crisis at least as serious as the one that began in late 1973 in Australia and I advise you to get rid of me. I do not intend to say that the fault is yours, mine or anyone else's, simply that I see the signs of mental illness which I recognise from before... I do not care whether you believe it or not, I know it to be so... Do not be loving or caring or sentimental. I am doing what I can for three children I love and am trying to establish financial viability as best I can.

---

102 6 & 7 May 1975

103 Two years later it would re-emerge during the Queen's Silver Jubilee as *The Valley and the Hill*.

104 *Psalms of the Elements*, responsorial psalms for unison choir, congregation and organ, a commission from The United Church of Canada, Toronto.

105 8 June 1975

The letter enclosed a cheque for 1,000 Canadian dollars. He expected to return to England that July.

> But I neither wish our marriage to be repaired, nor I suspect do you. We can love each other better from a distance and cope more rationally with all our problems.

He moved back to New York, where he could breathe and be himself again. 'Funny how New York represents so much to me,' he had written not long before. 'It is the world, civilisation, beauty and anguish; the grief of the world and its hub.'[106] The whole city, he now told friends, was 'gorgeous', 'beautiful and stimulating'. Weinberger's John Schofield received further details:

> I have been living in down-town Manhattan which is a delicious pleasure. Hectic and humid. New York is like fresh air after the antiseptic horrors of Canada – after a week there I was out of my tree – I owe my current sanity to New York, Washington and to loving friends, so I am at peace and working like you wouldn't believe. Nobody here is negative and I find my masochism and general insecurities disappear along with my Puritan hang-ups… I had a beautiful afternoon with Aaron Copland. Did I tell you?[107]

In New York he stayed with Larry Smith, a young American musician, studying at the Juilliard School, with whom he had been friendly for the past four years.[108] Ambitious to be a composer himself, Smith was delighted to share his tiny flat ('it was a one-room student digs, really'), which for a while would be Malcolm's regular New York resting-place:

> I was about twenty at the time. Malcolm would sometimes help me as a teacher, but his life was so complicated that he seldom could do more than just react to whatever I had written. Although he must have been twice my age, sometimes I felt that I was the parent – helping him as best I could to sort out his life, getting him to bed if he had been drinking too much.[109]

Malcolm's New York life was as chaotic as it was pleasurable. Letters to Dolly in late June, addressed to 'Darling Doll' and 'Darling Dollink', pretended that all was well: he was working phenomenally hard to safeguard the family's future; Mario Bois had again most kindly offered them all the use in August of

---

106 MW to Dolly Williamson, 19 February 1975

107 30 June 1975. The constant references made to great musical productivity at this period are misleading. Malcolm's completed works in 1975 consisted of a large number of psalms and hymns, many episodes of *Churchill's People*, his Van Gogh piano album for young players and two French cassations, *La Terre des Rois* and *La Colline et La Vallée*. He completed no major works, the two on which he tried to make progress – the Harp Concerto and *Les Olympiques* – were not to be completed for another year.

108 Smith recalls: 'I first met Malcolm in Fort Wayne, Indiana, at a concert and ended up going out to dinner with him. Thereafter I had an intense (but not sexual) relationship with him until 1983. I went to see him in Louisville, Kentucky, when he wanted some help with accompanying. In 1973 I was with him in Ohio, where he came to play and do some teaching. This provided some income for him and he had various relationships with young people.' (August 2005)

109 August 2005

his country home or Paris flat; Dolly should not worry about 'the alcohol business' – he had only had problems in Toronto because it had been such a nightmare. To Richard Toeman, however, he wrote ambiguously:

> You do not need to know about my present troubles, which are soluble, but Dolly deserves all sympathy at this time.

By early July he seemed to have forgotten the letter sent from Canada, and told Dolly optimistically that 'alcohol does not appear to be a problem after all'. His absence from home he justified by the need to stay well: 'Do try to understand, even if you think I am being tiresome'. By mid-July, however, he brought up again their earlier decision to separate, and this time suggested it should be with a view to a divorce. He wrote to her:

> Remember that I love you, whatever happens. Remember also that I am thinking of all those who are depending on my survival for their survival… Please help me and even love me if you can…[110]

At the same time he confided to John Schofield:

> In the present unhappy state of my private life I intend to stay in the USA from next autumn. I have asked Dolly to divorce me or take separative action as she deems best. It is a sad fact that here, as in France, I enjoy magnificent health without any pills or worries which cause headaches. I feel very sorry for her, but in the former situation it was myself I was sorry for. Perhaps at last I'll be able to face the world honestly as what I am.[111]

Malcolm returned to England in August, loosely based at East Sheen, and drinking very heavily. Eventually, on Yom Kippur Eve, 14 September, two years of uneasy vacillation finally ended. The unwitting witness to the final act of Malcolm's long marital drama was one of his most talented composition pupils, John Hawkins, who arrived for a lesson in Hertford Avenue to discover that, while Dolly was out with the children at the synagogue, Malcolm was busying himself for departure. He apologised to Hawkins for the lack of a lesson. He was leaving Hertford Avenue for good, he told him. A friend's car was outside, already fully packed. Moments later Malcolm precipitately departed, leaving Hawkins alone in the house, waiting behind with the unenviable task of telling Dolly that Malcolm had finally left her:

> Her reaction was very calm. She gave little away. As if she was expecting it.

Dolly remembers the moment too:

> We came home to find John white-faced, asking the kids to go upstairs. 'I want to talk to your mother.' The kids went upstairs and came right back and sat on the stairs. They thought that Malcolm must have died. John took me into the living-room. 'What's wrong?' I asked. 'Malcolm's left you,' he said, very upset, almost shaking as he spoke. 'What do you mean, he's left me? How do you know?' 'Somebody he knew came and collected him in a beige Volkswagen.' That was something of a relief. I

110 15 July 1975

111 18 July 1975

knew that meant his old boyhood friend from Melbourne, Edward Brown, and at least he'd be safe with him.

The next morning the situation turned almost to farce. The telephone rang. It was an authoritative voice, wanting to speak to Malcolm urgently. 'I'm sorry,' said Dolly. 'He's not here right now!' The voice at the other end, correct and official, was not to be gainsaid. When could he expect to speak to him? How could Dolly know? Three days? Three months? Three years? Never? She parried as best she could: 'It will probably be best for Malcolm to ring you when he returns.' 'No,' replied the authoritative voice, 'I'll ring him. When might I expect to find him at home?' 'Well, he should be back by 6.00 on Friday,' said Dolly, giving herself three days to find him.

Eventually, 'by a miracle', Dolly managed to contact Malcolm just in time to persuade him to return to answer the call. He turned up at Hertford Avenue half-an-hour early and, when the phone rang precisely at the agreed hour, 6.00 pm, he shut himself in the front room, his old study. Dolly waited patiently until, an hour later, he emerged, flushed and excited.

'Anything important?'

'Yes, quite important, really! That was Lord Maclean from Buckingham Palace.' Malcolm took a step back, to steady himself by the door.

'The fact of the matter is: they want me to be the new Master of the Queen's Music!'

12 SIMON

Australia, 1975

DOLLY WAS ALARMED, Malcolm euphoric. It was seven o'clock as she began one last verbal battle to keep him from what she believed would be disaster. He was at his best, she argued, as a large fish in a small pond; he wouldn't see the pitfalls and wouldn't know his place. The glare of publicity, too, which the post would inevitably bring, was the very last thing he and the family needed at this time of personal crisis. Malcolm was unmoved, seeing his future somewhat differently, as a large fish in a large pond. 'I want this more than anything I've ever wanted in my life,' he kept repeating. With the new-found confidence and prestige which the entrée to Buckingham Palace would bring him, he could truly fulfil himself; he had reached emotional and professional melt-down; he needed support not criticism, the approbation of the country, not the carping of East Sheen. The debate carried on and on, until, at four in the morning, Dolly finally realised there was nothing more to be said and they went to bed. The next morning Malcolm hurried from Hertford Avenue to begin his new life.

Dolly's immediate reaction to the situation was one of 'raw fear', her emotional distress compounded by practical problems like meeting the next round of bills, many of which were considerably back-dated. She had no idea of Malcolm's whereabouts, though she knew he was scheduled later that September to fly to New York on his way to Australia, where he was to be filmed for the BBC Television documentary *Malcolm Williamson Down Under*.

Dolly, therefore, did not expect to see Malcolm again for some time. Only five days later, however, she met him at a 75th birthday reception which Boosey & Hawkes were hosting for Aaron Copland at Brown's Hotel, Mayfair. She had not wanted to attend, but Richard Toeman had encouraged her to do so, to keep up appearances. 'I'll go as a fly on the wall!' she agreed at last. 'Nothing else!'

In the event, she found herself considerably more central, on the top table next to the guest of honour, with Peter Pears nearby. Malcolm, placed on a lower table, was not best pleased. Copland was *his* friend, not hers, and he loudly expressed his displeasure. Worse followed. In the middle of dinner, he rose uncertainly to his feet, staggered over to a good vantage point and started haranguing everyone for not welcoming Copland more warmly. It was nothing short of disgraceful… Absolutely no-one had yet said what a great composer Aaron was… So he was now going to make amends! Various attempts were made to quieten him as he began his eulogy, but it took time before he was persuaded to resume his seat. A little later there was another, equally embarrassing, incident, still remembered by Tony Fell, who as Managing Director of Boosey & Hawkes, was the party's host:

> Suddenly Malcolm got up again and came charging over to Peter Pears, went down on his knees and started sobbing. It was evidently intended as a public demonstration of thanks to Peter for the contribution he and Britten had made to his royal appointment. Eventually someone managed to drag him off, and Peter quietly suggested that Malcolm should be found a taxi and taken home.[1]

Three days later, the Copland fiasco quite forgotten, Malcolm was writing affectionately to Richard Toeman from Washington, thanking him for an enjoyable farewell lunch:

> My dear friend,
>
> …I cannot praise highly enough the sympathy and understanding you showed me; and I have deep gratitude that it has brought me nearer to you; and whatever the future holds, and although we are not currently bound contractually, I feel that we can anticipate a more deeply productive relationship together.[2]

That Malcolm was able to apologise fulsomely for past rudenesses was an indication of the sense of well-being which the royal appointment had given him:

> You have had more rough treatment from me than gratitude. Probably more abuse for the poor printing and proof-reading of earlier times than appreciation for the excellent presentation and greater care that obtains currently; more criticism for the promotional failures than thanks for the promotional successes. It is not rare that composers treat publishers like this, and I am aware that I am more demanding than most; but when one has to survive in a world that does not owe one a living one is ceaselessly demanding because, in my life at least, there has never been enough money to feel secure, never enough time to think through my musical ideas. And we the dissatisfied can be cruel, I know it...

[1] August 2005. One story goes that Britten, having declined the office himself on the grounds of ill-health, said 'Ma'am, you have no choice but to choose Malcolm Williamson'. This differs, however, from Donald Mitchell's recollection of being rung up by Britten and asked for a short list of possible Masters as he'd been asked to make some proposals: 'I can't remember my short list, but it didn't include Malcolm Williamson, as I was proposing older composers. A day or so later Ben rang again: "I think it's high time we had a Master of the Queen's Music who came from the Commonwealth. That's why Malcolm Williamson has come to my mind."' (June 2005)

[2] 25 September 1975

Only months before he had been crippled by professional self-doubt. Now, with the imprimatur of Buckingham Palace, he had swung strongly the other way, as with great frankness he chronicled his personal problems, as he saw them:

> …I have had to carry the burden of a spectacular creative musical gift (this is not Modesty Day) through a childhood with parents (fine people certainly) who expected things I could not find in my character to actuate. Dolly, a finer person dare I say than either of my parents, without realizing, expected the same. It has not been fun to suppress my native wish for the love of men, and for the solace of alcohol and of drugs that would remove the pain of a deep knowledge of my inadequacy. And this I have attempted to do since puberty, while trying to avoid musical meretricity.

With his new sense of well-being he was able to see himself acting altruistically.

> My departure to Canada this last June and my remaining in North America were, in part at least, to hide from a world that seemed to me to be asking more than I could provide. Every way forward was a cul-de-sac. My main motive in wishing to have Dolly divorce me was to give her a better chance and my children as well, with someone adequate to the father-husband role. In some ways it is disastrous that she, poor girl, wishes to stay by me in full knowledge of all.

Choosing to forget the recent chaos his drinking had caused, Malcolm cheerfully assured Richard Toeman that there was no danger from alcohol in his future life. The dangers would rather come from 'self-disapprobation'. In this context he again rejoiced in the new appointment:

> The bombshell of this last week from SW1 brought out the initial impulse in me to say 'Stop, stop, I don't deserve it! You've got the wrong guy!'[3] But it is a step towards the recovery – and I am determined to recover – from a horrible mental illness that began in 1973 in Australia and grew progressively worse throughout the Churchill affair….. I am (thanks to the Atlantic crossing and thanks to OUR breakthrough) in better form. In Australia I shall be taking well-proven specialist medical, psychiatric and spiritual treatment and I have regained a little of that valuable quality called HOPE. The more I gain of real hope the better I can serve humanity and music.

He was intent that his new musical initiatives would be appropriate to his elevated position. He intended to orchestrate *Pietà* ('one of my most effective and good pieces, but unlikely to accomplish anything substantial in its present form') and take a new look at *Lucky-Peter's Journey* ('the problem is how to do the re-writes since I have serious doubts as to whether collaboration with the

3 Ironically stories persist that by some bizarre error the Palace did appoint the wrong Malcolm, and that Malcolm Arnold was in fact the intended choice. Composer Ian Kellam remembers: 'I was at Downing Street just after Bliss had died and I asked Harold Wilson who was going to be the next Master of the Queen's Music. He said he didn't think it was much to do with him but a few days later then I had a telephone call from a secretary at No 10 and she asked me for my suggestions for who might take on the job. I said there's no point in asking Britten because he's too ill and Tippett wouldn't have been right. We need somebody who could rise to it, and that would be Malcolm Arnold – he would be my obvious choice, and they said "Fine".' (July 2006)

original librettist could be considered and would serve to good purpose.') Both of these excellent ideas came to nothing.

There was only muted celebration at Weinberger's over his appointment. Although it would undoubtedly be a boost to sales, his proud vision of serving 'humanity and music' suggested he did not have things in proportion. Gerald Kingsley and John Schofield both felt that Malcolm would be pulled unhelpfully in different directions:

> On the one hand he would be the champion of the people, sounding off against privilege and the establishment; on the one hand, he would be fawning on Princess Margaret and the Queen Mother…[4]

They were worried when Malcolm, in the first flush of his enthusiasm, outlined to them a highly ambitious plan that the Queen, in her coming Jubilee, should set up a centre for research into how music could help the severely handicapped. Richard Toeman attempted to instill caution:

> Your idea about setting up a scheme of therapeutical musical research is very exciting.
>
> I have a feeling that this is the sort of thing you will have to plan very carefully and thoroughly with the powers-that-be before announcing its inauguration... You will have, please God, many many years in which to originate, nurture and fulfil such important projects, and I am sure you would not want to let them be known about until they are planned and OK'd in every detail…[5]

Malcolm was already in New York when his appointment was officially announced at the beginning of October 1975. He was staying, as he usually did, with Larry Smith in West 55th Street, and it was from there that he gave some of his many interviews.[6] The lack of space mattered little in that Malcolm would spend most evenings and many nights in the gay areas of Greenwich village, vigorously asserting his new independence. It was an eventuality which John Schofield feels was inevitable, despite Dolly's best efforts:

> Shortly before the break-up Malcolm would often ring me up to say how much his work was being affected by his domestic situation; that he was struggling to write when in the middle of rows with Dolly. I used to marvel that he could write at all, given the state he was in. It makes you believe in God in a way. A bit like Mozart, who at the end of his life writes K595, a work of ineffable calm. How could he write it, when he was in such a state? I felt the same about Malcolm, who was going through incredible trauma, because Dolly was a very strong character.
>
> But, in spite of all the things he said about her, she really was the best thing for him, kept him on the rails, had a really positive influence on his life. She was the only person who could get the better of him in an argument.
>
> Malcolm, however, for all his bisexuality, was principally gay, and he reached a point in his life when he couldn't suppress it. He couldn't live the suburban domestic

---

[4] May 2005

[5] 1 October 1975

[6] He also used the Boosey & Hawkes New York office.

> life any more; he had to get away from it. The love-hate thing had been going on for years.[7]

The inevitability of the break-up did not lessen its destructive potential. Malcolm was Master of the Queen's Music because of all the achievements in his years with Dolly. He could, therefore, be said to have accepted the post under false pretences, for the Queen had appointed the workaholic of East Sheen, not the troubled pilgrim asserting his newfound freedom in the gay bars of New York. There might well be a reckoning.

For the immediate moment, however, he basked in the pleasures of celebrity. The first congratulatory cable was from Richard Rodney Bennett. Others came flooding in, and he was much moved by what he later described as 'a great wave of love'. From the reports in the papers it is clear that much of the old confidence had returned:

> The new Master of the Queen's Music has already decided on his first composition: a piece to mark the Queen's Silver Jubilee in 1977. From New York, where he is seeing his publisher en route to Australia, Mr Williamson said this morning: 'I think this would be most appropriate and I'll be discussing it with Her Majesty just as soon as I return in November. I'm very interested to hear her tastes in music… I imagine I'll be kept pretty busy, as I don't regard it in any way as a sinecure…'[8]

He was proud, he told reporters, to be following in the line of Elgar, Bax and Bliss; to be the holder of an office which went all the way back to the reign of Charles II, when the Master provided musick for the monarch at dinners, banquets and state ceremonies. He refrained from disclosing his disappointment at the paltry honorarium of £100 a year and the disruption to his plans of settling in New York, now that the royal post demanded his continued residence in Britain. He had even had to clear with the Palace his absence while filming in Australia.

The hour-long BBC television documentary was, like the royal post, the culmination of everything Malcolm had achieved in his partnership with Dolly; the result, too, of delicate negotiations in which she had played a helpful part. As the recently appointed Master of the Queen's Music, of course, he was now a figure of even more interest, and the BBC, in sending out the experienced director Kenneth Corden with a large support team, was investing generously in the project. The documentary would film Malcolm on his return to Sydney, Melbourne and Canberra, visiting places of his youth and discussing the impact which his Australian background had exerted on his music. He would be shown directing his cassations and playing with the Melbourne Symphony Orchestra. This splendid celebration of his achievements, however, could not have come at a worse moment, and he was extremely nervous about it, full of insecurities and drinking heavily to compensate. A brief reunion with Bessie in Sydney did

---

7 February 2005

8 Londoner's Diary, *Evening Standard*, 3 October 1975

nothing for his equilibrium. She had hardly warmed to Dolly over the years, but was even less impressed with talk of separation and divorce.

The finished television film comes over as a lively portrait of an opinionated but edgy forty-five-year-old.[9] It opens, with unintentional irony, with Malcolm playing his First Piano Concerto, his present for Lorenzo. Piano works abound, with the talented Melbourne GP, William Kimber, joining Malcolm in extracts from both the sonata and the concerto for two pianos. There are lengthy sections from the television production of *The Violins of Saint-Jacques*, just completed by ABC, including the lilting aria 'I Have Another World to Show You'. Malcolm's serious organ music is contrasted with his popular church works, and there is strong emphasis on the social uses to which Malcolm is putting his cassations. He is seen, most impressively, working on *The Moonrakers* with the children of the Koomarri School. The Koomarri children are involved again in a service at the tiny Catholic church of the Sacred Heart, Tuggeranong, where, with Malcolm on the harmonium and help from a few strong adult singers, the children concentrate magnificently in making a contribution to Malcolm's settings of '*Miserere Domine*', 'The King of Love' and 'I Will Lift Up Mine Eyes'. In a totally different setting, a Channel 10 television studio in Sydney, he shows himself as able a performer with adults as children, handling the audience with great finesse as he takes them through part of a cassation on the Mike Walsh Show.

There are insights into important friendships: interviews, for example, with Hazel Reader,[10] the eighty-one-year-old Sir Bernard Heinze,[11] Ken Healey and Yehudi Menuhin. But some of Malcolm's problems are also on view. Kenneth Corden, the director, interested in the way many Australian critics were denigrating Malcolm for living abroad, shows extracts of Malcolm struggling at a press conference and trying to pre-empt criticisms with a patriotic preface:

> So, ladies and gentlemen, perhaps to anticipate a question people may ask, I'd like to say before anything else that when *The Times* of London in the Court Circular announced this appointment and used as its first words 'Australian-born', I've never had such a proud moment in my life.

This is greeted with desultory, tepid applause. And the question duly follows:

---

9 It was shown as part of the BBC2's 'The Lively Arts' series on 31 October 1976 (with a repeat on BBC1 on 15 August 1979).

10 Malcolm and Kenneth Corden stayed with Hazel and Ralph Reader at Melrose Valley Farm for the duration of the filming in the Canberra area. A large tank in the grounds, built for water conservation and fire fighting, was used to show Malcolm swimming, and the Readers' grandchildren and their friends were thrilled to march across the farm with a donkey for a powerful rendition of the *Procession of Palms*.

11 Malcolm's insistence, however, that Heinze should conduct the Melbourne Symphony Orchestra is said to have caused problems in that the legendary Australian musician was in anything but total control of proceedings. However that may be, he was certainly articulate on interview.

> Malcolm, you've spent most of your working life overseas. Do you still consider yourself an Australian?

Corden gives Malcolm a 'voice-over' to express his frustration:

> If there is anything to attack, the Australian press will attack it with a lack of compassion, a lack of kindness, which seems to me unique.... I've long ago given up worrying what the Australian press say about me for my lack of patriotism. I've been upset and distressed too many times.

One of Malcolm's greatest critics, Maria Prerauer, is shown justifying her 'piranha' nickname:

> Well, congratulations, Malcolm, on becoming Master of the Queen's Music! It's actually confirmed my belief that it isn't always the *best* composer who becomes Master of the Queen's Music or the best poet who becomes Poet Laureate.

Malcolm, aware of the camera, responds cautiously:

> We know this happens, but when the Master of the Queen's Music is chosen it is the opinion of Her Majesty and her advisers that they choose the person who will best do the job, Maria. This does not mean that I am considered the finest composer in Great Britain. Just somebody who will serve best to do the job.

But this is not enough to divert the 'piranha' from further attack:

> – Well, as you know, I have never been one of your fans!
>
> – Yes, kind friends always send me your bad notices!
>
> – I feel your work is often a miscellany of other composers, ordinary tunes with a few wrong notes put in to make them sound more interesting.

At this point, Malcolm comments in another 'voice-over':

> Maria has always in print perpetually pushed me down in ways that I consider almost less than decent. She has indulged in what I would consider *personal* attacks on my very soul.

A few further sallies follow:

> – You really do have the guts, Maria, to make yourself as unpopular as you make yourself?
>
> – I'm not in criticism for popularity. I do have a plimsoll line for myself, where I measure music. Whether it be above or below.
>
> – And mine in particular you find below the plimsoll mark?
>
> – Not always, but often! I think what is furthest below the plimsoll mark are those do-it-yourself pieces, where you have people rushing around flapping their arms at dawn and being roosters or kangaroos.
>
> – Be fair! You walked out of the single performance!
>
> – I walked out because I wouldn't bow down to God Malcolm Williamson!

This potentially damaging attack is carefully undermined by the use of music clearly well above most people's plimsoll marks. Elsewhere Corden's sympathetic direction allows Malcolm's natural enthusiasm full impact in descriptions of his Australian past, particularly his early life at St Mary's. Sydney, where Malcolm no longer feels welcome, is mostly omitted, though Corden, acting as narrator, stresses the Opera House's present disinterest in his work.

The one thing which Corden could not manipulate in Malcolm's favour is his drinking. His thickened waistline and occasionally slurred speech are undisguisable, and there is a revealing section when Malcolm is seen wandering high up in the Blue Mountains. Behind him in all directions, as far as the eye can see, stretches unspoilt tree-covered national park – towering sandstone plateaux either side of the plunging gorge of the Megalong Valley. Malcolm, however, instead of expressing admiration, commences a long, passionate diatribe attacking the beauty of his surroundings because (of all things) they haven't experienced suffering:

> We Australians regard this as absolutely God's own country, the most unspoilt and marvellous thing that ever happened, and in some ways it is, because it is physiologically so remarkable. I just wish I could appreciate how remarkable it is. It won't be remarkable for me until man has attempted to destroy it, and man has attempted to preserve it, because it is in danger of being destroyed.

He explains that he finds the Maritime Alps more 'fulfilling' because soldiers like Hannibal once crossed them; and Israel more inspiring, 'because its rivers have flowed with blood'. He then goes off on a huge tangent, somehow managing to bring in André Gide, Benjamin Britten, Vaughan Williams, Utrillo and Mount Rushmore, before his peroration, a further attack on the Megalong Valley:

> For all its grandeur it has an insatiable cruelty, a total inconsideration for man's history, and it cannot interest me nearly as much as the anguish, the deep horror that has happened in similar places with perhaps loftier peaks, with perhaps less sensational varieties of green, with less spectacular volcanic stones, but the places where life has been lived, where life has meant pain, where life has meant innumerable cruelties.

The viewers might well have wondered whether the valley really was insatiably cruel, just because it had never been a battlefield, but Malcolm speaks so mellifluously and with such great authority that he brooks no denial, lulling the viewers into placid acquiescence.

The programme ends strongly with contralto Loris Synan singing Malcolm's sombre setting of 'Crossing The Bar', accompanied by many images of ever darkening Australian skies. It is all in stark contrast to the poseur high up in the Blue Mountains. Corden is reminding us of the serious musician, encouraging viewers to think back to Malcolm's comment earlier in the programme, 'The greatest privilege that God has given us is the privilege to die'.

Death was very much on his mind during the filming. For the Melbourne sequences he was staying at Eltham, on the outskirts of the town, where an old friend of his, Professor Richard Downing, had a country home. Downing, a popular and urbane character, was not only Dean of Economics at Melbourne University but also, and most importantly, the Chairman of the ABC. He had married ten years earlier, at fifty, but prior to that had lived with his gay partner, the composer Dorian Le Gallienne.[12] Two weeks after Malcolm's arrival, right in the middle of filming, Downing died from a sudden heart attack. Malcolm was devastated, as Cecily Huckfield, who was working with him, recalls:

> Malcolm was very sensitive indeed, so much more so than most other famous people. And when Professor Downing died, who was such a good friend to him, Malcolm cried like a baby in my arms.[13]

His response to the tragedy was to plunge into an alcoholic binge, which continued after the filming had been completed. He stayed for a while with William Kimber, who had agreed to put him up for a few days only for him to stay well over a month.

> We couldn't get rid of him, and we were very keen to, for when Malcolm was on a binge, he was at his least attractive and capable.[14]

It was during this particularly bad period in Melbourne that Malcolm met up again with Simon Campion, the organiser of the Music In The Round weekend at Chirnside House two years earlier and still working in Melbourne as a music teacher and cathedral organist. Simon saw at once the extent of Malcolm's crisis and did his best to help him, in the first instance addressing practical problems like the need for somewhere to live. Professor Max Cooke of Melbourne University's Conservatorium was involved:

> Simon came round and asked me if I would do a great favour: 'Would you allow Malcolm to have your house for a while?' I agreed to do this, but only for a week, while we were away. When we arrived back, however, Malcolm hadn't gone. And he wouldn't go! We asked him to leave and he refused, using terrible language! During our week away he had drunk all my best wine and made quite a mess. He also used my phone to make many international calls. It was not a happy time.[15]

Amid all the mayhem Simon Campion continued to look after Malcolm, who slowly began to appreciate the devoted nature of the support. William Kimber recalls one unconventional expression of a developing affection:

> After leaving me, he and Simon went to stay with Max Cooke who told me that Malcolm had pissed 'I love you, Simon' in the sand on a Melbourne beach. They came back to stay with me for a short while, before going on to see Malcolm's mother

---

12 Malcolm had first met Downing and Le Gallienne twenty-five years earlier, when he had fled from home to Melbourne. Le Gallienne, who died young, wrote in the tradition of Vaughan Williams.

13 November 2006

14 June 2006

15 July 2006

> in Sydney. Malcolm was a real mess at this time; his social sins were great – and all because of the alcoholism.[16]

Simon's life and background had combined to give him the resilience and insight to cope with Malcolm in his lowest moments. He was a first-generation Australian, born in Perth but said to be descended from William the Conqueror. The family's home for several centuries had been Danny Park,[17] near Hurstpierpoint, Sussex; his grandfather, Sir William Campion, had been a distinguished soldier in the First World War, a member of the London Stock Exchange and MP for Lewes before becoming Governor of Western Australia in 1924. Like Malcolm, Simon had converted to Catholicism as a very young man. He started a medical degree at the University of Western Australia, transferring to an arts course, before, in 1961, entering the Jesuit Theological College at Melbourne. He stayed with the Jesuits thirteen years, and in the late 1960s, as part of his training, he took a four-year degree at the University of Melbourne in music performance, with the organ and piano as his instruments. This new musical life outside the Jesuit community eventually decided him not to enter the priesthood.

Simon, like Malcolm, was at an important turning-point in his life. It soon became clear that Malcolm's needs might answer his own, the expressions of love even be welcome. Malcolm himself, despite the excesses of his present drinking binge, was well able to appreciate the qualities of his new companion. He was caring and undemanding, better able to cope with the minutiae of life and eminently helpful in sorting out his final Australian commitments. Simon's Jesuit training had usefully inculcated fortitude, though his business skills were less pronounced. As his friend the writer Gerard Windsor has commented:

> Simon always reminds me of an absent-minded professor. He could be very forgetful, and might not always get to the point.[18]

---

[16] June 2006. Kimber particularly remembers Malcolm's energy. He could not stop still. One moment the two of them would be rehearsing at the piano; the next, with a quick 'Hold on a moment, Bill', he'd be leaping to the telephone to ring up Robert Helpmann about a ballet or the ABC about a concert. Despite the drink problem and the chaos he left behind him everywhere, he still achieved a considerable amount during his stay in Melbourne, and Kimber's memories are full of affection: 'He enlivened all our lives with his dynamism, his acerbic wit and, above all, his acute sense of humour. We were rehearsing with John Hopkins on one occasion, who, as a Seventh Day Adventist, urged Malcolm very strongly to go easy on the alcohol. Malcolm thereafter would always have a large glass of orange juice ostentatiously to hand when working with John. The only trouble was that it would be liberally laced with brandy...'

[17] Rented out for six months to Lloyd George, it had briefly became part of British history when, in 1918, the War Cabinet agreed the terms of the Armistice offered to Germany. Danny's was sold in 1957, when it became a retirement home.

[18] 18 March 2006

Like Malcolm he was an accomplished talker, taking pleasure in erudite and witty conversation. His practical music skills helped him understand Malcolm's compositional and performing life.

Having delayed his intended return to England in November, Malcolm would ideally have stayed on convalescing with Simon, but the Lord Chamberlain made it clear that the Queen was expecting to see him in early February to confirm his position. As he told Richard Toeman, in a fairly bland summary of his Australian visit, he was still far from well:

> My time here has been packed with musical triumphs and deteriorating health; but after all had been done, I was packed off by my six doctors to rest. The recuperative period should be ongoing but alas because of obligations in London I shall leave Australia in fairly rocky shape, altho' better than recently. The days of swimming and jogging, exercise, sleep, under supervision, worked miracles on the weeping wreck who limped in to a studio to supervise the superb recording of the 2nd Symphony with the Melbourne Symphony under Cavdarski; this being the last obligation.[19]

Simon had been central to the whole recuperative process. To part from him at this important moment was unthinkable. So Malcolm asked him to come back to England with him, as his musical assistant. Simon's life had already been a series of new starts; in middle age he needed to settle down; to become the partner of such a well-known personality was to make sense and use of all his own musical training and prowess. Not only could he assist and perhaps inspire a great composer, but his own career as an organist might prosper from the association. So he accepted.

Although money was short, Malcolm and Simon decided to continue the process of recuperation by making a holiday of the flight home, with several pauses en route. 'Only a little selfishness will save me… I have to rest,' Malcolm told Richard Toeman, who was currently enjoying an unusually long period in total favour. He planned to reach England at the end of January. He would travel across the Pacific 'by slow stages with my assistant and valued saviour, Simon Campion, who is to be my assistant in England'.[20] Malcolm's dread of facing his family had led him to having extensive sessions of psychotherapy:

> I need to handle problems of considerable dimensions and to achieve a certain tidiness ultimately. Not too easy…. Dolly knows not too much of things! She has been wonderful. I've written her with pain…

He ended on a note of optimism:

> I rather hope for a working future, particularly after I heard the 2nd Symphony well played and decided that I was possibly a composer with a future. Incidentally also a superb recording of the *Six English Lyrics* with orchestra!

One of their Australian friends, pianist Ronald Farren-Price, remembers their departure:

---

[19] 7 December 1975

[20] 23 December 1975

> The decision for Malcolm and Simon to go off together seemed to happen very quickly. At that time my parents were staying with us and Simon came round to the front door to say goodbye. My mother's words afterwards were 'He seemed so excited – just like someone going off on his honeymoon.'[21]

By the end of December Malcolm and Simon were enjoying their first stop, at Noumea, the capital of the French territory of New Caledonia. From the Hotel Ile de France Malcolm wrote to Richard Toeman very happily:

> My dear Richard,
>
> My reclamation has begun and what a difference! I can see the degree of hypertension (or whatever it is called) after a week in New Caledonia where I am learning to sleep again and willing myself not to work, and my companion, Simon Campion, has been a life-saving influence, forcing me to swim, exercise and giving me the prescribed pills.
>
> I thought all had come to an end last Thursday when after a bicycle ride of several miles around the Isle of Pines the bike skidded on a curving hill on a dirt road and I had an impressive fall. I am covered with scars and suspect a broken rib. We are flying off to Hawaii for ten days of this compelled rest (aren't you all cross with me? Hawaii? The Beach Boy Hotel?) But I have much recovery to do and it is very serious.
>
> Thank God for my strong heart (just checked) and my stamina. The trouble about this sort of malady, caused in the first place by overwork and various emotional tensions leading to pills to keep one going – then emotional collapse, tears, a deeper sense of inadequacy and then physical collapse from fatigue, is that nobody really sympathises with unanswered letters, incomplete works commissioned and so on. Simon is slowly but very efficiently straightening all out.[22]

There was a further report from Honolulu, though this time the latest account of his state of health was augmented, probably at Simon's instigation, by an attempt to re-establish a working relationship with his publisher:

> All well and positively recuperative except for the capricious pain under collarbone from the cycle spill. It occasions me great discomfort. However, sunshine, sleep and surf do wonders…
>
> I need to talk long to you about our future together. I wonder if Weinberger's want me back and if so on what terms; also if B & H want me, & in either case what the various wisdoms are…
>
> …I appear to be a good risk health and career-wise provided I can continue my recuperation and have a buffer against the world.
>
> …Expect me late January. I rely on you to support Simon who will need to work closely with you.[23]

As part of the therapy of recovery from depression, Simon had been gently directing Malcolm's thoughts towards his first projects as Master of the Queen's Music. He also encouraged Malcolm to arouse Weinberger's interest in them:

---

21 September 2005

22 29 December 1975

23 3 January 1976

> My memory is rather hazy of the last two months in Australia, so I cannot recall if I told you of my works to come, including a big orchestral work for the LPO under Haitink for USA tour of 1976 with 6 performances guaranteed there, and a work for the 3 Choirs Festival for 1977 for the 250th anniversary. As well as the tv opera...

He also had some vague plans involving France's most distinguished actor, Jean-Louis Barrault:

> In my non-activity I've neglected the whole *Growing Castle* – Paris – Jean-Louis Barrault affair. The *Jeunesses Musicales* & Barrault are anxious to plan on this – *Le Songe* – and I'd hate nothing to happen. It's envisaged for 1977 with a French cast, a tourable production to begin in the petite salle at the Theâtre D'Orsay and to tour – in conjunction with cassations... The British Council is inclined to help, but I cannot cost it and do the needed detailed work. Mario [Bois] is in the dark (not knowing the opera) and alas since Castle Opera cannot be said to exist, it may all collapse. Can you see what can be done? The British Council man in Paris is Henry Merrick-Hughes... I shall try to settle it when I go to Paris in Feb (13th?)... Jean-Louis is all enthusiasm...

Barrault, then in his mid-sixties, was an unlikely ally. The esoteric *Growing Castle*, too, was hardly the most obvious companion to the cassations. It sounded an ill-considered scheme, and nothing came of it.

From Hawaii they made their leisurely way to New York via Los Angeles and Florida. Malcolm briefly considered the possibility that Simon should stay in New York for a few days while he faced the '*foudres londoniennes*' alone.[24] Instead the two of them flew across together, having arranged that they would stay with Dolly for a short while in Hertford Avenue, before travelling to France to direct some cassations. The journey was not without its problems, the airport authorities at New York twice refusing Malcolm permission to board because he was so drunk. Dolly, perplexed at the latest development, awaited Malcolm's return with mixed feelings:

> He had told me he would be bringing his new 'musical associate'. I went out to Heathrow to pick them both up. Malcolm was the worse for drink, yet on the way home in the car he asked whether I had any brandy. I must have looked startled. 'I don't want the children to see me like this,' he explained. He seemed under the impression that the brandy would sober him up...[25]

With Peter home from school for the weekend, Dolly found the whole situation extremely difficult. Quite what was she to say to the children?

> In those days bisexuality wasn't much spoken about. This development was something of a shock, although I should have seen signs. But you don't see what you don't want to see sometimes.

Peter, now fifteen, was vaguely puzzled:

---

24 'London thunderbolts'

25 20 August 2006

> I wasn't quite sure what was going on… I learnt what was going on long after it had gone on![26]

The *ménage à trois* lasted two painful weeks, though, in retrospect, to Dolly it seemed a nightmare of much longer duration:

> The whole situation was absolutely dreadful, but Malcolm and I didn't really have discussions about it. I don't think he wanted me around very much. I was for looking after the house and the children. (Our *au pair* had long since gone). What I remember of Simon is a lot of arrogance, assuming that he was now in his proper place. He assumed, for example, that the car would be there for his use. He came to me one morning and said 'Where are the keys to the car?' 'What car?' 'The car you have. Malcolm said I could use it whenever I wanted.' 'Well, actually,' I replied, 'It's my car! Bought and paid for by me and in fact you can't use it! You'll have to make other arrangements!' Invitations came in for first nights, and at the beginning Simon said I would have to get another ticket and come with them because it would look bad if I wasn't there. I didn't and I wouldn't.

Malcolm's thoughts were centred on only one event, his visit to Buckingham Palace on 3 February 1976, when he was received by the Queen and confirmed as Master of her Music.[27] With Simon left behind at East Sheen, Malcolm was driven by Dolly for his twelve o'clock appointment, arriving punctually, smart and sober:

> We were admitted through two sets of great gates and I was directed to a parking place. Malcolm went in alone, and I waited in the car. Like a chauffeur, though inappropriately dressed in jeans, and therefore quite startled when a Palace official appeared at my window, shortly before Malcolm returned, to apologise profusely (and impeccably, as they do) that I hadn't been invited inside, as they hadn't realised I was waiting in the car. I wish I could recall Malcolm's comments afterwards, but I can't. Probably because I disapproved of the whole exercise, still feeling that the appointment would be a disastrous step both for Malcolm and his musical career.[28]

The Palace visit over, Hertford Avenue had served its purpose, but there were to be another three excruciating days for Dolly before the strangely unreal situation came to an end. Even amongst all the melodrama, however, there were moments of farce. Early one morning, for example, the phone started ringing. Dolly went into the sitting room where Simon was sleeping on the sofa. The telephone was not in its usual place, so she shook Simon to wake him up. 'Where's the telephone? It's ringing and I can't find it!' Simon sat up. 'Oh, I hid it because Malcolm threw it at me.' Dolly looked at him and noticed a bump on his forehead. 'Oh my God!' she cried. 'No! no!' replied Simon hastily, reading her thoughts. 'That's congenital'. He got up and retrieved the phone from where it had been hidden, in a shopping bag hanging on a high hook in the hall.

---

26 August 2006

27 'Music' finally began to replace 'Musick' (which Bliss had re-introduced).

28 August 2006

Dolly again acted as chauffeur as Malcolm and Simon set off to France to fulfil the commitment with *Jeunesses Musicales*.

> I drove them to the airport. I also found some French francs – a couple of hundred pounds' worth that was all – that Malcolm and I had left over from a previous trip, because I thought they wouldn't have any money. I took them to the airport, gave them the francs, dropped them off and that was that.

A few days later she discovered that what little money there should have been in the bank wasn't there any longer. The emptiness of their joint account seemed symbolic, an expression of the way Malcolm's practical and emotional needs had totally swept her and her children aside. Malcolm was now looking towards bright new horizons; for the more realistic Dolly, the immediate prospects were bleaker.

III

The Queen and the Duke of Edinburgh watch
The Valley and the Hill, *Liverpool, 1977*

13
THE SILVER JUBILEE
London, 1976–77

MALCOLM HAD BEEN IN CONFIDENT, expansive mood in his first official audience with the Queen at the Palace. He guessed that the Silver Jubilee of 1977 would come up in conversation, and, determined to make a good first impression, had several proposals ready of works which he would be privileged to dedicate to her: a grand opera, a children's opera, a choral orchestral work and a symphony. The Queen declined the grand opera, but graciously accepted Jubilee dedications for the rest. She herself mentioned another possible project. The poet laureate, John Betjeman, had written a Jubilee hymn. It had been suggested that Malcolm might care to set it to music. He agreed with alacrity and left the Palace in high excitement. Shortly afterwards he collected an additional commission, for a BBC series on the House of Windsor.

He had, he thought, plenty of time for it all. The Jubilee hymn would be performed in February a year hence; the children's opera and large choral work the following summer; and the symphony nearly two years away, at the climax of the long Jubilee year. He already had started on two of the projects. He had been planning since 1953 a *Mass of Christ The King* and working on it seriously since its acceptance for the Three Choirs Festival in 1977. Likewise, in the course of his work with *Jeunesses Musicales*, he had already written a cassation based on the 23rd psalm, *The Valley and the Hill*, which would merely need amplification and orchestration. The only work on which a start had not yet been made was his Fourth Symphony.

In his enthusiasm he probably did not pause to reflect that, with the exception of the troubled *Hammarskjöld Portrait*, he had completed nothing of major significance for three years; that two commissioned scores, *Les Olympiques* and the Harp Concerto, on which he had struggled in that period, now urgently needed his attention; and that he would have to acquire private or public sponsorship to pay for the many hours of work to be put in on the royal commissions. There was also the problem of finding somewhere to live. But that was a problem for another day. For the next two months he and Simon would be on the road in France, earning some money taking cassations around schools.

They started at a provincial town, about two hours by train from Paris:

> My tour began at Chateauroux, a not too interesting Indre et Loire town, but with as high a standard of music education as I've found in France, or maybe anywhere… 2,200 children this last week built Stone Walls – 9 seances [performances], endless receptions that almost killed me – truly the kindest people on earth, the French… I wish I had not overtired myself seeing Jean Marais in *Les Miserables* – three and a half hours in a draughty cinema – live, not celluloid, but not good… On Sunday Simon and I shared playing the Grande Messe in a packed church…[1]

Wintry weather affected their two weeks at Lille, where they stayed at the Hotel Moderne ('Moderne? You should see it!'[2]). Then illness struck:

> A very disagreeable bout of bronchitis last Friday, which reached the flower of its maturity as I stood for 75 minutes in a glacial Belgian wind outside Lille Station while Simon searched for taxis, has gripped me. The doctor has ordered a week's rest…. Simon took my place, so performances of the *Snow Wolf* went on… In the meantime I take pills and suffer…[3]

Despite his new optimism – Mario Bois was investigating the possibility of doing all the cassations on national television – his travels in France were dogged by worries. Malcolm's illness led *Jeunesses Musicales* to cancel the second week at Lille and query the arrangements for Pau, but Malcolm swiftly recovered and, indeed, was soon in excellent spirits, even able to return briefly to the dark complexities of the Harp Concerto:

> I am composing with new energy and seriousness… Pau and Lourdes – in fact Les Basses Pyrenees altogether – are divine…[4]

And when he continued the letter at 3.40 a.m. in the morning, he was still quite positive:

> I am again insomniac… we've had excellent sessions at the casino here... Tomorrow we have 480 kids in the morning and 883 in the afternoon… Seven sessions to go….

When these were over, they refreshed themselves at Lourdes, before quickly crossing the Pyrenees for a short holiday in Cantabria. They loved the capital, Santander, with its charming old quarter, distinctive Spanish architecture and the attractive long beaches. Not far away lay Santillana del Mar, where, at the Collegiata, the most admired Romanesque church in Cantabria, Simon gave the first performance of a short organ work which Malcolm had composed for him, a Fantasy on 'O Paradise'.[5]

---

[1] MW to Richard Toeman, 15 February 1976. Berlioz's *Grande Messe* was a work Malcolm had long admired. The bisexual Marais was a strikingly handsome actor, who, in his younger days, had been Jean Cocteau's lover.

[2] MW to Richard Toeman, 15 February 1976

[3] *ibid.*

[4] MW to Richard Toeman, from the Hotel Roncevaux, 1 March 1976

[5] 13 March 1976. The work is dedicated to 'the citizens of the Province of Santander, Spain'.

The title was appropriate to the mood of the moment. Malcolm, caught up in the creation of his own new life, had assumed that he and Simon would briefly return to East Sheen while settling down to look for somewhere of their own, and was not best pleased (as he told Richard Toeman) when Dolly vetoed the suggestion:

> You may know by now that my personal life is not on a happy footing. Dolly has asked me not to return to Hertford Avenue after the French tour. Whatever the rights and wrongs I wish she had not chosen this time to be difficult. Personally I shall be delighted by a separation but it is a bad time for me to be away from my children and I should be grieved to be away from them.[6]

Dolly had every intention of being 'difficult' if that meant saving her children from further trauma. Malcolm had chosen a future with Simon, but had yet to face up to the consequences of his actions. Dolly had accommodated his wilfulness for many years, adapting and compromising her own life in the process, but would do so no longer. Malcolm's feelings for Simon would not be paraded in front of the children. The children's futures were the chief consideration, and one of her first actions was to take legal advice:

> Eventually it evolved that I was to have £50 a week, but getting it was just terrible. Then there were the school fees, a considerable sum of money. Our lives were being torn apart and I was determined the children were going to stay on at their schools. I made threats. I said I would create the most terrible scandal if the school fees weren't paid! One of my lawyers said, 'Don't worry about the school fees! I'll chain you to the gates of Buckingham Palace with a sign across your chest! The school fees *will* be paid!' And he did pay them. I had a couple of summer meetings with him just to finalise it all, with a lawyer to help…[7]

Dolly's current life was far from easy:

> I was threatened with cut-offs from all the utilities. People would come to the house to cut me off, and I would say, 'Come in, have a cup of tea and let me explain!', and after I'd promised that the debts would be paid eventually, they were usually very nice about it and kindly refrained from cutting us off… But all in all it was a hopeless situation, and finally a friend said 'You'll have to divorce him'. I waited a year and then started proceedings. He was very, very upset. He told me to hold on and I'd be Lady Williamson!

For the children, even though they had become used to seeing very little of their father, the new situation was as distressing as it was perplexing. Peter in his five years at boarding school was visited only once by his father:

> That was the only time, I think, that I saw him sober after 1975. And even after I left school – three years after he became Master of the Queen's Music – I didn't see a great deal of him. Occasionally we had some pretty horrendous meeting (amusing, perhaps, to look back on) when he was completely trashed from drink. When he went on a bender, he really went the whole way.[8]

---

6 Letter from Pau, 1 March 1976

7 January 2005

8 May 2005

It was not that his children weren't often in his thoughts. Postcards continued to drift in from various parts of the world. From Chateauroux he sent Peter a picture of the Chateau de Nohant, George Sand's home.

> I thought you might like to see the writing-room of George Sand, where I was last week. Chopin, Liszt, Delacroix & others were regular visitors…[9]

Malcolm also sent Tammy and Clare a postcard of George Sand:

> Girls! Don't lose this – it is evidently the only photo taken of George Sand – towards the end of her life. When photography was young, but she was not. Love, Malcolm.[10]

From Biarritz, where Malcolm and Simon paused on their way to Santander, Peter was sent a postcard of Lourdes Cathedral. Strangely, it was not signed by 'Dad' or 'Malcolm':

> I send you this because, against my better judgement, I was very impressed. I was bathed in the sacred waters and quite incredibly there was no feeling of temperature but a great feeling of well-being. Miraculous healthy cures have taken place here. Yrs M.W.

Such a formal ending can have only one possible explanation. Anxious to get all protocol right in his new royal role, he had been reading up books on etiquette and discovered that the correct procedure with postcards was to use just the initials.

As Master of the Queen's Music he was soon a household name. Within months, for example, he was a castaway on Desert Island Discs, his choice of music including Britten, Vaughan Williams, Messiaen, Stravinsky, Mozart and some Williamson.[11] His luxury, a puppet theatre, was less predictable than his book, the plays of Strindberg.

As Master of the Queen's Music he found it even easier to ask favours of friends, an important consideration for a pair without a home. Through the kindness of well-wishers, Malcolm and Simon were soon moving into a flat in Chiswick for a short stay.[12] The working conditions there were far from ideal, but Malcolm managed to complete a Piano Trio commissioned by the Cheltenham Festival in memory of Arthur Bliss.[13] That apart, he struggled to find the necessary focus. He had, for example, been trying to write a Suite based on *The Violins of Saint-Jacques*, which had much potential as a concert work. 'It's a huge job,' he confided to Richard Toeman, 'and I do wonder if I will get it done.[14]

9 16 February 1976

10 Posted from Lille, 21 November 1976

11 Britten: *Les Illuminations* (Pears/Goossens); Vaughan Williams: Symphony 9 (Boult); Messiaen: *Communion Messe de la Pentecoste* (Messiaen, organ); Stravinsky: *Symphony of Psalms*; Mozart: Symphony 40 (Britten/ECO); Williamson: Violin Concerto (Menuhin/Boult); Williamson: *From A Child's Garden* (Cantelo); Brahms: Symphony 2 (Boult/LPO).

12 Sharon Road

13 First performed on 22 June 1976

14 He didn't.

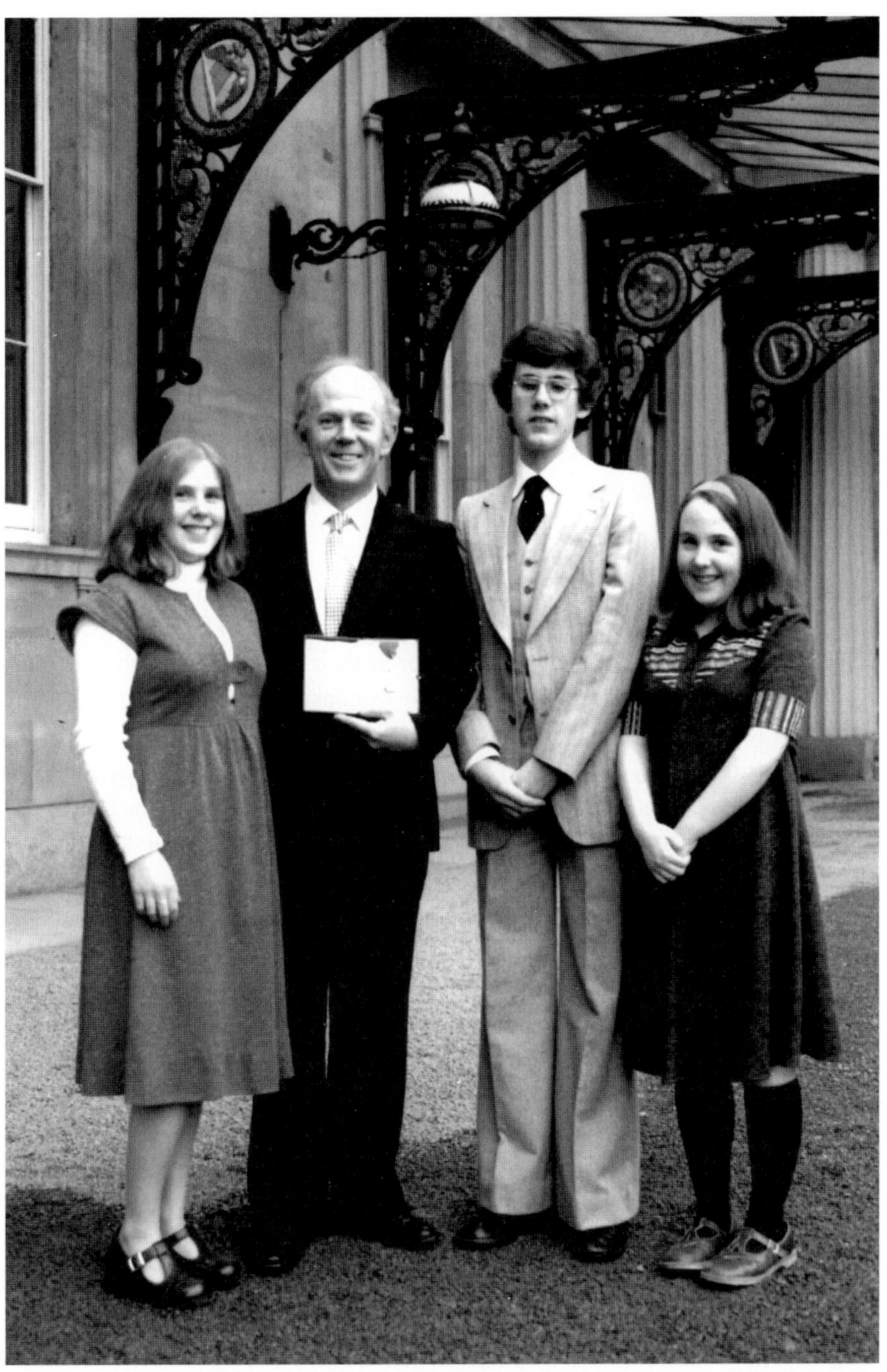

Collecting the CBE with the children, 1976

There is just too much to do and I feel like weeping at the years ahead, although they look rosy.'[15] Small presents for friends were a different matter. When Lizzie Lutyens celebrated her seventieth birthday that July, Malcolm wrote her a three-minute piano piece, *Ritual of Admiration*. Later on, at one of her 70th birthday concerts, he and John Amis sat alongside her on a panel answering the audience's questions between works. She hated such situations as much as Malcolm loved them. When her new work, *Mare et Minutiae*, was applauded in error five minutes before the end, she promptly rose and took her bow. 'It's not the end!' the leader of the quartet hissed. 'Oh yes it is!' she replied grimly, and left the platform. Malcolm's friendships so often ended in disarray, but he and Lizzie Lutyens remained devoted to each other, their friendship even surviving the famous moment at a party when Malcolm, desperate to demonstrate a particular lift in *Swan Lake*, chose Lizzie as his Odette, raising her to the heavens as he executed a nimble step or two. Alas, he proved no Nureyev and they collapsed in an ignominious heap.

Malcolm's new-found devotion to Benjamin Britten persisted after his appointment, and when Britten unexpectedly accepted a peerage, Malcolm sent 'delighted congratulations and deepest love.' Two weeks later he and Simon were staying with Nancy Evans and Eric Crozier at their home near Aldeburgh. Life with the Croziers at Church Field Cottage was considerably more gracious than in Sharon Road, Chiswick, and he was soon angling for a return visit.

> Simon and I are due to lunch with Ben on July 10. Is it conceivable that we might invite ourselves over after that? I know that Simon would love to see you both again, as would I. Perhaps he might have an exploratory hour on the church organ…[16]

Malcolm had discussed with Nancy Evans the possibility of a Swinburne song cycle, but in view of mounting commitments, it was perhaps fortunate it never came to anything.

He had made early progress on the first and easiest of his Jubilee commitments, a setting of Betjeman's hymn, though he had tailored it to the requirements of the Moreton Morell summer school rather than the Royal Philharmonic Orchestra. The *Warwickshire Music* magazine reported:

> The rest of the final morning was spent with Malcolm's newest composition, hot from the writing desk of room 4, 'Jubilee Ode', written to verses by the poet laureate: a people's chorus or *ritornello* accompanied by flute, harp and guitar interspersed with solo verses for soprano and bass – instantly sing-able, with Malcolm's great gift for a good tune…[17]

---

15 1 March 1976

16 25 June 1976

17 Philippa Whitaker, Spring 1977, p.7. During this summer school in 1976 there was also a performance, only the second ever, of the Piano Trio, Simon playing the piano part. Malcolm had recently orchestrated *The Terrain of the Kings*, which was performed in this guise for the first time.

He was less painstaking in the continuing saga of a possible television opera for the BBC. Humphrey Burton had gently sent back his draft outline of *The Document of Adam*, explaining that it would be too costly and that he had doubts whether such a mystical theme would come over well on the small screen. Burton was happy, however, to pursue the idea of an operatic version of Strindberg's *Easter*, long one of Malcolm's most cherished projects. He alternatively suggested that Malcolm might write in a lighter vein, something to 'enwrap the nation in some way':

> Observing in 'Down Under' the success of your work with young people, I suddenly felt your television opera should be avoiding symbolism and allegory like the plague and aiming instead to make the feet tap, lips smile and the heart turn over.[18]

Could there not, added Burton, even be a part for the viewers to sing in their homes? It was an imaginative idea, very suited to Malcolm's talents, but he no longer wanted to do *Easter*, let alone set the nation singing in front of their televisions. He was determined to write about the holocaust, a subject in keeping with the dignity of his new position, and Burton's constructive letter went unanswered for six months.

He had another route to the holocaust, via the Harp Concerto, which had been inspired by the Tomb of the Unknown Jewish Martyr in Paris, but he had struggled to come to terms with it for nearly three years. He therefore went to see the London psychiatrist Dr Joan Gomez, who had helped him before, when suffering from writer's block, and whose healing methods included the use of hypnotism. It was a therapy he liked and, more importantly, in which he had great faith. 'You *will* be able to finish the Harp Concerto,' Dr Gomez told him persuasively. And he did.

She proved a helpful friend in other ways. When a sudden crisis arose in September 1976, with the need to vacate the flat in Chiswick, Dr Gomez offered Malcolm and Simon a small flat on Thornton Hill, Wimbledon, owned by a relation who was not currently using it.[19] It would be theirs for the next six months, and rent was not required.

But at the time of the move Malcolm was rushed to hospital in a state of collapse, and kept in to undergo (though not successfully) some alcohol aversion treatment. While he was there his thoughts turned guiltily to his family, and he wrote to Peter, who would shortly be sixteen:

> My dear Peter,
>
> How are you? I long to see you round about your birthday and have written to Dolly to see what we can arrange. You can tell me about your O-levels and what is going to happen now.
>
> As I have been in hospital I've been out of touch with most of the world; but I expect to be around for the weekend and then on; so may we meet?

---

18 5 July 1976

19 17 Thornton Hill

> Did you see the last night of the Proms when some of my music was played?[20] I was allowed to go and quite enjoyed it. Sir Charles Groves did a great job on it....
>
> I have more work to do than I can keep up with, so I'm glad to have had the necessary hospital care and to be well again...[21]

Soon afterwards Malcolm was settling in at Wimbledon. An insight into life there comes from Australian writer Gerard Windsor, a friend of Simon's from the days they were at Jesuit College together. His short story 'The Life of a Man's Man' describes a visit Windsor made to the Wimbledon flat at Simon's request.[22] Although classed as fiction, the story, says Windsor, was a true description of that visit.

The flat, approached up stairs and entered through two 'puny' pinewood doors, greeted him with the smell of cooking fat and stale cigarettes. The kitchen and bathroom were chilly linoed rooms, fifty years out of date, 'with enough dust and detritus and disregard for hygiene to inhibit any urge I might otherwise have felt to touch and use...' The sitting-room was dreary and dun, with cheap furniture; its carpet was worn and dirty, its walls bare. A small piano was loaded with papers, crockery and ashtrays. Various brown tables and low bookcases were scattered with manuscripts, scores and books, nearly all of which seemed to have been covered in matching brown paper. All in all, wrote Windsor, it was 'a glimpse of life in the raw'.

Unsurprisingly, in such a difficult working environment Simon struggled in his secretarial duties. When he informed the BBC of Malcolm's change of address, he initially gave them the wrong number, and in confirming the contract for *The House of Windsor* he used a typewriter which employed red and black ribbons indiscriminately. Such things, though very minor in themselves, tended cumulatively to confirm the rumour already beginning to circulate that all was not well with Malcolm.

Because the Wimbledon flat was so lacking in amenities, Malcolm was quick to persuade his neighbours and old friends John and Ursula Alldis to let him and Simon take over their home in nearby Wool Road while they were away for three weeks in Devon. It would be particularly helpful as Paul Jennings was scheduled to come down for a *Radio Times* interview.[23] The borrowed house duly impressed Jennings, who began his piece with a lyrical description:

> The road leading down to the one where Malcolm Williamson lives offered a falling vista of trees, three receding parallel horizons of them. It might have been in Hampshire: in fact it was in Wimbledon. A good, classy, quiet neighbourhood for

---

20 The orchestral suite from *Our Man In Havana.*

21 22 September 1976

22 Gerard Windsor: *Memories of the Assassination Attempt* (Penguin Australia, 1985) pp. 109-123

23 A popular personality and humorist, Paul Jennings wrote regularly for *Punch* and *The Observer*.

> composing: country quiet in London, handy for Palace and Abbey. So this is where the Master of the Queen's Music has settled down, I was thinking as I rang the bell.[24]

Malcolm appeared, immaculately tidy, playing the perfect host:

> 'Do come in. We're all eating chicken in the kitchen.' (It was three o'clock). 'I've been working all night, sleeping this morning … would you like some coffee?' 'You've stumbled into a nest of Australians,' said Simon Campion, an Australian organist, giving me the coffee.

By the time Paul Jennings had been given a quick resumé of the more printable sections of Malcolm's life, he had realised that he was not, in fact, in Malcolm's home.

> 'Yes, this is John Alldis's house. He's in Scandinavia or somewhere. My children are in America. They're coming back later this year. John has performed a great deal of my work. I wrote the *Procession of Palms* privately, at a time of despair and anger about capital punishment, but John said he must record it – can anyone work the radio … the gramophone?' We took our coffee into a room with a big glass-topped table, indoor plants, a grand piano. He sat down and played a Lennox Berkeley prelude: clear, resonant, crisp, French-sounding. 'How wonderful to have written that – oh, I like to live with a key signature…'

Malcolm was putting on his usual good show, and Paul Jennings was clearly impressed:

> Malcolm Williamson is a man utterly without the mask that most men (let alone creative artists) present to the world. His thoughts flash and subside, with sparks of allusion, tailings-off, recurrent grand central themes, darting side-flashes of wit, like a turning bird's wing in his own music, particularly in its Messiaen moods. 'Messiaen said *Je suis musicien surtout catholique* and that's what I am. I became a Catholic when I was 20. It was terrible. I can't imagine any other idea of life…

From Messiaen Malcolm rapidly moved to *Procession of Palms:*

> 'Now this idea of the Palms' (by now Simon Campion had found it, first track on a record called *20th Century Music for Worship*; it was first performed in Canterbury Cathedral) 'you've got the procession *Ride on in Majesty* – a bit jazzy – then the verse and response from the altar.' A strange, beautiful echoing canon for counter-tenor and soprano, like Gabrieli in modern dress: then a Blessing of Palms, flowing and Brucknerish, followed by a wild cheering Hosanna. 'But they're going to kill him. It's everyone's cruelty. My cruelty, your cruelty. We're all cruel…!'

It was a good cue for an erudite digression with a little name-dropping:

> 'There's a marvellous play by Henri de Montherlant – I read French most of the time, but God, I'm ignorant: Trudy Bliss produced an effortlessly right quotation at a dinner and I thought it was Eliot and it was Shakespeare – well, in this play, *The Master of Santiago*, there's a medieval Spanish monk-knight, a war hero, who is asked why he has gone off wars and the burning of heretics. He says 'I have seen God in his mantle of war, *dans son manteau de guerre*, holding out his arms' – like a palm tree, with dead warriors hanging from his arms, that's how those palm trees looked to me.'

---

24 'Music Is For Everyone', *Radio Times*, 30 October 1976

Paul Jennings gently turned the discussion away from palm trees. Did Malcolm mind, he asked, that so many critics tended to bracket his inspiration with that of other composers? Was his 'eclecticism' a problem? Malcolm's response was less than totally frank:

> 'Of course not! I like more music than any other composer I know. Arthur Bliss once said to me 'I hear you react against traditional music', but I don't really. I've never reacted against Stainer – well, what about this? –' (he played a bit from *The Crucifixion*) 'or Vaughan Williams or anyone.'

The interview moved on to what he was currently writing. Malcolm's eyes sparkled:

> 'Come and look at this: I was struggling with it last night.' On the piano was the Kyrie of a mass of Christ the King. 'The Feast of Christ the King was only created in modern times. I'm very interested in it: what we need is this gentle authority of God. See: the soprano (she'll be April Cantelo) calls out higher each time, above the choir, *Kyrie eleison*, have mercy on us – come on, you're in a choir, let's have a go! We stumbled through it, I sight-reading, Malcolm in his awful composer's voice, Simon Campion no Gigli either. I felt Malcolm wanted the photographer to join in too.

It was a good interview. Malcolm, it seemed, was getting on with the commission for the Three Choirs Festival, still ten months way. And photographs in the *Radio Times* showed him looking spruce, if a little tired.[25] The house, in the background, looked immaculate. It did not stay that way long. Nor did the work on the Mass of Christ The King persist. Within days of the interview Malcolm was binge-drinking, damaging the house in the process and upsetting the neighbourhood. Ursula Alldis still remembers the scene of devastation to which she and John returned:

> They had absolutely wrecked the house. We were quite appalled. They'd wrecked it! We had hidden all the drink at Simon's request, but there was one cupboard in the dining room that I forgot. Apparently Malcolm found some vodka there and that started the whole thing off. The place was filthy. It smelt to high heaven. We were so distressed.[26]

The binge ended after a few days when neighbours found Malcolm lying in the road outside the house and summoned an ambulance. Lennox and Freda

---

[25] One of the photographs was later used for the cover of a double LP issued by EMI (First Symphony, *Sinfonia Concertante*, Violin Concerto and *The Display*).

[26] February 2006. John's memories of Malcolm, however, have remained very warm: 'He was a rogue! A highly likeable rascal! I always thought of him as a rogue because, in the nicest possible way, he manipulated people if he possibly could! He had such 'scandale' all around him. He used to say a lot of things he really shouldn't have said. A terrible gossip! Wicked! And such energy! It was as if he was spinning around in circles at high speed all the time. Exhilarating! I liked him immensely. I really fell for him.' Ursula has similarly amused memories: 'He used to come in dramatically and quietly declaim, "Chi-ick!" – for some reason he always called me Chick – "Chi-ick! I'm very i-ill! Have you got some asp-ir-in?" We were for ever running around after him! He was one of those people with a talent for getting others to do things for them!'

Berkeley, hearing that he had been rushed to hospital, intervened to ensure the best possible treatment. He was soon writing calmly and cheerfully to Freda from Westminster Hospital:

> My dear Freda,
>
> I cannot begin to tell you how grateful I am to you and to your family for your patience kindnesses and help. It is through your intervention that I am having the real help that I so badly need in a psychiatric hospital under Rodney Long and through him Dr Joan Gomez.
>
> Since you have heard me and, I expect, Simon speak of the present besetting problems there is no need to reiterate them. Enough to say that I am being superbly looked after by these two doctors, and through Rodney's goodness I have a small private room with a desk where I can work.
>
> The treatments are not pleasant but are evidently as effective and sophisticated as modern psychiatry can realise, and I am deeply grateful...[27]

When news of Malcolm's latest collapse reached Bessie in Sydney, she caught the next plane to London. Malcolm responded positively to seeing her and elicited some useful financial aid, as he relayed to Freda Berkeley:

> My mother has appeared, is in good form, and is disposed to be helpful; so circumstances improve. Simon is buying an old car.

From hospital Malcolm wrote to Peter, remembering his birthday with a card. For the moment there could be no present:

> Money is short at this difficult time but will I hope become easier soon, so you will not mind waiting...[28]

He had been allowed out of hospital to judge a competition for young conductors:[29]

> With a first prize of £5,000! I'd have liked to award myself the money, but the Master of the Queen's Music is supposed to be rich...

The appointment, he conceded, had its problems:

> I have a terrific burden of work which shows no sign of decreasing. A hell of a lot is 'honour and glory' stuff i.e. no money attached.

On leaving hospital, he was at last able to acclimatise himself to life back in Dr Gomez's Wimbledon flat, and he was not at all dismayed by the flat's Spartan appearance, which appealed to his bohemian spirit. After all, he argued, many of the great composers had known poverty. 'In the present situation,' he wrote to Janet Canetty-Clarke, 'the flat is a boon, although lacking piano and any aids to listening to music.'[30] Shortly afterwards they acquired a small piano and a cheap record-player.

---

[27] 1 October 1976

[28] 1 October 1976

[29] At Fairfield Halls, Croydon, 1 October 1976.

[30] 8 October 1976

With Graham Wade, Warwick

The need for money was paramount, dictating a working schedule which hampered fulfilment of his jubilee commissions. In September 1976, for example, he was again engaged in Warwickshire as composer-in-residence at the summer school for music teachers at Moreton Morell Agricultural College. It was a long way from the Albert Hall and Buckingham Palace, but here, as Dolly had suggested, as a big fish in a little pond, he found some form of peace, thoroughly enjoying participating in concerts and always playing with as much passion and commitment as in a major concert hall.

Malcolm's popularity at summer schools only tended to plummet when he began to coerce people to copy out parts of his latest work, a task which could take many hours. This summer it was turn of the Harp Concerto, *Au Tombeau du Martyr Juif Inconnu*, having its long-awaited first performance that November,[31] at the Queen Elizabeth Hall, with Yuval Zaliouk, his host and guide in Israel, conducting the London Mozart Players, who had commissioned the work.[32] The harpist was Martine Geliot, the French winner of a recent Harp of David competition in Israel, Malcolm having lost the services of the dedicatee Marisa Robles.[33]

Malcolm's programme notes, so much fuller than usual and a token of the importance he attached to the work, give full details of the background inspiration. Several years ago, he wrote, when he had been idling around the Seine, he saw a sign pointing to the *Tombeau du Martyr Juif Inconnu*. He was so fascinated that he went down several tiny streets to seek whatever this tomb might be. He found a tall, impressive granite building with a caution to the passer-by, written in large French and Hebrew letters, to remember those who

31 17 November 1976. The concert was one in a series of 'Composer's Choice', in which Malcolm in Betjemanesque style talked about his choices, which included Britten (Prelude and Fugue in 18 parts), Mozart (Adagio and Fugue in C minor), Bliss (*Music for Strings*) and his own 2nd Piano Concerto in which he was the soloist. Shostakovich's *Two Pieces* had to be dropped at the last minute for lack of time.

32 With the Arts Council and the ever-supportive Australian Music Association

33 Marisa Robles was taken aback by the stark nature of the work: 'I was very busy with my chamber ensemble and travelling and he was going through such a bad time that I didn't eventually play his concerto. It is a very distorted and unhappy work – he was very unhappy when he wrote it – and I just didn't like the piece!' (August 2005)

had made their final journey to the death camps in various parts of Europe during the Second World War:

> In front of the building was a flagged courtyard and, in the centre of the courtyard, a large bronze monument with the names of the death camps inscribed. It was curiously beautiful to look at in spite of the tragedy so vividly evoked. I watched through the locked iron gates, while outside in the streets little French boys wearing Star of David medallions about their necks, collected coins from passers-by for the 'Freedom from Hunger' campaign… It was one of those occasions that a composer hopes for which occur rarely, when, instead of sitting at his desk trying to think of an idea, an idea comes full-blown like a rose into his mind and the piece of music, the very sounds of the harp and the string orchestra, came to me there and then. The very modality around the note E all came to me in a flash. Not the whole work, but the basic material of the whole idea for the piece…

Central to the conception was the Jewish harp, the harp of the Old Testament, David' s harp, a harp born 'to sing and cry almost with the sad consoling passions of a ghetto violin'. It asserts itself in a long, dark opening: a figure of lamentation, first heard with half the cellos and half the double basses in unison against very low Es from the rest of the basses and very high Es from the upper strings (with the harp playing a cadential figure). Two further themes follow, one jagged and Stravinsky-like, expressing violence and protest, the other a dissonant rising harmonic figure. 'If you care,' wrote Malcolm, 'you can visualise the trains travelling across Europe with their prisoners encased in them.' In the craggy discords, Malcolm declared,[34] a train can be heard going over the points leading up to a camp.

As the movement progresses the three themes combine, disintegrate, pile up and develop. It concludes with a contrasting, lovely coda. The suffering and lamentation are at end. Instead there is balm. Arpeggio figures in the harp accompany a return of the theme of lamentation, only this time resolved tonally in a chorale-like passage of great beauty. Yet there remains a sense of tension – the harmonies never quite coalesce. This coda (as Malcolm later explained) represents the love of man for man, which can transcend suffering, ennobling and conquering it. Malcolm is here expressing the consolations of martyrdom, and in this sweetest of bitter-sweet codas it is hard not to believe he is expressing too the love he felt for Simon.

The second movement brings a short contrast: a fast, feverish, whirling scherzo. The high-spirited brightness of the spiralling figures, wrote Malcolm, reflected the toys of the children in the ghetto. There is also a sense in this chattering music of the resilience of an oppressed people:

> There is something of the Semitic fierceness about the music along with some of the 'devil-may-care' humour which one finds in the Jewish world, be it in Israel or on Broadway in New York. It is said that as Hebrew scholars were going on their final journey from this world in the Gas Chambers they were still disputing on the spiritual

34 To Weinberger's Gerald Kingsley

finesse of certain texts in the Bible such was their pre-occupation with the world of the spirit.

Finally there comes an Adagio in which the earlier material is refined to simpler textures. At last there is consolation for the martyr and a place in heaven with the angels. Unlike the heaven in the finale of his lst Symphony, *Elevamini*, the reception here is necessarily a little muted:

> As one listens to the Adagio harmonically one feels that even the angels eat bitter herbs of sorrow which for centuries the Jews have eaten ritually and actually. The idea behind the scalic theme that opens the movement is that of Jacob's ladder in the spiritual sense, the ascent of the martyr into heaven, and the second subject, very richly coloured harmonically with multi-divided strings, is the welcoming embrace of the angels for those who have suffered.

As in the first movement Malcolm reserves the best for last. The welcoming embrace of the angels is reflected in serenely tonal music: long held notes, accompanied by the harp sparkling with a chattering figure. All becomes virtually motionless, long pedal notes underlining the ethereal atmosphere. The harp comments finally with chords laden with emotion, and the concerto sinks to an achingly beautiful conclusion. The most impressive of all Malcolm's many moving studies in martyrdom, the work is masterly in its exploration of the potential greatness of the human spirit in the face of overwhelming cruelty, and, in celebrating the bravery of the unknown Jewish martyr, Malcolm transcends the boundaries of Jew and Gentile and speaks to everyone.

It proved, on the whole, a critical success. Paul Griffiths of *The Times* was predictably hostile, declaring it 'weak in shape and ideas', but then Griffiths's allegiance lay with the avant-garde about whom he wrote prolifically.[35] A very different response came from Nicholas Kenyon in the *Daily Telegraph*:

> In addition to the recognisably Semitic intervals which underpin all three movements there is indeed an elegiac heavily brooding atmosphere throughout. Not even a central scherzo, fleeting though it may have been, can banish the mood… This is one of his most outstanding recent works. [36]

Edward Greenfield in *The Guardian*, after suggesting parallels with Bartok's Music For Strings and Celesta 'not only in the actual sound but in the elliptic mode of argument and its intensity', believed it heralded 'a new tone of voice for the composer, a reconciliation of his sharply differentiated easy and difficult manners of the past'.[37]

The work soon attracted several other harpists, the most notable of whom was Osian Ellis:

> I remember doing it at Southwell Cathedral and Malcolm made a speech before I played it. He was very moved by the spirituality of its content. He spoke a lot about

---

35 His books on Boulez and Electronic Music were shortly to be published.

36 18 November 1976

37 18 November 1976

it and what it meant to him. The Jewish overtones. Before I played it for the first time, he came over and had tea. But he talked so much that we hardly had any time to go through the music...[38]

The Harp Concerto somehow transcended the chaos of Malcolm's existence. Perhaps, indeed, such a study of martyrdom drew strength from his own embattled life, the self-inflicted struggle with poverty and drink. The deleterious effects of the alcoholism were all too apparent, and friends like Ian Partridge, who had known Malcolm years earlier at the time of *English Eccentrics* and the John Alldis Choir, were shocked on meeting him:

I happened to pass him on Wimbledon Hill. I didn't recognise him. It was so sad. I was going up and he was coming down and I walked past him and suddenly thought 'That's Malcolm!' We did have a few words, but he was in a very bad way. The wonderful enthusiasm of his had all gone. The eyes were dead.[39]

Tony Fell, managing director of Boosey & Hawkes, was similarly shocked:

Soon after I took over the job, towards the end of 1974, less than a year before he became Master of the Queen's Music, I asked Malcolm out for a meal. He was slim, trim, highly intelligent and really good company. His regression after the appointment was really rapid.[40]

It was inevitable that Buckingham Palace soon became aware of his problems. In early December 1976, for example, Malcolm's Epiphany Carol was featured in a royal concert. Sweetly melodic, it has the power to charm the dourest breast, but, alas, something went very badly wrong, Malcolm turning on his publishers in fury afterwards for sending him a flawed version 'with wrong notes and a confused organ part'. In his current alcoholic haze, he is more likely to have caused the crisis himself. An early opportunity of impressing the Royal Family had clearly been lost: 'My work was greeted by the Princess in icy silence!'[41]

Malcolm's erratic behaviour was becoming more and more a subject of amusement in the musical world. A long-standing friend in the business remembers being summoned to Wimbledon one day in early 1977, with bizarre consequences:

He rang me up one day – 'Will you come over? I've got some supper for you.' So I got there about half past six and banged on the door. I waited a long time. Simon clearly wasn't around. Suddenly the door opened. 'Who is it?' He was wearing a dressing gown and nothing else. 'Have a drink,' he said as he flops on the sofa, exposing everything. 'I'd better be off,' I said. 'Didn't I say we'd go to dinner?' 'Yes, you did indeed invite me over for a meal!' He changed into a jogging outfit. Then his face fell. 'I don't think I've got enough money.' 'How much do you want?' 'Another ten quid.' So I gave him a tenner and off he went with it. He came back twenty

38 August 2005

39 August 2005

40 August 2005

41 MW to Richard Toeman, 23 December 1976

> minutes later with a Chinese Takeaway. His face falls again. 'Oh damn, I meant to get something to drink with it.' 'I'll go,' I said. Out I went and came back ten minutes later to discover he'd eaten all the food. He couldn't have eaten all day – he'd only just got up! Next thing I knew he'd sat down on a sofa and dozed off. So very quietly I let myself out.[42]

There were even more distressing stories:

> He used go around in far from clean clothes – and he smelt. And he wondered why he wasn't picking up trade. On Wimbledon Common and places like that. He could sometimes almost be taken for a tramp.[43]

Simon's position was extremely difficult, but he loyally stayed with Malcolm, helping as much as he could, but soon realising that whether he condoned or criticised the drinking – and he tried both approaches – it was going to make little difference.

Gerard Windsor's autobiographical story 'The Life of a Man's Man' sheds light on the relationship. Windsor had visited the couple in the early months of 1977, the Queen's Silver Jubilee year. His first sight of the composer was of him lying drunk on the floor, vaguely conscious but for the moment unable to speak. 'We have a visitor,' comments his 'remarkably forbearing, even gentle' friend to him softly. There is no response from the floor. Windsor remarks that it is sad to see the composer so reduced. The friend reflects for a moment, as if measuring the statement's sincerity. 'It'll do him good to see you,' he says at last. Later, after the composer has stumbled off into the bedroom, Windsor comments that at least he seems quite docile. 'No mood can be relied upon to last,' says the friend, adding that it is the range and unpredictability of the moods which are so wearing. Asked why he puts up with them, he shrugs his shoulders. 'You do a lot for genius.' Later on the composer rallies, finds his feet and loses his temper. He empties a pot of pea-soup, being heated by his friend, onto the floor. The chicken and chips (which his friend had just gone out to buy) he heaves out of the window, plate and all. And finally, to the extra-loud sounds of an Aaron Copland LP, he sets fire to the bedroom.

It is clear where Windsor's sympathies lie. In the final scene, in a hospital, the composer is an all-demanding, manipulative monster. Windsor takes him on, suggesting his partner has become nothing but a doormat or nursemaid, just stopping short of adding 'when he's not the object of unwanted and bilious lechery'. 'I love him,' replies the composer stubbornly. 'I really do. And it is the only time he has ever been loved.' But Windsor will have none of it. Shortly afterwards he urges the friend to have a break for a while, leaving the composer to himself that evening. 'Stay with me!' comes the anxious cry from the bed. 'Stay with me!' Windsor points out to the hesitating friend that there's a competent hospital staff, only for the cries of anguish to intensify. 'I need you.

---

42 September 2005

43 The same friend of long-standing

You'll stay with me, won't you?' 'Well,' says the friend, giving in, 'Just this once.'

Simon, then, gladly accepted his difficult supporting role, strengthened by his proud belief that he was in the daily presence of musical genius. His role also brought some reward for his own musical ambitions. Only the month before, for example, he had played one of the two pianos in a recording of *The Brilliant and the Dark* made specially to celebrate the coming Silver Jubilee.[44] Simon tried hard to make Malcolm see that it was music that mattered most in their relationship, not sex. To the sexually charged Malcolm, possessive and quickly jealous, Simon's feelings were hard to understand and distressing. So explosive was the early relationship that in the first year of their life together Malcolm made three suicide attempts. These seem to have been genuine attempts to kill himself with a drugs overdose, rather than mere cries for help. Twice he had come very close to success, or so, at least, he assured Freda Berkeley, who at this stage had assumed the role of Mother Confessor:

> The taking of overdoses was never premeditated, but impetuous, following on black despair. I made my act of contrition and hoped then to sleep. The last time I was found by chance. Until you have done it you do not know the feeling, the balmy sleepiness and abnegation of responsibility, and if it's cowardly you don't care. You trust in a wise God and hope never to wake again. Maybe it's a form of madness?[45]

Frustration over Simon, he said, was the primary cause. He could cope with poverty, the prospect of divorce and cramped living quarters, but not with what he described as 'cock-tease'. It was a situation which had been going on for over a year, said Malcolm, and it was this which had driven him to excessive drinking and consequent hospitalisation. If there was to be a future, it would have to be one with a 'satisfactory love-life with Simon, combined with hard work, lots of sex and avoidance of alcohol to enable me to pursue the God-given Christian vocation.'

Two days later he wrote to Freda Berkeley again, a little calmer and more thoughtful:

> Nothing in this world is ideal but the loving (in every sense) companionship that I once had with Simon was the happiest and most productive thing that I ever had; and the change in him really coincides with his leaving his country. Although he had no home he had a neat (if lonely) life with an excellent job and it's tough that, first crack out of the box, he collides with someone as difficult as I am. One way or the other I hope to live it through, although too often the pain blinds one's sense of proportion… I'm going to phone Simon now. I spoke with him last evening and as always he is excellent at making love by post or phone. My intentions of being firm were really

44 The recording, under the auspices of the *Reader's Digest*, was made on 11-12 December 1976, Antony Hopkins conducting the English Chamber Orchestra. The soloists were April Cantelo, Norma Procter, Alfreda Hodgson and Sally Le Sage. Janet Canetty-Clarke was the other pianist.

45 24 January 1977

> crushed by his lovingness – if only he'd stop being so much of a bedroom-preacher…[46]

Malcolm's letters to Freda Berkeley were written from a friary where he had been brought, raging drunk, in order to find the necessary peace to complete the orchestration of the Jubilee Hymn, which was to be sung in the Albert Hall in the presence of the Queen in less than two weeks' time. Malcolm was used to retreating into friaries and monasteries, and they had been very good to him over the years at this particular one, but he waspishly entertained Freda Berkeley at its expense:

> Possibly I may settle in but so far the love and compassion of Christian queens in their scapulars is driving me crazy. The fellas, all camping about and being hair-shirted and chaste I find infinitely depressing. They are so like projections of what Simon must have been in his Jesuit days.
>
> If God has called me to chastity, the call has been too faint for me to hear; and I cannot bear the Christian love which seems to be forgiving me for my shortcomings – I've had enough of that from Simon. The horror of the chaste camp community life may diminish in the days to come, but my present feeling is that I want to get out, fuck someone blind and get as drunk as a coot.

After a further two days he was still feeling satirical:

> I'm going crazier than ever! This joint is pure Iris Murdoch (The Bell) or do I mean Muriel Spark? It's the Conversion of S. Paul today and after an hour's liturgical camping around among the incensed pretties I just wished S. Paul had never converted… Anglo-Catholics are not for me! Oh God, where is Hell? In this entirely comfortable guest-house are i) people with frightful nervous collapses ii) wayfarers, as they call them and iii) intense Anglican lads tuning in to the good life as lived by S.S. Francis & Clare of Assisi. No wonder people take to vice of various sorts![47]

Just a week later[48] Malcolm conducted his Jubilee Hymn with the Royal Philharmonic Orchestra at the Albert Hall in front of the Queen and a crowd of five thousand, an event which attracted all the more attention because of the simple words, described by one MP in Parliament as 'absolutely pathetic'. The five verses were certainly simple:

> In days of disillusion,
> However low we've been,
> To fire us and inspire us
> God gave to us our Queen.

And after each verse came an equally simple chorus:

> For our Monarch and her people,
> United yet and free,
> Let the bells from ev'ry steeple
> Ring out loud the Jubilee.

---

[46] 26 January 1977

[47] 28 January 1977

[48] 6 February 1977

Betjeman had been worried about the poem all along, writing to his wife:

> The commonplace verses I have written for the Jubilee have pleased the Master of Music, an Aussie, and been passed to the Queen. They are not at all good, just like a Christmas Card. But they have to be comprehensible to the T.U.C. and natives of Africa.[49]

He told Tom Driberg that Malcolm had cheered him up by saying the words were the kind he wanted as they left him the gaps he needed.[50] Malcolm managed to maintain a tactful façade in public, and, when cross-examined on 'The World This Weekend', loyally refused to join the criticisms, though some time later he was to admit that the setting of Betjeman's hymn had been 'like trying to knit with spaghetti'.

The Hymn was sung at the royal entertainment by the fine choir of Trinity School, Croydon, whose director, David Squibb, found Malcolm extremely eccentric:

> I got as big a choir as I could – over a hundred, including some staff and former choristers – for the Jubilee Hymn. Malcolm came down to the school. There had already been a lot of fuss in the press about Betjeman's words, so the BBC sent some crews down. At one point Malcolm asked part of the choir to do something and some other boys were talking and he turned round acidly: 'How dare you talk when I'm talking to these people. Haven't you got any manners?' It was a real show of temperament, and, of course, was captured on TV. Malcolm was very spontaneous and sensitive and nervy. But the hymn worked well.[51]

The Jubilee Hymn did Malcolm's reputation no good at all, his involvement in an enterprise derided by many as jingoistic and sycophantic calling his artistic integrity into question. It was known that he openly longed for a knighthood – he had been made CBE early on, in 1976 – and his participation in the Jubilee Hymn was seen, fairly scornfully, as a determined step in the right direction. There was greater sympathy for the short organ work, 'The Lion of Suffolk' which he wrote for Benjamin Britten's memorial service at Westminster Abbey.[52]

At the beginning of March 1977, six months before the Mass of Christ The King was to be performed in Gloucester Cathedral as the centrepiece of the 250th Three Choirs Festival and as an official Jubilee salute to the Queen, a press

---

49 John Betjeman, *Letters*, Vol 2, p.512

50 *ibid.* p.504

51 June 2006. David Squibb had first come across Malcolm in 1973 when doing *The Red Sea* at the Croydon Festival with the Trinity School choir and orchestra: 'I went over to his house at East Sheen, and tried hard to get his views on the orchestral arrangements, but he refused to be drawn. 'Use what you can! It's entirely up to you,' he said. Came the day of the concert, and Malcolm rushed up. 'The orchestra's hopeless – nothing like I imagined – come back here this evening two hours before the concert and I'll put it all right.' He changed virtually everything! What the trumpets were playing the clarinets took over and vice versa etc etc. Fortunately they were very able youngsters and it all worked. But I felt a bit miffed – and I didn't really think the changes made any difference at all!'

52 Played by Stephen Cleobury in the presence of the Queen Mother, 10 March 1977.

June Mendoza's fine portrait, Wimbledon 1977

conference was called in the Piccadilly offices of the Arts Council to publicise the event. Malcolm, asked to attend to make a progress report on the new work, arrived late and astonished everyone by launching into a passionate tirade. His feelings towards the Arts Council, he said, were ones of 'total disgust' because of their lack of support! He had asked for £5,000 and received nothing! It was simply 'one more humiliation in a long list of humiliations' he had suffered from the Arts Council over a great many years…![53]

Malcolm's frustration was understandable. He had no private means to tide him over the many months' work which his Jubilee commitments would entail. He needed financial subsidy early on, so that he could free himself of other work to fulfil these important, though unpaid, projects, and the Arts Council was an obvious first source of funding. Failing, in the first instance, to elicit any financial support for the Mass of Christ the King, he had no recourse but to carry on travelling around earning whatever money he could, wherever it was offered. He was even scheduled to spend ten days in America that summer to direct yet more cassations.

53 Boden: *The Three Choirs Festival*, p.228

All this needed to be said carefully and calmly. Instead, disastrously, Malcolm enlarged his tirade, commenting darkly about sinister 'reprisals' made by the BBC and Arts Council on composers who dared to stand up against them:

> I am speaking very much for the senior composers, many of whom have knighthoods and other distinctions, and have to behave like English gentlemen when applying for financial help. There is, of course, this vexed Anglo-Saxon habit of glossing over matters concerning money!

He then moved back to the Mass, warning that it might well not be finished on time:

> The lack of financial support for me to write this composition has impeded work on it very much. I hope somehow the difficulties will be solved and that it will be possible for the work to be presented. At the moment I have serious doubts about it. Given the concentration that goes into it, one is receiving less than a bus conductor gets pro rata…

The work had only gone ahead, he said, because the Johnson Wax company had promised £2,000,[54] and the Royal Philharmonic Orchestra (whose President Malcolm had recently become) had lent £1,000.

The press reported the outburst widely and luridly. John Cruft, Music Director of the Arts Council, made a grumpy statement in response:

> I am sorry Malcolm Williamson did not discuss with me the things troubling him rather than astonishing a gathering in this building who had come to hear plans about the 250th Choirs Festival.[55]

It would have been better to let the matter drop, but that was not Malcolm's style. Asked if he had anything to say to Mr Cruft, he drew a deep breath:

> Mr Cruft's assumption that I starve and behave like a good little boy to protect the Arts Council's anonymity and at the same time write an enormous work is very unhelpful...[56]

For the moment, despite the unfortunate outburst, there was still a chance of a satisfactory outcome. Later that month he completed on time the BBC radio commission for *The House of Windsor*. He offered, indeed, more music than was needed, and, in his enthusiasm, created out of it an eight-minute Suite with short movements like 'Waltz of the Royal Princesses', 'Windsor at Dawn' and 'The Queen at Westminster'.[57] But this attractive Suite, though in due course published, was ignored by both the Palace and the musical world.

It is doubtful, of course, whether an immediate £5,000 grant from the Arts Council would have entirely solved his Jubilee year crises in a period which contained so much personal turbulence. In early May 1977, for example, he and Simon moved from Wimbledon (where, says Dr Gomez, he had run up 'an

---

54 The firm's ultimate contribution would be £3,500, including printing costs.

55 *Evening Standard*, 3 March 1977

56 *ibid.*

57 There were three programmes in the end, not four, broadcast in April and May.

enormous telephone bill'),[58] to rent a flat in the newly-built Ben Jonson House in London's Barbican. It seemed a sign of greater financial stability, and just prior to the move Malcolm had spent time on a health farm,[59] even though he was currently telling Peter that he was 'in drastic debt'. Most promisingly, after seven years without any film work, he had secured a contract for a project about which there was much optimism, *Watership Down*.[60] He wrote to Peter:

> There seems no end for the work I have to do for Jubilee Year, and the most that I can hope for is that by August the biggest jobs will be done. These include music for the film of *Watership Down*. Did you read the book? I didn't until I was asked to do the film and then it was something of a labour… The film of *Watership Down* is very beautiful and rather transforms the book. The allegorical aspects are emphasised. It's all done with animation and marvellous artwork. The voices are people like Zero Mostel and Ralph Richardson.[61]

Once settled in the new flat, Malcolm found himself only weeks away from the Liverpool performance of his pageant-opera, *The Valley and The Hill*. Most of the music had long since been sent up to Liverpool to be distributed among the city's junior schools, for, in a remarkable entertainment for the Queen, all 17,000 of the ten and eleven-year-olds in Liverpool and its surrounding districts were to participate in the singing. Nonetheless, there was still some orchestration to be done for the first and last of the eight sections of the pageant and, unfortunately, Malcolm was committed to his regular visit to the Holme Cultram Festival, where he and Elizabeth Lamb were giving a recital at Cartmel Priory (Williamson and Brahms) and he was also to direct a cassation, *The Terrain of the Kings*. Elizabeth Lamb has vivid memories of the occasion:

> Simon needed a break and didn't come, but told us the situation was so tense we were not to hide the drink! So Malcolm drank a lot! Indeed, he was somewhat the worse for wear at the recital and unfortunately the Dean found a bottle of spirits he had left on the vestry table. The Dean was so cross that Malcolm very nearly didn't do the second half of the programme![62]

These commitments over, Malcolm implored Elizabeth to let him stay on at her home in an attempt to solve his pageant-opera crisis. If he could work there for a week, from the 9th to 16th of June, he might yet complete the orchestrations before the day of the pageant, the 21st. Malcolm's love for drama was probably

---

58 May 2006. Dr Gomez worked at the Westminster Hospital. 'Malcolm used to come to see me in my flat in Weymouth Mews, just behind my practice in Harley Street. He would ring me and say he was in a pickle... He began coming to me well before he became Master of the Queen's Music. He saw little of Dolly during the later stages of the marriage; he used to unburden himself to me about her...'

59 Enton Hall, Guildford

60 A few years earlier, in the last period of constant creativity, Malcolm had written several film scores: *Crescendo* (1969), *The Horror of Frankenstein* (1969) and *Nothing But The Night* (1970).

61 25 February, 1977

62 September 2005

appeased by such brinkmanship, and he may well have derived much pleasure from playing on the anxieties of his hosts, thereby receiving their full attention:

> He would do no work until he had been to Mass! Then he would start on a regime of mint tea at regular intervals, which helped him concentrate. The dining-room table was fully extended and he had manuscript paper all over it. As he would finish one page my husband would take it to Oxenholme Station and someone would pick it up and take it on to Liverpool. In the evenings we would be up to 3 or 4 in the morning singing through each section to see whether it would work.

Part of the pageant-opera would be sung to live accompaniment, but most of it would be sung or mimed to pre-recorded tapes, played over a series of tannoy speakers. It is well documented that all the recorded material had been prepared months beforehand. He was clearly late with some of the orchestrations for live performance within the cathedrals, but, in 'singing through each section to see whether it would work', Malcolm would seem to be over-elaborating the drama.

Somehow Malcolm and Simon managed to fit in a rapid visit to Germany to see the premiere of his cantata *Les Olympiques* at the Ruhr Festival,[63] before they travelled up to Liverpool the day before the Queen's visit. The Master of the Queen's Music might have been expected to stay at one of the city's grander hotels, but instead he and Simon were put up, free of charge, at a girls' physical education college. The next morning they visited the scene of the pageant, the connecting route along Hope Street between the Catholic and Anglican Cathedrals. The area was already full of scaffolding and gathering crowds, bus upon bus disgorging excited children arriving for final rehearsals. By the time the pageant began in the middle of the afternoon, this small area was tightly packed with 30,000 people, over half of them participants.

A reporter from the *Liverpool Weekly News* recorded the scene at midday:

> Outside the Metropolitan Cathedral thousands of schoolchildren who had rehearsed for months danced excitedly in the sunshine under the abstracted gaze of teachers, determined to see that all went well. Inside, the blue cool of the Cathedral did nothing to dispel the rising tension as the great occasion neared. Those fortunate enough to get through the ranks of police and stewards could listen as the slowly filling cathedral thrilled to the sound of hundreds of schoolchildren's voices in last-minute rehearsal. 'That was absolutely marvellous!' said musical director and conductor Michael Bush. 'Let's do it again!'[64]

It was a case of glorious organised chaos, but fortunately there were plenty of glossy programmes on hand to lend some stability to proceedings. They contained a succinct account of what was about to happen:

---

63 The presence of the Master of the Queen's Music at the Ruhrfestspielhaus in Recklinghausen near Dusseldorf was all the more unusual as this summer festival had been established after the Second World War for a working class audience, bringing international theatre, music and dance to a heavily industrial region.

64 23 June 1977

> The Pageant is sung and danced by those very children on whom our hopes for the future are built. The Pageant lasts forty minutes and is a musical and dramatic interpretation of Psalm 23. It is conceived in four parts, representing Spring, Summer, Autumn and Winter. The over-riding colours for the scenery of the four parts are respectively green, red, gold and blue. Each of the scenes is acted and sung by the children from one Junior School in Liverpool together with a choir from a neighbouring Junior School. The eight scenes of the opera are linked by a Refrain sung by all the Junior School children lining the route between the two Cathedrals. The scenery in Hope Street and St James Road has been designed to suit the grand scale of this unique operatic performance.

St Cyril's School had the daunting task of starting off the pageant-opera inside the futuristic Catholic cathedral (just ten years old, like many of the children), singing and dancing through the first scene, accompanied by the Liverpool Youth Orchestra. Expectancy was raised by the Queen's late arrival – her car had been slowed by the large crowds thronging around it – and one over-excited school which started a loud chorus outside the Cathedral of 'You'll Never Walk Alone' was quickly silenced, yet, as the Queen and Prince Philip were ushered into the building by Archbishop Worlock, the cheering would not have disgraced Anfield. Inside, tumultuous applause greeted the royal arrival and, after the National Anthem and the Jubilee Hymn, the pageant (for which Malcolm had also written the text) commenced with 'In The Winter Barn', the cathedral suddenly full of hungry lambs and smiling shepherds. The shepherds begin:

> Each Winter we have promised Spring to the new-born lambs.
> Now once again their eyes are strong as the Spring returns.
> In Autumn all the barns were filled with a Winter's food.
> But now the food is all but gone yet the grass appears.

The shepherds (subdivided into three groups of parts) reassure the lambs that they will lead them out of the barn safely and sing a rousing anthem:

> Open wide the door of the barn.
> See the sunlight streaming.
> Open wide the door to the sun,
> See the green grass gleaming.
> Open wide the door on the world,
> See the Springtime flowers growing.
> See the mountains skip with joy,
> See the pleasant waters flowing.[65]

One quick recapitulation follows, before the sheep, with their guardian shepherds, begin their joyful yet dangerous journey through life.

The first part over, the royal party emerged from the Cathedral into the bright sunlight, Malcolm's music on the tannoys temporarily drowned by the cheering, as 'to scenes of unbridled joy a sunny Liverpool welcomes their monarch'.[66]

65 *The Valley and the Hill*, Campion Press, 1990

66 *Liverpool Weekly News*

The Queen and Prince Philip enjoying The Valley and the Hill *in the Catholic cathedral and along Hope Street, Liverpool*

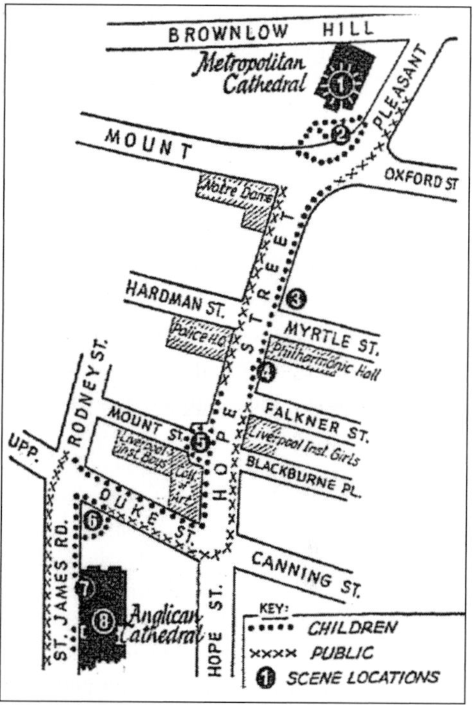

The royal route

Then came the big moment for many thousands of children. After an introductory fanfare it was time for all the sheep ranked en masse between the two cathedrals to sing the refrain:

> We shall fear no evil, we shall fear no evil.
> Though we pass through the Valley of the Shadow of Death, we shall fear no evil.

The refrain was then repeated, the better singers, as shepherds, offering a counter-melody.

The first of six outdoor scenes then unfolded on the grass verge outside the cathedral, Hunts Cross Primary School taking responsibility for ‘In the Spring Green Pastures’: the sheep, afraid of the natural landscape, are given confidence by the shepherds, who introduce them to friendly dogs and small birds. The shepherds afterwards direct the flocks onwards towards the summer lands and tell them not to be afraid.

The waiting thousands then lifted their voices again with 'We shall fear no evil!' as the Queen and Prince Philip travelled in an open Range Rover at the front of a small cavalcade down Hope Street. They stopped at the Liverpool Clinic car park, for the third section, 'Towards the Shadows': The spring pastures have become parched, the rivers dry. Losing courage, the dogs and small birds have gone on their way. The shepherds direct their flocks into the Summer lands, again urging them to have no fear.

The Queen and Prince Philip were driven onwards down Hope Street, passing the Philharmonic Hall before stopping for the fourth section, 'In The Valley of the Shadows', staged outside the Liverpool Design Centre. Here, in a scene both dramatic and amusing, eagles, vultures, scorpions, serpents and lizards threaten to kill the sheep, the singers being given opportunities to make suitably predatory noises.

> Scorpions lurk in the rocks.
> Serpents glide over the ground.
> High in the rock-face above
> Eagles and vultures abound,
> Waiting to devour us.
> Nowhere can safety be found.
> Lizards emerge from their holes.
> Vultures and eagles await,
> Anxious to devour us,
> Glaring with anger and hate…

The shepherds quickly save the sheep, reminding the predators at the same time that they too are God's creatures. Predators, shepherds and sheep join in a song of peace.

On again the Queen travelled, as flags, banners and handkerchiefs waved and massed children's voices raised the refrain 'We shall fear no evil'. The fifth section took place at the junction of Hope Street with Mount Street, where Paul McCartney's old school, Joseph Williams Primary, presented 'The Descent to the Harvest Plain': harvesters are at work, as the Shepherds and Sheep look down on the golden fields of Autumn. The sheep receive a good welcome and offer their fleeces in gratitude.

The sixth scene, 'At the Feasting Board', took place just round the corner of Mount Street, where Upper Duke Street crosses St James Road: The feasters are interrupted by sinister skeletal figures representing Death. As the sheep cower in terror the shepherds raise their rods and staffs high in the air and angels appear from above and stand between the figures of death and the sheep. The figures writhe and fall to the ground.

Finally, as 'We shall fear no evil' rose yet again to the clear blue skies in even greater volume, the Queen's cavalcade, with Malcolm and John Betjeman in cheerful attendance, reached Sir Giles Gilbert Scott's Anglican Cathedral, where under the towering Gothic entrance Bishop David Sheppard was waiting to greet them, before the children of Ranworth Square Junior School presented 'At The

Foot of the Night Mountain' on the steps, the shepherds helping the sheep, harvesters, dogs and small birds up a stony mountainside.

Inside the Cathedral the mountain-climbers discover that they are beyond the sun and the moon, and have entered the House of the Lord. In a masterly finale Malcolm incorporates his own setting of 'Lead Kindly Light' and the pageant comes to a rousing conclusion with a two-part version of 'Open Wide the Gates of the Sky'. After some appropriate words from Bishop David Sheppard and another rendition of the National Anthem and the Jubilee Hymn, the Queen and Prince Philip left the Cathedral to the sound of its pealing bells.

After it was all over, Malcolm and Simon met friends for a drink, one of whom was violinist Brian Brown:

> As we entered the pub Malcolm said to me 'Name any spirits and mix them in one glass!' He had a number of these lethal concoctions, despite the fact that later that evening he was meeting the Queen at a reception on the Royal Yacht Britannia. But then he had this remarkable ability to sound fairly sober even when he was drunk![67]

The pageant had been the most enormous success.[68] The next day, interviewed by the *Liverpool Daily Post*, Malcolm was full of gratitude:

> It was a superb performance. I could not believe the precision of it all and the quality of the organisation. I was also astonished by all the outdoor scenery. The Queen indicated to me last night during the reception how pleased she had been by the performance.[69]

It had all ultimately depended, of course, on huge commitment from large numbers of music teachers in the participating schools, as well as the far-sighted Merseyside education authority, and, above all, Michael Bush, who as Assistant Music Adviser to the Liverpool Education Committee had supervised and cajoled for months beforehand. But the grandiose concept which had provided the Queen with such an original Jubilee experience was Malcolm's. Its triumph was a vindication of his musical judgement, and, indeed, of his royal appointment.[70]

---

67 July 2005

68 In distinct contrast to the very genuine mass enthusiasm displayed in Liverpool for the royal visit, the media sometimes favoured a more detached view. *The Times*, for example, in reporting the Liverpool pageant, gave it the headline 'Pageant For the Queen on Edge of Slum Site'. Penny Symon's report gave as much coverage to the slums as the pageant: 'As the Queen watched a musical pageant in Hope Street, Liverpool, she could also have seen, if she had glanced to the left, one of the city's most derelict and neglected areas...'

69 23 June 1977

70 *The Valley and the Hill* does not need such elaborate treatment. It can be staged very simply, working equally well in a confined area. It is particularly relevant in a multicultural society. As Malcolm explained in a production note: 'The psalm was chosen as a basis since it is in the Jewish, Christian and Islamic traditions. It may also be seen as part of the heritage of the spiritually uncommitted. The allegorical character of the psalm places it outside remembered time which means, in practical terms, that we can legitimately juxtapose Bedouin shepherds, French grape-treaders, African, Dutch or Indian harvesters, and Australian sheep-shearers, for example...'

The success of the Liverpool Pageant unfortunately did not translate itself into effective work towards the urgently needed completion of the Mass of Christ The King, now only two months away. Malcolm had made a bad misjudgement. The drama of the situation was this time more than he required. Larry Smith, his American friend who happened to be over in England, did his best to help in the growing crisis:

> I was often in the Barbican flat when he was trying to get the Mass finished – it was a time of total desperation. I helped him orchestrate it, even writing the notes sometimes – though Malcolm would tell me which ones! It was not an easy time. Malcolm was a very complicated person to deal with – so needy and yet so difficult.[71]

There was no problem with the vocal score. But there was a serious lack of orchestrations. The Mass had been conceived on a large scale, lasting for well over an hour, its sixteen movements contained in five sections: the Introductory Rite, the Liturgy of the Word, the Liturgy of the Eucharist, The Rite of Communion and the Concluding Rite. When the conductor John Sanders called a Royal Philharmonic orchestral rehearsal in London, he was shocked to discover that he could not even make a beginning as no parts had arrived. Instead, therefore, he began rehearsals of *The Dream of Gerontius*, and half-way through this rehearsal Simon arrived with about two-thirds of the work.

During the next few days extra sheets of music were sent piecemeal by train to Gloucester. Malcolm himself arrived on the day of the performance to deliver additional sheets, before hiding himself away in a feverish attempt to write more. Donald Hunt recalls finding Malcolm smoking furiously 'in the Monks Lavatorium area of the cloisters', orchestrating and writing out parts:

> Of course he didn't get it finished and was in quite a state over it. He was drinking too. He was obviously feeling very guilty.[72]

John Sanders called an extra, eleventh-hour rehearsal, during which extra pieces of manuscript were rushed in by Simon. Half-way through John Sanders, a mild man, decided enough was enough. They would tolerate no more late additions, but perform only what they had rehearsed satisfactorily. This meant the total exclusion of the three of the sixteen movements, the Gloria, the Psalmus Responsorius (The Lord is my shepherd) and the Credo.[73] The Agnus Dei, dedicated with the Queen's permission to Benjamin Britten, was performed with organ accompaniment.

On hearing this decision Malcolm went berserk. There was a noisy incident shortly afterwards outside the Cathedral when Malcolm told anyone who cared to listen that there would be no performance at all! He was not prepared to have

71 August 2005

72 June 2006

73 Malcolm's distress at the missing sections was understandable in that his setting of 'Dominus Me Pascit' (The Lord is my Shepherd), as later completed, is one of the very finest sections of the work. The Credo too is an emotional centre-piece.

his music performed in the format suggested by John Sanders! Physically restrained, he was led away and heavily sedated. But he had recovered sufficiently to take a bow at the end of the work, ashen-faced, drawn and dishevelled, a cigarette hanging from his lips.

April Cantelo, one of the four original soloists, remembers greatly enjoying singing the Mass, despite all the panic surrounding it:

> The sound in the cathedral was wonderful and the sections which were completed – the vast majority of the work – went very well indeed. I had friends there in the audience who knew nothing of the problems and really enjoyed it. We all felt so sorry for Malcolm, who looked terribly ill.[74]

The critics too were favourable. William Mann wrote in *The Times*:

> It would be idle to assess Mass of Christ The King until it is performed complete. I can only assure those readers who spurn Williamson's simplistic music (its invention all the stronger because it has to be instantly performable) that the new mass is an elaborate composition, grand and often surprising, for all that the choral music draws on ecclesiastical traditions, especially on plainsong. It makes a jubilant and variegated noise, approachable yet demanding concentration… The solo vocal music, such as we heard of it, gave uplifting scope to April Cantelo's easy, pure high tones and Philip Langridge's fluent mellifluous tenor. Loris Synan displayed an impressive high mezzo register. The bass part was ably taken by Geoffrey Chard.[75]

Nonetheless damage had been done. In the media, celebrity-baiting was now a matter of course. The Queen herself in her Silver Jubilee year was mocked by the Sex Pistols, whose derisive 'God Save The Queen' quickly became the country's best-selling record. Her Master of Music's failures were widely lampooned, one BBC 'satirist', for example, announcing, 'And now, ladies and gentlemen, we are proud to introduce a new composition by Malcolm Williamson, Master of the Queen's Music'. Just one single note followed. Malcolm had just created a Kyrie of surpassing beauty; a Sanctus and Benedictus infused with supreme rhythmic passion; a *Pater Noster* of such melodic delicacy that few listeners were not deeply moved. But all that counted for nothing in a Britain which looked upon people's misfortunes as material for mass entertainment.

There were now just three months before the premiere of the 'Jubilee' 4th Symphony, but still Malcolm found himself impeded by all manner of other things. He had, for example, promised a new work for some of his Moreton Morell friends who ran a semi-professional orchestra, the Beauchamp Sinfonietta, of which he was President. In mid-October the orchestra had been engaged to play in St Edith's Church, Monks Kirby (near Rugby) which was celebrating its nine hundredth anniversary. Larry Smith was coming over from America to conduct a work of his own which he had dedicated to Malcolm.[76] The

---

74 April 2005

75 27 August 1977

76 *Apogees for String Orchestra*. Smith, still only in his early twenties, was grateful to Malcolm for having helped him with it in New York the previous autumn.

second half of the programme Malcolm had promised to conduct, as it would contain a 'new' short work, *Concertante for Organ and Strings*.[77] Simon was scheduled as the organist, and would also be playing a Handel concerto. However, at the last minute both Malcolm and Simon withdrew, Larry Smith conducting the premiere instead, for by that time the Jubilee Symphony was in a state of crisis.

A four-movement symphony, lasting around twenty minutes and based on the key of E (for Elizabeth), had been promised for the Queen's concert on 8 December, with four further performances scheduled by the LPO under Bernard Haitink. All four movements were titled – The Dawn of the World (*largo*); Eagles (*allegro vivo*); The Prayer of the Waters (*lento*); The Throne of the Rock – but by mid-October the Oxford University Press, who were to publish the work, had received nothing. Word began to seep out that there were problems, and at the end of October, when *The Times* featured NEW JUBILEE SYMPHONY IS NOT READY as a headline on its front page, Malcolm made the brave announcement that 'there was every danger in the world that it will not be completed'. The third of four movements was 'ready to go off' and the first, he said, would be ready in a week.[78]

The third movement finally arrived at OUP on 7 November, a month before the concert, by which time Malcolm and Simon had taken themselves off to the Camargue in the hope of a better working atmosphere than at the Barbican. The fourth movement arrived at OUP on 22 November (sixteen days before the concert) and the second movement on the 29th, just nine days before. Of 'The Dawn of the World' there was no sign, and preparations began to be made to play just the three movements. A week before the concert *The Times* informed its readers:

> The new symphony has not been completed in time for its premiere before the Queen at the Royal Festival Hall this Thursday and only three of the four movements will be performed in the concert. Mr Williamson explained yesterday that although he had planned his Symphony No 4 as an 18-minute work, it had grown under his hands until it had become 'an enormous work' lasting more than half an hour. He has been staying in the Camargue, working with little sleep to complete the work, but the orchestration of the first movement has not been finished. The London Philharmonic Orchestra will see the score for the first time today and rehearse the work under Bernard Haitink each day until the concert.[79]

These rehearsals, however, did not occur, because of a lack of orchestral parts. On 3 December, five days before the concert, Robin Langley of OUP was

[77] It was not a new work, but a re-working of an old piece. A year later, when Larry Smith was married at St Margaret's Westminster, it was played at the wedding, this time under the title of Ochre, with Simon playing the organ part. (2 September 1978)

[78] 'First' was possibly written in error for 'second', since the first was incomplete on the date of the concert.

[79] Martin Huckerby, December 1977

casting around in all possible directions for copyists, and attempting meanwhile to placate an extremely anxious conductor concerning the first rehearsal, planned for just two days before the concert:

> Dear Mr Haitink,
>
> I realise that your patience and goodwill have been sorely tried, as have ours, over this matter, but I may assure you that we will do everything in our powers to ensure the accuracy of the orchestral parts. We will undertake to keep the composer away from the Tuesday rehearsal as requested. I look forward to meeting you on Tuesday when we will have a full staff on hand to deal quickly and efficiently with any difficulties which may arise.

Alas for the OUP's brave efforts, Haitink rehearsed the three movements of the Jubilee Symphony on the Tuesday for just twenty minutes before deciding to remove it from the concert. The next day news broke of the Symphony's withdrawal:

> PREMIERE OF UNFINISHED SYMPHONY CANCELLED
>
> The saga of Malcolm Williamson's Jubilee symphony has finally ended, at least temporarily, with an announcement yesterday that its premiere tomorrow night has been cancelled. Although only three of the four movements have been completed, Mr Williamson said on Monday that those three parts would be given at the premiere before the Queen and the Duke of Edinburgh. However, he changed his mind overnight and announced yesterday that it would be improper to perform only part of it.
>
> The London Philharmonic Orchestra received the score only yesterday, but a representative of the LPO said the reason for the cancellation was not that the players were unable to learn the work in time; it was the composer's decision…
>
> The Queen is still to attend the concert tomorrow night, despite the demise of the symphony. Instead of Mr Williamson's work she will hear Elgar's *Cockaigne – In London Town*.[80]

A statement was issued by the London Philharmonic management that Malcolm had felt it would be improper for the work to be performed until it could stand as a whole.

> Both Mr Haitink and the orchestra are very disappointed by this decision. They wanted to perform the work and the time was right for it. It was something of a challenge.

Eric Bravington, the LPO's managing director, was quoted as saying that in his thirty-eight years' association with the orchestra no commissioned work had previously failed to appear on time.

On the day of the concert *The Times* sent their reporter along to the Barbican to interview Malcolm, whose fulsome apology was published under the heading of

MASTER OF THE QUEEN'S MUSIC BLAMES WORK PRESSURE FOR FAILURE TO FINISH SYMPHONY

80 *The Times*, 7 December 1977

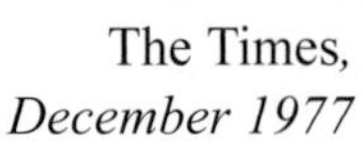

The Times,
December 1977

‘Currying favour with the Royals again I see, Malcolm...’
WILLIAMSON JUBILEE SYMPHONY CUT
Marc

Malcolm refused to speak of his decision to cancel the symphony, which increases speculation that the cancellation was forced upon him after Haitink gave up on the work in rehearsal. Christopher Austin, who discussed the symphony with Malcolm several years afterwards, certainly believes that this was the case:

> Malcolm told me that when Bernard Haitink made a decision not to conduct it, he was given a choice. Either the LPO would announce that the conductor had refused to conduct the work, or he, Malcolm, could say that he wished to withdraw it, to add a further movement...[81]

While the media revelled in Malcolm's misfortune, other composers staunchly refused to give them further lurid copy. Michael Tippett declared that he had once missed a deadline by a whole year; Nicholas Maw said he had been working for three years already on a LSO commission and it would not be finished for another two years. ‘In a large work there might be as many as 900 sheets of manuscript paper to fill,’ declared Stephen Oliver, ‘and we're still using the same notation system as in 1550. It's like copying out a Dickens novel in

[81] 6 May 2005

long-hand…' But nothing much helped. The probing into Malcolm's failure was merciless. Reporters went rushing round to the Barbican:

> Even though the Queen will not get to hear Malcolm Williamson's unfinished symphony tonight the composer was still trying to complete it this morning. 'I'm at my desk working,' he told me from his London home, 'that is my job.'[82]

Malcolm and Simon left England just as soon as they could. Mario Bois had offered them sanctuary at his country home south of Paris and from there, shortly before Christmas, Malcolm let the press know that he was planning a year's sabbatical. He would complete the two royal works before the spring, after which he would undertake no further commissions for a considerable while. The subsequent headline

Mr MALCOLM WILLIAMSON TO TAKE SABBATICAL NEXT YEAR

further damaged him. It was, in a way, an admission of failure and inhibited future commissions. The Master of the Queen's Music, after only two years in the job, would be forced more and more to look abroad for work.

The public relations disasters of 1977 were largely avoidable. The biggest damage at Gloucester was not the exclusion of three items from a long work, which would have caused no great stir, but the unintentional comedy which Malcolm and Simon provided as they rushed around delivering extra pieces of manuscript in the forlorn attempt to save the situation. Malcolm's drunken tirade outside the cathedral would not have taken place if, weeks before the concert, a calm decision had been made as to which sections would not be available. The dithering right up to the moment of performance was disastrous. Simon could hardly be blamed for his inability to head off the catastrophe; even Dolly would have struggled in the alcohol-inflamed situation. The only people capable of preventing the debacle, the Festival authorities, for the best of motives forbore to make the decision which might have minimised the adverse publicity.

Damaging as events surrounding the Mass were, it was the non-appearance of the Jubilee Symphony which caused Malcolm's career irreversible damage in Britain. Although he himself had publicly declared many months before the concert that the work was unlikely to be finished, no cut-off date was ever mooted nor were there any alternative arrangements until the very last minute. It is hard to understand why.

It is clear from Eric Bravington's curt comments that the London Philharmonic management felt hugely let down, and understandably so. Without Malcolm's Jubilee Symphony their concert in honour of the Queen suddenly looked silly, their Brahms and Rachmaninoff offering nothing other than an uncomfortable reference to the Queen's distant kinship with those not wholly satisfactory Kaisers and Tsars. The orchestra *needed* the Jubilee Symphony which it had funded. Moreover, its Dutch conductor had just been knighted for

82 Londoner's Diary, *Evening Standard*, 8 December 1977

all he had done to bring the orchestra up amongst the finest in the world. Their reciprocal gesture of thanks had been badly sabotaged by Malcolm's inability to meet a very generous deadline. Unsurprisingly, the orchestra was subsequently to take no notice at all of Malcolm's three-movement Jubilee Symphony when later published. It was too painful a reminder of a very public embarrassment.

The Jubilee Symphony fiasco took away much of Malcolm's confidence and reputation for good. It was such a very public humiliation, with so little sympathy or understanding. When a composer has serious problems and cannot complete a work on schedule, he needs support not vilification.

14 COMPOSING IN CONCRETE

The Barbican, 1977–81

THE FLAT IN BEN JONSON HOUSE in the Barbican had been acquired in a mood of much optimism in May 1977, with the major events of the Jubilee year still to unfold. Malcolm had been awarded a CBE in 1976. A successful Jubilee Symphony might result in a knighthood, coming in the immediate wake of the Jubilee Hymn, *The Valley and the Hill* and an organ tribute to Britten, *Lion of Suffolk*. It had seemed a good time, therefore, to move out of the flat in Wimbledon into something more appropriate to a Master of the Queen's Music.

The redevelopment of the Barbican had been going on for fifteen years. By 1977 several of its residential towers were in use, but the Barbican Centre itself was merely a building site waiting to be transformed into the largest arts complex in Europe, its amenities to include a 2,000-seat concert hall for a resident orchestra. By moving into the Barbican, Malcolm and Simon were staking a useful early claim in Britain's boldest musical development since the Festival Hall, hoping that in the fullness of time Malcolm might turn into the Barbican's composer-in-residence. The worryingly expensive rent was the only drawback, but there were local schools where, if necessary, Simon could find employment.

Ben Jonson House had been completed in 1973. It was the longest block in the Barbican, on its northern edge, a low-rise building with only seven residential floors. The flat was on three different levels, the central floor being open-plan, with views to Finsbury to the north and the Barbican Centre site to the south. Few who visited the flat, painted throughout in an insipid green, remembered it with much affection. It was 'new but sterile, its only virtue being its brightness'; and 'as empty of food as of furniture, mainly characterised by the many piles of music'.[1] Malcolm, however, had convinced himself that he would find inspiration there. In the course of one interview he commented:

[1] Larry Smith and Valerie Thurston (2006)

> It is the ideal place to compose. I compose in concrete. I need it. I work on 14 trestle tables near the light, the rain and the wind and it is delicious.[2]

Initially Malcolm spent only limited time in the Barbican. In the immediate crisis over the completion of the 4th Symphony, he had taken refuge in France, a country in which he always felt comfortable and where, he believed, there was greater tolerance towards homosexuality. (In France, he once suggested to Tammy, being gay had never had the same stigma as in London. He cited Oscar Wilde as a case in point, living out his final years there.)[3] Malcolm was lucky to be able to recover from the Jubilee traumas in Mario Bois' chateau in the village of Montceaux-les-Provins, south of Paris. From there, after a long period of silence, he resumed contact with Bessie:

> I've been living in France since October with a brief and disastrous fortnight back in London when the horror of Bernard Haitink and my Fourth Symphony occurred. He did not even bother to rehearse the three existing movements properly; it was clearly beyond him.[4] It all hit national headlines, some favourable, others not. Of course the Australian press minced me as I have learned to expect. At the height of the barrage Dolly got me by phone and lammed into me once more. Lizzie Lutyens also. The gutter press broke the Barbican security twice, and were held at bay by Simon.[5]

Malcolm and Simon had spent Christmas at Montceaux together with the whole Bois family, and on New Year's Eve, so Malcolm related to Bessie, he and Simon had talked over the past year, keeping up their morale by reminiscing over the successes: the Queen's delight with the Jubilee Hymn and the Liverpool children's pageant-opera; the good reviews of the Mass of Christ The King; Malcolm's reception by Cardinal Hume at a concert in Westminster Cathedral; conducting the Royal Philharmonic Orchestra at the Banqueting Hall, Whitehall, in the presence of the Kents; the opportunity to play the Organ Concerto again at the Proms with Adrian Boult (now eighty-nine), and its fine reception; the performance by Kerstin Meyer, the Swedish mezzo-soprano, of *Les Olympiques* at the Festival of the Ruhr; his six talks on radio on the history of the Master of the Queen's Music;[6] EMI's announcement of a double LP of some of his most significant works; and the continued rise of his royalty income from an increased number of broadcasts.

Later that January, while Simon returned 'to attend to things in London', Malcolm stayed on in the comfortable chateau. 'Isolated from the world, I work

---

2 *Daily Telegraph*, 29 April 1978

3 25 March 1980

4 This is grossly unfair to Haitink, unable to hold his first rehearsal until two days before the scheduled performance.

5 10 January 1978

6 The recordings were made at the Golders Green Hippodrome between July and September 1977, the busiest time of the Jubilee year, Malcolm making several cancellations because of illness. Simon wrote to the BBC (30 September) thanking them for their infinite patience and courtesy shortly before the programmes were broadcast.

like a demon'.[7] He was writing what turned out to be his one work of 1978, a short orchestral piece called *Fiesta*, and two months later he was in Geneva for its first performance, his only disappointment that money was too tight for Simon to be with him, for, as he told Bessie, Simon had been very involved in its orchestration. It is clear from this letter that the fiasco of the Jubilee Symphony still weighed heavily on him:

> I've had five days here – my first time in Switzerland since 1950. It's incredibly expensive. I'm the guest of the gramophone companies[8] in this luxurious hotel as the Orchestre de la Suisse Romande gave the premiere last night of my new piece *Fiesta*. It was a terrific success. Perhaps one day the Australian press will register things of mine that succeed, and not invent lies and make a meal of the things that don't. However I am happier to have the support of Her Majesty than that of the Covells and Prerauers of this world...[9]

Malcolm always accentuated the positive when writing to his mother, and *Fiesta*, in fact, was one of his least successful efforts, the carnival spirit undercut by dissonance, a repetitive dance tune struggling ineffectively to shake off the glum serial writing, the oppressive atmosphere reflecting the great difficulty he had in completing the nine-minute work. He was still suffering from post-Jubilee trauma, and later, back in the Barbican, he was incapable of completing the film score for *Watership Down*, which, after much acrimony and recrimination, was largely written by others.[10] Simon had done his best, fending off producers and copying out neat versions from Malcolm's untidy manuscript, but it was not enough. The creative spark was not there. Interviewed on television, Malcolm gave some insight into his current feelings:

> Writing a piece of music is like an enormous physical weight on your shoulders. And then, when you've finished, the spring, which has been winding tighter and tighter inside you, suddenly goes whoosh! As a composer, you open up the door of memory. If the music simply isn't coming, you can be a very irritating person to be near. If the music begins to pour out, I find myself still being very irritable, until I can get the first sketches down... There's such a hurry to get the music down on to the score paper that, if the pen goes dry and you have to spend precious time refilling it, you can get into a frenzy...[11]

---

7 MW to Bessie Williamson, 10 January 1978

8 *Fiesta* was commissioned by the International Federation of Producers of Phonograms and Videograms, celebrating a hundred years of recorded sound; it was premiered by Wolfgang Sawallisch at the Victoria Hall on 14 March 1978.

9 From the Hotel des Bergues, Geneva, 15 March 1978

10 Malcolm only managed the Prologue and Main Theme. Most of the score was written by Angela Morley. Mike Batt and Art Garfunkel provided the very popular 'Bright Eyes'.

11 From an interview on ITV with the well-known Canadian chat-show host, Elaine Grand, March 1978. The programme included recent film of scenes from *The Red Sea*, well presented by the Trinity School, Croydon.

After probing questions about the Jubilee year, he was asked whether it was true he had actually said that he would rather be somebody other than Malcolm Williamson. Yes, he replied, it certainly was:

> I'd like to have these weights off my back. I'd like to be a beachcomber. And not to be writing music. Anything's better.

It was a striking admission for someone who, only two years earlier, had taken over his royal post with such enthusiasm.

It partly reflected the way he was being hounded by the media. Every time, it seemed, a work of his was performed, his personal life was also mentioned. At the time of the premiere of *Fiesta*, for example, the *Daily Mail*, under a jokey headline of UNFURNISHED SYMPHONY IN A FLAT, tried hard to embarrass him:

> The touchy Australian Malcolm Williamson, balding Master of the Queen's Music, has moved into a spacious flat in the Barbican, leaving his Battersea[12] home to his wife of 18 years and their three children. On the prospect of divorce his wife Dolores says: 'I don't want to talk about it just now.' Recently in trouble for failing to complete work in time for musical deadlines, Williamson is now nursed through his creative traumas by his youthful personal assistant Simon Campion, who also lives in the Barbican…[13]

A little later, under the heading A HARMONIOUS COLLABORATION, the same reporter went further, no doubt savouring words like 'organ' and 'stimulate':

> Brought together by their passion for the organ, Malcolm Williamson, Master of the Queen's Music, is forging a rewarding association with younger fellow Aussie musician Simon Campion. Following the separation from his wife Dolores, Williamson has been stimulated by the presence of Campion, whose virtuosity on the Melbourne Cathedral organ (1972-75) prior to his emigration to Britain is fondly recalled. Now they work together from a flat in the Barbican, where Malcolm tells me 'Simon looks after my musical affairs'…[14]

It was no wonder that Malcolm, as the media's whipping-boy, wanted to give up the writing of music and become somebody else. Interviewed by the more sympathetic Ann Morrow, the *Daily Telegraph*'s Royal correspondent, he was quite open about his current 'sabbatical' away from composition:

> The paralysing inability to complete the Jubilee Symphony had been sheer hell.. 'I would be poised in that moment between the brain conceiving and the notes going down on paper and the phone would ring asking me to judge a brass band competition. I thought it was my ruin… I thought indeed that I was finished'. He is now on a year's sabbatical, mainly spent in France drinking camomile tea '*pour les heures calmes*'. During his difficulties he went to Lourdes, and ever since he has worn two medals round his neck.[15]

---

12 Facts were again less important than innuendo.

13 20 March 1978

14 8 August 1978

15 'The Music Master', 29 April 1978

This time Malcolm expressed a different alternative to composition. Instead of being a beachcomber, he would like to find a post in an English department of an Australian university where he could 'talk about his favourite poets and novelists'.

Malcolm's detailed study of a select group of French writers like Gide, Proust and de Montherlant was all part of the important process of coming to terms with himself and what had happened to him since the official break-up of his marriage three years earlier. His current preoccupation was André Gide, who, significantly, had left his wife in middle-age for a 16-year-old boy,[16] the two embarking on a long pilgrimage together lasting up to Gide's death. In his novels Gide is much concerned with the concept of personal freedom, particularly as it relates to the world's moral and puritanical restraints. How best to be fully oneself? How best to be true to one's own sexual nature, without betraying one's sense of values?

Malcolm was also fascinated by Gide's exploration of what does, and does not, represent Christian love. In the *Symphonie Pastorale*, for example, which Malcolm had re-read several times, a Swiss Protestant minister falls in love with a blind girl, just fifteen years old, and wrestles with the rights and wrongs of his situation. Should true love, outside marriage, be condemned? It depended, suggested Malcolm to Tammy, on which version of 'Christianity' one followed:

> Christ himself never particularised one type of love; not only did he not condemn illicit love, but he condemned condemnation. It was S. Paul in the *Epistle to the Romans* who renewed the Judaic moral code for Christians and condemned adultery and homosexuality and so on. The unhappy pastor in the *Symphonie Pastorale* tries to cling to Christ and bypass S. Paul.... The problem is that you cannot, in the Christian context, divide the Bible...

Malcolm's current 'sabbatical' gave him less incentive for staying sober, for when he was working he always kept clear of alcohol. Yet even in 1978, when bouts of drinking proliferated, his letters to his mother still recounted periods of sobriety when he would take daily swims and even sometimes visit a gym for a workout. At such times he was at his most engaging, as the writer Ann Morrow had discovered:

> Lunch at a grill near Smithfield was the composer's choice. Wondering what it would have been like meeting Handel or Vivaldi, I was unprepared for the first sight of the Master of the Queen's Music. A small, tousled fair-headed figure in sneakers, bare-chested and eyes brimming with chlorine after a swim, he opened the taxi door and asked if I had enough money. His charm is enormous. He has a deceptive diffidence and a sharp wit... He says he tends to do things in excess. He smoked endlessly and during lunch drank Perrier, refusing anything stronger...[17]

On his bad days he presented a very different persona. Stories of excessive drinking abound. Weinberger's Martin Dales was a regular visitor to the Barbican flat during this period:

> Malcolm and Simon were always hospitable and sociable – and very generous with the gin. But Malcolm was extremely temperamental, to put it mildly. I remember being at a recording session at the Maida Vale studios[18] when Malcolm was so

[16] Marc Allegret, the future film director

[17] *Daily Telegraph*, 29 April 1978

[18] *In Place of Belief*, Studio 2, 12 July 1978.

> distraught he was throwing piano stools all over the place! 'Oh fucking hell, I want to re-write this!' and so forth...[19]

Drink led to him performing uncharacteristically erratically, misled by the belief that a bottle of brandy would always sober him up. On one occasion, having started an organ recital poorly, he startled his audience by stopping and announcing, 'I played that rather badly! I'll play it again!'[20] When an old Australian friend, Ken Healey, called in at the Barbican and mentioned in conversation that Father Augustine Watson, Malcolm's confidant in Canberra, had just died, Malcolm rushed out of the flat, bought three bottles of vodka, and drank them all. Mario Bois remembers an evening in Paris when he and his wife were talking with Malcolm into the early hours and drinking cognac. At two in the morning they left him downstairs, promising he would drink no more. Next morning not only had he finished the bottle of cognac, but a second one too.

His friends tried hard to help him. Gerald Kingsley, who for several years looked after his interests at Weinberger's, invited Malcolm to join his wife and children on a weekend break to Alfriston, in an effort to sober him up. At first Malcolm seemed in good form, his usual provocative self:

> We stopped for some tea on the way down. The restaurant had some innocuous background music playing and Malcolm at once imperiously summoned the manager. 'I'm a composer,' he said, 'I insist that the music's turned off!' They turned it up louder.[21]

At Alfriston all went well. Malcolm was immaculately behaved. But just before it was time to leave the hotel, it was noticed he was missing:

> I went to his room. He wouldn't answer the door. Eventually I had it opened. And there he was, lying on the floor with a bottle. He said he'd met somebody in the bar who'd never heard of his music... He always blamed other people... Things were never his fault...

Malcolm's shrewd understanding of human nature didn't help him. He saw all too clearly that the deep affection he felt for his children was mocked by his withdrawal from their daily life, and, however much he pretended otherwise, however much he intellectualised with the help of Gide, he was all too aware of his betraying them at a most important period in their lives. These feelings were all the more acute at times when, to his great anger, public interest in his divorce led to their names being paraded in the newspapers. When the Mass of Christ The King was given its first complete performance in a high-profile London concert, the *Daily Mail* used his impending divorce as an opportunity to express his relationship with Simon more bluntly, regardless of the children:

---

19 Martin Dales had the job of helping along the Mass of Christ The King. 'It was a nightmare. I was for ever on the telephone. It did absolutely no good!'

20 The story is told by Christopher Morris, briefly his publisher at OUP.

21 February 2005

> IF MUSIC BE THE FOOD OF DIVORCE
>
> Good news and bad news for Malcolm Williamson, Master of the Queen's Music – his Mass of Christ the King will at last be performed complete and his wife, Dolores, is divorcing him after 18 years. Since the Spring Malcolm has been sharing a Barbican flat with organist Simon Campion, while his American wife has remained at the family Battersea home with their children – Peter, 17, Tamara 16 and 13-year-old Clare.[22]

Three days after this appeared, Malcolm was writing to Peter, distractedly jumping from topic to topic:

> I have been going dotty with various things including flu... Losing Grandma[23] is still something I'm not yet recovered from and, over and above everything, hits me afresh many times a day. In short, I've been fighting to keep on top, and all I ask is for your tolerance and understanding about lack of mail. I think of you constantly, miss you perpetually, and wait daily for that dreadful scrawl of yours to come flying through the mail slot…
>
> We went to a party at Nicole's last Saturday, and the memory I carried away with me was of their amazed, staring faces as they caught sight of me actually dancing to rock with a suave Frenchman with one tooth missing…
>
> I've resigned from the AMA as two years on a committee is enough. Am taking a few days off next month to go first on a three-day Good Food Guide inspection tour in Suffolk…
>
> Bessie, your grandmother that is, is at this very moment winging her way in this direction. Duck everybody! She apparently is going to Holland (more diamonds?), then to Norfolk (lucky everybody) and presumably hits London in good time for Daddy's Mass of Christ the King, completed praise be…[24]

Bessie's impending arrival was something both to please and alarm Malcolm. That August he had written to her from the Barbican:

> Dear Bessie Wum,
>
> How are you? I've just spoken to Marion and learned that you have booked to come here for several months which is marvellous. You can of course stay here if you wish. It's not too bad and is very central. Simon and I are going on a cruise to earn some money and have a holiday free on the QE2, the 21st/29th October, so the apt. is yours for that time, apart from your being here with us when you want... There is so much work to do and so little cash. Simon has been like a right arm and works 25 hours a day for my music. All the more reason for a holiday in October![25]

It was hardly the warm response Bessie had anticipated, as she soon made clear. A month later, therefore, the cruise cancelled, Malcolm made amends:

---

22 10 October 1978

23 'You will be sad to know,' he wrote to Bessie, 'that Dolly's mother, Mrs Daniel, died in a New York Hospital on August 15th. She was ill for about a month and Dolly and the children were in New York seeing her daily for the last two weeks...' (14 September 1978)

24 13 October 1978

25 19 August 1978

> It will be wonderful to see you here. I cannot have made it clear that you are welcome in London whenever you want… For goodness' sake, stay here whenever you like…[26]

It was ominously foggy as Bessie flew in to Norwich from Frankfurt on 25 October, to stay with Marion and her family at Overstrand, on the Norfolk coast near Cromer. Malcolm dutifully travelled up for a couple of days, and a week later they were all down in London where, at Westminster Cathedral, his Mass of Christ The King was given its first complete performance.[27] The day was made perfect for both Bessie and Malcolm by the Queen Mother's presence.

Bessie stayed on afterwards in Ben Jonson House, which speedily led to rising tensions. On one occasion a heated exchange resulted in her sweeping out of the sitting-room and settling down on the stairs to complete her knitting. Marion writes:

> When the usual 'honeymoon period' was over, and Bessie was no longer giving Malcolm the attention he wanted, they were soon arguing, as Bessie tried to tell Malcolm how to run his life, which he didn't like. Mother never accepted Simon and felt that Malcolm should have gone back to Dolly. Anyway, things got worse and worse that visit and on 18 November Malcolm was rushed into hospital, having taken an overdose of mother's pills.[28]

He survived, and Bessie returned to Norfolk, while Malcolm and Simon visited Lourdes. 'I feel miraculously better as a result of taking the waters,' he reported to her. In early December he was back in London, but gently making it clear to his mother that a further visit from her would be inappropriate:

> We returned to find the heating in the apartment broken and the phone cut off. We are still trying to get these things rectified. Glad that you are not here to suffer the cold![29]

Diane also arrived in Norfolk in mid-December and Malcolm was expected to join the family gathering on Christmas Eve (though Simon would be staying with his cousins). Much to everyone's disappointment, however, Malcolm failed to appear, and Bessie did not see him again before her flight back to Australia in mid-January. Bessie had been contemplating a permanent move to England, but Marion's imminent return to Australia and Malcolm's unpredictability dissuaded her.

Several months after Bessie's departure, Malcolm's long 'sabbatical' came to an end and, in April 1979, he began a period of renewed creativity, working for a year with the same kind of relentless application which had characterised his life in the 1960s. Significantly this reappearance of his former self began at a time of reassurance about his children, the same month in which he informed Bessie proudly:

---

26 14 September 1978

27 3 November 1978, with the Three Choirs Festival Chorus and the Royal Philharmonic Orchestra conducted by Charles Groves.

28 November 2006

29 5 December 1978

> I lunched with Tammy last week, and she looks gorgeous. She's doing French, German, Latin & Russian and seems to have a great gift for languages. I'm lunching with Clare on Tuesday, which will be a pleasure. She is also a joy. Peter has a beard and is about 6′1″ tall!! He has turned out wonderfully at 18, very serious and hard-working, but also amusing…[30]

The musical breakthrough came about via a commission from a youth orchestra. During his time with Dolly Malcolm had been involved in many local music festivals, and on one occasion the East Sheen Choral Society, conducted by John Michael East, had given a concert of his psalms. East also conducted the Brent Youth Orchestra, a group of young musicians whose impressive talents were a credit to the local education authority's support of music in its schools.[31] In 1979, when the orchestra was looking to commission a work to celebrate its tenth anniversary, East approached Malcolm about the possibility of a symphony. Malcolm was at once interested, but would not accept until he had heard the orchestra in person, wanting to know its strengths and weaknesses:

> We were very strong in wind players and percussion, though the strings were more stretched. Malcolm, suitably impressed overall, agreed to the commission, declaring that he would not in any way write down to the young players, but, rather, write to their strengths. This meant some interesting percussion, plenty of things for the flutes, oboes, bassoons and much choral writing for the brass. His only concessions were to limit his usual practice of dividing the strings and to adopt a single time signature (5/8) for the entire piece.[32]

Malcolm also insisted that East should understand the background to the new work:

> He arranged for me to see a friend of his who ran a bookshop in Richmond. There he played me recordings of all of Malcolm's previous symphonies. Malcolm was keen to get my reactions to them.

The symphony's deep spiritual theme, honouring St Bernadette of Lourdes, played its part in inspiring Malcolm's creative renewal.

> Lourdes meant a lot to him. He used to go there annually. He knew an Australian couple – the Metcalfes – who ran a travel agency called St Peter's Pilgrims so they would arrange for him to go to Lourdes at the drop of a hat…[33] He went for a cooling off or quietening down there during the writing of the symphony. When he went to

30 14 April 1979. He also wrote of a TV show that he had done in Bristol for Easter, in which Simon played the organ 'very creditably' and he conducted a choir of ninety and also accompanied April Cantelo.

31 East was currently a lecturer in music for the extra-mural department of the Universities of London and Surrey. The Brent Youth Orchestra's first conductor, Muriel Blackwell, the Borough's Music Adviser, was another key figure in the commission and had done much to stimulate serious music-making in all of Brent's junior and senior schools.

32 John Michael East, April 2005

33 It was an important friendship. Mary Metcalfe told East how wonderful Malcolm was to her son – 'when his birthday came up Malcolm wrote a piece for him'.

> Lourdes he didn't just take the waters, he was right there, wheeling the stretchers and helping. It wasn't just a pretty holiday thing for Malcolm. He was very involved!

The symphony was given the sub-title *Aquerò*, 'that thing', the word in Languedoc dialect used by Bernadette to describe the apparition of the Virgin Mary. Like the Second Symphony, the Fifth could also be considered a tone poem, this time in the form of a meditation on the events at Lourdes in 1858. Although the symphony has no actual programme, in his notes to the first audience Malcolm gave some specific indications of the content:

> As a symphonic entity the work is a broadly developing drama of ideas. At the outset, soft high strings suggest sunrise in the Pyrenees, and soon the horns are heard playing a long chant-like melody. Above these forward-moving elements is a circular figure for flutes and glockenspiel, and another for clarinets and vibraphone, characterising the eternal and celestial revolving above the earthly dynamic. Two further elements constitute the entire material of the symphony: a sequence of rich, slow chords suggesting the Apparition, and a long, wide-ranging melody which refuses to fall into a harmonic cradle.

The Symphony was written over a period of eight months.[34] Geoffrey Elborn, a young writer who had met Malcolm three years earlier when researching his biography of Edith Sitwell and had since become a great support and help, remembers Malcolm's outstanding powers of concentration and endurance:

> On one occasion I sat up with him three days and three nights in a row, to ensure he wasn't interrupted in his orchestrating; he took one short rest – it was just an hour or so before he came down again – and he told me to do the same, but I didn't, for I was too afraid I wouldn't wake up. I provided him with a great deal of coffee. There wasn't a drop of alcohol anywhere. He could work with such resilience, because his energy was so phenomenal. I suspect it sprang from his paradoxical nature, the clash of many opposites; he needed those opposites to create this remarkable energy.[35]

For John Paul East the creative process was fascinating:

> Malcolm was in touch with me the whole time. As soon as the work began to appear, we started rehearsals, several of which Malcolm attended. The first bits of music didn't obviously fit together or into anything, and I was crossing my fingers… I used to go to the flat at the Barbican, and he came to me once or twice… He would sometimes phone me up at 4.30 in the morning to talk about it! There were periods when he was interrupted and unable to work at all…

---

[34] It was written between early May 1979 and early January 1980. Its first professional performance was given by the BBC Welsh Orchestra under Norman Del Mar (November 1980). John Paul East writes: 'Malcolm and I went down to Cardiff for the rehearsals. It was fascinating to see my four months' work being done by professional players in six hours!' There was also an early performance at the Sydney Opera House by Patrick Thomas and the Sydney Symphony Orchestra (4 July 1981).

[35] March 2007

One interruption, for example, was his appearance at the 1979 Proms, playing his two-piano concerto with an important new friend, Moura Lympany. They also played it at Nottingham, Haddow and the Edinburgh Festival, and so delighted was Moura Lympany with this new addition to her considerable repertoire that she donated a new television to the Barbican flat.

An even bigger interruption began in late August 1979, when Prince Philip's uncle, Earl Mountbatten, was assassinated on his boat in Ireland. Malcolm at once rang up Gerald Kingsley at Weinberger's to tell him that the Fifth Symphony was postponed indefinitely.

> He was furious at the killing of Mountbatten. Absolutely furious! He had met him, and liked him enormously, and the assassination made him very angry indeed. He was beside himself with rage![36]

Geoffrey Elborn remembers Malcolm's state of shock:

> Every single piece of music had some germane event or religious experience motivating it. For example his tribute to Lord Mountbatten, a highly emotional response to the assassination. The night Mountbatten died, Malcolm was extremely upset. We went out and ate egg, bacon and chips at two in the morning at an all-night café in Smithfield Market. He was very upset, and at such times he could never disguise his distress – he'd simply burst into tears.[37]

Out of his tears at Mountbatten's martyrdom came a ten-minute work for solo violin and string orchestra, *Lament in Memory of Lord Mountbatten of Burma*, a deeply brooding and austere meditation on the seeming disinterest of the divine will in human affairs. No Master of the Queen's Music can have offered so personal and poignant a tribute. But it does not make for easy listening, the violin constantly aspiring towards the lyricism of Delius, only to be undercut by the orchestra's savagely dissonant expressions of despair, and finally sinking into defeated acquiescence. Possessing much of the catharctic power of an ancient Greek tragedy, the *Lament* is a starkly arresting expression of the pain of martyrdom.

The *Lament* over, Malcolm returned with relief to the Fifth Symphony, its completion in early January 1980 allowing East four valuable months for final rehearsals:

> There was much difficult stuff in it and I knew if we did what we usually did – sit down and have a play-through – it would be a disaster. So I took sectional rehearsals, and although it was difficult in the first weeks, gradually, as the players got hold of one section, I would fit it together with another… In the end it all fell into shape and they began to enjoy the symphony and be very proud of it. Malcolm came to a number of the later rehearsals, and was both critical and encouraging. He knew exactly how to deal with young people. 'Watch the beat!' he would cry! 'Watch the beat!'

---

36 Gerald Kingsley, February 2005

37 March 2007

Simon had been quietly in the background throughout the whole long creative process and East felt his support was crucial:

> I liked Simon and we got on very well. Inevitably there have been times when people have found he got between them and Malcolm. But where would Malcolm have been without him? He was ever present, organising things and encouraging Malcolm to stay on the straight and narrow. I don't think the Fifth Symphony would have happened, if he hadn't been there.

The Barbican was proving a far from ideal place of work. Though Malcolm made use of its space to erect his fourteen trestle tables in the main room, he found the thin walls a disadvantage and was constantly oppressed by extraneous noise. He wrote to Diane:

> The apartment has been a nightmare for months with general pneumatic drills and cranes going 8am–5pm seven days a week and our nice but musical neighbour Jim playing his quadraphonic Elgar and V Williams on the other side of the wall in the evenings. The strain sent me for a week to a Benedictine monastery on the Isle of Wight.[38] This was wonderful, but it was all day and half the night composing interrupted for meals and some eight short services in the Abbey which one is expected to attend. This is edifying and quite moving, but no vacation.[39]

It was in the final stages of the symphony's creation that Malcolm first met Valerie Thurston, another helpful friend at a time of need. Valerie, Director of Music at the Barbican-based City of London School for Girls, had been in the process of mounting *The Happy Prince* in November 1979 when she was told by a parent that Malcolm was living nearby:

> We invited him, and he attended all four performances, which was remarkable as he was working hard at the time and was very tired.[40]

He was so tired, indeed, getting only three hours' sleep a night, that when Valerie invited him and Simon round to her flat (also in Ben Jonson House) to a dinner party with her headmistress, Miss Lily Mackie, he ignominiously fell asleep. He had been keeping himself awake, he later admitted, by various stimulants, his compositional problems compounded by other commitments including those of organist at a local Catholic Church in Islington, where he and Simon worshipped and assisted:

> That evening I was propped up on strong tea, cigarettes and pernod to get me on through one job after another; and so it continued (not the pernod but the others) until last week. Christmas Eve, for example, was composing all day, stopping to practise for and to play Midnight Mass, listen to a friend[41] in sorrow until 5.00 a.m., then Xmas Day giving a Beethoven to Bartók and Berkeley piano recital in a psychiatric hospital etc etc…[42]

---

38 Quarr Abbey

39 12 January 1980

40 June 2006

41 Ronald Senator, whose wife was very ill.

42 MW to Valerie Thurston and Lily Mackie, 13 January 1980

Far from being offended, the ladies were anxious enough about his state of health to suggest a week's holiday, which, with the school's financial assistance, Malcolm and Simon took in middle of January 1980. Only days after the completion of the symphony, they were relaxing in style in a terrace apartment beside a swimming-pool at the Sheraton Hotel, Madeira. They were so exhausted, wrote Malcolm, that he slept non-stop for the first fourteen hours and Simon for seventeen.

Malcolm had intended to confine his holiday activities to swimming, sunbathing and reading Iris Murdoch and his latest discovery, Fay Weldon, but such were his feelings of gratitude that he began writing a piece specially for Valerie Thurston and her City of London girls, a Mass for three-part choir accompanied by simple two-part instrumental textures, dedicated to his favourite saint, Bernadette. Completed in just three weeks after his return,[43] The Little Mass of St Bernadette was first performed at the City of London Girls' School on 26 November 1980.[44]

Before the first performance of the Mass, Malcolm's other homage to Bernadette, the Fifth Symphony, received its premiere at Brent Town Hall.[45] News of its completion aroused some ironic comment in the media. *The Times*, for example, greeted it with the headline FINISHED FIFTH. And it was quick to point out how very dramatically Malcolm had fallen in the musical hierarchy:

> That famous unfinished symphony by Malcolm Williamson which was not completed in time for his royal premiere during the 1977 Jubilee celebrations is still unfinished. But the composer has already completed another symphony, his fifth, and the premiere is scheduled for April 23. Given Mr Williamson's position as Master of the Queen's Music it might be expected that the premiere would be a glossy occasion presented by a leading orchestra. Instead the symphony will be performed at Brent Town Hall, in north-west London, by the Brent Youth Orchestra, who commissioned it… And the unfinished Fourth Symphony? The composer said he was still working on one movement. He does hope to complete it eventually.[46]

It was, indeed, a comedown of significant proportions. Whereas the Fourth had been commissioned by the London Philharmonic Orchestra with money from the Arts Council, the Fifth was to be premiered by schoolchildren and funded by the Kilburn Grammar School Old Boys Association. If this troubled Malcolm, he

43 He did, however, write out a full score in the summer. The title of a 'Little Mass' referred technically to a work without a Credo. In its proportions it is far from little.

44 The Mass, written in the twentieth-century equivalent of plainchant rather than in the popular style of earlier, Beaumont-inspired works (like the Mass of St Andrew), was performed with great aplomb by the 'City' girls and enjoyed considerable popularity.

45 23 April 1980. Malcolm's homage to St Bernadette paid off. On his visit to Lourdes in 1980 a knee which had long troubled him was, he believed, cured by its exposure to the holy water.

46 7 February 1980. The Fourth Symphony's projected first movement was never written – it was presumably too painful a topic to address – and the other three movements have yet to be performed or recorded.

didn't let it show. Anyway, he liked working with young people. They were important. They were the future.[47]

Malcolm was already at work on a new, more immediately prestigious project involving the Scottish Baroque Ensemble, a relationship which Gerald Kingsley had carefully fostered. The orchestra had initially approached Weinberger's to see if Malcolm might re-arrange the National Anthem for an opening by the Queen of the Queen's Hall in Edinburgh. Kingsley suggested to Leonard Friedman, the orchestra's conductor, that if he wanted that favour he should include some Williamson in the concert, and so the *Lament for Lord Mountbatten* received its first performance most appropriately in the presence of the sovereign. It was an occasion not without incident.

Although Friedman was to conduct the *Lament*, Malcolm was conducting the National Anthem. So when Gerard Kingsley met him off the train at Edinburgh station, he prudently enquired whether he had remembered to bring his dress clothes with him. He hadn't. Kingsley, therefore, took him along to Moss Bros only to discover that all white tie and tails of the appropriate size had already been hired out. 'Ah well,' said Malcolm. 'There may be a way out. My Scottish great-grandfather came from Fife.' A day later Malcolm was looking particularly dapper as he stood in his kilt in front of the Scottish Baroque Ensemble in the Queen's Hall, waiting for the arrival of Her Majesty and the royal party. Gerald Kingsley, sitting at the end of her row, noticed the look of surprise on the Queen's face, as she took her seat. 'Surely that can't be Malcolm in a kilt!' she commented quietly to the Lord Lieutenant. '*Can* it?' Malcolm was certainly magnificently attired, glowing as brightly as David Niven's Bonnie Prince Charlie. Unfortunately, however, the kilt did not fit him with customary Moss Bros exactitude, being at least two sizes too large, and as he flung himself around on the podium, extracting the last ounce of emotion out of his newly arranged anthem, it began a steady, downwards descent. Luckily, after much effort, he succeeded in upholding his modesty.

The Scottish Baroque Ensemble, impressed with the austere *Lament*, quickly asked Malcolm for something with which to celebrate the Queen Mother's 80th birthday.[48] His *Ode For Queen Elizabeth* resulted, a five-movement work full of melody and good-humoured Scottish allusions, perhaps the sunniest piece

---

47 Stanley Sadie's review in *The Times* began with an atmospheric recreation of the opening: 'It begins as a representation of a Pyrenean dawn: soft blurs of string sounds against solemn sustained lines for the horns and trumpets, jangling interjections from the percussion. There is a hint of the timeless mysteries of Nature, a tone of awe, heightened by the deep sombre lines in the heavy brass: akin to Messiaen's contemplations, if less grandiose. This gives way to busier textures, artfully laid out in interchangeable blocks of sound: all written not only with a keen ear but also a keen eye to the young players' needs for security in numbers and for rewarding music to play.' Overall, thought Sadie, it was an impressive *pièce d'occasion*, one which a professional orchestra should surely take up.

48 Sponsored by Johnson Wax Arts Foundation and the Scottish Arts Council

Malcolm had written since the 1960s.[49] Christopher Austin, who has strongly championed this strangely neglected work, writes:

> It's a brilliant divertimento for strings. The Alleluia, the slow movement, is breathtakingly beautiful. The first run-through I ever conducted of the Alleluia completely changed the atmosphere of the room. It is so simple yet so potent it takes hold of you and your environment immediately. Not much music does that. It has to be very special.[50]

Malcolm conducted the first performance at a private party in Edinburgh at Holyrood Palace.[51] Such grand occasions, unfortunately, tended to bring out one of his worst traits, an over-elaborate devotion to royal protocol. Several players still remember that hardly any time was spent on the music in rehearsal because he was too busy inculcating correct behaviour in the presence of royalty. The more irritated the orchestra became, the more detailed his homily.

Despite the lack of final rehearsal, however, the piece proved highly successful and Malcolm was still in a state of euphoria when later that evening he wrote to Richard Toeman:

> Imagine my delight when after the performance Her Majesty, the dedicatee, rose from her seat and came to me with outstretched hand and spoke with great warmth and gratitude!!! At the party later she spoke in much detail of the work; and I wish that I could say our professional music critics retained as much of a new work as the great lady demonstrably did. Both she and the Queen were terribly pleased that it is built on E B-L (L=A), Elizabeth Bowes-Lyon… The Queen observed that it was a personal tribute written from the heart where it might have been formal and impersonal. Naturally my relief was great![52]

Bessie too was given a full account:

> I've had a year of non-stop writing, but somehow excellent health, exercise, diet and sobriety keep me going. My big orchestral work for the Queen Mother's 80th birthday went marvellously. I conducted it at a private party in the presence of the Queen, Prince Philip, Princess Margaret, Prince Charles and the Queen Mother herself. Can you imagine how pleased I was afterwards when the great lady came up and took my hand and said the warmest things and then wrote me a letter of great appreciation.[53]

Malcolm's letters to Bessie of this period contained several references to his dealings with the Royal family:

> – I had the great pleasure of talking to the Queen Mother at the Royal Garden Party. She is very beautiful and has great charm. She is very young for her 78 years…
>
> – The Queen Mother and I are becoming good friends – we drank whisky out of the same double-handled cup…

49 Friedman's cooperation and expertise were much in evidence, as the work was only completed one week before the scheduled first performance.

50 April 2005

51 3 July 1980

52 6 July 1980

53 9 December 1980

– The Queen Mother's conversational skills are highly impressive. She introduced me to an eminent physiologist with the words 'I do think – don't you? – that mathematics, chemistry and music have a lot in common.'

– I had a long talk with Princess Margaret last Thursday. She is very well again and is in fine form. She is very amusing…

Malcolm's relationship with Princess Margaret seemed particularly strong. She would occasionally ring him up and invite him round to enjoy a glass or two of whisky and play piano duets together. Edward Greenfield remembers being invited by Malcolm to a concert given by Rostropovich at Windsor Castle where 'Malcolm and Princess Margaret were drinking scotch like mad!'[54] A Mass on which Malcolm had been working for three years with the Princess in mind, the Mass of St Margaret of Scotland, was dedicated to her on its completion in 1980.

The Holyrood performance was followed by a successful public premiere of the Queen Mother's *Ode*,[55] Leonard Friedman including the piece regularly in his programmes thereafter, together with several other Williamson works. Malcolm was fulsome in his praise of his publishers and, in writing to Richard Toeman, seemed to have forgotten all his previous bitterness:

I am so grateful to the House Weinberger. John Schofield removed all worry from me, and saw to it that clear, accurate parts arrived on time. No time was lost in rehearsal. When I reached Edinburgh Leonard had received enough of the score to keep him busy. When we had rehearsed the first three movements once, the parts for the remaining two were there and a couple of tiny errors in the parts (due in part to mistakes in the score) were corrected in seconds in the coffee break. So top marks and thanks to the publishers for maximum efficiency and cool heads in a difficult situation.[56]

This period of content and success was epitomised by Malcolm's friendship with Moura Lympany, who not only played his double concerto with him on many occasions, but also took his 2nd and 3rd piano concertos into her repertoire. Moura Lympany, like Malcolm, loved France, and had acquired a home in the village of Rasiguères, near Perpignan, where in 1981 she was to create her first Festival of Wine and Music. In August 1980 Lympany lent Malcolm and Simon a cottage in Rasiguères for a two-week holiday, Malcolm idyllically happy in the Pyrenean countryside, Simon a little anxious about the new term about to commence at the City of London Girls' School, for he was now assisting in Valerie Thurston's music department, and, as Malcolm reported to her from Rasiguères, taking it very seriously:

Simon is studying hard for the new term's work. We had a splendid evening on Shostakovich's 5th Symphony, but he is a bit panicked over things that have to be done in London before school and wants to return earlier than Saturday.[57]

---

54 May 2006

55 Hopetoun House, Edinburgh, 25 August 1980

56 6 July 1980

57 Geoffrey Elborn comments: 'Malcolm was very devoted to Shostakovich – he played Shostakovich a great deal when he wasn't writing any music himself, or if he wanted a break...' (March 2007)

Now that Simon was no longer acting as Malcolm's full-time assistant, but instead was the one earning a regular income, the balance in their relationship had altered, as Malcolm was to acknowledge:

> Formerly he took great care of me. Now I have my heart and mind involved in spurring him on to make a success of teaching as he badly wants to. I'll be heart-broken if the teaching has to stop because of my exorbitant demands, or for any other reason.[58]

Their partnership had by now lasted five years, a remarkable time in the context of Malcolm's volatile temperament, their deep friendship based on a shared vision of life as a Catholic pilgrimage. Financial hardship, though scarcely anticipated and far from welcomed, gave them a different perspective on the riches of this world. It could make simple pleasures, like those at Rasiguères, idyllic:

> We went up the hills at midday and picked blackberries which are now stewing along with pears from Moura's tree. Marvellous weather. In a week here I've done more work than in months in the Barbican…[59]

But the pilgrim life was rarely to be lived without some small crisis. Even Moura Lympany's Pyrenean cottage would not come problem-free:

> Moura's cottage is two tiny rooms, one above the other with a ladder. There is a tiny kitchen annexe. It is however delightfully furnished and very comfortable. The first days were a bit of a nightmare with a boy staying here who wouldn't leave. This all meant sleeping-bags on floors and the boy coming in after 1.00 am and nobody having room to move. He went last Tuesday after taking his turn on the floor. That night there was a thunderstorm and the roof let in a cascade. Simon was bailing out the top room with a washing-up basin 1am-4am. Since then it's been fine and warm. The roof-man eventually came and with splendid Gallic spirit said that nothing was wrong…

1980 was by far the happiest and most productive of the Barbican years. Malcolm had re-found himself professionally, and had little need of alcohol. He had re-established some form of relationship with the children and, in the wake of the completed divorce, found himself less bitter towards Dolly. Instead of dubbing her, as before, 'perfectly dreadful' and 'causing much distress' he was able to write that 'being divorced makes it easier for me and Dolly to get on'.[60] He was also deriving great pleasure from his relationship with the royal family, fully restored after the embarrassments of the Jubilee year, and, with the successes of his *Lament for Lord Mountbatten* and *Ode to Queen Elizabeth*, he was again, and with good reason, believing that a knighthood could soon be his. But it was a fragile kind of happiness and it did not last. Only a few months into

58 MW to Valerie Thurston, 23 August 1980

59 *ibid.*

60 MW to Bessie Williamson, 9 December 1980. His letters for the past two years had been full of recrimination against the manoeuvres of Dolly's divorce lawyers.

1981 his world was disintegrating in a series of perceived slights, arguments and self-made disasters. The catalyst for all this mayhem was a single event, the marriage of Prince Charles and Lady Diana Spencer in July 1981.

The wedding of the heir to the throne might reasonably have been expected to involve the Master of the Queen's Music in some capacity. But, instead, Malcolm was totally excluded. Charles may well have felt that, four years on from his mother's Silver Jubilee, a Williamson commission was a risky commodity, but, anyway, Malcolm was a member of his mother's household, not his own. So he asked the Welsh composer William Mathias, who had written for his investiture at Caernarvon, for a wedding hymn, an important commission which would be heard on television worldwide by nearly a billion people.

The media were quick to highlight Malcolm's discomfiture. Under a heading DISCORDANT NOTE TO ROYAL MUSIC, the *Evening Standard* made much of it:

> Prince Charles seems to have snubbed Malcolm Williamson, the Master of the Queen's Music. I understand that Williamson has curiously not been asked to write a piece of occasional music to celebrate the Wedding in July. Although the bearer of the honorary title would normally expect to be hard at work in preparation, Williamson is singularly absent from the palace's plans... The ceremony at St Paul's will I understand include a set of responses specially composed by the organist Christopher Dearnley... Williamson's exclusion has certainly come as a surprise to the musical establishment...[61]

Two months later, shortly before the wedding, Malcolm featured in *The People*:

> NO ROYAL DISCORD
>
> Malcolm Williamson is sorely displeased by reports that he has been snubbed by Prince Charles... The reports, he says, that his nose was put out of joint are simply not true. Yesterday in between explosive sneezes brought about by hay fever to which he is susceptible, Mr Williamson said; 'I knew what the music for the wedding was to be long before it was announced, and I approved fully of the arrangement. Some hurtful things have been said about myself and John Betjeman being left out of the arrangements, but as appointees of the Queen's Royal Household it is impossible to reply to them publicly.'[62]

Privately, however, Malcolm was unable to conceal how badly he felt let down, grumbling to friends that the only thing the Queen had asked for since the Jubilee was a list of Australian guests for a Garden Party.[63] Nonetheless, Malcolm of his own accord presented Charles and Diana with a gift, a delightful song, 'Now Is The Singing Day', the words translated by his friend Dr Albert Friedlander (a well-known London rabbi) from the Hebrew 'Bridal Dialogue' of *The Song of Songs*. The first verse appropriately focused on Charles:

---

61 27 April 1981

62 24 June 1981

63 Don Westlake, June 2006

> Your prince is riding through the streets
> To his espousal time…
> Crowned by his mother rides he forth
> To bells' encycling chime
> Attended by his paladins
> Bright guards about his way
> Bedecked with swords, white plumes, with gold,
> Now, now, now is the singing day.

The second verse, Diana's, was especially poignant :

> Her armour is her loveliness
> Her hair is lambent gold;
> Her captive willing prince submits
> Rejoicing to be won.
> Arise my love, my fairest one,
> Arise and come away.
> Arise my love, allume the world,
> Now, now, now is the singing day.

It was a very special gift, a miniature of real quality, but for some reason it seems not to have been appreciated by its recipients, and, though Malcolm recorded it three years later with the soprano Sybil Michelow for an album of Jewish music, it has otherwise suffered complete neglect. One of his most moving songs, written out of a mixture of admiration and despair, it deserves better.

Deeply upset at the seeming rejection of the song, which had been presented on behalf of London's Jews, Malcolm resorted to damaging drinking bouts, and he needlessly fell out with Leonard Friedman, whose championing of his music with the Scottish Baroque had been doing him great good; he also broke with the local Catholic church, where Simon only recently had directed the Mass of the People of God; he upset the BBC, two important record companies and many other influential figures in the music world. Most rash of all was the final severance of the long-standing professional relationship with Richard Toeman at Weinberger's.

In January 1981, outraged at Toeman's very reasonable refusal to pay expenses for some not very promising promotional work in Paris, Konstanz and Vienna, Malcolm foolishly resorted to a letter as tasteless as it was grossly unfair:

> Dear Richard,
>
> If your sexual technique is like your human behaviour it must be very enjoyable. You clearly relish having me beg you for help rather like the foreplay, and your pompous refusal of help when you have insulted me with brilliant volleys of spite is obviously of orgasmic satisfaction.

There followed an ill-advised invitation to end the relationship:

> Find another victim. You have humiliated me once too often… I cannot muddy myself further by toadying to your ego trips… Please no more letters or phonecalls to me. I have only contempt for your glacial cruelty and for the spite that you clearly enjoy. It is simply pathetic that you have to reassure your manhood by torturing others…

A self-pitying tirade followed:

> I have no money. A life's work of music has sat on Weinberger's shelf because you always knew best, and nothing was until recently [the coming of Gerald in 1979] exploited with intelligence or competence. Had you listened to me or even discussed matters with me I should not find myself at 49 years of age without a real income and the prospect of only a UK income … like Adolf Hitler you love absolute power…[64]

This appalling letter, full of untrue allegations, signalled the end of his time at Weinberger's, though he remained on good terms for several years with Gerald Kingsley and John Schofield, and indeed Richard Toeman never lost his strong affection for him. Toeman had been good to Malcolm in the difficult Barbican years, publishing his works, though few promised big returns,[65] but he had a business to run and Malcolm's continual abuse was intolerable. Weinberger's continued to promote his music in their catalogue, but Malcolm's already floundering career would quickly disintegrate without the outlet of an established publisher.

He was now, for all his abilities and achievements, perceived more and more as an eccentric figure of fun. It was a situation of his own making. His appearance at the Bromsgrove Festival in 1981, where he was a featured composer, was typical, as its organiser, Donald Hunt, recalls:

> Malcolm was a key guest for the 21st Festival. He was with us about a week. He played the 2nd Piano Concerto, participated in his piano quintet and helped on a production of *The Happy Prince*. We sang his new Mass of the People of God in St John's Church.[66] He had promised us programme notes but none came. He offered, instead, to speak for a few minutes. So he went up into the pulpit, wearing his Jewish skull-cap, and proceeded to speak for nearly half an hour![67]

The skull-cap was just one of a number of props which Malcolm was now beginning to favour in public, as he courageously sought to convert the world to a more inclusive social and religious outlook. He also wore the gay badge of a pink triangle at many functions, including Buckingham Palace garden parties. In publicly espousing such causes as gay rights and inter-racial harmony, he was well before his time. Thirty years later, such a stance would have been helpful rather than damaging.

Another typical piece of self-harm occurred at Leeds, where, in the summer of 1981, he was engaged to spend a week inspiring the students of the City of Leeds College of Music. He was also to participate in two concerts, one of which

64 21 January 1981. Richard Toeman, despite the vitriolic forays which eventually led to the dissolution of their professional partnership, remained deeply attached to Malcolm and his music. Shortly before he died, in 2005, he had specifically requested that Malcolm's setting of 'Crossing the Bar' should be sung at the conclusion of his funeral.

65 The Fifth Symphony, the *Lament for Lord Mountbatten*, *Ode for Queen Elizabeth*, the Mass of St Margaret, the Little Mass of St Bernadette and three Fanfares.

66 29 April 1981

67 January 2006

would feature the English premiere of Three Fanfares for Brass, Percussion and Organ. It sounded a good week, but Malcolm arrived without the parts for the Fanfares, and so he co-opted students and staff in the laborious job of copying out his music, fraying tempers in the process. The week culminated in a concert at the Civic Hall, the presence of the Master of the Queen's Music inspiring an occasion of great formality with many local dignitaries, including the Mayor. Disliking the stuffy atmosphere, Malcolm decided to preface his concert with a plea for social tolerance. 'I am Jewish,' he began. 'And Catholic. And Moslem. And Hindhu. And Buddhist!' The audience, which had been struggling to come to terms with his informal dress – a kaftan tunic and a yarmulka – giggled uncomfortably. They were even more uncomfortable when three hours later the concert showed no signs of ending, Malcolm warming to the task of playing and introducing his own music, intent on giving good value.

He had stayed the week with Joseph Stones, the College's Principal. After the final concert, in the middle of a late meal with the family, Simon suddenly appeared to the consternation of Joseph Stones, who was not expecting him and did not have a spare room. 'Oh, don't worry,' said Malcolm. 'He can sleep with me.' The comment went down badly. Malcolm responded testily, thumping the table and inadvertently showering several people with coffee. The argument quickly escalated until Malcolm stormed out of the house with Simon. They had no money for a hotel. So Simon, having just driven up to Leeds, found himself driving back again to London through the night…[68]

In the confused situation of 1981 even Malcolm's relations with Simon were not always easy. In February, for example, frustrated that Simon was not coping with important letters, he had enlisted the aid of a typist at the City of London Girls' School. But, as he informed his trusty confidante, Valerie Thurston,

> Simon searched for those letters for an hour before I plucked up courage to tell him that I'd had Jane type them. He was justifiably cross. But I'm cross that he's too busy to put a handful of cheques in the bank (we're so overdrawn every penny helps). Then Simon searched for an hour for the brass-organ works that were mislaid. I am at fault I know; but I cannot work under the stress of temper… as you said, we need organisation here…

His only major composition in 1981 was a song cycle[69] in honour of the Yugoslavian dictator, Tito, which some people in high quarters interpreted as a deliberately provocative gesture from the Master of the Queen's Music, whereas Malcolm genuinely (if naively) admired Tito, proudly hanging his portrait above his desk at the Barbican. But for all his admiration, the cycle was proving a terrible struggle, as he told Valerie:

> The tension caused me to write whole passages of violas and cellos in *Josip Broz Tito* in the wrong clefs in the wrong bars and I had to take tranquillizers just not to

[68] As related later to Graham Wade by Malcolm

[69] A setting of Walt Whitman's poems for baritone and orchestra

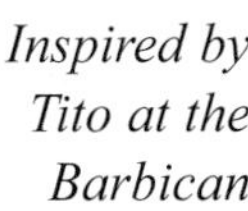
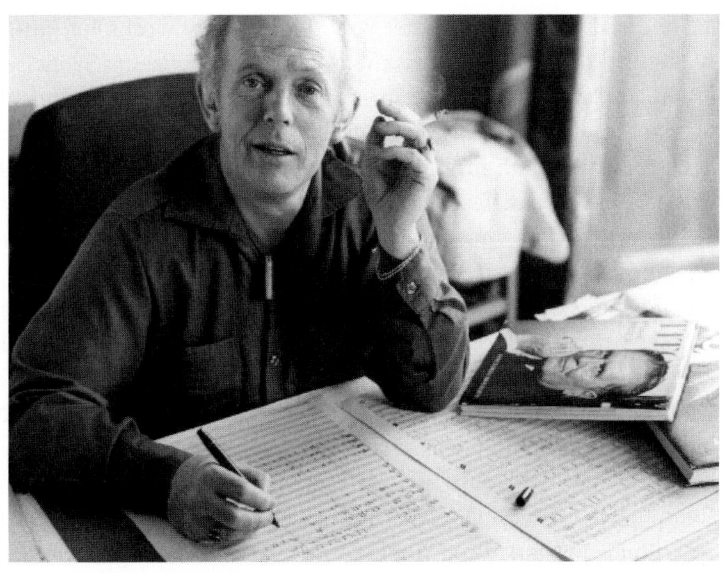

Inspired by Tito at the Barbican

> explode. It doesn't matter whose fault it is. I am a difficult person – but composers are. Simon is a saint of patience, loyalty and dedication but takes on too much and tries to follow it all through conscientiously…[70]

Relentless travels in search of money were also unsettling, Malcolm most inventively contriving to see the world at others' expense. In a twelve-month period he visited Bordeaux (for cassations), Banff, Canada (for its Music School of Continuing Education), New York (for promotions), Paris (for discussions on more cassations), Skopje, Yugoslavia (where Vanco Cavdarski and the Skopje Chamber Orchestra played his Tito tribute), and Aldeburgh (for a broadcast performance of the same work).

After travelling around the world directing, playing and listening to his own music, Malcolm, when back at the Barbican, naturally believed his music should be central to everyone's lives. Valerie Thurston came to find that, inspirational though his association with the school's music sometimes was, there was danger of suffocation. She, moreover, was for ever at his beck and call:

> When I did his works he would give me terrific backing, but he expected me to do nothing but Williamson! Malcolm could be very demanding – he would ring me at any time of day demanding I go over to the flat and help him sort out some music. Normally I was teaching, and I couldn't! He would ring up at six in the morning, asking if I had any coffee! On one occasion he asked me over for my opinion on a particular cadence in another Mass he was writing, the Mass of St Margaret. 'Should it go like this or this?' he asked.[71]

70 20 February 1981

71 June 2006

Valerie had dutifully sung her way through new works for him, organised trips of City girls to join in cassations at Villefranche-sur-Saone, embellished his empty larder with pots of marmalade and home-made chocolate cakes, but eventually, like so many good friends of his before her, was hurt to find the accustomed warmth turning cool without good reason, as he and Simon slowly drifted away in a different direction.

So often Malcolm was his own worst enemy. One of his most important positions in 1981 was his Presidency of the Royal Philharmonic Orchestra, and Gerald Kingsley, mindful of this connection, had been working quietly for many months behind the scenes to achieve a fitting concert with the RPO to celebrate Malcolm's 50th birthday that November. Knowing how easily Malcolm could upset concert arrangements, Kingsley had been careful to keep Malcolm in the dark until everything was fixed. Moura Lympany would play his 3rd Piano Concerto and Malcolm himself would be the organist in Saint-Saëns' Third Symphony, a work he loved. The concert, which Charles Groves would conduct, was going to start with Sibelius' *En Saga.* Not long after the RPO sent this programme to him, however, he was ringing up Gerald Kingsley's home at two-o'clock in the morning:

> 'Do you know what time it is, Malcolm?' said my wife. He ignored the question. 'I need to speak with Gerald.' So I picked up the phone at the side of the bed, not exactly fully *compos mentis*, and a voice said, 'Do you know what fucking key *En Saga*'s in? 'No, Malcolm, no idea. 'E flat major! And do you know what fucking key my concerto is in?' 'Yes, Malcolm. E flat major.' 'Well then, fucking *En Saga* is not to be in the fucking programme! We're not having two pieces the same key! That would be disaster. An absolute fucking disaster!'[72]

Malcolm then started interfering. Charles Groves was telephoned about the problem of keys, and a letter sent to the RPO suggesting *En Saga* be replaced with *Tapiola.* A month later Malcolm wrote again, this time suggesting an all-Williamson concert. When Simon followed this up with a query as to why this suggestion had, as yet, received no reply, the orchestra's chairman told them[73] that the anticipated loss on the birthday concert was no longer sustainable and he would be discussing with Charles Groves and Moura Lympany a new programme involving more traditional composers. Malcolm, outraged, responded to this disappointment in the only way he knew: he resigned as the orchestra's President.

In July 1981, shortly after the cancellation of his 50th Birthday concert (and, ironically, just a few months before the Queen opened the Barbican Centre whose noisy construction he had looked down upon for the past four years), Malcolm left Ben Jonson House for good, to spend time in Australia. Malevolent gossips suggested that he had been sent dramatically into exile, having offended

[72] February 2005

[73] Gerald Kingsley, 10 July 1981

Buckingham Palace, various wild stories circulating as to the exact nature of his offence. One of the more outrageous was promulgated by *Private Eye*:

> There was a time when no royal party was complete without the giggling presence of Sir[74] Malcolm Williamson, the Master of the Queen's Music. But owing to some astonishing behaviour the composer has fallen seriously from grace... While Williamson's habit of addressing Princess Margaret on things sexual always irritated the Queen, his chief crime was to gate-crash a private party at Windsor Castle and pinch the Queen Mother's bum. Williamson is frantically searching ways of winning back Brenda's favour, but it is understood that she is adamant.[75]

This was probably all nonsense.[76] Malcolm's departure was not a sudden one at all. He was moving to Australia to research the problems of mental illness in the young, for which he had the support of a university fellowship and bursary.

The gossip, however ill-founded, was certainly understandable. It seemed odd for the Master of the Queen's Music to uproot himself from England to pursue scientific research in Australia. It was not generally known that, as a composer without a publisher and with serious financial problems, Malcolm could not afford to turn down the opportunity of subsidised accommodation, wherever it might be.

He made the journey out alone – 'Simon is consoling Keith in London... albeit with my blessing. The insatiable Keith had a rough ride and needs love and support...'[77] But Simon would fly out to join him in August. Malcolm in the meantime, having quickly shaken off the disappointments of the summer, was determined to enjoy himself, especially at his first port of call, Ystad in Sweden, where Weinberger's Gerald Kingsley had negotiated several performances of *Our Man in Havana*. Such was Malcolm's enthusiasm that he spent his composer's fee many times over by staying in a hotel for two weeks beforehand, generously coaching the singers and orchestra for free, as they prepared to mount *Havana* in a 'beautiful little opera house in the Fenice manner'.[78] Kingsley was regaled with vivid progress reports, Malcolm pretending great anguish over the problems of his conductor:

> Whole sections sound post-Stockhausen... Last night he said to me, 'Each day we rehearse where we crashed the night before' – but he crashed last night as many times as the RAF in World War Two...

74 Probably a mistake rather than a joke. It was often thought that Malcolm must have received a knighthood.

75 5 November 1982

76 Geoffrey Elborn, who wrote a biography of Princess Alexandra around this time, is adamant that the comments by *Private Eye* were totally fictitious; that Malcolm was never drunk or rude; and that Malcolm enjoyed excellent relations with the Royal Family throughout his tenure of the post.

77 MW to Gerald Kingsley, 17 July 1981

78 MW to Gerald Kingsley, 9 July 1981

However, Ystad itself was 'neck deep' with attractive 'Vikings', and Malcolm loved all his singers, Hawthorne being positively 'the hottest thing since fried bread'. He also had fun playing the Chopin E minor concerto on two pianos with the daughter of the composer Moses Pergament. All in all, Ystad seemed a good omen for the new life in Australia. 'God knows what horrors Australia holds,' Malcolm wrote cheerfully to Gerald Kingsley. 'It may also have many delights. But at least, I hope, some gelt, since it is poverty forcing me out there.'[79]

[79] MW to Gerald Kingsley, 9 July 1981

15 ADRIFT AT FIFTY

Australia, 1981–83

MALCOLM WAS TO WORK for a month at the Australian National University, Canberra, before moving to the University of New South Wales' medical school, Sydney, where his year-long studies would be funded by the Ramaciotti Foundation, a charity established to further biomedical research. It was a wonderful opportunity to acquire a deeper scientific knowledge to underpin his therapies for the mentally handicapped. But musical commitments and the ever-pressing need to make money would regularly divert him from these researches. He was committed, for example, to involvement in parts of the large celebration the ABC was organising for his fiftieth birthday, a series of over fifty concerts and broadcast recordings (which would quite eclipse the arrangements being made for Percy Grainger's centenary). He was under contract, too, to make several recordings, notably with Barry Tuckwell in Hobart. There were also two major commissions – for a cantata and a symphony – which he needed to honour.

Both these commissions attracted him. The cantata, *The Cradle of Hope of Peace*, would allow him full scope to inveigh against the horrors of war. It was to be written for an important gala concert in Bristol in the summer of 1982, when the International Society for Musical Education would be flying in children's choirs from all over the world. Malcolm had already assembled an impressive array of material: Edmund Blunden's poem 'August the Sixth' on the dropping of the atomic bomb on Hiroshima; Edith Sitwell's 'Three Poems of the Atomic Age'; and any number of English, French, Russian, Hebrew, Latin, Swedish, Japanese and Serbo-Croat texts, including part of Tito's speech on disarmament to the United Nations. Malcolm was constantly coming up with ever more interesting ideas, putting off the writing of the piece as he explored them.

The same completion date awaited an even grander project, a symphony to mark the 50th anniversary of the Australian Broadcasting Corporation. Malcolm's Sixth Symphony was to be no ordinary work, but one specifically written for use as a television film. Moreover, this format would allow all seven of the ABC's orchestras to be involved, each being filmed in its own city as it played its allotted sections, so that every single orchestral musician employed by the Corporation would feature in its fiftieth birthday jamboree. In addition to the film of the seven orchestras playing their individual pieces, the programme would also include footage of town and country scenes typical to each state, Malcolm acting in a consultative capacity to ensure that the imagery was appropriate to the music.

Those commissioning the work saw the symphony as 'a liturgy in homage to the tradition of culture and learning in the ABC, the University of Australia'. This high-minded aim led Malcolm to relate the work to one of Plato's philosophical discussions which currently preoccupied him, namely the relationship between *stasis* (repose) and *dynamis* (movement) and, in particular, the way in which *stasis* evolved out of *dynamis* in the creation of the world. Malcolm intended his symphony to show musically how *stasis* might evolve from *dynamis*. He told his friends that the solution, if there was one, lay in the destruction of the tyranny of the bar line, something which Messiaen and Stravinsky, like the medieval composers before them, had already achieved. It was an idea with which he was to continue to wrestle:

> At the end of the two great classics of our time, Messaien's *Turangalila Symphony* and the *Symphony in Three Movements* by Stravinsky, you feel that there has been a still point in your moving world and not a work moving forwards while you, the auditor, are still… A complex chord by Messiaen, held for ever, sets up an acoustic vibration that, if you look at it on paper, seems to be static, but it sets up an acoustic tension that gives the impression of force, *dynamis*. Movement in stillness is terribly important. There is all the difference in the world between writing very slow music, like a Bruckner or Mahler slow movement, and the stillness so wonderfully described in Plato – the creative force that made the world in *stasis*.[1]

Malcolm had much on his mind, therefore, as he flew from Sweden to New York on the second stage of his latest Australian adventure. There he had discussions with a charity[2] involved in access to the arts for the mentally handicapped and with several brain experts, before flying on to Canberra to take up the short fellowship organised for him by Hazel Reader. He was soon gaining further practical experience at the Koomarri School and adding to his already copious notes on psychogenetic and perinatal brain insult, while the stimulating academic atmosphere of the Australian National University inspired him to venture beyond medical research and lecture on Ibsen and Strindberg. He was much flattered by the attendance at these lectures of Professor Manning Clark, the distinguished historian, and his Swedish wife Dymphna. It was not long before Malcolm was on close terms with the Clarks and regularly visiting their

[1] MW interview with Belinda Webster, 'A Word With Malcolm Williamson', ABC Radio *24 Hours*, November 1991

[2] Hospital Audiences

Canberra home, which possessed one of the finest pianos in the Capital Territory. Clark had retired as Professor of History at the University but was working hard on his six-volume History of Australia, begun twenty years earlier, the most ambitious account of the country ever undertaken.

Through the Clarks Malcolm quickly enlarged his literary contacts, forming strong friendships with Leonie Kramer, the Professor of Australian Literature at Sydney University, and the Clarks' son, Axel, who was lecturing in the English Department at the ANU and had just published a definitive book on the Australian poet Christopher Brennan. These contacts led Malcolm away from medical research to further literary studies, and he rapidly acquired a detailed knowledge of the poetry of David Campbell and the fiction of Henry Handel Richardson. He was naturally anxious that Bessie should benefit, and that her taped books for the blind should be as fully representative of Australian history and literature as possible. That August he wrote to her:

> Dearest Mme. Whunme,
>
> Dymphna Clark expects you to contact her when you are ready. She's thrilled about what you're doing. Of course you can go direct to Manning, it's just that the great man is so busy that Dymphna will take all the information and give it to Manning at a moment when he's at his most receptive... You must read Manning's 'The Quest for an Australian Identity' (in 'Occasional Writings & Speeches'). And read David Campbell, a very great Australian poet...[3]

Malcolm was in the highest of spirits, loving the academic atmosphere, the sunshine and the constant concerts put out for his 50th birthday. Gerald Kingsley was given a glimpse of Canberra's attractions:

> If you could see this glorious country! Summer has just begun. You'd want to bottle the Mediterranean sunshine. The university parks are radiant with sub-tropical trees and the tiny streams flowing thru' the country are fresh. I'm composing fruitfully but I don't know why. Maybe because the weather is so baking and the ABC is beaming out hours, literally, of my music and the *Radio Times* tells me that it is similar in Great Britain and I feel that it is worth going on. I am deeply grateful to you for all that you have done for my music...[4]

Malcolm's Creative Arts Fellowship at Canberra ended (with a concert of three of his concertos) in September 1981, allowing him a three month gap before he began his research in Sydney. Simon was by this time out in Australia, he and Malcolm recording the Double Piano Concerto with Barry Tuckwell and the Tasmanian Symphony Orchestra, one of five of Malcolm's concertos recorded that month by ABC. Malcolm told Gerald Kingsley:

> Simon, by his air economy ticket, must return to London on October 5th. Also he is teaching and, poor guy, will be winding up the Barbican apartment, after which I hope he will return to Australia. He played the piano very well here. Tuckwell is conducting marvellously. At present I have no plans to return to the UK. There is neither money

[3] Undated letter

[4] 3 December 1981

to go back to Europe nor money or prospects there. I am sorry to be missing Christ the King…[5]

The Mass of Christ The King was to be telerecorded at a concert at the Festival Hall in October, and screened later on BBC television on Malcolm's 50th birthday. Frank Shipway, who conducted the Philharmonia, recalls his considerable involvement:

> Gerald [Kingsley] had been asking me to do the Mass for some time, when the opportunity of doing it for Malcolm's 50th birthday turned up. I said that I'd take it on, on condition that I could re-orchestrate it! Malcolm by this period had become very careless. For example he'd written for trumpets in Bb. But, for no particular reason, he wrote for trumpets in D in one movement, but then forgot about halfway through. There had been a number of performances when no one noticed (even Malcolm!) One trombone passage was unplayable! One of the choruses was written in 5/8 but was virtually impossible to sing. I rebarred it and it became so much easier (it sounded absolutely the same of course!) He did idiotic things sometimes – the final chorus was pretty heavily orchestrated and he wrote the chorus part (in harmony) so low that it would never come through clearly. I made the whole choir sing in unison and gave the harmony to the orchestra.[6]

In the end Malcolm did not miss the concert, Weinberger's kindly providing the air fare. It should have been a very happy occasion. Shipway drew an inspiring performance from the Philharmonia, his massed choirs and soloists.[7] Malcolm, however, was unsettled from the moment he entered the hall and noticed, to his great surprise, that the organ shutters were open. During the performance Shipway's various alterations, about which Malcolm had heard nothing, fuelled his mounting anger and at the end, as he rushed onto the platform, immaculately dressed, to take the applause, he completely ignored Shipway. Later that evening the two men happened to meet in a Festival Hall lift, and Malcolm again cut him. For Gerald Kingsley it was a disappointing conclusion to a fruitful collaboration:

> Frank had done a lot of Malcolm's music, including a considerable amount of BBC work. His idea of some organ continuo, to give some bass support, was essentially a very helpful idea. But Malcolm never forgave Frank for 'tampering' with the score.[8]

During this short return to England Malcolm recorded a birthday interview on BBC radio with Michael Oliver. He initially created a good impression, talking enthusiastically about his medical work:

> I'm branching out from composing to working intensively on research into treatment of the severely intellectually handicapped and retarded. I'm being given facilities to work with babies, schoolchildren and 'unteachable' children, adults in psychiatric hospitals and intellectually subnormal old people in geriatric hospitals.

---

5 20 September 1981

6 January 2006

7 Jill Gomez, Anne Howells, Robin Leggate and John Shirley-Quirk

8 15 June 2006

Sociability, he declared, could be slowly achieved 'through music, mime, words, narrative, detached meaningless gesture and a whole world of fantasy, as you have in opera'. But Malcolm never learnt the wisdom of thinking carefully before blurting out his true feelings, and the interview was marred by an outburst about his rejected (and highly reject-able) television opera, *The Testament of Adam*:

> I want to go back to a television opera that the BBC commissioned years ago when John Culshaw was in charge of BBC television music... and he, great, sensitive man that he was… bullied me in the nicest possible way into making a full-size operatic idea from it. Then he went and people at BBC television, people who were very good friends, said 'This is the most horrible idea ever, throw it in the dustbin!' It's still there in the BBC archive. And I haven't a single friend except Culshaw, who's no longer alive now. Everybody hates it, except Culshaw and me, but I'm determined to do it as soon as I can hire myself a beach house in Australia and work at it because it demands to be born.

Asked what was so horrible about the 'horrible idea', Malcolm said he didn't know. His opera was simply 'a long-range protest against the subtler forms of fascism'. The heroine, a mezzo-soprano, was a mixture of Kirkegaard and Alexander Pope:

> She is hunch-backed and lame. And by a diabolical chance becomes transformed into somebody beautiful at the end by the machinations of a Hitler figure.

With Simon Campion

Soon afterwards, still smarting about the rejection of his hunch-backed heroine, Malcolm said his goodbyes to Simon and returned to Australia. There he speedily relaxed as he engaged in a series of visits to different cities to hear or play his music. Back in Canberra, where Hazel and Ralph Reader had organised a big 50th birthday party, he wrote to Richard Toeman as if the problems of the past had never existed:

> My dear Richard,
>
> While I thank you and your colleagues for deeply appreciated messages, let me thank the firm for twenty years of adventurous and fruitful collaboration. I do hope you will agree that since December 1961, when I first visited Dougie Foss's office in Crawford St, quite a bit has happened. Seeing the *Radio Times*, enjoying a crowded concert in Melbourne's Great Hall while the ABC put out 2 and a half hours of my music, while Donald Hunt was doing *Xst the King* in Worcester, while I receive telegrams from UK, Eire, Sweden, France, Germany, USA, Africa and my own Australia, I feel that the collaboration has not been without meaning… Don't think that I don't realise and appreciate the colossal amount of diligence the firm put into what is happening across the world.[9]

A few weeks later he was back in Canberra after a round of travels, still writing to Richard Toeman contentedly:

> Contrary to my intentions, I am sitting in one of my two universities writing music into the night. It's worth going on with. I have a beautiful picture of a menorah on the desk and my crucifixes on the wall… For a long time I've been in a different city each week and next week it's the *Pas de Quatre*, *Symphony for Voices* & *Winter Star* in Melbourne. *Julius Caesar Jones* is here after Xmas, and so on...[10]

Malcolm next moved to Sydney, renting a flat at Elizabeth Bay,[11] far enough away from Blues Point Tower to feel unthreatened, Malcolm managing to see just enough of Bessie to keep their relationship unruffled. His letters to her are full of the sharp repartee they so much enjoyed years before. On his 50th birthday, for example, Bessie had inadvertently sent a telegram wishing him a happy 55th. 'It's a little ahead of its time,' he responded, 'like the late works of Beethoven. May I keep it among my souvenirs, or do you wish to file it for re-use?'

At Sydney Malcolm much enjoyed working under Dr Robert Walsh, the Dean of the Faculty of Medicine at the University of New South Wales, 'a magnificent boss', who set him 'no end of neurological and similar work' to produce the necessary back-up for his theories.[12] Malcolm's Fellowship also allowed him to

---

[9] He was also delighted that Frank Shipway's Mass of the Christ The King, played on television by the BBC at the time of his birthday, had been well received, *The Times* declaring that he 'may have produced that rarity, a new large-scale choral work which could become part of the popular repertoire'. The Mass, said *The Times*, was being taken up by choral societies all around the country, 'perhaps as an alternative to all those Messiahs'.

[10] 2 December 1981

[11] Roslyn Gardens

[12] MW to Robert Solomon, 2 November 1986. Dr Michael Armstrong writes: 'Walsh's

travel widely, even to New York, where his mentors included the Australian-born Nobel Prize Winner, Sir John Eccles, and several of his followers working on the split-brain theory. Study of the human brain eventually led Malcolm to the study of crocodiles:

> I discovered something about the 'split brain theory' which puts into question the probably inaccurate dividing line between cognition and instinct. At the lowest (or rather oldest) end of the scale, I fell among people across the world, some involved in the mind-brain debate, which led me to other people who have observed quite amazing cognitive abilities, highly selective behaviour in the most ancient extant creatures on earth – the crocodilian order. This puts into question the very important and criminally wrong assumptions about the 'mentally handicapped', and, in a worthwhile society, leads us to research the intelligence potential of many condemned and institutionalised people.[13]

Peter, now at university, was given a good brief on crocodiles:

> You may think me crazy but for my neurophysiology work I'm doing a study of the crocodilian order, the oldest extant reptiles, whose physiology and behavioural patterns are several million years out of step with the commonly accepted Darwinian concept of evolution. I discover that little work has been done in this field. This country is a great place to study both the Estuarine and Johnsonian crocodiles and they have a lot to teach us about human brain behaviour.[14]

Thereafter Malcolm's research advanced on two fronts, as he attempted to wed his studies in the cognitive powers of the most primitive reptiles with those of handicapped (and often non-verbal) human beings. He became a regular visitor to Sydney's Natural History Museum, and so all-consuming was his work at the University that he had little time to spend on the cantata or symphony. Both began to look like lost causes when, in March 1982, just three months before the deadlines, he spent five weeks in France working for *Jeunesses Musicales*.

As Simon was still occupied in London, one of Malcolm's closest allies at the BBC, the producer Ann Kirch, drove down to Angoulême, Bordeaux, to assist him, together with a young pianist, recommended to Malcolm by Weinberger's, Jonathan Still. Within only minutes of their arrival, however, Malcolm had fallen out with Ann Kirch on the subject of the incomplete *Cradle of the Hope of Peace*, and so badly that she was soon driving home. That evening, determined not to let the problems over the Bristol cantata spoil his return to France, he settled down

---

background was in pathology. I doubt if he offered any particular ongoing supervision of Malcolm's work. I think he just engineered the Ramaciotti Fellowship for him and let him have his head.' Armstrong still remembers vividly Malcolm's passionate commitment to the practicalities of musical therapy, citing the television programme on his work at Koomarri. 'Malcolm was totally engaged, focusing intensely on one very severely disabled boy. At a crucial point Malcolm cried out, in total admiration, "You very wonderful boy!". It was a shock, a lovely shock, to be confronted with his utter regard for the boy, a human being unlikely ever – before or since – to have been so acclaimed.' (April 2007)

13 MW to Robert Solomon, 2 November 1986

14 25 January 1983

calmly to explain to Jonathan the music to be used next day: the cassation he had recently written in French, *Le Pont du Diable*,[15] *The Moonrakers* and *The Red Sea* (both translated into French by Mario Bois). For Jonathan it was the beginning of a precious relationship:

> From that moment on we really became best friends, and it lasted until Simon got difficult about it – mind you, Malcolm could get difficult too! Our time in Bordeaux could not have been happier. We spent hours and hours sitting in restaurants talking about his work. He was so witty, such a wonderful conversationalist that it was quite overwhelming to be with him. His language was often like a mixture of two of his favourite authors, Evelyn Waugh and E F Benson. It was Malcolm at his very best. He wasn't drinking at all – in fact, I didn't even know that he did drink.[16]

They were joined for a while by Tammy, on vacation from studying languages at Bristol University, and she has similarly happy memories of Bordeaux. They were lucky, she recalls, to be staying with a wonderful Angoulême family, the Picards, actors who lived in a beautiful house in the country.

> The Picards were lovely people, civilised and calm. They were much amused by Dad's French, not because it was incorrect, but because he pronounced everything with such dramatic relish. They loved this exuberance and the way he tended to dominate meal-times with his rich fund of stories...[17]

Malcolm did some work on the symphony while in France, but when he met up with Simon, back in Australia, he had to admit that the situation with *The Cradle of the Hope of Peace* was unpromising: just a quarter had been sketched out, none of it orchestrated. In the circumstances it was probably not helpful when, in June 1982, he and Simon accepted a ten-day visit to Japan, funded by the Japanese Foundation, to attend a production of *The Happy Prince* in Tokyo, and coach a school choir in Hiroshima which was scheduled to participate in *The Cradle of the Hope of Peace* at the Bristol gala. In the event, Simon coached the Hiroshima choir, to allow Malcolm a little extra time for writing, but there was no last-minute attempt at salvaging the cantata, for Malcolm was now working feverishly on an entirely new project.

When, earlier that month, he had been playing the organ at the funeral of his 'darling friend and mentor', Bernard Heinze, who had died at eighty-seven, he had promised Lady Heinze that he would produce a small orchestral work for an ABC concert just three weeks later. Even without the Japanese visit this would have been a highly rash commitment. As it was, each day in Japan was filled with

---

15 *The Devil's Bridge*, commissioned on his previous visit by the Comité d'Animation Culturelle d'Angoulême, was to be the last cassation he wrote.

16 December 2005. Jonathan Still stresses that Malcolm's hard-drinking reputation has become exaggerated: 'People know him as a drinker, but he did not touch alcohol for very long periods. The trouble was that when he was drunk he was so obnoxious that it tended to stay in your memory!'

17 April 2005

memorable sight-seeing, from Shinto ritual dancing to the glories of the Imperial Gardens of Kyoto, and Malcolm grew deeply involved with Japan, which he thought 'breathtakingly beautiful' and the 'adorable'[18] Japanese. He was also most distressed by a visit to two Hiroshima hospitals treating survivors of the atomic bomb:

> One woman, as a child, crawled into the area around the hypocentre to look for her baby sister who was of course incinerated. The effect on her, 36 years later, is that she can neither sleep nor stay awake. She has had 32 skin grafts, the pectoral bone removed (it was shattered), tendons of the hands rebuilt, fingernails removed... Another woman whose face melted on the left side into her shoulder has had surgery to detach what was left of her face from the shoulder... Over the years her face has been rebuilt... I should like Mrs Thatcher, Reagan and others to see these things. These are the children who did not die at the time or within the two years of maximum radiation consequence. And yet the fatuous hysterical belligerent lying of Whitehall, the Kremlin, Washington continues! Tito foresaw all this. Tito was right, may God keep his lovely spirit![19]

He was left little time for his memorial to Heinze, yet somehow he managed to complete it:

> Lady Heinze's words 'You'll do it, you'll do it!' were ringing in my ears all the way across Japan... I was obliged to stay up all night, night after night, writing the work, a big orchestral piece – 8 and a half minutes of Presto for quadruple woodwind, 6 horns, 4 trumpets, 4 trombones, tuba, harp, 6 percussion 15-part strings for a concert in Sydney Opera House on July 1st. By some miracle it got written, but the writing in planes, trains and hotels took its toll...[20]

No doubt the emotion of the moment carried it through to the 'radiant success' Malcolm claimed for it, but, stripped of its emotional background, *In Thanksgiving – Sir Bernard Heinze* fails to make much of an impact, despite a theme of some stature asserting itself from time to time through the general celebratory mayhem.

---

18 MW to Jonathan Still. Much of the work was written at the Hotel New Otani, Tokyo, and the Park Hotel, Kyoto.

19 MW to Jonathan Still, 2 August 1982

20 *ibid. In Thanksgiving – Sir Bernard Heinze* was the opening work in the ABC's 50th Anniversary concert, a very grand occasion graced by the Governor-General. It fulfilled yet another commission which Malcolm had been struggling to meet, Heinze's death giving him the necessary emotional focus. (The chief theme was based on BTH – Bernard Thomas Heinze.) Dr Michael Armstrong writes: 'I recall with horror Malcolm's departing for Japan about two weeks before the concert with little or nothing on paper. It proved one of those classic instances where the score was delivered to the orchestra [Sydney Symphony] with the ink barely dry. The first recorded version cut the duration of the first performance by almost a minute! Malcolm was working under such pressure that immediately after the work had been performed and he'd taken his bow, he rushed out of the Opera House to continue composing.' ABC later used the work in its coverage of the Queen opening the new Parliament House in Canberra in 1988.

With Jonathan Still

A few weeks later came the inevitable fiasco at Bristol, but Malcolm, half a world away, showed little concern, commenting to Jonathan Still:

> I do hope that it was done with piano four-hands… so long as the Hiroshima kids got to sing I don't care about anything else…

Others did, and Malcolm's failure to honour this commission effectively finished his career in Britain, *The Times* mocking him as 'living up to his reputation as the musical equivalent of the Advanced Passenger Train'. The *Bristol Evening Post*, under a headline COMPOSER LETS DOWN FESTIVAL OF MUSIC, reported 'international musicians' being 'stunned' by the failed commission, for which Malcolm had been given a full two years. Children had been flown in to the gala from around the world, and the Bedfordshire County Youth Orchestra had been expecting to accompany the various choirs:

> But last night's capacity audience at the Colston Hall was told that the work had not been received. The agreed fee for the work was about £1,500 from the Arts Council and £2,000 from the Hinrichsen Foundation, although some of the cash had a completion clause attached… The piece was played as a piano duet at very short notice by Professor Raymond Warren and Kenneth Mobbs of the university music department, but instead of lasting a full hour the work only ran for fifteen minutes.[21] Conference organisers were deeply upset.[22]

It was all the more ironic that, in Australia, Malcolm's praises were being loudly sung at this time. Michael Brimer, Ormond Professor of Music at the University of Melbourne (Bernard Heinze's old position) invited him to participate in Melbourne's first Percy Grainger Centenary Concert, where he played his own Third Piano Concerto,[23] and was later made an honorary Doctor of Music by the university. Brimer remembers him being on his best form at the ceremony:

> He made a brilliant speech and had everyone in the Melbourne Concert Hall in the palm of his hand. He was particularly moving on the subject of music therapy. He had

21 Another report offered a different statistic: 8 minutes completed out of an expected 25.

22 29 July 1982

23 The programme notes particularly pleased Malcolm: 'Grainger's hopes for world recognition of Australian musical composition have certainly been achieved by Williamson... Grainger would also have admired Williamson's ability to present his own compositions on the concert platform.'

> the most wonderful brain, and, as a raconteur, when in full flight he was unstoppable. It was a most memorable and happy occasion.[24]

Two weeks later, in Sydney, Malcolm received a similar honour from the University of New South Wales. His strong desire for a title had at last been appeased. He might not yet be Sir Malcolm, but Dr Williamson was very definitely an encouragement.

Domestically, however, Malcolm was hardly showing the *gravitas* appropriate to his new status. There were some wild bouts of drinking and, as Gerard Windsor remembers, this led to mounting arguments with Simon:

> Things blew up in Sydney in 1982. They were staying at Potts Point, where Malcolm was enjoying several young men, and he threw Simon out. Simon stayed for a while with my wife and me. He seemed more concerned at Malcolm's tax being done properly than anything else, and had brought all the papers with him.[25]

Out of this unhappy fracas, an important and very helpful friendship resulted with a young Sydney psychiatrist, Dr Michael Armstrong:

> I first met Malcolm in 1982 when he and Simon briefly separated – I think in a jealous spat over some young man they both knew – and a mutual friend thought that as a psychiatrist I might be able to help mediate. In fact, they got back together within a day or so, and I became included in their circle. I was never Malcolm's therapist, although I did steer him in the direction of getting help. I eventually got to realise that Malcolm had become infatuated with me. I never reciprocated this love, although I certainly found him loveable (among other things!) and as a younger man was immensely flattered by his friendship.[26]

Malcolm left Sydney shortly afterwards when the opportunity for practical work in music therapy at the University of Melbourne encouraged him to take a six-month lease on a flat owned by the Jesuits.[27] Simon, himself a Jesuit in Melbourne for many years, stayed with him, their recent problems having been quickly resolved.

Malcolm was particularly proud of the clinics he ran in Melbourne under the aegis of the University's School of Medicine, and of the lengthy thesis he was hoping to complete by March 1983. His letters grew increasingly full of technical language:

> My little world is simply teaching techniques for materially and perimately brain-injured people; and that takes in for a beginning neurophysiology, non-invasive neurosurgery, philosophy of mind, hemispheral transfer, corpus callosum,

---

24 May 2005. Eileen Joyce was being honoured with him. Malcolm wrote warmly of her, both seemingly having forgotten the argument over his First Piano Concerto in the late 1950s.

25 December 2005

26 February 2007. Armstrong remembers the transient separation occurring prior to the visit to France, 'a tension introduced at the very beginning of this difficult year.' He questions the extent of the drinking: 'I don't recall drinking being an issue. If it was, then it must have been a very brief episode, because to my memory he wasn't drinking at all in the later months of 1982. He was just too seriously busy.' (April 2007)

> commissural behaviour and material non-detectable virology. I have spent ages on the relationship between the cortex of the 23 crocodile species and the paradoxical behavioural patterns…[28]

In his work he had much contact with the nuns of Abbotsford Convent, who helped him in his clinics. Excited by their enthusiasm Malcolm hit upon a plan of turning the convent into a Music Therapy institution and, in that cause, went rushing round the city, trying to find ten wealthy women prepared to donate $200,000 each. It all came to nothing, but the nuns were so supportive they even loaned Malcolm and Simon a car for three weeks…

Despite this support Malcolm was spending less time on his researches than he had hoped. The demands of the Sixth Symphony, for example, meant that he and Simon were travelling relentlessly between the major cities. In late August 1982 he wrote to Bessie:

> Since we spoke I've been to Brisbane, also Perth and Sydney. Tomorrow it's four days in Adelaide, then six in Sydney, then Melbourne again. I've finished composing my almost hour-long symphony at last!! Went to Sydney in time to hear Sir Charles Mackerras give a superb performance of my *Sinfonietta*. Did you hear it?[29]

Malcolm had been working on the Sixth Symphony for the ABC's Golden Jubilee since before his arrival in Australia the previous summer, the completed manuscript telling of work at New York, Banff, Sydney, Hobart, Paris, Brisbane, Banbury, Melbourne, Angoulême, Villefranche, London, Tokyo, Hiroshima and Canberra. A forty-five-minute work of seventeen sections, divided among seven orchestras and written at odd times in odd places all over the world, could so easily have turned into an utter shambles.[30] Malcolm's remarkable memory helped ensure it didn't. The symphony's conductor, Paul McDermott,[31] would tell of an occasion when a couple of pages of the full score went missing, forcing

27 Stafford Street, Abbotsford

28 MW to Richard Toeman, 12 January 1983

29 30 August 1982

30 Malcolm seemed to thrive on distractions. 'I felt terrifically bucked last week,' he wrote to John Schofield, 'as I sat at my table orchestrating while Simon watched a movie on TV, and suddenly I realised that it was in French. I'd been listening to it without watching and it never occurred to me that it was not in my native tongue...' Friends have commented on Malcolm positively encouraging conversation when he was transcribing onto full score. 'The orchestration was in his head already. He would often be telling jokes, as he worked away, or even discussing other music.' (Bryan Youl, March 2007).

31 McDermott had been a leading member of the Melbourne Symphony Orchestra for many years. A great friend, who had been involved with Simon in creating Melbourne's 'Music in the Round' project, he had come out of retirement to conduct the symphony, but tragically died on the day he was scheduled to hear the edited recording. There had been great difficulties in finding a conductor to undertake the massive project. At one stage Malcolm thought he might have to do it, and he did indeed conduct the first rehearsal with the Sydney Symphony Orchestra. At the first break, however, the Concertmaster very gently suggested, much to Malcolm's relief, that it was too complex a work for an amateur conductor.

Malcolm to write them out again, as best he could. A little later the missing pages were re-discovered, and McDermott was impressed to discover that Malcolm's 'copy' was absolutely identical, note for note, with the original.

Malcolm also had the happy inspiration to adopt a plainchant theme – a deliberate quotation from Debussy's *Martyrdom of St Sebastian* – from which the whole work took its being.[32] The shrewd unifying idea even won Roger Covell's approval:

> Williamson's solution, a brilliant one in the circumstances, has been to go out to one of the oldest structural devices in Western music, the *cantus firmus*. This involves nothing more recondite than the repetition of a basic theme (sometimes buried in the inner parts, or spaced out so that it is hardly recognisable) as a kind of thread or spinal cord throughout the piece.
>
> The *cantus firmus* theme is first heard on orchestral horns, a rather grand and simple formulation, appropriate to what has been described as the first transcontinental symphony. I have not seen a score... but it is my strong impression that the central theme is never absent from the score in one form or another from then on... The advantage of the *cantus firmus* method is that the responses to the theme can themselves become the basis of continuous variation... The achievement, against all the odds, is impressive.[33]

The scoring throughout the symphony is unusual and arresting. In the sections for full orchestra[34] large percussive forces often hold sway, introducing an unstable, volatile and sometimes brutal sound world, as Malcolm, in search of *stasis* in the midst of *dynamis,* sweeps the listener forwards. Interlaced with these great swathes of sound are ethereal sections in which the Platonic ideal of movement in stillness is created with the help of some unusual instrumental combinations: glockenspiel and harp; flute and muted trumpet; strings divided into twenty-five parts; flutes and tuba, accompanied by four marimbas, a solo piano and two organs...

Richly textured and full of invention, deeply satisfying both emotionally and intellectually, the Sixth Symphony is one of Malcolm's finest orchestral works. Yet the intended filmed performance on television never materialised, only a solitary radio broadcast being given, in 1986, a full four years after the Jubilee.[35] Since then this exhilarating symphony has languished in obscurity. With some

---

32 Gabriele d'Annunzio's play, to which Debussy supplied the incidental music, emphasises the Emperor's love for the third-century martyr, blending pagan narcissism with Christian masochism, Sebastian telling the archers 'Whoever wounds most deeply loves me more'. The climactic nature of the Sixth Symphony would seem to owe as much to the sexual undertones as the need to provide each of the orchestras with strong conclusions.

33 *Sydney Morning Herald*, 1 October 1986.

34 Orchestral requirements are massive: four flutes, piccolo, four oboes, cor anglais, four clarinets, bass clarinet, four bassoons, double bassoon, six horns, four trumpets, four trombones, two tubas, timpani, six percussion players, harp, piano, organ and strings.

35 29 September 1986, ABC FM radio.

careful editing it could be played by a single large orchestra, but this has yet to happen.

One of the musicians most closely connected with the symphony, percussionist Richard Mills, suggests that the four-year gap was the result of the ABC's inefficiency:

> After all the recordings were made, they just didn't get it edited – ABC's David Harvey was notorious – if you didn't get anything done before lunch, you could forget it, because they would all repair to a pub called King Arthur's Court and get pissed. David Harvey – or 'Griselda' as Malcolm called him (he had a nickname for everyone)[36] – was a brilliant man, but wouldn't get things done. So it just never got edited. It was finished all right, but never edited. In the end, all they had to show for all that effort, all that filming John Widdicombe did, was the simple sound recording.[37]

But Mills also remembers that it was 'absolute chaos to get the symphony written in time' and when the turn came for the Queensland Symphony Orchestra to record a section, the music turned up at 4.00 in the afternoon for what was to have been a full day's rehearsal.[38]

This is a hint of the real reason for the ABC's loss of interest in the symphony, its late arrival, over which, it seems, the Corporation generously decided not to make a public fuss. The symphony should have been recorded and filmed in time to be shown on 1 July 1982, the 50th anniversary of the ABC's first official broadcast, but it wasn't even nearly ready by then. In October, for example, four months after the intended premiere, the symphony was still being recorded:

> Yesterday the Melbourne SO did the opening section of my Liturgy of Homage – Symphony No 6. Now it's all sound recorded. We have to do the sound mix in Sydney next week, then the TV synchronisation is nearly completed.[39]

A month later, in a letter to Peter, Malcolm made it clear the project was far from finished:

> Since by its nature it must be video-recorded – seven orchestras playing in a succession of seventeen sections – there's much work to do in fusing and balancing sounds and sights. There is much commuting. Most of this is in Sydney, I now

---

36 ABC's Harold Hort, for example, was 'Hortensia' and Richard Mills 'Mitzi'.

37 June 2006. Mills had asked Malcolm for a percussion concerto: 'And that's why there's so much percussion in the 6th. I showed him how to set it all up. In the recording I'm multi-tracking all those marimbas! We didn't have that many in Australia at the time!' Widdicombe was the project producer and co-ordinator.

38 John Widdicombe later stated: 'He often finished sections of the work a day before they were recorded, which, because none of the orchestras played from anything but copies of Williamson's manuscript, made it a nightmare from the librarians' point of view. At times he was writing parts in the taxi on the way to a session...' (ABC's *24 Hours* magazine, September 1986)

39 MW to Gerald Kingsley, 26 October 1982. He took the opportunity of trying to interest Weinberger's in the 6th: 'Here, he said casually, is a new symphony without a publisher, but with score, parts and disc and video...'

> discover, after moving to Melbourne for my work with the mentally retarded. However driving across Australia is glorious and the ABC pays for that...[40]

And even seven months after the Jubilee, in January 1983, though the score was at last complete, Malcolm was telling Peter about future filming:

> I've finished my gigantic symphony and we're busy putting it together for TV. This is a huge job, as I have to do an ecological programme and then we (i.e. the ABC and myself) have to find suitable film across the vast continent either from archives or we go out to shoot it. The bureaucratic delays mean that it can't go out on TV until later this year...[41]

All, however, was not advancing as well as Malcolm would have his correspondents believe, for, eight months on, as late as 8 September 1983, he was confiding to a friend that

> the last bit of my gigantic symphony for the ABC is to be recorded in February [1984] in Melbourne...[42]

It was unsurprising, therefore, that the ABC eventually fell out of love with the never-ending project, so that, in the end, there was just a single broadcast of the edited sound-tape.

In August 1986, just before the symphony, subtitled 'Liturgy of Homage',[43] received this much-delayed broadcast, Malcolm wrote the ABC some background notes. They offer a useful overview of this important work:

> The assembling of the sections of the work was a long process. It was exciting to go from capital to capital of Australia, recording the music piece by piece, and then assembling it in Sydney. What was remarkable was that the orchestras of Sydney and Melbourne do not have it all their own way in terms of executive excellence: in the virtuoso and elaborate music that I had composed, the orchestras of Brisbane, Hobart, Adelaide and Perth, as well as the National Youth Training Orchestra, acquitted themselves superbly well.

---

40 11 November 1982

41 25 January 1983. Tammy too was given a full update at this time: 'I finished my massive symphony for all Australia's eight [sic] orchestras and had a hectic time going from state to state recording it. I played piano and organ in some parts of it. It lasts three-quarters of an hour. The televising is almost completed – i.e. the TV of the orchestras, but on top of that I now have to do an ecological video scenario with Australian nature symbols and urban life. It's very badly paid. I tend to get free plane and car rides, hotel expenses paid, but slender fees! So, at the end of the day, little in pocket. However, this is a world-wide kvetch...' (30 January 1983) The cost to ABC was considerable. Richard Mills believes that Malcolm's expenses at Brisbane (including all the phonecalls) came to $100,000.

42 MW to Enith Clarke Compton

43 Calling the symphony 'an act of prayer and devotion and homage to Australia', Malcolm identified thirteen sections of the symphony with different parts of the Catholic Mass. The Melbourne SO, for example, is given the *Introit*, *Kyrie* and *Gloria* in the first section, the Tasmanian SO the *Collect* in the second. This liturgical programme would seem an over-elaboration, and was probably unhelpful to the symphony's cause.

> The late Paul McDermott flew round and round the continent preparing the entire work, at times having to go onto the conductor's stand when the ink of this or that section was scarcely dry; and he miraculously held the entire structure in his head, while the players in the individual orchestras must have been at times mystified that they were recording sections of a work whose totality they could not envisage.
>
> Much technical work of a highly sophisticated nature was required where, for example, the full power of the Sydney Symphony Orchestra, including the organ, had been recorded in the Opera House, and was juxtaposed with a chamber-music-like section using half the Tasmanian Symphony Orchestra recorded in the Hobart Odeon Cinema.[44] The acoustic balance had to be achieved by technical means to prevent, or at least minimise, the dislocation of resonant values as the sound moved from one venue to another. I heard a trial recording late in 1985 and was happy with the result. The listener can tell when the sound moves from one orchestra to another, but this is quite deliberate, and the ABC technicians have so worked the sound quality that neither is Hobart disadvantaged for Sydney, nor the other way about.
>
> There are two sections marked 'Interludes' in which members of various orchestras were recorded in different cities, after which their sounds were imposed upon each other with exact synchronisation. In one section the flutes and tuba from Brisbane are playing with the strings of Perth, with the composer playing the piano in Sydney and the Sydney Opera House organ, and, with all this, layer upon layer of percussion recorded by the brilliant Richard Mills, at that time with the Brisbane Symphony Orchestra…[45]

There is still, however, much mystery surrounding the background to the Sixth Symphony and Malcolm's deteriorating relationship with the ABC at this period. The Corporation's decision to cancel, suddenly and without explanation, a scheduled televised performance of the Mass of Christ The King certainly supports the hypothesis of a serious altercation. There was also an unfortunate clash in the early months of 1982 when Malcolm became embroiled in a national debate about the building of a dam in the Tasmania Wilderness and the damage it would do to the Franklin River.[46] As Master of the Queen's Music he was a useful ally to the environmentalists' cause and he was soon on radio and television declaring trenchantly that he had warned the ABC that he would withdraw permission for the performance of his Sixth Symphony, if the Tasmanian players taking part in it were

---

44 Sometimes there were problems with venues. John Widdicombe recalled difficulties at Melbourne: 'The beginning of the piece involves an organ with the orchestra and, after the first session in Robert Blackwood Hall, we realised the organ there was not powerful enough for the sound we wanted. We then recorded this section in the Victorian Arts Centre Concert Hall, but it transpired that the orchestra had not played in the hall before, and, as well, the technical results were less than successful due to our unfamiliarity with the Centre's equipment. Finally, a third attempt, in the Melbourne Town Hall, was a success...' (*24 Hours*, September 1986)

45 Gloucester, 19 August 1986

46 Strong public hostility towards the dam eventually led, in 1983, to the defeat of Malcolm Fraser's government, Bob Hawke quickly cancelling the project, and the Tasmania Wilderness becoming in due course a World Heritage Site. Malcolm had followed the dictates of his conscience and, at a cost, played his part in this important environmental victory.

not replaced by players from other orchestras. The threat was later withdrawn, but the damage it caused was not so easily undone.

Such professional crises were mirrored by personal ones. Malcolm tended to lose friends as readily as he made them, and in 1983 there was an unfortunate falling-out with Hazel Reader. Her husband still recalls it with distress:

> Malcolm's behaviour was very reprehensible. My wife was very fond of him – we both were – and she did a very great deal to help him. She was largely responsible, for example, for his 50th birthday events in 1981. She did all the negotiating with the Managing Director of the ABC. But he behaved so abominably to her, was so very rude, that all our warmth was destroyed. His homosexual tendencies seemed to affect his behaviour. I was very angry and I have never quite got over it.[47]

As Malcolm grew older and the drink became more of a problem, his bouts of irascibility increased. Richard Mills remembers Malcolm at the time of the Sixth Symphony as

> a fabulous man, someone with great heart and generosity of spirit, who enriched everyone who knew him. He delighted in the human predicament in all its permutations.

But there is a coda:

> It has to be said that he also had a fantastic capacity to piss people off.[48]

In January 1983, as Malcolm turned his thoughts to a return to England, which Buckingham Palace had indicated would be a good idea, he had another falling-out with Simon. 'I do not wish to see Simon for a very long time, if ever,' he wrote to Michael Armstrong, who had himself just given Malcolm a new idea, a religious work commemorating his late uncle.[49] There was a quick reconciliation, however, before Simon headed for London, while Malcolm spent time in America, from where he wrote to Armstrong:

> Miss you sorely! Thank you so very much for taking me to the airport. It was the loveliest goodbye from Australia! I had a divine time in Washington. An old love of mine, also a Michael, and I resumed an affair as if no time had passed… The days in Philadelphia were magic with Sean [Deibler] and his friends. He's done more for my music than I knew. He's heaven. New York's panic this season is horrifying – Acquired ID – (forgotten what it stands for) but you get it, and it leads to pneumonia and carcoma and you die…[50]

---

47 Ralph Reader, July 2006

48 June 2006

49 This developed into *A Pilgrim Liturgy*, a cantata for mezzo-soprano, baritone, chorus and orchestra (completed in August 1984). The Right Reverend Alan Abernethy Dougan had been the long-serving Principal of St Andrew's College, Sydney. Malcolm wrote to his nephew of him: 'Everything that gets in the way of my writing the piece annoys me, since the urge, fed by your ideas, is so strong. You inspired me about Moderator Dougan... you had already given me clues towards a saint of rich life, a man with his priorities in order, whose end was peace...'

50 28 March 1983

In New York, for all the other diversions, Malcolm was still maintaining his interest in musical therapies, attending lectures at The Columbia University Medical School and delighting in a three-hour meeting with Dr John Schaeffer, the neurologist at New York Hospital, which led, the next day, to discussions with Michael Gazzaniga, famous for his research in the 1960s into the complexities of the split-brain.

So the period ended as it had begun, with a confused mixture of musical and scientific ambitions. His most significant achievements in both fields frustratingly ended in disarray: he had made considerable progress in his medical researches, but not to the point where he could publish his findings and suggestions; and though he had completed a wonderful symphony, his *Turangalîla* (as Bayan Northcott dubbed it), there was no immediate prospect of its performance or publication.

Simon had gone ahead to find temporary accommodation before they planned the next stage in their pilgrimage. They faced the future together with optimism, their biggest worry the lack of a publisher, both for the new symphony and the as-yet-untitled cantata for Michael Armstrong's uncle. Weinberger's, despite Malcolm's overtures, were clearly still reluctant to take on anything more. Various proposals in other directions had been disappointingly unproductive. It was a new and very disagreeable situation for Malcolm after thirty years of taking publication for granted. As he re-crossed the Atlantic, he tried to drive the thought away, but it stayed with him obstinately. The Master of the Queen's Music without a publisher! It was as unthinkable as it was humiliating.

Dr Williamson

16 CHASING RAINBOWS

Sandon, 1983–88

THE FLIGHT FROM AUSTRALIA had been so hastily arranged that most of their belongings (their piano included) had been left behind for future recovery. Simon had found an apartment south of the Thames, close by Brixton Prison, 'a temporary stop-gap with hellish music coming through every wall'.[1] Socially disorientated by his Australian adventures, Malcolm needed psychiatric encouragement – perhaps further hypnotism – to resume his public role in England as Master of the Queen's Music, but he was clearly soon enjoying it:

> Joan Gomez has been very helpful. I've felt very shy appearing at London's jazzier occasions, but she and Simon have rather pushed me. Last night I went to the Royal Academy banquet, one of the occasions of the year. It was good to be met by a wave of love by the Buckingham Palace people and by Lords Carrington, Goodman and so on, by Richard Attenborough and the starry creatures who inhabit these London realms. It's all a little unreal – not the people, but the ambience of mutual protection and privilege; occasions where the 'successful' get together… Still, it's the world, and I am persuaded that it is more productive to swan around these affairs than to write more music at home…[2]

Meanwhile the question of a permanent home was about to be resolved:

> Simon has made a brave search and has found a farmhouse in Hertfordshire rather near Cambridge. A lease has to be looked at and signed so that we can move.

A couple of weeks later, in early June 1983, they travelled up to Hertfordshire to begin a new and very different phase in their lives together. Beckford House in the hamlet of Green End (population 92) was not really a farmhouse at all but a modern building, standing by itself overlooking open fields in a narrow, winding lane going nowhere, next door to a flourishing pig farm owned by their new landlords. The sleepy village of Sandon (population 190) was a mile away, its main focal points an fourteenth-century church and a well-known saddlery.

---

1 MW to Michael Armstrong, 24 May 1983

2 *ibid.*

Out of necessity they had acquired a second-hand car and, as Malcolm had never learned to drive, Simon began his long career as the chauffeur without whom Malcolm had no connection with the outside world. The closest shops were three miles away at Buntingford. The Moon and Stars, their nearest 'local', was two miles off in Rushden village. It was five miles to Royston, over twenty to Cambridge.

Initially the delights of rural life far outweighed the inconveniences. 'Come and see the country gentlemen in their new retreat,' wrote Malcolm cheerfully to a good friend, Richard Womersley.[3] And to another, Gerald Kingsley:

> This place is gorgeous… Kingsleys may come and stay – 4 bedrooms, 2 bathrooms, 2 loos, 2 horses in the garden and 2,000 retired army men in the village and 2 much stickey-beating![4]

For Malcolm, who had lived most of his fifty-one years in towns like London and Sydney, the initial impact of life in the Hertfordshire countryside was considerable. Suddenly the roar of traffic had been replaced by the sound of cows and pigs, and, for a while, at least, it was as strange as it was 'gorgeous'. Yet, as Malcolm informed Bessie after less than a month there, the placid atmosphere might not be wholly conducive to hard work:

> I'm sitting in one of the house's two living-rooms, next to the double doors looking out onto the garden and the fields. It's very England, and as such enchanting. It provokes idleness, which Simon and I have to fight to counteract.[5]

A month later he was worrying Bessie by his seeming preoccupation with household chores and village life. He had previously mentioned a new piano work, in memory of Yugoslavia's President Tito whom he so admired, but it was no longer in his immediate thoughts:

> It's strange that living in the country here Simon and I now find visiting London a disagreeable experience. Perhaps the country is a cop-out, I don't know. Village life is seductive, but it's funny in its blinkered view of things. We have no Mrs Mop here. It's a helluva lot of work. The English summer has decided to be benign, so housework is enjoyable. This is also unfortunate as it puts off real work, and in the country there seems to be more time than there is…[6]

A further month on, it was clear that Malcolm was reacting to lack of stimulus. He told a friend:

> The scenery's fantastic here, but I'm going bananas. I long to get back to Australia. This place has no cutting edge. Everyone's slow. If friends visit, and they do, I'm

---

3 6 June 1983

4 Undated and somewhat obscure letter, July 1983. The village, he always claimed, was a hotbed of retired Colonels. The horses must have found their way into the garden in error. They were not usually there.

5 10 July 1983

6 5 August 1983

Beckfield House, Green End

Sandon

> cooking and cleaning forever. People come for several days and this in itself is delightful, but there's nothing to do except go for long country walks.[7]

Malcolm began to slow down, turning in on himself and becoming fascinated by the minutiae of village life:

> We are living in a very unsettled way here. It is very remote, and one gets the habit of waiting on the postman. He comes mid-morning with the post and *The Times*, stands outside the door, if he thinks he is unseen, has a read of the paper and looks at the addresses and stamps on our letters…[8]

Malcolm's insights about the postman continued. Bessie was soon to learn that 'Poor Kevin is not allowed to wear his CND badge when on his rounds in this politically right-wing part of the world'. It was all part of Malcolm's growing involvement in local gossip, which centred on The Moon and Stars, an attractive

[7] MW to Enith Clarke Compton, 8 September 1983

[8] MW to Bessie Williamson, 20 September 1983

little pub considerably the more colourful for his presence.[9] Meanwhile the music suffered. In 1983 he did not complete a single work, his first totally barren year since boyhood.

His family and friends struggled initially to understand the motives for the move to the country, struck by the seeming incongruity of the situation. But soon the real thinking behind it emerged. In the country, where the rent was cheaper, Malcolm and Simon could have more space, and this was all-important now that they had taken the bold decision to solve their greatest problem by self-help. Once fully settled near Sandon, Simon would become Malcolm's new publisher.

The recent emergence of computerised desk-top publishing had made such a venture possible. Simon might not know much about it but he could quickly learn. Of course they both realised that the creation of Campion Press would be a gamble; that money would be extremely tight if Simon could no longer go out to teach; and that, however modest their initial ambitions might be, they would nonetheless involve significant costs. Both of them were extremely excited at the idea. For Simon, now in his late forties, it was a chance to become a figure of real significance in the musical world, giving his life a new focus and distinction; his relationship with Malcolm would be subtly altered, their partnership more evenly balanced. For Malcolm it was a pleasure to make such a public commitment of trust and loyalty to the man he loved, and it was also an attractive means of showing Weinberger's (the scapegoats for all his problems) how to do their job.

Malcolm's spirits rose dramatically as the planning began. He had grown very depressed at how marginalised his music had become, telling Gerald Kingsley

> The Britten works go out daily on the radio. They are promoted by an immense publicity machine for which I once worked. I have for three months studied the amount of British contemporary music going out on radio, TV and concert; there is an immense lot. But not anything of mine.[10]

Now, however, with Simon taking on the publisher's role, he was optimistic that things would improve.

Not all his friends agreed. There were several who thought the decision foolhardy. Pianist Jonathan Still, for example, recalls the dismay he felt on first hearing the news:

> It was such an enormous job which Simon was taking on, and one for which his previous life had not really prepared him. How much office experience, for example, did he have? And how could he, a single-handed novice publisher, hope to achieve more than a whole office full of experienced people? [11]

---

9 A former barmaid there remembers him, twenty years later: 'Oh yes! He used to come in quite a lot! Very lively he was!' And she bursts into peals of laughter. (October 2005)

10 7 September 1983

11 December 2005

Jonathan Still was also worried that the personal relationship might impede the professional needs:

> Simon had to be hard-nosed about things, to be tough with Malcolm, to shut him up in a room with no booze, if necessary, and tell him to get on with the music!

Jonathan's frustrations were all the greater in that he felt that Malcolm could still regain much of his former prominence. He was not, at that stage, a lost cause:

> In my view it was lack of promotion which had most to do with the tailing off of Malcolm's career. There was a big shift in his later years to accessibility in classical music, and I really think that Malcolm's many tuneful works could have got him out of hock – any publicist should have been able to sell Malcolm's music on the basis of its tunefulness, its dance qualities. But Simon had too big a job, and one for which he was not really suited…

The founding of Campion Press, however, gave Malcolm precious new hope, which in due course was to express itself in a burst of effective writing, even though it was to take time before Malcolm broke through the anxieties which beset him. The early months at Sandon had been eased by bank loans, but further help towards the needs of Campion Press was unforthcoming, the Bank taking fright at the recent sharp drop in Malcolm's royalties, and the situation further complicated by Dolly making legal moves to recover owed alimony. In the autumn of 1983 Malcolm, overwhelmed by anxieties, needed psychiatric help in Fulbourn Hospital, Cambridge.

For a while, on his return, Malcolm could concentrate only on non-musical enthusiasms. Although he never completed his Australian university thesis on music therapy for the handicapped, the subject was still important to him. In 1984, as President of the British Society for Music Therapy, he delivered a paper in London on 'The Search For Tactile Response to Music in the Non-Verbal Child' containing many illustrations from his own experiences. A new friendship, with Dr Bob Champion and his wife Phyllis, who lived not far away in Fulbourn, was a further powerful stimulus to this interest, as he explained to Bessie:

> Simon and I had (and have) a tragedy nearby with friends of ours, the Champions. Of their three children the 2nd and 3rd are victims of a rare form of gargoylism called Sanfilippo Syndrome, which is a congenital condition perceived only in the 4th or 5th year of life. The body and mind waste away, and death occurs in early adolescence. David, aged 13, died late October, and Richard, aged 10, is in poor condition… We drove to see Richard at the home where he is in Aberdeen, and where David died… Richard is comfortable, and evidently happy. Much time is spent getting him to walk, and inducing him to be active with his body. But it is a race against time. There is no control of bodily functions, no speech, and very little awareness of the outside world…[12]

Malcolm had known David for only a few months before his death, but Phyllis Champion remembers the immediate impact Malcolm made on both her children and later with other mentally handicapped children at Fulbourn Hospital.

---

12 Late November 1983

> Malcolm had a tremendous capacity to meet people at their own level, whatever that was. He could break through barriers which bemused most helpers. He held the children enthralled simply by being his own uninhibited self, someone who was always going to do the unexpected! He would, for example, happily lie on the floor and make roaring noises at them! He also had an unerring instinct for knowing how to approach people by music for whom words didn't work.[13]

Malcolm's long-held enthusiasm for academic life was also given an outlet when Gerald Kingsley engineered his appointment in 1983 as visiting Professor of Music at the University of Strathclyde. He was soon giving his first lecture, 'Is Music Science?', attending a performance by the university jazz orchestra and rehearsing some of his own chamber and choral works. Malcolm held the post for four years, gave several more lectures, participated in a number of concerts, and, not always being completely sober, raised a few eyebrows.

Malcolm also had contact with other universities, particularly the Classics Department at Bristol, as he pursued his researches into Plato. Greek philosophy became a consuming passion and Malcolm naturally assumed that it was a subject which interested everyone. Peter, for example, received several long letters about Plato. One particularly lengthy one concerned Malcolm's latest thinking on the Myth of the Line in Book Six of *The Republic*,[14] and from there Malcolm moved on to the all-absorbing Simile of the Cave:

> I have been sketching in my mind a ballet on this theme. I don't know if I shall ever write it, but, as I am a composer, I can better study something by attempting to use it and to trace my creative lines of thinking through it.[15]

He had already enjoyed 'very fruitful' discussions on the subject with Iris Murdoch ('an eminent Platonist') and Bristol's Professor John Gould.[16]

---

13 September 2005. The Champions were very musical. Bob played the flute, Phyllis the clarinet, and it was not long before Malcolm was involving all the children too in music-making. Simon was later to publish *The Champion Family Album*, which contained 'A Song to David', 'A Chime for Richard' and 'A Waltz for Bob'. In addition to its flute and clarinet parts, there was any amount of percussion for David and Richard as well as a guitar part for their sister Clare. Granny was given the important job of helping the boys strike their various percussion instruments.

14 '... It is just as curious that Professor Julia Annas should call Plato to task for not mentioning that two sections of the Line had always to be equal, as it is that they should be equal. There seems to be no internal reason why the divisions and subdivisions should be specifically unequal, particularly since the basest and noblest sections, as prescribed by Plato, can be larger or smaller, higher or lower. I am fascinated to see that the various illustrators always make the noblest section the largest and the highest. Since Plato mentions first the lowest state, why do people transcribing it not put it at the top, or, if horizontal, not on the left, where we write from?...' (17 September 1983)

15 17 September 1983

16 Gould was author of *The Development of Plato's Ethics*. Although Malcolm had talked to Iris Murdoch at several functions, it was only now that he began to get to know her well. He had been 'dazzled' by her new book *The Philosopher's Pupil*, he told Michael Armstrong. 'We have been in correspondence in an extended way. I am invited to see her in the autumn.' (10 September 1985)

Despite such interests, because he was not writing music Malcolm felt far from settled, the severity of the first winter in Sandon increasing anxieties about its remoteness. 'I wonder if living in the country is bad,' Malcolm mused to Bessie. 'There seems to be such isolation that one falls to worrying about things that one can do little about.'[17] Life, he declared, was a treadmill. He hankered after the Australian sunshine and was toying with the possibility of a job in Perth in social welfare with the handicapped. He was also contemplating applying for a grant 'for research in mental retardation in NSW for the calendar year of 1984'.[18] By Christmas, however, he was more cheerful. The villagers were mounting his cassation *The Winter Star* in the local church and it was also being put on at Buntingford. His feelings of isolation had also been softened by an invitation from Mrs Thatcher at 10 Downing Street:

> The PM was very kind to me. I've always found her icy cold, but she has such charisma. Ten minutes with her, and I'd do anything for her, against my judgement. Lobster, chicken, gooseberry fool for lunch.[19]

Christmas allowed Malcolm and Simon an opportunity to spend time with Bob and Phyllis Champion:

> My little Richard Champion has had his 11th birthday and is doing amazingly well. I was able to do a lot with him. A young doctor from NSW called Seth Grant also worked wonderfully with him.[20]

In the New Year Malcolm made several breakouts from the country. First he braved deep snows in Scotland to deliver eight seminars at the University of Strathclyde (not on music but French literature), and stopped off at Huddersfield to supervise a two-day music teachers' workshop on *The Red Sea*. Next, when a Sandon policeman found himself in trouble with his superiors, Malcolm took him off to France 'where a friend of mine lent us a house'. Devoted as he was to Simon, he still appreciated having time away from him: 'It was a marvellous break. I had the chance to be myself and to think with some detachment.' He remained as inventive as ever in arranging expeditions despite an overdraft so severe that his cheques were being stopped. When the Peabody Conservatoire in Baltimore mounted the USA premiere of Mass of Christ The King in May 1984, Malcolm funded a few weeks' holiday by giving some well-paid lectures on the east coast. By the time he reached Baltimore, where, in addition to coaching a huge choir from the Johns Hopkins University, Malcolm demonstrated his theories of musical therapy at the university's medical school and the John F Kennedy Institute for Handicapped Children, he was in an extremely hyperactive state, drinking heavily and acting eccentrically. The *New York Times* correspondent, sent to interview him, was not at all impressed:

17 November 1983

18 MW to Michael Armstrong, 5 November 1983

19 MW to Bessie Williamson, 12 December 1983

20 MW to Bessie Williamson, 6 February 1984

> It sends an obviously intended message about the folky timbre of the British monarchy these days that a shambling, extroverted Australian like Malcolm Williamson can be appointed Master of the Queen's Music...[21]

Malcolm, described as 'a grey-haired, balding, chain-smoking 53-year-old of modestly Falstaffian proportions and immodestly lively manners', was quoted at length on the Royal Family, his inept remarks an indication that he was less than totally sober:

> Mr Williamson said of the Queen that 'Her Majesty is not known to be very musical' but is 'very democratic'. 'She was not going to appoint someone who would eat peas with his knife, you know, but I suppose it's a sign of the times that she appointed an Australian'. Mr Williamson told a somewhat startled dinner audience of the Baltimore chapter of the English-Speaking-Union that, 'Her Majesty is a benign monarch. I think that if we did away with the monarchy in Britain in favour of a republic, Her Majesty would be the first President.'

Such visits abroad, while not doing his relationship with Buckingham Palace much good, certainly helped stimulate the creative muse, and a foray to Yugoslavia shortly afterwards led to no less than three new works. At long last, given the stimulus of a two-week visit to Belgrade, Skopje and Zagreb in March 1984, Malcolm at last completed his long-intended work for solo piano extolling the virtues of Tito, *Himna Titu*.[22]

Tito's years in charge of Yugoslavia had become for Malcolm a kind of Utopia, with Tito as ideal a ruler as Plato's philosopher-king. History, of course, hardly justified this hero-worship, and Malcolm's outspoken support for the Yugoslavian dictator exposed him to considerable ridicule. But Jonathan Still, whose Serbo-Croat studies, made him one of Malcolm's most valuable allies in his various Yugoslavian projects, can understand the sincerity and enthusiasm of his commitment:

> Yugoslavia before all the recent troubles was a very beautiful place. Malcolm loved it, felt comfortable in it, and was inspired by it. He admired the people just as much as the country. Some of the Yugoslavs he knew were outstanding, wonderful people... As regards the politics, Malcolm took a simplistic view, admiring Tito for his independent stance, fighting against both fascists and communists. The subsequent, very bloody disintegration of Yugoslavia after Tito could to some extent justify Malcolm's admiration of a strong ruler, exhorting the brotherhood of man.[23]

Malcolm gave the first performance of *Himna Titu* at a concert at the Australian Embassy, and subsequently broadcast the piece on Radio Belgrade. He had also made a commitment to orchestrate the work for the Macedonian conductor Vanco Cavdarski to broadcast with the Belgrade Symphony Orchestra.

---

21 Ben Franklin, 6 May 1984

22 A fairly sombre work, despite the inclusion of one of the songs sung by Tito's partisans in the fight for freedom. He also played works by other Australians: Peter Sculthorpe, Roy Agnew and Dorian Le Gallienne.

23 December 2005

Cavdarski was alarmed to discover on Malcolm's arrival that the orchestration had not yet been finished. Having worked with Malcolm in the past,[24] Cavdarski knew what he was up against and was determined not to be defeated. The story goes that he pre-empted Malcolm's intentions of visiting the hot springs in the mountains around Belgrade by shutting him in his hotel room, locking the door and stationing guards outside. Malcolm hastily completed the orchestration and Cavdarski duly broadcast[25] the work (now titled *Cortège for a Warrior*).

While in Yugoslavia Malcolm conceived a second new work, *White Dawns*, a short song cycle for low voice and piano, using four poems by Kosta Ratsin, a Macedonian patriot who had fought and died in Tito's battles with the Germans.[26] And the influence of Macedonia, then part of Yugoslavia, also played a part in Malcolm's Seventh Symphony, the first of his three major Sandon works.

The four-movement Seventh Symphony, a commission procured by friends in Melbourne, was partly subsidised by its youth orchestra, The Chamber Strings of Melbourne,[27] and partly by the State of Victoria, keen for a work to celebrate its 150th anniversary. In early January 1985 the symphony was given a controversial premiere in Australia House, London, when the young orchestra (its ages ranging from sixteen to twenty-three) was on a European tour. Malcolm's outraged account to Bessie of the premiere was not wholly accurate:

> They [The Chamber Strings of Melbourne] had had the temerity to write ahead to Australia House to ask them to get the national critics, which they did. The youthful players turned up in London having failed to learn one of the movements of the work. I offered to go to London to coach them in the few remaining days before the concert, but the offer was declined as they were sight-seeing… Three of the four movements were played, and very badly, and I was abused in *The Times* for being late with the music…[28]

24 He had, for example, conducted the premiere of *Tribute to a Hero* as well as the ABC's televised version of *The Violins of Saint-Jacques*.

25 March 1984

26 *White Dawns* was first sung by Sybil Michelow in a concert at the University of London in 1985 in support of a Yugoslav Studies Fellowship in memory of Marshal Tito. Antony Sanders, who accompanied Sybil Michelow at this premiere, has very positive memories of it: '*White Dawns* is not Malcolm in his tuneful vein, but it's gritty and written with tremendous integrity. There is a wonderful chant at the opening and then the Serbian dance-like music, after which he contrasts the two – very effectively. The ending is particularly beautiful. All in all it's a super piece! Malcolm gave a talk before the performance, but he'd had a bit too much to drink and talked, outrageously, at great length.' (October 2005) Antony Saunders also gave *Himna Titu* its first British performance at this concert and Brian Rayner Cook sang *Tribute to a Hero*.

27 Dr Alexandra Cameron, the ninety-five-year-old doyenne of the orchestra, recalls that the connection with Malcolm occurred through Music-in-the-Round. 'He had in fact wanted to include the Melbourne Youth Choir in his Mass of Christ The King at Gloucester Cathedral, but the score arrived too late for the choir to take part.' (November 2006)

28 11 January 1985

The conductor, Christopher Martin, has very different memories of the occasion. Far from arriving on time, the music was sent out to Australia late, bits at a time, the rhythmically complex second movement not arriving until the orchestra was about to set out for Europe. Moreover, the writing all through was extremely sophisticated, making no concession to the youth of the players, so Martin decided not to play the work on tour:

> When we got to London, I phoned Malcolm and told him. He pleaded with me to do it! The critics, he said, would slay him! When I remained adamant, he pleaded all the more, getting crosser and crosser. Eventually I gave way, at least to the extent of performing three of the four movements, and said I would preface this performance with some explanatory words. After all this, it was snowing on the night of the performance and he didn't turn up…[29]

The critics, unfortunately, chose to ignore Martin's comments and condemn Malcolm's waywardness. The bad press was all the more ironic in that the Chamber Strings of Melbourne subsequently demonstrated on several occasions that the Seventh Symphony, played in its entirety by an orchestra which has given the challenging score enough time and care, is a fascinating and highly attractive salute to the beauty of Australia. It certainly deserves to be much better known.

The first movement, in turns mysterious and dramatic, owes its inspiration to Glenrowan and other areas in Victoria associated with Ned Kelly and his gang (the music suggesting that Malcolm saw the infamous bushranger more as folk hero than thug). The second movement, the one not played at Australia House, is a gloriously sinuous Macedonian dance, written to celebrate Melbourne's Macedonian community. The anguished yet lovely third movement reflects the natural beauty of such places as the Dandenong Mountains and Wilson's Promontory. It would also seem the utterance of an expatriate who regrets leaving his homeland, but no longer has the means to return – music from the heart of a fifty-two-year-old who had recently written:

> My nostalgia for Australia becomes greater and greater. I'd like to enjoy life in the climate of my own country. All the romance of Ye Olde has gone. But Simon this month will collect our things from Melbourne and Sydney and have them sent back. This is the end of Australia for us on any permanent basis. The inevitability does not lessen the pain…[30]

The fine concluding movement is the second with Yugoslavian influence, taking its start from a short organ work which Malcolm had written and played at a Macedonian-Australian wedding in Melbourne.

Six months later came the second of the three major works of 1985, the ballet *Heritage.* It was eighteen years since the premiere of Ashton's *Sinfonietta*, and

---

[29] November 2006

[30] MW to Bessie Williamson, 14 July 1984. Primarily, however, as Simon Campion explained in a programme note several years later, the third movement was 'a lament for a beloved friend'.

over ten since Malcolm's falling out with Helpmann over *Perisynthion*. This time – in keeping with his professional marginalisation – the ballet was to be danced not by professionals but by children – from the West Midlands Youth Ballet – but, as with the Seventh Symphony, this made little difference to Malcolm. There would be no patronising concessions to youth.

The high-spirited Phyllis Kempster, a lady well into her sixties who had run her own ballet school in Solihull for many years, had founded the West Midlands Youth Ballet in 1975 and now ran it with one of her former pupils, Morwenna Bowen. Prominent among its patrons was the well-known environmentalist David Bellamy, whose life had been guided by two passions, botany and ballet. For the company's tenth anniversary Bellamy had devised a scenario based on his recent book, *The Queen's Hidden Garden*. The plot, involving the wild life in the grounds of Buckingham Palace, seemed an ideal project for the Master of the Queen's Music, so early in March 1984 Bellamy came down from Bishop Auckland to Sandon to discuss the idea with Malcolm. Fellow enthusiasts, they at once liked each other and agreed that the ballet, *Heritage*, would be performed in sixteen months' time; there was a commissioning fee of £5,000. Bellamy still views the ambitious venture with cheerful nostalgia:

> Malcolm was not the easiest person to get work out of! He drank too much! But I had wonderful meals at his house which he cooked himself. I commissioned an eighteen-minute work from Malcolm but he came up with about fifty minutes' music! It was so good that we did three performances. He was magic with the kids and even danced with them – you couldn't keep him down – his rapport with the young dancers was totally magical.[31]

Bellamy's simple scenario was ideal for a young company: caterpillars ask the Queen's flowers if they can feed from their leaves but are denied permission. Desperately hungry, they turn to the weeds for food, and this time the request is granted. A Red Admiral, needing a stinging nettle on which to lay her egg, finds none and dies. Meanwhile, oblivious of the dramas of life and death all around her, the Queen is holding a Garden Party…

Malcolm, who could never resist altering a scenario, at once decided to universalise this story. The Queen was turned into a King and made the central character, to be danced by William Tuckett, later to distinguish himself at the Royal Ballet. The death of the Red Admiral became 'the death of all beautiful, loved creatures'. The moment when the King carried the dead insect downstage had as its subtext Malcolm holding Rebecca's coffin in a Surrey graveyard. Malcolm, indeed, became so involved with the implications of the ballet that he sent Phyllis Kempster Virginia Woolf's short story 'Death of the Moth' 'as a profound meditation on helplessness in the face of death', and began to see the story in terms of religious allegory:

> The Haughty Flowers are like the Pharisees in the Temple, proud, elegant, richly coloured and disdainful. The Red Admiral is like the Dove out of the Ark that has

31 August 2005

> nowhere to lay its head. It is also indicative of the Holy Child, rejected from the Inn, but with a seminal message to leave on Earth which will be understood only after its death… The Parable of the Sower is strongly suggested with the weeds….. The Queen herself suggests Our Lady, the Eternal Feminine, the Earth Mother….[32]

As the project progressed, Malcolm and Simon were soon regularly visiting Phyllis and her daughter Jayne at the Warwickshire village of Claverdon. There were occasional reciprocal visits to Sandon, the first one, as Morwenna Bowen remembers, quite tense:

> He tried to phone us to say we couldn't go, but we were already en route! Malcolm put on his little skullcap, sat at the upright and played Sunrise – it was something of a surprise! Not at all a conventional sunrise, but quite a discordant sound! All those flowers had become haughty and pretentious people, really quite aggressive. The caterpillars we identified with at once, for they sounded like caterpillars. But the flowers were quite harsh![33]

Malcolm, disappointed in their reaction, asked tartly whether they wanted 'a silly short piece' or something that would live on in posterity. 'At least in seventy-five years' time people will know the value of this piece!' Phyllis, however, instead of being cowed, responded with spirit, and Malcolm, delighted to have a new sparring partner, at once became confident and accommodating.

> Malcolm was always trying to find excuses as to why he couldn't finish the music. He was at a very low ebb and really finding it very hard to write. But Phyl got through to him, gave him new heart. 'You must marry me Phyl!', he would cry! She so enthused and inspired him that it seemed Simon become a little jealous.[34]

Simon, however, was as enthusiastic about the ballet as Malcolm and totally involved in its development. In early January 1985, for example, Malcolm wrote to the Kempsters:

> You will see I have removed one pas d'action and transposed the pas de trois and the Dance of the Green Leaves; also have given the Guardian Flowers a little more to do, and brought the Haughty Flowers on briefly. Most of this is Simon's idea, and we've talked it through over and over…[35]

There were, inevitably, huge panics as the performances at the University of Warwick neared. The third act was completed first, the rest very late indeed. Telephone bills soared, and the Kempsters were constantly woken for earnest discussions at 4.00 am. It was a great help that Malcolm had persuaded the young Israeli conductor Omri Hadari to take charge of the amateur orchestra.[36] Hadari's

32 MW to Phyllis Kempster, 11 December 1984

33 Morwenna Bowen, October 2005

34 *ibid.*

35 28 January 1985

36 The Warwickshire-based Beauchamp Sinfonietta, founded in 1971 by violinist Brian Brown. Malcolm was its President. Omri Hadari's friendship went back to a broadcast and recording of *Sinfonietta* he had given with the Queensland Symphony Orchestra for the ABC

Angela Betts and William Tuckett of the West Midlands Youth Ballet, before performance at the Royal Albert Hall

professional ballet experience proved invaluable – the dancers only heard the orchestrated score for the first time at the dress rehearsal.

The performances went well[37] and Malcolm was euphoric. It was 'a wild success,' he told Peter, and Bellamy was 'a great guy'. An extract, performed later at the Albert Hall in a gala for World Peace, was equally successful. Malcolm's terse score, interpreted with great feeling by Phyllis Kempster's choreography, has always impressed Omri Hadari:

> The organization of all the leitmotifs to fit the story, its characters and events, as well as the relationship of them to each other, in contrast and juxtaposition, was all done with such craftsmanship. The originality of the harmonies and rhythms, which both often serve as leitmotifs on their own, were characteristic of earlier Williamson and here used so perfectly, creating just the right atmosphere as well as telling the story. With its unusual orchestration and highly complex score *Heritage* is indeed a masterly work, which can stand on its own right on the concert platform.[38]

The success of *Heritage* strengthened Malcolm's commitment to Phyllis Kempster and her company. He was soon organising workshops at their local church and, as Jayne Kempster recalls, he even started enquiring about properties to rent in the locality.

---

five years earlier, Malcolm ringing up afterwards to congratulate him. Hadari came to *Heritage* with a detailed knowledge of Malcolm's music. 'It needs patience and time. It is highly complex. It needs to be understood properly, to be performed with great care...' (August 2005)

37 The first performance was on 4 July 1985.

38 August 2005. A year later Hadari recorded *Homage* for the ABC with Tasmania Symphony Orchestra.

> Malcolm on our doorstep! Perish the thought! But it was all part of the obsessive nature. He had to drink. He had to smoke. He did everything to excess. He insisted on one occasion of taking the whole company to a Jewish gala for Alicia Markova at Covent Garden. And, for some reason all the children had to be dressed in white! He paid enormous attention to detail...![39]

Malcolm had helped organise the event for the Spiro Institute for the Study of Jewish History and Culture. Later, he wrote of the occasion to Bessie:

> The 75th birthday tribute for Dame Alicia Markova at Covent Garden that I thought up and spoke at was an absolute triumph. The great lady wafted onto the stage[40] like a dream and talked of her career and her friendships with Ravel, Stravinsky, Diaghilev, Balanchine and so on. It was one of the great evenings of one's life.[41]

At the height of his enthusiasm he even tried to interest Phyllis in founding a National Youth Ballet of Great Britain,[42] which would tour the country by coach. Though this would have meant the end of Phyllis' ballet school in Solihull, he believed it a price worth paying. Jayne became alarmed for her mother, who had collapsed from overwork shortly after *Heritage*:

> For the next three years he was really pushing Phyl, taking over her life a bit…all sorts of projects… And mother wasn't getting any younger…

He pushed her very hard on one new project in particular: *The Young David*, a short ballet which was to use an old score of his, *Pas de Quatre*, and showcase the talents of William Tuckett as King David. Malcolm was not only providing the music but also the somewhat limp scenario:

> The young David, who is adored by the girls of Israel, is expected back from his latest triumphs as a victorious warrior and defender of Israel against the Philistines. The two maids-in-waiting are waiting in girlish excitement for his appearance. They run to tell Michal that he is expected. She joins them, but stands a little back from them, as befits the dignity of a princess…. David enters. First he describes his exploits in battle. The girls chatter at his manly beauty and his valour in war. Michal pays homage to him. He is moved by her beauty and they dance a big *pas de deux*. Finally, in marriage clothes, David and Michal plight their troth. The maids-in-waiting dance about in ecstasy.

The Kempsters were given precise details of the setting and costumes to be provided:

---

39 October 2005

40 The event was held on a Sunday evening in the Crush Bar, where, in fact, there would have been no 'stage'. Claus Moser, Chairman of the Royal Opera House, opened the evening, Clement Crisp interviewed Markova, and Malcolm concluded proceedings.

41 16 June 1986

42 The idea, in itself, was a good one. Three years later Jill Tookey founded the National Youth Ballet of Great Britain, albeit on somewhat different lines from those envisaged by Malcolm.

> A bare stage with film projections on the cyclorama of ancient and modern Israel in black and white and sepia to set off the brilliantly coloured costumes in royal gold, purple with a predominance of Israel's national colours of sky-blue and silvery-white.

The whole enterprise seemed more a vehicle for showing off King David than giving the audience lively entertainment, and it was probably a big relief for the Kempsters when William Tuckett was accepted by the Royal Ballet School and *The Young David* was indefinitely postponed.

Less than two months after the performances of *Heritage* Malcolm had another premiere, the only one of national importance in his Sandon years, the cantata *Next Year in Jerusalem*, sung at the Proms by Heather Harper in late August 1985. The commission had come about through a chance meeting with Heather Harper and Robert Ponsonby (Controller of BBC Music) in Australia in 1982, when Heather Harper was successfully singing *Hammarskjöld Portrait* on tour, and Ponsonby proposed the BBC commission another Williamson cantata for her.

It was Heather Harper's Argentinian husband, Eduard Bennaroch, who suggested to Malcolm the poems of a fellow-countryman, Jorge Luis Borges – a contentious idea in the year of the Falklands War. But Borges' poems had immediate appeal for Malcolm who loathed everything about the war and was in despair when Mrs Thatcher won a sweeping election victory in its aftermath. ('Unless the Prime Minister is put in the confinement of a psychiatric hospital where she belongs,' he wrote to Peter, 'it could be the last election before the end of the nation.')[43] He was also able to combine his hatred of Mrs Thatcher with his respect for all things Jewish, for Borges, an admirer of Jewish culture, had written his 'Three Poems For Israel' to mark the triumph of the Seven Days War after centuries of Jewish humiliation and persecution. For his title Malcolm chose the passionate cry from the Passover service, 'Next Year in Jerusalem', expressing not just the desire for a return to the promised land, but also to peace within the human spirit.

Although Malcolm found the spirit of the cantata so congenial, Eduard Bennaroch remembers that the writing proved anything but easy:

> Malcolm was a very charming and warm person, but insecure and subject to pressures outside his control. Time started running very short – and eventually he said he couldn't complete the work and Heather should sing Strauss's Four Last Songs instead. I read him the riot act and in the end he produced the work in time…[44]

One cause of delay was a period spent in Fulbourn Hospital for psychiatric help, Malcolm going in as a national health 'guinea pig' under the watchful eye of Sir Martin Roth.[45] Dosed with lithium carbonate and lorezepan, Malcolm gradually

---

43 10 June 1983. He continued: 'I wrote to Keith Vaz. He polled some three and a half thousand in Richmond-Barnes which is a fine effort in that Tory hell-hole.'

44 July 2005

45 Professor of Psychiatry at Cambridge University, a specialist in the care of the various manifestations of anxiety.

recovered confidence, but for several weeks was not alert enough to write music:

> I feel quite extraordinary, as if I am outside myself observing myself. This comfortable detachment feels dangerous to me.[46]

And, tired of being 'a lovely and calm person' who had recovered his 'temperamental equilibrium', Malcolm refused medication for several weeks, though staying under the hospital's overall care. Progress on the cantata, even so, remained slow until help came from an unexpected quarter. He and Simon were visiting dear friends, Sybil Michelow and her husband, Dr Derek Goldfoot, who was terminally ill. Aware of Malcolm's current problems with *Next Year in Jerusalem*, Goldfoot promised he would try to eat (something he was then finding extremely difficult) if Malcolm promised to return to work. Malcolm responded by working day and night for three weeks, sleeping very little and confining himself to house and garden. His daily routine became such a mechanical process that, as he told Peter, the first morning after the cantata was completed he still leapt from his bed at five and 'rushed automatically to the desk, peering over the juice and coffee at the manuscript'.[47] Not long afterwards, the night before Derek Goldfoot died, Malcolm visited the Goldfoots' home with Simon, gratefully bringing down a newly-composed *Vocalise*, based on his friend's initials.

> Derek kissed us and told us that he loved us very much. I gave him the Blessing of Aaron that I have the power to give. Simon said prayers outside the sick-room, then Simon and I played the accompaniment in the music room while Sybil sang the *Vocalise* by the bed, holding his hand the while.[48]

Even with the cantata written, the final run-up to the concert was not without its dramas. Visiting Heather Harper's house one day to rehearse the work, Malcolm decided he would go into the garden to greet the family's white German sheepdog. Eduard Bennaroch realised at once there could be problems:

> Bianca was a very protective dog. We knew Malcolm might be in trouble as soon as he flung open the kitchen door with a great deal of unnecessary drama. Bianca came pounding in, making a beeline for Malcolm. 'Sit down, Malcolm!' cried Heather quickly. 'Sit down! It's safer!' 'Nonsense! replied Malcolm, 'Dogs all love me!' Two seconds later Bianca leapt through the air and bit him in the goolies.

---

46 MW to Michael Armstrong, 6 June 1985

47 27 July 1985. In the same letter Peter was given an interesting insight into the relationship between what his father was writing and reading: 'Don't you find that with each project you have a book to read which seems to change its character after the project is complete? I do; and during the scoring of the last movement of this last work I was reading Iris Murdoch's *A Word Child*... I finished the music and had not finished the book. It felt suddenly very self-indulgent to finish the Murdoch, but I did.' He had now moved on to Gabriel Garcia Marquez's *One Hundred Years of Solitude*. 'I sit shivering in Sandon reading about the torrid jungle conditions of South America...'

48 MW to Michael Armstrong, 21 August 1985

Heather Harper had more than this temporary setback to worry about. From the moment she saw *Next Year in Jerusalem* she felt it was wrong for her voice, more suited to a mezzo than a soprano. She likewise felt the orchestration too heavy:

> It was a struggle for me to get through the orchestra especially with all that overwhelming brass. I remember saying that even Birgit Nilsson wouldn't be able to cut through it![49]

However, Malcolm's rich Straussian treatment of Borges' poems was well received by the audience, and the work, as broadcast, sounded well-balanced and attractive. Malcolm was delighted, and told Bessie that it was one of the biggest successes of his life;[50] Heather Harper had sung superbly and the Ulster Orchestra under Bryden Thomson was very fine; 'There were balance problems, which maddened me, but the BBC overcame them.'[51]

Next Year in Jerusalem was the final work of this two-year burst of creativity, Malcolm's most productive period since he had left Dolly. In twenty months he had somehow forced himself to complete ten works[52] – a determined response to the needs of Campion Press and a level of creativity which he would never again be able to match. With *Next Year in Jerusalem* he had written himself out, and within days of the Prom, exhausted and out of control, he retreated again to Fulbourn Hospital. Heavily sedated, he wrote to Bessie:

> Professor Roth is starting me on some different medication, and I am being observed for my reactions. I tried this morning to write some notes, but can't get the pen to obey me, and I feel as happy as a sand-baby, so this may be no good either... Anyway, it's very restful. There is a pleasant room, awful hospital food, and on the whole agreeable people. The exception are two old ducks who are always first to the trough, and fight over milk for their tea… I don't know how long I'll stay here…[53]

It was September 1985, and he was not to complete another major work for four years.

Despite all the frustrations and bouts of depression Malcolm derived considerable comfort from Sandon, finding village life seductively entertaining. Jonathan Still, staying for a while at Beckford House, was surprised to discover just how involved Malcolm had become in his own small and enclosed world:

> It was a bit like *The Archers*! He'd be obsessed with the latest gossip: who was having an affair with whom – funny stories about cleaners – he knew all of the tittle-tattle and

49 July 2005.

50 The concert took place on 20 August 1985

51 5 September 1985

52 Other works included a final film score, *The Masks of Death*, a Sherlock Holmes adventure for television. 'It looks lousy,' he wrote to Bessie, 'but stars Anne Baxter, John Mills, Peter Cushing and other big names, so it may succeed on its own level.' (14 July 1984) He also completed *A Pilgrim Liturgy*, the full-scale cantata honouring Michael Armstrong's uncle, Alan Dougan, which he had begun in 1983; and *Lento for Strings*, a beautiful little piece in memory of Paul McDermott.

53 5 September 1985

> could caricature people beautifully. There was someone, for example, who was a snob about English grammar and who used to get very annoyed when he would say, deliberately, 'between you and I' Malcolm found everything so very entertaining! Nothing was mundane! He would turn everything into a comedy or tragedy! His comedies were as hilarious as the tragedies distressing.[54]

Dawn Dodd-Noble, the owner of Sandon Saddlery, remembers chiefly the comedies:

> Everything he did was fun! One Xmas, he gate-crashed a party I was giving. 'I promise you I will be good!' he said to me. 'I will sit at the piano and play whatever people want.' It was not long before everyone was dancing…[55]

Sandon proved a rich source of material to feed his natural talents as a raconteur. One of his favourite stories featured a New Year's Eve dinner party at which an extremely right-wing lady declared that history may have misrepresented Hitler and his treatment of the Jews. Highly incensed at such rubbish, Malcolm picked up his plate, sent his spaghetti bolognese hurtling across the table and scored a direct hit. Amid considerable uproar the historical revisionist, now looking like something from *Bugsy Malone*, was gently led away to a bedroom by her hostess and helped out of her ruined dress. Seconds later, however, she came rushing back into the dining room in her underclothes, in an even greater state of outrage, hysterically complaining that she had just been propositioned. Malcolm, by this time full of contrition for misusing his spaghetti, gallantly joined Simon in saving a delicate situation by wrapping her up and escorting her home, only for there to be further hysterics when she could not find her front door key. Her husband, she wailed, would not be back for hours! What on earth was she to do? They decided to force an entry, Simon resourcefully finding a ladder and making a brave ascent to a first floor window, where, to his considerable surprise and alarm, he was greeted, less than welcomingly, by the lady's husband, who had apparently not gone out for the evening after all…

Such were Malcolm's high spirits that Jonathan Still at first thought that in Beckford House he had at last discovered his Utopia. He was in wonderful form, both funny and inspiring. There was domestic bliss too, Malcolm's rapport with Simon very clear to see. But then Still found the atmosphere slowly changing. The emphasis on the comic faded, and the dramatic took over:

> When they fought, they really fought! And if Malcolm was drunk it got even worse. The arguments (often violent) were about Malcolm's drinking and other domestic matters rather than music. One day, leaving the house and walking down the road to get out of the atmosphere, I heard this awful blood-curdling screaming, and thought that someone must have been stabbed. I felt an idiot afterwards when I realised I'd just walked past a pig farm! But the animosity was sometimes of an intensity that

---

[54] December 2005. Geoffrey Elborn recalls the amusement Malcolm took in discovering that the local Women's Institute was gossiping about his collection of tea towels.

[55] September 2005

> made me deeply anxious. Even at quiet moments there was terrible tenseness underneath.[56]

Although the drinking was the major cause of upset, Still believed that there were other underlying tensions which it brought to the surface:

> It was difficult for Simon to handle the drink problem. There were times when he refused to buy alcohol. There were other times he would hide it. Malcolm would sometimes say he wanted a drink and Simon would say 'No!' only to relent after more pressure. 'OK! Have a bloody drink!' They would normally only argue on occasions when Malcolm had somehow managed to get hold of some alcohol. It wasn't quite as simple, however, as Malcolm being drunk and therefore arguing. Once he was drunk, he reverted to type, and Simon too. Malcolm let out all his frustrations against what he saw as Simon's manipulation, and Simon let out all his frustration at Malcolm's drinking. Once they engaged, they couldn't let go. It was ghastly. Maybe it was because of a lack of emotional engagement in other ways that they got involved in these ghastly arguments…

At such times Jonathan Still questioned the whole relationship:

> Sometimes I wondered why on earth they stayed with each other. It became clear that Malcolm had convinced himself that Simon was his saviour. He believed he loved him – I think he probably did in many ways – but Malcolm, in fact, really didn't really need a full-time saviour. I'd seen him in France, for example, quite capable of looking after himself. The drinking surely emanated from frustration. Not just about music and not working so much any more, but the great longing he had for conversation and sex. Freda Berkeley once said to him, 'You know what's wrong with you, Malcolm? It's not drink, but cock!' He used to love telling that story!

Malcolm's frustrations over writer's block were lessened by local musical involvement. In 1986 he wrote to Bessie:

> Last Monday afternoon I played for a funeral – a man I didn't know, but son-in-law of Elsie, the local midwife (aged 84). Dare I say that I did a very good job with the service, and Elsie thanked me in the churchyard. Si and I have occasionally played for weddings and funerals for friends and to show village solidarity. Imagine my surprise when a cheque for all of £6 came from the vicar, and to cap that a phonecall from him, saying how marvellous it all was. So I may eventually be launched in Sandon![57]

He and Simon had early on formed a church choir called Village Voices, which sang not just at Sandon but at several other small local churches, notably Rushdon and Wallington. It was an opportunity to enjoy themselves with music they particularly liked. They would celebrate spring, for example, with Lennox Berkeley's *Ode du Premier Jour de Mai*. Malcolm's own works naturally loomed large, an early service featuring *The World at the Manger,* the *Te Deum* and many of his psalms. The gentleness of the ambience and the sense of timelessness which pervaded these country churches brought back to Malcolm memories of his father. At long last, for George had been dead for nearly twenty years,

[56] December 2005

[57] 7 February 1986

Malcolm began to understand him and reflect on his unassuming life of service. At the time of the Seventh Symphony's first performance, for example, he wrote to Diane:

> George (RIP) was much in my mind last week. We had a village concert in the little church here with 45 singers and organ, me playing, Simon conducting. People all came out in the blizzard, and it was a great success. Among other things we did Dad's *Te Deum*, which used to make him proud as a peacock. I wish he were alive to know HIS piece, which he used to hear at S. Martin's, Killara, is sung in UK, USA, Canada and elsewhere. However, he knows about it where he is, I expect, although he has better music and has higher concerns...[58]

There was great support for Village Voices, and Malcolm welcomed the choir's devotion. On one occasion he turned up at the church for the usual practice and asked whether they would be prepared to sing at a memorial concert. 'Yes, of course,' replied Village Voices. 'When is it?' 'In an hour and a half,' said Malcolm.

One of Malcolm's biggest (and most reasonable) grumbles was that so little of his highly attractive church music was in regular use around the country. It was a topic with which he regularly taxed Richard Toeman:

> I see in all the churches hereabouts, where the Tories meet to congratulate the almighty, Rutter and other OUP and Novello works on every pew, every choir loft! Alas, absolutely nothing of mine![59]

Some of his early church music, like *Procession of Palms*, was, of course, still being sung around the world.[60] That more was not still in evidence was perhaps a failure of marketing, but Malcolm could hardly blame Weinberger's for lack of promotion, when he was constantly vilifying them, publicly as well as in private. The creation of Campion Press, moreover, accompanied by continual (if fictional) contrasting of Simon's achievements and Weinberger's failings, only exacerbated the situation.

Campion Press was inevitably a struggle from the outset. Malcolm and Simon needed to be in London in the heart of the musical world. The more they busied themselves with local music-making, moreover, the less chance there was for Campion Press to achieve professional credibility. One of Simon's first publications, *Songs for a Royal Baby*[61] (six poems by Mary Wilson attractively set with piano accompaniment in 1979) exemplifies the inherent problems. The songs, dedicated by the approval of the Queen to Prince William, Prince Harry

---

58 11 January 1985. He dedicated the *Te Deum* to George in 1962.

59 14 January 1985

60 'Last Sunday was Palm Sunday,' he wrote to Bessie in April 1984, 'and *Procession of Palms* seemed to be being sung all over the country. It has achieved the status of a classic by a long-dead composer, and I meet people who look older than I who sang it as children! There's more where that came from if the bloody publishers would just get the stuff off the shelves and market it...'

61 Initially in celebration of a single baby, Peter Phillips.

and all her other grandchildren, should have been of considerable public interest, properly deserving a launch in London. Instead, in 1985 Malcolm and Simon introduced the songs in a programme at the Royston Arts Festival.[62]

It was at this concert that Malcolm and Simon first met the eighty-year-old composer Elisabeth Poston. They would often visit her at Rooks Nest House, not far from Sandon on the outskirts of Stevenage, the childhood home of E M Forster made famous in his novel as Howard's End. Elisabeth Poston's own career had fallen away after the war when she was no longer regularly in London, but Malcolm saw no warning signs and was optimistic about Campion Press, which he considered the only means of securing his professional future. More and more music publishers, he told his Sydney friend Michael Armstrong, were operating from outside London in the green belt. But in his case it was not just the publisher who was out of sight but the composer as well, and one who was becoming less and less assertive:

> The emotional situation between Simon and me is turning curiously. I've not been as far as the end of the lane in three weeks, and as I cannot drive I'm obliged to ask Simon to drive me, which I hate to do when he is busy. On the other hand I long for at least the liberty to please myself if I go and buy a cask of wine or have an orgy of book-buying in Cambridge. As Campion Press grows, and the activity becomes more feverish (I have such a debt of gratitude for this), Simon becomes more and more his own man, and I become more and more like a little boy asking permission to live. It's all my attitude, not Si's fault. It is also for me to correct. I am so lucky in him, but I slide into the state of living by his permission. All too easy and comfortable.[63]

A month later Malcolm returned to the same theme:

> It would be unfair to say that Simon dominates me, but he has been very assertive and discouraging about my going anywhere without him. He is a tiger for work and his Campion Press is progressing very well… For weeks and more my only contact with the outside world was with the grocer, milkman, cleaner et al. who come to the house. I ought not complain since Campion Press is Simon's creation for my music. He has no idea that living in sexless conjunction with him is difficult for me. But I keep telling myself that what he does out of affection is more profound than an erotic relationship would be; but why not both? Anyway, so it is! As he develops self-assurance, so I adjust (or try to) to this new relationship.[64]

Michael Armstrong, as a psychiatrist, was so anxious about Malcolm's expressions of frustration, claustrophobia and depression, that he very generously decided to take decisive action, funding a two-month round-the-world trip for him. While Simon worked away in snow-bound Sandon on preparing the materials for the premiere of an orchestrated version of *Songs for a Royal Baby* to be given by the University of Kent Chamber Choir at the end of

---

62 It was such a sudden decision that Lady Wilson did not have enough notice to attend the performance.

63 MW to Michael Armstrong, 26 July 1985

64 MW to Michael Armstrong, 21 August 1985

January, Malcolm enjoyed himself in the USA (his travels including Los Angeles, Pasadena, Washington, Virginia and New York) before basking in the sunshine at Sydney, Melbourne and Port Macquarie. Malcolm's stay with Bessie went particularly well. He told Marion afterwards:

> I enjoyed my time with Bessie enormously. She does enjoy that beautiful home and keeps herself fruitfully occupied. While knowing that she has eyesight problems, I can only admire the more all that exacting work she does, particularly the tapestry. We caught up on lots of things and laughed a great deal. The one uncomfortable moment (physically) was when the neighbourhood pest paid a surprise visit, and Bessie, moving like a racehorse, said 'Quick!' and I had to hide in a very hot laundry until Bessie called out 'All clear!'[65]

The visit marked a new shift in his relations with his mother. On his return he began writing regularly to her and there were helpfully frank exchanges on his alcohol problems. Bessie even proposed his spending half the year in England and half in Australia, volunteering to help with housing in New South Wales.

The visit was all the better for the absence of alcohol. 'My ceasing to tipple,' Malcolm was later to report, 'was effortless, like the turning off of a light switch.'[66] He even survived the tedious flights drinking only milk. Poor Simon was meanwhile working day and night on the orchestral parts for *Songs of a Royal Baby* and was utterly exhausted by the time of Malcolm's return. 'I sat on a Heathrow trolley with my luggage for three hours,' Malcolm told Michael Armstrong. 'Si had overslept.'

Depression at having to return from the Australian summer to the English winter re-started his drinking. Although he was later to describe the premiere of the orchestrated *Songs For a Royal Baby* at the Chapter House of Canterbury Cathedral as 'a spectacular triumph', he let himself down badly. The University of Kent's choirmaster, Andrew Fardell, who much admired him, was shocked by the condition in which he arrived:

> I'd asked him if he would give a lecture in conjunction with the performance, but it couldn't have gone worse. With his quick brain and sparkling wit, Malcolm could be a superb public speaker. Alas, his lecture was absolutely terrible, hugely long and wildly rambling. At one point he shouted at two old ladies who were getting up to leave after about an hour! They were only going for their bus![67]

The Canterbury affair heightened the tensions between Malcolm and Simon. A few days afterwards Malcolm was reporting:

> Simon has just emerged from the shower and given me a lecture on the pure life without alcohol or medication. I could really scream!!![68]

---

65 2 February 1986. Bessie had recently exchanged the Sydney flat for a house at Port Macquarie.

66 MW to Michael Armstrong, 28 January 1986

67 March 2006

68 MW to Michael Armstrong, 28 January 1986

Such arguments would always only be temporary. Soon they were busily involved together on a scheme for Campion Press (with help from Sandon Saddlery) to present the Queen with a de luxe, leather-bound copy of *Songs For a Royal Baby*. It was a generous idea, particularly when their finances were so strained. Malcolm was currently blaming a 'new and very disagreeable bank manager' for failing to notice that they owed seventeen months' rent.[69] At the same time he had a VAT demand and a final tax notice that was bigger than his annual income. 'It is clearly a mistake but will have to be paid.' Cash was so short that sometimes there was not enough money for travel to London for appointments at the BBC.[70] When they ran out of oil for the central heating, it couldn't be replenished as terms were cash-on-delivery; meanwhile they were being threatened with the disconnection of the telephone:

> As a last desperate measure Simon wrote to the Bank asking permission to pay something on account to keep the telephone on. The Bank Manager was on the phone at 8.30 saying 'Pay the telephone bill'. Simon therefore had to drive to Cambridge, put a cheque in the hands of Telecom and try to get them to reverse the disconnection instruction.[71]

To add to their miseries there were problems with a recalcitrant car.

> Coming home in the small hours of Sunday night we were just outside a remote Bedfordshire village when the exhaust pipe buckled and would have jack-knifed if Simon had not been driving so slowly. We had to telephone (for Si a long walk in the cold on a country road to a phone) and wait for help (thank God for insurance), which eventually came. The pipe was patched to get us home – 4.30 a.m.! The car's batteries are flat or something, and each time it is used the car has to be rolled up the drive into the lane to the top of the little hill.[72]

These Sandon crises were exacerbated by waning royalties from the works of his most productive years. 'My quarterly royalties,' wrote Malcolm to Richard Toeman in September, 'have shrunk like unbleached calico.'

Life at Beckfield House was accordingly very spartan, particularly in winter. In the middle of a big freeze, in February 1986, Malcolm wrote to Bessie:

> It is cruelly cold and has got colder. A TV weatherman says he's afraid to go into his local pub in case someone hits him in a rage. There is much snow impacted over hard ice; everyone seems to be slipping. I always felt galoshes were prissy, but I'm glad to have them for once. The water pipes are freezing and bursting, the central heating

69 MW to Peter Williamson, 1 December 1985. Malcolm's letters to his children often contained news of his latest, direst financial crises. Some aspects of these crises may have been exaggerated in that his Sandon landlords, Guy and Valerie Butler-Henderson, have absolutely no memories of rent arrears: 'He was always very precise and charming. Payments of rent were spot on.' (June 2006) Their son Charles played the saxophone, and Malcolm wrote him a short Concertino. 'It was in fact rather too difficult for him, but we got someone else to play it!'

70 MW to Tammy, 6 April 1986

71 MW to Tammy, 16 April 1986

72 MW to Michael Armstrong, 9 April 1986

> breaking down, and no plumber available, and gales blowing through the cracks in the doors. Looking on the brighter side, the fence fell down last autumn, half of it is repaired and the wood from the old fence is useful as firewood for the one fireplace in the house.[73]

When Jonathan Still sent him a fan heater, Malcolm wrote in gratitude for the timely gift:

> The heating in this joint went on the blink last week and we were ready to die of hypothermia except for a couple of electric fires and Simon (like Captain Oates) going out into the snow for firewood.[74]

A day later there seemed promise of better things:

> Two dishy numbers turned up yesterday and laboured for hours with all the heaters, boilers etc. Then the spokesman came and said 'I've two bad pieces of news for you. One, there's an electrical fault and we can't fix your boiler. Two, the loo basin downstairs has come off its moorings and we can't fix that either.'

It was hard for Simon to make progress with Campion Press in such trying conditions. Malcolm reported to Bessie:

> Simon works terribly hard. He's bringing out some of my things beautifully printed, but he needs an assistant-secretary. There's too much for one person to do, and it needs an injection of capital. He has a good head for finance, but whatever Mrs Thatcher may say it's not easy to start a small business. The clerical work alone, sending out invoices, doing promotion, packing music, responding to orders, all takes one person's time…[75]

Musical friends like Phyllis Champion would help him from time to time but essentially Simon was on his own. Malcolm claimed (and, indeed, believed) that the Press was flourishing, his devotion to Simon and criticisms of Weinberger's debarring him from seeing the broader picture. He told Jonathan Still irrationally, 'I feel as if I am coming back from the dead.'

Sometimes he saw the funny side of their embattled situation:

> I had an idea last night that seems to me good. It is that until we can afford help with Campion Press we ought to invent a name – I mean a fictitious employee – and write letters, and make phone-calls where necessary, using that name. Simon rather objects to this morally. I frankly can't see much difference between this and certain publishing firms where real names are used, and office space occupied, by people who do fuck-all anyway, and might as well be fictitious.… I was going to consult you about a name. It needs to be a name that is translatable into European languages, like Simon's which sounds OK in French, German etc and possibly a name that can be spoonerised to sound filthy – like Gomez's colleague Rodney Long, which inevitably becomes Long Rod…[76]

---

73 23 February 1986

74 27 February 1986

75 12 February 1986

76 MW to Jonathan Still, 17 April 1976

The relationship with Weinberger's was now quite tense, and Simon, in writing to them, would adopt a formal tone, anxious to sound as business-like as possible. When parcels arrived at Beckfield House from Weinberger's, he politely asked them not to use his private address, but write instead to 'Campion Press, Sandon, Buntingford', the inference being that this would reach the business premises, whereas, in fact, all mail addressed in this way was (by arrangement with the Post Office) collected from the helpful ladies at the Sandon Saddlery.

The much maligned Weinberger's continued to give Malcolm support. In 1985 they paid his air fares for a promotional trip to New York as well as a subsistence allowance for a stay in Vienna, where they stirred up the British Council on his behalf and organised an interview on Vienna Radio. When Malcolm wrote to Weinberger's in 1984, asking if they would hand over the copyright of *Tribute to a Hero* to Campion Press, Richard Toeman responded generously.

> We have conferred here about your wishes regarding *Josip Broz Tito*.[77] In view of your particular commitment to Tito's country, and also of the special situation concerning the orchestral material, we are quite willing to release the copyright in the work to you…[78]

Further requests for release of copyright, however, were refused. Eventually, after much discussion on the subject, Malcolm asked his lawyer, Lord Goodman, to take action against Weinberger's at a tribunal for the recovery of all his works which, he claimed, were not being properly promoted. John Schofield explains Weinberger's position:

> When they came at us through Lord Goodman, we tried to broker some financial deal. Our position was: 'Fine, find another publisher, and they can buy the stuff from us'. We had invested hundreds of thousands of pounds in him. He wanted us just to give it back! Of course he didn't have any money, and he couldn't find a publisher who was willing to take this on… So we offered to have some kind of relationship with Simon, whereby he would do some promotion and we would administer things, for he had no ability to do that, and we'd split the publisher's share… We tried all sorts of things to try to broker some deal to help, but Malcolm wanted it all just given back to him![79]

Weinberger's had no wish for legal confrontation, but felt that capitulation was in nobody's best interests.

> I said to Richard Toeman, 'If Malcolm can find another publisher, fine… but this music is too important just for us to let it go. If it goes to Malcolm, it is going to get lost in some barn! All the material's going to disappear, and it's too important for that… It's got to go to a proper home, or stay with us.' So that was that. Case over. Malcolm then stopped contacting us. And we didn't ring him.

77 As *Tribute to a Hero* was originally called.

78 30 November 1984

79 February 2005

This final break with Weinberger's came at a time when Malcolm was winning more headlines than commissions. When another royal wedding came along in 1986, the *Daily Mail* ran a story WHY THE PALACE IS CALLING THE TUNE, which was quick to explain that the Royal Family had again 'snubbed' him:

> Buckingham Palace has announced that even if Williamson produces a trendy composition in time for Prince Andrew's wedding to Sarah Ferguson next month it will not be used. A Palace spokesman confirmed diplomatically: 'I would find it most unusual if a piece by Mr Williamson were included because I don't know where it would fit into the arrangements. He did not contribute to the Prince of Wales' wedding.'
>
> But Simon Campion, a close friend of the shy Williamson, revealed 'Yes, he is writing something, but I'm afraid he cannot give you any details.'[80]

There were, in fact, none to give. Malcolm was fighting off another bout of depression, to which his exclusion from the royal wedding had certainly contributed. He told Bessie:

> I've been snubbed by the Anglican musical establishment. There is always a quite indecent scramble for prominence on such occasions and frankly I don't care; but the press ring almost daily and I have to avoid answering the phone! The happy couple wouldn't know what music was being done, but there's money in it for the publishers and the wide-awake ones hop into it…[81]

With no commissions coming his way, Malcolm continued to communicate his frustrations to Michael Armstrong in self-absorbed letters of great detail,[82] conscious perhaps that the response would come not just from a friend but also a psychiatrist:

> I really feel like going out and getting tight. I think that, by hook or crook, I'd just do that, except that I'd have to ask Simon to drive me, and he'd object. The effect is extraordinary. Sexual frustration, life in a remote country village, no medication, all made worse by Si saying that I'm easy to live with these days, add up to my losing enthusiasm to write music or to live in any active way. Simon is such a wonderful

---

80 15 June 1986

81 16 June 1986

82 Sometimes he would find relief from his own problems by bemoaning the state of the world: 'We are so much in the hands of bestial people in UK, as in USA. Mrs Thatcher has the sauce to say that we must continue trading with South Africa because the only other place where we can obtain certain metals is USSR (the assumption being that USSR is evil), and then there is the cry that if we censure the South African regime there will be revolution and that the Russians will sweep in. Is it possible that the Russians are as bad as the present Afrikaners? It is a melancholy thought that with the immense financial advantage of the British Tories, and their unbelievable selfishness, the next election will see another massive advertising campaign, USA-style, which will sweep them back to power yet again. The thought of it is too much. I recall two Nixon elections in USA where his name was on every lamp-post, and many simple folk knew that name and that name only. I was also there when Reagan got in. Ditto. Makes you wonder if the world is worth continuing to live in. Plato writes of the philosopher who is the best ruler because he is a reluctant one. Where is one such now?' (MW to Michael Armstrong, 1 July 1986)

> companion, and a loving selfless guy, but my virtuous life, although he doesn't know it, is due to my being confined here where I live by his rules. If I am to be a teetotaller, I'd like it to be because I choose to be so. I fear a violent breakout inside me.[83]

He went on to draw parallels with the poet Swinburne, who had poured out his best work when living in a 'wild, gay, fetishist and druggy' way, only later to be taken in hand by 'a nice, good man' and lose the spark of creativity. In his own occasional walks down Sandon's silent lanes, he pictured Swinburne, breathing in the pure bright air of Putney Hill, deserted by his muse.

> I thank God for as wonderful a companion as Simon; but I think we'll both go bananas if we continue too much longer in each other's pockets, detached from the world. Open-air walks in the biting winds are not fun; the phone, as an escape-valve, is prohibitively expensive, and we seem to live too much by permission of each other. The areas of the 'unsaid' become larger. Isolated country life, with neither daring to hurt the other's feelings, is tension-making. Still, being alone is worse.[84]

On another occasion he wrote:

> Excessive dependence on the saviour causes the saviour to call the tune, and we end up living by his permission, doing what he approves of, and vice versa. I get screwed up about asking for anything that requires Si to drive me anywhere, but without that I can't go anywhere. He works hard, and in my interest, and can't always stop to chauffeur me to a train. All phone-calls resonate thru the house, and the least curious person cannot avoid hearing everything which can lead to a negative view being expressed by Si after the phone has been put down. Then hours of tension.[85]

AIDS was another source of tension. The disease, which had only been identified three years earlier, became big news in 1985, when 'Rock Hudson's death gave AIDS a face'.[86] Malcolm had been shocked to hear that Rudolf Nureyev might be the latest sufferer.[87] Casting around helplessly for a response, he had made a tentative start on a choral work,[88] for possible fund-raising in the fight against the epidemic, though, as he explained to Michael Armstrong, he had his doubts about the practicalities:

> The cause is eminently worthy, but such a compositional venture would need to have enormous pre-publicity and then finance and the commercial machinery to market the work everywhere and to have packaged and marketed record-albums etc. Leonard Bernstein has done something (as conductor) along these lines. He has a world reputation as a conductor and composer, and the courage to take a risk that came off.

---

83 15 April 1986

84 17 April 1986

85 1 July 1986

86 Actress Morgan Fairchild

87 'I'm reading Rudi Nureyev's autobiography, written at the age of 24. The triumph over odds of a Tartar peasant boy is deeply impressive. He seems to have discovered gayness only late and in the West. He certainly made up for lost time since. There are rumours Rudi has AIDS. Pray that he has not...' (MW to Michael Armstrong, 26 August 1986)

88 Early sketches for what was to become, in 1992, *Requiem For A Tribe Brother*.

> But the amounts of money to be made seem to be in the realm of legend if it is to be worthwhile.[89]

In his letters he was ironic about the changing media response towards the disease – 'It is fascinating to see the reaction of society: fag-beaters usually hunt in packs, and the big media guys, when appearing solo on TV, have to appear sympathetic' – drawing bitter comfort from changing public perceptions now that the epidemic was said to be afflicting people outside the gay community:

> Maybe this will do something to change the ostracising of gays and shut the traps of Pharisees like Mrs Whitehouse… Maybe it will also bring to the attention of the most obtuse that there are many different lifestyles in the human condition…

He brooded constantly on his own situation:

> Sometimes I wonder if the very unsatisfactory state of my love-life with Simon is caused by his fear of AIDS, or is just his total lack of interest in me in that way. Whichever it is, I have patches of suppressed misery and frustration. However, the bonds of love between us are deeper than ever after 11 years, so I am certainly more fortunate than many.[90]

The dividing line between happiness and frustration was clearly a narrow one:

> I think we feel like fighting for Campion Press rather than committing suicide, but, even if not seriously, the word suicide crops up often in this house – which indicates a sense of feeling that there is no way out. In the car recently Si said something beginning 'If Campion Press has to be scrapped…' which turned my blood to ice.[91]

It was a spring and summer of ever deepening depression – 'I hold impotent rages inside myself,' he told Bessie, 'but sometimes I think that it's just a childish desire to control a world that I can't control'. Binge drinking led to another period in hospital. Bessie, as usual, was told only half the story, that he had simply been drinking wine and orange juice. Nonetheless he did furnish her with some details of life at Fulbourn:

> I'm in an 18-bed ward with some tragic cases around me. One guy died, and two others are likely to pop off at any time. This is depressing except the guys are very cheerful. Worse thing is the noise all day and all night... I read a lot between meals, thermometers, the eternal round of dreadful cups of tea...What I want to discover is why I drink...[92]

He was never to discover the answer. But the antidote to depression was work, and it was through Fulbourn Hospital that he met two new friends who helped him make an important breakthrough after a year of writer's block. Arnold Feinstein was a leading Cambridge immunologist with a passion for classical music and literature, who was in Fulbourn at the same time as Malcolm, likewise recovering from depression. They quickly became good friends, and his

---

89 27 August 1985

90 *ibid.*

91 9 April 1986

92 10 June 1986

wife, the novelist and poet Elaine Feinstein, recalls their acting together like naughty schoolchildren:

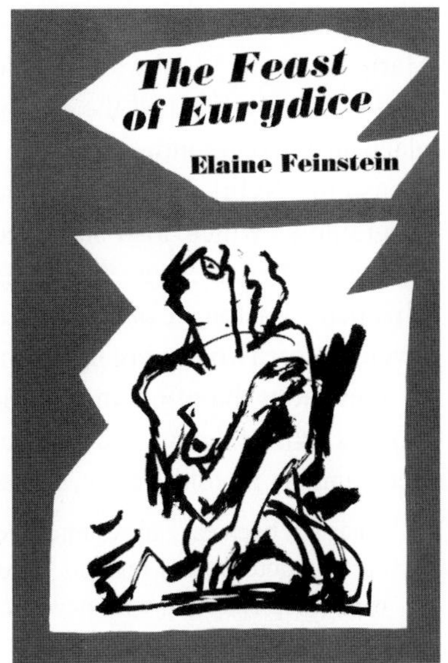

> I went in every day to see Arnold, and would see Malcolm too, in the adjacent bed. There never seemed to be anything wrong with him, but there never seemed to be anything wrong with Arnold either, who had gone in very distressed.
>
> Malcolm took a great interest in me when he learnt I was a writer. He loved women writers. Through me he met Fay Weldon and Bernice Rubens, and he was absolutely taken with them – not in love, that's the wrong word – he was obsessed with them and he was a mad telephone caller of them![93]

When Arnold Feinstein left the hospital Elaine gave Malcolm a copy of *The Feast of Eurydice*, her most recent poems, offering a new slant on the classical myth, told from Eurydice's point of view rather than Orpheus's. Malcolm was soon at work setting them for female voice, and as Elaine's son Martin was just starting out as a professional flautist, Malcolm added flute and percussion to his piano accompaniment, thereby creating an appropriately classical atmosphere. *The Feast of Eurydice* is a dark work, as dark as Eurydice's sombre reflections on the transience of life and the brave futility of the creative artist, symbolised by Orpheus's solitary head, floating down the river, apart from its body but still singing:

> I think Malcolm caught the shape of the emotions, the melancholy and the crushing disappointment. It's a lovely piece, but I always felt a little ambiguous about it, for poets traditionally dislike their words set to music. Music always wins! Your own control is gone completely. Very early on, for example, he created one very attractive, sprightly little piece, which he played to me at Sandon. It had a really lively tempo, and I was horrified, for the poem was not like that to me at all, so I did a recording for him of all eight poems in the shape that I imagined them… That seemed to be helpful.[94]

The work (which, significantly, he dedicated to Bessie) was given its first performance at a concert Malcolm and Elizabeth Poston organised at the Berkhamsted Civic Centre to celebrate Simon's 50th birthday, every work on the

---

93 July 2005. Elaine Feinstein came to know both Malcolm and Simon well: 'Malcolm was incredibly articulate. It was difficult actually to get a word in when he was talking. I felt for Simon in a way. He did all the looking-after part, and Malcolm did all the talking. Malcolm talked a great deal more than people had the time for, but he didn't repeat himself and he wasn't boring. People loved his anecdotes.'

94 Elaine Feinstein, July 2005

programme being published by Campion Press.[95] The accomplished soprano Marie Hayward Segal was the soloist, coping magnificently with the fact that the work was only finished the day before the concert. The celebration, which took place just five months before Elizabeth Poston's death, also featured Martin Feinstein, Sybil Michelow and Jonathan Still. Malcolm introduced the programme, which also included Poston's *Re-Creations* and his own *White Dawns* and *Adoremus* and ended with a delightful birthday present from Elizabeth Poston, *Campion Carillon*, which, very appropriately, was 'an invention for two to play upon one piano'.

Inevitably the effort of completing the thirty-five-minute *Feast of Eurydice* took its toll. Malcolm had been existing on coffee and cigarettes without much sleep and, as he told Bessie, it was hard to relax in the immediate aftermath:

> It has not been easy to resume sleep patterns and to get my body right… After you rev up so much to do a big job, when it's finished your brain is still wildly active and won't stop spinning with new ideas.[96]

In addition, worries and distress came crowding in on him. Bob and Phyllis Champion's son, Richard, who had defied his predicted lifespan of just ten years, was now, at thirteen, very ill; news had just arrived that Claire Motte, Mario Bois's ballerina wife, had succumbed to cancer in her forties; Peter Pears' death, meanwhile, brought a poignant reminder of old friendships and uncomfortable reflections on what might have been.[97] Malcolm had also suffered personal disappointment on two material losses: his failure to acquire a commissioning fee[98] from the Regional Arts Council for *Eurydice*; and his inability to raise a mortgage on a house in Buntingford, which he and Simon hoped to buy ('a splendid manse built in 1860, solid as a rock') until his bank manager declared no mortgage company would be interested, so low was his income. On top of all this, so at least he asserted, he was having to keep on the alert to escape the assiduous attentions of a Mr Flowerdew, a representative of the Bankruptcy Court…

---

95 4 October 1986. By 1986 Campion Press was looking after Elizabeth Poston's new and unpublished works.

96 2 November 1986

97 He wrote to Michael Armstrong: 'Today is Peter Pears' funeral. I felt that I could not bear to go to Aldeburgh (even if the car were operative)... I loved Peter greatly, and owe him a lot. If only the world knew what a life he had in coping with Britten, who was not easy, to put it mildly.... Peter was handsome, charming, intelligent, ruthless, and, as the architect and guardian of the Britten empire, dedicated to one thing... Peter was to be feared in regard to Ben and his music. It was sacrilege not to worship at the shrine, right down to the last semi-quaver, and those who 'overstepped the mark', to use Peter's own expression, woke up to find their careers blocked... I mourn Peter as a friend and as a marvellous musician, but though I received more kindnesses from Ben than most people did (even if he did cruel things to me as well), I felt that his empire did many bad things to British music; that there were many human casualties...' (9 April 1986)

For a while Malcolm resorted to living on brandy, arriving none too sober for a first session with his new psychiatrist in Cambridge, 'a slender dishy youth', who was much surprised to be asked to supply a mattress, upon which Malcolm settled comfortably. Alas, his young father confessor was firmly heterosexual, and though at subsequent sessions he readily blushed at Malcolm's more outrageous declarations of admiration, he too proved one more disappointment. Too much brandy led to twenty-four hours in hospital, where, to his bemusement, Malcolm found himself playing hymns to 'long-term incurable and profoundly psychotic people' before being sent home 'sober to the old sexless world with a Simon who is becoming increasingly fractious and overworked…'[99]

As the constant recipient of Malcolm's daily crises and frustrations, it was hardly surprising if Simon himself showed signs of strain, labouring under the usual heavy workload as well as the constant pacification of their creditors. His feelings, therefore, could be all too well imagined when Malcolm announced, just before Christmas, that he badly needed a break alone and was proposing to go to Paris. When Simon, not unreasonably, suggested that this would be an extravagance, Malcolm shared his perplexities with Michael Armstrong:

> While I devoutly hope to spend the rest of my life with Simon, and while Campion Press is my lifeline, it is also his lifeline, and his life is very precious to me. He was never physically attracted to me, although I have always been so to him. The long periods of proximity with chastity drive me mildly crazy, although I adore him nonetheless.
>
> I have the opportunity to go to Paris and have Mario's house for two weeks, and there are many good reasons for my going to Paris. With the Campion Press workload there are reasons for him to stay here. However, he expresses desolation at the idea of two weeks' separation, and this leaves me with the choice of not going to Paris, or having him come with me, leaving urgent work behind undone. Anyone with half an eye can see that, with my history, the frustration plus the suppressed annoyance at Simon's pointlessly coming to Paris will spark off an alcoholic episode. While I do not propose to roam Paris in search of street love, the maddening feeling of being monitored for my own good will drive me spare...[100]

Common sense eventually prevailed, and Malcolm stayed at Sandon, but, as he pointed out mildly to Bessie, 'the lack of any break, even when the best of friends are always together in a house in the remote countryside, can be a strain.'[101] To please Simon and his doctor, he took himself off to Alcoholics Anonymous, but did not persevere. ('It puts alcohol at the front of one's mind,

---

98 Just before the recital the Regional Arts Council had held out hopes of a £2,000 commissioning fee, but the offer was withdrawn, according to Malcolm, as it was against their statutes to commission existing works. 'So in the end I wrote this very large work for nothing.' (MW to Michael Armstrong, 29 October 1986)

99 *ibid.*

100 14 December 1986

101 2 January 1987

which is the last thing I want.') He was pent up, frustrated, thoroughly out of sorts and ready for an explosion. It duly happened that January.

As Master of the Queen's Music Malcolm had agreed to speak in Maidstone at a press launch to encourage Kent industries to support orchestral music in the county. In addition, however, he indulged in a tirade against the government's betrayal of the arts, suggesting that someone 'ought to bite the tits off Richard Luce', the Arts Minister, and declaring Mrs Thatcher 'a bitch'. These comments were of course widely reported in the national news, and in Parliament a Tory MP called for his resignation as Master of the Queen's Music. ('With a name like his,' commented Malcolm darkly, 'Mr Dick MP would have done better to remain in decent obscurity.')[102] He at once wrote to Mrs Thatcher and the Queen, to apologise, and fully intended to make amends in a radio interview. The right words, however, just wouldn't come:

> I see Mrs Thatcher as an admirable person, but she has done an incalculable disservice to medicine, education and the arts… I should not have used the word 'bitch'. Perhaps it should have been 'snake', which has a high level of self-preservation.

This provoked another round of vivid headlines. The *Daily Mirror* was typically succinct: MAGGIE'S A SNAKE, SAYS QUEEN'S MAN.[103]

The Queen's man was now viewed by Buckingham Palace as a distinct public relations liability and there was some uneasiness when it was learnt that Malcolm had been invited to Russia by the Union of Soviet Composers, one of a thousand delegates at a Peace Conference[104] organised by Mikhal Gorbachev. *Glasnost* was under way, but the West was still looking with suspicion upon Russian protestations of peace. Fay Weldon, a fellow delegate, had been told by the Foreign Office that it would all be *Mir*, *Mir*, *Mir (*peace, peace, peace) while the Russians secretly prepared for war.

Malcolm nursed no such reservations and was only too happy to speak on behalf of socialist solidarity. He enjoyed showing off his hastily acquired Russian and basking in the aura of celebrity which surrounded Moscow's Hotel Kosmos. In some ways it was more like a Film Festival:

> Over there was Norman Mailer chatting with Yoko Ono. Through the lobby strode Gregory Peck. Claudia Cardinale was a stunning sight in a tailored black-and-white striped suit. Peter Ustinov moved grandly about, with all the bearing and intonation of one of his best-known characters, Hercule Poirot. 'I can't believe it,' said an awed American tourist as she gawked around the lobby of the Kosmos Hotel. 'This could be Hollywood'…[105]

Malcolm had come on two particular personal missions. The first was to hand over as a gift to the children of the Bolshoi Ballet School a specially composed

102 MW to Robert Solomon, 28 January 1987

103 24 January 1987

104 'For A Nuclear-Free World. For the Survival of Humanity',

105 *Time* magazine

divertissement, Springtime on the River Moskva. The Bolshoi had been in England the previous year, dancing at Birmingham, where Malcolm and Simon watched them through the generosity of Phyllis Kempster. Enormously impressed, Malcolm went to Moscow laden with scores, recordings and gifts. *Springtime on the River Moskva,* written for two pianos, is a delightful little piece, full of vitality and exciting cross-rhythms. Unfortunately Malcolm's attempts to contact the Bolshoi's Galina Ulanova failed, and though he left his various gifts with the High Commissioner of the Australian Embassy, who later confirmed sending them on to the company, he never received any acknowledgement.[106]

Malcolm's other mission was to make contact with some of the beleaguered Soviet Jews forbidden emigration to Israel. This was hardly an activity to please his official guides, so, in the best James Bond tradition, he slipped away from his hotel and headed for his secret destination, only for things to go very wrong. According to Tammy, who heard the story from her father,

> He hailed a cab and the driver took him for a long drive out into the middle of nowhere and dumped him in the snow… and he had to hike, with just a thin jacket on, till he eventually found a police station and convinced them that he needed help. The cab driver took a hundred pounds off him![107]

Peter heard a similar story:

> He left the hotel, where Graham Greene was also staying, eluded his escort, got a cab, but then was taken for a ride and dumped…[108]

From subsequent comments Malcolm himself made about the escapade, it sounds as if he might have been lucky to survive. Alone in a snowy and mountainous landscape, he began walking uncertainly in the direction of what he hoped would be civilisation. Eventually, in a somewhat surreal encounter, he met some fellow human beings:

> I stood to one side on a mountain path in the snow to let a woman with children pass. As I doffed my cap and greeted her in my kitchen Russian, I fell into a snow drift, but she didn't see me.[109]

The snow-drift, it seems from another account, was quite deep:

> I fell into a snow-filled ravine in the Russian countryside and somehow got myself out again. The Soviet police, when I found them, said that it was quite impossible, so we all piled into a police van and found (by great good luck) the place, where it appeared an elephant had dropped from the skies, and there was my pack of Marlboro

---

106 Perhaps the gifts should have been sent formally to Yuri Grigorovich, the Bolshoi's long-time Artistic Director, but Ulanova, at seventy-seven, was still acting as ballet mistress and involved with the school.

107 April 2005

108 April 2005

109 MW to John Duhigg, his former Latin teacher at Barker College, 28 April 1987

> cigarettes. The delicious young Soviet cops (terrific, like all country people) said that nobody had ever emerged in such circumstances before.[110]

The KGB, called in by the delicious young cops, were less impressed by Malcolm's exploits. Records told them that back in England Malcolm had connections with a highly seditious Committee of Women for Soviet Jewry. He was clearly up to no good, and it was not long before he was bundled onto a plane heading out of Moscow.

The visit to Russia, which subsequently inspired some of his funniest stories, could easily have ended in tragedy. Three months later one of Malcolm's hands still showed signs of frostbite. It was also an extremely unhelpful diversion from the most prestigious commission he had received since the Queen's Silver Jubilee ten years before. The Sydney Opera House Trust had asked him for a large-scale work for the Australian Bicentenary commemoration of January 1988: a work for narrator, chorus and orchestra celebrating the nation's 200-year history, to be a focal point for a royal visit on Australia Day. The deadline of mid-December 1987 was still some nine months away, but so far Malcolm had nothing to show except his outline plan. The work was to be called *The True Endeavour* and in its survey of Australian history it would stress urban despoliation of rain forests and aboriginal homes as well as the need for 'makarrata', reconciliation between peoples and also between man and his environment. The idea of using a narrator had been imposed on him by the Opera House:

> I can't really bear music and the spoken word simultaneously, as it is impossible to absorb both at the same time. My present thinking is to have proses read between the music sections, and I am raiding the rich mines of the great Manning Clark for suitable stuff. [111]

Three months later, in May 1987, with *The True Endeavour* not much advanced, Malcolm went out to Australia by himself for a two-month visit, which again was paid for by kind friends. This time the initiative came from Robert Solomon, who had been a pupil with him at Barker College in the 1940s and had since distinguished himself as an athlete, a Rhodes scholar, a lecturer at the University of Tasmania and an MP in the Australian Parliament before recently accepting the chair of English at the University of New South Wales. After a gap of many years the two had been back in touch and, when Barker College built a new music school, Solomon persuaded the headmaster to invite Malcolm to open it. Malcolm was much taken with the idea, felt that an expenses-paid trip around the world was too good to reject, and believed that, as before with the Sixth Symphony, he might find inspiration for *The True Endeavour* by travelling around Australia.

---

110 MW to Robert Solomon, 12 March 1987

111 MW to Robert Solomon, 20 April 1987

With Robert Solomon in Sydney

He arrived in Sydney on 31 May, dramatically and ignominiously led off the plane in handcuffs. His business class ticket had unfortunately allowed him free drinks, and his behaviour on the later stages of the journey had become so belligerent that the Sydney Airport police had been asked to deal with him as soon as the plane landed. He was subsequently taken to a Catholic hostel where he spent the next four days.

Robert Solomon was eventually able to pick him up and drive him to their old school, Barker College, Hornsby; there the honoured guest seems to have said all the right things, opening the McCaskill Music Centre with aplomb and giving several fascinating lessons. He was full of pride when his carefully organised greetings from the Queen and the Archbishop of Canterbury arrived in time to add further lustre to the opening ceremony. His relationship with the Queen naturally aroused much interest and, in the course of a very garrulous talk to the whole school, he couldn't resist supplying a few insights:

> The Queen is a very private person, and very beautiful, like her mother and sister. The blue of those eyes is quite astonishing, and she has a very sly and very subtle form of humour. She will sit with her legs crossed – like this – and she'll say something murderously funny while swinging her ankles, but her face won't smile at all. She's often so funny that I find myself doubled up with laughter, and yet she just waits, obviously very gratified, but not showing that she thinks what she's said is funny at all. It's her own private form of humour.

He had insights too about the Queen Mother:

> She is also enormously witty and amusing, a very kind person as well, and I have often wondered if I'm the only person to whom she has sung the National Anthem. She sang it for me one afternoon at a Garden Party. She said 'Not a bad tune, is it?' She sang it and she danced – she's got the legs of a young girl – and so she did a rather lovely dance while she sang it.

Afterwards he made some light-hearted observations on his own royal role:

> There are no duties as such, except when there are contentious matters, like 'God Save The Queen' arranged by Stockhausen arousing angry letters from Pitlochry saying 'How dare the Queen be subjected to this?' Such letters are sent to me. I also get lots of letters from school kids on scruffy bits of paper, ripped out of exercise books. 'Dear the Queen' or 'Dear Your Highness, I am doing a thesis for my A-level on Music of the Stuart Courts and would you please supply me with all the information.' Of course, I have to answer them all with scrupulous care!

After the Barker College celebrations were over, Malcolm stayed in Erskineville, Sydney, for over a month with the Solomons. He was drinking again but at least Robert Solomon had taken the precaution of hiding his wine cellar in a garden shed. He and Malcolm arrived home as the rest of the Solomons were watching 'Alf' on television, a series about a furry alien who moves in on an American family. Malcolm immediately became the Solomons' Alf, their furry alien. Like a creature from another planet, he was distinctively different. He carried around his CBE, for example, in a small black case, taking it out to wear at mealtimes together with his AO[112] and various Russian medals of which he was also inordinately proud.

A riotous time ensued, which Malcolm later cheerfully likened to 'the rise and fall of the Roman Empire'. There was a mixture of relief and anti-climax at Erskineville, when Malcolm eventually moved on to a Catholic retreat, the Holy Family Parish Centre at nearby Manoubra, where he intended to concentrate hard on *The True Endeavour*. From there he wrote gratefully to Robert Solomon:

> My dear friend,
>
> Am installed and am working up a storm for the Bicentenary effort. With luck I'll deliver a movement today. It's no small thanks to your kindness and patience that the creative dam burst again. Now I must maximise the shining hour which began under your hospitable roof…[113]

---

112 In January 1987 Malcolm had been made an Officer of the Order of Australia for his services to music and the mentally disabled. It is sometimes suggested that this honour was the Australian substitute for a knighthood, but there were higher honours, the AC (Companion of Australia) and (up to 1986) the AK for Knights and AD for Dames. Joan Sutherland, having been made an AC in 1975 became Dame Joan in 1978. Charles Mackerras, having been knighted in 1979, later became an AC. It is wrong, therefore, to suggest that in Malcolm's case the AO precluded a knighthood.

113 24 July 1987

Malcolm (r) waits to speak at the opening the new music centre, Barker College

Unfortunately the drinking continued, and his noisiness and late night telephone calls caused the nuns and priests to unite in urgent representations to the Reverend Father. The older nuns in particular found it hard to cope with his passionate entreaties that they should throw away their sticks and walking aids, as 'Lourdes will provide!' Robert Solomon, trying to make contact with Malcolm, experienced a very tight-lipped priest at the other end of the telephone:

– Hallo! Is Malcolm Williamson within calling distance?
– No, he's not.
– Do you know when he will be, Father?
– No, I don't. He's persona non grata.
– Oh dear! What on earth has he done, Father?
– Let's simply leave it at that.

And the phone went dead.[114]

Malcolm, meanwhile, was fortunate to be admitted to Prince Henry Hospital, not far from the Solomons, at Little Bay, where it was discovered he was suffering from inflammation of a gland in the brain, a condition exacerbated by drinking. For the five days he spent there in the wards Malcolm proved a popular figure with

114 'The Maroubra effort,' explained Malcolm to Bob Solomon later, 'reflected less Catholic Christianity than bourgeois respectability. I am very grateful to Father R.D. who is himself cliff-hanging there as guest and outsider to the Irish-Australian whisky-priest tradition. I did not create a crisis. The darling nuns were afraid I might. And the middle of night telephone drama was like Saki's *The Unrest Cure*.' (6 August 1987)

both fellow patients and nurses, though stories suggest that he was something of a handful, 'like a mischievous elf, with that glint in his eye'.[115] At one stage the nurses, at their wits' end, put him on a drip. 'Gracious!' remarked a doctor. 'Does he really need it?' 'No, of course not!' replied a nurse. 'But *we* do!'[116]

It was Malcolm's good fortune that there was a young doctor at the Prince Henry, the one who had diagnosed the brain problem, who knew Malcolm's work and was himself an outstanding pianist. Realising that Malcolm needed somewhere quiet to concentrate on the Bicentenary commission, Dr Bryan Youl was also in an ideal position to help:

> I was a registrar in charge of admissions, neither a junior nor a senior person at the hospital, and also doing my neurology training there. Malcolm needed a quiet base, so I told the hospital administration that I had received a very important visitor, a cardiologist from South Africa! Would it be OK for him to use one of the doctors' apartments? They were delighted. It would be good for the hospital to house a leading cardiologist! It was no ordinary doctors' quarters, into which Malcolm moved. The Prince Henry (since demolished) was on the Pacific Ocean, between a couple of holes in a golf course, with the most beautiful views imaginable. So he had a fantastic room. But I was always very nervous about being found out.[117]

One day early on Malcolm was interviewed on a national radio programme, and, on being asked his feelings on his return to Sydney, he began by stating how wonderful it was to wake up in the morning every day, draw his blinds and look out across Little Bay. Youl was most alarmed:

> The only two buildings he could have been referring to were my doctors' quarters or the Little Bay penitentiary.

Fortunately the remark went unnoticed, so the new cardiologist stayed on.

It was not long before he had fallen for the charms of a young shop owner nearby, and he quickly dubbed Bryan Youl 'Prince Charming', though disappointed to discover that he was firmly heterosexual. Malcolm impressed at Prince Henry, Youl remembering him not only for his great musical skills but also as a most caring person. He stresses in particular his generosity ('He never seemed to have much disposable cash, but whatever he had was always at the disposal of those who needed it'); his compassion ('He was always so very thoughtful about local families with difficulties'); and his commitment to friends ('He gained a doctorate for the aboriginal rights' fighter, Kath Walker, by persistently lobbying the Chancellor of Macquarie University'.) He could not have been more generous or painstaking in sharing his musical knowledge. He took a great interest in Bryan Youl's musical education. When, for example, they heard a piece of Delius together, *Brigg Fair*, Malcolm sent him an 8-page letter

---

115 Robert Solomon's son-in-law, Phil Clarke

116 The story comes from Phil Clarke, who regularly acted as Malcolm's chauffeur around Sydney. He remembers how caringly the nurses responded to Malcolm's wilful good humour.

117 March 2007

afterwards with a penetrating analysis of the work. Similarly on learning that Youl was teaching himself French prior to a move to a Paris hospital, Malcolm gave him unstinting help:

> He seemed to have the born linguist's understanding of the structure of the language. He acquired specific neurological vocabulary at a huge rate.

This most attractive side of his character was the one, in Bryan Youl's view, which was predominant, and the popular conception of Malcolm as an inveterate drinker is, in his view, erroneous.

> He was generally someone who did not drink alcohol. My recollections of him overall are of someone who was teetotal. Of course he had his problems, and they were big, important ones. But he didn't go near alcohol when he was working, for really long periods. When he was composing at Prince Henry, for example, he had a perfectly pinned manuscript paper on a draughtsman's curved surface. Everything about the operation was immaculate.[118]

For a period, then, Malcolm made good progress with his important commission. Soon after his arrival at Prince Henry he told Robert Solomon:

> Everything in my life seems to about-turn to good effect. The splendid young doctor Bryan Youl said that I had done brilliantly, yanked me out of the hospital and into the private medicos' quarters, had me play him Brahms and he played me Chopin...[119]

He was expected to return to England at the end of his two-month stay, but after a mysterious crisis at Sydney Airport ('There was a fuck-up by Qantas, a dreary mistake...') he decided to stay on in Australia. He travelled north to stay with Bessie at Port Macquarie, and he was soon relaxing with a drink or two at the tourist haven of Flynns Beach. Initially Bessie was delighted at Malcolm's stated intention to settle down quietly with her to complete his important new work, but it was not long before there were problems and the mood at Port Macquarie quickly changed. Feelings of inadequacy which his mother often aroused compounded his current urge for alcohol. Marion, who was now working north of Port Macquarie as a physiotherapist at the hospital at Macksville, started receiving distressed phone-calls from her mother:

> Their relationship was such that there were often big problems. It wasn't love and hate exactly, because there wasn't any hate, but there was certainly great love and other, strongly contrasting emotions. Bessie was in high dudgeon on the phone, telling me that Malcolm was drinking and being difficult, and a family conference was needed![120]

---

118 March 2007. Geoffrey Elborn agrees: 'The drinking could be exasperating, but it didn't go on for ever, and he could stop when he wanted. He didn't attempt to work then. Work was quite separate. Drinking was simply time off. And afterwards he would go back to work as if nothing had happened. (March 2007)

119 6 August 1987

120 July 2005

Marion, who was about to undertake an eight-hour drive to Sydney for a conference there, duly called in at Port Macquarie, to find all far from well:

> Malcolm was fairly drunk and Bessie in tears, saying she couldn't cope. It seemed a good idea to take him to Sydney, as he had a doctor friend there who might help. I intended to stop off overnight at Newcastle to see Diane. Malcolm was agreeable to come with me, as long as he could take his vodka, so we set off on what proved anything but a pleasant drive in the dark with Malcolm talking non-stop rubbish, before we stopped off at Diane's.

Diane, who was working as a hospital secretary at Newcastle, agreed to take over responsibility for Malcolm as he was clearly not in a fit state to travel the next morning, allowing Marion to attend her conference.

> So he stayed with me! He pretended he was having long drinks of orange juice, but in fact they were heavily laced with vodka. I really didn't know what to do, and in the end I took him down to the James Fisher Hospital in Newcastle. I think he realised he needed help at this stage… That might have been the last time I saw him, when I left him there. Such a lonely figure with his funny Russian hat on, and all his badges and things, carrying a bag with very few clothes, telling everyone his address was Buckingham Palace! I'd thrown out all his bottles…[121]

After a few days in the James Fisher Hospital, Malcolm was well enough to take the train up to Bessie at Port Macquarie before returning to Sydney. There he settled down at the King Henry Hospital, as Bryan Youl's guest, with the same delightful view of the Pacific. While there he completed a section of *The True Endeavour*, 'a movement relating to rain forests which, as you may imagine, means millions of notes.'[122] He then worked on a wedding present for Robert Solomon's daughter, Tamsin, and her fiancé, Phil, his devoted chauffeur. Malcolm's head was still full of *Springtime on the River Moskva*, so he decided his present to the young couple would be a short continuation piece, *Pas de Trois*, which had the advantage that he could play it at the wedding on two pianos with Bryan.[123]

The calm was unfortunately interrupted by another crisis, Malcolm learning that his old piano teacher in Melbourne, Ada Corder, had died. A former pupil of

121 July 2005

122 MW to Robert Solomon, 7 September 1987

123 *Pas de Trois*, written overnight and completed at 6.00 am on the morning of the wedding, is a charming andante with a brief 'programme' attached: 'Three moorhens glide down the river as the sun rises. The young Cossa watches them. He throws twigs at them; the water bubbles; but they prefer minnows.' Phil believes Malcolm had intended to take the piece further, and certainly the young Cossa (or Cossack) could be the intended hero of a children's ballet, set by the river Moskva, which was never written. The two pianos are marked throughout BY and MW, the dedication 'For Tamsin and Phillip, with love from Bryan and Malcolm'. The mystery of the *Pas de Trois*'s connection with *Springtime on the River Moskva* was further heightened when the Campion Press edition of the latter was prefaced with the dedication: 'For Tamsin and Phillip, Students of the Bolshoi Ballet'...

For Tamsin and Phillip
6.ix.87
with love from Bryan
and Malcolm
PAS DE TROIS
(Three moorhens glide down the river as the sun rises. The Young Cossa watches them.)
Andante piacevole
PIANO
B.Y.
M.W.
(echo)
poco dim
cresc.
dim.
sempre cresc.
(the water bubbles.)
(they peck at the twigs.)
(but they prefer minnows)
legato
mf dim.
p dim.
Malcolm Williamson July/September 1987
Erskineville / Port Macquarie / Little Bay N.S.W.

With Tamsin Solomon

With the wedding present for Phil and Tamsin Clarke. Bryan Youl looks on.

Schnabel and hugely respected, she had lived to ninety-three, but Malcolm was so upset that he rushed from King Henry Hospital to Tamsin and Phil's new home where he steadily worked his way through bottles of champagne left over from the wedding before collapsing and being returned to the hospital. As soon as he had recovered, he sped to Melbourne, staying with Bill Whitfield, a pianist friend for over thirty years and a fellow Corder pupil, taking over his telephone as he 'organised' the funeral, in the process booking at least two symphony orchestras to play Fauré's *Requiem*. It took considerable time to sort out all the confusion, and Bill Whitfield subsequently hid his telephone, taking it with him if he went out. Malcolm's eccentric behaviour at the funeral was long remembered:

> At Ada's 'lying-in-state' Malcolm asked to be left alone with her. He put on his Jewish prayer cap and knelt by the body, reciting the Rosary loud enough to be heard in the next street. Then he rose to his feet unsteadily and flicked the veil off Ada's face – he was about to kiss her, when another of her former pupils came strutting in, and with a cry of 'Don't you dare desecrate the dead!' rushed up to the coffin and pushed him away. A sharp exchange followed.[124]

124 February 2007

Malcolm insisted on playing the organ at the funeral, although he was in no state to do so:

> With a bottle of brandy in his pocket he went up to the organ loft and began playing a Bach Chorale Prelude. The priest tried to begin the service, but Malcolm wouldn't stop playing. Something of an argument eventually broke out. Malcolm wanted to give the eulogy too, and when the priest started on it, he shouted from the organ loft 'Damn priest, hogging the pulpit!'

Outside the church Malcolm's determination to pay proper homage to Ada continued:

> At the graveside there were many nuns and mothers-superior in attendance. Malcolm seized hold of a spade and began shovelling earth furiously onto the coffin, though much of it splattered the nuns who had to take evasive action. Malcolm was eventually taken away, still in a highly distressed state.

When the day came for the reading of Ada's will, Malcolm was again overwrought, demanding Bill Whitfield allow him three shots of brandy in his coffee. When Whitfield cautiously prevaricated, Malcolm was furious. 'The Queen herself pours gin down my throat!' he shouted, and flung the coffee-filled cup at his host. Not long afterwards he fell and hit his head badly. After a doctor was called, both he and Malcolm ended up sitting on the floor together, as Malcolm read the doctor his favourite Kath Walker poems.

Eventually, when the Whitfields could finally take no more, they gently suggested he return to Sydney. Instead, he turned to other Melbourne friends. Michael Brimer remembers his great surprise at finding Malcolm at the front door at eight o'clock one morning, a small suitcase in one hand, a cardboard cask of wine in the other, and a second cask under his arm. 'Can I come and stay?' he asked. He stayed a couple of days, drinking 'determinedly' and bringing a young writer home with him one evening. *The True Endeavour* was never mentioned.

His early morning departure, to catch a plane to Sydney, was as sad as his arrival. Malcolm sat in the back seat of the Brimers' car together with a suitcase, a wine-cask and a glass, but as Judith Brimer was delivering her young son to school he refrained from drinking:

> On the journey to school Malcolm told our son, John-Michael, one funny story after another, keeping him in fits of laughter the whole way. As soon as John-Michael got out, Malcolm poured himself a glass of wine and downed it, while Judith was turning the car to head for the airport. She accompanied him to the departure counter and managed the checking-in and boarding so that no-one noticed that he was under the weather. We knew he was going to stay with a doctor friend in Sydney who would look after him, but it was really was awful to see him like that, and knowing how much he hated himself.[125]

Malcolm left for England in mid-October, two months before the expiry of the Opera House's deadline. At Prince Henry Hospital he had just completed a

125 Michael Brimer, August 2005

movement called 'Ode to Those who Died in Vietnam'[126] playing it through to Bryan Youl on his last evening. By the next morning, however, it had disappeared, and Phil, who as usual was helping out as Malcolm's taxi driver, remembers terrible crises, he and Tamsin spending hours trying to retrieve the lost manuscript:

> We searched everywhere, looking for the music in the garbage, for example, but couldn't find it. He blamed me for its loss, which was a little unfair! It would not surprise me if Malcolm left it around after playing it on that creaky old upright in the doctors' quarters.[127]

Youl thinks this likely:

> Malcolm used to do most of his composing in a public area with fantastic unimpeded views out to sea, and it's very possible that the cleaners might have found it lying around and thought it was not important.[128]

Vietnam does not feature among the work's seven movements, so the Ode was never found. When Phil finally picked Malcolm up from the hospital to take him to the airport, despair over the manuscript's loss made the departure all the bleaker:

> He was as pissed as a parrot, blaming me for everything, and dressed in a grey tracksuit, grey pullover and a large grey beret. It was a grey late evening too. Everything was grey… He looked like a very bad-tempered garden gnome. I think he was cross because we still liked him…

There was a moment of truth when he sobered up and told Phil and Tamsin that he hated being liked purely for his music; he wanted to be liked for himself; to recover his own identity as a human being and discard the outward shell of Williamson the composer, Master of the Queen's Music. But it was only a brief moment of calm. The furry alien was spirited to the end, his anger suddenly sparked into fierce exchanges with the staff of Qantas, as Phil and Tamsin sorted out the details of his flight. They ushered him away from the check-in, still protesting, bought him a large breakfast, and saw him into the departure lounge.

> We told him he was being so bad-tempered that if the plane didn't take off, we were going to push it till it flew!

Despite all the crises of this grey evening, they stayed and watched Malcolm's jet accelerate up into the night sky and away over Botany Bay, before going back to Prince Henry, where, torches in hand, they fruitlessly resumed sifting through the garbage…

It had been 'a great wrench to leave Australia', Malcolm wrote to Robert Solomon, when he eventually arrived back in Sandon. The stops at Los Angeles and New York (where he met Clare) were brief, and the return to England

---

[126] No such movement is mentioned in the Williamson catalogue.

[127] September 2005

[128] March 2007

spectacular as 'the plane bounced into Heathrow'. He had arrived the evening of the famous hurricane of 1987, the worst in Britain for two centuries, when winds of around 100 mph did enormous damage, destroying fifteen million trees. The terminal was in pandemonium and Simon had been delayed. Reunited, they endured a hazardous return to Hertfordshire:

> Roads had become lakes, trees were across them, wires were down. I don't know how many fatalities.[129]

Fortunately, apart from the uprooting of one tree and a roof blown off a shed, Beckfield House had survived. Malcolm himself, however, began to feel more and more like one of the uprooted trees. Robert Solomon received details of his problem:

> I am in the grip of an apparently long-term depression since I returned to the UK. It's all an odd feeling since it's not paranoid or psychotic and I can stand outside and objectify it.[130]

He was aware that the depression was related to guilt: at his inability to concentrate fully on *The True Endeavour*; at the five months away from Simon ('I left Simon with scarcely tolerable burdens while I lived largely on the goodness and charity of others');[131] and at his frustrations with the continued presence of Simon's elderly mother, who had been staying at Beckfield House since before his departure to Australia.

There were now barely two months left for the completion of *The True Endeavour* and the continued presence of Nieza Campion was distracting him. He told Robert Solomon:

> It is difficult for me to work while the old girl is spouting her political views which are diametrically opposite to what I believe in… I am trying through my music to realise a vision, and the old girl's attitudes are disturbing. Result: Simon is torn in two. Devotion to mum and trying to fence me off so that I can meet my deadlines.

A little later, with only six weeks left to complete what he now described as his '30-minute protest work', he began to consider leaving Sandon:

> I've suggested to Simon that I spend time in a Benedictine Monastery, but Simon forbids this so forcefully that I cannot consider it.

So he stayed on in Beckfield House, where there were ever new impediments to progress:

> What a life! Yesterday we went to get haircuts and somehow the house keys got lost. The next door neighbours, who have a duplicate, were out, so a day was spent in cold frustration, until they returned. Life seems at the moment to be more mists than mellow fruitfulness…[132]

---

129 MW to Robert Solomon

130 3 November 1987

131 *ibid.*

132 MW to Jonathan Still, 5 November 1987

Robert Solomon was given more details of the deepening mists: he had lost confidence in the value of psychiatric counselling; in trying to write music, he felt utterly defenceless, armed only with pen and blank paper; and he resented any assertions that his drinking was a major problem:

> I can objectify my own depression; it is not psychotic and certainly not alcoholic (which reminds me, I'll dong the next person who tells me to keep off the bottle…) but seems to relate at least in part to climate. Three bad summers in succession and long biting winters between seem to have sapped much of the British spirit.

Malcolm seemed to seize any diversion which would ease the current crisis. Elizabeth Poston had died last March while working on a book of Christmas Carols, and Malcolm accepted a lucrative offer from her publishers to complete the work, though it involved writing a long introductory essay and setting over thirty carols. It was very much a labour of love, the essay allowing him to pay affectionate homage to a dear friend in most carefully polished prose. Of one of her most famous carols, for example, he wrote:

> The persistent tale of Elizabeth's having composed 'Jesus Christ the Apple Tree' in a garage while waiting for her car to be repaired exists in as many versions as a popular carol, and while Elizabeth would undoubtedly have corroborated every version of the tale, it is no more likely to be founded on fact than Neale's words for 'Good King Wencelas'.[133]

The continued presence in Beckford House of Simon's mother, nearly blind but determined to be helpful, did not make Malcolm's pressing commitments easy to fulfil. He set out his frustrations in a letter to Jonathan Still:

> Simon is worn to a frazzle and he and I are in a state of truce – just. He has receded to a guilt-ridden infant state, and is coping by superhuman strength, and maybe it is a successful test of my love for him and of his for me that blood has not been shed.[134]

Attempting to preserve his sense of humour, Malcolm itemized the causes of some of the rows that day:

> (i) Should the sausages be grilled or fried, because Nieza [Simon's mother] wanted to be helpful but can't manage the grill. (ii) Simon, in her view, is a failure as a business-man because he was so long on one phone-call – it was about the Xmas Carol book. (iii) Nieza refused to have supper and stomped up to bed. Simon said 'OK. Goodnight'. She was down again and hungry after I'd made supper for two and put it on the table, so Si made her a salmon dish which she insisted on supervising and so overcooked it. (iv) She made it clear that she was suffering through the 'Perfect Spy' thriller on TV because she couldn't see. (v) Simon typed an urgent letter for the 8.45 Stevenage collection. The row over whether or not he ought to drive to Stevenage PO caused him

---

133 *A Book of Christmas Carols*, p.13. There were some delightful insights into projects he and Simon had shared with her towards the end of her life: 'Around the age of 80 Elizabeth Poston fought one-woman battles with the telephone system and the municipal authorities who closed down her road in Hertfordshire for repairs. In both cases she astonished every-body by emerging victorious...' (*ibid.*)

134 19 November 1987

> to miss the post, and, anyway, he couldn't find a stamp – another crime on his charge sheet. (vi) Simon watched the late night movie and Nieza lay in bed at the other end of the house upstairs (once my office) hearing voices (TV) and thought it was burglars…

And so it went on…

The True Endeavour was beyond retrieval and it hardly mattered that there was an excursion to London in late November, which included the annual St Cecilia Service in aid of the Musicians' Benevolent Fund, for which a few months earlier he had written a lengthy and attractive setting of Mary Wilson's devotional poem *Galilee*.[135] It was a day of mixed emotions as Malcolm later explained to Lady Wilson:

> Sitting in the car in the traffic jam, I felt like Marie Antoinette in a tumbril. Then at the church I was coolly told that one of the choirs (Westminster Abbey) had communally collapsed with 'flu… But Galilee was brought off quite wonderfully. So from my Marie Antoinette acceptance of my forthcoming execution in the early morning, I found myself last night praising and thanking God for what seemed to be a triumph.[136]

Ian Kellam, a friend since the 1950s, remembers Malcolm coming to this concert from an audience at Buckingham Palace. Mary Wilson had expressed the hope that Malcolm would arrive with news of a knighthood but Kellam himself thought this would be unlikely. There was a rumour, he said, that on one occasion the Master of the Queen's Music had used inappropriately colourful language in the Queen Mother's presence, after which a knighthood was never a possibility.[137] When Malcolm arrived, resplendent in his Open University robes[138] and proudly wearing a Moscow Arts Theatre badge, there was indeed no news of the coveted award. 'He looked so lost at the concert,' remembers Kellam. 'Washed out and ever so tired.'[139]

The success of *Galilee* was a pleasing contrast to the frustrations of *The True Endeavour*, on which Malcolm now gave up, turning instead to more of Mary Wilson's poems. Just two weeks before the expiry of his deadline, he wrote to her in considerable exultation:

> There must be some God-like spirit abroad. There is. Beat this: last night, sick to death of working on my big Australian bicentenary piece, I turned from it to what really tempts me – 'Easter in St Mary's Church' and in the late hours a talent (too good to be my own) gave me an opening melodic phrase of, I think, great and immediate beauty. I saw in my mind the church, the people, the flowers as evoked by your poem.

---

135 It was sung by the choirs of Westminster Cathedral, the Chapel Royal and St Paul's, conducted by Richard Popplewell, who remembers it as 'a good piece' and that Malcolm was very generous with his praise afterwards. (August 2005)

136 19 November 1987

137 Other friends, however, strongly refute all such rumours of improper behaviour, believing that Malcolm's relationship with the Royal Family remained cordial throughout. 'If he erred at all,' comments Geoffrey Elborn, 'it was only because at times he was sycophantic.' (March 2007)

138 He had been made an Honorary Doctor of the Open University in 1983.

139 July 2006

> You know that great feeling you get when you write a real smackeroo? Maybe a line, maybe a phrase. Nobody can then rob you of the elation thereby given!
>
> One swallow doesn't make a summer, and the opening phrase that so pleases me of 'Easter in St Mary's Church' is, I fear, also a challenge to make the rest of it as good. I tried it out on Simon, who grabbed its beauty (dare I say that?) but, playing Devil's Advocate , said, 'Yes, but it cannot be a companion to 'This Christmas Night' because of the secular element'.[140]

A week later Malcolm and Simon lunched with the Wilsons in London before going on to the House of Lords. Although they were late arriving ('We left tons of time to be with you at the moment agreed, and then sat helpless in Birdcage Walk in what felt like a petrified taxi-rank!'), it proved a memorable day. Though it was eleven years since Harold Wilson had retired as Prime Minister and he was now struggling severely with Alzheimer's, Malcolm's enthusiasm, admiration and conversational skills brought out the very best from him. Later Malcolm wrote to Mary Wilson:

> It was a super relaxed luncheon… a thrill to be at table with a great man and to find him such a genial companion with the sagacity and humility of the really great…[141]

And so the deadline for *The True Endeavour* came and went. Six weeks later, on 26 January 1988, Prince Charles and Princess Diana were the guests of honour at the Sydney Opera House for the celebration of the 200th anniversary of the landing of Captain Arthur Phillip's eleven ships at Sydney Cove. After speeches on the forecourt, a flypast and a re-enactment in the harbour of Captain Phillip's arrival, the dignitaries, who might have been listening to *The True Endeavour*, instead heard Douglas Gamley's *Overture of Colonial Themes, based on British folk tunes*.

But Malcolm still had a few friends in influential places who believed in him. Although the Bicentenary celebrations commenced in January, they embraced the whole year, and an October date was offered Malcolm for the premiere of *The True Endeavour*, its venue still the Opera House forecourt. With several weeks' work ahead of him, if he was to finish it, Malcolm took himself off to a clinic for a dry-out, suffering the agony of DTs. He was afterwards able to write triumphantly to Robert Solomon:

> Hiya! Today I finished *The True Endeavour*. The monster narrator-chorus-orchestra work for October 23rd. For many reasons, among them your immense, generous hospitality, I can now, as I put the last staccato dots, the last dynamic markings, say 'Thank you, Bob, for giving me friendship and a roof – and caviar, which helped that work be written'.[142]

It took another two months before the manuscript was finally delivered to the Melbourne Symphony Orchestra in April 1988. All seemed well. Malcolm might

---

140 27 November 1987. 'This Christmas Night' was a Mary Wilson carol which he had set ten years earlier and was now revisiting.

141 November 1987

142 5 February 1988

yet make an Australian come-back, for the seven-movement work[143] would cause a considerable stir with its striking theme of the nation's past errors and future needs. With the addition of well-chosen texts from Manning Clark, Malcolm's view of Australian history promised to make him a champion of the radical left. But by August he was indulging in a furious argument with the Sydney Opera House for changing arrangements against his wishes. Robert Solomon was given some details:

> The arrangements for the Oct 23 are a fuck-up to the point of genius – venue is now the Opera House not the forecourt; without my permission they've changed the conductor from Dobbs Franks with whom I prepared the work to Iwaki, who, being Japanese, will undoubtedly make a good job of Professor Clark's fine text with narrator and chorus; they've failed to ask Ruth Cracknell, Michael Johnson and Mr Justice Kirby to narrate and have engaged some dim-wit to superimpose a 'pageant' (whatever that may mean) on my work. I know of no other country where a nationally important artistic centre high-handedly overrides the author's wishes.[144]

Malcolm's furious recriminations proved too much. At the last minute the work was withdrawn from the concert. The orchestra, it was said, had not had sufficient time to rehearse. Hiroyuki Iwaki, a conductor of much experience with strong Melbourne connections, could hardly be blamed for his reluctance to proceed with the piece. Malcolm had been too extreme and too public in his views and had paid for it. *The True Endeavour* still waits for its first performance.[145]

The only Australian Bicentenary celebration in which Malcolm was actively involved was a quiet one in Warwick, England, where Phyllis Kempster had been persuaded that for 1988 the West Midlands Youth Ballet should mount an all-Australian programme. Not only was *Heritage* revived, but there was a first performance for *The Cave*, his ballet on Plato's myth, set to his Concerto for Wind Quintet and 2 Pianos, a project which Malcolm had been trying to place professionally for some time, having discussions about it with Beryl Grey, Maina Gielgud, Kenneth MacMillan, Michael Corder, and Robert Cohan.

Heritage was again a big success, but *The Cave* struggled to make an impact even on a friendly audience of proud parents, much to Malcolm's disappointment. It was hardly Phyllis' fault – Plato's Myth of the Cave was never going to

143 The seven movements are Southern Cross Above Gondwana; Aboriginal Australia; Barcarolle of the Disinherited Country; The Rain Forest – Urban Despoliation; Threnody for Murdered Aborigines; The Past and the Challenge; Mateship – Whitlam's Vision – Makarrata.

144 17 August 1988

145 It features in the 1992 Campion Press catalogue, but other than that is completely unknown. 'The reason for its current unavailability,' says Tony Gray, 'is that Malcolm was beginning to have doubts about it, and so Simon won't let it out.' (March 2005)

be a crowd-pleaser, Malcolm's static scenario imposing impossible restraints on the choreographer.[146]

The time had come for another parting of the ways. Malcolm's relationship with the West Midlands Youth Ballet had become very strained. Phyllis Kempster, now over seventy, had started on a third Williamson work for the Bicentenary, to be called *Salute* and based on the *Sinfonia Concertante*, only for illness to intervene, whereupon Malcolm showed less sympathy than might have been expected. In his fiery determination to turn amateurs into professionals, he had become an unyielding taskmaster, and his excessive demands on Phyllis were no longer tolerable. In 1989 the West Midlands Youth Ballet began a new life without him.

Jayne Kempster and Morwenna Bowen remember Malcolm, however, with deep affection and sympathy:

> – Malcolm would have so liked to have been a dancer! I remember him with his arms high in the air crying 'This is what the Sun should be doing!'
>
> – He had such enthusiasm and talent! So many problems too. On one occasion Simon had to lock him in the car because he was not in a fit state to speak to the dancers.
>
> – In the end there were several vindictive letters, incredibly small-minded. But Phyl would always rise above such things: 'Well, Malcolm, I suppose I shall have to be like Christ and take the blame for all of this!'
>
> – Four o'clock one morning the phone rang and it was Malcolm accusing us all of being Vestal Virgins! Poor Malcolm was never at rest. Extremely trivial things could upset him. People inevitably pulled away.[147]

There had to be a reckoning. It came in the late autumn of 1988, not long before his fifty-seventh birthday, when Malcolm had a stroke severe enough to lose the use of a hand temporarily. He wept tears of frustration as he attempted to play one of his favourite show pieces, Chopin's Opus 25 *Etudes*, 'with a disobedient right hand'.[148] He claimed that the doctors had told him it was simply the result of overwork, but in this, as in many other things, he was misleading himself, fooled

---

146 The first of the three scenes was set in an underground cave, in which a group of prisoners were sitting: 'They are chained together by their necks and ankles. Behind them on a walkway are a group of Puppets, manipulated by unseen hands. In the middle of the cave is a fire whose light causes the Shadows of the Puppets to be projected against the back wall of the cave. The Prisoners are perfectly happy to sit watching the Shadows they imagine to be real. One Prisoner, who is ultimately to become Plato's ideal Philosopher-Ruler, breaks his chains and, slowly and painfully, gets to his feet. He turns and sees the Puppets and eventually the fire, and thus realises that the fire is causing the Shadows which are mere illusions, and not the reality that Prisoners had thought them to be. With resistance to the pain in his eyes caused by the firelight, the Philosopher-Ruler passes, as if drawn by unseen forces, to the mouth of the cave through which a greater light shines. The Prisoners and Puppets remain indifferently where they are.'

147 October 2005

148 MW to Alexander Sverjensky's widow, Enith, 10 March 1989. Two days earlier he had written to her: 'I am just off to Toronto where the National Ballet of Canada is doing a ballet on the 3rd Piano Concerto. Have had a tiny stroke affecting my right hand. Improving...' It is sometimes said that Malcolm had suffered a small stroke much earlier, around 1975, but there would seem to be no evidence for this.

by his body's great resilience to years of mistreatment. Although he was to recover the use of the hand fairly quickly, he would never be the same pianist again. It was a worrying conclusion to a difficult final year at Beckford House.

The Sandon years had ended in disappointment. In 1984 and 1985, at the height of his belief in the prospects of Campion Press, Malcolm's creative life enjoyed a brief revival, and he had written three outstanding works, his Seventh Symphony, *Next Year in Jerusalem* and *Heritage*. The three final Sandon years were a poor contrast, a few minor works leading to *The True Endeavour* which merely confirmed what most people already thought, that he was a spent force.

Malcolm's inaccessibility is often cited as an important factor in his steady decline. Kenneth Pont, for example, the director of the Mayfield Festival in Sussex, relates that it was his inability to get in touch with Malcolm which, in 1986, ended the fruitful Williamson connection with the Festival:

> Perhaps Simon Campion was over-protective. Perhaps Malcolm was ill. I very much wanted him to continue at the Festival, but eventually I gave up trying to make contact. Also, at that time I was Editor-for-Schools at OUP and I was desperate for Malcolm to write some more cassations, which we were very keen to publish. But I simply couldn't get through.[149]

It is unlikely that Malcolm would have been able to respond to any such commissions. In 1987, for example, Fay Weldon produced, at Malcolm's request, a libretto for a one-act children's opera. *A Small Green Space* sounds perfect for his purposes, an ecological tale of a young boy who wanted a bomb site turned into a nature reserve, not a car park. But much as Malcolm admired Fay Weldon, he was unable to produce a score.

By 1988 several of Malcolm's friends were expressing dismay about his quiet life in the country. Elaine Feinstein was typical:

> He came to see us in London on several occasions, Simon always with him. Sometimes to lunch, sometimes to dinner, sometimes to parties. He was always a great asset, always had something to say and loved people. But one of the great tragedies, I always thought, was that he was stuck in the depths of Hertfordshire. What on earth could he be doing there? He couldn't have had many friends around him there. People might have remembered him if he'd been in London.[150]

But a return to London, however desirable, was no longer a financial option. The pilgrim life demanded low rents. It even demanded they leave Sandon when they were offered the use of a house on the outskirts of Stevenage on terms too good to turn down. But it was no ordinary offer. Elizabeth Poston had lived many years in Rooks Nest House. On her death she had bequeathed[151] it to a nephew, and when he was suddenly posted abroad, he offered it to Malcolm and Simon. It was now to inspire one of the last outstanding works which Malcolm had left in him.

149 October 2005

150 July 2005

151 She also left some jewellery for Malcolm, which she very much hoped he would wear.

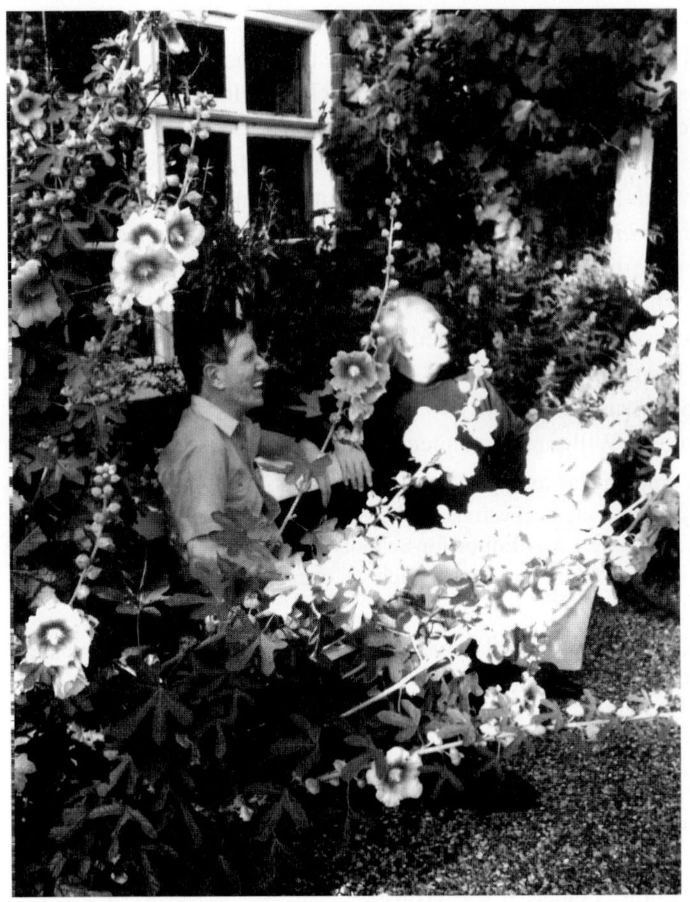

With Michael Kirby outside Rooks Nest, 1987

Piano duet with Johan van Ulcton in Rooks Nest, 1987

17
A SINGLE DAWN
Brisbane, 1989

MALCOLM STAYED AWAKE AND CRIED for much of his first night at Rooks Nest. 'This new house depresses me,' he was later to explain to Bessie. 'It is quite 400 years old, the oldest parts...'[1] There were too many ghosts. For centuries it had been known as 'Howards', after a family which had farmed there, just outside Stevenage, being renamed Rooks Nest only on the demise of the Howards in the 1880s. Rented out by its new owner, it included among its first tenants a delicate child, the future novelist E M Forster, who in 1910 immortalised it in *Howard's End*, using the childhood home he always loved as a powerful symbol of the life of the spirit bravely challenging materialistic values. He had modelled its owner, the sympathetic Ruth Wilcox, on the wife of a local Stevenage stockbroker, Clementine Poston, and four years later, by a strange but appropriate quirk of fate, she herself moved into Rooks Nest,[2] along with her daughter, the future composer Elizabeth Poston.

Malcolm that first night felt like an intruder. The much admired Elizabeth, who had lived in the house for seventy-three years, was everywhere: Elizabeth the friend of Peter Warlock and Ralph Vaughan Williams, whose *Sweet Suffolk Owl*, the song which brought her fame in the 1920s, was composed there; Elizabeth, the broadcaster, who in the Second World War had sent out messages from the BBC to occupied France in musical code; Elizabeth the folk song enthusiast, who only recently had begged him to scour the highways and byways of Russia to augment her collection; Elizabeth the friend, who at her death had lovingly appointed Simon as her literary and music executor; Elizabeth the nature lover, whose *Ariel and Ferdinand*, incidental music from *The Tempest*, had been written to accommodate the sounds of real birds and livestock. (Who else but Elizabeth would have chased around the Hertfordshire countryside

[1] 2 January 1989

[2] It had by now acquired the title Rooks Nest House, to distinguish it from the adjacent Rooks Nest Farm.

seeking a cock that crowed in D Major?) It was not surprising that Malcolm wept instead of slept. He had never before lived in a house with such deep resonances.

The move had been left largely to Simon, who ferried their belongings the five miles from Sandon over several weeks, for Malcolm was still suffering from the effects of the stroke and was low in spirits. A Cambridge psychiatrist had recently diagnosed Seasonally Affected Depression, brought on by lack of sunlight, but that was only a small part of his troubles. Shortly after arrival at Rooks Nest Malcolm wrote to Jonathan Still:

> I'm going through a bad patch… Simon is working hard enough for a dozen people. I am little help. The predicted post-stroke weakness is upon me. I am only sustained by friends and a belief in my music.[3]

The unhappy saga of *The True Endeavour* was, of course, a contributory factor to the depression, and it had also affected Simon badly, for he had been working long hours single-handedly producing vocal and orchestral parts, right up to the moment of cancellation. That Malcolm believed the responsibility for the fiasco lay in an argument between the ABC and the Opera House perhaps alleviated a little the sense of sour anticlimax. He told Bessie:

> I cannot but wish that *The True Endeavour*, on which I worked under your roof, had come out as scheduled. I suffered a delayed reaction to the shock of the last-minute cancellation, and am quite disgusted…[4]

He had aged considerably. One early visitor to Rooks Nest, who had never met Malcolm personally before, was surprised at his appearance:

> His face was puffy and he was smoking a lot. He looked as if he'd taken a bit of a pasting over recent times. He was corpulent in shape and flamboyantly dressed – with a highly floral shirt. There were newspapers everywhere, and ashtrays and glasses. The house was homely and comfortable, but full of detritus. He was utterly charming and very funny, though at the same time he seemed to be working out whether I was friend or foe...[5]

It was not long, however, before Malcolm began to appreciate the charm of Rooks Nest, 'a Poston-Forster shrine… packed with furniture, much of which is antique and nearly all broken, chipped or cracked…'[6] By the terms of the lease nothing in the shrine was to be removed or re-arranged and, as every cupboard seemed full, there were soon piles of books and music on the floor. Rooks Nest, with its narrow passages and staircases, its oddly sited connecting doors, and its three floors and basement full of treasures old and new, had the atmosphere of an enormous, maze-like Aladdin's Cave:

> The three vast living-rooms downstairs are magnificent, likewise the five bedrooms upstairs and the vast gardens not to mention the downward sloping meadows of the

3 18 January 1989

4 2 January 1989

5 Jeremy Taylor, June 2006

6 MW to Bessie Williamson, 2 January 1989.

Forster country with the lights of Stevenage on the horizon... The loft is crammed with God knows what – including letters of Delius, Peter Warlock, Vaughan Williams et al. Worth, I believe, a small fortune. Simon has taken a guess that it will take quite three years to go through it. With help Simon is bravely going through drawers. You couldn't imagine the elastic bands, cellotape, old Mrs Forster's night cap, bodkins, bits of embroidery, empty ballpoint pens. One cupboard is full of candles, for example. The kitchen is miniscule... a sort of rusty saucepan museum. There is enough china and crockery for dinner for 50 but nowhere to sit and eat it. On one wall of the tiled breakfast room hang some sort of assemblage of instruments that looks like an Indian or Caribbean orchestra![7]

Malcolm particularly liked the secluded gardens, with their old apple trees, rose beds and borders of huge red tulips, so full of memories of Elizabeth, tall and stately, always elegant even in her most casual gardening clothes. It was not long before he was exploring its theatrical potential:

The garden has a flagged patio set high and with 2 entry-exit possibilities. It is tolerably smooth, and on the grass rising to it people could sit. The huge hedge behind is a natural cyclorama. *Pace* weather, we could have a dance manifestation in the spring, if we could get people.[8]

Encouraged by the dramatic possibilities of Rooks Nest, Malcolm took to wearing flowing kaftans and colourful African headgear.[9] His growing reputation for eccentricity coupled with the fame of the house resulted in several newspapers sending reporters to Stevenage. The *Evening Standard*'s Janice Morley was fascinated by Malcolm's Aladdin's Cave:

The small lobby with its wood-panelled walls and blue plates is the first and last sight of order and convention. Forster's mother Lily would have muttered at the unruly arrangement of furniture and possessions now scattered on an interior landscape of fading Fifties colours – beige walls and brown furniture loose-covered in purple, orange and yellow. The large inner hall is dominated by an inglenook, though the fireplace was long ago taken away by Lily after a ferocious row with the landlord. In its place is a large dark wood mantelpiece, holding memorabilia of the house, postcards and Williamson's pictures of Vaughan Williams and Forster alongside photographs of his own handsome family. Other walls are for some of the contrasts in his life. On one side are five studies of a haystack by East Anglian artist Alan Burgess, on the other, aboriginal pictures above a huge desk heavy with sheet music, papers and notes...

Other interviewers commented on Elizabeth Poston's piano, boxes of Poston-Forster letters and much memorabilia of Malcolm's: a Cecil Beaton study of Edith Sitwell, some Russian dolls (a gift from Lindsay Anderson whom Malcolm had met in Russia) and a small statue of the Virgin which Malcolm had brought back from Italy. On a work-table there was a painting by Richard Champion; on

7 MW to Jonathan Still, 18 January 1989

8 *ibid.*

9 This also reflected his involvement in local support groups, helping Africans and other immigrants settle in Stevenage.

a desk the first chapters of a book he had started on the novels of Bernice Rubens alongside voluminous notes on musical therapy for the handicapped; and, gaping from a shelf in the entrance hall, any number of model crocodiles.

Malcolm enjoyed playing host at Rooks Nest and although his knowledge of Forster, who died in 1970, was almost entirely second-hand, he would never let his interviewers down by a too scrupulous respect for facts. He would talk of 'that shy old maiden gentleman, a sweet darling old don' who kept coming back to Howard's End 'like a ship at the end of a rope', as if he knew him well; and he always made much of Forster's old nursery, the middle bedroom on the second floor which had become Simon's office. As a guide, Malcolm usually gave a polished performance. One typical response found him 'a gentle, amusing, discursive, mischievous man, hugely curious...' By seizing the initiative, talking fast and taking his visitors round the house at great speed, he was less vulnerable to penetrating questions. To the readers of the *Evening Standard* he was working as effectively as ever:

> He worked, he explained, in both the drawing and dining room: 'One to sketch and compose, the other to orchestrate. I keep four works going at one time and I like to move from one room to the other. I must have changes. I must even have changes of furniture. I never choose one chair to sit in; I sleep in different beds, on the sofa sometimes.'[10]

It is true that he always liked to keep more than one work going and, as generalisations, the comments were accurate, but he currently had no work in progress. For over a year, since the completion of *The True Endeavour* in the spring of 1988, Malcolm had written nothing. Of his last summer at Sandon he wrote to Bessie:

> My will-power and concentration seem to have gone... For weeks I've been roaming about, feeling terrific, but working for no more than a few minutes.[11]

Both he and Simon visited London to try acupuncture from a highly recommended Vietnamese doctor. Malcolm found it more therapeutic than Simon, but the creative muse failed to return.

In the first months of 1989, as he settled into Rooks Nest, Malcolm was particularly frustrated that he was having problems with another important work for Australia. Back in 1987 he had accepted two Bicentenary commissions, the second, *The Dawn Is At Hand*, a choral work for Queensland. As with *The True Endeavour*, he had missed his original Bicentenary deadline, but had generously been given a later performance date (in this case October 1989). However, he had not touched it for a year, only one of the five movements was written, and the performance was now only months away. At a time when he was seldom being commissioned, it was not a project to surrender lightly. Moreover, its subject

---

10 Janice Morley interview

11 31 July 1988

matter – the aboriginals – meant a great deal to him. But prospects of completion looked minimal.

Help arrived from an unexpected source. A dynamic young lady, Rebecca Hossack, who had come to London from Melbourne the previous year, had bravely opened up a gallery in Fitzrovia for the promotion of the great passion in her life, aboriginal art. When, in the Spring of 1989 Malcolm heard about the gallery, he at once travelled down to London to meet her. It was an important encounter for both of them, and Rebecca Hossack remembers it vividly:

> Malcolm was quite remarkable! More passionate about aboriginal people than anyone I had ever met! At the time most people in this country were hardly aware that the aboriginals even existed, but Malcolm had this blazing concern for them, beyond anything I had ever encountered. So it was love at first sight! And from then on, until he was too ill, we used to have daily phone-calls, many lasting as much as an hour.[12]

Malcolm was so thrilled with the gallery and everything that Rebecca was trying to achieve that he energetically devoted himself to furthering its cause. In these early weeks he came to cherish the work of Robert Campbell junior, whom he telephoned in Australia several times just to discuss 'Aboriginal Musicians', the painting in the gallery he most admired. He urged all his many friends and acquaintances to come and see it, and Robert Campbell's paintings soon started selling in good numbers, and Rebecca Hossack's highly adventurous project looked much more secure. It was not long before Malcolm's promotional efforts soon extended to other fields; he spent considerable time, for example, haranguing publishers into accepting aboriginal artists as illustrators.

Rebecca rarely saw Malcolm with Simon. He would usually come down to London on his own, often giving the impression of a naughty boy out on a spree. He seemed so delighted with the simple things of life that she quickly came to realise the very considerable privations his poverty was forcing upon him:

> When he came to dinner with my husband and myself, he used to eat so much! Non-stop! One night he came with a pile of books: philosophy, biology, crocodiles, opera, everything… and he clambered up the stairs to the flat above the gallery, sat on the floor, spread all the books out, had a huge plate of spaghetti and then did not stop talking till one o'clock. He was mesmerising. With amazing plans for the aboriginal people. Really profound.

Over several subsequent plates of spaghetti Malcolm explained to Rebecca the whole background to *The Dawn Is At Hand*, and, in particular, the development of his important friendship with the aboriginal rights leader, Kath Walker. It all began, he told her, when he was over in Australia in 1987 and was introduced to a lady called Melba, an aboriginal campaigner and 'working class saint', who fired him with indignation at the way racial prejudice still operated in the country. Had he by any chance, Melba asked, read the poems of Kath Walker? He hadn't. Within two days, however, he had read everything Kath had

---

12 December 2005

ever written and was full of excitement, realising her poetry ideal for a musical setting. Next day, by the strangest of coincidences, a friend from Brisbane, Kevin Power, approached him on behalf of the Queensland State and Muncipal Choir about the possibility of his writing a choral work for the Bicentenary year. Had he by any chance, asked Power, read the poems of Kath Walker? It was only minutes before they were shaking hands on an agreement.

But there was one snag: Kath Walker was known to dislike her poetry being tampered with in any way. So Malcolm went to see her at Moongalba, on North Stradbroke Island, where she ran her well-known Education and Cultural Centre.

> With two musical colleagues I flew to Brisbane and then took the ferry over to Stradbroke Island. We drove the dusty roads through the lush and lusty tropical vegetation to a cluster of tents and caravans among the trees. A small dainty woman, elegant in a cerise dress and hat which would command admiration in any fashionable street in the world, came to greet us. Although photographs had made the face familiar, nothing prepared us for the beautiful aquamarine eyes that bespeak innocence, intelligence and wisdom. Kath led us to the veranda and offered us cucumber sandwiches, tropical fruit and tea. In a clearing nearby was a fire of wood and stone being heated for their evening barbecue… Although time seemed to have stopped, none was wasted in preliminaries. We realized that we had the total acceptance of a loving, candid and indomitable woman.[13]

In due course they discussed her six books of poems. Malcolm had arrived with a list of his choices, which Kath Walker took and quickly reassembled. Malcolm, usually so self-assertive in the choice of his texts, at once accepted her version because everything she said made perfect sense. He eventually left the Moongalba Centre fired with enthusiasm and laden with passion fruit, the poems racing through his mind.

The friendship was consolidated in Sydney, where he met Kath and her son Vivian after a performance of *The Rainbow Serpent*, a piece of aboriginal theatre which they had devised and in which Kath, although sixty-seven, not only recited, but sang and danced. To Malcolm 'she showed the effortless grace of a teenager'.[14] Soon Malcolm was persuading Kath to resume her tribal name, Oodgeroo Noonuccal, and he was being invited to become an honorary member of the Noonuccal tribe, taking the name of 'Malcolm of the Makarrata'. When Kath received an honorary university degree, Malcolm wrote a small celebratory piece for brass quintet for the occasion.[15] He also interceded with the Queen on her behalf when she upset Buckingham Palace by returning her MBE as a protest at continued discrimination against aboriginals.

---

13 From Malcolm's introduction to the collected poems of Kath Walker, published in 1996 under the title *The Dawn is at Hand*, which, in addition to being the title of Malcolm's cantata was also that of her second book of poems, published in 1966.

14 Introduction to Kath Walker's *The Dawn Is At Hand*, p.14

15 *Ceremony For Oodgeroo*

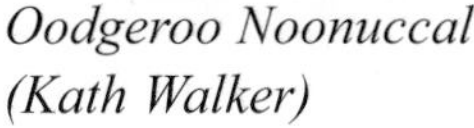

Oodgeroo Noonuccal
(Kath Walker)

Vivian and Kath Walker
on North Stradbroke Island

> I laid Kath's poems before Her Majesty without telling Kath that I was doing so. 'The quality,' said the Queen, 'is indeed deeply impressive.' Her Majesty is now devoted to Kath's work.[16]

It was an exciting, moving story that Malcolm told Rebecca Hossack in the little flat above the art gallery. But he omitted to mention that he had long since come to a halt on *The Dawn Is At Hand* and its chances of completion were negligible. Rebecca had naturally assumed from the enthusiastic way he spoke about it that all was progressing well, and he found it hard to tell her otherwise. There was only one solution. In the late spring of 1989 Malcolm settled down soberly at Rooks Nest to face his problems. Progress at first was slow, his powers of concentration fitful. His task, to write the final four-fifths of what was in effect a choral symphony, would have taxed any composer, let alone a struggling one. But with daily calls to his muse in Fitzrovia and many all-night sessions in August and September, Malcolm eventually completed the score, Simon just committing the final parts to the computer in time for the two of them to fly out to Brisbane, bringing their materials with them. Both knew that the work had great potential.

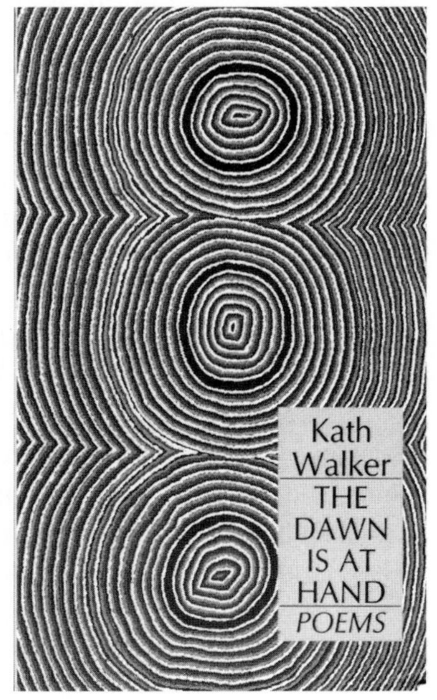

Kath
Walker
THE
DAWN
IS AT
HAND
POEMS

The opening movement, as gritty and uncompromising as Kath herself, is the least attractive of the five, reflecting Malcolm's earlier depressed state. The first of its three poems, 'The Dawn Is At Hand', is presented

[16] MW speaking in an ABC radio interview, October 1989

with dignity by baritone and chorus, its constant movement between dissonance and consonance suggesting the humiliations of the aboriginal past and the optimism of the present. The soprano solo 'Let Us Not Be Bitter' offers the same contrast, but a little more warmly, before the chorus and four soloists present the demands of the 'Aboriginal Charter of Rights'[17] with strong rhythmic vigour, the prevalent dissonance finally overwhelmed in a defiantly tonal conclusion.

It is the highly moving second movement that proclaims the inspiration which Malcolm received from Rebecca Hossack and her art gallery, as three poems explore the meaning of the death of one member of a tribe within the context of a continuing life cycle. In the gloriously atmospheric 'The Curlew Cried' (divided up between soloists and chorus) Malcolm takes the listener to a sacred aboriginal site, which is vividly alive with the sounds of wild life. Here the curlew, considered by the aboriginals to be their brother, warns the encampment of a coming death in the tribe by crying three nights in succession. 'Have courage,' cries the curlew (who will later escort the soul of the departed to the land of the dead), 'death is not an end… Death is kindly and your friend.' 'Tree Grave' (a soft, reassuringly diatonic passage for baritone and chorus) describes the funeral rites beside a sleepy lagoon, which is very delicately depicted. The deceased is lonely and afraid; he needs the prayers of his tribe brothers

> When the night winds whisper
> Their ghostly tune
> In the haunted swamp-oaks
> By the Long Lagoon.

From this gentle and unashamedly romantic section rises seamlessly the 'Dawn Wail For The Dead', a lovely hymn in which soprano and tenor weave delicate elaborations around the chorus's statement of the main melody. The poem tells of the camp at early morning. As the tribe members wake, they participate in a communal 'wail for the dead', mourning for the past in order to draw hope for the future. Eventually it is time to move on and resume the business of everyday life:

> They are remembered.
> Then it is over, life now,
> Fires lit, laughter now,
> In a new day calling.

Malcolm begins this epilogue with a poignant oboe solo; the curlew melody then returns and there are more soft bird-calls, before, in a dramatic conclusion, a fortissimo chorus leaves behind the dark, misty world of the curlew and returns to the world of the living. It is a wonderful conclusion to a beautifully integrated second movement, full of characteristic cadences and unexpected harmonic twists and turns, a real *tour de force*.

---

[17] A poem written for presentation at the 5th Annual General Meeting of the Federal Council for the Advancement of Aborigines and Torres Strait Islanders, 1962

The expectations now raised are fully met in the final three movements. The third, based on a single poem, 'Assimilation – No!', explores with bitter-sweet melodic lines the needs of the oppressed people. The tone is again cautionary. In saying 'yes' to integration the aboriginals are not to forfeit their own identity; their past is precious and somehow must be preserved. The movement begins and ends with a powerful image, effectively entrusted to the chorus: if you pour a pitcher of wine into a river, there will soon be no sign of the wine, only the river. 'Assimilation – No!' gives the work its emotional core, both musically and textually.

The fourth movement, 'We Are Going' (for soprano, baritone and chorus), takes on the cautionary argument a stage further. Not only must the aboriginals hold onto their culture, but be aware that it is in a frail state. There is precious little left of the old ways! First Malcolm has the choir in unison singing a chant-like melody as weary aboriginals trudge into a town where the white immigrants have taken over their old bora ground and turned it into the community refuse tip. Next, a declamatory section, with some harsh dissonance – a response to the outrage of the tip. Then comes a musical *coup*, a heartfelt passage of rare beauty, as out of the dust, weariness and confusion soars the soprano with her defiant message to the dying race. 'We are as strangers here now, but the white tribe are the strangers.' The movement ends in a long-sustained diminuendo of great pathos – 'The bora ring is gone; the corroboree is gone; and we are going' – a deeply moving expression of what it means to belong to a long-oppressed minority.

After a startingly powerful link passage, contrasting despair and optimism, the final movement features two poems, each prefaced by orchestral interludes. 'United We Win' is extremely optimistic: there is 'mateship' now; the good white hands stretch out to grip the black; there is at long last strong hope that racial discrimination will cease. But Malcolm refuses to be triumphalistic, preferring the music to emphasise the current distressed situation of the aboriginals as 'fringe-dwellers' and the 'last representatives of a dying race'. This, however, is the prelude to 'A Song of Hope', a rich and highly melodic tune of uninhibited emotional appeal, in which Malcolm at last accedes to the triumphant conclusion the text demands. The soprano soars over the chorus in the first stanza: 'Look up, my people!' The baritone is in similarly inspired dialogue with the chorus in the second: 'Now brood no more!' Both soprano and baritone then weave sinuously around the chorus as they sing of the destruction of racial discrimination: 'So long we waited!' The culmination, the final stanza dedicated to a new Dream Time,[18] brings in all four soloists and chorus in what must be one of the most emotionally rousing choral ensembles since Verdi. The passage is full of poignant suspensions, glorious harmonic side-stepping, and unabashed climaxes.

[18] The Dream Time, or Dreaming, relates to the creation of the universe and the period when the aboriginals lived freely in Australia before the white man's arrival, or, as Malcolm put it, 'a crude and cruel eruption for which ignorance alone can be blamed'... 'Coffin ships came bearing gifts of alcohol, lying and disease hitherto undreamed of in the Dreaming.' (Introduction to Walker: *The Dawn Is At Hand*, p.9)

It is followed by a superbly atmospheric coda, featuring the same arresting seven-note ostinato figure, suggestive of dawn, with which the work opened. As it softly dies away, the baritone makes one final reflection: 'To the generations of the past, the sorrow; to the generations of the future, the happiness.' The music sinks to an awed silence, but, far from choosing a comfortable resolution, Malcolm ends the work with a whispered, challenging question mark.

The Dawn Is At Hand is a great Australian work of art, an emotionally and intellectually powerful plea for the values of multiculturalism, expressed by two of the country's most original and passionate talents. It is all the more successful in that, like Kath Walker's ambition for the aboriginals, it blends, but does not attempt to assimilate, two very different traditions. Malcolm wrote in his language, Kath in hers. Malcolm was at pains to explain why there were no didgeridoos or aboriginal drummings in his score:

> Specific aboriginal musical devices are not in my tradition and culture, so I haven't used them. When Stravinsky was setting Shakespeare to music, he never ceased to be the twentieth-century Russian-cum-French-cum-American master that he was. Roger Quilter's Shakespeare was that of Edwardian England. Words and music of two traditions can intermarry.[19]

Malcolm and Simon arrived in Australia with just ten days to spare before the concert on 20 October at Brisbane's Performing Arts Centre.[20] Despite the extremely limited time for rehearsal, Dobbs Franks (conducting the Queensland Symphony Orchestra) and Kevin Power (directing the Queensland State and Municipal Choir) were well versed in Malcolm's music, understood and admired it, and were accordingly cautiously optimistic. Their confidence, however, quickly turned to panic, when it was discovered that Simon's computer disc, which should have contained all the vocal and orchestral parts, had nothing on it at all. Dobbs Franks refused to cancel the performance (the most obvious option) and instead, with Power's strong support, sent the orchestra and choir home for the first two rehearsals so that they could manually copy out their own parts.

There was a further setback when, the night before the crucial final day of rehearsals, Malcolm was given a bottle of whisky which started him off on a drinking bout, and he was so inebriated next day that he could say nothing useful. Debbie Price, the Queensland Symphony Orchestra's publicist, who had invited Malcolm and Simon to stay at her home, experienced the full impact of this binge, despite emptying down the kitchen sink each and every bottle she could find:

> There was an almighty crash in the house! I rushed to see what it was and couldn't believe my eyes! Malcolm had somehow fallen through the sitting-room wall – 'The Malcolm Williamson Memorial Void' I called it afterwards! He was very embarrassed afterwards![21]

19 ABC radio broadcast, 20 October 1989

20 The soloists were Sandra Hahn, Lauris Elms, Ronald Stevens and Raymond Myers.

21 December 2005

Greta Williams, who also worked for the Queensland Symphony Orchestra, remembers him in similar vein:

> He was a charming and lovely man, but drinking very heavily… At the final rehearsal Dobbs summoned me with an SOS: 'Get him off the stage and out of the concert hall!' I tried to take him to the Green Room – on the way we passed the bar – he said he wanted a drink and I said it should be coffee – but that was my mistake – he spilt it everywhere![22]

There was one more problem. In 1989 Australia was still far from accepting itself as a multicultural society. The socially inclusive message of *The Dawn Is At Hand*, therefore, was controversially radical. Kath Walker's programme of reform, demanding a reappraisal of social and political attitudes, also stressed the aboriginal anxieties at the way man was abusing nature, long before problems like global warming were being taken seriously. 'Kath was a tough cookie,' recalls Dobbs Franks, 'and many white people didn't like her work at all.'[23] Indeed, it was so unpopular that half the Queensland choir resigned on learning what they were expected to sing, giving Kevin Power the very difficult job of finding suitable replacements at extremely short notice. Power remembers with wry humour the fury with which one singer resigned, rushing into his office and hurling the score across his desk.

The Brisbane press seemed equally uneasy at the Walker-Williamson crusade. In one interview Malcolm had only just begun to speak out on the subject of mistreatment of the aboriginals – 'As the world becomes more and more a global village, there is less room for prejudice, insularity and parochialism'[24] – when he was cut short and questioned very fiercely about the prejudice, insularity and parochialism exhibited by the aboriginals. The same newspaper, two days later, gave the concert scant coverage, despite the local interest it aroused.

Fortunately goodwill and optimism were much in evidence in the concert hall for the performance, which was remarkably good, given the many difficulties surrounding it. Dobbs Franks and Kevin Power had been quite outstanding in their leadership of the project, the packed audience responding most warmly to the magnificence of their achievement. Seldom can a standing ovation have been so deserved. Malcolm himself presented a dignified figure that evening, seemingly quite sober. Richard Mills, playing with the Queensland Symphony Orchestra, remembers him 'coherent and almost child-like'. Wearing his favourite sweater featuring the aboriginal flag, Malcolm spent the evening in the close company of Kath and Vivian Walker, both smartly dressed in aboriginal red. He would not quickly forget the occasion, remaining deservedly proud of it:

> Kath and I had unwittingly made history. Never before had an Aboriginal poet and a Caucasian composer collaborated in so vast a work. We stood together holding hands

---

[22] December 2005

[23] September 2005

[24] 20 October 1989

in the royal box to acknowledge the deafening applause which seemed to last almost the whole length of the work and for scheduling reasons was eventually curtailed by the national radio. It was shortly after this that the overtly racist government of Queensland, which had for so long been a scarcely concealed scandal, fell.[25]

In excellent spirits, Malcolm enjoyed the rest of his stay in Brisbane, doing his best to make amends for the pre-performance mayhem. (He gallantly bought Debbie Price a bust of Tchaikovsky to make up for the hole in her wall.) As he made his way to Melbourne, where he was to receive the prestigious Bernard Heinze Award,[26] he was optimistic that he had written a work which all right-minded Australians would take to their hearts. 'The Song of Hope', in particular, had a relevance and an immediacy which could make it very popular. There seemed every prospect that *The Dawn Is At Hand* would find its way into the choral repertoire.

Instead, it was to endure a long period of total neglect. Damaged by his tarnished public image, and with no stronger promotional body behind it than an impoverished one-man outfit in the depths of the English countryside, *The Dawn Is At Hand* was not to be given another professional performance in his lifetime.

25 Introduction to Kath Walker's *The Dawn Is At Hand*, p.14

26 Professor Michael Brimer, who made the speech of presentation, remembers Malcolm in excellent form that day. His speech of acceptance was short and pithy, and he took the opportunity to reply to those critics for ever blaming him for being an expatriate: 'I am more proud than I can say that I can *flout* those people who say I am an expatriate! I am obliged to live in Great Britain because I have the honour of being part of the royal household of Great Britain. I am nonetheless very much an Australian and this wonderful honour reaffirms my lifelong Australian identity.'

18 THE FINAL FLING

Howard's End and Royston, 1990–95

ALTHOUGH MALCOLM WAS HAPPY to be back at Rooks Nest, he did not relish his return to Mrs Thatcher's Britain. Her 'philistinism' still irritated him, and his criticisms of her government's unwillingness to back the arts with liberal subsidies were all the more bitter with the continued paucity of commissions.[1] Yet he still had a few friends in high places. John Drummond, for example, the BBC's Controller of Music and Director of the Proms, had been sufficiently impressed by *Next Year in Jerusalem* in 1985 to offer Malcolm another Proms commission, and it was to this that Malcolm turned his thoughts in the first months back at Rooks Nest. Drummond had asked Malcolm for a flute concerto for James Galway in 1991. The more Malcolm weighed up the possibilities, the more excited he became. By including a chorus with the flute and orchestra, he had the perfect means of expressing the truths of Plato's Myth of the Cave musically. There was plenty of time for such an ambitious concerto, a full nineteen months…

1990, however, proved a barren year, except for one work, inspired by the death of Lennox Berkeley. Although there had been nearly a thirty-year age difference between them, Malcolm always felt very close to Berkeley and had been much encouraged by him, particularly in the 1950s, when he had come to know Berkeley well through their mutual friendship with Benjamin Britten. Berkeley, who, like Malcolm, was a fine organist and pianist, also converted in

1 Occasionally friends would bring commissions. Flautist Martin Feinstein and guitarist Richard Hand, for example, keen to develop their own repertoire, visited Rooks Nest in 1990 to discuss the possibility of a work. 'Malcolm played the piano and said outrageous things,' remembers Hand, 'about every single person you could think of. He was rather the worse for wear. He later came to Blackheath to hear the first public performance of the short piece he wrote for us, *Channukah Sketches*.' (August 2005)

his twenties to Catholicism. Malcolm much admired his music,[2] and wrote very passionately about it in an obituary notice in *The Independent.*

The opportunity to pay a practical tribute to Berkeley came from John Michael East, who ten years earlier had conducted the Fifth Symphony with the Brent Youth Orchestra, and now, as Director of Music at St Etheldreda's Church, London, commissioned from Malcolm a *Missa Brevis* with which to celebrate his church's 700th anniversary. Malcolm at once determined to take a Berkeley theme as his starting point and was soon busy on it at Rooks Nest, from where he wrote emotionally to Freda Berkeley:

> As I work on my Mass dedicated to Lennox, and based on the theme of the 2nd movement of his 4th symphony, I am more than ever profoundly impressed by the great mind of Lennox crystallised in his music. You see, copying it out, rather in the manner of renaissance students apprenticed to the great painters, one sees it in an even deeper dimension than any amount of listening can reveal.[3]

Despite the enthusiasm and affection Malcolm felt for the Mass, its writing still proved immensely difficult and, as East recalls, he only just met his deadline:

> We had the first performance scheduled at a big Mass[4] which Cardinal Basil Hume was to attend. It was extremely hair-raising as the work nearly didn't get finished in time, coming from Simon page by page. There were also problems about payment, Simon wanting to receive the money before he delivered the manuscript. It was fairly traumatic, all in all, even if the choir eventually sang the difficult work with considerable success.[5]

2 He particularly liked the Piano Sonata ('absolutely faultless, a stupefying masterpiece, not a bad note in it'), the 2nd and 3rd Symphonies, the Piano Concerto and the 2-Piano concerto. After a memorial service to Berkeley he wrote to his widow: 'Darling Freda, Tuesday was a most beautiful day that none of us will ever forget. There is something of a spiritual completeness in the celebration of a great man's life in our metropolitan cathedral with the beautiful Benedictine Latin con-celebration. This is not a letter of condolence but rather a letter to say a thank you for Lennox's life and music, and for your marvellous part in it. How lucky you are to have shared a life with a very great saint, and a very great composer. Being vain myself, I was flattered when Monseigneur Wheeler spoke of Lennox's founding a dynasty. This was my phrase in *The Independent*, and Simon naughtily nudged me when it was said: but it is in every sense true. One piece of evidence was in Michael, who read most beautifully and the composer of a lovely and creditable work. We were so glad, and Lennox in Heaven must have shared the joy of a piece of Michael's being included...' (23 March 1990)

3 undated letter, c. May 1990

4 2 July 1990.

5 July 2005. Malcolm took umbrage that Dolly wasn't at the performance: 'Today's Mass at S. Etheldreda's Church went very well. It was humbling but enjoyable to be writing music in harness, so to speak, with Lennox. Lady Berkeley had hoped very much that you would be able to attend, and arrived early to welcome you; but she is aware that you are busy and did not have your diary when she asked you. I was sorry not see you since I believe that you'd have liked the two-composer work, which was very well performed, and I should like to have presented you to the Cardinal. Many of your friends were there. May I suggest that you send Lady Berkeley a card explaining your schedule problems?' (2 July 1990)

With The Myth of the Cave concerto still an anxiety he could not for the moment address, Malcolm was grateful for an attractive diversion that summer, performances of *English Eccentrics* at the Trinity College of Music. It was a small reminder of the fine operas of the 1960s which had been almost completely forgotten in England. Several critics were impressed by the work's quality, the ever supportive Edward Greenfield leading the way:

> Had the opera *English Eccentrics* been written by a trendier composer than Malcolm Williamson it would no doubt have been hailed as a masterly example of music-theatre, written ahead of its time. That is clearly how it should be seen now, a sparkling, offbeat entertainment that in this brilliantly economical production by Keith Warner for the opera group of the Trinity College of Music made a perfect end-of-term entertainment, both hilarious and touching…[6]

Such sympathetic comment was all the sweeter for its comparative rarity. More typical, that summer, was a probing feature in the *Daily Mail* over Malcolm's lack of productivity:

> Composer Malcolm Williamson finds himself molto agitato with those who harp on about his not writing enough Royal music. Next month sees the Queen Mother's 90th birthday, the Princess Royal's 40th, and Princess Margaret's 60th. But none of these events has prompted a new composition by Australian-born Williamson. 'Why indeed should they?' asks Williamson's friend and publisher Simon Campion. 'Being Master of the Queen's Music is an honour, but there are no formal duties attached. In any event, a composer doesn't write music unless it is going to be performed, and you only know something will be performed if you are asked to write a piece by, say, an orchestra or ballet company. Even at this late stage Williamson would be happy to compose something if commissioned – but he hasn't been.'[7]

However carefully Simon put the case for the defence, it would not be enough, for in a society where widespread affluence encouraged a greater cynicism towards privilege and tradition, the Master of the Queen's Music was an obvious target for ridicule. The same year, for example, the *Evening Standard* ran a piece on Malcolm's interest in crocodiles, but, by leaving out its relationship to his researches into mental health, contrived to make him sound very silly indeed:

> Malcolm Williamson, the Master of the Queen's Music, has developed a peculiar passion for crocodiles. Whenever friends return from foreign travels, he insists that they bring toy crocs back for him. His close friend, publisher Simon Campion, tells me: 'He collects ornamental crocodiles, artefacts, pictures and books to do with crocodiles. In fact, he has become extraordinarily knowledgeable about reptiles in general.' Williamson, 59, has been producing royal tunes since 1975. Sadly his annual honorarium of £100 won't buy him a real crocodile.[8]

Nor would it buy basic necessities. There might have been more sympathy for Malcolm in the media had it been known to what straitened circumstances he had

---

6 *The Guardian*, 18 June 1990:

7 30 July 1990

8 31 December 1990

now been reduced. He could no longer live off his commissions and royalties, and so difficult was the situation at Rooks Nest that friends had even begun to negotiate some discreet assistance from the Musicians' Benevolent Fund.[9] Struggling in his music, Malcolm tried to utilise his talent for the written word, and, though the rewards for his time-consuming book reviews were minimal, it boosted his flagging morale to see his name regularly in print and to be able to support writers in whom he was particularly interested. The Czech novelist Ivan Klima, a Jew who had survived a Nazi concentration camp as a boy, was one favourite; another Henrik Stangerup, the Danish novelist and film director, whose important trilogy of historical novels was inspired by the philosopher Sören Kierkegaard, the father of existentialism. Malcolm enjoyed analysing these books, for one of Kierkegaard's formulative influences was Plato. He was writing from a similar position of strength in giving a warm commendation to Peter Dickinson's *The Music of Lennox Berkeley* ('genius out of tune with the voice of Britain'). Malcolm's writing in the Rooks Nest period was at all times incisive and illuminating, his obituary notices full of generosity and insight. Of Aaron Copland, for example, he wrote:

> 'Inspiration is the antithesis of self-consciousness,' wrote Copland, but his own music is the antithesis of this statement. What on paper was soberly planned and deliberate became in performance the spontaneous impetuosity of a sure-footed athlete, the explosive violence of a libertarian crusader, or sublime self-forgetting mysticism. Copland was a radiant paradox, but his music is its solution…[10]

That summer of 1990 Rebecca Hossack, wishing to thank Malcolm for his support, brought up to Rooks Nest a party which not only included one of Australia's great aboriginal painters, Clifford Possum Tjapaltjarri, but also an American millionaire and his wife, well-known as generous patrons of art and music. Everything went very well initially. It was a hot day and they all sat out in the garden as Malcolm played through *The Dawn Is At Hand* and reduced several of the party to tears at the conclusion of the 'Song of Hope'. At lunchtime, however, Rebecca discovered there was a problem:

> I looked in the fridge and all I could find was a little lump of cheese in silver foil. That was it! Nothing else! Malcolm and Simon were entertaining a millionaire, whose goodwill might be extremely helpful, and there was nothing for lunch! The crisis, of course, was quickly averted. We went out and bought a picnic meal, but it said a great deal about Malcolm and Simon's unworldliness and lack of basic resources.[11]

---

9 Support from the MBF had been discreetly going on for a while. On one occasion, in 1988, the Fund not only sent Malcolm money ('a generous cheque, but a drop in the overdraft ocean') but organised 'a much-needed break on a 40-acre estate in mid-Wales – self-contained flat, maid-service, all facilities to compose and/or walk in the stately grounds'. (MW to Bessie Williamson, 22 August 1988)

10 *The Independent*, 4 December 1990

11 December 2005

In the Poston shrine, 1992, surrounded by his own latest interests
(John Freeman)

Unworried by this small domestic crisis, Malcolm was in sparkling form, and when Clifford Possum declared his great admiration for the Queen, he was told arrangements would at once be put in place for him to meet her. Rebecca imagined this was something which would be forgotten the next day.

> But not a bit of it! ! We were invited to Buckingham Palace, and Clifford had a private audience with the Queen. He was absolutely thrilled and went around saying 'This is my number one day'! Malcolm just stood there beaming. He was so pleased to have been able to bring this about.

The cost of keeping up appearances as Master of the Queen's Music had for several years added significantly to Malcolm's overdraft, but to have resigned

With Clare

The garden at Rooks Nest

would have been an admission of defeat and, as such, was unthinkable. On attending one of the many royal galas at Covent Garden which came his way, he reflected wryly:

> It is important to show up, even in a vast crowd. Always funny, turning up for such a lavish event, followed by supper at the Savoy, when you don't know if you can pay for the petrol for the trip to town, the utilities are about to be cut off and the grocer is owed hundreds.[12]

The contrast in other people's lifestyles was sometimes hard to bear. When a circular letter came from the Palace offering members of the Royal Household a holiday cottage to rent in Cornwall, he remarked sadly to Bessie that the cost per week was more than the Palace paid him per annum:

> I thought it was from some poor fish at the Palace, wanting to make a few pennies, but it's evidently the not-so-poor Prince Charles who collects the rent. It's the Palace assumption that everyone's as rich as they are.[13]

On the other hand, he still derived great pleasure from participating in royal functions, and though he would prevaricate over the acceptance of invitations, the call of society usually defeated the need for economy. Of a visit to Claridge's, where a reception was being held for the Mayor of Westminster, he wrote:

> I wanted not to go, but to telephone excuses. Simon asked me if the reception was important, and I said 'Yes'. It was important to be seen at such things, but I felt disinclined to go. However, I went.[14]

And of a function at the Royal College of Music:

> Tonight I'm going to London to visit the Queen. It's an occasion that I'd love to avoid, but I'm in the presentation line, so there's no avoiding it. Funny world. It means dressing up, laundering, searching for black socks that match, polishing shoes in order to face traffic jams and parking miles from the spot, and trying to find a taxi that I cannot afford, for an evening that I know the Queen will hate as much as I shall.[15]

In November 1990 his fifty-ninth birthday coincided with several official functions, necessitating an expensive weekend in London. This was made all the more exciting by the current political intrigues, as Michael Heseltine led the bid to topple Mrs Thatcher, a manoeuvre Malcolm watched with eager anticipation:

> I personally dislike them both, trust neither, but I'd give a lot to see Mrs Thatcher given the push. She has done, and continues to do, incalculable damage to this country. Lots of people here still think that Britannia rules the waves, and cannot wait to go to war with Saddam Hussein…[16]

Malcolm enjoyed a busy day as Master of the Queen's Music: accompanying

---

12 MW to Bessie Williamson, 5 November 1986

13 MW to Bessie Williamson, 12 February 1986

14 MW to Bessie Williamson, 13 January 1990

15 5 November 1986

16 MW to Bessie Williamson, 15 November 1990. For many years he had been going on about the 'incalculable damage' wrought by Mrs Thatcher. Four years earlier, no doubt on the very flimsiest of evidence, he cited the Queen as a fellow critic: 'Madame Thatcher has done incalculable damage to education, medicine, the arts and more. It is well known that the Queen loathes her, but of course can do nothing...' (17 September 1986).

Dame Janet Baker at the Musicians' annual service in Westminster Cathedral; attending 'a grand, but not good luncheon' in the City of London; and finally, delighting in the formality of a royal concert at the Albert Hall. ('As always it was enjoyable to have time with the Queen.') By contrast, the next day, he was back in the role of the impoverished composer, 'tramping London looking for manuscript paper in the rain, without any luck'. He and Simon met in the evening, celebrating his birthday with 'a not good meal in a chilly restaurant'[17] in which the main topic was the continuing political crisis. Early the next day Mrs Thatcher, choosing not to stand for a second leadership ballot, ended her eleven years as Prime Minister.

Music and literature, however, were Malcolm's current concerns rather than politics, and that weekend in London his head was full of the Proms commission for James Galway on which he had at last made a start, with only seven of his nineteen months left. As with the Berkeley Mass, he had needed an emotional charge to overcome lack of confidence, and this time it came in the form of the final illness of Richard Champion, the Sanfilippo Syndrome sufferer, who against all the odds had somehow survived several crises, but now, at fifteen, was finally dying. Malcolm sorrowfully noted the day of his death – 26 November 1990 – on the fourth page of the short score, which, three weeks later, was ready to be sent to James Galway. He still had the big task of the whole of the orchestration ahead of him, but he had at least warded off his immediate crisis.

It was only a temporary burst of musical activity and Malcolm was soon busying himself with more book reviews. Poetry by Ruth Padel and three books on Modigliani were followed by his views on a new translation of Plato's *Theaetetus* and the autobiography of Dorothy Hewett ('that wonderful Australian woman, a big and bouncy girl from W A, a one-time communist, and on Australian TV a firebrand and a charmer').[18] Of all his many reviews of this period perhaps the one on Modigliani was the most self-revealing. Under the heading of 'Does a great artist have to be a good man?', he not only offered a shrewd analysis of the painter and sculptor whose life was blighted by alcohol and drugs, but a very personal summing-up:

> He extracted joy from miserable environments, pursued his conception of Truth and, even dying, was a generous man. Despite lack of appreciation he obeyed his inner creative voice...

Malcolm's current literary life turned his thoughts once again to his father:

> I recall that one of George's ambitions for me was that I should be a journalist. It was, sadly, one of his ambitions for himself. I still have absurd guilt about him; but I have to say in my own defence that every article I write I read to several people, including Simon, and take advice, and then often alter things. Dad used to ask for advice from me, and then not take it, just get very cross. I wonder what might have happened with his writing. Iris Murdoch, possibly the finest living writer in English, wrote 13 novels before she got one published…[19]

17 MW to Bessie Williamson, 26 November 1990

18 MW to Bessie Williamson, 20 November 1990

19 *ibid.*

In addition to book reviews Malcolm was now writing poetry and had made a start in 1987 on an autobiography, for which Elaine Feinstein had found him a publisher. He was planning, he told Bessie, to paint a very dramatic and semi-factual picture of a deprived childhood. The book would begin with a backwards count from 10 as his hypnotist brought him out of a trance, and contain verse as well as prose. Despite his initial enthusiasm, however, he made only slow progress; the project had an unpromising title, *This Long Disease, My Life,* a quotation from Alexander Pope.

It was not a good idea to include his poetry for it was so intellectual as to be largely incomprehensible to the non-specialist. Tammy was sent several of her father's more considered poems, devotedly keeping them safe despite the perplexing subject matter. One poem, for example, 'On Seeing Harry Weinberger's *Positano Triptych*', which Malcolm dedicated to Iris Murdoch, was a confusing mixture of ancient Greek science and an entertaining pursuit of opposites. It begins:

> I have been there.
> I had to know
> That There was Here –
>
> The foldant Where
> I sought to go
> Far from the Near
>
> Aptotic year
> Of static flow –
> Strife moons both steer.

The later stanzas are even more obscure.

Perhaps Malcolm felt a need to impress the important literary figures with whom he was in daily contact; perhaps too his children, in whose academic achievements and careers he continued to take great pride and interest. It was now fifteen years since he had walked out of the family home, and time had not lessened the guilt. Meanwhile the bitterness between him and Dolly had slowly disappeared, to be replaced by a certain fondness. On the occasions they attended the same gathering he would always make a point of spending time with her. Dolly, who had resourcefully built up several new careers for herself within the classical music industry and was now living in a flat in Maida Vale's Randolph Avenue, never remarried.

One such reunion had occurred in 1990 at Peter's wedding. Although Malcolm sincerely admired Peter's successes at university and as a teacher of mathematics, and was also genuinely enthusiastic about Brenda, his future daughter-in-law, he was quite unable to cope with the maelstrom of emotions the event seemed to provoke, and, as the wedding approached, Peter found his father impossibly difficult:

> He would ring up advising against marriage one moment, and the next he'd be contacting the priest to say his services were no longer required as he'd be providing

With Dolly at Peter and Brenda's wedding

> a priest of his own! It was intolerable! And when I suggested he stopped interfering, he took considerable umbrage![20]

The day before the wedding Peter had a phone-call from Simon, urging him to talk to his father or he would not be attending. So Peter paid a quick visit to Rooks Nest:

> He was sitting in an armchair wearing, if memory serves me right, a pair of underpants and nothing else, very much the worse for booze. I said 'If you're in this state I'd very much rather you stayed away.' And he said, 'I know how to deal with this better than you do. What I'm going to do is to drink two bottles of brandy and I'll be absolutely fine!' He must have done that because halfway through the wedding ceremony the door opened and in he waddled with Simon in support. He was as drunk as a lord. Fortunately half the congregation was Irish, and they respect somebody who really can go for it! In some photographs he's like the Tower of Pisa.

[20] April 2005. Dolly too was the recipient of several directives: 'Having been reared in ecclesiastical matters I do know something about these ceremonies, and I have made tentative enquiries from Father Michael Hollings (who did Lennox's Requiem in the same church) and who is a close friend of Albert Friedlander. I am assured that, if asked, Michael and Albert can fix a suitable liturgy which will please everybody. I had hoped that my new Mass on themes of Berkeley could be done in harness with what Dymphna Nolan [Brenda's mother] proposes, as well as my Jewish Wedding Hymn with Albert's text...' He was distressed that Dolly was sending out invitations without consulting him. He mentioned two people, rumoured to have been invited, whose presence would mean 'I shall with deep grief withdraw from our son's wedding ceremony musically and personally'. (23 June 1990)

At Peter's wedding

Dolly remembers standing in the receiving line with him:

> Malcolm kissed every woman, hugged every man, and in between he would kiss and hug me; he was just gone.[21]

Malcolm's relationship with the other strong woman in his life, Bessie, had continued to blossom.[22] The mother who had so dominated him in his boyhood and adolescence was doing so again, even from across the world; she was someone who had devotedly made her home his shrine, a seemingly ageless source of support. It was a terrible shock, therefore, to be told by Marion and Diane that Bessie could no longer cope by herself but needed institutional care. Unable at long distance to appreciate the seriousness of Bessie's dementia, he revolted at the whole idea. Initially, too, Bessie sounded anything but incapable. For a while she was even giving elocution lessons to the nurses and organising everyone in sight in her characteristic way. Michael Brimer, visiting her at the nursing home, was extremely surprised to discover that she had made arrangements for him to give a piano recital:

> All of the inhabitants of the home were sitting waiting in the lounge, the staff as well, to hear me play! In spite of the fact that she was there because of her dementia, she stood up and introduced me to the audience, getting all the bits of my 'history' correct. It was delivered with wonderful enunciation and humour. She was a real 'Auntie Mame'![23]

In late 1990, however, just after Malcolm had finished the short score of his Galway commission, Bessie suffered a stroke and for a time was unable to talk coherently. Malcolm, distraught, took himself to bed and spent Christmas Day quietly weeping. The thought of Bessie incoherent amid strangers preyed on his mind and he wrote to Marion:

> It may seem brutal but may it, please God, be her last Christmas on earth. She always hated Christmas and she won't know it's Christmas anyway. I have ghastly visions of

---

21 April 2005

22 The turning point had been her late acceptance of Simon. In 1987, during his stay at Port Macquarie, he had been delighted that she held her peace when told 'the happiest eleven years of my adult life have been with Si'. It was the start of a genuine truce on a vexed subject, and now, in her old age, Bessie could again do no wrong.

23 August 2005

> decorations, funny hats and even crackers that misguided nurses may be putting up in Bessie's home…

Bessie, however, survived the crackers and funny hats and made such encouraging progress that a little later, on her 85th birthday in February 1991, Malcolm was sending her a rallying call:

> Happy Birthday, Bess! You're the star. Stay shining. We all need your sparkling radiance! Simon joins me and the grandchildren in sending lots of love and good wishes.[24]

Bessie rose to the challenge. A starring role she had always fancied, and now she began to deliver high-quality speeches down the telephone: her life was intolerable in her present home; only he, Malcolm, understood and loved her; and if he could do nothing to save her from an intolerable imprisonment she might have to consider drastic last resorts. It was hardly the kind of 'sparkling radiance' Malcolm had been looking for, but it certainly captured his undivided attention. Although he was much preoccupied with a production of *The Valley and the Hill* at the Stevenage Arts & Leisure Centre (involving four hundred local children), he began to plan a secret flight to Australia, unknown to his sisters, to assess Bessie's 'imprisonment' first-hand. Robert Solomon was given some details:

> Having talked a third time to Bessie, I am both easier in my mind and more disturbed. Easier, because her mental health is excellent and her physical health very much better than anyone dared hope… disturbed, because of what emerged from a conversation which concerns her immediate environment and her motivation for living. It does appear that I can help her, provided I am myself not distressed, by people or booze...[25]

His plan was to fly in to Newcastle, where Bessie was currently living, close to Diane. But he would not tell Diane or Marion ('Bessie's very wish'); instead he would stay secretly at a Newcastle motel before spending a few days with Robert Solomon, who was sworn to secrecy.

Fortunately nothing ever came of this wild cloak-and-dagger scheme. He could not afford a ticket, and his credit was poor. In the end he had to settle for 'solving' poor Bessie's problems as best he could by telephone, which seemed to involve calls to most of the neurologists and geriatric specialists between Perth and Newcastle.

Malcolm's worries over Bessie's illness ensured that he would not complete the orchestration of his Proms commission on time. Elaine Feinstein watched on, like many friends, in helplessness:

> It was a disaster! He was going to do it, going to do it, going to do it! And then he hadn't done it! Simon was certainly pressurising him to do it. But that may not be the right way to go. I don't know.[26]

---

24 9 February 1991

25 28 March 1991

26 July 2005

In early May 1991 John Drummond announced that, by mutual consent, the premiere of the new flute concerto, scheduled for the Proms in late July, was being cancelled. The work, he said, had outgrown its original intentions, having turned into a large-scale ballet score, of which the concerto was now just the opening movement.

This was true. The short score which Malcolm had sent James Galway was really not a concerto at all, its subtitle, 'A Myth for Dancers', suggesting a wider remit than the concert hall. Galway was expected to double on the alto flute and piccolo; a chorus of prisoners, meanwhile, came in towards the end of the piece, singing of the finding of the first map, north of Babylon; a man doing his football pools on the night train to Larisa; mankind hiding 'in the yellow spice of the acacia' and 'accepting the stigmata of educator, doctor and rail time-table'. The music, which was highly chromatic with complex rhythms and ever-changing metres, was certainly very challenging, but Malcolm had allowed his enthusiasm for Greek philosophy, existentialism and modern poetry to run wild. The piece worked neither as concerto nor ballet, and the lack of orchestration provided a merciful release from what promised to be an embarrassment at the Proms. The newspapers were understandably ironic at this latest cancellation, Michael White setting the tone in the *Independent on Sunday* with the heading COMPOSER NOTED FOR THE SOUND OF SILENCE.

'Even Schubert finished some pieces'
– Independent on Sunday, *5 May 1991*

For all the brave talk of the large-scale ballet score (which was never written), this latest setback destroyed Malcolm's self-esteem, so that he could not even respond to the death from AIDS of Kath Walker's son, Vivian, Kabul Oodgeroo of the Noonuccal tribe. Vivian Walker had sent Malcolm a copy of his latest play a few months before his death, warning that it would be his last, and the two had thereafter kept in touch by telephone until the final days. When Kath gently queried the possibility of a musical tribute, Malcolm revisited the sketches he had made of a possible AIDS fund-raiser, which he hoped would be a good starting-point. He soon had a title, *Requiem for a Tribe Brother*, and he planned for it to be sung in the open air at Vivian's grave in front of Kath's house on Stradbroke Island. He himself would play a portable electric harmonium. But these plans all came to nothing; his muse had deserted him.

1991 was a totally barren year. On his sixtieth birthday, in November 1991, he was well treated in Australia, the ABC broadcasting over forty programmes of his music. In Britain, by contrast, he was largely ignored. Friends rallied as best they could. Bayan Northcott wrote an appreciation in *The Independent*, in which, after noting that the London Philharmonic Orchestra would be playing his overture *Santiago de Espada*, he deplored that it was 'an anniversary our other major orchestras, opera and record companies have unanimously chosen to ignore'.[27] The lack of interest, wrote Northcott, was all the stranger in that the 1990s were more conducive to Malcolm's stylistic breadth than earlier decades:

> The pity of all this is that where Williamson's works are now heard, they tend to sound better than they did. To Sixties ears, preoccupied with notions of stylistic purity and technical innovation, his music often seemed unacceptably eclectic; in today's pluralism it is, paradoxically, easier to appreciate the unifying sensibility behind, for instance, the brilliant motley of his operatic review *English Eccentrics* or to accept that distinguished addition to the Prokofiev-Walton tradition, the Violin Concerto, for its own memorably elegiac worth.[28]

Northcott, in his spirited defence, reminded readers of the great wealth of works awaiting rediscovery, making a special plea for the 3rd Piano Concerto, the *Sinfonietta* and the first two symphonies:

> Yet potentially the biggest wow of Williamson's eight symphonies to date – were it to arrive at the Proms, say, under the baton of Simon Rattle – could well prove the Sixth…

Such strong endorsements could have been very helpful, had Malcolm been in a condition to build on them. Instead, careless of his reputation in a way very reminiscent of the wild 1950s, he did his own cause enormous harm. A *Musical Times* feature on his 60th birthday was typical of a series of disastrous interviews which left readers in no doubt that his life had been wrecked by alcohol.

Chris de Souza, in writing up his interview for *Musical Times*, began with the preliminary telephone call:

> 'It really *is* Howard's End,' Malcolm Williamson told me of the house he lives in when I phoned to fix an interview. The call took 70 minutes, and probably gave me enough irrelevant material to doubt if I could ever get him to concentrate on important issues.
>
> I had plenty of basic questions: 'What does the Master of the Queen's Music do?' 'Why don't you produce more music for Royal occasions?' 'Why do you never seem to finish new pieces?' 'How do you feel about the incessant jibes?'[29]

When de Souza visited Howard's End, tape recorder in hand, he found Malcolm 'already fairly merry'.[30] There was no sign of Simon, though they had company for their meal and discussion, a refugee from Kazakhstan called Islam, apparently one of a number of Jewish musicians Malcolm was currently involved

---

27 9 November 1961

28 21 November 1991

29 *Musical Times*, November 1991. Even in serious musical circles, Malcolm was of most interest as the failed royal retainer.

30 November 2006

in trying to rescue from the Soviet Union. Precisely what Islam was doing in Howard's End was not clear. ('You can either live in an ivory tower,' explained Malcolm enigmatically, 'or live life on the streets.') Malcolm himself looked much older than de Souza had expected, and was so drunk that a meaningful conversation was out of the question. De Souza, therefore, let the tape recorder run as Malcolm rambled on inconsequentially, his words coming slower and slower, the sleepier he became. Some of Malcolm's opinionated and confused comments, when reproduced in *Musical Opinion*, were at once appropriated by *Private Eye* for its Pseuds' Corner feature. It is easy to see why:

> I write music *because* of the human condition. It is the most sublime non-verbal communication with the human being, before he was born – after he'll die, as he struggles through life, as Kirkegaard has marvellously delineated. And of course, leaning on Plato – everyone leans on Plato, even Aristotle…

His attempt to talk seriously about religion ended in comedy:

> The hound of heaven pursues me, Chris. I go to Lourdes every year and have recourse to the Blessed Mother at the Grotto. I went there this present year to tell the Blessed Mother that I was an atheist, I did not believe in God, and I made a novena of baths, of masses, of Holy Communion, and spent a lot of time at night at the holy grotto talking to the Blessed Mother – this is really what my music is about. It is not for me to comment on whether people see it as that or not, but music is life, life is music. I had occasion to say to a student, 'You have a choice. Either the world's your oyster, or your oyster is the world.' And regrettably I feel that many people feel that their oyster is the world…[31]

Soon after Malcolm's sixtieth birthday, it was announced that Andrew Lloyd Webber had been asked to provide some music for an event at Earl's Court, to be televised world-wide, celebrating the 40th anniversary of the Queen's accession. The *Sunday Times* ran an investigative feature, at this seeming slight to the Master of the Queen's Music, quoting a comment allegedly from 'a palace insider':

> We just forgot about Mr Williamson. He's not really at the forefront of people's consciousness.[32]

Understandably upset, Malcolm was unable to keep quiet when asked for his views. 'I'm not an athlete,' he told one reporter, 'but I would run 100 miles rather than listen to *Cats*!' 'But,' replied the reporter ingenuously, 'Isn't Mr Lloyd Webber's music absolutely everywhere?' 'Yes,' said Malcolm, 'and so is AIDS!' He warmed to his theme:

> The difference between good music and Lloyd Webber's is the difference between Michelangelo and a cement-mixer. But the comparison breaks down to an extent that there is an element of creativity in a cement-mixer.[33]

---

31 *Musical Opinion*, November 1991

32 19 January 1992

33 London newspapers, quoted by the *Sydney Morning Herald*, 21 January 1992

Later, told that Andrew Lloyd Webber had been hurt by his attack, Malcolm plunged on recklessly:

> I wish that the feeling of hurt will go into his music – it needs it. His father wrote abysmally unsuccessful oratorios and Andrew is not fit even to tie his bootlaces…

Appearing on BBC2's *Behind The Headlines* he still had more to say:

> The Queen will offer a silent prayer to God that she is not obliged to extend her very considerable intellect upon concentrating too hard on something absolutely fatuous.[34]

Lloyd Webber, to his great credit, contacted Malcolm, told him how much he had admired his music since first playing it at school, and invited him to *Sunset Boulevard.* A dramatic conversion took place, Malcolm subsequently seeing the musical another four times. But his new-found interest in *Sunset Boulevard*, *Cats* and *The Phantom of the Opera* was not newsworthy. A composer cracking up made for much better copy. *The Observer* was intrigued by the 'inner turmoil' visible beneath Malcolm's cheerful façade, its reporter encouraging him to bare his heart; to confess that he pined for 'the cosy academic position that has never quite materialised'; to quote an uncle who used to declare lugubriously, 'One door shuts and another slams in your face'; and, finally, to admit, 'I keep wishing not to go on. I find it very hard to write a piece of music…'[35]

The media wouldn't leave him alone. He was such good value. Even when attempting to project a positive public image, he tended to over-compensate with hyperbole. Asked by a reporter what he thought of Michael Jackson's latest album, *Dangerous*, Malcolm struggled to find enough superlatives:

> I'm bowled over! It is so beautiful. My one fear is that people may underestimate its value. He belongs to the next century. He's been born before his time. He's way ahead of everybody else. When we have gone to our makers, his music will be relevant. He is writing about the human condition, about the world. His music has a subtext that is eternal.[36]

Many people, of course, would have agreed with him; the album was to sell twenty-nine million copies worldwide; a single, with an important message, 'Heal The World', was to emerge from it. But serious musicians, on the whole, simply sniggered.

His many loyal supporters fought on. One of them, Peter Broadbent, whose Joyful Company of Singers had already won a Choir of the Year competition with Malcolm's choral suite from *English Eccentrics*, celebrated Malcolm's sixtieth birthday with a concert at Southwark Cathedral in which Williamson featured along with those other Masters of the royal music, Byrd, Bax and Elgar. Malcolm attended, clad colourfully in Ghanaian kaftan and fez, and afterwards, in a convivial post-concert session in a pub, mentioned to Broadbent his old idea of *Requiem for a Tribe Brother*, which he felt might work very well for an

34 30 January 1992

35 23 February 1992

36 *Today*, 22 April 1992

unaccompanied choir of such quality. Broadbent was at once interested, sought out funding and quickly acquired a commission for Malcolm from the Gustav Holst Foundation. Having had to return the fee to the BBC for the flute concerto, Malcolm was all the more eager not to pass up this opportunity. With terrible pangs of guilt he remembered his promise to Kath Walker about Vivian. Kath herself was now no longer well. It was time to assert himself, to regain something of his old concentration. And he did, by starting at the very end, with Vivian's ascent to heaven, In Paradisum, and by associating its beginning melodically with The Song of Hope, the triumphant conclusion of *The Dawn Is At Hand.* As Kath's choral symphony ended, so Vivian's requiem would begin. Once started, his love for Vivian took over. He was now, as he confided to Janet Canetty-Clarke, under compulsion to complete the work:

> Nothing but my death could release me from my promise to Vivian's mother and brother to write a Requiem for unaccompanied choir for that lovely and remarkable boy…[37]

Interruptions fortunately no longer mattered, for there were to be several.

The first and most considerable was the move from Rooks Nest, following the unexpected return of Elizabeth Poston's nephew from abroad in August 1992. Malcolm was not best pleased. In addition to his concerns about the Requiem, the house comfortably accommodated the ever increasing storage requirements of Campion Press and the large number of papers and books they had accumulated over the past seventeen years. To move them somewhere else would be a huge undertaking, particularly as there was little rationale in the whereabouts of specific items.[38] There was also his affection for the place and its genuine celebrity appeal, which had increased considerably that year with the release of Merchant-Ivory's *Howard's End.*[39] So when his last day at Rooks Nest House arrived, Malcolm went out into the garden and in a fit of pique knocked the apples off the trees.

It had taken some time to find somewhere new, as Malcolm confided to a friend:

> The goose chases are as wild as nightmares. I cannot credit some people's houses; and you've known the black depression, haven't you, of slumping in an armchair after long days of looking at houses, each more bizarre than the other?[40]

---

37 16 October 1992

38 Antony Gray, for example, remembers one particularly intriguing storage room: 'I was interested to learn of two piano sonatas which, according to Weinberger's catalogue, were unpublished. Enquiring about them one day at Howard's End, I was pointed by Simon in the direction of a laundry room. It was full of an amazing collection of things, including bits of manuscript and pieces of music. At Simon's invitation I spent three days looking through this room. All in all I found sixteen completed but unpublished works, including the two piano sonatas. Malcolm seemed thrilled by these discoveries...' (August 2006)

39 Even though a house near Henley-on-Thames was substituted for Rooks Nest, the film-makers finding the rooms of the original too small for use.

40 MW to Janet Canetty-Clarke, 21 August 1992

There could not have been a more striking contrast between the space and old world charm of Howard's End and their new home, a modern four-bedroom house at the end of a cul-de-sac on the outskirts of Royston, so modern, in fact, that Malcolm declared 'it ill accords with our shabby furniture after Rooks Nest where everything was old and shabby'.[41] It made financial sense to be in a town, it was helpful to be on a direct rail link with London, and Royston was twelve miles closer to Cambridge than Stevenage had been. Although the new home was physically less isolated than Rooks Nest, it would not be the same kind of magnet for visitors, and more and more in Royston the two would rely on themselves for company.

Simon took the initiative for the actual move, arranging for Malcolm to stay for two weeks with the artist Alan Burgess and his family (at Royden, near Harlow), to avoid too much disruption[42] to the Requiem. There Malcolm somehow transcended all the earthly problems and anxieties which beset him to celebrate, with great sensitivity and discrimination, heavenly joy and peace, and, though focusing on the untimely death of a single friend, he universalised his grief, and the Requiem became, to a large extent, the work he had envisaged several years earlier, a message of deep sympathy for those whose lives had been prematurely curtailed by AIDS.

Malcolm's morale in the difficult final stages of its composition was much boosted by the enthusiasm of the young Australian pianist Antony Gray, and as soon as he had successfully met his deadline he thanked 'dearest, inspiriting Tony', for 'strong, sage, forceful support' as well as 'affection and non-judgemental patience'.[43] Antony believes this mostly refers to Malcolm's occasional anxieties about the gay background to the work:

> He wasn't exactly afraid about writing a work strongly connected to an AIDS-related death, but there were certainly some worries about it in the house generally, and perhaps I offered a bit of calm on the subject. He was certainly grateful for what support I could give him, and he wrote a dedication to me in the score above one of the movements, though I'm not sure if it made it into print![44]

At the first performance at St John's, Smith Square[45] Gray amused Malcolm with the gift of a Body Shop sweatshirt with a Mostly Men logo on it:

---

41 *ibid.*

42 Alan Burgess remembers Malcolm in excellent form, spending most of his time upstairs working steadily on *Requiem For a Tribe Brother*. His concentration survived not only the move to Royston but also several days spent with Simon in Bucharest as guests of the Romanian government, attending the Constantin Silvestri Festival where the Second Symphony was much admired. 'Did I tell you,' he asked Bessie, 'that my second symphony had a triumph in Romania? It was done at a concert, then broadcast and televised twice.' (19 November 1992) 'My visit to Romania,' he wrote to his sisters, 'was quite wonderful... Of course Bucharest is battle-scarred after their revolution, but it is a very beautiful city and the people are a delight.'

43 November 1992

44 December 2006

45 19 October 1992

> He was delighted with what he called 'his beautiful, brave chemise', thinking it initially a little risqué, though he came to wear it a great deal.

Requiem for a Tribe Brother, the last of many works inspired by Malcolm's staunch Catholic beliefs, proved one of his very finest. Each of the Requiem's ten sections shows great surety of touch. The introit (*Requiem Aeternam*) has a strength and atmosphere which rivals the introduction of Britten's *War Requiem*; the *Kyrie* is a ravishing intimation of the prospect of heavenly peace – just three words spun out into two and a half minutes of exquisite prayer for divine pity; *Pie Jesu* is thrillingly operatic, *Agnus Dei* a study in purity, *Lux Aeterna* a bold expression (through the blend of two sopranos) of the striving for higher things; *Libera Me*, strongly rhythmic, provides an apt preparation for *In Paradisum*, Malcolm's sweetly melodic and highly emotional farewell to Vivian Walker, his much loved tribe brother.

Although the overall effect is one of great simplicity, stylistically the work is far less conservative harmonically than might first appear. Christopher Austin writes:

> At any given moment the harmony may seem familiar, only to be diverted into some unexpected region. This is one of the keys to Malcolm's unique tonal/modal harmony. It's always beautifully conceived for voices – but the level of chromaticism also makes it a challenging sing. The Kyrie, for example, though luxurious with all its suspensions, nevertheless covers a very wide tonal field. It is by no means commonplace, even while it serves up what seem like tonal suspensions. Overall, there is a dialectic between two harmonic areas, one stark, as embodied in the drones and semitone dissonances of the Introit, and the other richly saturated with thirds and chromatic sidestepping that might ultimately be founded on Malcolm's love of Broadway. And why not?[46]

As Malcolm settled down in Royston, the Requiem successfully behind him, it was almost a relief that there were no further commissions or commitments in the immediate future. He had time for reflection, to look back beyond recent vicissitudes to take pride in all that he had achieved in the forty years since he had first come to England, full of self-belief and ambition. Simon, meanwhile, was as busy as ever, ensuring that Malcolm's newest works were available in print, his heavy workload lightened by the assistance of an engraver, Michael Fowler, who lived locally. But there was never to be tranquillity for long. Even from secluded Royston Malcolm continued to make headlines for the wrong reasons. He ill-advisedly let slip, for example, his view that Benjamin Britten was 'a back-stabber'. There is a much-told story of Malcolm on the telephone in one room at Royston, making highly indiscreet comments to *The Independent* about Britten, and Simon in another room imploring Bayan Northcott to try to get the newspaper to pull the story.

A wonderful diversion from the personal grievances which provoked such unhelpful outbursts came with the arrival of his first grandson, Josef Daniel

46 August 2006

Williamson, of whom he was at once obsessively proud. ('I have to keep reminding myself,' he wrote to Marion and Diane, 'that I am not Josef's father, only his grandpa!') Josef's latest triumphs were quickly relayed to all the many people he would invariably telephone each day, the highly expensive morning ritual of speaking to friends becoming more important to him than ever at Royston. Iris Murdoch[47] was a constant recipient of his latest intelligences, as John Bayley remembers:

> Iris was a very kind lady – she disliked long telephone calls and so it was the most remarkable act of self-sacrifice that she would regularly speak to Malcolm for up to an hour or longer. I would be gesticulating to her to get off the phone, but she would go on listening to all he wanted to say. It was usually about philosophy, poetry or music…

Whatever had been discussed in one conversation, would often be explored further in the next. Bayan Northcott was often part of the chain:

> Phone-calls would come out of the blue, early in the morning, and it was usually great fun, but you never quite knew what was coming. Some of them would be very coherent, following up things in the media. Some of them were absolutely fizzing with indignation from something he'd read – or one or other of his *bêtes noirs*… he had an awful lot of them… and he could be rather scatological. Occasionally he'd just ring up and say 'Bayan, I've another funny for you,' and one of those terrible jokes would be produced. And one would lead to another. Some of them one would have heard already several times. Eventually he'd get on to somebody else.[48]

Alexander Goehr might sometimes be that person:

> Malcolm would often phone me, somewhat lengthily, to tell old jokes with a few new ones, but he always told them well. If he hadn't drunk too much, he would be extremely witty. He'd be rambling on about what Lizzie Lutyens did twenty-five years ago, or talking of the very gifted John Lambert with whom he was very close for a time…[49]

Alternatively there was Brian Shaffer:

> He would often ring and engage in very long phone calls – sometimes two hours! He would also like to visit and you knew these visits would also be very long! He would talk about his latest interests – Iris Murdoch (he was very distressed by her growing illness), some philosophical point, boys with genetic problems, the latest book he'd

47 Malcolm had immersed himself in Iris Murdoch's difficult philosophical works, full of Plato, Freud and Sartre, though he did admit to finding *The Sea, The Sea* hard going. Over the years he treated each new novel with devotion, until, in 1993, *The Green Knight* disappointed him. He had revered its predecessor, *The Message to the Planet*, and was surprised that others might struggle with it: 'Out of personal loyalty Simon laboured through about 50 pages, and fell back defeated, lacking even the curiosity to battle on. I without effort have luxuriated in this masterpiece of some 550 pp. a number of times.' (MW to Antony Gray, 25 June 1992)

48 October 2005

49 January 2005

> been reading. He couldn't switch off. He was great unless he became drunk – he'd be very difficult to manage then – would go over the top.[50]

Then there were calls to Australia. Robert Solomon was one of the Sydney recipients:

> Malcolm would telephone occasionally and at length, usually well lubricated. When I felt the bill was becoming excessive and he was on the third round of jokes about the Royal Family et al., I would try to cut him off, which he resented. As often as not, Simon would be in the offing, fretting about last month's telephone bill for a thousand pounds…[51]

At the time of the move to Royston Malcolm was still able to telephone Bessie, though it was hardly a satisfactory process. One moment she would be urging him to come out to Australia, settle in Port Macquarie and start a publishing company. The next she would be refusing to talk to him, flinging the receiver away, and Malcolm would be left anxiously soliloquizing before hanging up in great distress. As he explained to Marion:

> My calls to her start with a 5-minute honeymoon, in which she rubbishes everyone mercilessly, and does her great actress bit (at which she will always be superb). After this she tries to persuade me to rescue her from the home in some lunatic scheme. Then she flops and stops talking, later reviving long enough to blame me for all her troubles past, present and future…[52]

She was so unpredictable, he told Marion, that on her death bed she would probably suddenly sit up and go into the sleep-walking scene from *Macbeth*.

The unsatisfactory phone-calls to Bessie stopped in June 1993 when she suffered a serious stroke, from which it seemed she might die. When Marion rang up Malcolm with the news, he wept for a week, and for months thereafter, like an aboriginal, he would cry at dawn each morning in a form of ritual lamentation. This lasted until late in 1993, when one early dawn he heard Bessie telling him, quite severely, not to be so foolish. But his distress at her helplessness did not lessen. Eventually, when he could bear it no more, he wrote to Marion and Diane on the subject:

> One person close to me, Ursula Vaughan Williams, told me that she went through a similar prolonged thing with her father. I do not know how to convey this except in her own words. She 'gave him permission to die', and in the briefest time he lay back and died peacefully. Ursula asked me to pass this on to you.
>
> Can we help wondering if the habit of almost 90 years of caring and worrying about family and others keeps the heart and breath going when almost everything else has packed up? Can you 'give her permission' to slip away?[53]

[50] July 2005

[51] September 2005

[52] 2 February 1993

[53] 23 June 1993

Bessie, however, whether invited to slip away or not, resolutely fought on. Indeed, to an extent she recovered. In October 1993 Malcolm wrote:

> My poor old mother drags on in a nursing-home. She shows no sign of decline but the mind is gone and she is a skeleton (a breathing one).[54]

As such she remained Malcolm's chief preoccupation, inspiring some of the highly allusive poetry he was currently writing. One poem, 'Black Bess Is White', was to be included in the autobiography he was still contemplating.[55] The style may be perversely obscure, but the key thought – that Bess should now be allowed the dignity of death – comes clearly through the first verses of this long poem:

> All sempiternal rest, dear Bess; accept not loss of
> dignity! Redeem your priddy priestly pride.
>
> Damn you, you gods whose Jewish duty don't;
> A lioness' body blind awake in sleep. The wordlost
> Body fails and flails;
>
> Giver of strength, and stronger for that, you now
> must plead to the weak, the fools of false gods.
>
> Listen to the Ixionic dignity, Prometheus unbound,
> The wheels. The woes of piteous chains, the obvious
> obseen, the evident unfound. The Sisyphic will not
> stop rolling.
>
> O burgled dignity, O ache of being obliged – the state
> You hated most in a life ebb of breath nor wave
> its beat!
>
> Goddam you gods, free her to stand in parity
> With Michael! There is no archangel, no Michael,
> until she, my first, last, only Bess create
> Him yet again.[56]

Marion and Diane, coping with the practicalities of their mother's long illness, were on the whole relieved that Malcolm did not come out to Australia

---

54 MW to Robert Solomon, 6 October 1993

55 It was never completed.

56 This was one of his easier poems. The obscurity of Malcolm's poetry is better illustrated by 'Musicanal to the Castle Perilous' (October 1993), which starts:

> Four Watermans, Besser than she-ppor goats
> Knowing ungods they make gay love the gayer.
> Deaf to blind sobs they leave Sabrina feyer
> That they may grope the demiurge in notes.

It ends with Adam kissing Cain, but it is hard to work out what happens in the middle. Tammy sees the obscurity of her father's poems as typical of his interest in word play: 'He also adored complicated crosswords, and was extremely good at them. I never saw him look anything up and he seemed very familiar with the various setters' devices and delighted in working out the puns...' (March 2006) to complicate things. He often rang them to ask if he should. Perhaps it would be better, they advised, to remember her as she was. It would be distressing not to be recognised by her.

The gloom of 1993 was intensified by Kath Walker's death[57] and his own illness. His problems began when he fell over in the street, a fall compounded by another shortly afterwards, though he made light of it all in a letter to Marion:

> I have short-term amnesia resulting from a terrific slither on the invisible black ice in the next street to ours, which caused a fall on a loose carpet on the staircase here, which made me bang my head on a bookcase at the foot of the stairs… My pal Iris Murdoch in Oxford fell in similar circumstances and thought that she had suddenly become senile or had Alzheimer's Disease. The amnesia recedes but slowly and there is nothing to be done except wait…[58]

Bessie meanwhile had moved into a world of her own, sleeping for much of the time. Malcolm began to come to terms with the situation. He at last realised too, with gratitude, just how much Diane and Marion had put into the exhausting task of supporting a mother who no longer recognised them. He reminded himself that Bessie had always said to him that she looked forward to death, seeing it as a dark blanket of sleep covering her and bringing her peace.

Malcolm's anxieties for Bessie had played a big part in the collapse of his creative powers, and, having finally reached an acceptance that nothing more could be done for her, he briefly re-found his muse. In 1994-95 he completed his five last works, very different from each other in scope, yet sharing one similarity: they all reflected important friendships. The first work, for solo harp, came about through Malcolm's interest in musical therapy. Through Bob and Phyllis Champion Malcolm had met the outstanding Welsh harpist, Elinor Bennett, who, like the Champions, had two boys with the Sanfilippo Syndrome, both dying within months of each other. Malcolm's friendship, both before and after this double tragedy, is remembered by Elinor with deep appreciation:

> Malcolm used to ring up for hours at a time! It was particularly helpful in that he had such knowledge of the Sanfilippo Syndrome and related illnesses. He was immensely kind and wonderfully supportive. For many years he was a very important part of my life.[59]

There had been much talk of his writing her a piece, but nothing happened until Elinor, with a concert coming up in the Purcell Room in 1994, asked again. Perhaps, she gently suggested, he could write something in memory of her boys, Alan and Geraint? Malcolm began at once on a Harp Symphony, starting the work most unconventionally with a reading of Rupert Brooke's 'Day That I Have Loved'.[60] All four movements are technically challenging.[61] The second

57 He wrote a moving obituary in *The Independent* that September.

58 2 February 1993

59 August 2006

60 He had set the poem for low voice eight years earlier.

61 The first movement proved so difficult that Elinor Bennett has plans to arrange it for two harps.

movement is based on a Welsh tune, the third is a tango, ('because my daughter was spending some time in Patagonia') and the last, with tolling chimes, is a specific memorial to the two boys.[62]

The Third String Quartet, also completed in 1994, originated through Audrey Ellison, who for a time acted as Malcolm's agent. She was also working for the Australian String Quartet (led by William Hennessy), and neatly managed to organise a commission from the Birmingham Chamber Music Society for both her clients, the ASQ undertaking to play Malcolm's new work in concerts in England as well as recording it at the ABC's Adelaide Festival. The piece, which lasts just ten minutes and is cast in one movement, is serially based, the chief motif undergoing considerable exploration and development. William Hennessy, who had met Malcolm in Hobart some years earlier and gone with him to meet the Governor of Tasmania during the crisis over the Franklin River dam, remembers Malcolm as a man 'full of contradictions, raw as a rough diamond yet full of warm humanity'. He writes of the quartet:

> It is a work of great intensity and integrity, robust yet delicate and sensitive. There's something of Schoenberg in it. Beethoven and Tippett too. When we did some rehearsals with Malcolm, he was less interested in the detail of the piece than its overall atmosphere. What he was fighting for was the major gesture. [63]

The main event of 1994, however, was the completion of a fourth piano concerto. The idea had first arisen in the middle of the 1980s when he became friendly with the Wolff sisters, Marguerite and Dorothy ('Dolly'). Marguerite was a well-established concert pianist, a former pupil of Louis Kentner and a friend of Arthur Bliss, whose works she strongly championed. Her younger sister, Dolly, also a talented pianist, became particularly friendly with Malcolm when they were working together in a voluntary capacity to help Jewish musicians emigrate from Russia and settle in England. In 1987, however, at the height of Malcolm's interest in Russia, Dolly died. Malcolm thereupon impulsively told Marguerite that a work he had already been promising to write for her, a Scherzo for Piano and Orchestra, would now be developed into a Concerto in D, the key chosen specially for Dolly, in whose memory he would write a beautiful slow movement. He would be tailoring the concerto, he told Marguerite, 'like a Saint Laurent ball gown,' a particularly apt simile for Marguerite who was famous for her glamorous dresses.

Marguerite was delighted with the concerto when it finally arrived and still looks upon it with affection:

> It's the best of all his concertos! When he finally finished it there was considerable excitement! Cheltenham was very interested. Very much so. But it needs a great deal of rehearsal – it is very difficult piece for all concerned…[64]

62 Elinor Bennett gave the first performance of the *Harp Symphony* in February 1994.

63 August 2006

64 July 2006

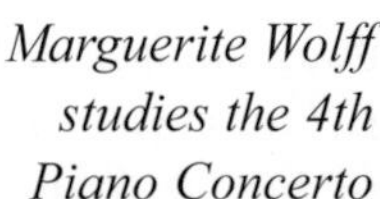

Marguerite Wolff studies the 4th Piano Concerto

The concerto's prospects suffered a setback when Malcolm threw a tantrum over Marguerite playing at a memorial service for an agent he disliked. Disappointed in her hopes to work with him in the preparation of the piece, something she felt was very necessary, Marguerite put off negotiations with concert managements over the premiere. The concerto still awaits its first performance.

This might suggest the work is flawed in some way, but that is not the case. It is a fascinating piece, the lyrical slow movement, Dolly Wolff's memorial, containing one of Malcolm's great tunes, though the prevailing atmosphere is typically bitter-sweet. Of the strongly contrasting outer movements, the first is lithe and highly rhythmical, a confession of a lifelong admiration for Stravinsky, and as immense a challenge to the pianist as the Third Concerto of 1962. It begins with great dissonance, the piano announcing itself by hurtling down in a thrillingly complex, cadenza-like introduction. The last movement is an arresting Tarantella, saturnine and sinister, very different from the high-spirited Tarantella which closes the *Sinfonietta*.

A smaller orchestral work, *With Proud Thanksgiving*, achieved, by contrast, two performances in 1995. Written for the celebrations of the first fifty years of the United Nations and played in a concert at Geneva, it is a strangely sombre piece, less in keeping with the celebration than its dedication, to Harold Wilson, whose death occurred during its composition.[65]

The climax of 1995 and, indeed, of his whole career was the symphonic song cycle *A Year of Birds*, which, despite the problems of *The Myth of the Cave* four

---

[65] Malcolm's friendship with the Wilsons went back a long way. Twenty-five years earlier, well before he became Master of the Queen's Music, Malcolm attended several dinners given by the Wilsons at Downing Street: for the Romanian premier, Ion Maurer, in 1969; for the Yugoslavian President, Mitja Ribicic in 1970; and, the same year, for the young Swedish Prime Minister, Olof Palme, whose radical agenda Malcolm much admired and whose assassination greatly distressed him.

years earlier, was premiered at the Proms, thanks to the imperturbable John Drummond.[66] Using as its text twelve short poems by Iris Murdoch[67] associating the months of the year with specific birds, it is a work on which he worked, on and off, for eight years.

He was still at Sandon when he started discussions on the project. A year later, in 1989, just after the move to Rooks Nest, he was intending a premiere in Oxford, where Iris Murdoch lived, the work to be dedicated to her mother, a keen amateur singer. He had sketched it all out, he announced, had finished four of the twelve poems and was speaking every morning to Iris Murdoch about it. It was a project about which the Queen herself was excited: 'It was not for nothing that the Queen made Iris a dame. Her Majesty is no fool.'[68] But the Oxford premiere didn't happen and it was to be another six years before the work was finished.[69]

The extremely slow progress suggests that it may have been a project he couldn't bear to finish, one that was too important to him, as an ongoing act of homage to both Iris Murdoch and Olivier Messiaen (whose *Catalogue d'Oiseaux* he admired and regularly played). He himself also had a very personal relationship with these poems, as someone who every dawn would feed the birds in the back garden (and, at Sandon, had shooed away the neighbours' ginger tom, whose regular arrival at this critical moment, was not, he suspected, totally accidental). Malcolm may well have also sensed that *A Year of Birds* was going to be his last major work. If so, why the need to hurry?

A month before the concert, in July 1995, Malcolm received a visit at Royston from Robert Solomon, who was planning to write his biography.[70] It already had a title – 'Her Majesty's Grand Eccentric' – and chapter headings, and the visit was intended to take it further. 'Prepare for concentrated labour,' Robert had warned him. 'If you can lay your life out on the dining room table, so much the better.'[71]

66 19 August 1995.

67 Iris Murdoch's *A Year of Birds* was first published in 1978. When a new edition of the poems was published in 1990 with wood engravings by Reynolds Stone, Malcolm reviewed it enthusiastically for *Country Life*. (1 November 1990)

68 There was talk of a further collaboration, a chamber opera, *Acestos – Above the Gods*. The two would often meet at April Cantelo's Oxfordshire home, so that they could hear and discuss the latest settings for *A Year of Birds*. 'I thought the settings were very beautiful and imaginative,' remembers April. 'Iris's short condensed poems seemed to suit him very well. He had a different feel for each.'

69 It was close enough to completion at the time of his visit to Bucharest in 1992 for him to suggest a premiere there, at the next Silvestri Festival, in 1993, though it never materialised.

70 Four years earlier Malcolm had written to Robert Solomon: 'I want you to do the book on me quite badly and the fact that you are outside music is a big plus!' Various approaches to Australian publishers had been made unsuccessfully. It was now thought the book might be easier placed with a British publisher...

71 7 June 1995

Unfortunately in the run-up to *A Year of Birds* there was considerable tension at Royston which seemed to affect the reception Solomon received:

> The travel arrangements had been carefully made, but when I arrived at Royston Station there was no-one there to meet me. I rang Simon, and he came to pick me up, though in a surprised kind of way – they seemed to have forgotten about me.[72]

The spare bedroom was being used by Simon's engraver, Michael Fowler, who was involved in the urgent job of feeding the notes of the song cycle into a computer. So Solomon slept on a sofa. Malcolm, half his mind on proof-reading the emerging parts, talked away happily about his life, though for every reminiscence there were usually three bawdy stories. It soon became clear to Solomon, however, that there were now problems with the whole idea of a biography.[73]

> Malcolm was still extremely keen. He spoke warmly about a recent book I'd done. But Simon pointed out that I wasn't a musician. I wasn't the right person for the job.

It was an uncomfortable visit.

> Malcolm's behaviour during this visit wasn't impressive. He'd done a rehearsal at a church and someone had arranged to pay him. But he was discontented about the payment – Simon said 'don't worry' but Malcolm got on the phone to this woman and was very abusive. He and Simon were really at odds over this, Malcolm being very unreasonable.

A very difficult few days came to a predictable end:

> I had a brief, blazing row with both of them, for (in their decidedly old-womanish opinion) failing to give a belatedly unveiled and ageing video of Malcolm at the Proms the close attention it deserved, while I was packing to catch my train.[74]

The video was of his last Proms premiere, ten years earlier, *Next Year in Jerusalem*:

> They didn't feel I was giving it proper attention. 'What happened? You didn't see it!' I said I did see it, though it was difficult to concentrate as I was packing at the time. Anyway, they reckoned I'd missed something and they got really huffy. I blew my top. It was an example of a very wide range of behaviour that you could expect from Malcolm.[75]

Back in Sydney, Robert Solomon wrote a conciliatory letter, enclosing a new nine-page synopsis of the proposed biography. He ended:

> Thank you for your hospitality, and my apologies for tantrums, however provoked. I am not used to being told what I saw or thought. I cannot understand why Simon thought I would be with you for a day only, in view of long-standing advice and my letter of 7th June + phone. Regards to him. Shalom.[76]

---

72 September 2005

73 'It was clear that Simon didn't want me to write Malcolm's biography,' wrote Robert to Gerard Windsor, shortly after Malcolm died.

74 Robert Solomon to Gerard Windsor, 11 March 2003

75 May 2005

76 17 August 1995

There was no response from Royston. Solomon's good wishes that Christmas likewise were not reciprocated. Indeed, he never heard from Malcolm again. The proposed biography was therefore not written. Another opportunity for reviving interest in Malcolm's flagging career had been lost.

Fortunately this sad saga was not an omen for the premiere of *A Year of Birds*, which was an outstanding success. The soprano Alison Hagley rose to the occasion magnificently, as did the BBC Concert Orchestra under Barry Wordsworth. At the end of the performance, to great applause, Malcolm (in his aboriginal and African finery) took Iris Murdoch by the arm and led her onto the platform.

'She looked pretty lost,' remembers Bayan Northcott. 'She didn't quite seem to know where she was.' But it was a wonderful evening, with a fine party afterwards at the Australian Ambassador's residence nearby. Dolly, who had attended the concert as an IMG representative of Richard Stoltzman, the soloist in Copland's Clarinet Concerto, had a chance to congratulate Malcolm, who wrote to her affectionately afterwards:

> It was great to see you at the Proms, and looking very beautiful! It was inevitable that we were so rapidly divided in the crowd… I was pleased that you liked my piece, and I can return the compliment by saying how very much I admired Richard Stoltzman. Aaron's concerto is a favourite of mine…[77]

There were several excellent reviews. Hilary Finch, for example, wrote most supportively in *The Times*.

> This is a major, verdant work from Williamson. Almost unrelievedly rhapsodic, a full orchestra's graphic season-painting, bright with birdsong (Williamson did not study with Messiaen for nothing) supports abundantly melodic writing for the voice. Murdoch's poetry is a real children's garden of verse, with both the simplicity and resonance to get any composer's sap rising.[78]

The good reviews were very well deserved. *A Year of Birds*, a genuinely symphonic work, developing the themes from the soprano's songs within extended orchestral passages, is attractive at first hearing and, like all fine music, reveals more and more of itself on further acquaintance. It is Malcolm at his most

77 28 August 1995

78 22 August 1995. The review highlighted the way the work's three movements, each 'through-composed' like a Puccini or Strauss opera, split the year into strongly distinct sections: 'Williamson's first tableau also seems to recall another poet's vision: Edward Thomas's rook's-eye view of winter passing in a half-thawed land. Broad, slow-moving strings are brushed by cymbal and harp and a high piping piccolo yields to vocalising which forms into words as a real rite of spring gets under way. Spring then warms into summer in a waltz of merry-making, raucous with trumpet and timpani. June blazes in multi-layered orchestral hyperactivity worthy of Mahler, while the first three repetitive notes of the blackbird's song spur voice and orchestra into the dog-days. Alison Hagley revelled in it all, finding a new bloom in her voice for the season of mists, 'water like glass' and an owl crying. After an orchestral recreation of the hurricane of 1987 comes the benediction of the Christ child, a piping robin and back to vocalising as the world winds down.'

characteristic, exemplifying all the various traits which combine to produce his unique sound: exciting rhythmic complexities; the drama of constant tensions between the tonal and the chromatic; vivid use of percussion; glorious outbursts of rich, post-Straussian chromatic harmonies; the arresting nature of unusual key changes and unexpected phrase endings; and the rich colouring which comes from his many-layered orchestral writing, most notably in the divided strings. It is the work of a composer who has carefully assimilated many of the major influences of his century – Messiaen, Stravinsky, Britten and Richard Strauss – on the way to achieving something truly memorable and original.

A Year of Birds brought Malcolm welcome comfort at a difficult time, briefly reviving some hope in the future, and when, that November, he celebrated his 64th birthday, he cheerfully assured Dolly that, thanks to his excellent health and strength, he could once more become 'a promising young composer'. Everything, he told her, suddenly seemed so much easier. But these hopes were short-lived, vanishing abruptly when the BBC's abbreviated presentation of the concert on television totally excluded *A Year of Birds*. There would be no more first performances. His long career was over. And his glorious finale, *A Year of Birds*, eight years in the making, would not be performed again in his lifetime.

19 THE CURLEW'S CRY

Royston, 1996–2003

THE LAST FOUR MAJOR WORKS, *A Year of Birds*, *Requiem for a Tribe Brother*, the Fourth Piano Concerto and *The Dawn Is At Hand*, were all in their different ways reminders of the transitory nature of life. There were further reminders for Malcolm and Simon as the year ended. In November 1995 Simon flew out to Perth on news that his mother was very ill and shortly afterwards Malcolm reported to Diane:

> It is with great grief that I tell you that Simon's mother died in Perth on November 11th. He was with her for the last 48 hours or so. It was another stroke, and she was blind, but mentally in full command of herself. She recognised him by his voice and by much feeling of his face. She said a little, he talked to her a lot, and was present when she went peacefully into her last earthly sleep.[1]

Bessie meanwhile lingered on. Malcolm, writing to Dolly of Nieza Campion's death, gave her the latest situation:

> Bessie, who is about to hit 90, is dotty. She is skeletal but wolfs down marshmallows. The doctor says 'At her age why not?' Diane sticks by her, even though she sleeps through most visits. She has forgotten her children and grandchildren, but cuddles photos of Josef saying, 'This is my son, Peter'. She is evidently happy in this odd dimension. I have done my grieving, I think. I wish only that across the miles she was aware of our marvellous children and grandchildren, but there can be no return…[2]

The letter contained more distressing news:

> Another reason for my writing is that in the week of Simon's mother's death, Michael Fowler, Simon's Campion Press colleague, and I worked night and day writing, printing and faxing 2 organ pieces for him to play in Oz at the Requiem. Just hours

1 13 January 1996

2 7 December 1995

> later, Michael, driving in the small hours to hospital, died of a massive heart attack in the car. He was 45.[3]

Michael Fowler's expertise had been a great asset for several years in the production of professional scores; he had been responsible, for example, for the engraving of *The Valley and the Hill* in 1990, perhaps the most attractive of all the Campion Press editions. He and Malcolm had been working in Royston up to 4.00 in the morning, before Fowler, feeling unwell, had decided to drive himself the twelve miles to a Cambridge hospital. The police later woke Malcolm to break the news of Fowler's death. Simon, having played the organ pieces at his mother's Requiem Mass, rushed back to England and played with Malcolm at the service for Michael Fowler, before returning to Australia to help sort out his mother's estate. As in *A Year of Birds*, November had been a very sombre month indeed, and for both Malcolm and Simon it marked the start of several taxing years.

With Simon abroad and all restraints therefore lifted, Malcolm responded to the tragedy by drinking unrestrainedly. One good friend, meeting him for a meal at a Chinese restaurant in this difficult period, was alarmed on arrival to find him already the worse for drink and ordering treble gins and tonic. The meal proved a desperately sad affair:

> He would take a mouthful of food, transfer it to the side of his mouth, carry on talking, have a swig of drink, cough, and when you thought that everything was going to come up any second now, with the whole restaurant waiting expectantly, it did.

Called away from the table, the friend returned to find Malcolm sitting with his face caked in rice, seemingly unaware that he had just fallen forward into his food. The bill for drinks at the end of the meal was immense, and, when the time came to leave, Malcolm was unable to stand, a couple of Chinese waiters having to lift him out of the restaurant and into a waiting car.

The inability to walk was not totally drink-related. By late 1995 Malcolm had been having circulatory problems in his left leg and for several months either side of Christmas he had been unable to walk unassisted. Although he assured Diane[4] that 'vascular claudication has not been definitely diagnosed', he was sufficiently frightened by his doctors to try again to stop smoking. ('I hope that this, if it is the cause, will clear it up.') He had attempted to do so a year earlier ('chewing gum, hypnosis, pads – nothing works')[5] but without his cigarettes he felt strangely lethargic, and, depressed already by being confined to a sugar-free diet, was more in need of an alcoholic charge than ever.

---

3 Antony Gray recalls: 'Michael was a lovely old thing, a great fan of Malcolm's, and no threat to Simon because there was absolutely no ego involved. He was also outside the musical establishment. He took Malcolm on a holiday to France for a week or so, mainly, I think, to give Malcolm and Simon a break from each other. He was a big man, perhaps a bit of a loner, but very friendly. It was a real blow when he died.' (December 2006)

4 13 January 1996

5 MW to Dolly Williamson, 15 August 1994

Malcolm was in no physical or mental state, therefore, to capitalize on the success of *A Year of Birds*. Nonetheless he had several projects which he considered as works in progress: the re-arrangement for piano trio and chorus of a piece written for cello and chorus; a passacaglia for two pianos; and a fifth piano concerto, which he dearly wished to write for Antony Gray.[6] It would be in the key of C, he decided, but he lacked the necessary concentration, his first efforts producing nothing more than a couple of themes.

Even at this late stage he harboured his old ambitions to write an opera on Strindberg's *Easter*. For the past fours years Simon had occasionally driven him to Henley-on-Thames where he worked on it with his collaborator, Myfanwy Piper, Britten's librettist for *The Turn of the Screw*, *Owen Wingrave* and *Death in Venice*. The widow of John Piper, Myfanwy was now well into her eighties. 'Age drops away when I am with her,' wrote Malcolm.[7]

Unable to work effectively himself, Malcolm enjoyed the compensation of having young musicians around him whom he could encourage and entertain. As a raconteur he was as good as ever. Antony Gray remembers conversations suddenly veering from an analysis of a crocodile's brains to the use of the word 'then' in 'to Carthage then I came', the quotation from St. Augustine in Eliot's 'The Waste Land'. Less intellectual were his unvarnished comments on famous personalities in the music business. Of one contemporary Australian virtuoso he declared, 'What a shame he plays the piano with a tomahawk'; of another, less showy player: 'He needs to have a love affair, be a bit wild in his private life, do a bit of bed-hopping!'; of a pianist who never stopped talking of her important connections: 'If you try to tell her to bugger off, you might just as well be addressing a rhinoceros.' His views on his fellow composers were equally lively. 'I have a blanket love of Delius, a qualified love of Elgar, while I cannot see why Janacek bothered to write his music down at all.' He was extremely eloquent about 'the ambidextrous' Britten.

Morgan Hayes remembers several visits to Royston where Malcolm held court with great aplomb:

> He was unforgettable. Hugely engaging! Gin would be flowing (though Chris [Austin] and Tony [Gray] would see to it that Malcolm's was drowned in tonic). After a meal – with Chris sometimes doing the cooking – we would sit around and chat. Malcolm, perhaps a little like Lizzie Lutyens in her old age, could be very antagonistic towards contemporary composers, criticising Tippett unmercifully for lack of technique. He could also be very direct. On one occasion he was talking about Strindberg and he stopped in mid-flow to ask me if I was gay.[8]

---

6 'For ages I've wanted to write a bravura piano concerto for Tony Gray,' he wrote to Rebecca Hossack in July 1995, 'and against all good sense (financially) I've begun.' Shared Australian roots cemented the friendship. Gray, who had studied with Geoffrey Parsons, one of Malcolm's contemporaries at the Sydney Conservatorium, recorded Eugene Goossens' complete piano music on Malcolm's encouragement.

7 MW to Marion and Diane, 23 June 1993

8 June 2005

Malcolm with young friends including Christopher Austin, seated bottom right

Malcolm with Teresa Cahill and a member of the Brunel Ensemble

On one visit Hayes showed Malcolm his recently written Violin Concerto:

> Though it was not his style, he at once saw beyond the stylistic. He had a great sense of timing and told me that a particular high dramatic note on the violin was reached too soon. He was always very astute.

Malcolm much valued this new role of elderly guru, and was particularly delighted that Christopher Austin should include his works in concerts with his Bristol-based Brunel Ensemble, a connection which had begun in 1994 with a performance of *Lament in Memory of Lord Mountbatten*.[9] Austin in turn was delighted at Malcolm's interest:

> Not only did Malcolm come to performances of his music, but to other concerts as well, getting Simon to drive over from Royston to Bristol, which is quite some way. Malcolm absolutely adored a piece of Simon Bainbridge's; he was also thrilled by Diana Burrell's *Bronze*. He was always so involved – when we did a Lutyens premiere in 1996 along with a piece by Raymond Warren, at the pre-concert talk I was giving with Raymond Malcolm was asking quite complex philosophical questions!

9 The Ensemble received its name two years earlier when fifty musicians came together under Christopher Austin to record the first draft of Will Todd and Ben Dunwell's *Isambard Kingdom Brunel*. Its public debut followed in 1993.

In November 1996 his sixty-fifth birthday was ignored by London concert managements, but Austin and the Brunel Ensemble staged a celebratory concert at Clifton Cathedral, performing the Seventh Symphony and *Hammarsjköld Portrait* (with Teresa Cahill as soloist).[10] Many messages of goodwill in the souvenir programme added to the sense of occasion. Bayan Northcott, for example, listed his favourite works:

> Thank you, thank you for the hieratic First Symphony, the exotic Second and the grandly synoptic Sixth; for the touching Violin Concerto and the uproarious Third Piano Concerto, for the unsettling *Sinfonietta*, the engaging *Pas de Quatre*, the tightly argued Piano Quintet, the visionary *Next Year in Jerusalem*, the endlessly inventive *English Eccentrics*… and for so much else from your diverse, imaginative, learned, colourful and, not least, practical pen. And looking forward confidently to the day when other performing groups besides the Brunel Ensemble, and other organisations besides the BBC, will recognise a master in our midst who has given so much, and who still has so much to give…

Simon meanwhile highlighted Malcolm's refreshing unwillingness to conform to convention:

> You are the master of the unexpected, delighting, entertaining, disconcerting, infuriating, the challenger of shibboleths, the hammer of convention. You are the extrovert with a fund of ribald stories. You are the contemplative, giving us *Hammarskjöld Portrait*.
>
> Journalists have made you the scapegoat of your profession. You are inconvenient: a gadfly. Yet the complete catalogue of your works is formidable and it continues to grow…

One of the most unusual tributes came from the young Thomas Adès, who offered a short musical quotation from his opera *Powder her Face*, in which one character sang 'He's heaven' and another, in agreement, 'Perfect heaven'. Fay Weldon, meanwhile, summed up delightfully:

> Dear Malcolm, original of all originals, may life never turn down quieter paths! Why should it?

Malcolm was deeply moved by the whole occasion. Smartly attired and characteristically sporting an AIDS awareness ribbon and a colourful African fez, he was presented at the end of the concert with a signed poster of the event, before launching unexpectedly into a long speech, which (much to Christopher Austin's relief) could not have been faulted for its impeccable good taste.

---

[10] The concert took place on 15 November 1996, six days before his birthday. Teresa Cahill remembers learning the cantata in the original Swedish: 'It was a tall order! But it's a work of very high quality. Especially the fast stuff. Christopher is a very fine conductor and directed a wonderful performance. Malcolm was very keen afterwards to do Iris Murdoch's "Agamemnon – Class of 1939" for me. Simon spent a long time explaining the poem, and Malcolm giving me a very comprehensive analysis of the Greek. The project thereafter was continually on and off.' (November 2006)

Though forgotten by most concert managements, Malcolm was still remembered from time to time by the media. The most inflammatory attack in 1996 came from *The New Statesman* in which Dermot Clinch's 'Off with his Head!' showed impressive Ciceronian rhetoric, though better suited perhaps to a genuine Catiline than a hard-pressed composer deserted by his muse:

> Williamson has, to put it charitably, kept his head down in his noble office. John Betjeman, as Poet Laureate, brought poetry a little closer to the nation's heart. Ted Hughes has been less lovable, but has kept the flame of occasional poetry flickering. Malcolm Williamson, by contrast, has relegated music to the back-burner of the public's attention! Where has the Master been when music needed him?[11]

As Malcolm had been neither funded nor encouraged to write for the royal family for over a decade, it was somewhat hard for him to be blamed for inactivity, let alone for failing his country in its hour of need. Nor was it Malcolm's fault that the post-war education system had produced a nation whose musical needs, on the whole, did not stretch much beyond the Rolling Stones or the Spice Girls.

Malcolm had so often been criticised unfairly for his lack of productivity that the attacks no longer hurt with quite the same intensity. Moreover, he had other, more pressing worries, particularly as regards his health. Shortly before his 65th birthday he had confided to 'dearest' Dolly:

> Last Thursday I had a shock which has given me pause to think. For over a year I thought that I had vascular claudication in the calf of my left leg. I was told that this could be due to my heavy smoking. With your help (and my own determination) I had a second go.[12] Now I've not had a cigarette for four months and am down to middle-size patches. I have infrequent nicorette sprays and now almost no withdrawal symptoms. To this degree I am very lucky. The shock was from my very good GP who did some preliminary tests, and it seems probable that I have Parkinson's Disease. The following day a specialist from Addenbrooke's Hospital in Cambridge confirmed it…[13]

He felt quite well, he told her, but had only limited control over his legs:

> I can shuffle, not really walk, but my legs rush forward independent of me, and I am therefore obliged to pull my body after them. This is unsatisfactory, as the running shuffle can, and often does, go its own way, leading me into a wall or door. I'm developing techniques to combat that. The local Red Cross has lent me a walking-stick…

He was anxious that news of his illness should stay within the family – 'This is because I could lose work' – and remained very grateful that his brain was not in any way affected.

However, in the late spring of 1997 he suffered another stroke, which sent him back to Addenbrooke's, though he was at pains to play down the seriousness of this newest setback when later writing, in a shaky hand, to his sisters:

---

11 9 June 1996

12 He also made good use of Quitline ('an excellent phone service – you can ring them when you feel like screaming!')

13 16 August 1996

> I am getting over some sort of illness – partly physical and partly mental, which has affected my walking and my thinking. I leave out words and misspell other quite simple ones and have been to and from hospital like a ping-pong ball. It all began the year before last and things got worse… Everything is improving (including slight diabetes) except my left leg (vascular claudication). I am going though an odd stage, as memory returns slowly, but with blanks, and I have had to learn to write again...[14]

Over the years he had done his best to scorn all intimations of mortality. He and Bessie had often joked about the deaths of the famous, offering from time to time their own candidates for 'death of the month'. Levity lessened the pain. On the death of Lizzie Lutyens Malcolm told Bessie: 'Considering her life-style, I'm amazed she lasted to 73'. On Robert Helpmann: 'There'll be a nation-wide hunt to find someone with something charitable to say about Bobbie!' On Eileen Joyce: 'Nobody knew how old she was, because she said she was found by nuns in some bushes!' He remained defiant even after Bessie's loss of contact with the world. In 1996 as a tribute to one of his idols, Ella Fitzgerald, he sang 'Ten Cents a Dance' down the Royston telephone to a bemused Iris Murdoch.[15] But he could find no defiance at the loss that year of a dear friend Mary Sandbach, a Swedish scholar of much distinction and the first recipient of the Strindberg Prize,[16] nor, in early 1997, of Myfanwy Piper, whose death ended whatever hopes he nursed for *Easter* and whose obituary in *The Guardian* was to be one of his final pieces of published writing.

Malcolm was himself recuperating in hospital in Cambridge, when, in the middle of June, the news he had expected for the past eight years arrived. Bessie, at ninety-one, had finally died. Malcolm wept all night. He was still devastated when, two weeks later, back at Royston, he wrote to Marion and Diane:

> I was sorry that Bessie did not have a Catholic send-off. She spoke of it many times to me and swore me to secrecy at Port Macquarie. It was certainly her wish, but [at] a distance I was not prepared [to] fight about it. I did see Monsignor Donnelly about it in Port but lost touch. She and I often climb[ed] those endless steps to the cliff top. She sat and meditated in the Lady Chapel while I said the Rosary before the Pietà.[17]

This was hardly tactful, but he was in no mood for tact, his mind in turmoil, finding it hard to come to terms with the reality of his loss. Suffering all the Nietzschean confusions of a son dominated by an all-powerful mother – a relationship Iris Murdoch had written about most perceptively – Malcolm kept reproaching himself for keeping away from Bessie in her final years. Unlike Simon, he had not visited his mother at her time of need. And so he asked his

---

14 1 July 1997

15 This was no sudden whim. He had rung up a friend, Ken Bailey, bemoaning the death of 'Dr Fitzgerald' (as he always called the singer) and asking him to send over a copy of the sheet music, so he could give a complete performance.

16 'I'm writing a tribute for *The Independent*,' he told Bessie. 'She was a lovely dainty lady. I'm amazed to discover she was 89.' (15 November 1990)

17 1 July 1997

sisters for a few mementos, to serve, as it were, as holy relics, icons he might venerate to help assuage the guilt: an attractive tapestry of *Giselle*[18] which Bessie had embroidered; a little replica of Michelangelo's Pietà; and a triptych which Father Donnelly had once blessed for her:

> I'd treasure a memory of Bessie. Nothing will erase the true memories of Bessie which are beautiful. We had a memorial service in our Synagogue in London, which was very beautiful. Peter and [I] were together at the front. Several people (including Dolly) were late, but considering the London traffic in London [sic] I was amazed that [they] managed to arrive at all.

Distress over Bessie tipped the balance of his own precarious health, and less than two months after her death – on the day before Princess Diana died in Paris – Malcolm suffered a major stroke, while visiting friends in London.[19] One early hospital visitor was Richard Womersley:

> He spent the first two days after the stroke at the Royal Free Hospital, Hampstead. I went to see him. He couldn't speak and his mobility was restricted. I had to speak whatever came into my head. Fortunately I'd just been to a concert which included his piano trio, so I was able to tell him all about that. It was obvious from the eye contact that he could follow every word. And that he wanted to hear more. So I told him about the rest of the concert – there was a Shostakovich trio in it. Suddenly he started singing the last movement of this piece. He couldn't speak a word, yet he could sing! And he was note perfect.[20]

A long period of hospitalisation followed in Cambridge. Another friend, Jonathan Still, found him seriously impaired in speech but active in mind.[21] Gwenneth Pryor was surprised how little of his personality had been destroyed by the stroke; that it still shone out, even in enforced silence; and that he could communicate effectively just with his eyes. Clare, likewise, visiting her father in hospital, found him slow and slurred in speech, but undimmed in spirit, attempting anecdotes and mimicry as of old. By this stage he had become addicted to the television.

---

[18] Diane writes: 'Mother took up tapestry when her sight was poor and did about nine pieces in all. She would sit at the tapestry frame for thirty minutes at a time, with a special magnifying glass and light, and stitch away until her eyes couldn't cope. She would have a break and then go back and stitch some more.' (December 2006)

[19] 30 August 1997

[20] December 2005. April Cantelo experienced the same phenomenon: 'After he'd had his stroke we tried having telephone conversations. It would be painfully slow, but then he would remember some tune and sing it and immediately everything flowed. He would sing an excerpt from one of the operas. Suddenly the tongue worked and everything. He was very brave in his disability, struggling to get words out and really trying to make progress...' (April 2005)

[21] For a long time Still struggled to understand what Malcolm was trying to say to him. Eventually he worked out it was French – 'Quelle âge as-tu?' – a shared joke: 'When we were in France some twenty years earlier there'd been a very amusing man called Monsieur Quellard, whom Malcolm had nicknamed "Monsieur Quelle-âge-as-tu".'

I remember him crying over a particularly moving episode of *The Waltons* – he was an incredibly emotional man.[22]

Eventually Simon was able to bring Malcolm back to Royston. It was the beginning of a new phase, in which Simon, as a full-time carer, had to make compromises with his commitments to Campion Press. Sessions of physiotherapy and speech therapy were organised, and improvements were slowly achieved, although the impairment in speech was always to remain. The frustration for Malcolm, who so loved to talk, was enormous, but he bore it with an uncharacteristic calm. Tammy was much impressed:

One of the curiously uplifting things about Dad in his afflicted state was how incredibly accepting he seemed about his new limitations, particularly his speech problems. Once he and Simon found the right therapist, he worked very hard and achieved quite a lot. But it was his apparent lack of frustration which impressed me. It didn't make him not want to be understood. He just got on with the situation without making a fuss.[23]

The relationship between Malcolm and Simon altered significantly in this last period together, as Elaine Feinstein observed:

Before the disabling stroke which made him totally dependent on Simon, Malcolm was quite bossy. He made the decisions about where they went and what time they left. Now, however, the balance shifted. The loss of dominance had the usual effect of making the patient hate his carer, while at the same time clutching at him. Nothing that Simon did was right. Malcolm, for example, would remember a story he wanted to tell, and perhaps produce one word with great effort. And then Simon, who knew the story, would tell it for him, but never satisfactorily as far as Malcolm was concerned. It was a difficult situation for both of them.[24]

At least they enjoyed a greater sense of security when Simon accepted the opportunity of buying the house in Royston they had hitherto been renting. Antony Gray remembers it as quite capacious and very well lived in:

There were four bedrooms upstairs, two of which Simon used for the business, and the other two they slept in. Downstairs there was a large living room on the right of the hall, with two alcoves, one of which had a piano in it and the other some bookshelves. On the left of the hall was a small room, where, after his stroke, Malcolm slept, with a kitchen-dining area behind. There was a large garden, and I used to mow the grass every so often. I also used to do mountains of washing-up when I went out there… Simon had a homehelp for a short while. After she left, he wanted to clean up before he employed another one, which he never did, so it just got worse and worse. The house was full of towering stacks of old newspapers, *Readers' Digests* and computer magazines, which Simon would buy and then never have time to read, and would keep for when he did have time. The garage was completely full of boxes of the same that he'd brought from Rooks Nest. In the end it was quite difficult to get around. There was a path between the stacks from Malcolm's bed to the lavatory and

22 July 2006

23 March 2006

24 September 2005

> another to his chair in front of the TV. There were also stacks of junk mail which Simon wanted to go through before throwing out...[25]

The pressures on Simon were unrelenting, his responsibilities all the more challenging as he was temperamentally more scholarly than practical. Peter's wife Brenda remembers a time when several of the electrical appliances had broken down at Royston:

> I asked him why he didn't get them fixed, as things like cookers and heaters were essential items! Simon was attracted by the philosophical implications of my statement. 'You say they're essential, but what exactly do you mean by that?'[26]

Peter recalls some spirited exchanges arising from their different approaches to time and responsibility:

> He'd ring up and say 'Can I drop Malcolm off so I can go and see my cousins in Putney?' and, because his time-keeping was often extremely erratic,[27] I'd reply 'Please do, but it would help if you would arrive by so-and-so and leave by so-and-so.' He'd respond as if I was being wholly unreasonable. 'So you're going to put Malcolm out on the doorstep are you?' And, regardless of what I'd said, he'd still arrive two hours late and come back to collect Malcolm similarly late. It was a different way of looking at life! He once said to me, 'I really need a break from Malcolm! And there's some work I have to attend to in Australia. Could you come up to Royston and stay with him?' When I pointed out that, much as I'd like to help, as a full-time teacher I couldn't do so during term time, he couldn't see my reasoning. 'But he's your father!'[28]

Only the family and a very close circle of friends were aware of the extent of Malcolm's illness, which Simon, conditioned by years of defensive manoeuvres against the inquisitive media, decided to keep out of the press. Unfortunately this served to upset friends who felt they were being inexplicably excluded or, if they knew of the illness, deprived of the chance of giving him encouragement. Ken Healey, who had first met Malcolm in Canberra thirty years earlier, was one of those disappointed:

> My last visit to see Malcolm in England was absolutely disastrous. It was after the major stroke and Simon wouldn't allow me to see him. He seemed in denial of Malcolm's illness, liking to think everyone would imagine Malcolm was getting better.[29]

---

25 December 2006

26 July 2005

27 Bayan Northcott recalls one vivid example of carefree time-keeping: 'Robin Holloway had kindly organised a lunch for four of us. In addition to Malcolm and Simon there was old Howard Ferguson who was in tremendous form, wonderfully urbane. It was quite a riotous occasion. But Malcolm and Simon were so enjoying themselves they just never went. They were still there by the evening, and Robin was getting slightly desperate, as it was Christmas Eve or something, and they had eaten him out of house and home! And showed no signs of going. Malcolm was so happy to be slightly off the leash. One just got that sense. He seemed ever so pleased to be out of Royston.' (October 2005)

28 July 2005

29 May 2006

At Royston: with Simon (above) and Marion (below)

Rebecca Hossack was another:

> Sometimes I would ring Malcolm up and the phone would be answered by Simon, who would say 'No, I'm awfully sorry but you cannot speak to him' There were times when I had something exciting to tell Malcolm, and it was extremely upsetting that I couldn't speak to him.[30]

It seems likely that had Malcolm resigned as Master of the Queen's Music in 1997 on the grounds of ill-health and had the extent of his illness been fully

30 January 2006

known, the benefits would have outweighed the disadvantages. The devotion Simon gave to him over this period would likewise have been better recognised. Even as it was, there were those, like Elaine Feinstein, who felt an unequivocal appreciation:

> It was awful for Simon. And I thought he behaved very well in very difficult circumstances. He had a great deal to do. He was supposedly operating his Press, and doing the shopping and cooking, and looking after Malcolm – from picking him up from the floor to all sorts of intimate difficult jobs, all of which he did without complaint.[31]

Christopher Austin, likewise, stresses the sacrifices Simon had to make:

> A lot is often said about how much Malcolm craved the stimulus of company and musical performance and what a shame it was for him to be cut off in Royston, and so on. While this is true, it must be remembered that Simon needed those things too and isolation in Royston, with all its complex causes, was a burden for both of them.[32]

Up to and including Malcolm's seventieth birthday, there were occasional forays to London and beyond. Simon took him down to Gwenneth Pryor's London home, for example, for discussions with Antony Gray (about to record the complete solo piano works in Australia) and Piers Lane. Gwenneth remembers Malcolm being 'alert and astute, antennae moving in every direction!' It was clear that such meetings with fellow musicians were highly therapeutic.

With this in mind Christopher Austin raised the possibility of Malcolm writing music again in some form or other:

> I suggested to Simon many times that, if original composition was physically impossible, then orchestrating *The Myth of the Cave* with me as his amanuensis might be a way to get things going again. Or, alternatively, *White Dawns*, setting it for voice, harp and strings, for a Brunel concert. But after initial enthusiasm, the idea was quietly dropped.[33]

Other mooted ideas – performances of the unperformed Fourth Symphony and Fourth Piano Concerto and a commission from Brunel for a work for the Queen's seventieth birthday in 1996 – were all found to be 'too problematic':

> The Queen's seventieth birthday commission really seemed to be going somewhere, when out of the blue Simon told me that while it was a good idea in principle, 'our composer doesn't have an idea for a piece', so that was that. I was never told this directly by Malcolm, and sometimes I wondered whether these ideas were knocked into touch because Simon, busy as he was looking after Malcolm, was worried about his ability to produce the materials…

Christopher Austin gives an interesting insight into the day-to-day pressures on Simon, which may have played their part in his unwillingness to explore such

---

31 May 2005

32 April 2006

33 August 2006

At Peter's with Dolly and Simon Campion

Grandfather accompanies

Malcolm and Simon

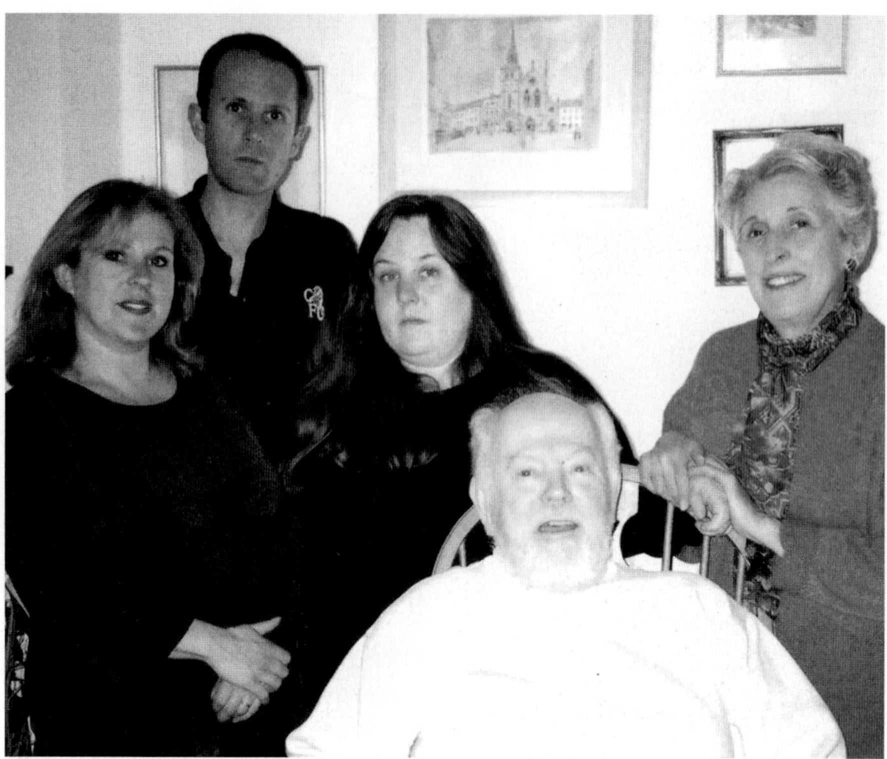

With the family

bold initiatives. In 1999, two years after Malcolm's major stroke, Austin was invited to join the pair on a short holiday to Cornwall, combining the chance to use a friend's cottage with visiting Tammy and her family. The intended time of departure was Saturday lunchtime, but such were the problems of organising Malcolm that it eventually took place late Sunday afternoon. The long journey that evening was further lengthened when a wrong road was taken out of London, so they eventually arrived at their destination well after midnight, a day and a half late. Their first actions were to attempt, unsuccessfully, to get the heating working to rid the cottage of damp.[34]

Austin's most vivid memories of the holiday concern the constant battle being fought by Malcolm and Simon over how much Malcolm was allowed to drink:

> Being denied alcohol was what annoyed Malcolm most, the issue being his autonomy as a person in the face of his steadily declining physical condition. His acceptance of

[34] Malcolm meanwhile had an opportunity to begin his holiday reading. 'The books packed away in his suitcase,' recalls Christopher Austin, 'included Wittgenstein and Murdoch (a paperback novel plus *The Sovereignty of the Good*) as well as Ronald Duncan's not uncritical book on Britten. There was manuscript too – he was still keen on the proposed vocal symphony he wanted to write for Tessa Cahill and the Brunel Ensemble, a setting of Iris Murdoch's "Agamemnon, Class of 1939".' (June 2006)

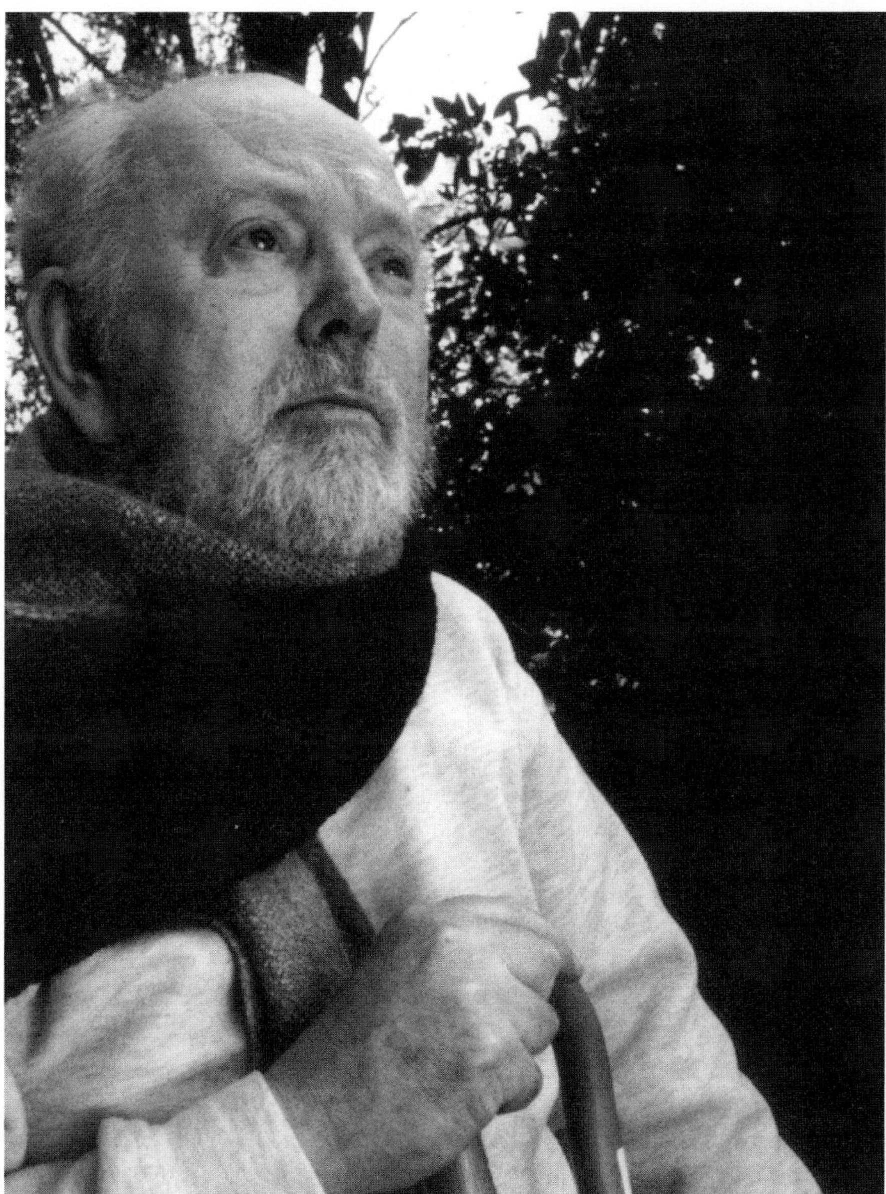

> the danger of drinking heavily, with the real possibility that it was going to kill him, seemed the most potent way in which he could assert control over his own destiny…

After a windswept morning in St Ives, they lunched 'in a rather prim restaurant' where Simon wished Christopher Austin to 'drink enough of the bottle of wine to ensure Malcolm didn't have too much'.

> I felt for both of them: Simon as the harried carer and Malcolm as the man whose self-determination had been totally compromised by the stroke of 1997. I felt, as often before, in the middle of a battle of wills.

After lunch they drove to Truro to see Tammy and her family, which, for Austin, was the most stress-free part of the trip:

> I saw immediately that Tammy was her father's daughter: the mischievous humour, the openness, and the immediate warmth she showed me, a stranger.

For Tammy too there are happy memories:

> Simon drove the three of them over from the cottage for supper and they stayed the evening, seeing the kids before they went to bed. Malcolm's speech was impaired, but he could talk a bit and be more or less understood. It was a lovely evening.[35]

The next day an unexpected emergency led to Austin making his own way home earlier than anticipated:

> To be truthful, I was a little relieved to get out; not because I didn't want to spend time with them, but because I couldn't cope with the stress that they would induce in each other. Simon's selflessness in caring for Malcolm was absolutely extraordinary, but it led to this struggle of wills. The same issue was present in Royston long before the stroke, but in Cornwall the situation was more disconcerting than ever.

The duty of care, then, was far from easy. By the time Simon came to drive Malcolm one last time to Claverdon, for Phyllis Kempster's funeral in November 2000, he had been nursing Malcolm for three hard years, drawing strength for current vicissitudes from his Jesuit training, the knowledge that he had never been more needed and the comfort of past happiness. The funeral, for all its inherent sadness, was for both of them a reminder of pleasures shared in better times. Vivid memories of *Heritage* returned, and the important spirit of hope which Phyllis's young dancers had engendered. Malcolm and Phyllis had been in touch again in recent times, and Malcolm was determined, though confined to a wheelchair, to be present to say his goodbyes. Simon helped him take Communion and later, outside in the Claverdon churchyard, they sprinkled earth together on the coffin. 'It was very good of Malcolm to come when he himself was so unwell,' said Jayne Kempster afterwards. 'He has such a kind heart.' But it was good too for Malcolm to gain strength from the ghosts of the past as he faced up to the uncertainties of the future.

The next year he reached seventy, an anniversary which might have gone by unnoticed but for Christopher Austin and Antony Gray, who both organised birthday concerts. Christopher Austin's concert with the BBC Concert Orchestra was recorded at the Hippodrome, Golder's Green, and subsequently broadcast on BBC Radio 3. The programme mixed popular successes like the Third Piano Concerto (Piers Lane as soloist) and the orchestral suite from *Our Man in Havana* with unusual works: the first London performance of *With Proud Thanksgiving* and the first British performance of the never-danced ballet *Perisynthion*.[36] Just before the concert started, in which Austin was giving a short

35 August 2006

36 *Perisynthion*, as challenging to play as it is glorious to hear, required more rehearsal time than Christopher Austin was allocated. It was therefore not played at the concert, but rehearsed separately and added to the eventual broadcast.

introduction to each piece, he asked Malcolm if he could help him with the Binyon poem from which *With Proud Thanksgiving* takes its title. He knew the first two lines:

> With proud thanksgiving, a mother for her children,
> England mourns for her dead across the sea.

But what came next? Malcolm, his eyes filling with tears, very slowly, but clearly, told him:

> Flesh of her flesh, spirit of her spirit,
> Fallen in the cause of the free.[37]

Two days later at the Wigmore Hall, on Malcolm's actual birthday, came the second concert, for which Antony Gray had organised a very full programme of chamber works and song cycles performed by young professionals, including, most appropriately, two Australian sopranos for *Celebration of Divine Love* and *From a Child's Garden*. Gray himself played the Second Piano Concerto, while a first performance was given to *Three Songs*, written at Sandon in 1986.[38] There were specially composed tributes from Peter Sculthorpe, Michael Finnissey, Ross Edwards, Morgan Hayes, John McCabe, Andrew Toovey and John Carmichael, Peter Sculthorpe also contributing affectionate reminiscences in the programme.

It was a highly emotional occasion, not just because, as Paul Conway was to write next day in *The Independent*, it showed 'the extraordinary quality of all these scores', but also in that it offered so many people who had shared some part of Malcolm's pilgrimage, a sense of a journey reaching its completion in love and affection. April Cantelo's abiding memory is of Malcolm's bravery:

> At the end of the concert he was wheeled forward, but he put aside his chair and, helped by Peter, walked to the end of the platform to take his applause. Incredibly brave.[39]

Tammy was similarly moved.

> The concert concluded with Happy Birthday celebrations. Tony Gray had organised the most magnificent tribute. Dad was totally aware throughout, and enjoyed it, and afterwards there was a reception sponsored by Australia House – a wine and finger buffet in the basement. Loads of people turned up whom we hadn't seen for years. It was a wonderful conclusion and thrilled Dad to bits…[40]

---

37 Austin quotes this as an example of Malcolm's ready empathy, his ability to relate emotionally as well as intellectually to the subject in hand.

38 Settings of Brooke's 'Day That I Have Loved', Herrick's 'The White Island' and Marvell's 'The Mower to the Glow-worms' were performed by Roderick Williams and Antony Gray.

39 April 2005. April Cantelo had asked Malcolm what he would like for a 70th birthday present. 'A recital, please,' he replied, whereupon, with pianist David Lewis, she recorded a birthday CD for him, choosing pieces which over the years had meant a great deal to both of them and together covered the seven ages of man, beginning with two songs from Malcolm's *From a Child's Garden* and ending with Mozart's *Abendemfindung*: 'It is evening. The sun has gone down and the moon gleams. So do life's hours pass as in a dance... Soon life's pilgrimage will end for me and I shall fly to the land of rest...'

40 April 2006

Peter was likewise grateful:

> It combined the two things Dad liked best, which was being around people – especially musicians who loved his music – and being able to get his hands on a certain amount of drink, though this of course Simon rationed. Simon seemed to be having a pretty good time himself.[41]

The evening ended in one final act of kindness, which epitomised the whole occasion. It was provided by Marie Hayward, the soprano who fifteen years earlier had given *The Feast of Eurydice* its premiere:

> I was in the audience clapping enthusiastically when I suddenly thought Malcolm and Simon might enjoy a full meal after the busy post-concert reception. So I rushed home by taxi to prepare a suitable feast! They came back afterwards and we had a wonderful time. It was, in fact, to be the last time I saw Malcolm. He couldn't speak well at all, but Simon translated for him.[42]

Malcolm's determination to write more music was fired by these birthday concerts, and in their wake he started immediately planning a new symphonic song cycle. Only days later, however, he suffered a further stroke, which this time affected his mouth and throat muscles, as well as his lungs. Though he returned to Royston, he was a complete invalid, requiring round-the-clock care.

Six months afterwards, however, he made a rare visit to London to attend the opening of a new courtyard at the Royal Academy of Arts by the Queen as part of her Golden Jubilee celebrations. Taken inside Burlington House in a wheelchair, he was much moved that the Queen made a particular point of speaking to him. It was a big occasion, billed as 'the most sensational gathering ever of Britain's arts world',[43] one of those glitzy parties Malcolm had always so much enjoyed, its six hundred guests ranging from Dame Cleo Lane to Griff Rhys Jones, Sir Simon Rattle to Dame Vera Lynn, Barry Humphries to J K Rowling; Dame Shirley Bassey to Baroness Thatcher and Vanessa Redgrave, the Mrs Wilcox of Merchant-Ivory's *Howard's End*. There was a lively choice of music – a jazz quartet, a gospel choir and Jools Holland, and, as the Queen turned on the new fountains in the courtyard, they were dramatically 'choreographed' to Handel's *Water Music*. News-film footage shows Malcolm alert and interested in everything around him, his wheelchair facing Sir Malcolm Arnold's. The only sadness in this glamorous outing, embellished with so many Knights and Dames, was the reminder that he himself had not achieved the knighthood he had once assured Dolly would be his…

That summer he met his sister Marion on two final occasions. She had come over to see her first grandchild, Tara, whose parents were living in south Buckinghamshire. Marion's husband Brian had recently died, and she was not

---

41 April 2006

42 July 2005

43 *Evening Standard*, 22 May 2002

70th Birthday celebrations at the Wigmore Hall with Richard Womersley and Antony Gray

With Dolly at the Wigmore Hall

certain she could cope with 'the difficulties and heartache which often accompanied contact with Malcolm'.[44] But eventually she rang:

> I spoke with Simon and said I would like to come and see them. He said it would be better if they came to visit me at Cliveden. This was not going to be easy, for several

44 January 2007

With Marion, 2002

> reasons, but we arranged a time for their visit. Malcolm seemed frail and old and could not walk far, but although his speech had considerable difficulties, it was not diminished in quantity. We had a pleasant meal, though the length of their stay caused problems with the baby. Simon rang the next day to say they had enjoyed their visit and would like to come again. We were just off to Norfolk so I suggested I call in to see them en route. I was told this wasn't possible as the house was not suitable for a young baby, which I took to mean the house was probably in a worse mess than it had been when I last visited and stayed with them.[45]

Up in Norfolk, however, Marion rang again to suggest calling in on the way down:

> Once again Simon refused, proposing instead we meet for lunch at a hotel. Though, as usual, they were late arriving, we had a pleasant lunch. I was allowed to drive them back to their house, but was not invited in, so we said our farewells outside. I had said goodbye to Malcolm so many times in my life, thinking I wouldn't see him again, that this time didn't seem much different, even though logic suggested it was likely to be our last meeting.

Four months later, in late November 2002, Malcolm had yet another stroke.[46] This time he remained in Addenbrooke's, and Simon's life now became a daily vigil at Malcolm's bedside. For Tammy, down in Devon with her family, it was a great help to receive Simon's detailed daily bulletins. One particular day, however, Simon sounded anxious, commenting that, if she was thinking of coming up from Devon, now would be a good moment.

> When I got there I was relieved to find the alarm was over. Simon was his usual calm self. I had been nervous about seeing Malcolm, unsure how to hide my reaction if I was shocked. He was hooked up to various machines and couldn't sit up very well in bed, but his eyes were the same; twinkly, inquisitive; lively. I had made a photo-montage of him with his grandchildren so I held it up for him and talked him through the various occasions. I could see him reminiscing along with me, giving the odd

[45] 8 July 2002. Marion left for Australia a week later.

[46] 10 November 2002

> chuckle, which was difficult, as his throat wasn't working well. There was more chuckling later when Simon read some P G Wodehouse to him.[47]

Malcolm's final stay in Addenbrooke's lasted three and a half months. The nurses in the ward were extremely encouraging. Charts were put up outlining his 'progress', real or imagined. There were one or two sessions of physiotherapy, when Malcolm held on to parallel bars, but it exhausted him very quickly and was not repeated.

Tammy's last visit was particularly distressing. Malcolm had just been moved to a new ward, in Simon's absence, and looked terrified:

> Malcolm's distress was heart-breaking. We both stood by the bed trying to make Dad feel relaxed about his new surroundings, while everything settled down around him. That was my last sight of my father. I kissed and hugged him, then stood at the foot of the bed (while staff fiddled with equipment beside him) and mouthed 'I love you'. He blew me a kiss. I walked into the Relatives' Room and burst into tears.

Malcolm had been given a simple keyboard on which messages could be typed out, for his mind was still as quick as ever. One morning, when he was very weak, a consultant asked him if there was anything he could do to make him more comfortable. Malcolm pointed to the tube in his neck and then typed 'Get this fucking thing out of me'. Each letter had been an effort of will. The consultant felt the expletive said a great deal about Malcolm's will to live.

But the situation had become hopeless. Just a few days before Malcolm died, Tammy and her family were booked for a holiday abroad. She rang the hospital from the airport.

> We had a brief chat with Simon before he held the phone to Malcolm's ear. I could hear him breathing, listening attentively. He hadn't spoken for some time, so I was used to this kind of 'conversation'. I felt it important my kids should say 'hello' to him and tell him they loved him which they willingly did. Kids being the way they are, they easily accepted that he couldn't speak.

Peter was making the journey between London and Cambridge regularly in the final stages:

> In the last weeks Dad was in extreme pain and really having a really terrible time. He hadn't been able to take food for ages. He'd been fed by drip. Everything went out through a tube and in through a tube… he couldn't communicate. He was having his throat regularly vacuumed out… There was no physical pleasure left to him, only pain… Eventually it started coming towards an end, and thank God it did.[48]

He alerted Dolly to the deteriorating situation:

> Peter rang me early one morning. He had been up at Addenbroke's in the middle of the night. 'Dad's not doing very well,' he said softly. So I rang Simon and said 'I gather Malcolm may be close to death? I'm coming up by train.' 'I'll meet you at the station,' he replied. I said, 'Please, no! I'll take a taxi.' At the hospital Simon and I

---

47 April 2006

48 December 2005

> had a quick word first. He didn't say Malcolm was dying. I'm not sure that he knew. He was still optimistic. I was there for quite a few hours. Malcolm was conscious, and glad to see me. I'm sure he knew exactly what was going on.[49]

One thing discussed by Dolly and Simon was whether or not to risk disturbing Malcolm with the wordly news that Clare, who was currently in Florida, had had a baby, named Jake after Dolly's father. They decided they should. Malcolm by this time had little ability to be expressive. When told about Jake, however, he slowly opened his eyes, wider and wider, communicating his delight. He died just a few hours later, grateful for the absolution of the last rites he had so hoped Bessie might take, embracing at the last the God whom he had, in his own idiosyncratic way, served so faithfully.

Malcolm died on 2 March 2003, a time when all the newspapers were full of the impending American and British invasion of Iraq. Nonetheless, as Master of the Queen's Music, he attracted many full and, on the whole, laudatory obituary notices. There were, of course, the inevitable comments about missed deadlines, but the highlights of Malcolm's career were also carefully documented. 'Gifted composer who sought a reconciliation between the popular and the intellectual in his music,' stated *The Times* heading. 'Controversial composer out of tune with the establishment,' declared *The Guardian*. The *Daily Telegraph* was a little wider of the mark. 'Composer of more than 120 works who became a somewhat underproductive Master of the Queen's Music.' Other parts of the media were less sympathetic. 'I don't want to sound callous, but, quite frankly, it's good he's gone,' commented one critic brusquely on the radio.

Even in death Malcolm was still regarded in some parts of the press as fair game for a cheap laugh. Miles Kington's 'By Royal Command' in *The Independent* was a particularly cruel piece of satire, noting his partaking 'fondly of the bottle' and suggesting a silly reason for 'why he never seemed to write any music for the Queen'.

The funeral took place in Cambridge at the Church of Our Lady and the English Martyrs.[50] Simon had selected the music and readings with great care; Peter Broadbent conducted The Joyful Company of Singers; Peter gave the address. Malcolm would have been hurt by the lack of royal representation, but the presence of Ursula Vaughan Williams, in Robin Holloway's words, 'conferred a metaphorical benison more impressive, maybe, than the real thing'. The service (as Holloway later reported) proved an unexpectedly uplifting experience:

---

49 December 2005

50 A Memorial Service was also held in Sydney, at St Canice's, Elizabeth Bay, at which Diane delivered a touching address on the brother she had lost some years earlier. Marion remembers the sudden surprise of Malcolm's death: 'Although it was obvious on my visit nine months earlier that Malcolm was in a poor state, it was a shock to us when he died. We were never told that he was in hospital. We only heard he was seriously ill a few hours before he died. I find it hard to forgive Simon for that...' (January 2007)

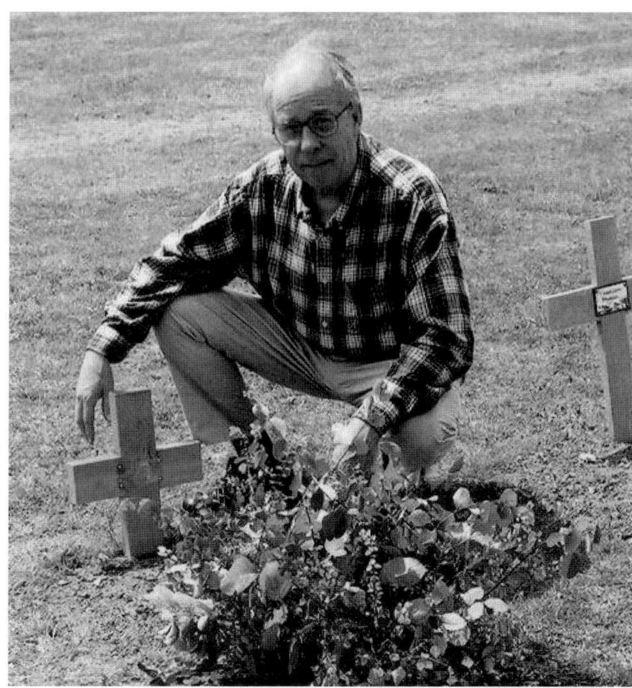

Simon Campion at Malcolm's grave, Fulbourn

A potentially harrowing occasion was softened by Malcolm's mitigating muse. The large congregation was regaled by an excellent professional choir in movements from *Requiem for a Tribe Brother*; and joined lustily in the *Sanctus* from one of his folk-masses and four of those wonderful/awful hymn tunes, occupying a no-man's land somewhere between Ivor Novello, Palm Court and *Hymns, Ancient and Modern*, thoroughly vulgar without becoming cheap, resourceful, even artful, in making so much out of so little, spreading warmth and comfort (the police had ejected a vagrant who sought these things, just before the service began: Malcolm would have let him stay on, and would have given him all his spare change to boot); the occasion became suffused with euphoria that, along with the solemn liturgy and a funny, touching address, brought the man himself into uncanny proximity.

The saddest reflection a few days later is that our musical culture abetted his innate self-destructiveness in making so little of so much! The times are out of joint when gifts of this order cannot be properly valued, fruitfully channelled, fully used.[51]

Tammy also remembers the therapeutic effect of Malcolm's 'mitigating muse' at the service:

We were standing on arrival with the coffin at the back of the church, and suddenly *Procession of Palms* started up – it was so unexpected – Simon picked up song-sheets, passed them round, and we all joined in the singing – 'Ride on, ride on in majesty!' – and what was a deeply horrible moment was suddenly transformed into a swirling daze of great emotion and vivid memories – Dad writing it and proudly playing it to us – and amid all the tears there was Dad, alive, young and wonderfully creative…[52]

51 *The Spectator*, 29 March 2003

52 May 2005

The burial took place not far from Cambridge, in St Vigor's churchyard in the village of Fulbourn, which Malcolm had known well. He and Simon had both played the organ in the attractive little thirteenth-century church; and the two Champion boys, the suffering of whose final years Malcolm had tried so hard to alleviate, were also buried there. Vigor himself had been Bishop of Bayeux in the sixth century, so there was a French connection which would have pleased Malcolm. As Master of the Queen's Music he had always delighted too in the church's royal connection, an effigy of the chaplain to King Edward III.

But above all it was the peace of the place, a pilgrim's peace, which seemed so appropriate. Fulbourn churchyard is a long way from 'the haunted swamp-oaks by the long lagoon', yet it has much of the tranquillity of the old aboriginal burial site Malcolm had so movingly depicted in *The Dawn Is At Hand.* Kath Walker and Vivian might be at rest half a world away, but the gentle greens and browns of the Cambridgeshire countryside, stretching away towards the Gog and Magog Hills, unspoilt acre after acre, have in their own way something of the majesty of the glowing golds and blues of North Stradbroke Island. Far from the intrusive noise of traffic, the birds around the Fulbourn churchyard only have to compete with the odd cowbell when making their music.

It was March, but the sun, which Malcolm had so loved and needed, was shining. The interment over, friends and family made their way reflectively to the nearby home of Phyllis and Bob Champion, where stories about Malcolm soon began to be quietly enjoyed. In the large, walled garden chatter and laughter grew steadily stronger. For all the sadness of Malcolm's absence it was a joyful, sustaining occasion and, like most of Malcolm's parties, it went on a very long time.

A hundred yards away, dusk eventually settled around the churchyard in respectful silence. Even Iris Murdoch's birds for the month of March, the doves, were no longer to be heard complaining 'that love is pain'.

Elsewhere, of course, little had changed. In London, excited crowds were making their way to the Festival Hall; there was opera at the Coliseum, dance at Sadler's Wells. Across the world, in Sydney, the Opera House would soon be readying itself for a fresh day's admirers; the Harbour Bridge for its day-long cavalcade. Blues Point Tower was already glinting in the early sunshine. Across the water, up in the Botanical Gardens, attendants were idly spearing yesterday's litter, and soon ambitious young musicians would be scurrying past on their way to the Conservatorium.

LIST OF WORKS
(Chronological)

Key to publishers:

B	Boosey & Hawkes
B*	Mario Bois
C	Campion Press
N	Novello
W	Weinberger
WC	Warner Chappell

OPERAS

A Haunted House (1951, un)
Early competition entry: 1-act chamber opera based on Virginia Woolf short story

Our Man in Havana (1962-63, W)
Superb 3-act opera (once much admired) from Greene's novel, premiered at Sadler's Wells

English Eccentrics (1963-64, C)
Zany 2-act chamber opera, Sitwell-based, premiered at Aldeburgh, delicately scored

The Happy Prince (1964-65, W)
Delightful, once hugely popular 1-act opera based on the story by Oscar Wilde

Julius Caesar Jones (1965, W)
Ambiguous 2-act opera for children and adults, set in garden in London's suburbia

The Violins of Saint-Jacques (1966, W)
Richly melodic 3-act opera for Sadler's Wells, his masterpiece, from Leigh Fermor's novel

Dunstan and the Devil (1967, W)
Brittenesque 1-act opera, written originally for church performance in Cookham Festival

The Growing Castle (1967-68, W)
Esoteric and astringent 2-act chamber opera, based on Strindberg's *A Dream Play*

Lucky-Peter's Journey (1969, W)
Second Strindberg opera, tuneful 3-acter, but a spectacular disaster at the Coliseum

The Red Sea (1971-72, W)
Lively 1-act, do-it-yourself opera, written specifically for use by young people

Easter (1990s, Un)
Unfinished opera, his third using Strindberg, with libretto by Myfanwy Piper

CHILDREN'S OPERAS (Cassations)

The Moonrakers (1967, W)
The first cassation, written to bring the idea of opera to children, much performed

Knights in Shining Armour (1968, W)
A second 7-minute piece for the Brighton Festival, equally popular in its day

The Snow Wolf (1968, W)
A sister piece to the above, equally lively, premiered at the same event

Genesis (1971, W)
Biblical fun, an American commission, singers encouraged to bring saucepan lids

The Stone Wall (1971, W)
Big hit at last night of Proms, a short but epic confrontation at Hadrian's Wall

The Winter Star (1973, W)
Much performed 20-minute Biblical cassation, commissioned by Arts Council

The Glitter Gang (1973-74, W)
Thought-provoking, pro-Aboriginal 11-minute tale of the Australian gold rush

The Terrain of the King (1974, B*)
20-minute piece, set in Provence, featuring bulls, horses, birds and man (the enemy)

The Valley and the Hill (1975-77, C)
Superb 50-minute religious 'pageant', written for 15,000 Liverpool children at Silver Jubilee

The Devil's Bridge (1982, C)
First performed in France, 20-minute cassation with strong moral, based on local French legend

ORCHESTRAL

Theme and Variations (Divertimento in Bb major) (1947-48,un)
Student work: 6 variations (on a sophisticated theme) for large orchestra

Lento for Orchestra (1949, un)
Early work, thought to be lost

Scherzo for Orchestra (1949, un)
A lively movement, alternating 3/4 with 5/4, dedicated to his teacher Alexander Sverjensky

Symphony No. 1 (*Elevamini*) (1956-57, B)
A passionate Catholic's glimpse of heaven (in 3 movements) first played by Boult and LPO

Santiago de Espada (1957, B)
Popular overture, also championed by Adrian Boult, telling story of St James

Piano Concerto No. 1 (1956-58, B)
Cheltenham Festival commission, premiered by Hallé, Barbirolli and dedicatee Clive Lythgoe

Sinfonia Concertante (1958-60, B)
For 3 trumpets, piano and strings (originally Laudes), dedicated to Dolly Williamson

Piano Concerto No. 2 (1961, B)
Archetypal sparkling Williamson, Australian prize-winning concerto for piano and strings

Concerto for Organ and Orchestra (1961, W)
Bravura piece, dedicated to Adrian Boult, and premiered by him and LPO at the Proms

Piano Concerto No. 3 (1962, W)
A virtuoso's delight, ABC commission, premiered with style by John Ogdon in Sydney

Our Man in Havana Suite (1965, W)
A follow-up to the successful opera, always one of the most popular concert works

The Display ('A Dance Symphony') (1963-64, W)
Commissioned and choreographed by Helpmann, danced worldwide by Australian Ballet

The Merry Wives of Windsor (1964, W)
Incidental music for Royal Shakespeare Company production

Sinfonietta (1965, W)
For Boult, New Philharmonia and Radio 3's inaugural concert; later used by Royal Ballet

Concerto for Violin and Orchestra (1964-65, W)
For Yehudi Menuhin and Bath Festival, dedicated to Sitwell, championed by Neville Cardus

Concerto Grosso (1965, W)
BBC Proms commission, premiered by Colin Davis and LSO, dedicated to Yuval Zaliouk

Symphonic Variations (1965, W)
Dedicated to Richard Rodney Bennett, BBC Edinburgh Festival commission

Sun into Darkness (1966, W)
Full-length ballet, premiered at Sadler's Wells by Western Theatre Ballet

Epitaphs for Edith Sitwell (1966, W)
A string arrangement of the organ piece based on a phrase from the Violin Concerto

Symphony No. 2 (1968-69, W)
Dark, 1-movement work, hinting of Messiaen, celebrating Silvestri and BSO anniversary

A Word from Our Founder (1969, W)
Written for a Hoffnung Festival, but later withdrawn

Symphony No. 3 (The Icy Mirror) (1972, W)
Sombre choral work, words by Ursula Vaughan Williams, for Cheltenham Festival

Concerto for Two Pianos and String Orchestra (1972-73, W)
For Australian Council, challengingly dissonant except for ethereal slow movement

Perisynthion, (1973-74, W)
Dramatic ballet score, written for Robert Helpmann, as yet unperformed

Concerto for Harp and String Orchestra (1973-1976, B*)
Intense tribute to holocaust victims, for Marisa Robles, commissioned by London Mozart Players

Symphony No. 4 (1977, C)
Commissioned by the LPO for Queen's Silver Jubilee, still awaiting a performance

The House of Windsor Orchestral Suite (1977, C)
Seven short pieces based on music written for the television series

Fiesta (1977-78, C)
Swiss commission, a perplexingly dour celebration of 100 years of recorded sound

Ochre (1977, C)
A five-minute work (in serene C major) for orchestra or organ and strings

Azure (1978, C)
Arrangement by Brian Brown of wind piece ('Music for a Quiet Day')

Fanfarade (1979, W)
In celebration of the 10th anniversary of the Open University

Symphony No. 5 (*Aquerò*) (1980, W)
Inspired by St Bernadette and Lourdes, written for the Brent Youth Orchestra, challenging

Ode for Queen Elizabeth (1980, W)
Delightfully sunny and Scottish 5-movement tribute to one of his Royal Family favourites

Lament in Memory of Lord Mountbatten (1979, W)
Deeply brooding memorial (for violin and string orchestra) to IRA victim

In Thanksgiving – Sir Bernard Heinze, (1982, C)
Heartfelt tribute to one of MW's kindest mentors and inspirations

Symphony No. 6 (1982, C)
An Australian masterwork, huge, vivid and (amazingly) still awaiting first live performance

Symphony No. 7 (1985, C)
Extremely attractive and approachable 4-movement work, written for Melbourne Youth Strings

Cortège for a Warrior (1984, C)
Inspired by devotion to Tito and Yugoslavia, an orchestration of piano work, *Himna Titu*

Lento for Strings (1985, C)
Simple and beautiful short tribute to Melbourne violinist and conductor, Paul McDermott

Heritage (1985, C)
Ballet set in gardens of Buckingham Palace, based on idea by botanist David Bellamy

Bicentennial Anthem (1988, C)
British and Australian national anthems, orchestrated for Australian Bicentenary

Bratsvo – Brotherhood (1988, C)
Very short, rare work for military band, celebrating Tito's imposition of brotherhood

Concerto for Flute ('Myth of the Cave') (1990, un)
An intended flute concerto for Galway that grew into an unwieldy ballet with chorus; no performances to date

Piano Concerto No 4 in D (1991-94, C)
A scintillating late work, as yet (alas) unperformed, written for Marguerite Wolff

With Proud Thanksgiving (1995, C)
Serious, moving tribute to the United Nations and former Prime Minister Harold Wilson

VOCAL and CHORAL

Hannacker mill (1946, un)
A song with words by Hilaire Belloc

Two Songs for Middle Voice and Piano (1947, un)
A student work, presently lost

A Cycle of Love Songs (1947, un)
The young Joan Sutherland, a fellow student, gave an early performance of these songs

Nocturne (1948, un)
Britten influential in this imaginative setting of nocturnal poems for tenor and orchestra

My Phillis (1950, un)
Setting of Robert Burns' poem, now lost, first performed at Sydney Conservatorium

Two Motets (1954, C)
Schoenbergian in style, and his first work to be published

Aye, Flattering Fortune (1956, un)
Equal lst (with Arnold Cooke and Rodney Bennett) in competition judged by Peter Pears

Meditations for SATB (1956, un)
Setting of three religious poems by Emily Coleman, dedicated to choirmaster Louis Halsey

The Fly (1957, C)
An imaginative competition setting of William Blake, another equal lst from Peter Pears

A Vision of Beasts and Gods (1957, B)
6 (difficult) poems by the colourful George Barker for song cycle commissioned by Pears

With this ring (1960, C)
Little-known song, words by Alex Graham

Ode in Solitude (1960, un)
For baritone and piano

Symphony for Voices (1960-62, W)
Deservedly popular unaccompanied work (for John Alldis choir), using James McAuley poems

Celebration of Divine Love (1963, N)
Fine, lengthy song cycle, using James McAuley verses again, written for Barbara Elsy

The Boar's Head (1964, N)
An arrangement of the traditional carol for SATB

A Young Girl (1964, W)
Sitwell poem set for unaccompanied choir, first conducted by Louis Halsey

Three Shakespeare Songs (1964, W)
For April Cantelo and Julian Bream at the Edinburgh Festival (but piano an alternative to guitar)

A Christmas Carol (1964, W)
A short setting of G K Chesterton and dedicated to Owen Brannigan

North Country Songs (1965, W)
Arrangements of four traditional songs, commissioned and premiered by Owen Brannigan

The Brilliant and the Dark (1966, W)
Wonderful hour-long 'operatic sequence for women's voices' – triumphed once – could do so again

Six English Lyrics (1966, W)
Tuneful and deservedly popular song cycle for low voice and piano or string orchestra

A Canon for Stravinsky (1967, Tempo)
One of 12 very short works as a Homage to Stravinsky, for unaccompanied SATB

Mowing the Barley (1967, W)
Britten conducted the song's first performance, at opening of the Queen Elizabeth Hall

From a Child's Garden (1967-1968, W)
Delightful song cycle: 12 settings of Robert Louis Stevenson, for high voice and piano

The Death of Cuchulain (1968-71, W)
A difficult, but effective work (text: Yeats) for 5 singers and percussion

Hallo Everybody (1969, C)
24 simple songs for students learning English

Sonnet (1969, W)
A capella work, words by Oscar Wilde, first performed by the John Alldis Choir

In Place of Belief (1969-70, W)
Superb, deeply-felt song cycle (using Lagerqvist poems) for six-part chorus and 2 pianos

The Musicians of Bremen (1971-72, W)
Grimm's fairy tale, set for the King's Singers, ingenious and hilarious

Love, the Sentinel (1972, W)
For chorus *a capella*, taken from Tennyson's *In Memoriam*

Ode to Music (1973, W)
Attractive choral setting of words by Ursula Vaughan Williams for Robert Mayer celebration

Vocalise in G Minor (1973, C)
Written for Hazel Reader, who inspired the 50th birthday celebrations in Australia

Hammarskjöld Portrait (1974, B)
Proms commission for soprano and string orchestra, 30 minutes of archetypal serious Williamson

Les Olympiques (1976, B*)
Symphonic cycle for mezzo-soprano and string orchestra, with defiantly gay subtext (de Montherlant)

This Christmas Night (1977, W)
Carol with words by Mary Wilson

Jubilee Hymn (1977, W)
Silver Jubilee text by Betjeman resulted in heated exchanges in the House of Commons

National Anthem (1978, W)
An arrangement for the opening of The Queen's Hall, Edinburgh (for SATB and orchestra)

Songs for a Royal Baby (1979, C)
Charming settings of poems by Lady Wilson, dedicated to the Queen's grandchildren

National Anthem (1980, W)
An arrangement for SATB and strings

Now is the Singing Day (1981, C)
Poignant song, very personal marriage gift to Charles and Diana – a devout Jewish commission

Tribute to a Hero (1981, C)
For baritone and orchestra (words: Whitman), honouring Yugoslavia's Josep Broz Tito

Cradle of the Hope of Peace (1982, C)
Choral work (piano accompaniment) – a project only partly completed

A Pilgrim Liturgy (1983-84, C)
Large-scale work for choir and orchestra, celebrating saint-like Sydney academic

Next Year in Jerusalem (1985, C)
Powerful symphonic song cycle for soprano and orchestra, encapsulating Jewish aspirations

White Dawns (1985, C)
Four astringent settings for low voice and piano of poems by Kosta Ratsin (Macedonian patriot)

Vocalise in G Major (1985, C)
Written for Sybil Michelow's husband, a great friend, Dr Derek Goldman

The Mower to the Glow-worms (1986, C)
Setting of poem by Andrew Marvell

The White Island or Place of the Blessed (1986, C)
Setting of poem by Robert Herrick

Day that I have Loved (1986, C)
Setting of poem by Rupert Brooke

The True Endeavour (1987-88, C)
Large-scale (unperformed) work for speaker, choir and orchestra; meant for Australian Bicentenary

The Dawn Is At Hand (1987-89, C)
Superb (but, as yet, only once performed) choral symphony, celebrating aboriginal aspirations

A Year of Birds (1987-95, C)
Final Proms commission, superb cantata for soprano and orchestra (words by Iris Murdoch)

CHURCH

Mass for SATB (1956, B)
Dedicated to American friend, Emily Coleman

Adoremus (1959, B)
Christmas Cantata: very tonal, but beginning with some Messiaen-like bird song

Dawn Carol (1960, WC)
For unison voices and organ, with colourful harmonies, dedicated to Peter Williamson

Ascendit Deus (1961, WC)
A cantata for chorus and organ, written for Manchester Cathedral

Tu es Petrus (1961, WC)
A cantata for speaker, SATB and organ

Agnus Dei (1961, W)
Simple, effective and gloriously tuneful, archetypal popular Williamson

Dignus est Agnus (1961, WC)
A motet for soprano, chorus and organ

Procession of Palms (1961, W)
For SATB choir and organ/piano, deservedly popular, full of very singable tunes

Easter Carol (1962, W)
Highly vivacious, immediately accessible

Jesu, Lover of my Soul (1962, W)
A typically attractive hymn setting, 'light church music' with an extra touch of class

Harvest Thanksgiving (1962, W)
Dedicated to Ursula Alldis, extremely attractive and full of rhythmic vitality

Let them Give Thanks (1962, W)
For SATB choir and organ, a short work written for Canterbury Cathedral

Wrestling Jacob (1962, N)
Rhythmically involved anthem for soprano, SATB and organ, dedicated to Barbara Elsy

The Morning of the Day of Days (1962, W)
8-minute Easter Cantata, dedicated to Fr Beaumont whose *Folk Mass* was a huge inspiration

Planctus (1962, W)
A monody for men's voices, set to 11th century words by mediaeval philosopher Peter Abelard

12 New Hymn Tunes (1962, W)
Settings with popular appeal

Te Deum (1962, W)
Attractive work, dedicated to his father, the Revd. George Williamson

Six Christmas Songs for the Young (1963, W)
Simple and effective settings dedicated to Peter and Tamara Williamson

An Australian Carol (Nativity) (1963, N)
For SATB and organ, with words by Australian poet James McAuley

Epiphany Carol (1963, W)
Archetypal popular Williamson, in its graceful beauty – solo soprano/treble, SATB chorus and organ

Good King Wenceslas (1963, N)
An arrangement for SATB and organ

Ding Dong Merrily on High (1963, N)
An arrangement for unaccompanied SATB

Six Evening Hymns (1964, W)
For unison voices and organ

Mass of Saint Andrew (1964, W)
Devotional piece in popular style, with a Lord's Prayer to make Richard Rodgers jealous

A Psalm of Praise (Psalm 148) (1965, W)
For unison voices and organ

Carol Arrangements (1969, W)
4 carols arranged for double choir, commissioned by CBS Records

I Will Lift Up Mine Eyes (1970, W)
Anthem for the Queen's visit to St Stephen's Presbyterian Church, Sydney, a gift to the Minister

Cantate Domino (Psalm 98) (1970, W)
Written for Westminster Choir College, Princeton, where he worked for a year

Te Deum (1970-71, W)
For SATB, organ and optional brass

Six Wesley Songs for the Young (1971, W)
Written for the choir of Colet Court, Prep School to St Paul's Boys, London

O Jerusalem (Psalm 122 – No. 2 of *Carols of King David*) (1972, W)
For unison choir, congregation and organ; very accessible

Together in Unity (Ps. 133 – No. 3 of *Carols of King David*) (1972, W)
For unison choir, congregation and organ

Who is the King of Glory? (Ps. 24 – No. 4 of *Carols of King David*) (1972, W)
For unison choir, congregation and organ

The King of Love (Ps. 23 – No. 5 of *Carols of King David*) (1972, W)
For unison choir, congregation and organ

Canticle of Fire (1973, W)
Major work for SATB choir and organ, written for American Guild of Organists

The World at the Manger (1973, W)
Delightful 20-minute Christmas cantata – should be as popular as Britten's *Ceremony of Carols*

Communion Hallelujahs (1974-75, M)
In the lighter *Procession of Palms* style, written for organist John Rose

16 Hymns and Processionals (1975, C)
For unison voices accompanied by piano or organ

This is my Father's World (1975, Agape)
A gentle and popular-style anthem for SATB and organ

Love, Dove and Above Chorales (1975, C)
24 chorales for voices with piano, organ or guitar accompaniment

Mass of St James (1975, C)
For union voices and piano or organ

Psalms of the Elements (1975, B)
20 responsorial psalms each dedicated to a friend

Mass of Christ The King (1970-78, W)
70-minute masterpiece, standing comparison with *A Child of our Time* or Britten's Requiem

Mass of St Margaret of Scotland (1977-80, W)
For congregation, optional SATB choir and organ, dedicated to Princess Margaret

Kerygma (1979, W)
An anthem marking George Thalben-Ball's 60 years as organist of the Temple Church

Three Choric Hymns (1980, W)
Dedicated to Sir James Plimsoll, the distinguished Australian diplomat

Little Mass of St Bernadette (1980, W)
For unbroken voices and organ (or instruments), a thank-you to the City of London School for Girls

Mass of the People of God (1980-81, W)
A Plainsong Mass written for the Bromsgrove Festival

Galilee (1987, C)
For SATB chorus, fine setting of words by Mary Wilson

Easter in St Mary's Church (1987, C)
A Scillonian song by Mary Wilson

A Book of Christmas Carols (1988, C)
31 arrangements of popular Christmas tunes

Our Church Lives (1989, C)
For SATB choir and organ, a collaboration with Susan Sayers

Mass of St Etheldreda (1990, C)
Challenging Missa Brevis, inspired by Lennox Berkeley

Requiem for a Tribe Brother (1992, C)
Most moving (and largely tonal) 30-minute memorial to AIDS victim

WIND and BRASS

Canberra Fanfare (1973, W)
Written for opening of the Canberra Theatre by the Queen

Music for a Quiet Day (1973, C)
An arrangement for Concert Band of the fourth movement of *Mass of a Medieval Saint*

Adelaide Fanfare (1973, W)
Written for the Queen's visit to Adelaide

Konstanz Fanfare (1980, W)
Rather more than a fanfare, a 5-minute salute to the German city.

Richmond Fanfare (1980, W)
A salute to Surrey's Richmond, first performed in Germany

Fontainebleau Fanfare (1981, W)
An 8-minute salute to a city he much admired

Fanfare of Homage (1988, C)
Tiny work for military band.

Ceremony for Oodgeroo (1988, C)
For a brass quintet to play when Kath Walker received doctorate at Macquarie University.

Fanfares and Chorales (1991, C)
2 short fanfares for Glaxo Pharmaceuticals

CHAMBER MUSIC

Minuet for Violin and Piano (1947, un)
Student work, in Db major, with simple textures in the piano

Study for Unaccompanied Horn (1947, un)
For friend and fellow student at the Sydney Con, Barry Tuckwell

String Quartet No. 1 *Winterset* (1947-1948, un)
Inspired by his violin studies at the Sydney Con

Nonet (1949, un)
For wind, strings and harp

Lento for Seven Wind Instruments and Piano (1953, un)
A single movement work written in 20 days, gently serial

String Quartet No. 2 (1954, un)
An essay in fairly strict Schoenbergian style

Concerto for Soprano, Oboe, Cor Anglais, Cello & Organ (1957, un)
A somewhat bizarre combination, written for a Wilfrid Mellers summer school

Trio for Clarinet, Cello, and Piano (1958, un)
Harrison Birtwistle played clarinet at its Aldeburgh premiere; dedicated to Imogen Holst

Variations for Cello and Piano (1964, W)
Demanding, both technically and intellectually; later turned into ballet, *Spectrum*

Concerto for Wind Quintet and Two Pianos (8 Hands) (1964-65, W)
Written for Rawsthorne's 60th birthday – deeply intellectual, astringent and rewarding

Serenade (1967, W)
Colourful and poignant three-movement piece for flute, piano and string trio

Pas de Quatre for wind quartet and piano (1967, W)
Attractive, thoughtful and unfairly neglected, originally written for New York ballet workshop

Pas de Deux (1967, W)
The third movement of *Pas de Quatre*, a gorgeous occasional piece for clarinet and piano

Piano Quintet (1968, W)
Two Adagios frame large-scale Allegro Molto in bitter-sweet work

Partita for Viola on Themes of Walton (1972, W)
BBC Television commission, first performed by its dedicatee, Yehudi Menuhin

Pietà (1973, W)
A work of dark, melancholic beauty for soprano, oboe, bassoon and piano (text: Lagerkvist)

Piano Trio (1975-76, W)
Sombre memories of Sir Arthur Bliss, his predecessor as Master of the Queen's Music

Champion Family Album (1984-85, C)
Simple pieces written for the children of close friends

The Feast of Eurydice (1986, C)
Dour setting (for voice, flute, percussion and piano) of Elaine Feinstein's challenging poems

Concerto for Charles (1987, C)
A work (for saxophone and band) for next-door neighbours' son – by no means easy

Channukkah Sketches (1990, C)
Duet for flute and guitar

Day that I have loved (1992, un)
4-movement 'symphony' for solo harp, written for Welsh virtuoso Elinor Bennett

String Quartet No 3 (1994)
An intense, delicate and robust work in 1 movement, an Australian String Quartet commission

PIANO

Great Lady Waltze [*sic*] **(**1942, un)
Tribute to a much-loved grandmother, written when he was just ten

Two Part Invention for Piano (1947, un)
A student work from Williamson's days at the Sydney Conservatorium

Variations for Piano (1953, C)
Written while studying with Elizabeth Lutyens, so strongly serial

Piano Sonata (1955-56, B)
Commissioned by Britten for Aldeburgh, a striking homage to the neo-classical Stravinsky

Piano Sonata No. 2 (formerly *Janua Coeli*) (1957 rev. 1970-71, W)
Neo-classical Williamson, a Cheltenham Festival commission in memory of Gerald Finzi

Piano Sonata No. 3 (1956, un)
Written for the fortepiano, a modern take on the world of Haydn

Toccata Americana (1959, un)
Humorous token of appreciation to Dolly Williamson

Four Pastorals (1960, un)
The four seasons in great clarity intended for orchestration

Travel Diaries (1960-61, C)
5 sets of effective and colourful miniatures depicting famous landmarks, ideal for teaching

Ballet for One (1961, un)
Piano reduction of work for Royal Ballet's David Blair

Piano Sonata No. 4 (1963, un)
A 2-movement work with Tippett and jazz influences

Five Preludes for Piano (1966, W)
Impressionist images from Wordsworth sonnet, its complex sonorities testing technique

Sonata for Two Pianos (1967, W)
Serial and severe, archetypal intellectual Williamson

Haifa Watercolours (1974, C)
Written after inspirational Israel visit, the pictures often dark with eastern tints

The Bridge that Van Gogh Painted and the French Camargue (1975, C)
Ten further pictures, related to the Haifa watercolours, though drawing on Provencal themes

Ritual of Admiration (1976, C)
Short work for Elizabeth Lutyens' 70th birthday, serial but lyrical

Himna Titu (1984, C)
Introspective homage to Tito, incorporating songs of Yugoslavian patriots

Springtime on the River Moskva (1986, C)
Short and rhythmically lively divertissement, for 2 pianos, a present for the Bolshoi Ballet School

Pas de Trois for piano duet (1987, Un)
A wedding present for Australian friends, but again with 2 pianos and the river Moskva

ORGAN

Epithalamium (1955, un)
A wedding present for Louis Halsey

Fons Amoris (1955-56, N)
Strongly medieval, reeking of Messiaen, successfully premiered at Festival Hall

Everyman (1956, un)
Nineteen pieces of incidental music for a production of the morality play

Résurgence du Feu (Pâques 1959) (1959, B)
Histrionic piece, written when organist at St Peter's, Limehouse

Variations of *Veni Creator* (1959, un)
The score is presently lost

Symphony for Organ (1960, N)
35-minute work, dramatic, original and difficult, written for Allan Wicks

Vision of Christ Phoenix (1961 rev. 1978, B)
10-minute blockbuster, written for the re-opening of Coventry Cathedral

Elegy – JFK (1964, W)
6 minutes of meditation on President Kennedy's assassination

Epitaphs for Edith Sitwell (1966, W)
Short and not so sweet, premiered by Simon Preston in the Aldeburgh Festival

Peace Pieces (1970-71, W)
6 highly emotional statements, first performed in Washington DC by the composer

Little Carols of the Saints (1971-72, W)
5 beautifully crafted meditations, gift for Newark-based organist, John Rose

Mass of a Medieval Saint (1973, C)
First performed in St Thomas' Church, New York

Organ Fantasy on *This is My Father's World* (1975, C)
Based on the anthem

Organ Fantasy on *O Paradise* (1976, C)
First performed by Simon Campion in Spain

The Lion of Suffolk (1977, W)
6-minute tribute for Britten's Memorial Service at Westminster Abbey

Offertoire from the *Mass of the People of God* (1980-81, W)
Commissioned by the Manchester International Festival

MUSICALS

No Bed for Bacon (1958)
Book and lyrics by Sherrin and Brahms, produced at Bristol Old Vic in 1959

Make with the Mischief (1958)
Delightful score for unperformed Sherrin-Brahms version of *A Midsummer Night's Dream*

Trilby (1959-61)
Some fragments survive from this unperformed musical based on George du Maurier's novel

FILMS

The Timber Getters (1949)
An early Australian documentary about demolishing trees

Inland with Sturt (1951)
Reconstruction of Charles Sturt's expedition down the Murrumbidgee River, New South Wales

Arid Land (1960)
A film produced for UNESCO

The Brides of Dracula (1960)
Hammer horror at its best, a lusty vampire romp with Peter Cushing

Thunder in Heaven (1964)
Travel documentary set in Nepal, narrated by Ann Todd

North Sea Strike (1964)
Oil documentary, the first of several with this title, and the least well-known

September Spring (1964)
BP film on scheme for harnessing waters of the Snowy Mountains for hydro-electric power

Rio Tinto Zinc (1965)
Documentary which has seemingly disappeared without trace

Crescendo (1969)
Hammer Films thriller, LSO playing the score, Clive Lythgoe and Tubby Hayes the soloists

The Horror of Frankenstein (1970)
Hammer horror classic, directed, produced and written by Hammer supremo Jimmy Sangster

Nothing but the Night (1972)
Christopher Lee produced crime thriller, with Lee, Peter Cushing and Diana Dors

Watership Down (1978)
Only the titles music and prologue of this major film hit

The Masks of Death (1984)
TV movie, Sherlock Holmes caper, with Peter Cushing and John Mills (Dr Watson)

BIBLIOGRAPHY

Allen, John (ed.), *Entertainment Arts in Australia*, Paul Hamlyn, Dee Why West 1968

Alomes, Stephen, *A Nation At Last?*, Angus & Robertson, North Ryde 1988

Alomes, Stephen, *When London Calls*, CUP, Cambridge 1999

Ashby, Margaret, *Elizabeth Poston, composer*, Friends of Forster Country, Stevenage 2005

Ashby, Margaret, *Forster's Country*, Flaunden Press, Stevenage 1991

Bainton, Helen, *Facing the Music*, Currawong, Sydney, 1967

Barker, George, *A Vision of Beasts and Gods*, Faber & Faber, London 1954

Baume, Michael, *The Sydney Opera House Affair*, Nelson, Melbourne 1967

Bellamy, David, *Jolly Green Giant*, Century, London 2002

Bellamy, David, *The Queen's Hidden Garden*, David & Charles, Newton Abbot 1984

Blake, Andrew, *The Land Without Music*, MUP, Manchester 1997

Bliss, Arthur, *As I Remember*, Thames, London 1989

Boden, Anthony, *Three Choirs*, Sutton, Stroud 1992

Braddon, Russell, *Joan Sutherland*, Collins, London 1962

Braga, Stuart, *Barker College*, John Ferguson, Sydney 1978

Brahms, Caryl & Sherrin, Ned, *Too Dirty for the Windmill*, Constable, London 1986

Brahms, Caryl & Simon, S.J., *No Bed for Bacon*, Hogarth Press, London 1986

Brook, Donald, *Singers of Today*, Rockliff, London 1949

Brown, Nicholas, *Richard Downing*, Melbourne University Press, Melbourne, 2002

Callaway, Frank & Tunley, David (eds.), *Australian Composition in the Twentieth Century*, OUP, Melbourne, 1978

Carpenter, Humphrey, *Benjamin Britten*, Faber & Faber, London 1992

Chitty, Susan (ed.), *Antonia White, Diaries, Vols 1 & 2,* Constable, London 1991 & 1992

Clark, Axel, *Christopher Brennan*, Melbourne University Press, Melbourne 1980

Clark, Manning, *Occasional Writings & Speeches*, Collins/Fontana, Sydney 1980

Clarson-Leach, Robert, *Marguerite Wolff*, Artmusique Publishing, London 1985

Coleman, Peter, *The Heart of James McAuley*, Wildcat Press, Sydney 1980

Collins, Diane, *Sounds From The Stables*, Allen & Unwin, Crows Nest NSW, 2001

Colt, C F & Miall, Anthony, *The Early Piano*, Stainer & Bell, London 1981

Covell, Roger, *Australia's Music*, Sun Books, Melbourne 1967

Cox, David, *The Henry Wood Proms*, BBC, London 1980

Cracknell, Ruth, *A Biased Memoir*, Penguin, Ringswood (Victoria) 1997

Dickinson, Peter, *The Music of Lennox Berkeley*, Boydell Press, Woodbridge 2003

Drefus, George, *Being George – and Liking It*, Allans, Richmond 1998

Dunn, Jane, *Antonia White*, Jonathan Cape, London 1998

Elborn, Geoffrey, *Edith Sitwell*, Sheldon Press, London 1981

Evans, Lindley, *'Hello, Mr Melody Man'*, Angus & Robertson, Sydney 1983

Farson, Daniel, *Limehouse Days*, Michael Joseph, London 1991

Farson, Daniel, *Never a Normal Man*, HarperCollins, London 1997

Farson, Daniel, *Soho in The Fifties.* Michael Joseph, London 1987

Feinstein, Elaine, *The Feast of Eurydice*, Next/Faber, London 1980

Fraser, Robert, *The Chameleon Poet*, Cape, London 2001

Gill, Lydia, *My Town. Sydney in the 1930s*, NSW Library, Sydney 1993

Glendinning, Victoria, *Edith Sitwell*, OUP, Oxford 1981

Glock, William, *Notes in Advance*, OUP, Oxford 1991

Goossens, Eugene, *Overture And Beginners*, Methuen, London 1951

Green, Candida Lycett (ed.), *John Betjeman Letters Vol 2*, Methuen, London 1995

Greene, Graham, *Our Man in Havana*, Heinemann, London 1958

Hammond, Joan, *A Voice, A Life*, Gollancz, London 1970

Harries, Meirion & Susie, *A Pilgrim Soul*, Michael Joseph, London 1989

Headington, Christopher, *Peter Pears*, Faber & Faber, London 1992

Hopkins, Antony, *Beating Time*, Michael Joseph, London 1982

Joel, John, *I Paid the Piper*, Howard Baker, London 1970

Kavanagh, Julie, *Secret Muses*, Faber & Faber, London 1996

Kennedy, Michael, *Adrian Boult*, Hamish Hamilton, London 1987

Kennedy, Michael, *The Life of Elgar*, CUP, Cambridge 2004

Kitcher, Barry, *From Gaolbird to Lyrebird*, Front Page, Melbourne 2001

Larson, Randall D, *Music from the House of Hammer*, Scarecrow Press, USA, 1996

Leigh-Fermor, Patrick, *The Violins of Saint-Jacques*, John Murray, London 1953

Lutyens, Elizabeth, *A Goldfish Bowl*, Cassell, London 1972

Lympany, Moura, *Moura Lympany: Her Autobiography*, Peter Owen, London 1991

McAuley, James, *Collected Poems*, Angus & Robertson, Sydney 1971

McEwen, John (ed.), *The Colony Room Club 50th Anniversary Art Exhibition*, London 1998

Martin, George, *Twentieth Century Opera*, Dodd, Mead & Co, New York 1979

Mason, Colin, *Music in Britain 1951-1962*, Longmans & Green, London 1963

Moore, Jerrold Northrop (ed.), *Music and Friends*, Hamish Hamilton, London 1979

Moorhouse, Geoffrey, *Sydney*, Weidenfeld & Nicolson, London, 1999

Moraes, Henrietta, *Henrietta*, Hamish Hamilton, London 1994

Murdoch, Iris, *A Year of Birds*, Chatto & Windus, London 1984

Murdoch, James, *Australia's Contemporary Composers*, Macmillan, Melbourne 1972

Noonuccal, Oodgeroo and Kabul, *The Rainbow Serpent*, AGPS, Canberra 1988

Peter Darrell Trust, *Man of Tomorrow*, PDT, London 1998

Poulton, Alan (ed.), *Alan Rawsthorne*, Bravura, Kidderminster 1984

Poston, Elizabeth & Williamson, Malcolm, *A Book of Christmas Carols*, Simon & Schuster, London 1988

Protheroe, Jacqueline, *Thank You For The Music*, privately printed, Farnham, 2003

Radic, Therese, *Bernard Heinze*, Macmillan, Melbourne 1986

Rosenthal, Harold, *Sopranos of Today*, John Calder, London 1949

Routley, Erik, *Twentieth Century Church Music*, Herbert Jenkins, London 1964

Rubens, Bernice, *When I Grow Up*, Little, Brown, London 2005

Russell-Cobb, Trevor, *Paying the Piper*, Queen Anne Press, London 1968

Salter, Elizabeth, *Robert Helpmann*, Angus & Robertson, Brighton 1978

Salter, Elizabeth, *Edith Sitwell*, Jupiter, London 1979

Sametz, Phillip, *Play On!*, ABC, Sydney 1992

Sculthorpe, Peter, *Sun Music*, ABC Books, Sydney 1999

Seabrook, Mike, *The Life and Music of Peter Maxwell Davies*, Gollancz, London 1994

Shaffer, Anthony, *So What Did You Expect?* Picador, London 2001

Shaffer, A & P, *Withered Murder*, Macmillan, New York 1956

Shaffer, Peter, *Five Finger Exercise*, Hamish Hamilton, London 1958

Sherrin, Ned, *A Small Thing – Like an Earthquake*, Weidenfeld & Nicolson, London 1983

Sherrin, Ned, *Autobiography*, Little, Brown, London 2005

Sherry, Norman, *The Life of Graham Greene Vol. 3*, Viking Penguin, New York 2004

Simeone, Nigel & Mundy, Simon (ed.), *Sir Adrian Boult*, Midas, Tunbridge Wells 1980

Sitwell, Edith, *English Eccentrics*, Dobson, London 1958

Sprigge, Elizabeth, *The Strange Life of August Strindberg*, Hamish Hamilton, London 1949

Thorne, Les, *North Shore Sydney*, Angus & Robertson, Sydney 1968

Vaughan, David, *Frederick Ashton and his Ballets*, Dance Books, London, 1977

Vaughan Williams, Ursula, *Collected Poems*, Albion Music 1996

Walker, Kath, *The Dawn Is At Hand*, Marion Boyars, London 1992

White, Antonia, *The Sugar House*, Eyre & Spottiswoode, London 1952

Williams, H A, *Some Day I'll Find You*, Beazley, London 1982

Windsor, Gerard, *The Harlots Enter First*, Hale & Iremonger, Sydney 1982

Windsor, Gerard, *Memories of the Assassination Attempt*, Penguin, Ringwood 1985

INDEX

C

D

E

F

G

H

I

J

K

L

M

(continued overleaf)

T

U

V

Y

Z